B'day 2003

B'day 2003

By Donald J. Heimburger

By Donald J. Heimburger
Layout by Marilyn M. Heimburger

Some of the material in this book was previously published in *Railroad History*, No. 133. Specifically, the entirety of Chapter 1, entitled "The Wabash: Steel Rails Link the Heart of America" and "Troubled Times Beset the Wabash," page 8-24, previously appeared in *Railroad History*, No. 133, as "The Wabash Railroad" by William Swartz. "Guide to Predecessor Lines of the Wabash," pages 28-29, appeared under that title in the aforementioned issue. Finally, the "Wabash Locomotive Roster," pages 251-263, appeared in that issue as "All-Time Wabash Locomotive Roster" by William Swartz and W.D. Edson. All reprinted material is copyright, 1975, by The Railway and Locomotive Historical Society, Inc. and is reprinted by permission.

Library of Congress Card Number: 83-83067
ISBN 0-911581-02-2

Second Edition
Printed in the United States of America

Heimburger House Publishing Co.
7236 W. Madison Street
Forest Park, IL 60130

Dedication
To Mom, who grew up along the Wabash Railroad herself, and who has supported my interest in trains. May you be filled with happy memories of your childhood days in Sadorus, Illinois.

An early 1900s Wabash freight train waters up just west of Sadorus, Illinois at the Little Kaskaskia River. *Frank Sadorus, courtesy of The Champaign County Historical Archives of the Urbana Free Library*

Indiana Autumn—Wabash Railroad—1947.

Howard Fogg, courtesy Miner Enterprises, Inc.

Contents

Introduction

Wabash. The name brings back pleasant railroad memories. The railroad that took its name from a 475-mile river flowing through Illinois and Indiana is equated with automobile tonnage, perishable traffic and merchandise forwarder. The Wabash was the only railroad from Kansas City to Buffalo with a through east-west route avoiding big city congestion. Wabash also meant famous passenger trains such as the beautiful $1.5 million Budd-built *Blue Bird* which grossed $2.73 a mile and the seven-car *City of Kansas City* which ran round trips between St. Louis and Kansas City daily. Wabash meant big steam power like the O-1 Class 4-8-4 Northerns built by Baldwin, and the 1,500 horsepower EMD-built F-7A and B's that carried the bulk of freight in later years.

Certainly Wabash meant people—friendly railroad people doing their best to keep the nearly 2,500-mile "Heart of America" line running

smoothly and efficiently in both war time and peace time. The Wabash was one of the very first railroads to be revived from the effects of the 1929 Depression.

Wabash meant a strong, healthy railroad providing quality service to its customers.

FIRST IMPRESSIONS

My first impressions of the Wabash came at an early age because its St. Louis to Detroit mainline sliced right through Tolono, Illinois where I grew up. I don't recall the steam operations, but the diesels I remember well and with fondness. Early on Sunday mornings my paper route duties were delayed while I sat trackside and watched setouts and pickups between Wabash and Illinois Central trains in Tolono. Westbound Wabash trains left their consists at the last crossing in town and brought interchange cars to the IC. Sometimes they'd take half an hour to complete their moves,

and I sat there with eyes transfixed on the blue, white and gray diesels, sometimes with lashups such as F-7A's and B's, Geeps and FA-2's. My paper route suffered! The only thing I didn't like about Wabash trains coming through Tolono was when they didn't stop. I wanted to get a closer look at the trains, and always waved at the engineer, hoping he'd ask if I wanted a ride. I'd *never* turn down a cab ride.

While Wabash freight trains were fun to watch, I think everyone liked the passenger trains best. They meant people, and movement, and excitement. When they came through Tolono, I especially remember watching around the holidays how many cars they pulled. Often they had twice the number of passenger cars than usual, and they'd be a mix of the Wabash dark blue and Union Pacific yellow cars. And every once in a while I'd see a special train of 12 to 20 cars go through, probably a charter group. Wabash passenger trains were enjoyable to watch!

WABASH ERA ENDS

After a long, proud history, the Wabash era ended as a result of consolidation. It was a victim, if you will, of another, larger road needing it as a competitive edge against its competition.

When October 16, 1964 arrived, the Wabash began sliding into history. Its merger with the Norfolk & Western Railway signalled the end of a medium-sized independent railroad operating under the familiar Wabash flag. At the time of consolidation the Wabash was a 2,428 mile line operating in eight states and Canada—New York, Michigan, Ohio, Indiana, Illinois, Missouri, Iowa, Nebraska and the Province of Ontario.

Wabash fans like myself miss the old girl now, and as each year passes, we become more intent in our vow to preserve some of the glory and history of our favorite railroad. We pull out the old Wabash pictures and timetables more often for a look, and we wish we had taken more photos of Wabash equipment when we had the chance.

Our memories of the Wabash fade over time, of course, but this printed tribute to this once proud railroad will help keep our endearment to the Wabash Railroad alive and growing for a long time to come!

Donald J. Heimburger

Southbound *Blue Bird* at Englewood 63rd Street, Chicago in May, 1947.
Harold Stirton

Chapter 1

The Wabash: steel rails link the Heart of America

Late in October of 1964, the Wabash Railroad name was removed from train schedule boards, and the Norfolk & Western Railway name was substituted. With this symbolic act, repeated in dozens of stations over the Wabash Railroad, an era in railroading was ended—the *Wabash era,* a name proudly carried on locomotives and cars for more than a century was summarily swallowed up in a gigantic railroad merger and the Wabash, already a legend in cities and towns from Iowa to Ontario, took its place in history.

The Wabash Railroad's oldest section was rooted deep in Illinois history. More than 2,000 miles of mainline trackage which linked Omaha and Kansas City with Buffalo through six Midwestern states and part of Canada, became an integral part of the even greater N&W network which now reached halfway across the Continent to the Atlantic Seaboard. To be sure, the changeover in 1964 was not accompanied by any wholesale destruction or radical change. Equipment was reassigned and service continued much as before. But something once so meaningful had vanished. The red, blue and gold flag of the Banner Route was no longer displayed along the river valleys and prairies of the Midwest.

FINANCIAL DIFFICULTY

In financial difficulty during much of its history, the Wabash had the dubious distinction of being the first Class I railroad to suffer bankruptcy during the Great Depression in 1933. Nevertheless, the Wabash built a solid reputation in rail transportation. Under the able direction and efficient management of the Receivers, Norman Pitcairn and

An early Wabash 4-4-0 crosses a long trestle at Decatur with a five-car train. *Dick Wallin collection*

Frank Nicodemus, Jr., substantial recovery from the effects of the Depression was achieved by 1940. Pitcairn, directing operations from the Railway Exchange Building in St. Louis, undertook a track and equipment modernization program that paved the way for the fast passenger and freight service which was to characterize Wabash train operations for many years. "To Wabash" was to run fast at full throttle. Advertised as "Red Ball" freight service, the fast freight was responsible for pulling the Wabash out of the financial doldrums of the early 1930's. Seventy-mile-per-hour speeds on Wabash manifests were not uncommon.

Operating as it did in the nation's heartland, the Wabash coined the slogan *Heart of America.* The heart-shaped design depicting a rail network linking Omaha and Chicago with St. Louis and Detroit became nearly as well known as the famous Wabash flag with its *Follow the Flag* slogan. The Wabash Banner Route flag emblem was registered at the United States Patent Office in 1884, and in the late 1930's it received widespread publicity on the motion picture screen in many Midwestern theaters during promotional advertising of Niagara Falls excursion trains.

If the Wabash served the Heart of America, then St. Louis was the crossroads of the System. The Wabash was unique in that it served St. Louis both as a western and as an eastern road. In 1905 the Wabash was the first railroad to recognize and designate the city of St. Louis as a billing station for freight to and from points east of the Mississippi River, eliminating bridge tolls on freight formerly billed to East St. Louis, a practice which had for many years seriously handicapped industrial and business development in St. Louis. The previous year, the Wabash had firmly established itself as a prime passenger carrier in the St. Louis area when the Louisiana Purchase Exposition opened in Forest Park. The rallying cry that year was "Meet me in St. Louis-and come on the Wabash." The Wabash line running through Forest Park was utilized to capacity, handling crowds to and from the Exposition grounds. The railroad spent more than one million dollars on Exposition-related services including track and station facilities and new locomotives and cars. And as the St. Louis *Republic* pointed out, in the full page story on December 10, 1905, "the Wabash Railroad has put St. Louis 'on the map'." Later the Wabash built its own modern station at Delmar Boulevard, six miles west of Union Station. All trains eastbound or westbound stopped at Delmar. Eastbound trains circled round the City's north side and headed east to Illinois over the Merchants Bridge.

HISTORIC RIVERS

More than steel rails linking the Heart of America, the Wabash was bridges spanning historic rivers of the Midwest: the Maumee, the Wabash, Vermilion, Sangamon, Mississippi and the Missouri, where at St. Charles the spectacular 7,700 foot Pitcairn Bridge is still a masterpiece of railway engineering.

The Wabash was endless processions of fruit blocks eastward from Kansas City through the Hannibal cut-off. At Decatur, and such eastern Illinois prairie towns as Bement, Tolono and Sidney, fast moving manifest tonnage passed in a blur of speeding wheels. This traffic was met by tremendous westbound tonnages of automobiles and parts. Auto frames, stacked like cordwood in specially constructed gondolas, rolled out of River Rouge and the Detroit industrial complex down the Wabash corridor to assembly plants in Missouri. Early in World War II a new commodity was added to the heavy eastward traffic movement. Oil by the trainload moved over the line to east coast refineries nearly cut off from normal supplies because of submarine warfare.

In the heyday of the passenger train, the *Blue Bird, Banner Blue* and *Detroit Arrow* were no strangers to the annual Mile-a-Minute Speed Surveys conducted 35 years ago. And the immortal *Cannon Ball* running its last years between St. Louis and Detroit was a direct descendent of the famed *Continental Limited* which at the turn of the century provided direct, through service between St. Louis and Hoboken, N.J. via Buffalo and the West Shore Route. The *Wabash Cannon Ball,* listed in more prosaic terms in timetables as No. 1 and No. 4, downgraded by loss of mail contracts and equipment failure and neglect, managed to survive until the end of all service in 1970.

Of such was the Wabash. The passenger trains are gone and the flashing rods and thundering exhaust of Hudsons and Northerns are just a distant memory. But down along the Wabash Valley, down where the river winds through northern Indiana it is said, even today, if one will listen carefully he can hear the low, melodious sound of a steamboat whistle echoing across the Valley and the mighty rush of the engine speeding along with the *Wabash Cannon Ball.*

An old folksong *The Wabash Cannon Ball,* tells of a fabulous train that traveled from Atlantic shores to the Pacific. While the Wabash never reached either seacoast, more than a hint of truth is suggested by the song. Twice in a generation the Wabash was directly involved in attempts by the Gould interests to establish a transcontinental empire.

The Wabash was both beneficiary and victim of railroad power politics and the maneuverings of financiers and ambitious railroad barons of the late 19th Century. As President of the Wabash, Jay Gould took two railroads developing independently on opposite sides of the Mississippi River, having a common meeting point at St. Louis, and by construction and acquisition, forged a new railroad connecting St. Louis with six of the Midwest's largest cities.

But Gould left the Wabash a legacy of chaos. From the shambles of the eighties, the Wabash Railroad emerged to play a vital role in American rail transportation in the 20th Century. The early, difficult years proved to be a practical training school for seasoned, expert railroad men who went on to top executive posts: William Van Horn from Wabash Division Superintendent to Canadian Pacific fame; George Stevens to president of the Chesapeake & Ohio; James Herbert to president of the St. Louis-Southwestern and Charles Hays of the Grand Trunk. The Wabash Railroad history is a story of mergers, financial crisis and reorganization climaxed by the ultimate merger in 1964 that removed all trace of corporate identity.

LINES WEST OF ST. LOUIS

St. Louis in 1850 was a bustling city standing at the very gateway of the newly opened West, and her economy, like that of Illinois, was tied to and directly dependent upon river steamboat transportation. Upriver a few miles on the

The Northern Cross was the first steam line west of the Alleghenies and this stone at Meredosia, Illinois commemorates that fact. *Frank Yeakel*

NORTH MISSOURI RAILWAY.

Hon. BARTON BATES, President.   Hon. E. W. FOX, Vice President.   J. P. LAIRD, Gen. Superintendent.
H. H. WHEELER, Gen. Ticket Agent.   J. H. GAMMIE, Gen. Freight Agent, St. Louis, Mo.
J. B. MOULTON, Chief Engineer, St. Louis, Mo.
JAS. A. FELPS, Supt. East. Div., St. Charles.   G. H. CRAIN, Supt. West. Div. and Telegraph, Moberly.
E. I. BURRITT, Eastern Passenger Agent, New York City.

Going West					May 3, 1868.		Going East.			CONNECTIONS.
Acc.	Acc.	Exs.	Mail	Mls	STATIONS.	Mls	Exs.	Mail	Acc.	Acc.	
P. M.	P. M.	P. M.	A. M.				A. M.	P. M.	A. M.	A. M.	
5 00	10 00	3 15	7 30	0	...St. Louis 1 ...	304	10 30	5 15	3 45	7 45	At St. Joseph, With the Missouri River Packet Company's New and Splendid Steamers ; also, Daily Line of Stages for NEBRASKA CITY, OMAHA, and intermediate points.
5 19	10 17	3 32	7 48	4	...Bellefontaine ...	300	10 12	4 58	3 27	7 27	
5 40	10 33	3 48	8 04	10	...Ferguson	294	9 58	4 42	3 12	7 06	
5 55	10 44	4 00	8 14	14	...Bridgton	290	9 46	4 30	3 02	6 51	
6 15	11 00	4 15	8 30	19	....Brotherton ...	285	9 30	4 15	2 45	6 30	
6 30	11 20	4 45	9 00	20	...St. Charles 7 ...	284	9 00	3 45	2 25	6 15	
P. M.				29	....Dardenne	275	8 31	3 15	1 45	A. M.	
	12 15	5 21	9 40	33	....O'Fallon	271	8 20	3 04	1 28		At Kansas City and Leavenworth, With Union Pacific Railway (E. D.) for LAWRENCE, TOPEKA, FORT RILEY, AND POND CREEK.
	12 30	5 31	9 50	37	....Perrque	267	8 11	2 52	1 12		
	12 50	5 45	10 07	42	...Wentzville ...	262	7 58	2 37	12 50		
	1 15	6 00	10 24	48	....Millville....	256	7 41	2 18	12 19		
	1 30	6 09	10 34	51	....Wrights....	253	7 30	2 07	12 00		
	1 55	6 25	10 53	57	....Warrenton 3 ...	247	7 14	1 49	11 32		
	2 21	6 40	11 10	63	....Pendleton	241	5 57	1 30	11 05		At Terminus of U. Pacific Railway (E. D.), With Daily Overland Stages for DENVER CITY, SALT LAKE CITY, AND CALIFORNIA.
	2 41	6 52	11 27	67	...Jonesburg	237	6 45	1 15	10 45		
	3 02	7 05	11 46	72	...High Hill....	232	6 22	1 00	10 24		
	3 20	7 15	12 02	77	.....Florence ...	228	6 21	12 46	10 06		
	3 45	7 30	12 25	83	arr Montgomery arr	222	6 05	12 25	9 40		
	4 05	7 50	12 45	83	lve Montgomery arr	222	5 45	12 05	9 20		
	4 39	8 11	1 08	90	....Wellsville...	215	5 25	11 42	8 46		At Omaha, With Union Pacific Railway for CHEYENNE, and Western Terminus of Union Pacific Road, where connections are made with Daily Overland Stages for DENVER CITY, SALT LAKE CITY, AND CALIFORNIA.
	5 10	8 25	1 22	95	..Martinsburg ...	210	5 10	11 30	8 25		
	6 00	9 02	2 04	109	.....Mexico ...	196	4 35	10 53	7 04		
	6 20	9 16	2 20	114	...Thompson ...	191	4 22	10 38	6 35		
	6 55	9 40	2 45	122	Centralia Junction 4	183	4 00	10 15	6 05		
	7 00		2 50	122	Centralia Junction.	22		10 10	6 00		
	7 18		3 07	128	....Bush's	17		9 52	5 37		
	7 39		3 19	131	....Hickman ...	14		9 41	5 21		
	8 08		3 39	138	...Stephen's ...	6		9 23	4 52		
	8 30		3 57	143	arr Columbia lve	0		9 03	4 30		Palace Sleeping Cars run on all Night Trains! Baggage checked through Fares always as low as via any other Route! Daily Stage Lines are run from all principal Stations to all interior Counties and Towns. Tickets on sale at all the principal Railway Offices in the country. Call for Tickets via North Missouri Railway, and examine and see that such are given you.
	7 26	10 09	3 30	130	...Sturgeon ...	175	3 40	9 48	5 27		
	8 10	10 28	3 43	141	....Renick....	165	3 11	9 14	5 39		
	8 55	10 45	4 00	147	Moberly Junction 5	159	2 55	8 55	4 10		
	9 00		4 10	147	Moberly Junction	39		8 35	3 50		
	9 34		4 33	154	...Huntsville ...	32		8 12	3 16		
	10 05		4 54	161	...Clifton ...	26		7 51	2 45		
	10 36		5 15	167	...Salisbury....	18		7 30	2 14		
	11 07		5 36	175	...Keytesville...	11		7 09	1 43		
	11 29		5 49	179	.....Dalton ...	7		6 56	1 22		
	12 00		6 10	186	...Brunswick ...	0		6 35	12 50		
	9 17	11 00	4 18	152	....Cairo	192	2 39	8 36	3 26		
	9 40	11 15	4 35	157	...Jacksonville ...	147	2 20	8 20	3 04		
	10 15	11 45	5 05	168	arr Macon 6 lve	156	1 50	7 50	2 25		
	11 45	11 50	11 50		lve Macon 6 arr	156	A. M.	A. M.	1 15		
				165	...Mena....	12					
	11 30			180	arr.Atlanta. lve	0			12 30		
		1 45	1 45	202	....Brookfield ...	102	11 35	11 35			
		4 58	4 58	269	...Cameron 7	35	8 37	8 37			
		6 50	6 50	304	....St. Joseph 8 ...	0	6 45	6 45			
		8 00	8 00		...Kansas City 9 ..		5 45	5 45			
A. M.	A. M.	A. M.			ARRIVE	LEAVE	P. M	P. M	P. M.	P. M.	

CONNECTIONS.
1 Railways diverging from St. Louis. 2 Steamers to Nebraska. 3 Stages to all the towns on the Missouri River. 4 Connect with Branch to Columbia. 5 Connect with Branch to Brunswick. 6 Connect with Branch to Atlanta. 7 Connects with Hannibal and St. Joseph Railway. 8 Connects with K. C. & C. Br. of H. & St. Jo. Railway. 9 Connects with Missouri Valley Railway. 9 Connects with Union Pacific Railway, E. D.

The Fairbury, Pontiac & NorthWestern was a predecessor of the Wabash. *Robert Fiedler collection*

Missouri River stood the town of St. Charles, competing with St. Louis for prominence amid the swelling westward movement. On the same river 250 miles farther west the city of Independence towered over its tiny neighbor, Kansas City, on the edge of the Great Plains. Canal Fever, so prevalent in Illinois and Indiana only a few years before, had not made much headway in Missouri; but most Missourians still equated progress and growth with river transport, as they had since 1819, when the *Western Engineer* first steamed its way up the Missouri to Council Bluffs.

The potential of a railroad to tap the developing West appealed to a number of prominent St. Louis lawyers and merchants. In fact, the promoters envisioned three railroads, each using St. Louis as a base. One route, the Missouri Pacific, would follow the Missouri River west toward Kansas City. Another would build toward Iowa and the north. A third railroad, the St. Louis & Iron Mountain, would run southwest from St. Louis.

So it was that in March, 1851, a State Charter was granted to the North Missouri Railroad to build a line from St. Louis to the Iowa State Line. The railroad would consist of three divisions. The first division was a short distance of 19 miles from St. Louis to the east bank of the Missouri River opposite St. Charles; the second would run 148 miles in a northwesterly direction from St. Charles to a junction with the Hannibal & St. Joseph Railroad at Hudson, Mo.; the third division would complete 61 miles north from Hudson to Coatesville, Mo., on the Iowa Line.

Construction of the first division began in May, 1854, and by August 20, 1855, trains were operating to a ferry landing across the river from St. Charles where it was necessary to unload the freight cars, and passengers and goods crossed the Missouri by ferry boat. On February 1, 1858, North Missouri rails reached Coatesville and for the first time a railroad linked St. Louis with St. Joseph and Hannibal. The St. Charles ferry arrangement continued to hinder efficient train operation on the North Missouri during most of the Civil War years. The ultimate solution at St. Charles was, of course, a bridge—no small undertaking even in peace time. In 1864, as an interim measure, a railroad car ferry was placed in service which at least eliminated the task of transferring freight between cars.

From 1861 to 1865 the North Missouri was subjected to devastating attacks and raids by Confederate troops in the Missouri-Arkansas territory. Confederate General Sterling

The *Tolono*, a Toledo, Wabash & Western 4-4-0 built in 1866 by William Mason, poses at the Springfield, Illinois roundhouse in 1867. *Photo by Joe Lavelle, collection of William Swartz*

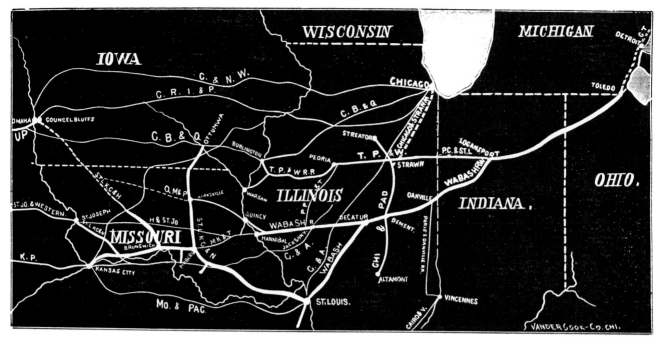

Map of the Wabash, St. Louis & Pacific. *Courtesy Railway Age, July 17, 1879*

Price issued an order in July, 1861, calling for the destruction of the North Missouri Railroad. Under Captain Bill Anderson, a small group of daring hand-picked cavalrymen were able to destroy every bridge in over 100 miles of line. The marauders also succeeded in doing extensive damage to track, cars and engines and burned fuel supplies and ties all along the railroad.

In another mission of destruction in 1864, Anderson burned two trains and seven stations. Near Centralia, Mo., in Boone County, more than 120 men were killed trying to stop the invaders and many were buried along the North Missouri right-of-way.

Following the Civil War the North Missouri began the work of rebuilding and expanding the railroad. In 1858 a charter had been granted the Chariton & Randolph Railroad to build a line west from a point on the North Missouri some 147 miles northwest of St. Louis. The Chariton & Randolph sold out to the North Missouri in 1864, before reaching its projected goal of Brunswick, and two years later the town of Moberly was established at the junction of the two railroads. Moberly, centrally located to all lines west of St. Louis, was selected as the site of extensive locomotive and car shops which would eventually employ nearly 1,000 men. A line known as the West Branch of the North Missouri continued the westward extension begun by the Chariton & Randolph entering Birmingham, 12 miles from Kansas City, in 1868. Construction of the long awaited Missouri River bridge began in 1869 following organization of the St. Charles Bridge Company, and in 1871 North Missouri trains were able to run through from St. Louis to Kansas City.

ST. LOUIS AND CEDAR RAPIDS

A through route to the upper Midwest region had long been the North Missouri's goal. The St. Louis & Cedar Rapids Railway was incorporated October 23, 1865, to build north from Coatesville into Iowa, and was to be operated by North Missouri under lease. Financial troubles plagued the line from the beginning, and by 1868 only

eight miles of track were finished. At this point the town of Moulton was established, named for the North Missouri's Chief Engineer. By 1870 an additional 35 miles was completed to Ottumwa. Although a reorganization in 1875 changed the name to St. Louis, Ottumwa & Cedar Rapids,

June, 1868 Official Guide. *Courtesy National Railway Publication Company*

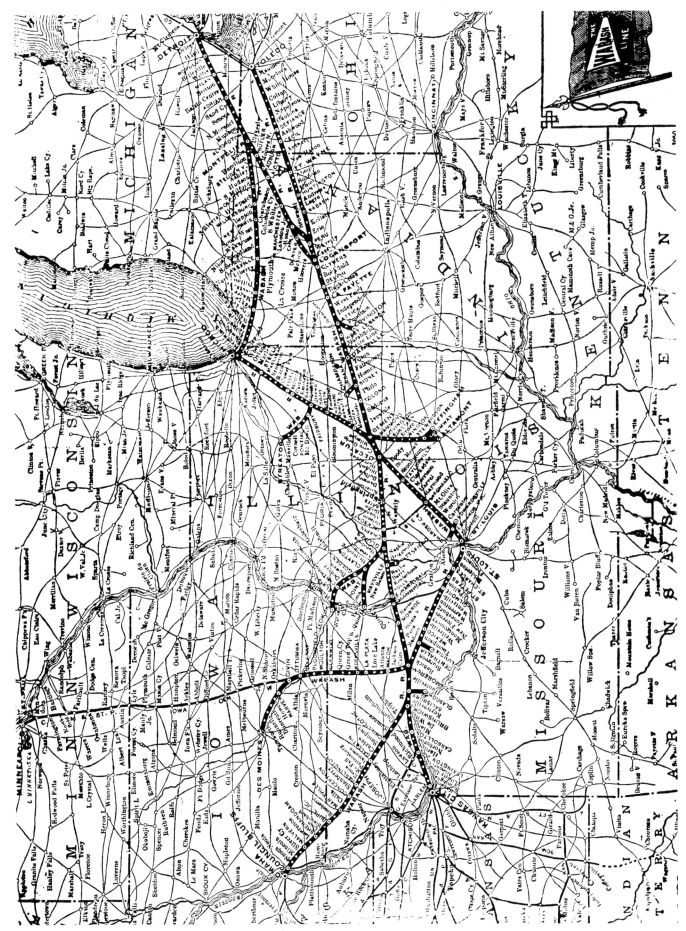

1890 Wabash system map from back of a waybill. *M.D. McCarter collection*

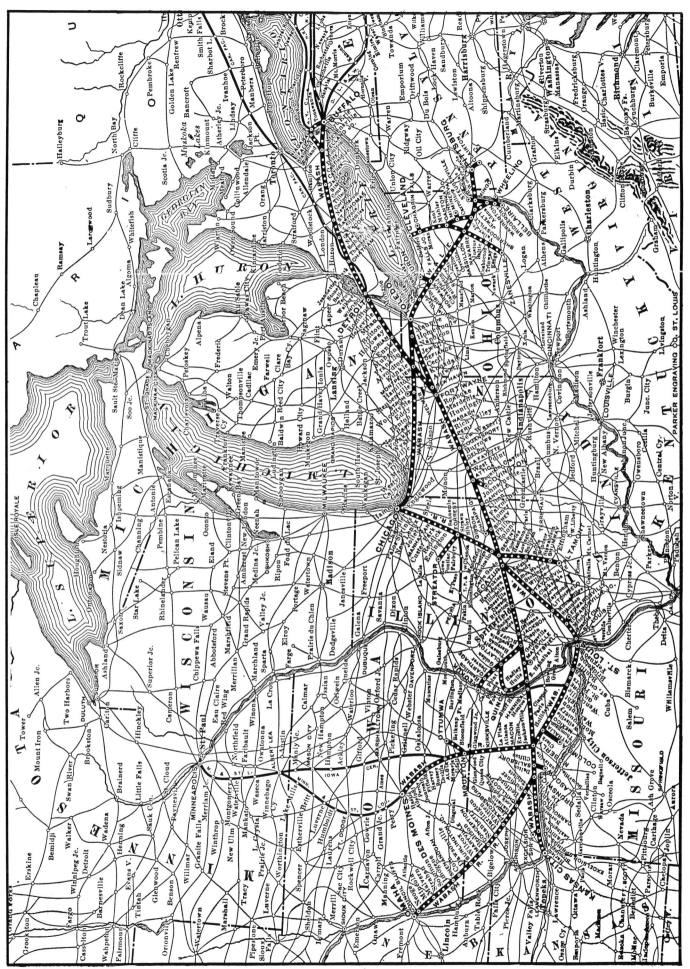

1908 map from public timetable shows Pittsburgh extension and ownership of W&LE. *Robert Fiedler collection*

Courtesy Norfolk & Western magazine

Pattonsburg, Mo., remained the end of track on the Council Bluffs line until 1878. On September 2, 1878, the Council Bluffs & St. Louis Railway was incorporated to close the gap of 143 miles. The pattern of control followed that of the Ottumwa extension in that the StLKC&N operated the Council Bluffs & St. Louis under lease. However, the lease continued under the Wabash, St. Louis & Pacific, and the Council Bluffs-Pattonsburg section retained a separate corporate identity until October 12, 1901, when the Wabash Railroad Co. purchased it. For some time prior to merger, Gould engineers were at work on the extension so that actual completion into Council Bluffs took place just one month before Gould officially gained control on November 10, 1879.

The topography of northwestern Ohio and northern Indiana indicated an ideal route for the new railroad and at the same time signed the death warrant of the Wabash and Erie Canal. The railroad would be built in a southwesterly direction from Toledo and would run through the valleys of the Maumee and Wabash rivers to Attica, 17 miles east of the Illinois state line. Leaving the Wabash valley at that point, the railroad would connect with the Great Western of Illinois at Danville. The proposed route closely paralleled the Wabash and Erie Canal, serving many thriving communities. The largest, Fort Wayne, was about mid-way between Toledo and Danville.

The Toledo Associates formed two companies in 1853. The Toledo & Illinois Railroad would build from Toledo to

Courtesy Norfolk & Western magazine

the St. Louis management decided against further extension to Cedar Rapids in favor of a line to Des Moines; but no progress would be made in this direction until the Gould merger.

Plans were set forth in 1870 to connect St. Louis with Omaha using North Missouri tracks east of Brunswick, Mo. The Brunswick & Chillicothe Railroad began the work, building 38 miles of line northwest from Brunswick by 1872. The St. Louis, Council Bluffs and Omaha completed 44 miles from Chillicothe to Pattonsburg in 1871, after which both lines were leased to the North Missouri. Also brought in under lease was the 21 mile Boone County & Booneville Railroad branch connecting Columbia to the main line at Centralia.

Shortly after completion of the St. Charles bridge, the North Missouri became insolvent. The reorganization produced a new name, reflecting the state-wide operations of the railroad. The St. Louis, Kansas City & Northern Railroad, incorporated January 2, 1872, began the final seven years of independent operation before joining the Wabash in 1879.

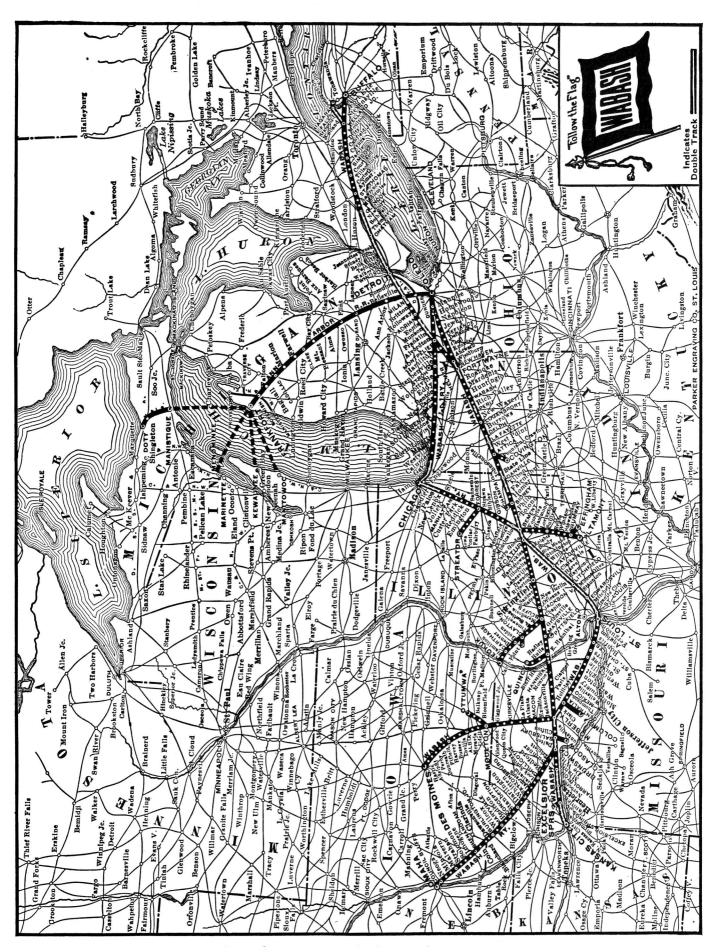

December 31, 1925 Wabash Annual Report map

15

Received, Brunswick Aug 13th 1872

Charles Nuckolls OF

ST. LOUIS, KANSAS CITY & NORTHERN RAILWAY COMPANY,

the sum of Twenty two Dollars,

in full for one calf killed June 15 & one heifer killed July 11/73

Charles Nuckolls

An early Wabash freight train with crew. *Dick Wallin collection*

This is the Springfield, Illinois roundhouse in the early 1900's. *Dick Wallin collection*

The following is a supplement to the history portion of the WABASH book. It follows the first paragraph, second column, on page 14.

Lines East Of St. Louis

When the first steam locomotive in the state of Illinois and the entire Mississippi Valley began to turn its wheels and emit puffs of smoke the cheers of admirers mingled with shouts and jeers from river men and "Canalers" who had gathered to watch what they hoped would be a fiasco. To the consternation of the frustrated "Canalers", the Iron Monster made a great hit with the townspeople and later in the day astonished the entire gathering by hauling a select group of citizens including the oldest inhabitant, Daniel Waldo, to the end of the eight miles of track and back again.

The date was November 8, 1838 and the place was the pioneer village of Meredosia, Illinois, on the east bank of the Illinois River. The Iron Monster was the *Rogers*, built in Paterson, N. J. and delivered to Meredosia by river packet. The ten ton *Rogers* was not much to speak of as a locomotive. It had no cab and had no whistle or bell. It had only a single pair of drive wheels. But that day in November, 1838 made history. The first train had successfully operated over the Northern Cross Railroad and the first section of track in what was later to become the Wabash was opened for business.

For Joseph Duncan, Governor of Illinois, the opening of the Northern Cross was the culmination of an eight year battle for more and better transportation for the state of Illinois. As early as 1830 Duncan, then a member of Congress, realized the possibilities in railway transportation to open up the Illinois frontier but he and his associates met with ridicule in every effort to obtain financing.

Canal proponents, men whose lives had been spent along the Ohio and Mississippi Rivers, strongly favored development of an inland waterway network using navigable rivers and constructing canals to connect the rivers with centers of commerce. Public opinion backed them and they pointed with pride to the Erie Canal in the East and the system of canals being built in the Great Lakes region.

But in 1834 Duncan persuaded the Illinois Legislature to pass the Illinois Internal Improvement Act. The Act authorized a study of the State's transportation system. Although the study committee's initial finding was in favor of canals, Duncan succeeded in forcing the approval of a steam railroad to be built with State funds and would extend from Quincy on the Mississippi River to Danville, a few miles west of the Indiana state line. Thus even as the "Canalers" were hailing the Legislative committee's decision for canal development, the death knell had already sounded for most canals in the Midwest.

Actual work on the new railroad was not begun until Nov. 1837 and construction was hindered by a shortage of labor and supplies and transportation problems. Iron rails had to be shipped from New Orleans by boat to St. Louis and re-shipped again up the Illinois River to Meredosia, designated as the starting point for the railroad. In the spring of 1838 the first shipment of rails reached Meredosia and track laying commenced on May 9th. Wooden sleepers one foot square were placed in the ground and across these, crossties were laid. On the ties were fastened wooden rails three inches wide tapering slightly at the top. Strap rail 5/8 inches thick and two inches wide was then nailed to the wooden rails.

Because the route surveyed for the railroad closely followed a pioneer trail across Illinois known as the "Northern Crossing", it was decided that the new railroad would be called the Northern Cross. By the end of 1838 rails had been pushed twelve miles east to Morgan City and on July 1, 1839 the first railroad advertising printed in the Mississippi Valley announced that three new passenger cars had been received and that extensive arrangements would be made to accommodate those wishing to see a railroad in actual operation.

The hard working *Rogers* waited in vain for the arrival of a companion engine, the *Illinois*, ordered from M. W. Baldwin. After considerable delay, the bad news reached Meredosia. The *Illinois*,

along with the locomotive *Indianapolis*, destined for the Madison & Indianapolis Railroad, was lost at sea on the long voyage from Philadelphia to New Orleans. In May, 1839 a second *Illinois* was completed at the Baldwin plant. Three months later this engine was unloaded at Meredosia and the Northern Cross scheduled two trips per day at a speed of six miles per hour between Meredosia and Morgan City.

On January 1st, 1840, track was completed to Jacksonville and for the next two years construction continued east to Springfield, where the first train was welcomed on Feb. 15, 1842. Although the state of Illinois operated the Northern Cross for nearly ten years, the revenues collected never came close to the original forecasts and discontent was growing in the halls of the State Legislature.

On May 13, 1842 the Northern Cross was leased to J. B. Watson and J. M. Morse for the sum of $10,300 per year. After two months of difficulty the operators asked for relief and the lease was taken up by S. M. Tinsley and Company who agreed to pay $10,000 per year for four years. The next four years saw a steady downturn in the fortunes of the Northern Cross project. Grading on the extension east from Springfield was suspended by the state for lack of funds. Repairs to the locomotives became difficult if not impossible since the nearest railway repair facilities were hundreds of miles away. By 1845 the locomotives had become so dilapidated that the Northern Cross was compelled to use animal power to move its trains, and for more than a year mules and oxen pulled two-car trains between Springfield and Naples making one trip each way daily.

In 1847 the state of Illinois decided to get out of the railroad business. On April 26, 1847 the Northern Cross was sold at auction for $20,000 to Nicholas Ridgely of Springfield. Ridgely and his associates, James Dunlap and Joel Mattison, immediately changed the road's name to the Sangamon & Morgan Railroad and embarked upon a rehabilitation program. The entire line of 57 miles was rebuilt and strap rails were replaced with U rails. In addition, new locomotives and larger cars were purchased and running time for the 57 miles was cut to five hours. At the same time Ridgely sold an interest in the Sangamon & Morgan to James Mather, also of Springfield. The partners agreed that with the steadily mounting rail traffic in the East and developing plans of eastern roads to tap the resources and business opportunities in Illinois and Missouri, it was of prime importance to get their railroad completed across the entire state.

To this purpose, Mather visited the financial centers in New York. While there, he negotiated the sale of the Sangamon & Morgan to Robert Schuyler, a leading railroad magnate. Included in the deal would be a new section of track being constructed toward Quincy from the west bank of the Illinois River at Meredosia to Camp Point, Illinois, a distance of 33 miles.

During 1850-1851 new T rails were laid over the entire Sangamon & Morgan, and rails pushed eastward to Decatur. On Feb. 12, 1853 the Sangamon & Morgan was renamed The Great Western Railway of Illinois. Locomotive shops were established in Springfield and route mileage increased to 180 when the Great Western reached Danville in 1855.

Meanwhile an enterprising group of Ohio and Indiana business associates headed by Azariah Boody met at Toledo, Ohio in 1852 to plan the organization of a railroad to move grain from Illinois and Indiana to the lakehead. Toledo was ideally situated as a rail center and the rapidly developing steamer traffic coming down the Great Lakes with cargoes destined for the Mississippi Valley region was required to make a long detour through Lake Huron and the Mackinac Straits to reach Lake Michigan. This route was open only nine months of the year and a transfer of cargoes from lake steamer to rail at Toledo appeared inevitable. Toledo and Maumee were already assuming a leading role as a center for grain handling and shipping and a railroad connecting the port of Toledo with the Mississippi River would be assured of a most favorable traffic balance.

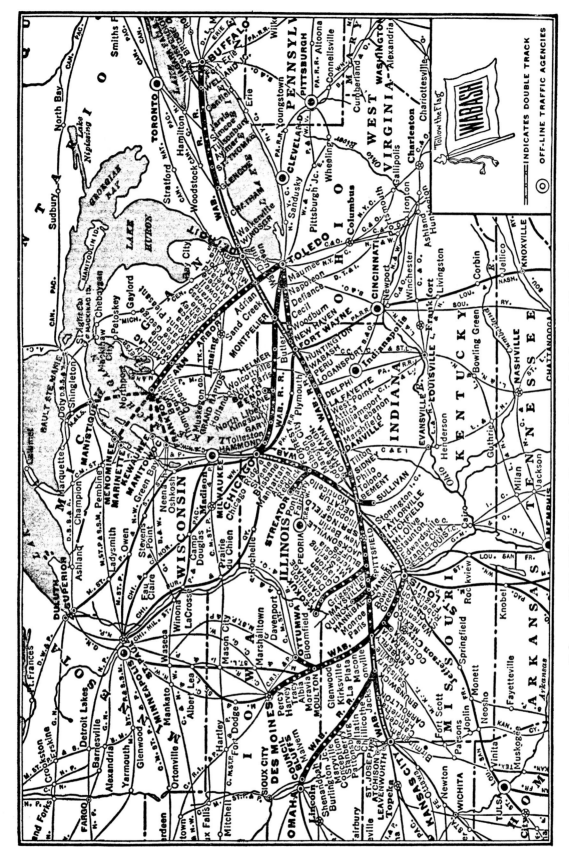

February, 1948 Official Guide. *Courtesy National Railway Publication Company*

17

RAILWAY EXCHANGE BUILDING
ST. LOUIS

Wabash depot, Huntington, Indiana. *Harold Conner collection*

the Indiana state line, while the Lake Erie, Wabash & St. Louis Railroad would continue the line across Indiana. This marked the first time that the name Wabash had been applied to the railroad. Construction out of Toledo began in 1854, and by early 1855 track was completed to New Haven, Indiana, east of Fort Wayne. Tracklaying proceeded southwest at a rapid pace, entering the Wabash valley east of Huntington. For the next 100 miles the railroad, first on the north bank, then on the south bank, was seldom out of sight of the Wabash River. Canal towns became railroad towns as terminals and yards were constructed in Fort Wayne, Peru and Lafayette. At Attica, the railroad approaching on a north and south alignment, swung sharply to the west, crossed the Wabash River for the last time and headed for the Illinois prairies and the link-up with the Great Western.

In accordance with the original plan of the Toledo Associates, the Toledo & Illinois and the Lake Erie, Wabash & St. Louis railroads were merged in the summer of 1856 to form the Toledo, Wabash & Western Railroad. The TW&W barely had time to order a few new locomo-

tives when a foreclosure action was initiated. Corporate reorganization on October 7, 1858, changed the name to the Toledo & Wabash Railway.

The Quincy & Toledo Railroad was organized January 31, 1857 to operate the Meredosia—Camp Point section and complete the Great Western's line to Quincy. By the end of 1857 an unbroken line of railroad had been completed between Toledo and the Mississippi River and work started on an extension to Keokuk, Iowa. To reach Keokuk, the Illinois & Southern Iowa Railroad was organized in February, 1857 and built 30 miles of track north from Clayton on the Quincy & Toledo to Elvaston, Illinois on the Toledo, Peoria & Warsaw Railroad. From Elvaston trains ran 12 miles on TP&W tracks into Keokuk.

THE GOULD REGIME AND UNIFICATION

Probably the most notorious individual in railroad history was Jay Gould: a wrecker of railroad finances, a stock manipulator, a schemer and an opportunist extraordinary. However, Gould's grandiose venture to put together a transcontinental railroad achieved one positive result. The Wabash Railway Company and the St. Louis,

The Wabash Railway Employees Hospital on North Broadway Street in Peru, Indiana. Photo taken by M.D. McCarter November 2, 1941. *William Swartz collection*

Branch Lines.

Read Down. **FORREST AND STREATOR.** Read Up.

72. Freight. Ex. Sun.	30. Ex. Sun.	32. Ex. Sun.	Miles.	Table 13	31. Ex. Sun.	33. Ex. Sun.	73. Freight. Ex. Sun.
AM	AM	AM			PM	PM	PM
......	......	11 30	0	Lv......**Chicago**.....Ar.	4 58	......	......
......	......	1 55	93	Ar....**Forrest 8, 9**...Lv.	1 55	......	......
6 30	7 00	2 10	0	Lv....**Forrest 8, 9**...Ar.	10 35	7 25	5 15
6 55	7 10	2 20	6	........Fairbury........	10 25	7 15	4 50
f 7 28	7 28	2 38	11	........Lodemia........	10 07	6 57	f 4 25
7 40	7 33	2 43	13	........McDowell........	10 02	6 52	4 15
8 25	7 43	2 53	17	........Pontiac........	9 52	6 42	3 55
8 55	7 55	3 05	21	........Rowe........	9 40	6 30	3 35
9 27	8 08	3 18	26	........Cornell........	9 27	6 17	3 18
..f...	..f...	..f...	28	...Manhattan Coal Co...	..f...	..f...	..f...
9 45	8 19	3 29	31	........Manville........	9 16	6 06	2 40
10 10	8 35	3 45	37	Ar.....**Streator**....Lv.	9 00	5 50	2 15
AM	AM	PM			AM	PM	PM

BEMENT AND ALTAMONT.

	71. Freight. Ex. Sun.	31. Ex. Sun.	Miles.	Table 14	30. Ex. Sun.	70. Freight. Ex. Sun.	
	AM	PM			PM	PM	
......	......	1 33	0	Lv..Danville 10, 10½, 21 Ar.	12 57	......	......
......	......	2 25	26	...**Sidney 10, 10½, 17**...	12 08	......	......
......	......	3 19	54	Ar.**Bement 8, 9, 10** Lv.	11 19	......	......
......	......	12 55	0	Lv..**Springfield 11**..Ar.	5 35	......	......
......	......	5 00	39	Lv.....**Decatur**....Ar.	1 30	......	......
......	......	5 40	59	Ar.**Bement 8, 9, 10** Lv.	12 50	......	......
......	7 45	5 45	0	Lv.**Bement 8, 9, 10** Ar.	11 05	5 45	......
......	8 00	5 56	4	........Voorhies.....Lv.	10 53	5 20	......
......	8 15	6 06	9	........Hammond........	10 43	5 00	......
......	8 40	6 20	15	........Lovington........	10 28	4 35	......
......	9 00	6 30	19	........Cushman........	10 18	4 15	......
......	10 08	6 40	23	........Sullivan........	10 08	4 00	......
......	10 30	6 55	29	........Bruce........	9 51	f 3 25	......
......	10 55	7 10	35	........Windsor........	9 36	3 10	......
......	11 20	7 25	41	........Strasburg........	9 21	2 50	......
......	f11 35	7 34	44	........Herborn........	9 12	f 2 35	......
......	11 45	7 42	47	........Stewardson........	9 05	2 25	......
......	12 10	7 57	53	........**Shumway**........	8 50	2 05	......
......	f12 30	f 8 12	58	........Blue Point........	f 8 30	1 25	......
......	1 00	8 25	63	Ar....**Altamont**....Lv.	8 20	1 10	......
	PM	PM			AM	PM	

ST. LOUIS AND HANNIBAL.

	51. Ex. Sun.	13. Ex. Sun.	Miles.	Table 15	50. Ex. Sun.	2. Ex. Sun.	
	PM	AM			AM	PM	
......	5 30	8 01	0	Lv.....**St. Louis**....Ar.	11 55	6 30	......
......	5 44	8 17	6	....Delmar Avenue 1....	11 36	6 08	......
......	6 08	8 35	12	........Ferguson 1........	11 10	5 51	......
......	6 33	9 01	23	......**St. Charles 1**......	10 40	5 30	......
......	7 04	9 29	36	........O'Fallon 1........	10 16	......	......
......	7 16	9 40	42	Ar.....**Gilmore 1**....Lv.	9 40	5 01	......
......	7 21	10 00	42	Lv. Gilmore 1 (St.L. & H.) Ar.	9 30	4 20	......
......	7 53	10 34	55	........Moscow........	9 00	3 45	......
......	8 06	10 47	59	........Troy........	8 48	3 30	......
......	f 8 22	11 06	65	........Davis........	f 8 29	3 07	......
......	8 38	11 24	71	........Silex........	8 14	2 50	......
......	8 51	11 44	77	........Whiteside........	8 00	2 28	......
......	8 59	11 57	81	........Eolia........	7 50	2 15	......
......	f 9 18	f12 17	88	........Cyrene........	f 7 32	f 1 55	......
......	9 32	12 35	95	......Bowling Green......	7 20	1 35	......
......	f 9 45	f12 51	101	........McCune........	f 7 05	f 1 04	......
......	10 07	1 16	109	........Frankford........	6 48	12 30	......
......	10 30	1 45	118	........New London........	6 26	12 00	......
......	10 45	2 03	125	........Oakwood........	f 6 10	11 35	......
......	10 55	2 15	128	Ar.**Hannibal 11, 19** Lv.	6 00	11 20	......
	PM	PM			AM	AM	

HELMER AND STROH.

	34. Daily.	36. Daily.	Miles.	Table 16.	33. Daily.	35. Daily.	
	AM	PM			PM	PM	
......	......	12 04	0	Lv......**Chicago**.....Ar.	5 00	......	......
......	8 20	......	0	Lv......**Detroit**......Ar.	......	8 50	......
......	12 10	5 10	0	Lv....**Helmer 12**...Ar.	11 30	4 30	......
......	12 40	5 40	4	Ar.......**Stroh**.......Lv.	11 00	4 00	......
	PM	PM			AM	PM	

REFERENCE MARKS.—† Daily, except Sunday. f Stop on signal.

The time from midnight to noon is shown by LIGHT-FACED figures, and the time from noon to midnight by HEAVY-FACED figures.

Read Down. **SIDNEY AND CHAMPAIGN.** Read Up.

	37. Ex. Sun.	35. Ex. Sun.	33. Ex. Sun.	31. Ex. Sun.	Miles.	Table 17	30. Ex. Sun.	32. Ex. Sun.	34. Ex. Sun.	36. Ex. Sun.	
	PM	PM	PM	AM			AM	AM	PM	PM	
......	6 35	2 30	12 25	10 10	0	Lv.....**Sidney 10**....Ar.	9 10	11 55	2 20	6 25	......
......	f 6 47	f 2 42	f12 37	f10 22	3	........Deer's........	f 8 57	f11 44	f 2 09	f 6 12	......
......	f 6 56	f 2 51	f12 46	f10 31	6	........Mira........	f 8 46	f11 35	f 2 00	f 6 02	......
......	7 06	3 01	12 56	10 41	10	........Urbana........	8 35	11 25	1 50	5 54	......
......	7 15	3 10	1 05	10 50	12	Ar..**Champaign 10**.Lv.	8 00	11 15	1 40	5 45	......
	PM	PM	PM	AM			AM	AM	PM	PM	

ST. LOUIS AND EDWARDSVILLE.

22. Daily.	36. Daily.	26. Daily.	34. Daily.	30. Daily.	Miles.	Table 18	25. Daily.	35. Daily.	29. Daily.	33. Daily.	39. Daily.
AM	PM	AM	PM	AM			AM	PM	PM	PM	PM
......	......	8 30	4 34	11 30	0	Lv......**St. Louis**.....Ar.	10 54	7 30	2 20	......	......
......	......	9 10	5 36	12 17	20	Ar...Edwardsville Junc..Lv.	9 45	6 39	1 27	......	......
7 12	6 42	9 47	5 38	1 29	20	Lv...Edwardsville Junc..Ar.	9 00	6 30	12 06	5 25	9 00
7 17	6 47	9 52	5 43	1 34	22	Ar.. **Edwardsville**..Lv.	8 55	6 25	12 01	5 20	8 55
AM	PM	AM	PM	PM			AM	PM	PM	PM	PM

MAYSVILLE AND PITTSFIELD.

39. Daily.	35. Daily.	33. Daily.	37. Daily.	31. Daily.	Miles.	Table 19	32. Daily.	34. Daily.	38. Daily.	30. Daily.	36. Daily.
PM	PM	AM	PM	AM			AM	PM	PM	AM	PM
......	......	......	5 00	5 00	0	Lv.....**Quincy 11**....Ar.	10 55	4 50	10 40	......	......
......	......	......	5 55	6 00	19	Lv.**Hannibal 11, 15** Ar.	10 00	4 05	9 43	......	......
......	......	......	7 24	7 14	53	Ar...**Maysville 11**..Lv.	8 45	2 38	8 27	......	......
8 35	2 45	8 50	7 35	7 15	53	Lv...**Maysville 11**..Ar.	8 35	2 30	8 20	7 09	7 15
8 50	3 00	9 05	7 50	7 30	59	Ar....**Pittsfield 11**...Lv.	8 20	2 15	8 05	6 54	7 00
PM	PM	AM	PM	AM			AM	PM	PM	AM	PM

ATTICA AND COVINGTON.

			37. Accom. Ex. Sun.	35. Accom. Ex. Sun.	Miles.	Table 20	34. Accom. Ex. Sun.	36. Accom. Ex. Sun.			
			PM	AM			PM	PM			
......	......	......	3 50	8 15	0	Lv..**Attica 10, 10½**..Ar.	12 59	6 00	......	......	......
......	......	......	3 53	8 18	1	........Peacock........	12 56	5 57	......	......	......
......	......	......	4 15	8 40	7	........Fountain........	12 25	5 25	......	......	......
......	......	......	4 30	8 55	11	........Nebeker's........	12 15	5 15	......	......	......
......	......	......	4 45	9 00	12	........Shelby's........	12 10	5 10	......	......	......
......	......	......	4 50	9 15	15	Ar....**Covington**....Lv.	11 59	5 00	......	......	......
			PM	AM			AM	PM			

ALTON AND EDWARDSVILLE.

28. Daily.	32. Daily.	20. Daily.	38. Daily.	24. Daily.	Miles.	Table 21	31. Daily.	45. Daily.	27. Daily.	37. Daily.	23. Daily.
AM	PM	AM	PM	AM			PM	PM	AM	PM	AM
11 15	4 35	6 20	8 20	8 15	0	Lv.......**Alton**.......Ar.	2 20	9 37	10 50	7 25	7 55
11 27	4 47	6 33	8 32	8 27	5	.......Wood River.......	2 08	9 25	10 38	7 13	7 43
f11 30	f 4 50	f 6 37	f 8 35	f 8 30	6	........Hartford........	f 2 05	f 9 22	f10 35	f 7 10	f 7 40
f11 31	f 4 51	f 6 38	f 8 36	f 8 31	7	.......Grassy Lake.......	f 2 04	f 9 21	f10 34	f 7 09	f 7 39
11 35	4 55	6 42	8 40	8 35	9	........Wanda........	2 00	9 17	10 30	7 05	7 35
f11 38	f 4 58	f 6 45	f 8 43	f 8 38	11	........Cotters........	f 1 56	f 9 13	f10 26	f 7 01	f 7 31
11 48	5 08	......	8 53	8 48	15	Ar....Edwardsville 18...Lv.	1 45	......	10 15	6 50	7 20
12 01	5 20	......	8 55	8 55	15	Lv....Edwardsville 18...Ar.	1 34	......	9 52	6 47	7 17
12 06	5 25	6 51	9 00	9 00	17	Ar...Edwardsville Junc...Lv.	1 29	9 05	9 47	6 42	7 12
10. Daily.	**50. Daily.**	**6. Daily.**	**12. Daily.**	**4. Ex. Sun.**		**To Chicago.**	......		**51. Daily.**	**11. Daily.**	**17. Daily.**
12 17	5 36	7 56	10 06	9 10	0	Lv...Edwardsville Junc...Ar.	......	......	9 45	6 39	7 12
1 03	6 40	8 47	11 00	9 55	31	........**Litchfield**........	......	......	8 39	5 48	6 21
1 42	8 00	9 45	12 00	10 33	64	........**Taylorville**........	......	......	7 32	5 03	5 30
2 25	9 00	10 35	12 55	11 20	92	........**Decatur**........	......	......	6 40	4 25	4 40
7 30	......	......	7 17	4 58	265	Ar......**Chicago**.....Lv.	......	......	......	11 30	11 40
		6. Daily.	**2. Daily.**	**4. Daily.**		**To the East.**	**9. Daily.**	**1. Daily.**			
......	......	7 56	9 13	9 10	0	Lv...Edwardsville Junc...Ar.	1 27	8 24	......	......	......
......	......	10 35	11 25	11 10	92	Ar......**Decatur**........	11 20	6 15	......	......	......
......	......	12 57	1 23	1 08	166	........**Danville**........	9 34	4 29	......	......	......
......	......	6 20	5 35	4 46	321	Ar....**Fort Wayne**...Lv.	5 18	12 20	......	......	......
......	......	10 25	8 45	8 15	429	Ar......**Toledo**......Lv.	......	9 00	......	......	......
......	......	......	5 45	......	679	Ar.....**Pittsburg**....Lv.	......	......	......	......	......
......	......	8 15	7 25	6 10	370	Ar... **Montpelier**...Lv.	4 05	11 10	......	......	......
......	......	......	10 00	8 50	467	Ar......**Detroit**......Lv.	1 30	8 20	......	......	......
......	......	......	9 15	8 10	698	Ar......**Toronto**.....Lv.	7 30	......	......	......	......
......	......	......	7 45	† 6 50	1036	Ar.....**Montreal**....Lv.	† 9 05	......	......	......	......
......	......	......	10 10	9 00	467	Lv......**Detroit**......Ar.	2 00	8 10	......	......	......
......	......	......	7 00	5 14	706	Ar......**Buffalo**......Lv.	8 30	2 15	......	......	......
......	......	......	8 00	5 00	....	Ar...New York (West Shore)..Lv.	......	2 00	......	......	......
......	......	......	7 45	......	....	Ar..New York (D. L. & W.)..Lv.	10 00	......	......	......	......
PM	PM	PM	AM	6 55	....	Ar...Boston (B. & M.)..Lv.	AM	12 30	AM	AM	PM

Branch lines from a June, 1908 Wabash public timetable. *Robert Fiedler collection*

Wabash commuter trains between Decatur and Chicago were Nos. 12 and 13. *Paul Slager*

Kansas City & Northern were merged and unified into one continuous line of 715 miles linking Toledo with Kansas City. The Wabash, St. Louis & Pacific Railroad Co., incorporated November 10, 1879, formed the central link in a chain of railroads in the Gould System that also included the Lackawanna, Missouri Pacific, Union Pacific and St. Louis, Iron Mountain & Southern. The 230 mile gap separating Detroit from the Lackawanna at Buffalo would be bridged, but not in Gould's lifetime.

Before the merger, in 1878, the Council Bluffs & St. Louis had been organized to build north of Pattonsburg, Mo., across southwestern Iowa and on into Council Bluffs. Farther east, tracks of the old North Missouri had reached Ottumwa, Iowa. Violating the terms of a traffic-regulating agreement known as the Omaha Pool, Gould rushed completion of Wabash rails into Des Moines and Council Bluffs. The Burlington, reacting with alarm at the invasion of its territory, promptly announced an extension of its line into Kansas City.

By the date of merger, completion of the Council Bluffs line was an accomplished fact; the line was opened October 11, 1879. A rather complicated series of maneuvers brought Gould to Albia, 70 miles from Des Moines. The Ottumwa route was bypassed. Consistent with Gould's policy of extending his lines by utilizing every available mile of existing track and minimizing new construction, he gained control of the Missouri, Iowa & Nebraska Railway and leased it to the Wabash. The MI&N ran west from Keokuk and crossed the Ottumwa line south of Moulton at Glenwood Junction, Mo. It controlled the Centerville, Moravia & Albia Railroad, a short line running between Centerville and Albia. The Des Moines & St. Louis Railroad was organized January 27, 1881, to build from Albia to the state capital.

When Gould acquired the MI&N, the west end of the railroad had reached Van Wert, 95 miles east of Shenandoah on the Wabash's Council Bluffs line. Thus, the MI&N served a twofold purpose in Gould's designs: half the route distance to Des Moines was secured and in addition, only 95 miles of construction was needed to complete the through route between Omaha and the Lake Shore connection at Butler, Indiana. To avoid direct confrontation with the Burlington, Gould compromised and the connecting link, known as the Humeston & Shenandoah Railroad, was built jointly by the Wabash and Burlington in 1882. Having brought the first Wabash passenger train into Des Moines

on November 6, 1882, Gould topped it off by adding the Hannibal & St. Joseph to his System.

Wabash presence in Des Moines was reinforced by the organization in 1884 of the Des Moines Union Railway. A joint enterprise of the Wabash and Milwaukee railroads, the DMU operation served more than 40 miles of industrial and interchange tracks in Des Moines.

On the eastern lines of the Wabash, St. Louis & Pacific, Gould moved toward Chicago from the south by purchasing the Chicago & Paducah Railroad. By 1877, the C&P had completed a 150 mile line running southeast from Streator, Illinois to Strawn, then south to Effingham and Altamont, and crossed the Wabash mainline at the town of Bement. The Bement-Strawn section was incorporated into the Chicago mainline. The Chicago & Strawn Railway was then organized to construct 90 miles north to Chicago & Western Indiana tracks near Chicago. A joint ownership agreement with the C&WI in 1880 gave the Wabash terminal facilities and trackage rights into the City.

Concurrent with the Chicago extension, plans were rushed to obtain an additional lake port and industrial connection at Detroit. Butler, Indiana was 110 miles southwest of the rapidly developing Detroit-Windsor complex where the Grand Trunk Railway channelled an enormous volume of freight traffic down from eastern Canada. Construction was done by the Detroit, Butler & St. Louis Railroad, organized February 11, 1880, and involved mileage in three states, mostly in Michigan. By the end of 1881, track was completed from Butler to Delray, near Detroit, where extensive yards were installed. Until the year 1902 when 26 miles of track was built connecting Butler with New Haven, the Wabash operated what was in effect a double line through northeastern Indiana. Trains bound for Detroit ran over the Eel River Division leaving the mainline at Logansport. Trains destined for Toledo continued on over the old TW&W mainline eastward through Fort Wayne. Trackage rights between Toledo and Detroit over the Lake Shore & Michigan Southern were in effect until 1902.

Development of the Detroit-Butler line into the main east and west traffic route signalled the decline in importance of the Toledo terminal to Wabash operations. After construction of a line between Toledo and Montpelier in 1901, the original line of the old Toledo & Illinois, from Toledo to New Haven, was gradually cut back to a branch line operation.

Troubled times beset the Wabash

Following the organization of the Wabash, St. Louis & Pacific in 1879, Gould brought in 10 small connecting railroads which the Wabash controlled under 50-year leases. Two of the lines, the Toledo, Peoria & Western and the Missouri, Iowa & Nebraska, accounted for more than 300 miles of the Butler-Omaha route. One line, the Indianapolis, Peru & Chicago, ran entirely in Indiana and linked Indianapolis and Michigan City with the Wabash at Peru. The Quincy, Missouri & Pacific connected northern Missouri with the Wabash at Quincy. In Illinois, four of the railroads formed an interconnecting network that linked Peoria with southern Illinois. These included the Cairo & Vincennes; Peoria, Pekin & Jacksonville; and Springfield & Northwestern. The Havana, Rantoul & Eastern and the Des Moines-Northwestern railroads were narrow gauge.

At its zenith in 1884, Gould's Wabash boasted of 3,549 route miles operated and the railroad extended from Omaha to Detroit on the east and from Spirit Lake, Iowa near the Minnesota line south to Cairo on the Ohio River.

By 1884 storm clouds were brewing over Jay Gould's Wabash, St. Louis & Pacific. Overexpanded, overcapitalized, and with juggling of assets to pay dividends, the Wabash System was unable to meet fixed charges. Although the Wabash route across Iowa reduced Omaha-Chicago distance by 100 miles, the line was never brought up to mainline standards. Gould's rate-cutting wars with the Burlington, North Western and Rock Island made profitability impossible. In a lightning turnabout, Gould sold the Hannibal & St. Joseph to the Burlington and leased the Wabash to the St. Louis, Iron Mountain & Southern. In May, 1884 the Wabash found itself without funds to make the required interest payment and defaulted. Unwilling to give up all control of the Wabash, Gould took the unprecedented, and unsuccessful, step of having himself appointed receiver. Probing the subsequent corporate smashup in 1885, the amazed receivers discovered that Gould's only holding was a handful of bonds. A dazed Wabash looked about and began to pick up the pieces. Unification of lines east and west was temporarily set aside. All 50-year leases were cancelled. This had the immediate effect of isolating the Des Moines line at Albia. Fortunately the Wabash still owned track to Ottumwa and arrangements were made for running rights over the Rock Island from Ottumwa to Harvey on the Des Moines line, a distance of 37 miles.

When the crash came and dismemberment began, the Wabash was forced to relinquish control of the 10 leased lines and hand them back to the former owners. Thus, out of a total of 551 locomotives owned by the Wabash in 1881, more than 100, including 10 narrow gauge engines, were acquired in the Gould takeover, and when the leased lines were disposed of in 1885-1888 they took with them their respective locomotives. During the five years of Wabash ownership the engines were renumbered and assigned Wabash numbers, but in the process, the identity of many engines was lost. The resulting enigma has plagued every locomotive historian and researcher who ever delved into the mish-mash of Wabash motive power.

THE YEARS AFTER GOULD

Lines west of St. Louis were reorganized March 8, 1887 under the name Wabash Western Railway. On May 18, 1887 the 143 mile section from Pattonsburg, Mo., to Council Bluffs, still controlled under lease, was reorganized as the Omaha & St. Louis Railway and operated until 1901 with its own locomotives. Lines east of St. Louis were divided into four sections by the state, under the receivership, and included Wabash Eastern of Illinois and Indiana, Toledo Western and the Detroit & State Line Railroad.

Seeking to avert total dissolution of the prostrate railroad and to substantially reunite the lines of 1879, a Purchasing Commission was formed in 1888. Here was no syndicate of

A K-4b No. 2705, a J-1 No. 675 and a B-7 No. 543 at Decatur. *Dick Wallin collection*

powerful financiers. The Commission consisted mainly of concerned individual investors and Wabash shippers whose businesses would rise and fall with the prosperity of the railroad. Believing profitable operation of the Wabash rested with new management, the Commission succeeded with its funding efforts. On May 27, 1889 a second and final unification of all lines east and west of St. Louis was effected by organization of the Wabash Railroad Company. The basic route of the Wabash was now firmly established. A new passenger train, the *Wabash Flyer,* was placed in service between Toledo and Kansas City running on a 23-hour schedule. With nearly 20 years of financial turmoil behind it, an optimistic railroad faced the 1890's that would bring the Columbian Exposition in Chicago and continued expansion of lines to the east.

In the three years ended with 1892, the Wabash took delivery of more than 60 new locomotives which greatly updated its roster of motive power and reversed a trend of the eighties wherein many Civil War era junkers were completely rebuilt.

During the Gould regime traffic interchange had been established with the Grand Trunk Railway between Chicago and Detroit, but by 1890 the volume of business increased to the point where the Wabash constructed its own line from Montpelier, Ohio to Clark (Gary), Indiana, thence by track lease for the remaining few miles into Chicago. However, a community of interest continued to exist between the Wabash and the Grand Trunk Lines into the late 1890's and resulted in Wabash operations taking on an international aspect.

WABASH ENTERS CANADA

The peninsula of Ontario between Windsor and the Niagara frontier forms a convenient, direct and relatively uncongested route between the Detroit and Niagara Rivers. Charles M. Hays, developing genius of the Grand Trunk System, began his career as a clerk in the Wabash Car Accountant's office and rose to become president of the Wabash. When Hays became president of the Grand Trunk, one of his first acts was to secure for the Wabash a joint section or trackage rights agreement giving it operating rights over the Grand Trunk from Windsor, Ontario to the Buffalo gateway at Fort Erie. Interchange track leased from the Erie gave the Wabash access to the city of Buffalo. The city of St. Thomas, roughly equidistant between Detroit and Niagara Falls, was selected as operating headquarters of the Buffalo Division and in March, 1898 Wabash trains commenced running in Canada.

Hays served as president of the Grand Trunk until April, 1912 when his death in the sinking of the liner *Titanic* brought a tragic end to a long railroad career. The agreement made between the Wabash and the Grand Trunk in 1898 remains in effect with successor lines Canadian National Railways and the Norfolk & Western.

Wabash Canadian operations are unique in that no physical connection exists between Detroit and Windsor. Rejecting the tunnel concept employed by the Michigan Central, the Wabash at first moved its cars across the Detroit River on Grand Trunk car ferries, then started its own fleet. Wabash car ferries eventually included the *Detroit, Manitowoc* and *Windsor,* each with the capability of blocking cars aboard and crossing the river in less than 45 minutes. Due to customs regulations which discouraged transfer of locomotives in and out of Canada, most Wabash engines were assigned permanently to the Buffalo Division. After 1920, all locomotive repair work was performed in Canada under contract with Montreal Locomotive Works, and later at shops of the Pere Marquette and Michigan Central in St. Thomas.

In 1898, the Wabash made a serious bid to enter the fast, through passenger train field with the purchase of five Baldwin Atlantics. These engines were soon placed on the Buffalo Division and teamed up with the big 4-4-0 "Greyhound" engines of the D-30 class to handle the newly inaugurated St. Louis to Buffalo *Continental Limited.* The first D-30, No. 651, was built at the Springfield shops under plans of Joshua Barnes, superintendent of motive power, and represented the last attempt by the Wabash to improve upon the American Standard design.

Coincident with the improvement in passenger service, routing changes were made in Indiana. To better utilize division point facilities at Peru, the Wabash built a nine and one half mile line north from Peru to the village of Chili, on the Eel River and 20 miles from Logansport on the Eel River Division. Thereafter, Detroit and St. Louis trains were routed via Peru and Chili. Upon completion of track between Butler and New Haven in 1902, the entire Eel River line was sold to the Pennsylvania and the 9-mile Peru-Chili section was acquired and operated by the Winona Interurban Railroad.

In Iowa, construction of 28 miles of new track in 1899 eliminated the circuitous route over the Rock Island that St. Louis-Des Moines trains had used for 20 years. The Moulton, Albia & Des Moines Railroad was incorporated to build the new line from Moulton to Albia and was then sold to the Wabash.

Success of the Baldwin Atlantics prompted the rapid acquisition of three additional groups of Atlantics in time to handle passenger business for the Louisiana Purchase Exposition at St. Louis and the new trains in the St. Louis and Chicago to Pittsburgh service occasioned by the opening of the Wabash-Pittsburgh Terminal Railway. Wabash train service to Pittsburgh began in 1904 using Wheeling & Lake Erie tracks from Toledo to Pittsburgh Junction, thence 60 miles to Pittsburgh over the Wabash-Pittsburgh Terminal's new line.

A thorough analysis of WPT operations has been made in John Rehor's *The Nickel Plate Story.* Suffice it to say that George Jay Gould, Jay Gould's eldest son, in an effort to revive the transcontinental dream of the eighties, organized the Wabash-Pittsburgh Terminal in 1904. The plan, while different in some respects, recalled the Gould schemes of 1878-1882. George Gould proposed to bring the Wabash to tidewater over the Western Maryland. As before, the Wabash formed the Midwestern link between Pittsburgh and Kansas City, and, as before, the outcome was receivership. Construction costs, largely borne by the Wabash, were astronomical. Much of the WPT's revenue base vanished when U.S. Steel renounced Gould's deal with Carnegie for steel traffic. The lengthy business depression following the panic of 1907 led to Wabash receivership beginning December 26, 1911. The WPT's 60 mile line west of Pittsburgh became the mainline of the Pittsburgh & West Virginia and most of the Terminal's 70 new engines were assigned to the Wheeling & Lake Erie.

The Wabash Railroad Company was sold at foreclosure on July 21, 1915, and with only a minor change in name, the Wabash Railway Company was incorporated on October 22, 1915. At the beginning of World War I the Wabash had only 80 modern locomotives on the roster and a tight motive power budget allowed the acquisition of only 45 new engines in the decade 1913 to 1923. The last new passenger engines the railroad would ever purchase were delivered in 1912. To economically bolster its passenger fleet, the Wabash started rebuilding Rogers 70-inch Prairies into Pacifics in 1916. The design was good and the lightweight J-2's performed well in both passenger and freight service for over 30 years. Twenty-five heavy Brooks Santa Fe's were delivered in the summer of 1917 to help move war time freight, but because of size and other restrictions, their service lives were confined mostly to the East St. Louis to Chicago line.

DECATUR SHOPS

After 1920, locomotive shop facilities were centralized at Decatur, hub of Wabash operations. Abandoned first was the 100-year-old Fort Wayne shop near the downtown area, surrounded by city streets and a General Electric factory complex. A bad fire hastened the closing of Springfield shops and by 1930 only a small amount of repair work was done at Moberly.

In the decade following the War, the phenomenal rise of the automobile industry brought changing traffic patterns to the Wabash and ushered in the Red Ball fast freight era. Concentration of the auto manufacturers in the Detroit and lower Michigan region placed the Wabash in a most strategic position astride the trans-Mississippi freight route; it was the only railroad that could offer direct freight service between the Buffalo gateway and Kansas City. Key trackage in this route was the 70 mile line between Hannibal and Moberly, Mo., former line of the Hannibal & Central Missouri, and operated jointly with the Missouri-Kansas-Texas Railroad since 1894. By 1923 the Wabash was running 90% of the trains and on August 1, 1923 a contract was negotiated with MKT leasing the 70 miles of track for 99 years, with option to purchase at any time during the lease. In 1944 the option was exercised and upon payment of $2,400,000 the Wabash assumed ownership on December 23, 1944.

The trans-Mississippi short line cut 50 miles from the Decatur-St. Louis-Moberly route, bypassed the congested terminals of St. Louis and Chicago and greatly enhanced the Wabash's role as a high speed bridge line between east and west. Balancing the predominantly westward flow of auto traffic, an ever increasing tonnage in perishables was blocked onto the Wabash at Kansas City. Generated in large part by the American Refrigerator Transit Company, one third owned by Wabash, most perishable business was destined for produce terminals in Detroit and Buffalo.

One more client was added to the already impressive list of automobile shippers when in 1926 an off-line connection was secured linking South Bend, Indiana with the town of Pine, eleven miles south on the Montpelier-Chicago line. The Wabash bought controlling interest in a short line bearing the unlikely name of the New Jersey, Indiana & Illinois. Incorporated at South Bend in 1902 and opened in 1905, the NJI&I Railroad was a creation of the Singer Manufacturing Company whose plants were located in New Jersey, Indiana and Illinois. Appropriately enough, the Wabash worked the little line with Mogul-type engines, and besides Singer and Studebaker business, it handled a large volume of interchange traffic.

ANN ARBOR CONTROL

In 1925 the Wabash acquired control of the Ann Arbor Railroad through stock ownership. Although managed from St. Louis, the Ann Arbor's corporate identity was preserved. There was no merger of motive power. Ann Arbor locomotive classes and numbers were changed to conform with those of the Wabash but separate lettering was maintained. The Toledo-based Ann Arbor operated 292 miles of mainline to Frankfort, Michigan on the eastern shore of Lake Michigan and intersected the Wabash at Milan, 37 miles from Detroit. Like the Wabash, the Ann Arbor derived a good percentage of revenue from auto and related industries. Its railroad car ferries plying Lake Michigan constituted a virtual floating bridge across the lake, forming a direct route to the Northwest that bypassed the congested Chicago Terminal. The Ann Arbor's four steamer routes made direct connections with railroads at Manitowoc, Kewaunee and Marinette in Wisconsin and Menominee, Michigan. One steamer route also served Manistique in the Upper Peninsula where the Manistique & Lake Superior Railroad, the Ann Arbor's isolated branch line, ran 38 miles of track north to Doty, site of extensive lumber mills and a connection with the Soo Line.

Preliminary surveys began in January, 1929 on what was to be one of the largest railway engineering projects undertaken in the United States—the replacement and relocation of the Missouri River bridge at St. Charles. Approval of plans for the new bridge was received from the Secretary of War and the Chief of Army Engineers in July, 1930. The bridge was designed to carry safely the 300 ton weight of the new Baldwin locomotives then being delivered and work was started in the summer of 1930 at a site one half mile downstream from the old bridge.

The nationwide plunge into the depths of business depression in 1931 not only halted work on the bridge, but in 1933 the Wabash became the first large railroad forced into receivership. Due in part to the overall involvement of the Army Corps of Engineers in the Missouri bridge project, the Federal Administrator of Public Works, Harold Ickes agreed to Federal financing in the form of a loan in the amount of $2,350,000. With the Wabash contributing $933,000 of its own funds, the Wabash-St. Charles Bridge Company was organized to complete the bridge which was opened for traffic in 1936.

The new bridge was impressive—and it was huge. The main channel span provided a clear opening of 600 feet for river traffic and a minimum clearance of 56 feet above high water. There were five great piers and four truss spans over the river proper, and the bridge was a mile and a half long. Seven miles of new approach track were built above flood plain, shortening route distance three quarters of a mile. In June, 1943 the Wabash purchased the St. Charles Bridge Co. and the Wabash-Hannibal Bridge Co. and assumed 100% ownership of both bridges.

Never burdened by an extensive branch line network, the Wabash ran only about 200 branch miles in 1930. More than 40 miles of this was eliminated with the abandonment of the southern end of the old Chicago & Paducah line. By 1938 track from Effingham north to Sullivan was torn up. Thirty-seven miles of the C&P's north end remain in service as the Streator branch.

PENNSYLVANIA CONTROL

Financial control of the Wabash was acquired by the Pennsylvania Railroad, through its subsidiary, the Pennsylvania Company, in 1928. Control was established through majority ownership of preferred and 99.29% of the common shares, subject to ICC approval, granted in 1932. Pennsylvania control of the Wabash lasted 36 years and came about as a result of the Wabash's financial alliance with the Delaware & Hudson during the abortive railroad consolidation frenzy of the 1920's. The D&H and Wabash jointly bought control of the Lehigh Valley about 1926 in a plan to form a new eastern trunk line system. By 1928 the Pennsylvania, mostly to protect itself, began to take an active interest in the alliance and bought in with the D&H to control the Wabash. The D&H soon withdrew from further participation in the trunk line plan and the Pennsy took over full Wabash control and that of the Lehigh Valley as well. Pennsylvania management and operational control over the Wabash was minimal, and few, if any, outward signs of Philadelphia influence were apparent.

The two railroads jointly operated the *Detroit Arrow,* one of the fastest trains in the country, making the 295 mile Chicago to Detroit run via Fort Wayne in five hours. The *Arrow* featured one of the last mainline assignments of Atlantic type locomotives on American railroads, requiring operating speeds of 90 miles per hour to maintain schedule. Main interchange points for Wabash-Pennsylvania operations were Fort Wayne and Logansport, and a familiar sight during the thirties and forties was the *Broadway,* the *General* and other trains detouring over the Wabash between Fort Wayne and Logansport when Pennsy's mainline was blocked by derailment.

In 1942, at Logansport, could be observed one of the many transportation dramas that unfolded as American railroads geared for all-out war effort. Thousands of tank cars loaded with critically needed oil moved east through Logansport. The old Eel River Railroad line, for many years a Pennsylvania branch, was pressed into mainline service to help move the oil and relieve congestion on the Wabash east end. Wabash K-4's and Pennsy N-2's labored day and night hauling 75 and 100 car blocks of tank cars.

The longest period of receivership in Wabash history drew to a close in 1941 with the approval of a reorganization plan authored by Wabash Treasurer and financial expert A.K. Atkinson who later became president of the company. All properties and assets of the Wabash Railway Company were sold for $31,000,000 on December 1, 1941 and in the final corporate reorganization, effective January 1, 1942, the Wabash Railroad Company took over operations.

DIESELS ARRIVE

Quietly, unobtrusively, diesel power appeared on the Wabash in 1939 and, as on most other railroads, the diesel came humbly, in yard service, almost unnoticed. A General Electric 44-ton steeple cab equipped with side rods was the pioneer diesel assigned to St. Thomas, followed by a steadily increasing stream of Alco, Baldwin and Fairbanks-Morse switchers. Steam's finest hour was yet to

come. World War II set the stage and Wabash steam turned in a magnificent performance. New passenger power and a new wheel type appeared as 3-cylinder K-5's entered the Decatur erecting shop and emerged as Hudsons painted Wabash Blue.

The first diesel road units were delivered in 1946 to the Moberly Division and were placed in passenger pool service with the Union Pacific pulling the *City of St. Louis* and the *City of Kansas City* trains between Denver and St. Louis. Although Decatur was still outshopping 41-year-old switchers with class repairs in late 1948, the steam era had run its course and the end was near. The summer of 1949 saw powerful three unit EMD's taking over manifest assignments and the *Wabash Cannon Ball* and the crack *Banner Blue* received diesels in the fall. By the end of 1953 the Wabash became totally dieselized with one notable exception. Fate—in the form of severe weight restrictions on the Illinois River bridge at Meredosia—decreed that the last stand of steam on the Wabash should occur at the birthplace of the railroad, on the original line of the Northern Cross. Ancient Moguls of 19th Century vintage plied the Bluffs-Keokuk branch for yet another two years until replacement in 1955.

Negotiations between the Norfolk & Western and the Nickel Plate Road began in 1958, and in 1960 the two railroads agreed to merge, with the successor company to be the Norfolk & Western. The Pennsylvania, looking at merger with the NYC and seeking a safe "home" for its Wabash investment, encouraged inclusion of the Wabash in the N&W-NKP merger. For the Wabash, the cost came high—its corporate identity. Stuart Saunders, N&W president, announced that the Wabash had been included in the merger plan and would be leased for 50 years. The proposal was put before the ICC on March 17, 1961. As for the Ann Arbor, the N&W wanted no part of it in the merger and it was pushed off onto the Penn-controlled DT&I. Including the Virginian, the Wabash-Nickel Plate addition brought the N&W route mileage to over 7,400 miles. Pennsylvania Railroad stock holdings in the N&W and the Wabash, the latter now at 99.5%, would be adjusted to a 32.1% interest in the new corporation.

ICC approval of the merger was voted almost unanimously on June 24, 1964, and on Friday, October 16, 1964, the Wabash Railroad, and a name first applied to a railroad and its locomotives 109 years before, was officially relegated to history. —*William Swartz*

No. 660 waits for passengers to load at Wabash, Indiana. *M.D. McCarter*

Chapter 2

Predecessor lines

CAIRO & VINCENNES RAILROAD
Locomotives 1871 to 1887

Organized in 1867 as the Morgan's Improvement Co., the line was completed in 1872. Operated by Wabash, St. Louis & Pacific under lease from 1881 to 1887. Name changed about 1880 to Cairo, Vincennes & Chicago and acquired by the CCC&StL Ry. in 1889.

Orig.	C&V No.	WStL&P No. 1881	1885	Specs.	Builder	New	CV&C No.	CCC&StL No.
				4-4-0 Types				
MI 1	1	540	1540	15x24-61	Baldwin 2389	3/1871	1	
MI 4	2	541	1541	15x24-57	Baldwin 2375	2/1871	2	
MI 5	3	542	1542	15x24-62	Baldwin 2377	2/1871	3	195
MI 6	4	543	1543	15x24-67	Baldwin 2524	7/1871	4	196
MI 7	5	544	1544	16x24-54½	Baldwin 2624	11/1871	5	
	6	545	1545	15x22-62	Grant	1872	6	193
	7	546	1546	15x22-62	Grant	1872	7	194
	8	547	1547	?	Grant	?	8	
P&D 1	9	533	1533	15x24-62	Baldwin 3653	9/1874	9	191
P&D 2	10	534	1534	15x24-62	Baldwin 3654	10/1874	10	192
P&D 3	11	535	1535	15x24-62	Baldwin 3671	12/1874	11	188
P&D 4	12	536	1536	15x24-57	Baldwin 3783	10/1875	12	189
P&D 5	13	537	1537	15x24-57	Baldwin 3950	7/1876	13	190,169
DSW 6	14	538	1538	16x24-63-76400	Baldwin 5007	3/1880	14	400,242,7011
DSW 7	15	539	1539	16x24-63-76400	Baldwin 4943	1/1880	15	401,243,7012
(a)	12	549	1549	16x24-63-76400	Baldwin 4795	9/1879	16	402,7013
	13	550	1550	16x24-63-76400	Baldwin 4793	9/1879	17	403,244
	19	551	1551	17x24-63	Grant	1880	19	405,246,7025
	20	552	1552	17x24-63	Grant	1880	20	406,7010
	21	553	1553	17x24-63	Grant	1880	21	407,7027
	22	554	1554	17x24-63-7600	Grant	1880	22	408
	23	555	1555	17x24-63-7600	Grant	1880	23	409
				17x24-63-81000	?	?	24	410,7067
				4-6-0 Types				
(a)	11	548	1548	16x24-54	Baldwin 3694	2/1875	18	404
				2-6-0 Types				
WStL&P	28			18x24-57	Baldwin 7792	1/1886	25	411,6352
WStL&P	29			18x24-57	Baldwin 7783	1/1886	26	412,6353
WStL&P	27			18x24-57	Baldwin 7789	1/1886	27	413,6354

(a) C&V 2nd 11-12 named *J.S. Morgan* and *A.J. Thomas*

CHAMPAIGN, HAVANA & WESTERN RAILWAY

This railroad was incorporated in February, 1861 as the Monticello Railroad. After reorganization about 1873, the name was changed to Havana, Mason City, Lincoln & Eastern. Leased to Wabash, St. Louis & Pacific in 1880 at which time 130 miles of line was in service from Havana to Champaign, and from White Heath to Decatur. Reorganization as Champaign, Havana & Western took place in 1886, and the line was merged with Illinois Central in 1888.

Orig. No.	CH&W No.	WStL&P No. 1880	1885	Specs.	Builder	New	ICRR No. 1888	ICRR No. 1890
				4-4-0 Types				
IB&W 18	?	400	1400	15x22-60	Rhode Isl. 165	4/1870	424	1469
IB&W 20	?	401	1401	15x22-60	Rhode Isl. 171	4/1870	425	1470
IB&W 32	?	402	1402	15x22-60	Rhode Isl. 372	11/1871	426	1471

CHICAGO & PADUCAH RAILROAD CO.
Locomotives 1872 to 1880

Incorporated March 19, 1872, the Chicago & Paducah acquired on June 15, 1872 lines of the Bloomington & Ohio River RR (35 miles from Bement to Windsor, Illinois) and the Fairbury, Pontiac & NorthWestern Ry. (31 miles from Streator to a point west of Fairbury, Illinois). By 1877 an additional 97 miles of track was constructed between Streator and Altamont-Effingham in the southern part of Illinois. The C&P was sold at foreclosure on April 6, 1880 and merged with Wabash, St. Louis & Pacific in June, 1880.

C&P No.	WStL&P 1880	No. 1885	Specs.	Builder	New	Rebuilt
				4-4-0 Types		
1	192	1192		?	?	1880 to A-3 0-4-2 (a)
2	193	1193	15x24-60-60000	Cooke 935	8/1873	1883 to A-3 0-4-2 (a)
3	194	1194	15x24-60-60000	Cooke 936	8/1873	1882 to A-3 0-4-2 (a)
4	195	1195	16x24-60-60000	Cooke 937	9/1873	1886 to D-22
5	196	1196	16x24-60-60000	Cooke 938	9/1873	
6	197	1197	16x24-60-60000	Cooke 940	9/1873	
7	198	1198	16x24-60-60000	Cooke 941	9/1873	
8	199	1199	16x24-60-60000	Cooke 942	9/1873	

(a) Trailing trucks removed from these engines prior to 1907.

DANVILLE & SOUTHWESTERN RAILROAD
Locomotives 1874 to 1887

Built originally as the Paris & Danville Railroad, the D&SW operated 103 miles of line from Tilton Jct. (Danville) to Lawrenceville, Illinois. Operated by Wabash, St. Louis & Pacific under lease from 1881 to 1887. Merged with Cairo, Vincennes & Chicago in 1888 and acquired by the CCC&StL Ry. in 1889.

Orig.	D&SW No.	WStL&P 1881	No. 1885	Builder	New	CV&C No.	CCC&StL No.
4-4-0 Types: 15x24-62							
P&D 1	1	533	1533	Baldwin 3653	9/1874	9	191 (a)
P&D 2	2	534	1534	Baldwin 3654	10/1874	10	192
P&D 3	3	535	1535	Baldwin 3671	12/1874	11	188
4-4-0 Types: 15x24-57							
P&D 4	4	536	1536	Baldwin 3783	10/1875	12	189
P&D 5	5	537	1537	Baldwin 3950	7/1876	13	190,169
4-4-0 Types: 16x24-63-76400							
	6	538	1538	Baldwin 5007	3/1880	14	400,242,7011
	7	539	1539	Baldwin 4943	1/1880	15	401,243,7012

(a) P&D 1-4 named *Danville, Paris, Marshall, Robinson*

DES MOINES — NORTHWESTERN RAILROAD
Locomotives 1877 to 1887

The three-foot gauge DM-NW was formerly the Des Moines, Adel & Western and ran from Des Moines to Spirit Lake with a branch to Boone. Leased to Wabash, St. Louis & Pacific in 1880. The Wabash organized and financed the St. Louis, Des Moines & Northern Railroad to bring the road from Waukee to Des Moines and build the Boone branch. There were six locomotives on the road when Wabash lost control in 1887.

Orig.	Type	Specs	Builder	New	WStL&P No.
? 1	?		?	?	? (a)
DMA&W 2	2-4-0	8x14	Porter 314	8/1877	?
DMA&W 3	4-4-0	11x18-42½	Pittsburgh 420	4/1880	?
DM-NW 4	4-4-0	12x18-42½	Pittsburgh 434	12/1880	?
DMA&W ?	2-6-0		Cooke 1092	1879	?
?	?		?		?

(a) Construction engine

HAVANA, RANTOUL & EASTERN RAILROAD
Locomotives 1876 to 1887

Organized by Benjamin Gifford of Rantoul, Illinois in January, 1876, as a three-foot railroad to run between LeRoy, Illinois and West Lebanon, Indiana. Original motive power was two locomotives placed in service in 1876. Leased to Wabash, St. Louis & Pacific on May 1, 1880. In October, 1886 the HR&E was sold under bankruptcy and leased to the Illinois Central. On June 3, 1887 it was merged with the IC as the Rantoul RR., and subsequently rebuilt to standard gauge. Disposition of the two Porter engines is unknown, but the two 4-4-0's were kept by the Wabash and rebuilt.

HR&E No.	WStL&P 1880	No. 1885	Specs	Builder	New	Disposition
1	200	1200	9x16	Porter 230	9/1875	?
2	204	1204?	9x16	Porter 235	10/1875	?
4-4-0 Types						
3	203	1203	11x22-44-32000	W.H. Bailey	12/1877	Reb.std.ga.253-
4	205	1205	11x22-44-32000	W.H. Bailey	2/1878	254 D-1 Class

INDIANAPOLIS, PERU & CHICAGO RAILWAY
Locomotives 1856 to 1887

The Indianapolis, Peru & Chicago had its origin in a strap iron railroad chartered in 1846 as the Peru & Indianapolis Rail Road and was built as a 73 mile extension of the Madison & Indianapolis Railroad north to a connection with the Wabash and Erie Canal at Peru. M&I locomotives operated the line until 1856 when the road was closed to replace strap with T rails and the first locomotives were acquired. After six years of receivership the railroad was reorganized as the IP&C Ry. in March, 1864.

The Cincinnati, Peru & Chicago Ry., organized in 1853, completed 28 miles of line between La Porte and Plymouth as part of a projected 88 mile extension north from Peru to Michigan City. After organization of the CP&C in 1856 as the Chicago, Cincinnati & Louisville RR, track was completed into Peru in July, 1869 and Michigan City in April, 1871. In May, 1871 the CC&L was acquired by the IP&C. Wabash, St. Louis & Pacific leased the IP&C in September, 1881 and operated the line until March, 1887 when it was sold to the Lake Erie & Western (later Nickel Plate). During the six years under Gould control, 10 Wabash locomotives were transferred to the Indianapolis Division and were included in the LE&W purchase.

Orig.	IP&C No.	WStL&P 1881	1885	Specs	Builder	New	Rebuilt	LE&W No. '87
0-4-0 Types								
	11	511	1511	14x22 44 50000	Cooke	1869	Peru '77	62
	14	514	1514	14x22 44 50000	Cooke	1870	Peru '81	63 to NYC Lines 4082
	15	515	1515	14x22 44 50000	Cooke	1870		61
4-4-0 Types								
P&I	1-2-				?	?		(a)
P&I	3	503	1503		?	?		(a)
	1	501	1501	16x24 60 69000	Grant	1873		84
	2	502	1502	16x24 61 70000	Pitts. 319	6/1875		79
P&I (b)	4	504	1504	13x22 60	Rogers 1023	6/1862		

LAKE ERIE & WESTERN RAILROAD,
"NATURAL GAS ROUTE"

MISSOURI, IOWA & NEBRASKA RAILROAD
Locomotives 1871 to 1887

Organized in 1869, the MI&N ran northwest from Keokuk to Albia, Iowa. Leased to Wabash, St. Louis & Pacific in 1880.

MI&N No.	WStL&P 1880	No. 1885	Specs.	Builder	New	
				4-4-0 Types		
1	455	1455	17x24-61	Pittsburgh 108	3/1871	
2	456	1456	17x24-61	Pittsburgh 110	5/1871	
3	457	1457		?		
4	458	1458		?		
5	459	1459		?		
6	460	1460		?		
7	461	1461	17x24-63	Cooke 1095	10/1879	
8	462	1462	17x24-63	Cooke 1096	11/1879	
9	463	1463	17x24-63	Cooke 1097	10/1880	
10	464	1464	17x24-63	Cooke 1098	4/1881 to Wab. D-19	

PEORIA, PEKIN & JACKSONVILLE RAILROAD
Locomotives 1864 to 1887

Acquired under lease by the Wabash, St. Louis & Pacific in 1881, the Peoria, Pekin & Jacksonville was incorporated June 11, 1863, and operated 83 miles of line from Peoria to Jacksonville, Illinois. The northern section of the railroad was purchased from the Illinois River Railroad at a foreclosure sale in 1864. During the years under Gould control, the PP&J formed part of the route of Wabash passenger trains between Chicago and Kansas City, via Peoria and Jacksonville. Properties of the PP&J were sold to the Chicago, Peoria & St. Louis Ry. Co. on June 28, 1888. The 40 mile section between Havana and Peoria became part of the Chicago & Illinois Midland Ry. after break up of the CP&StL.

PP&J No.	WStL&P 1881	No. 1885	Specs.	Builder	New	
				0-4-0 Types		
1	483	1483	15x22-48	Rogers 1690	2/1870	
2	484	1484	?	?		ex Chi. & R.I.
3	485	1485	15x22-60	Manchester 729	9/1875	(a)
				4-4-0 Types		
4	486	1486	14x22-60	Rogers 1174	7/1864	
5	487	1487	14x22-60	Rogers 1180	8/1864	
6	488	1488	15x22-60	Portland 124	3/1865	(a)
7	489	1489		?		
8	490	1490	15x24-60	Manchester 96	6/1867	
9	491	1491	16x24-60	Manchester 105	2/1868	
10	492	1492	16x24-60	Manchester 109	9/1868	
11	493	1493	14x22-60	Manchester 108	8/1868	
12	494	1494	16x24-62	Rogers 1672	12/1869	
13	495	1495	16x24-62	Rogers 1673	12/1869	
14	496	1496	16x24-60	Rogers 1936	12/1871	
15	497	1497	16x24-60	Rogers 1941	12/1871	
16	498	1498		?		

(a) #3 named *The Team*, #6 named *J.B. Clark*

QUINCY, MISSOURI & PACIFIC RR.

The QM&P line ran from West Quincy to Trenton, Missouri and was opened in 1879. Leased to Wabash, St. Louis & Pacific in 1880. Wabash records state that four locomotives were returned to the QM&P in 1888, but it is more likely that three were returned as the fourth engine, #410, was kept by the Wabash.

QM&P No.	WStL&P 1880	No. 1885	Specs.	Builder	New	
				4-4-0 Types		
1	407	1407		Manchester 376	8/1871	(a)
2	408	1408		Manchester 377	8/1871	(a)
3	409	1409	15x22-60	Rogers 2049	8/1872	
4	410	1410	16x24-64	Wabash RR	1881 to Wab. D-12	

(a)#1-2 named *Tom Jasper, Henry Root*

TOLEDO, PEORIA & WARSAW RR - TOLEDO, PEORIA & WESTERN RR.
Locomotives 1864 to 1887

Chartered as the Toledo, Peoria & Warsaw Railroad in February, 1863, the mainline ran from Effner, Indiana to Warsaw, Illinois and was opened in 1868. Sold under foreclosure in January, 1880 and reorganized as Toledo, Peoria & Western. In May, 1880 the TP&W was leased to Wabash, St. Louis & Pacific at which time a renumbering took place. The Illinois Railroad and Warehouse report of 1880 showed 44 engines on the TP&W (13 passenger and 31 freight). Wabash control of the TP&W ended in 1887.

Name of Engine	Specs	Builder		New	WStL&P No.
			0-4-0 Types		
Hercules		Rhode Island	390	5/1872	?
46		Rhode Island	677	6/1876	?
			4-4-0 Types		
Jacob Bunn		Portland	113	10/1864	?
John V. Ayer		Portland	114	12/1864	?
Portland	15x22-60	Portland	121	11/1864	?
Rushnell		Rhode Island	36	9/1867	?
La Harpe		Rhode Island	37	10/1867	?
Canton		Rhode Island	38	10/1867	?
Z. Secor		Rhode Island	70	9/1868	?
Judge Clifford	16x24-60	Portland	135	9/1868	?
J.B. Brown	16x24-60	Portland	139	9/1868	?
Falmouth	16x24-60	Portland	134	10/1868	?
Peoria		Rhode Island	72	10/1868	?
J.P. Drake		Rhode Island	73	10/1868	?
Ajax		Rhode Island	74	10/1868	?
Portland		Portland	140	11/1868	?
Gen. Merritt		Rhode Island	85	12/1868	?
Ft. Madison		Rhode Island	86	12/1868	?
Burlington		Rhode Island	88	12/1868	?
City of Nebraska		Rhode Island	89	1/1869	?
Ft. Kearney		Rhode Island	90	1/1869	?
Farrington		Rhode Island	91	1/1869	?
Bloomfield		Rhode Island	92	1/1869	?
Centreville		Rhode Island	93	2/1869	?
California		Rhode Island	94	2/1869	?

Oregon	Rhode Island	95	2/1869	?
Conjden	Rhode Island	98	4/1869	?
Mt. Aure	Rhode Island	104	4/1869	?
Beauford	Rhode Island	106	5/1869	?
Clarador	Rhode Island	107	5/1869	?

WABASH, ST. LOUIS & PACIFIC RAILROAD
Number Assignments 1880-1887

WStL&P 1880	Numbers 1885	Railroad
1-191	1001-1191	Wabash Ry.
201-202	1201-1202	Wabash Ry.
192-199	1192-1199	Chicago & Paducah
200,	1200,	Havana, Rantoul & Eastern
203-205	1203-1205	Havana, Rantoul & Eastern
207-213	1207-1213	Eel River Railroad
215-323	1215-1323	St. Louis, Kansas City & Northern
324-367	1324-1367	New for WStL&P
370-375	1370-1375	Secondhand from IB&W
376-399	1376-1399	New for WStL&P
400-402	1400-1402	Champaign, Havana & Western
403-406	1403-1406	Detroit, Butler & St. Louis
407-410	1407-1410	Quincy, Missouri & Pacific
411-454	1411-1454	Toledo, Peoria & Western
455-464	1455-1464	Missouri, Iowa & Nebraska
465-482	1465-1482	New for WStL&P
483-497	1483-1497	Peoria, Pekin & Jacksonville
499-532	1499-1532	Indianapolis, Peru & Chicago
533-555	1533-1555	Cairo, Vincennes & Chicago
556-576	1556-1576	New for WStL&P
577-584	1577-1584	StLKC&N and IB&W

Toledo, Wabash & Western
Locomotive Numbering

The Toledo, Wabash & Western numbers were kept through the reorganizations of 1877, 1879 and 1887 until final disposition.

In 1884-1885 all engines had "1000" added to their number, apparently as part of a numbering scheme to include all of the thousands of engines in the Gould System. The "1000" was dropped on most engines after 1887. This should not be confused with a renumbering done after 1898 where "1000" was added to the three-digit number of Buffalo Division engines. This was done to simplify train dispatching between Windsor and Niagara Falls.

Guide to Predecessor Lines of the Wabash

ANN ARBOR reorganized September 1896 from TOLEDO, ANN ARBOR & NORTH MICHIGAN. Control acquired May 1925 by Wabash.

BOONE COUNTY & JEFFERSON CITY opened October 1868, leased then to NORTH MISSOURI. Reorganized October 1873 as BOONE COUNTY & BOONEVILLE, leased in May 1875 to ST. LOUIS, KANSAS CITY & NORTHERN.

BRUNSWICK & CHILLICOTHE Organized 1870, completed 1872, operated by NORTH MISSOURI. Leased August 1878 to ST. LOUIS, KANSAS CITY & NORTHERN.

CAIRO & VINCENNES organized 1867 as MORGAN'S IMPROVEMENT CO. Leased 1881 to WABASH, ST. LOUIS & PACIFIC. Lease terminated April 1885, became part of CAIRO, VINCENNES & CHICAGO, later part of C.C.C. & St.L.

CHARITON & RANDOLPH chartered 1858, sold 1864 to NORTH MISSOURI.

CHICAGO & PADUCAH incorporated March 1872, opened 1877. Sold April 1880 to WABASH, ST. LOUIS & PACIFIC.

COUNCIL BLUFFS & ST. LOUIS incorporated September 1878, leased to ST. LOUIS, KANSAS CITY & NORTHERN, then to WABASH, ST. LOUIS & PACIFIC. Reorganized May 1887 as OMAHA & ST. LOUIS.

DANVILLE & SOUTHWESTERN organized 1881 to acquire PARIS & DANVILLE. Leased 1881 to WABASH, ST. LOUIS & PACIFIC. Lease terminated April 1885, became part of CAIRO, VINCENNES & CHICAGO, later part of C.C.C. & St.L.

DECATUR & EAST ST. LOUIS organized February 1867, completed 1870. Sold to the TOLEDO, WABASH & WESTERN.

DES MOINES, ADEL & WESTERN (3' gauge) reorganized October 1880 from DES MOINES & NORTH WESTERN. Leased 1880 to WABASH, ST. LOUIS & PACIFIC, but lease terminated 1887. Changed to standard gauge and sold December 1891 to DES MOINES, NORTHERN & WESTERN, later to C.M. & St.P.

DETROIT, BUTLER & ST. LOUIS incorporated February 1880, merged September 1881 into the WABASH, ST. LOUIS & PACIFIC.

DETROIT, EEL RIVER & ILLINOIS organized 1871, opened 1872. Leased 1877 to Wabash. Merged 1879 into WABASH, ST. LOUIS & PACIFIC. Sold June 1901 to PENNSYLVANIA as LOGANSPORT & TOLEDO.

FRANKFORT & SOUTHEASTERN acquired 1892 by TOLEDO, ANN ARBOR & NORTH MICHIGAN.

GREAT WESTERN OF ILLINOIS organized February 1853 to acquire SANGAMON & MORGAN. Merged June 1865 with QUINCY & TOLEDO, the TOLEDO & WABASH, and ILLINOIS & SOUTHERN IOWA to form the TOLEDO, WABASH & WESTERN.

HAVANA, MASON CITY, LINCOLN & EASTERN organized 1872, leased 1880 to WABASH, ST. LOUIS & PACIFIC. Reorganized 1886 as CHAMPAIGN, HAVANA & WESTERN. Merged 1888 into ILLINOIS CENTRAL.

HAVANA, RANTOUL & EASTERN (3' gauge) chartered April 1873, opened 1881 and leased to WABASH, ST. LOUIS & PACIFIC. Leased October 1886 to ILLINOIS CENTRAL.

HUMESTON & SHENANDOAH built 1882 jointly by the WStL&P and CB&Q. Merged May 1896 into CHICAGO, BURLINGTON & QUINCY.

INDIANAPOLIS, PERU & CHICAGO leased September 1881 to WABASH, ST. LOUIS & PACIFIC. Sold November 1886 to LAKE ERIE & WESTERN (part of N.Y.C., later N.Y.C. & St.L.)

ILLINOIS & SOUTHERN IOWA organized February 1857, merged June 1865 with GREAT WESTERN, the TOLEDO & WABASH, and QUINCY & TOLEDO to form TOLEDO, WABASH & WESTERN.

LAFAYETTE, BLOOMINGTON & MISSISSIPPI leased June 1871 to TOLEDO, WABASH & WESTERN. Lease cancelled 1876. Acquired 1879 by LAKE ERIE & WESTERN (part of N.Y.C.).

LAKE ERIE & FORT WAYNE formerly FORT WAYNE ROLLING MILL RR. Control acquired by WABASH about 1929.

LAKE ERIE, WABASH & ST. LOUIS incorporated August 1852, merged June 1856 with TOLEDO & ILLINOIS to form (first) TOLEDO, WABASH & WESTERN.

MANISTIQUE & LAKE SUPERIOR reorganized August 1909 from MANISTIQUE & NORTHERN. Control acquired by ANN ARBOR in April 1911.

MANISTIQUE & NORTHERN reorganized July 1908 from MANISTIQUE, MARQUETTE & NORTHERN. Reorganized August 1909 as MANISTIQUE & LAKE SUPERIOR.

MANISTIQUE & NORTH WESTERN reorganized about 1902 to MANISTIQUE, MARQUETTE & NORTHERN.

MANISTIQUE, MARQUETTE & NORTHERN reorganized about 1902 from MANISTIQUE & NORTH WESTERN. Reorganized July 1908 to MANISTIQUE & NORTHERN.

MISSOURI, IOWA & NEBRASKA organized 1868, leased 1880 to WABASH, ST. LOUIS & PACIFIC. Reorganized 1887 as KEOKUK & WESTERN, later part of C.B.&Q.

NEW JERSEY, INDIANA & ILLINOIS incorporated October 1902, opened 1905. Control acquired about 1926 by WABASH.

NORTHERN CROSS opened November 1838. Renamed April 1847 to SANGAMON & MORGAN.

NORTH MISSOURI (5'6" gauge until 1867) incorporated March 1851, reorganized January 1872 as ST. LOUIS, KANSAS CITY & NORTHERN.

OMAHA & ST. LOUIS reorganized May 1887 from COUNCIL BLUFFS & ST. LOUIS. Sold October 1901 to WABASH.

PARIS & DANVILLE organized 1874. Changed 1881 to DANVILLE & SOUTHWESTERN.

PEKIN, LINCOLN & DECATUR leased November 1871 to TOLEDO, WABASH & WESTERN, but lease cancelled 1876. Later acquired by ILLINOIS CENTRAL.

PEORIA, PEKIN & JACKSONVILLE incorporated June 1863. Leased 1881 to WABASH, ST. LOUIS & PACIFIC. Sold June 1888 to CHICAGO, PEORIA & ST. LOUIS.

QUINCY & TOLEDO incorporated January 1857, merged June 1865 with GREAT WESTERN, the TOLEDO & WABASH, and ILLINOIS & SOUTHERN IOWA to form TOLEDO, WABASH & WESTERN.

QUINCY, MISSOURI & PACIFIC opened 1879, leased 1880 to WABASH, ST. LOUIS & PACIFIC. Lease terminated August 1885. Reorganized 1888 as QUINCY, OMAHA & KANSAS CITY.

ST. LOUIS & CEDAR RAPIDS incorporated October 1865, reorganized 1874 as ST. LOUIS, OTTUMWA & CEDAR RAPIDS, which was leased October 1875 to ST. LOUIS, KANSAS CITY & NORTHERN. Consolidated November 1879 into WABASH, ST. LOUIS & PACIFIC.

ST. LOUIS, COUNCIL BLUFFS & OMAHA organized October 1870, completed 1871, when leased to NORTH MISSOURI.

ST. LOUIS, KANSAS CITY & NORTHERN reorganized January 1872 from NORTH MISSOURI. Merged November 1879 with WABASH RY. to form WABASH, ST. LOUIS & PACIFIC.

SANGAMON & MORGAN renamed April 1847 from NORTHERN CROSS. Renamed February 1853 to GREAT WESTERN OF ILLINOIS.

SPRINGFIELD & NORTHWESTERN incorporated May 1878. Leased 1880 to WABASH, ST. LOUIS & PACIFIC, but lease terminated, and sold June 1888 to CHICAGO, PEORIA & ST.L.

TOLEDO & ILLINOIS incorporated April 1853, merged June 1856 with LAKE ERIE, WABASH & ST. LOUIS to form TOLEDO, WABASH & WESTERN.

TOLEDO & WABASH reorganized October 1858 from (first) TOLEDO, WABASH & WESTERN. Consolidated June 1865 with GREAT WESTERN, the ILLINOIS & SOUTHERN IOWA, and QUINCY & TOLEDO to form (second) TOLEDO, WABASH & WESTERN.

TOLEDO, ANN ARBOR & GRAND TRUNK opened August 1881, consolidated June 1884 into TOLEDO, ANN ARBOR & NORTH MICHIGAN, which was reorganized 1895 as ANN ARBOR.

TOLEDO, PEORIA & WARSAW organized 1863, opened 1868. Reorganized January 1880 as TOLEDO, PEORIA & WESTERN, which was leased May 1880 to WABASH, ST. LOUIS & PACIFIC. Lease terminated June 1885.

TOLEDO, WABASH & WESTERN R.R. formed June 1856 as merger of LAKE ERIE, WABASH & ST. LOUIS and TOLEDO &

ILLINOIS. Reorganized October 1858 as TOLEDO & WABASH.

TOLEDO, WABASH & WESTERN RY. formed June 1865 as consolidation of GREAT WESTERN, the ILLINOIS & SOUTHERN IOWA, the QUINCY & TOLEDO, and TOLEDO & WABASH. Reorganized January 1877 as WABASH RY.

WABASH RY. reorganized January 1877 from TOLEDO, WABASH & WESTERN RY. Merged November 1879 with ST. LOUIS, KANSAS CITY & NORTHERN to form WABASH, ST. LOUIS & PACIFIC.

WABASH, ST. LOUIS & PACIFIC formed November 1879 from consolidation of StLKC&N and the WABASH RY. Reorganized March 1887 as WABASH WESTERN and the WABASH R.R. Both later merged.

WABASH R.R.* incorp. May 1889 to acquire part of WABASH, ST. LOUIS & PACIFIC. Later acquired WABASH WESTERN. Acquired October 1964 by NORFOLK & WESTERN.

WABASH WESTERN formed March 1887 to acquire part of WABASH, ST. LOUIS & PACIFIC. Later acquired by WABASH R.R.

*Poor's Manual 1888 lists Wabash Ry. as an operating Company.

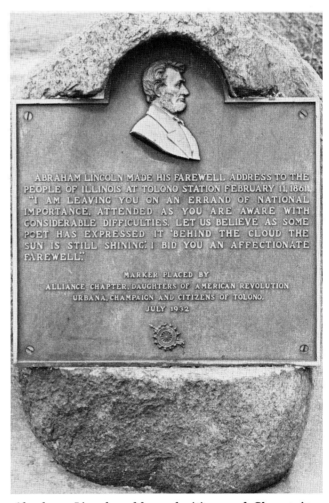

Abraham Lincoln addressed citizens of Champaign County in 1861 at the Wabash-Illinois Central station. This historical marker is located at the station. *Don Heimburger*

Chapter 3

The Wabash Railroad
A solid reputation in rail transportation

The Wabash merged into the Norfolk and Western Railway system on October 16, 1964. The merger added a modern, well equipped and well operated railroad to the N&W's expanding system. This chapter will describe Wabash operations in its final years as an independently operated railroad, specifically the years 1960-1964.

The Wabash physical plant during this period was in first class condition. Wabash management had traditionally prided itself on well maintained track, and all of the major Wabash lines had general speed limits of 79 m.p.h. for passenger trains and 60 m.p.h. for freight trains.

Lines between St. Louis and Moberly, Missouri; Hannibal, Missouri and Jacksonville, Illinois; Gibson City, Illinois and Chicago; and Logansport, Indiana and Ft. Wayne were generally single track with automatic block signals operated under timetable and train order rules. Between Hannibal and Kansas City; Jacksonville and Decatur; Bement and Logansport; Bement and Gibson City and Ft.

Wayne and Adrian, Michigan, traffic control system rules applied on railroad that was generally single track.

The lines from St. Louis to Bement and Adrian to Detroit were double track with automatic block signals. The balance of the lines in the United States were operated under "non-automatic block" rules, which is a version of a manual block system.

Wabash passenger service was unexcelled in its territory. The St. Louis to Los Angeles *City of St. Louis,* operated via the Union Pacific west of Kansas City, was a fine transcontinental streamliner, with dome cars, full diner, lounge car and through reclining seat coaches and sleepers to Denver, Los Angeles and Oakland. The stainless steel *Blue Bird,* operating between St. Louis and Chicago, also carried dome coaches and a parlor car, snack car for coach passengers, and one of the best diners in the nation.

Other Wabash passenger trains in the early 1960's were the *City of Kansas City,* a daylight round trip between St. Louis and Kansas City, the *Banner Blue,* which ran the other half of the two train daily service between St. Louis

Eastbound at 81st Street, Chicago, 4-8-2 in March, 1945. *Paul Eilenberger, collection of Harold Stirton*

and Chicago, and the *Wabash Cannon Ball* and *Detroit Limited* operating between St. Louis and Detroit. The *Wabash Cannon Ball* made the run in daylight hours, while the *Detroit Limited* ran overnight and carried a Pullman cafe-lounge and roomette/bedroom sleeper as well as deluxe coaches. A coach train ran overnight between St. Louis and Council Bluffs, Iowa, also handling freight cars between Berkeley, Missouri, Moberly and Council Bluffs.

The late 1950's had seen the demise of overnight trains between St. Louis and Kansas City, St. Louis and Chicago, and St. Louis and Des Moines. The Ft. Wayne to Toledo connection to the *Detroit Limited* had also disappeared during this period. While Wabash passenger traffic suffered during the post-war period, the Wabash never downgraded passenger trains or made attempts to discourage traffic. The service operated was first class in all respects to the end.

The Wabash in the early 1960's had four operating road divisions with headquarters at Moberly, Missouri; Decatur, Illinois; Montpelier, Ohio; and St. Thomas, Ontario. In addition, there were terminal divisions located at Kansas City, St. Louis, Chicago, Detroit and Buffalo. To describe Wabash operations during this closing period of its history as an independent road, let's take a look at each of the operating divisions.

KANSAS CITY TERMINAL

Kansas City was a major interchange location, and the Wabash yards at North Kansas City usually originated five through road trains daily, two for St. Louis and three for Decatur. The largest interchange roads were the Union Pacific and the Santa Fe, but interchange with at least a dozen other lines was important, too.

The Kansas City Ford assembly plant was located on the Wabash at Birmingham, and as many as four daily switch runs were operated from North Kansas City to serve Ford. The double track line between Kansas City and Birmingham was joint with the CB&Q, with the Burlington controlling the operation. This frequently caused conflicts between the two roads over priority attached to freight trains.

All Wabash passenger trains stopped at Union Station operated by the Kansas City Terminal Railroad Co., of which Wabash was one of the owners. Wabash transfer crews delivering cars to other lines used Kansas City Terminal tracks, and foreign line crews delivering to North Kansas City yard also utilized the Kansas City Terminal.

Wabash passenger trains, with the exception of the eastward *City of Kansas City*, operated over the joint Milwaukee Road-Rock Island trackage from Birmingham to Air Line Jct. (passing over the new Harry Truman Bridge in the process), the Kansas City Southern from Air Line Jct. to Sheffield, and the Kansas City Terminal Sheffield to Union Station, thereby bypassing the freight operation at North Kansas City. The eastward *City of Kansas City* used Kansas City Terminal trackage Union Station to the Hannibal Bridge across the Missouri River, thence joint Wabash-CB&Q trackage to Birmingham to permit straight through operation at Union Station, which eliminated the need to turn the train at Kansas City.

MOBERLY DIVISION

Through freight operations on the Moberly Division were normally five trains in each direction daily between Moberly and Kansas City, two each way daily between Moberly and St. Louis, three each way between Moberly and Hannibal (enroute to or coming from Decatur), one

Three freights at Decatur, Sept. 11, 1955. *Dick Wallin*

31

At Bement, Illinois, June 27, 1948. *M.D. McCarter*

each way daily between Moberly and Des Moines and tri-weekly service between Moberly and Council Bluffs. Through cars to and from Council Bluffs were handled on St. Louis-Council Bluffs passenger trains 211 and 214.

Branch line crews operated between Columbia and Centralia, Missouri, and between Moulton and Ottumwa, Iowa. The Columbia Branch crew made three round trips daily with a mixed train, connecting to mainline passenger trains at Centralia. The Ottumwa Branch crew served John Deere and Morell Packing companies at Ottumwa.

The Wabash entered Des Moines over the tracks of the Des Moines Union Railway Co., which it owned equally with the Milwaukee Road. The Des Moines Union switched Wabash and Milwaukee trains, served industries at Des Moines and interchanged with the other Des Moines railroads at the Iowa Transfer yard.

ST. LOUIS TERMINAL

Wabash passenger trains all originated and terminated at St. Louis Union Station, operated by the Terminal Railroad

Association of St. Louis. The Wabash also maintained its own station located north of Forest Park on the west side of St. Louis at Delmar Boulevard. Delmar Station was immensely popular, as it was located close to many of St. Louis' good residential neighborhoods and Washington University, thereby saving a trip downtown for Wabash patrons.

Wabash passenger trains to and from Chicago and Detroit used the Terminal Railroad Association "West Belt" line around the north side of St. Louis to allow them to make the Delmar Station stop, and they crossed the Mississippi via the Terminal Railroad Association's Merchants Bridge.

Through sleepers for Kansas City and Chicago were parked at Delmar Station for occupancy at 9:00 p.m., and were picked up after midnight by the overnight trains for these destinations. This service ended in 1960, with the last trip of *The Midnight* for Chicago.

Freight operations in St. Louis were centered around Luther Yard (in north St. Louis) and Brooklyn Yard (on the Illinois side). The Wabash also maintained small yards at Ewing Avenue, St. Louis (for interchange with the Frisco and Missouri Pacific) and at St. Louis Avenue (the St. Louis Produce Terminal). An extensive operation was based at Berkeley in north St. Louis County serving the Ford assembly plant and a large number of industries. Normally six switch runs operated daily to serve the Berkeley industrial complex and to operate between Berkeley and Luther and between Berkeley and Ewing Avenue.

Freight interchange operations on the St. Louis side were mostly via the Terminal Railroad Association, and on the east side were mostly via the Terminal Railroad Association or the Alton & Southern. The Wabash owned and operated a huge freight house at East St. Louis, which was used by Acme Fast Freight as a transloading facility for less-than-carload freight. This freight house could hold more than 100 40-foot box cars simultaneously, and inbound and outbound cars received expedited service.

The Acme freight house was switched at 6:00 p.m., and a switch crew handling about 40 cars would depart shortly thereafter for Luther Yard, stopping at Brooklyn to pick up

Tracks of stored 2900's at Decatur, April 24, 1954. *William Swartz, collection of M.D. McCarter*

Looking east at Decatur's Wabash yards. *Collection of Dale Doud*

A GP-9 handles a local through Jacksonville, Illinois in 1964. *J. David Ingles, collection of Louis Marre*

hot Ford loads and using Terminal Railroad Association trackage across the Merchants Bridge. These cars connected to train SK-1, which departed at 8:30 p.m. for Kansas City. SK-1 arrived at Kansas City at about 4:30 a.m. the next day, and blocks of cars were delivered to the Union Pacific and Santa Fe for their early morning trains to the West Coast.

The Alton & Southern interchange was at Mitchell, Illinois. Decatur to Brooklyn Yard trains set out cars for the Alton & Southern, and eastward cars were handled from Mitchell to Brooklyn by yard engine for incorporation in Decatur-bound trains.

DECATUR DIVISION

The operating heart of the Wabash was Decatur Yard, and system car and locomotive shops were at that location. Trains from and to St. Louis, Kansas City, Chicago and Detroit were classified at Decatur and cars made fast connections to outbound trains.

The Decatur car and locomotive shops did all heavy repairs for the system and handled inspections of all road locomotives. Rip tracks and enginehouses elsewhere on the system were restricted to performing only running maintenance, except motive power assigned to the St. Thomas Division received heavy maintenance at Ft. Erie, Ontario. These shops were well equipped, and were known for quality work.

Through freight operations on the Decatur Division nor-

mally were three trains in each direction daily between Decatur and Tilton, Illinois (to or from Peru), two trains each way daily between Decatur and Chicago, three trains daily each way between Decatur and St. Louis, and three trains daily each way between Decatur and Hannibal (to and from Moberly).

Decatur Division branch locals covered the Streator Branch from Forrest and the Champaign Branch from Tilton.

CHICAGO TERMINAL

The major yard of the Chicago Terminal was Landers, which was located on Chicago's southwest side. A subsidiary yard at 47th Street served the Acme freight house there and some interchange transfers.

The Wabash was an owner of the Belt Railway of Chicago, and transfers to BRC's Clearing Yard, not far from Landers, handled much of the Wabash's Chicago interchange traffic.

Dearborn Station was the Chicago home of the *Blue Bird*, the *Banner Blue* and the *Orland Park* local. Dearborn Station was operated by the Chicago & Western Indiana Railroad, which also operated a network of trackage on Chicago's southeast side. The Wabash was an owner of the C&WI along with the Erie-Lackawanna, Chicago & Eastern Illinois, Monon and Grand Trunk Western. The Santa Fe was a tenant at Dearborn Station. Needless to say, Dearborn Station ranked at the top of America's great stations during the passenger train era.

The Orland Park local was the Wabash's only commuter train. This train once operated between Decatur and Chicago, and was scheduled to arrive at Chicago in the morning and depart in late afternoon to allow people from Decatur and points enroute to spend the day on business in Chicago. The train was handling few passengers except in Chicago suburban territory when the Decatur to Orland Park portion was eliminated in the early 1960's. For a long time after the change, the train was deadheaded to Decatur each Friday night, returning from Decatur in the early morning hours on Monday, for the convenience of the crew (most of whom were Decatur residents) and to bring the engine and cars in for servicing.

MONTPELIER DIVISION

The Montpelier Division extended from Tilton, Illinois to Detroit and from Chicago to Toledo. Yards were located at Tilton (Danville), Lafayette, Peru, Ft. Wayne, Montpelier, Toledo and Adrian, Michigan. Dispatcher's offices were at Montpelier and Peru.

Though freight operations normally consisted of two trains daily each way between Montpelier and Chicago, three pairs of trains daily between Montpelier and Tilton (to and from Decatur), four pairs of trains daily between Montpelier and Detroit, a daily Toledo to Montpelier turn, and two daily Montpelier to Delta, Ohio turns. The Delta turns handled mostly Ford auto parts connecting from the Detroit, Toledo & Ironton enroute to Ford's midwestern and western assembly plants.

Local freights operating from Toledo and Ft. Wayne served the Toledo to Ft. Wayne line, which had important industries at Defiance, Woodburn and Napoleon. A major interchange with the Wabash-owned Ann Arbor Railroad was at Milan, Michigan. Other major interchanges were at Logansport, Indiana (PRR) and Huntington, Indiana (Erie-Lackawanna).

Wabash's yard operations at Toledo were important, and the road served the Anderson and Cargill elevators in the suburb of Maumee. These elevators were Toledo's largest, and the Wabash shuttled grain from them to load in vessels at Maumee River docks in Toledo in open top hopper cars. Important interchange operations at Toledo were with the NYC, PRR, Nickel Plate, Chesapeake & Ohio and Toledo Terminal.

Two Wabash subsidiaries were managed by the Montpelier Division—the Lake Erie & Ft. Wayne at Ft. Wayne and the New Jersey, Indiana & Illinois at South Bend. Each of these lines had one locomotive and operated under nonstandard labor agreements. The NJI&I connected with the Wabash at Pine, Indiana, about 10 miles south of South Bend.

The author served as an operating officer at Montpelier during part of the time covered in this chapter. Frank C. Flynn was division superintendent, and had been in that position for more than 20 years. Flynn was a strong manager and was particularly interested in the training of his younger officers. Flynn is remembered by a legion of operating officers, now scattered far and wide, as an exemplary executive and great railroad man. It is such people that made the Wabash the great railroad it was.

DETROIT TERMINAL

Wabash yards in Detroit were at Oakwood and the Boat Yard. Oakwood was the main terminal for road trains and had a large automobile loading facility devoted to Chrysler traffic. Transfer crews operated to the Boat Yard, where car ferries operating across the Detroit River were loaded and unloaded.

There were three car ferries in the Wabash fleet including the *Detroit,* the *Windsor* and the *Manitowoc.* The later two vessels were larger than the *Detroit,* and accordingly the *Detroit* generally was used only one shift per day unless volume dictated additional service. The two larger vessels handled about 28 40-foot cars, but the advent of longer cars, particularly 85-foot automobile parts and 89-foot automobile rack cars, severely cut effective handling ability on the car ferries.

The slips at the Boat Yard would accommodate two vessels simultaneously, and single slip docks at the joint Wabash-Canadian National yard at Windsor and at the Canadian Pacific yard at Windsor served the opposite ends of the run. It generally took 25 minutes to traverse the river, and then over an hour to unload and reload the vessel. The operation was cumbersome, especially during bad weather and during periods of high volume. The author remembers being called to service at Detroit during the middle of a particularly bad winter when over 500 cars were backlogged for movement across the river.

The car ferries were self-contained and equipped with fore and aft propellers. They carried radar equipment, and could navigate reasonably well under conditions of pea-soup fog and heavy ice. They needed all the help they could get, as their mission was to cross at right angles the world's heaviest trafficed waterway with lake vessels, foreign flag ships and hoards of pleasure boats passing in a never-ending parade.

ST. THOMAS DIVISION

This Canadian-based outpost of the Wabash system was headquartered at St. Thomas, Ontario, midway between

A 4-8-2 M-1 stirs the quiet setting at Pine, Indiana on October 26, 1947. *Harry Zillmer, collection of M.D. McCarter*

Detroit and Buffalo. The trackage was owned by the Canadian National, with Wabash having a long-term lease for its operation. The Wabash operated its own through freight trains, with all yard engines and local freight trains on the joint line being manned by the CN but handling the business of both companies.

Normal Wabash operations between Windsor and Buffalo were three trains in each direction daily. Trains changed crews at St. Thomas. The line was double track between Windsor and Glencoe, with the balance being single track. There were no block signals, but CN passenger trains using joint line trackage between Windsor and Glencoe on their run to Toronto operated at 80 m.p.h.

Motive power used by the Wabash between Windsor and Buffalo was built by General Motors of Canada at London, Ontario. It never was intermixed with power used west of Detroit.

The Wabash also had operating rights over the line to Niagara Falls, but discontinued its separate operation to the Falls after transferrring its Lehigh Valley and New York Central interchange to Buffalo in 1960. At the same time, the Wabash discontinued use of CN's Fort Erie Yard for interchange with the DL&W, Erie and Pennsylvania and moved across the river to become a tenant of the Delaware, Lackawanna & Western at East Buffalo.

BUFFALO TERMINAL

As described above, beginning in 1960, Wabash trains began crossing the Niagara River at Fort Erie and using DL&W tracks to DL&W's East Buffalo Yard. Soon after making this change, the DL&W merged with the Erie and became known as the Erie-Lackawanna Railway Co. The EL then proceeded to rebuild the East Buffalo Yard, and the resulting modern hump yard was named Bison Yard. The Wabash remained a tenant at Bison.

The Wabash maintained a small office at Bison Yard, housing a superintendent, assistant trainmaster and agent and their staff. Yard clerical personnel also were Wabash people, but all other operating personnel worked for the EL. All switch crews and mechanical personnel were EL people. Wabash road crews from St. Thomas manned trains entering and leaving the yard, but the EL performed all switching and interchange operations with the NYC, PRR, LV and South Buffalo Railway. The SB was a major source of Wabash traffic, as the Ford stamping plant was located on that line.

The greatest strength of the Wabash was its geography, linking major gateway cities such as Kansas City and Buffalo without passing through congested intermediate terminals. The Wabash was the only major line operating in both official Eastern and Western territories, and belonged to the rate bureaus in both territories. These advantages, good service, and a strong sales effort produced a good traffic base for the Wabash.

The automobile industry was far and away the most important source of Wabash traffic, with Ford accounting for about 25% of system revenues and Chrysler (which shipped only set-up automobiles on the Wabash) accounted for nearly 15%. Other major sources of traffic were grain, freight forwarder traffic and transcontinental perishable and lumber traffic.

For many years Wabash's traffic department was headed by John M. Barrett, vice president. Barrett was well known in national traffic circles and was a super salesman. He deserves much credit for the Wabash's success in its last years. He created a truly customer-oriented organization,

Wabash No. 2524, a 2-10-2, crosses Lake Decatur, on October 20, 1938. *Dick Wallin collection*

which was reflected in all aspects of the road's service, rate making and industrial development activities. Significantly, Barrett had been brought up in passenger traffic, which he headed before assuming system freight and passenger responsibilities.

The Wabash was operated as a fast, good service bridge route. Quality transportation, freight or passenger, was always its goal. That it survived in healthy condition to

play an important role in the strongest merger of the period is a tribute to Wabash people of all ranks.

Today, the Wabash is gone, but those who were associated with it will always remember the pride of its people that made it a fine railroad. *—E.A. Burkhardt*

E.A. Burkhardt was assistant to the General Manager of the Wabash from 1960 until it merged. He has also worked for the Great Northern, Rock Island, Santa Fe, New York Central, and Norfolk & Western. Currently he is vice president of transportation for the Chicago & NorthWestern.

Nos. 2253, a 2-8-2, and No. 1680, a 4-6-2 J-2, at Caledonia, Ontario on June 20, 1950. *Richard Ganger*

Chapter 4

Early Wabash steam locomotives 1867-1921

LEFT. Toledo, Wabash & Western No. 116 was built by the TW&W. The railroad was formed in June of 1856. No. 116 was photographed in Springfield, Illinois in 1867. *Joseph Lavelle, William Swartz collection*

RIGHT. Wabash No. 37 was photographed at Ft. Wayne in 1911. *George Sittig, collection of William Swartz*

BELOW. 0-4-2 A-3 Class steamer near Attica, Indiana was company-built in 1885. A few years later, she and her crew stop for a picture. *Collection of M.D. McCarter*

ABOVE. 4-4-0 No. 69 was a clean-boilered machine with a huge head-light, tall stack and large bell and domes. *B.R. Wood, collection of William Swartz*

RIGHT. We're at Peru, Indiana on August 19, 1912 as this sweet little 2-6-0 plys the rails. *Max Miller, collection of William Swartz*

BELOW. No. 148 was a Schenectady-built 4-4-0 of 1869 acquired by the Toledo & Western. *S.R. Wood, collection of Bill Swartz*

1900's Wabash train over "Noiseless Bridge" at Monticello, Illinois. *Collection of Robert Fiedler*

LEFT. No. 299, originally No. 90 of the D-17 Class, was acquired by the St. Louis, Kansas City & Northern. *George Sittig, collection of William Swartz*

BELOW. Ex-Wabash, St. Louis & Pacific No. 381 is a Class H-1 built by Rogers in 1881. Photo was taken at Decatur in 1882. *S.R. Wood, collection of William Swartz*

The year is 1912, a year after Wabash receivership and a couple of years before foreclosure. In 1915, the Wabash *Railroad* Company was changed to the Wabash *Railway* Company. The 4-4-0 Class D-29 Rhode Island-built steamer is at Toledo, Ohio. *C.E. Fisher, collection of William Swartz*

TOP. It's hustle and bustle at Chicago's Englewood Station in 1921 as No. 442 brings another train in. *Collection of William Swartz.* ABOVE. The year is 1899 and the place is St. Thomas, Ontario. Apparently the folks are celebrating *something. George Sittig, collection of William Swartz*

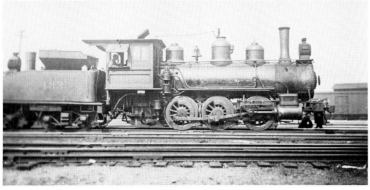

ABOVE. B-2 0-6-0 No. 433 is at Toledo, Ohio in 1912. She was built by Rhode Island in 1892. *C.E. Fisher, collection of William Swartz*

RIGHT. With a full load of coal in the tender, No. 477, a 4-6-0, steams up with a train at Ft. Wayne in 1911. The Ten-Wheeler was constructed in 1881 by Rhode Island and scrapped in 1916.

BELOW. This 4-4-0 is Wabash, St. Louis & Pacific No. 485. *George Sittig, collection of William Swartz*

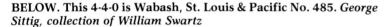

ABOVE. No. 566 is in Toledo in 1912; apparently the crew member coming down from the cab is wiping his brow. *George Sittig, collection of William Swartz*

LEFT. Stored Class D-30 Rhode-Island 1899-built 4-4-0 rests next to stored No. 657 which was built by Baldwin. *Photo by D.W. Youngmeyer, collection of Ross Grenard*

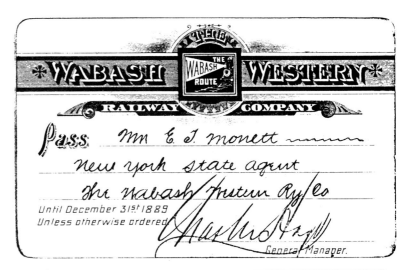

WABASH ★ *WESTERN* ★

THE WABASH ROUTE

RAILWAY COMPANY

Pass Mr E. T. Monett ~~~~~

New York state agent

The Wabash Western Ry Co

Until December 31st 1889
Unless otherwise ordered

Genera' Manager.

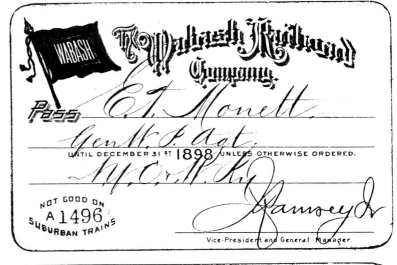

WABASH

The Wabash Railroad Company

Pass E.T. Monett

Gen'l W.P. Agt

UNTIL DECEMBER 31ST 1898 UNLESS OTHERWISE ORDERED.

N.Y.O. & W. Ry.

Ramsey Jr

NOT GOOD ON
A 1496
SUBURBAN TRAINS

Vice-President and General Manager.

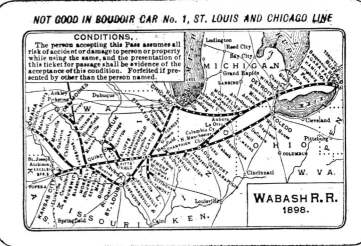

NOT GOOD IN BOUDOIR CAR No. 1, ST. LOUIS AND CHICAGO LINE

CONDITIONS.
The person accepting this Pass assumes all risk of accident or damage to person or property while using the same, and the presentation of this ticket for passage shall be evidence of the acceptance of this condition. Forfeited if presented by other than the person named.

WABASH R.R.
1898.

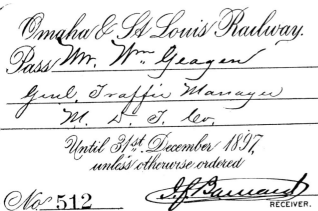

Omaha & St Louis Railway.
Pass Mr. Wm Geagen
Genl. Traffic Manager
O. & St. L. Co.
Until 31st December 1897,
unless otherwise ordered

No. 512

RECEIVER.

Wabash, St. Louis and Pacific Ry.

Pass W. Gragan

Gen. East'rn Agt. W.S.T.Co.

Until December 31st 1884 unless otherwise ordered.

Robt. Andrews

No. 1680.

Gen'l Supt.

Chapter 5

Wabash steam switchers

It's probably a hot day in pre-war St. Louis, as anyone who's ever been in St. Louis in the summer will tell you: the roof trap door is open. *R.J. Foster, collection of C.T. Felstead*

LEFT. Another B-6 0-6-0 made by Baldwin in June of 1904; this one is at Decatur on August 20, 1939. *C.T. Felstead collection*

It's almost hard to believe, once you've studied the two photos, that the engine is the same in both. The Wabash shop crews appreciably changed the appearance of No. 544 between 1914 and 1944. The Baldwin-built B-7 switcher had a robust crew in 1914! The 1944 photo was taken by William Swartz. *Photos from M.D. McCarter collection*

This 0-6-0 switcher is from a class that included Nos. 525 to 566, eight of which were from the Wabash-Pittsburgh Terminal. C.E. Winters took the photo in North Kansas City, Missouri on September 30, 1949. *C.T. Felstead collection*

No. 553 is a Wabash-Pittsburgh Terminal locomotive (No. 2213). You can see that the numbers had been changed on the tender. The locomotive is at Decatur in 1948. *William Swartz, collection of M.D. McCarter*

BELOW. No. 555 at St. Louis, in 1947. *R.J. Foster, collection of C.T. Felstead*

LEFT. This is No. 548 in 1948 at St. Louis. This locomotive was scrapped two years later. *R.J. Foster, collection of C.T. Felstead*

The second to the last engine in the B-7 Class, No. 565 is steamed up at Decatur in September of 1949. *P. Stringham, collection of John Nixon*

In June of 1948, No. 562 chuffs around the Decatur yards. *William Swartz, collection of M.D. McCarter*

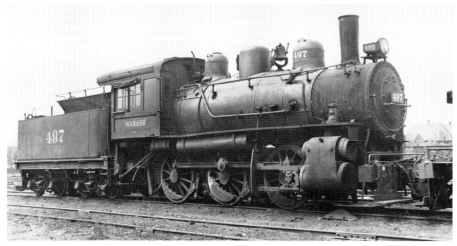

No. 497 0-6-0 of the B-8 Class at Decatur before the war. *R.J. Foster, collection of C.T. Felstead*

BELOW. The 0-8-0 Class C-1's consisted of Nos. 1501 and 1502, both rebuilt from I-2's (2-8-0's). This picture was taken just after it had been outshopped in December of 1946. *M.D. McCarter* BOTTOM. No. 1502 in Decatur before the war. *R.J. Foster, collection of C.T. Felstead*

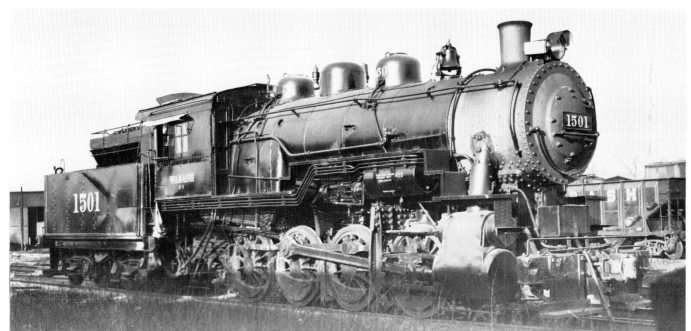

RIGHT. A Class C-3 0-8-0 at Council Bluffs in 1923. *Richard Ganger*

BELOW. This 0-8-0 is a handsome machine. June 1, 1952 at Springfield, Ill. *W.A. Peters, C.T. Felstead collection*

ABOVE. Sitting peacefully in Detroit on March 6, 1937 is this Class C-4. *Richard Ganger* LEFT. No. 1556 is assigned a transfer run. Taken at 21st Street in Chicago, September 28, 1946. *Paul Slager, collection of William Raia*

"Follow the Flag"
WABASH

Chapter 6

Steam
locomotives

4-4-0's through 4-6-4 Class P

FAR LEFT. The date is July 17, 1939 at Decatur and 4-4-0 Class D-30 No. 653 is simmering in the sun. The locomotive was built by Rhode Island in 1899. *Richard Ganger*

LEFT. Here's No. 653 again, this time in Chicago. *L.G. Issac*

BELOW. Last number in the series of D-30's, No. 659 was a Baldwin-built machine of 1899. It was scrapped in 1933, the same year this photo was taken. *R.J. Foster, collection of C.T. Felstead*

'T. ABOVE. No. 657 is a handsome Baldwin as she poses in Chicago on July 29, 1933. Notice the crewman's bag ngside the front trucks of the tender. It might be that No. 657 will be called out soon on a run. *R.J. Foster, collection of* . *Felstead* LEFT. It's 1929 in Chicago and the year before the Pennsylvania acquired the Wabash. *M.D. McCarter collec-*

Use the Wabash Triangle Service!

When you travel between Detroit and St. Louis, visit Chicago at no additional rail fare. Wabash tickets between Detroit and St. Louis are honored via Chicago in either direction. So, you can stop over in all three cities at the cost of a round trip between Detroit and St. Louis.

You can make your Wabash Triangle Trip by starting at either Detroit or St. Louis. You can go via Chicago either going or returning . . . or both ways. And there's no hurry about completing the "triangle." Your Wabash ticket is good for 90 days.

From September 26, 1948 Wabash timetable

Brooks made the E-3's for the Wabash in 1903. No. 619 was a beautiful example of them. *S. Davies, collection of C.T. Felstead*

It's 1938, only a year from arrival of the first diesel on the Wabash, howbeit only a yard engine. No. 621 seems unconcerned in July of 1938 as it prepares for another journey. *Robert Morgan, collection of Louis Marre*

WABASH RAILROAD CO.

AGENT'S STUB.

54 RIDE COMMUTATION TICKET.

SOLD TO

M *T. A. Pashle*

GOOD BETWEEN

Palos Park

AND

Chicago

................................Miles.

Issued *July 8* 190

Expires *Aug 8* 190

Rate per mile   Amount

.... $ *7.80*

No. 2635   Form C. 109.

Agent's stub from 1902. *Collection of Robert Fiedler*

BELOW. E-4 No. 606 was a Baldwin product of 1904; it was scrapped in 1947. *J.O. Riley, collection of C.T. Felstead*

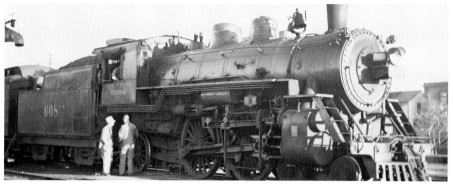

No. 608 is in Peru, Indiana on November 2, 1940 leading a string of varnish. Crew members chat beneath the cab while waiting at the station. *M.D. McCarter*

RIGHT. Here's No. 608 in December of 1937 at Chicago, looking proud and full of pep. *P. Eilenberger, collection of C.T. Felstead*

BELOW. This Schnectady-built E-5 reveals its Ann Arbor heritage above the "Wabash" stencilling on the cab with the initials "A.A" Photo was taken before the war. *C.T. Felstead collection*

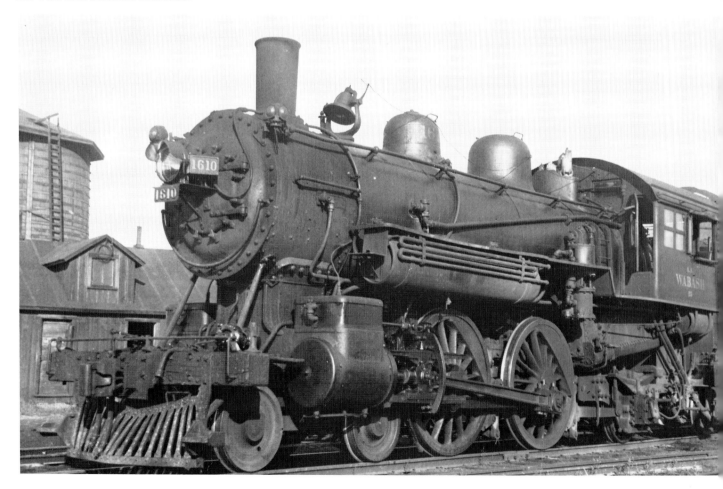

Form 78.

CHICAGO & PADUCAH R. R.

Report of STOCK KILLED *on Section* No. _September 12th_ 1877

Date Struck _September 12_

How much Injured _a little Injured_

Name of Owner _Fredrick Coole_

Kind of Stock _1 Steer_

Age _1 year old_

Whether Fence or not _not fenced_

Condition of Fence _No fence_

By what Train _No 1 going South_

On Curved or Straight Track _strait track_

Foreman's Valuation _not praised_

Appraisers' Valuation _not praised_

Names of Appraisers _not unny_

How disposed of _liveing yet_

REMARKS.

This citer is and likely to come rite but he want the damage paid as the stock got killed on him lately would & fence what he want fenced

Pat Keenan _____ *Foreman.*

N. B.—One of these Reports must be filled out and forwarded to the Superintendent's Office whenever any Stock is struck. All Stock killed in Towns or on Public Crossings, must be reported with full particulars.

The Wabash 2-6-0's of the F-4 Class were sporty looking locomotives as this picture of No. 569 attests. This engine was scrapped as late as 1955. *R.J. Foster, C.T. Felstead collection*

ABOVE. Just two years before being sold to the Museum of Transport in St. Louis, No. 573 works at Bluffs, Ill. *E. Lindquist, C.T. Felstead collection* RIGHT. No. 573 at Bluffs in 1948. *William Swartz, M.D. McCarter collection*

56

Equipped for the winter white stuff, No. 571 displays a snowplow at Bluffs, Ill. *W. Krawier, collection of C.T. Felstead*

WABASH RAILWAY COMPANY No. 252569

TREASURER ST. LOUIS, MO., FEBRUARY 1ST, 1917. $ 0 01

PAY TO THE ORDER OF *L. Arland*

Only One Cent ————— DOLLARS,

IN PAYMENT FOR WAGES JANUARY 16TH TO 31ST, INCLUSIVE, 1917.

PAYABLE AT
THIRD NATIONAL BANK, OR
STATE NATIONAL BANK
ST. LOUIS, MO.

NOT VALID IF DRAWN FOR MORE THAN TWO HUNDRED AND FIFTY DOLLARS

PAYMASTER

Old Santa Rides Wabash Train

DANVILLE, Ill., Dec. 26.—Santa Claus, who plays many roles, rode in a side-door pullman attired as a railway switchman on a special train consisting of yard engine, box car and caboose.

The train ran from Danville to nine Indiana towns on the forty-six-mile stretch of track between this city and Lafayette in a dire Christmas emergency, when it was seen that the last mail train on the Wabash Railway for points East was not going to have enough room for the Christmas mail that had accumulated here because of the storm.

There was to be a box car full of Christmas letters and presents left over. Night Yardmaster Lew Arland saw the predicament and having a houseful of kiddies of his own realized what a tough break a lot of other kiddies were going to get. There wasn't a road engine or a crew here to handle the train, so a switching crew was hastily pressed into service and the trip began.

A large sized box car was packed to the rafters with mail that could not be handled by the regular mail service. The crew with Arland in charge was from midnight until nearly daylight getting the presents to the various towns.

Both items, collection of William Arland

57

No. 573 now rests at the Museum of Transport in St. Louis. It is a Rhode Island-built product of 1899. Both photos taken in the summer of 1981. *Don Heimburger*

Collection of William Arland

THE WABASH RAILROAD CO.

F. A. Delano, W. K. Bixby, E. B. Pryor, Receivers

Office of General Superintendent

St. Louis, Mo., April 25, 1912.

Schedule for Yardmen

(Except Chicago Switching District)

Effective May 1, 1912

The following rates of pay, rules and regulations, apply to yardmen in the yard designated:

ARTICLE I.

(a) Rates of pay per hour:

	Day Foremen	Night Foremen	Day Helper	Night Helper
St. Louis	38c	40c	35c	37c
East St. Louis	38c	40c	35c	37c
Kansas City	38c	40c	35c	37c
Council Bluffs	38c	40c	35c	37c
Detroit	37c	39c	34c	36c
Toledo	37c	39c	34c	36c
Fort Wayne	37c	39c	34c	36c
Danville	37c	39c	34c	36c
Tilton	37c	39c	34c	36c
Decatur	37c	39c	34c	36c
Forrest	37c	39c	34c	36c
Springfield	37c	39c	34c	36c
Moberly	37c	39c	34c	36c
Stanberry	37c	39c	34c	36c
Peru	36c	38c	33c	35c
Montpelier	36c	38c	33c	35c
Lafayette	36c	38c	33c	35c
Quincy	36c	38c	33c	35c
Adrian	36c	......	33c	......
Streator	36c	......	33c	......

RIGHT. No. 756 renumbered to 576 is a Richmond locomotive which was scrapped in the late years, 1955. This is at Decatur in 1954. *Harry Zillmer, collection of M.D. McCarter*

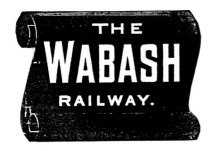

LEFT. It's spring, 1949, and in several months powerful three-unit diesels start taking over manifest assignments on the Wabash. No. 587 is at Decatur with a peeling stack and a smokebox. *Max Miller*

BELOW. Class F-7 No. 803 scurries a freight train down the Wabash tracks sometime in the early 1930's. *M.D. McCarter collection*

ABOVE. This F-6 rebuilt to an F-7 was transferred to the NJI&I. It's shown here at South Bend, Indiana in June of 1937. *Lamar Kelly, collection of M.D. McCarter*

LEFT. No. 826 in pre-war times. *R.J. Foster, collection of C.T. Felstead*
BELOW. Champaign, Illinois on July 26, 1937 finds No. 828 parked on a siding. *Lamar Kelly, M.D. McCarter collection*

No. 834 and No. 850 are both of the Class F-6, but the first is a Richmond engine, the latter a Baldwin locomotive. No. 834 was photographed nearly head on in August of 1939 at Streator, Illinois by Paul Slager. *William Raia collection* The No. 850 was photographed at Bement, Illinois on February 13, 1938. *M.D. McCarter collection*

BELOW. No. 1890 (originally No. 890) was photographed 45 years ago in St. Thomas, Ontario by Richard Ganger. This old picture shows the engine being stored.

The Wabash Prairies were sleek locomotives of the G-1 Class. No. 2014 built in 1906 idles near the water spout in Chicago before the war. *R.J. Foster, collection of C.T. Felstead*

LEFT. No. 2068 passes over someone else's tracks on a winter day. Note the three Wabash box cars behind the engine. *M.D. McCarter collection*

BELOW. 1907-built 2-6-2 looks in good condition at Decatur 31 years after being made by Rogers. It will be retired in 12 more years. *I.W. Oaks, C.T. Felstead collection*

ABOVE. No. 2075 and able crew bring a freight train up to the yard throat for a long journey; note full tender of coal. *M.D. McCarter collection*

One of the 2-6-2's that received new frames was this one, No. 2087. Richard Ganger took this photo on July 4, 1946 in North Kansas City.

From rear cover, 1955
Through your Wabash window.

...a ride on the

WABASH "Blue Bird"

Your Blue Bird "Sleepy Hollow" seat is the most restful ever built! All coach and Pullman passengers can enjoy Dome seats as well—no extra charge!

The Blue Bird's beautiful Observation-Parlor Car offers reserved chairs or a private drawing room. Deep-cushioned Dome and lounge seats at no extra cost.

THE NEW
WABASH
ST. LOUIS - CHICAGO
ROUTE

The only road that furnishes passenger service to and from the west and north end residence districts of St. Louis.

SEVEN PASSENGER STATIONS

FOUR IN ST. LOUIS: UNION STATION — DELMAR AVE. STATION
VANDEVENTER AVE. STATION — FLORISSANT AVE. STATION

THREE IN CHICAGO: ENGLEWOOD (63d St.) — FORTY-SEVENTH STREET STATION
DEARBORN STATION

EIGHT FAST TRAINS EVERY DAY

FOUR VIA VANDEVENTER, DELMAR, FLORISSANT AVENUES

St. Louis to Chicago		Chicago to St. Louis	
Lv. Union Station....	1 30PM 9 17PM	Lv. Dearborn Station 12 04PM	9 17PM
Lv. Vandeventer Ave.	1 38PM 9 23PM	Lv. Forty-seventh St. 12 14PM	9 27PM
Lv. Delmar Avenue..	1 45PM 9 32PM	Lv. Englewood (63d St.) 12 19PM	9 32PM
Lv. Florissant Ave...	2 00PM 9 47PM	Ar. Florissant Ave...	7 35PM 6 43AM
Ar. Englewood (63d St.)	9 14PM 6 44AM	Ar. Delmar Ave....	7 35PM 6 43AM
Ar. Forty-seventh St.	9 19PM 6 49AM	Ar. Vandeventer Ave.	7 42PM 6 50AM
Ar. Dearborn Station	9 32PM 7 00AM	Ar. Union Station...	7 57PM 7 05AM

FOUR VIA MERCHANTS BRIDGE AND ELEVATED

St. Louis to Chicago		Chicago to St. Louis	
Lv. St. Louis.........	8 30AM 11 32PM	Lv. Chicago.........	9 00AM 11 43PM
Lv. Washington Ave..		Lv. Forty-seventh St.	9 10AM 11 55PM
Lv. Granite City......	8 55AM 11 58PM	Lv. Englewood......	9 15AM 12 01AM
Ar. Englewood.......	4 43PM 7 43AM	Ar. Granite City.....	5 17PM 7 22AM
Ar. Forty-seventh St.	4 48PM 7 48AM	Ar. Washington Ave.	5 30PM 7 42AM
Ar. Chicago.........	4 55PM 7 59AM	Ar. St. Louis........	5 40PM 7 53AM

ST. LOUIS TICKET OFFICES

City Office, Eighth and Olive Streets
Union Station — Vandeventer Ave. — Delmar Ave.

CHICAGO TICKET OFFICES

City Office, 68 West Adams Street
Auditorium Annex — Palmer House
Dearborn Station — Forty-seventh Street
Sixty-third Street (Englewood)

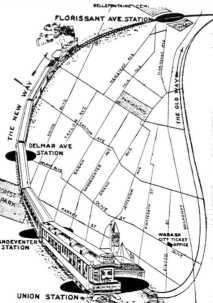

From October/November, 1911 Wabash Timetable

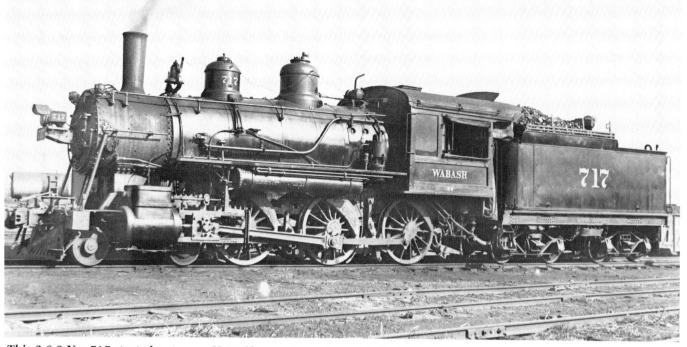

This 2-6-0 No. 717 started out as an H-10 Class and was later rebuilt into an H-9 Class locomotive. The engine was produced by Richmond in 1898. *R.J. Foster, collection of C.T. Felstead*

From June 18, 1939 Timetable

No. 642, a Baldwin Class H-12, at Ft. Wayne, Indiana on July 16, 1933. *R.J. Foster, C.T. Felstead collection*

The Moulton, Iowa depot needed moving, so why not by train? Ex-Omaha & St. Louis No. 600, now No. 257, does the honors. *Collection of William Swartz*

 WABASH ROAD OF THE MEN WHO MOVE THE GOODS

The I-2 Class of 2-8-0's were purchased from the DT&I in 1910; this one is at Decatur on October 23, 1950. *P.H. Stringham, collection of C.T. Felstead*

RIGHT. No. 2155 at Moberly, Missouri in May of 1949. *Charles Winters, collection of Louis Marre* BELOW. No. 2160 shows signs of use. *M.D. McCarter collection* BOTTOM. No. 2160 is running northbound at Streator, Illinois on November 30, 1946. *Paul Slager, collection of Harold Stirton*

RIGHT. An ex-Wheeling & Lake Erie engine, No. 2304, sports a short stack. Photo was taken before WWII in North Kansas City. *R.J. Foster, collection of C.T. Felstead*

No. 2313 I-3 with a wood caboose at Landers Yard in Chicago in June of 1937. *M.D. McCarter collection*

This is at 51st Street in Chicago in the spring of 1937; No. 2324 I-3 steams up. *M.D. McCarter collection*

Ex-Wheeling & Lake Erie I-3 is at Decatur in November of 1939. *Collection of John Nixon*

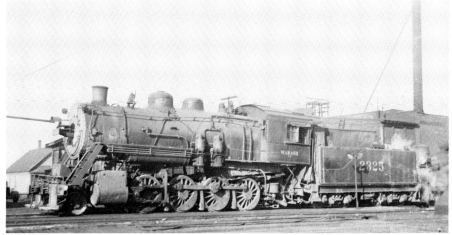

ABOVE. Christmas is only twenty days away in 1949 as two Wabash locomotives—No. 660 4-6-2 and a 4-8-4 pound the rails through Peru, Indiana. *M.D. McCarter*

ABOVE, RIGHT. No. 662 leads Train #4 between St. Louis and Detroit approaching Lafayette, Indiana. Photographer W.D. Edson recalls, "She was whistling continuously for one grade crossing after another" on that day in September, 1946.

RIGHT. No. 662 J-1 Class strolls into camera range for her protrait in Chicago on August 19, 1947. *Frank Smarz, collection of C.T. Felstead*

From 1939 Wabash Timetable

In February of 1912 Richmond produced the No. 663, and on April 17, 1948 Charles Winters photograped her. In 1953 she was scrapped. *Louis Marre collection*

The engineer on this passenger train looks content to have nearly 37,000 pounds of tractive effort at his command from No. 664, a J-1 4-6-2 passing Fort Street in Chicago. Date: March 23, 1947. *Louis Marre*

Clerestory passenger cars all, this Wabash flyer is an invitation to revisit the past. John Krause took this photo of No. 665 in September of 1948. *John Nixon collection*

From August, 1888 Timetable. *John Keller collection*

THE RECLINING CHAIR CAR.—These elegant cars are furnished with Reclining Arm Chairs, which can, with a touch, be transformed into comfortable couches, at any angle desired, with pillow and cushions complete. The Chair Cars are perfectly ventilated, and heated equally in every part during cold weather by hot-air furnaces; the windows are very large, and protected by elegant cloth hangings; rich Brussels carpets cover the floor, and the walls and ceilings are decorated and finished in the most artistic manner. They are provided with smoking and toilet rooms for the accommodation of passengers, and are run upon all the principal lines operated by this company. On the GREAT WABASH ROUTE between Toledo and St. Louis, Detroit and St. Louis, Chicago and St. Louis, Chicago and Kansas City, and Decatur and Keokuk, seats in these elegant cars are FREE to holders of first-class tickets, and they are attached to both day and night trains.

No. 666 sports clean safety stripes on the sides of the running boards in July of 1948 in North Kansas City. *Charles Winters, collection of Louis Marre*

J-1 Class No. 668 passes the Wabash Baking Company plant in Wabash, Indiana, filling the air with a few smells of its own. Date is June 23, 1934. *M.D. McCarter*

LEFT. No. 671 is a Baldwin-built J-1 of 1912. It's in Chicago on November 11, 1940. *Louis Marre*

BELOW. No. 671 leads a string of varnish over Wabash rails in this painting-like photo from the collection of Dale Doud.

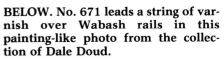

RIGHT. No. 672 in 1946. *Charles Winters, Louis Marre collection*

BELOW. C.T. Felstead was on Wabash property in Chicago on August 16, 1947 to take this photo.

BELOW. With bell in a horizontal position, No. 675 comes out swinging. *Richard Ganger*

The J-2 Class featured a bit more tractive effort than the J-1, but the drivers were smaller on the J-2's. No. 1677 is at Simcoe, Ontario on October 16, 1950. *Photo by J. Bowie, collection of C.T. Felstead*

No. 1677 a few years earlier in March of 1939 at Buffalo. The "sport" stripes are still visible in this photo. *Joseph Brauner, collection of Louis Marre*

With an old wooden water tank as a background, No. 1681 stands proud as she takes on water at Simcoe, Ontario on October 16, 1950. Drivers are 70″, boiler pressure is 215 pounds. *J. Bowie, collection of C.T. Felstead*

J-2 No. 684 plys the rails in 1948 with a three-car train of varnish. *Photo by John Krause, collection of John Nixon*

Long, sleek and in a word—fancy—J-2 No. 685 shows her beauty at Decatur on July 17, 1938. Note the tall Wabash shop chimney behind the tender. *Lamar Kelly, collection of M.D. McCarter*

The J-2's were rebuilt by the Wabash shops from 2-6-2's. Here, No. 692 sits at Ft. Wayne, Indiana on July 18, 1948. *M.D. McCarter*

Two years before it saw the torch, No. 694 with striping legible, was doing the honors in Chicago. Date: 9-4-48. Photographer: C.T. Felstead

No. 696 was rebuilt from a 2-6-2 in 1917 by the Wabash. She sits this winter day of 1948 in Decatur. *M.D. McCarter*

Last of the class, this J-2 gets a turn on the table at Moberly, Missouri on June 30, 1948. *William Swartz photo, collection of M.D. McCarter*

The K-2 Class 2-8-2's included Nos. 2201-2220. This 64″ drivered steam machine looks like it could handle quite a load! *R.J. Foster, collection of C.T. Felstead*

BELOW. No. 2210 in 1948. *Charles Winters, collection of Louis Marre*

LEFT. No. 2214 at North Kansas City in 1950. *Charles Winters, Louis Marre collection*
BELOW. Wreck-damaged No. 2214 at Decatur in May of 1939. *T.A. Radar, collection of M.D. McCarter*

Watering up at Chatham, Ontario on September 8, 1946! *Collection of John Nixon*

BELOW. No. 2253 passes a mail train at Jarvis, Ontario on Independence Day of 1949. *Richard Ganger*

BELOW. No. 2258, a K-3, was a Schenectady-born locomotive. R.J. Foster took this photo in September of 1947 at St. Louis. *C.T. Felstead collection*

ABOVE. No. 2261 is in Decatur, having been outshopped for Canadian service. The date is January 1, 1938. *M.D. Mc-Carter* BELOW. No. 2267 is at Chatham, Ontario in 1946. *Collection of John Nixon*

It's August 15, 1943 and this huge 2-8-2 Schenectady is barreling along to keep the nation's freight moving. *M.D. McCarter*

A K-3b with a booster poses at St. Louis on August 2, 1948. *R.J. Foster, collection of C.T. Felstead*

No. 2406, a K-1 that was Richmond-built, rounds a curve sometime back in the 1930's. Note the old tower in the left background with the signal attached. *M.D. McCarter*

No. 2435 was one of the Baldwin produced K-1's, and a pretty sight it was! *W. Krawier, collection of C.T. Felstead*

It's September 17, 1933 and we're in Niagara Falls on the Canadian side. No. 2456, a Pittsburgh produced steamer, rests while the crew chats about the up-coming run. *M.D. McCarter*

No. 2449 with 64″ drivers before World War II. *R.J. Foster, collection of C.T. Felstead*

CHICAGO TO PEORIA.

From August, 1888 Timetable. *John Keller collection*

Mls.	STATIONS.	Route	No. 5. Ex. Sun.	No. 1. Daily.	No. 3. Daily.
0	Lv. CHICAGO		8.25 am	2.45 pm	9.00 pm
8	" Western Indiana Jc.		8.58 "	3.20 "	9.35 "
17	" Worth		9.19 "		
26	" Alpine		9.36 "		
30	" Marley	Wabash Ry.	9.46 "	4.03 "	10.24 "
33	" New Lennox		f 9.52 "	f 4.09 "	
40	" Manhattan		10.05 "	f 4.20 "	
47	" Symerton		10.20 "	4.35 "	
53	" Ritchie		10.32 "	f 4.46 "	
54	" Custer Park	W.R.R.	10.35 "	f 4.50 "	f11.10 "
60	" Essex		10.48 "	f 5.00 "	f11.21 "
66	" Reddick	&	11.02 "	f 5.13 "	
72	" Campus		11.14 "	f 5.24 "	f11.50 pm
77	" Emington	P.	11.24 "	f 5.31 "	
84	" Saunemin		11.35 "	f 5.43 "	f12.14 am
93	Ar. FORREST	T.	11.55 am	6.00 "	12.38 "
93	Lv. FORREST		12.44 pm	6.05 "	3.35 "
98	" Fairoury		12.55 "	6.17 "	3.52 "
109	" Chenoa	W. & W.R.R.	1.17 "	6.37 "	4.25 "
118	" Gridley		1.34 "	6.53 "	4.55 "
125	" El Paso	Wabash	1.48 "	7.07 "	5.15 "
131	" Secor		2.01 "	7.20 "	5.35 "
139	" Eureka		2.15 "	7.34 "	5.57 "
146	" Washington		2.30 "	7.53 "	6.20 "
152	" Farmdale		2.45 "	8.03 "	6.40 "
157	Ar. PEORIA		3.00 pm	8.20 pm	6.55 am

No. 3 has Woodruff Palace Sleeping Car (Pullman pattern) attached, Chicago to Peoria.

2-8-2 No. 2462, a K-1, leads about a dozen cars and a caboose over Wabash rails near Cecil, Ohio on February 25, 1946. Oh, to see her runnin' again! *Photo by Paul Dunn, collection of John Nixon*

No. 2600 is a K-5, one of five such locomotives on the Wabash roster back in 1925. Anyone with a knowledge of the Wabash knows that this photo was taken at Decatur behind the locomotive shops. *Don Gruber collection*

LEFT. There were 20 K-4b 2-8-2's, all with boosters, starting with this handsome locomotive, No. 2700. Note the counterbalance on the third driver. *R.J. Foster, C.T. Felstead collection* BELOW. No. 2701 in 1950. *Richard Ganger* BOTTOM. Hartman, Indiana is the location for this doubleheader shot in 1942. *M.D. McCarter*

RIGHT. Slightly blurred, but No. 2722 looks good to the railfan eye anyway in May of 1943 at Hartman, Indiana. No. 2722 is a K-4. *M.D. McCarter*

No. 2730 2-8-2 leads freight train #99 south-bound through Auburn, Illinois in May of 1947. Just to be sure, someone chalked in "99" on the locomotive's front pilot beam. *Harold Stirton*

LEFT. Stored, No. 2733 looks forlorn in Decatur in September of 1934. *Richard Granger* BELOW. It's 1947 and big No. 2735 is chalking up another freight run at Moberly, Missouri. *M.D. McCarter* BOTTOM. Scrapped in 1950, No. 2503 Class L-1, works in 1947 at Chicago. *Arthur Johnson, collection of John Nixon*

No. 2503 deserves its own large portrait shot like this one, taken on June 22, 1947 at Brooklyn, Illinois. *R.J. Foster, collection of C.T. Felstead*

THE FAMOUS WABASH DINING CARS.

IF there was a "lacking ingredient" to the perfect happiness of the American traveler, it was supplied when the Dining Car became an acknowledged accessory to first-class train service and was generally adopted. There is now plenty of time to eat in comfort; the commendable rivalry between competing lines insures the best the market affords, and there is that indescribable charm and fascination which surrounds the situation as the passenger thus regales himself, while gliding over the country at the rate of forty miles an hour, that makes a meal in the Dining Car doubly enjoyable, and an experience always to be sought when occasion offers.

After a personal encounter with the Dining Cars of the "Wabash Route," a prominent journalist thus complimentarily remarks:

"These cars have evidently been constructed with a view of embodying all the best results of past experience in railroad cuisine and the modern excellence attained in car building.

"They are elegantly carpeted, and the seats are upholstered in stamped leather of beautiful design.

THE WABASH RAILWAY.

"No expense has been spared nor anything overlooked. The smallest details have received the most careful attention, and the result is the nearest approach to perfection to be found in this country.

"The table service is excellent, the attendance very prompt, the bill of fare equal to that of a first-class hotel, and the charges very moderate."

These cars are now running between Toledo and St. Louis, Chicago and St. Louis, and Detroit and St. Louis, serving all through trains.

THE KITCHEN

From August, 1888 Timetable. *John Keller collection*

We're working Landers Yard today as a part of the crew with 64"-drivered No. 2507, an L-1. We're a southbound freight getting ready to highball out of Chicago on February 13, 1939. *Paul Eilenberger, collection of Harold Stirton*

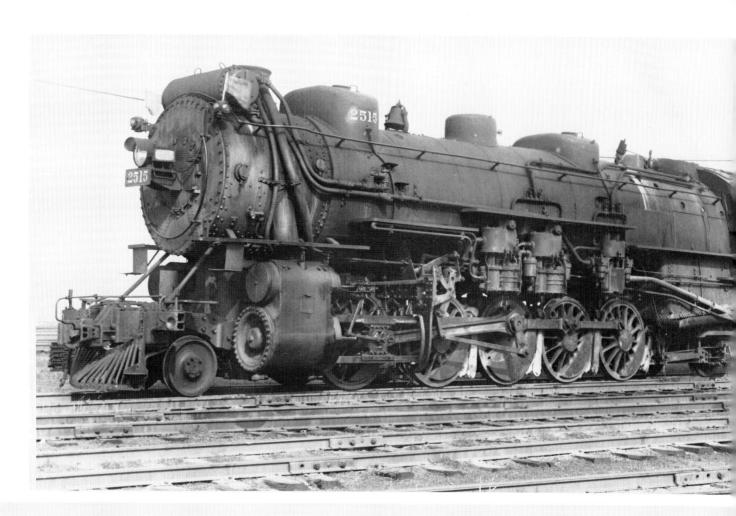

LEFT. Brooks-built Wabash No. 2515 was later sold to the Chicago & Illinois Midland. Here she works out at Decatur in 1947. *R.J. Foster, collection of C.T. Felstead* BELOW, LEFT. No. 2520 and No. 2919 (4-8-4) team up on #99 southbound at Ashburn, Illinois in August of 1948. *Harold Stirton*

BELOW. No. 2520 looks fine in October of 1947, in Decatur, but she was sold for parts only to the C&IM in 1959. *M.D. McCarter* BOTTOM. Here's No. 2520 again on April 24, 1949 in Decatur. *Don Gruber collection*

LEFT. Now we're talkin'! The M Class, that mammoth beast of 67,400 pounds of tractive effort, was pure Wabash! The first in the class, No. 2800, waters up in November of 1936 in Chicago. *Paul Eilenberger, collection of C.T. Felstead*

BELOW, LEFT. Racing like a sleek horse, No. 2804 pounds out the charge at Wabash, Indiana on April 3, 1943. *M.D. McCarter*

BELOW. A Baldwin locomotive, Wabash No. 2805 sets out cars at Logansport, Indiana on August 20, 1933. *M.D. McCarter*

No. 2805 in 1948 at Decatur is a picture of health. The M-1 is kept busy! *R.J. Foster, collection of C.T. Felstead*

No. 2808 stops for a refreshing drink at Hartman, Indiana on January 12, 1936 before continuing on. *M.D. McCarter*

No. 2809 and 2811 were built a month apart but eventually scrapped together in 1953. *M.D. McCarter and C.T. Felstead photos respectively*

LEFT. Logansport, Indiana comes under seige when No. 2812 and an O Class locomotive pay their respects to the city on November 23, 1935. *M.D. McCarter* BELOW, LEFT. No. 2815 is in Chicago in 1948 not far from C&WI tracks. *John Krause, collection of John Nixon* BOTTOM, LEFT. No. 2816 at Chicago in 1948. *C.T. Felstead*

No. 2816 isn't playing games in this March, 1939 photo. *M.D. McCarter*

No. 2817 begins to walk off with a freight train at Decatur in October of 1953. *R.J. Foster, collection of C.T. Felstead*

TOP. With weathering coated on its 70″ drivers, No. 2822 could use a wash. It's in Chicago in November of 1947. *C.T. Felstead*

TOP. No. 2823 is a powerhouse of strength. Here, she's at Brooklyn, Illinois in 1938. BELOW. The Class O 4-8-4's were 70″ drivered locomotives with nearly 71,000 pounds of tractive effort. *Both photos R.J. Foster, collection of C.T. Felstead*

No. 2901 worked almost exactly 25 years for the railroad that served the Heart of America before she was melted down. The engine has the original small stack. *R.J. Foster, collection of C.T. Felstead*

RIGHT. The 2900's had a stylized cab ladder and graceful lines all around. *Collection of Don Heimburger*

BELOW. We're near Peru, Indiana in 1943 as No. 2904 meets us just about head on, allowing her big drivers to churn the air in a mighty rush. *M.D. McCarter*

The mightiness of the Class O's becomes apparent by virtue of the smallness of the crew member atop the boiler. Chicago, June of 1948. *Richard Ganger*

Bell ringing out loudly, flags waving and engineer checking the view, No. 2907 makes its way in the late 1930's through Wabash, Indiana. *M.D. McCarter*

Billowing white smoke alerts everyone to the rush of another Wabash freight through Peru, Indiana in 1941. *William Swartz, collection of M.D. McCarter*

No. 2909 with a long freight thunders past. *Harry Zillmer photo, collection of M.D. McCarter*

WABASH RAILROAD
LINKING THE NATION
WITH "THE HEART OF AMERICA"

The 2900's. Even their class number—2900 Class—had a certain ring to it that meant power and might, that gave the locomotives an edge over other locomotives. No. 2914 rests its muscle at Brooklyn, Illinois before WWII. *R.J. Foster, collection of C.T. Felstead*

The Wabash comes back to us again in all its glory with this 1942 view at Peru, Indiana. No. 2915 and a sister locomotive move tonnage over the rails while the characteristic wooden water towers and cabooses salute the passing thunder. *William Swartz photo, collection of M.D. McCarter*

No. 2917 was wrecked in a boiler explosion on January 3, 1937 at Adrian, Michigan. It was rebuilt with a new Baldwin boiler. Thirteen years after the mishap, No. 2917 is hauling more Wabash freight at Brooklyn, Illinois. *E. Lindquist, collection of C.T. Felstead*

No. 2920 is at Decatur with a full load of coal in the tender and presumably a full tender of water as well on January 14, 1950. *W.A. Peters, collection of C.T. Felstead*

This black brute—No. 2924—lived a full life of steam, serving the Heart of America from January, 1931 to November, 1955. It will continue to operate almost a decade after this picture was snapped at Brooklyn, Illinois in 1946. *R.J. Foster, collection of C.T. Felstead*

FAR LEFT, TOP. Wabash Country! Imagine watching this O-1 coming down the track! *M.D. McCarter*

LEFT. No. 2923 is loaded with more than 70,000 pounds of tractive effort! *E. Lindquist photo, collection of C.T. Felstead*

The big 4-8-4's of the O Class were scrapped starting in October of 1955. By February of 1956, all of the class—Nos. 2900 to 2924—had been retired. The once-proud Baldwin-built 4-8-4's of the Wabash were relegated to history.

From August, 1888 Timetable. *John Keller collection*

TOLEDO, DEFIANCE & FORT WAYNE

To Kansas City, St. Joseph and Council Bluffs.

Miles.	STATIONS.	Route	No. 45. Daily.	No. 43. Daily.
0	Lv. TOLEDO		12.10 am	5 20 pm
36	" Napoleon		2.00 "	6 21 "
50	" DEFIANCE		2.47 "	6.47 "
51	" B. & O. Junction		2 52 "	6.50 "
71	" Antwerp		3.50 "	7.34 "
88	" New Haven		4.33 "	
94	" FORT WAYNE		5 00 "	8.17 "
109	" Roanoke		f 5.35 "	
118	" HUNTINGTON		5.57 "	9.01 "
125	" Andrews		6.10 "	9.15 "
137	" Wabash		6.45 "	9.33 "
150	" PERU		7.15 "	10.00 "
157	" Waverly		7.30 "	
166	" LOGANSPORT		7.50 "	10.26 "
172	" Clymers		8 05 "	10.43 "
180	" Rockfield		8 22 "	
186	" Delphi		8.35 "	11.07 "
203	" LA FAYETTE		9.20 "	11.40 "
205	" La Fayette Junction		9.45 "	11.50 pm
224	" Attica		10.28 "	12.22 am
233	" West Lebanon		10.47 "	
248	" Danville Junction		11.23 "	1.13 "
249	" DANVILLE		11.30 am	1.20 "
262	" Fairmount		12 08 pm	
269	" Homer		12.23 "	
275	" Sidney		12 36 "	
285	" Tolono		12.59 "	2.37 "
303	" Bement		1.41 "	3 10 "
323	" DECATUR		2.50 "	4 05 "
331	" Taylorville		3.36 "	4 57 "
384	" Litchfield		4.22 "	5.55 "
414	" Edwardsville Junction		5.15 "	6.50 "
436	Ar. ST. LOUIS		6.15 pm	7.45 am
462	Ar. HANNIBAL		+ 9.25 pm	10.40 am
473	Ar. QUINCY		+ 9.50 pm	10.45 am
488	Ar. KEOKUK		+11.45 pm	11.50 am
436	Lv. ST. LOUIS		* 8.25 pm	+ 9.00 am
459	" St. Charles		9.25 "	9.55 am
520	" Montgomery		11.20 pm	12.10 pm
528	" Wellsville		12 05 am	12.55 "
546	" Mexico		12.31 "	1.18 "
560	" Centralia		1.27 "	2.07 "
584	" Moberly		2.11 "	
605	" Salisbury		2.44 am	3.23 pm
623	Ar. BRUNSWICK		3 32 am	3.25 pm
623	Lv. BRUNSW CK.		5.25 am	4.59 pm
671	Ar. LEXINGTON JUNCTION		9.30 am	9.05 pm
744	Ar. ST. JOSEPH		7.10 am	8.30 pm
713	Ar. KANSAS CITY			
623	Ar. BRUNSWICK		2.45 am	+ 2.07 pm
661	" Chillicothe		4 02 "	
687	" Gallatin		4.55 "	
730	" Stanberry		6 40 "	
734	" Maryville		7.32 "	
766	" Roseberry		8 38 "	Via Kansas City.
799	" Shenandoah		9.33 "	
821	" Malvern		10 18 "	
847	" COUNCIL BLUFFS		11 35 am	6.25 am
849	Ar. OMAHA		12 05 pm	7.00 am

No. 45 has Free Reclining Chair Cars attached, Toledo to St. Louis, and Wagner Palace Sleeping Car, Toledo to La Fayette. Free Reclining Chair Car, Toledo to Quincy.
No. 43 has new Reclining Chair Car (seats free) and Wagner Palace Sleeping Car attached, Toledo to St. Louis and Palace Sleeping Car, Toledo to Quincy. * Daily. † Daily, except Sunday.

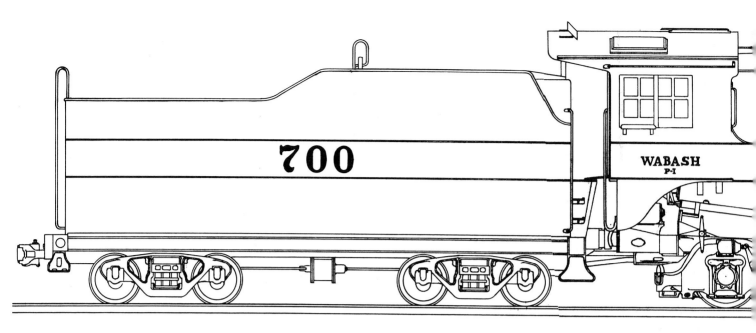

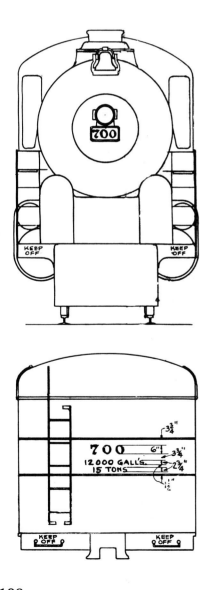

108

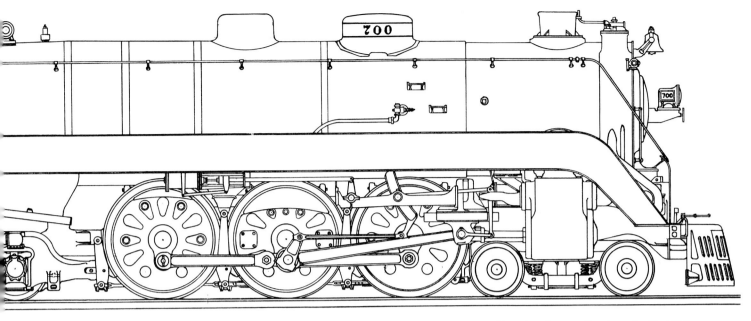

Drawing from collection of T.E. Nihiser

The Decatur-built 700's were the Wabash's answer to the modernization and streamlining of steam locomotive power on America's railroads in the 1940's. The 700's were originally the K-5 Class 2-8-2's. *Photo by R. Foster, collection of Don Gruber*

RIGHT. It's 1948 in Decatur and No. 700 (ex-2600) 4-6-4 with large 80″ drivers is in town with a train of varnish. *William Raia collection*

Richard Ganger found No. 704 awaiting assignment and captured its hulking frame on film.

PRECEDING PAGE, TOP. No. 702 has charge this day of one of the Detroit to St. Louis passenger runs. It's at Peru, Indiana now. *M.D. McCarter* BOTTOM. Photographer W.D. Edson sums this scene up: ''Converging on single iron with Train No. 1 about to cross over the Big Four and Monon through the interlocking at Lafayette Junction just west of town. Date is September, 1946. This little train had everything: a parlor-observation (open platform), diner, deluxe coaches, baggage car and RPO car, all powered by a colorful and handsome 4-6-4 with a steamboat whistle. Wabash-watching was a real experience!''

BELOW. No. 705 is dated by the ART reefer in the rear. *Richard Ganger*

The fires are dropped on the handsome 4-6-4's

BELOW. When new, we cheer things, we celebrate things. No. 706 is fresh from Wabash shops at Decatur, and the shop crew gathers 'round for a parting shot before the big 4-6-4 is let out on the mainline. *Collection of T.E. Nihiser* LEFT. One year into service, No. 706 is at Chicago at 63rd Street, Englewood Station. *Photo by John Krause, collection of John Nixon* ABOVE. Seeing anything *behind* the shop buildings at Decatur usually means it's on the rip track, that its useful life is finished. There is no celebration here on September 8, 1956, the year all the 4-6-4's were scrapped. *Richard Ganger*

WABASH

Chapter 7

Diesel switchers

Wabash No. 51 was a General Electric product of 1939. The D-3 B-B diesel switcher weighed in at 44 tons and developed 350 horsepower. It was subsequently sold in 1961 to Merrilees Equipment Co. Photo was taken September 9, 1956 by William Swartz. *M.D. McCarter collection*

BELOW. T.A. Rader caught No. 100 working at Ft. Wayne in June of 1941 about two years after it was built by Alco. The D-6 was eventually retired and scrapped in April of 1966. *M.D. McCarter collection*

ABOVE AND BELOW. Sister to No. 100, the 150 was built a year after in 1940. In these views, Henry Goerke found No. 150 in Adrian, Michigan in April of 1966 (top), and J. David Ingles captured it on film at Decatur in September of 1962. *Both photos from Louis Marre collection*

RIGHT. The Wabash purchased No. 1 from the Des Moines Union where it worked as their No. 1 as well. Louis Marre photographed the S-1 at Decatur.

LEFT. Another S-1, No. 151 was built in 1941 and was retired in 1966. Here it poses at Oakwood, Michigan in December of 1963. *J. David Ingles, collection of Louis Marre*

BELOW. No. 153 worked for the Wabash 22 years, then was sold in 1966. *J. David Ingles, collection of Louis Marre*

TOP. No. 157 basks peacefully in the summer of 1947 at Peru, Indiana after being manufactured by Alco earlier in the year. *William Swartz, collection of M.D. McCarter*

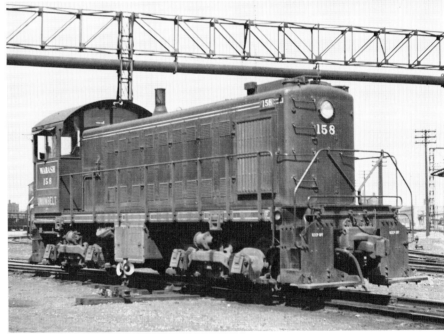

RIGHT. A Wabash switcher on the Union Belt of Detroit in mid-1951. *Elliott Kahn, collection of Louis Marre*

BELOW. An EMC SW-1 built in 1939 plys along switch tracks as part of its daily routine. The switcher later became No. 2 for the Bonhomie & Hattiesburg Southern. *Collection of Bruce R. Meyer*

ABOVE. With Detroit in the background, No. 103, an SW-1 600 hp switcher, shuttles cars along the waterfront. Louis Marre took the photo the day before Memorial Day in 1961.

LEFT. No. 111, another SW-1, poses for a photo against the familiar Decatur shop walls of the Wabash in April of 1964. *J. David Ingles, collection of Louis Marre*

FROM DETROIT TO THE SOUTHWEST, THE OFFERS

THE FASTEST, SHORTEST RAIL SERVICE TO ST. LOUIS AND THE SOUTHWEST.

RIGHT. A Baldwin model VO 660 built in 1941 is shown here involved in a derailment on July 25, 1950 at Decatur. Fifteen years later the engine was leased to the Lake Erie & Ft. Wayne and subsequently was retired in May of 1968. *Collection of Louis Marre*

RIGHT. It's 1947 and 40-year-old steam switchers are still being out-shopped with class repairs, but the diesel is already here and spreading. In two years the *Wabash Cannon Ball* and the *Banner Blue* will both receive diesels for headend power. The D-6 No. 201 is a Baldwin delivered eight months before this picture was taken in Decatur by M.D. McCarter.

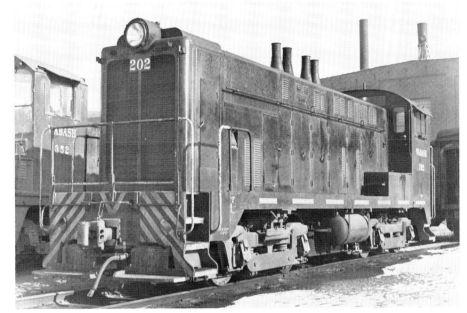

LEFT. No. 202 came out of the Baldwin shops in March, 1947, and along with its sister No. 201, served until March of 1964. It was the start of a new year—January 3, 1961—when Louis Marre photographed No. 202 at Decatur.

BELOW. GMD No. 123 was an SW-8 with 800 hp manufactured in December of 1950. Sixteen years later on May 30, 1961 it was still pulling its share in Windsor, Ontario. *Louis Marre photo*

LEFT. No. 124 in Decatur yards on July 27, 1966 after 15 years of service. *J. David Ingles, collection of Louis Marre*

the

Blue Bird...

From October 30, 1955 Timetable

Entertain while you travel!— *The club-like "Blue Bird Room" can be reserved for groups whenever 6 to 10 first-class tickets are purchased. Ideal for meetings, meals, refreshments . . . and perfect relaxation.*

LEFT. EMD-built No. 126 was manufactured in September of 1951. *Collection of John Nixon*

RIGHT. No. 132 sits and waits for N&W locomotives to engulf Wabash power in St. Louis on November 27, 1965. *Photo by The Garys, collection of John Nixon*

BELOW. No. 302 is a Baldwin product of 1944, model VO 1000. Photo was taken in 1946 at Peru, Indiana. *M.D. McCarter*

TOP. Only one of its kind, the No. 304 operated as a cabless booster unit for the Wabash. It was retired in March of 1964. The unit is on shop trucks in this photo taken September 1, 1963 in Decatur. Its model designation was DS 4-4-1000 B. *Louis Marre*

RIGHT. Nos. 300 and 304 team up for extra power in North Kansas City, Missouri in March of 1962. *Charles Winters, Louis Marre collection*

LEFT. Alco-GE S-2 No. 311 was recorded on May 21, 1951 at Delrey, Michigan, outside of Detroit. *Richard Ganger*

LEFT. Alco's 1000th diesel was this one—Wabash No. 317—a 1,000 hp S-2 built in June of 1944. M.D. McCarter took the photo of this engine four years later on July 18, 1948 in Montpelier, Ohio.

LEFT. Here's No. 317 again, but in January, 1966 after it had been around a while. Taken at Oakwood, Michigan. *Photo by Henry Goerke, collection of Louis Marre*

RIGHT. No. 320, an S-2 built in 1949, was photographed at Brewster, Ohio on February 19, 1967. *Photo by The Garys, collection of John Nixon*

BELOW. No. 322, an S-4, was one of three such switchers built in 1953. *J. David Ingles, collection of Louis Marre*

RIGHT. No. 347 was one of eight EMD NW-2 1,000 hp switchers delivered to the Wabash between 1940 and 1949; four were ex-NKP, ex-Wheeling & Lake Erie units. No. 347 eventually wound up on Des Moines Union lines where it became their No. 6. Tilton, Illinois is the location of this September 2, 1963 photo by Louis Marre

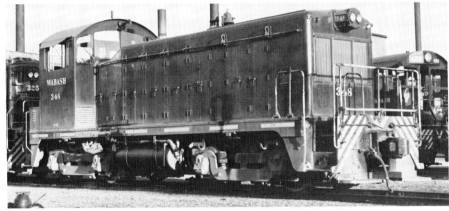

LEFT. No. 348, ex-NKP, ex-W&LE huddles among other switchers at Decatur in February, 1965. *J. David Ingles, collection of Louis Marre*

RIGHT. No. 352 is working at Brooklyn, Illinois in the spring of 1950, about a year after it had been delivered. *Photo by William Swartz, collection of M.D. McCarter*

BELOW. The Wabash Fairbanks-Morse diesels were distinguished by their high hoods. One year before the N&W merger, No. 380, built in 1946, works Decatur on September 1, 1963. *Louis Marre*

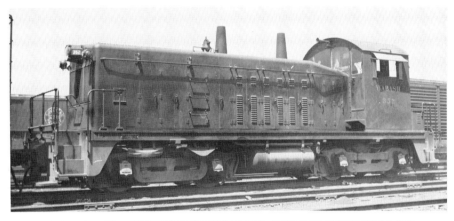

LEFT. Here's No. 380 again but in early 1948, two years after being constructed by F-M. The unit is at Decatur. *M.D. McCarter*

BELOW. No. 381 sits at Decatur (Brush) on February 14, 1965. *Louis Marre*

BELOW. The latest F-M in the series 380-383 to be retired (1970) was No. 382. *M.D. McCarter*

Fairbanks-Morse D-10 at Peru, Indiana in 1949. *M.D. Mc-Carter*

ABOVE. Lima-Hamilton 1,000 hp yard switcher No. 400 was a long, sleek machine, having started life as a demonstrator unit for L-H. The unit was later rebuilt to 1,200 hp. Photo date: August 3, 1963. *Louis Marre*

RIGHT. No. 306 was an S-12 built in 1951. Photo location: North Kansas City, Missouri. Date: August 3, 1963. Photographer: Louis Marre.

LEFT. EMD's SW-7 class boasted eight units on the Wabash, including No. 357. Photo was taken in May of 1953 at Peru, Indiana by M.D. McCarter.

BELOW. No. 361 at Oakwood, Michigan in October of 1966. *J. David Ingles, collection of Louis Marre*

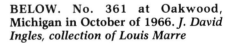

RIGHT. No. 371 at Decatur in March, 1965. *Louis Marre*

BELOW. The last unit in the SW-9 series was No. 374 (Nos. 363-374), and it was one of the last units of that series to be built in March, 1953. *Louis Marre*

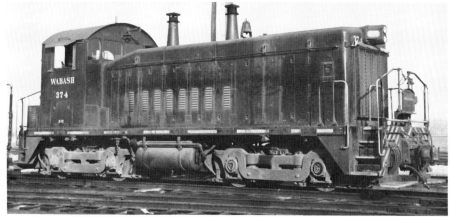

BELOW. We're at Toledo, Ohio in September of 1966 as Wabash Nos. 377 and 378 pull tonnage over Norfolk & Western trackage. Note the unique tower in center background. *J. David Ingles, collection of Louis Marre*

ABOVE. Still about seven years away from retirement, F-M No. 386 waits in Decatur in 1963 for merger happenings to occur. *Louis Marre*

RIGHT. Complete with safety striping, No. 385 is assigned to Decatur in 1963. *Louis Marre*

BELOW. Another broadside view of No. 386 in Decatur. *Bruce Meyer*

BOTTOM PHOTO. Lima-Hamilton No. 403 with its very square nose and large numberboards works out of North Kansas City, Missouri on December 22, 1960. *Louis Marre*

TOP TO BOTTOM. No. 404 on December 22, 1960 at North Kansas City; No. 407 which was ex-Lima-Hamilton demonstrator No. 1003 rebuilt with a 1,200 hp engine, as were the other D-12's; No. 409 also in North Kansas City on October 1, 1964, just 15 days from merger. *All photos, Louis Marre*

ABOVE. The 1,500 hp GP-7's were 34 strong on the Wabash, built between 1950 and 1953. Louis Marre caught No. 452 in North Kansas City on April 17, 1965. LEFT. GMD-built Geep in April of 1966. *Charles Winters, collection of Louis Marre* BELOW. EMD No. 456 on December 3, 1960 at Peru, Indiana. *H.N. Proctor, collection of Louis Marre*

LEFT. It's July of 1963, and photographer William Raia is sitting trackside in Chicago as Geep No. 458 rolls past on a transfer run to the Belt Railway of Chicago. It was a *hot* day, Bill recalls.

August, 1888 Timetable

RIGHT AND BELOW. Units Nos. 462 and 464 pose in the North Kansas City yard in the early '60's. *Both photos, Louis Marre*

ABOVE. No. 466 was slightly out of place on August 3, 1963 in North Kansas City surrounded by Lima/Alco units. *Louis Marre*

LEFT. It's New Year's Eve of 1958 at Jacksonville, Illinois and No. 469 does switching chores in the bleak winter weather. *Bruce Meyer*

BELOW. No. 479 idles at Lafayette, Indiana on May 23, 1964 with a lone caboose. *Louis Marre*

131

TOP. GP-9 No. 484 in the spring of 1962. ABOVE. No. 486 (and No. 485 out of sight) head up a Michigan RR Club excursion over the NJI&I at South Bend, Indiana on April 12, 1959. BELOW. No. 486 meets GTW 4901 and AA 21 all on AA track and all with football extras at Ann Arbor in October of 1959. *Top photos, Louis Marre; bottom photo, J.A. Pinkepank, collection of Louis Marre*

Road diesels

F-7 units are shown from low numbers to high numbers, irregardless of the 1961 re-numbering.

ABOVE. The F-7 EMD and GMD units were numerous on the Wabash. Here No. 621 leads a freight on February 3, 1965. *J. David Ingles, collection of Louis Marre*

BELOW. No. 630 in the dark blue and yellow paint scheme is at Oakwood, Michigan on Christmas Day, 1964 and two years before its retirement. *J. David Ingles, collection of Louis Marre*

LEFT. No. 643 sits at Oakwood, Michigan on July 22, 1961. BELOW. Leading the line-up at Detroit on October 31, 1961, is No. 650, followed by 681, 612 and 617. BOTTOM. No. 652 heads a freight at Jacksonville, Illinois in 1965. *All photos, collection of Louis Marre*

ABOVE. Springfield, Illinois, March 7, 1965. *J. David Ingles, collection of Louis Marre* RIGHT. No. 656 looks weatherbeaten in July, 1964. *Louis Marre*

LEFT. GMD No. 661 is at Windsor on December 30, 1965. *J. David Ingles, Louis Marre collection*

135

ABOVE. This GMD-built unit received an all blue paint scheme without the body stripes, says Louis Marre, who captured No. 662 on film the day before Memorial Day, 1961, in Windsor. LEFT. Another GMD locomotive, No. 669 on July 3, 1964. BELOW. This is an all-GMD set, including the sole GP-7, No. 453, taken at Windsor in October of 1966. *Both photos J. David Ingles, collection of Louis Marre*

You can see the headlight downgrade for about a mile and hear the murmur of diesel-electric engines and the track joints tightening. Before long it's upon you in its rushing glory. J. David Ingles was at Jacksonville, Illinois March 18, 1964 to record another freight train of automobiles. *Collection of Louis Marre*

RIGHT. No. 671 F-7A is preserved at Bellevue, Ohio at the Mad River & NKP RR Museum. The unit is a GMD. *John Nixon*

RIGHT. This GMD-built F unit was seen at Bellevue, Ohio in early 1965. The following year it was retired. *The Garys, collection of John Nixon*

BELOW. Wabash power was often lashed up in odd combinations such as this F-7, H-24, F-7, H-24 mix. J. David Ingles photographed the units on October 4, 1964. *Louis Marre collection*

NEXT PAGE. It's the 10th birthday of No. 688 which was built in July of 1951. In July of 1961, J. David Ingles caught No. 688 at Oakwood, Michigan. *Louis Marre collection*

TOP. Those great color and locomotive combinations made Wabash motive power-watching suspenseful. No. 698 and friends 629, 508 and 635 are at North Kansas City in July of 1964. RIGHT. No. 698 again at Orleans, Illinois February 14, 1965. *J. David Ingles* BELOW. No. 700 heads tonnage at north Decatur in March, 1964. *All photos collection of or by Louis Marre*

NEXT PAGE, TOP. The dust flies as a four-unit Wabash freight roars through Logansport, Indiana on September 4, 1963, with another unit in the hole. BELOW. No. 712 at Oakwood, Michigan in mid-1961. *Both photos, Louis Marre*

RIGHT. One of the last F-7 units to be retired was No. 704, which was sent to the scrapper in June of 1967. *Louis Marre*

ABOVE. Night falls on Wabash units at Decatur in September of 1964—including No. 717. The following month of that year night was to fall on the entire railroad. *Roger Meade, collection of Louis Marre*

LEFT. A Wabash inbound freight at 79th Street, Chicago, is crossing the Pennsylvania crossover and is about to clamor across the Baltimore & Ohio Chicago Terminal crossover in August of 1963. *William Raia*

The new Observation-Cafe Library Cars, Reclining Chair Cars, Day Coaches, Combination Passenger and Baggage Cars and Dining Cars recently introduced on the Wabash Line are gems of workmanship. They should be seen in order to be appreciated.

The new Day Coaches on the Wabash have broad vestibules, standard six-wheel trucks and steel wheels. They are finished in quartered oak, and have the half Empire deck. They are brilliantly lighted by Pintsch gas, all fixtures being especially designed. They are plain, but rich in finish and carpeted. It is a pleasure to ride in them.

RIGHT. The Wabash cuts through scenic country around Danville, Illinois such as surrounds this trestle and concrete approach near there. No. 724 walks a freight over the trestle on September 2, 1963. *Louis Marre*

LEFT. This three-unit ABA set was photographed on September 2, 1949 at Peru, Indiana by M.D. McCarter. No. 1100-A was renumbered in 1961 to No. 610.

BELOW. Montpelier, Ohio in the fall of 1949 with an ABA set showing the crisp front end of an A unit with coupler showing. *M.D. McCarter*

ABOVE. Delivered in 1949, we find No. 1105 and a B unit snuggled in a side track on August 2, 1953 at Peru. *M.D. McCarter*

RIGHT. It's mid-1950 at Delray, Michigan and No. 1141-A's paint looks good after a month on the Wabash. *Photo by P. Dunn, collection of John Nixon*

BELOW. New Paris, Indiana, station and tower allow No. 1141-A and its contents to parade between them in a shot by Harry Zillmer. *Collection of M.D. McCarter*

Niagara Falls, Ontario kept the GMD F-7 units on their side, the U.S.-built units on the opposite side. Taken the day before Independence Day in 1958 on the Canadian Falls side. *Louis Marre*

Wabash No. 1159-A at Niagara Falls, Ontario on July 3 in 1954. Close up, clean F-7's look handsome! *Collection of John Nixon*

It's January 1, 1960, and despite the occasion, 1159-A and train are in Windsor going about business as usual. *Bruce Meyer*

PREVIOUS PAGE, TOP. New Haven, Indiana, situated along the Maumee River, was one of the first Wabash towns inside the Indiana border next to Ohio. On April 14, 1960, No. 1180-A and two other units charge through town on their way to Ft. Wayne, a few more miles away. *Louis Marre*

PREVIOUS PAGE, BOTTOM. Mansfield, Illinois is north of Bement, and the countryside is cornfield flat. This westbound freight nears Mansfield on June 12, 1959. *Bruce Meyer*

WABASH RAILROAD

HOW THEY END UP! Above, on July 7, 1967, this is how EMD No. 3723 (nee 1188, renumbered 723) looked as Wabash lettering was phased out. *J. David Ingles, collection of Louis Marre* BELOW. The summer of 1981 at Decatur, a sister unit No. 3725 but built by GMD poses forlornly. This unit is now at the Monticello & Sangamon Valley Railway Historical Society in Monticello, Illinois. *Don Heimburger*

ABOVE. One of the classic Wabash locomotives was the FA built by Alco. Lashed between two F-7's is No. 814 at Oakwood, Michigan on July 9, 1961. *J. David Ingles, collection of Louis Marre*

RIGHT. FA-1 No. 1201-A and 1179-A butt noses at Decatur on the night of August 22, 1959. If this scene could only be repeated again now! *Bruce Meyer*

From November 12, 1930 Timetable

IMPORTANT WABASH PASSENGER TRAINS

to and from

St. Louis, Chicago, Detroit, Toledo, Kansas City, Omaha, Des Moines, St. Paul - Minneapolis

ST. LOUIS - CHICAGO
Banner Blue Limited
Chicago-St. Louis Special
Delmar Express
Midnight Limited

ST. LOUIS - KANSAS CITY
Pacific Coast Limited
St. Louis-Colorado Limited
Denver Express
Midnight Limited

ST. LOUIS-DETROIT-TOLEDO
Continental Limited
St. Louis Special
Midnight Limited

ST. LOUIS-ST. PAUL-MINNEAPOLIS
North Star Limited

ST. LOUIS-OMAHA
Omaha-St. Louis Limited

ST. LOUIS-DES MOINES
Des Moines-St. Louis Limited

CHICAGO-DETROIT
Midnight Limited
Detroit-Chicago Special

KANSAS CITY-DETROIT
Central States Limited

DETROIT-FLORIDA
The Southland

ABOVE. A handsome set of FA/FB's bask in the sunshine in July of 1950 at Peru. *M.D. McCarter*

BELOW. Almost exactly 1 year after being delivered, 1203-A has her picture taken at Decatur on March 8, 1950. *M.D. McCarter*

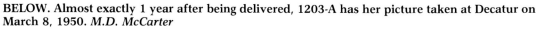

NEXT PAGE, TOP. Three FA units purr at Peru in 1957. *M.D. McCarter* BOTTOM. No. 1000 E-7A (renumbered 1002-A, then 1017) pauses at Moberly, Missouri on October 12, 1947 for passengers. EMD made the unit in 1946. *M.D. McCarter*

ABOVE. We're at Lafayette, Indiana on May 23, 1964 as No. 1001 EMD Model E-7A, a 2,000 hp passenger unit and her sisters have in tow a Wabash train of varnish. *Louis Marre*

BELOW. In an earlier day, May 22, 1949, No. 1001 is at St. Louis with the familiar gray, blue and white color scheme. *L.G. Issac*

The curious "arrow" at the top left of the nose of No. 1001-A is really just the shadow of the grabiron. *Collection of Louis Marre*

No. 1002 sits outside the Decatur shops in March, 1962 with the dark blue, silver and yellow paint scheme, presumably just new from painting. *R.R. Wallin, collection of Louis Marre*

ABOVE. Generating 2,250 hp, the E-8's were high-powered passenger units. No. 1006 is at Logansport, Indiana in the spring of 1950. *Elliott Kahn, collection of Louis Marre*

LEFT. The *Wabash Cannon Ball* is dieselized here with No. 1007, an E-8. Here it approaches the Wabash River bridge, westbound, after leaving Logansport on August 3, 1952. *W.D. Edson*

THIS PASS IS GOOD OVER THE FOLLOWING LINES:

Toledo to Hannibal,

Bluffs to Quincy and Keokuk,

Chicago to East St. Louis.

Bement to Effingham and Altamont,

Fairbury to Streator.

CONDITIONS.

It is expressly understood and agreed that the person accepting this Pass assumes all risk of personal injury and loss or damage to property which may occur upon the trains of the Company to the party while using the same. If presented by any other person than the individual named hereon the conductor will take up this Pass and collect fare.

I accept the above conditions.

....

EXCHANGE.

WABASH RAILWAY.

JOHN McNULTA, RECEIVER.

Pass Mr H. C. Wicker
Traffic Manager.
Chicago & N. Western Ry.

UNTIL DECEMBER 3ST 1888, UNLESS OTHERWISE ORDERED.

R154

RECEIVER.

1888 Wabash pass applies to lines east of Mississippi River. *Robert Fiedler collection*

THREE PHOTOS. No. 1009, built by EMD as their 10,000th unit, in June of 1951, glistens before us newly painted in the top photo, then in service on July 22, 1964, and finally, preserved at the Roanoke RR Museum in Roanoke, Virginia, in summer of 1969. *Collection of William Raia; Louis Marre photo; and Joseph Brauner, Marre collection, respectively*

No. 1017, formerly No. 1002-A and No. 1000, is at Wabash, Indiana in April of 1961. *Photo by H.N. Proctor, collection of L.G. Issac*

The Wabash 2,000-hp PA's were very "watchable" diesels. In a striking night scene at Decatur, No. 1052 (No. 1021) slumbers peacefully in July, 1964. *Roger Meade, collection of Louis Marre*

PA's and E-8's side by side at night in Decatur; the darkness hides some of their chipped faces. Bruce Meyer took the shot in August of 1959.

RIGHT. No. 550 and sister 551 were originally Fairbanks-Morse demonstrators TM-1 and TM-2. The FM engine noise was noticeably different than units of other manufacturers. Decatur, January 3, 1961. *Louis Marre*

LEFT. This FM unit, like two others, received three different numbers in its Wabash career. Notice the bold appearance of the sideframes and the muscular squareness of the hood. The H-24-66 was at Decatur on January 3, 1961 for this portrait. *Louis Marre*

RIGHT. No. 556 was 553A before the renumbering in 1961. In a depleted state when this photo was taken September 1, 1963 by Louis Marre, it was being used for parts to keep No. 557, the only serviceable Train Master, in operation.

BELOW. No. 597 Train Master leads a trio of Wabash F units and a Geep through Huntsville, Missouri on May 30, 1964. *J. David Ingles, collection of Louis Marre*

ABOVE. There were 105 Train Masters built for the U.S. Some say they were born too soon and too mighty (2400 hp) so they were phased out by the railroads. Decatur, 1961. *Louis Marre*

RIGHT. No. 594 also at Decatur on March 9, 1965. *Louis Marre*

BELOW. At Oakwood, Michigan in June of 1966. *J. David Ingles, collection of Louis Marre*

Wabash Line
World's Fair Terminal

The Wabash World's Fair terminal is an important undertaking and called for an outlay of $50,000 on the part of the Wabash Company for the station structure alone. Much time and thought has been given to the plan for the terminal, which is located directly in front of the main entrance to the Fair and through which a very large volume of the season's traffic will pass. In the arrangement of the tracks due provision has been made for handling the local, the through and the excursion business on rapid schedules, each independently of the other, and every precaution will be observed for safety. The Transit Company's terminal loop is located north of all the tracks of the Wabash at the World's Fair terminal, and, as will be seen by the diagram above, street car passengers will reach the main entrance to the Fair on a broad plaza passing under the Wabash tracks and thus avoiding all the danger of a grade crossing.

From September, 1904 Timetable

LEFT. The Wabash owned seven DL-640's, 2,400 hp low-nose four-axle road switchers Nos. B900-B906. The Wabash used the units, which were originally built for NdeM, as boosters. J. David Ingles caught No. B903 in 1965 at Decatur. *Collection of Louis Marre*

BELOW. B905 is at Landers Yard in Chicago in January of 1963. *William Raia*

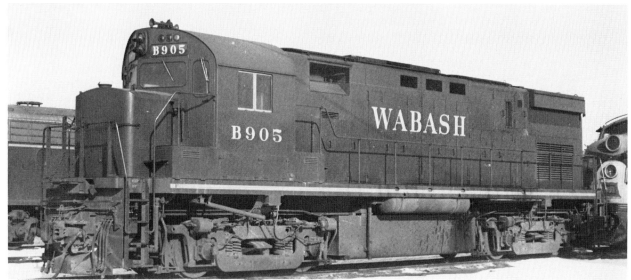

LEFT. Front end view of No. 509, a GE U25B of 2,500 hp. *Bruce Meyer*

No. 508 was one of 15 U25B's built for the Wabash on Alco FA trucks by General Electric. Two of these units could replace three conventional cab units. It's June 8, 1963 at North Kansas City. *Louis Marre*

BELOW. No. 511 at Decatur, 9-16-62. *Bruce Meyer*

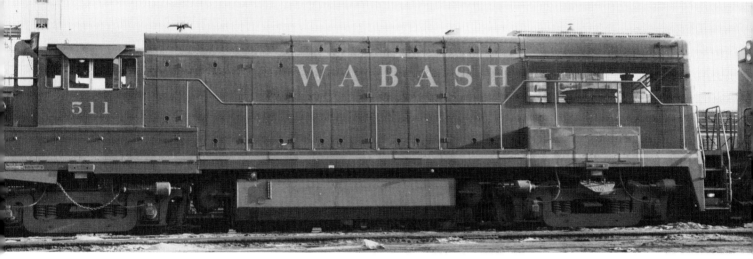

RIGHT. Three U25B's pull tonnage through Logansport, on April 20, 1963. *Louis Marre*

ABOVE. EMD-built GP-35 at Springfield, Illinois on May 30, 1964. *J. David Ingles, collection of Louis Marre* LEFT. No. 540 became No. 3540 in 1964 when the N&W took over the Wabash. *Charles Winters, collection of Louis Marre*

Decatur Car Repair Shops in 1927. Drawing by R. Brooks Stover

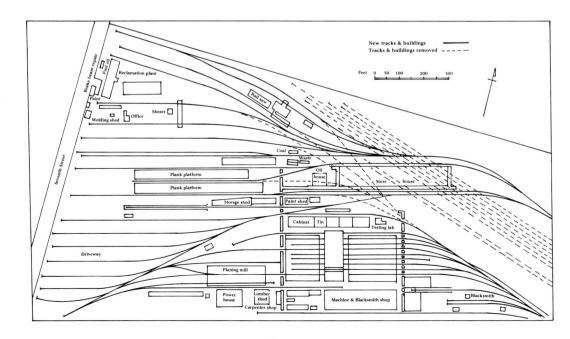

ABOVE. Unit No. 3542 carries the Wabash flag and name (on the side), but a smaller "Norfolk & Western" on the hood. October, 1966 at Oakwood, Michigan. *J. David Ingles, Louis Marre collection*

LEFT. Last of the series of GP-35's, No. 547 at Decatur in the late winter of 1965. *Louis Marre*

BELOW. Wabash-N&W No. 3541 at Conneaut, Ohio on June 6, 1966. *Photo by The Garys, collection of John Nixon*

After the N&W-Wabash merger

The Wabash started to fade on Friday, October 16, 1964.

Surrounded by N&W motive power at Decatur, the Wabash begins to fade into time on September 12, 1965. *J. David Ingles, collection of Louis Marre*

Norfolk & Western GP-35 units 1302-1308 were built by EMD in November, 1964 and ordered by the Wabash as Nos. 548-554. This one is at North Kansas City on April 16, 1965. *Louis Marre*

No. 1001, a DL-425, was built by Alco in November of 1964, but ordered as Wabash 582-589. It's spotted here at Bellevue, Ohio, July 5, 1974. *Louis Marre*

RIGHT. The old Wabash shop chimney still stands tall over the Decatur shops in the summer of 1981. *Don Heimburger*

BELOW. Imposing front view of No. 1001. *Louis Marre*

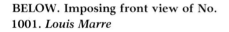

Builder's Plates
American Locomotive Company

0-6-0 No. 109 was a Rhode Island Locomotive Works product of 1891, surviving until 1931 on the Wabash. *Alco Historic Photos*

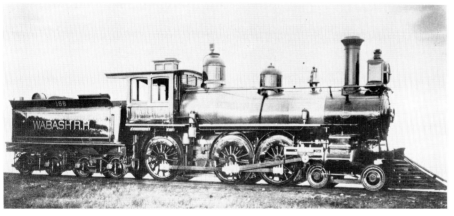

With 19x24″ cylinders and 64″ drivers, this Rhode Island Locomotive Works 4-6-0 is of the H-7 Class. *Alco Historic Photos*

NEXT PAGE, MIDDLE. No. 421 was built in November of 1892. It has large 70″ drivers. RIGHT. No. 325 is a Wabash, St. Louis & Pacific locomotive built in 1880 by Rogers. Later it was re-numbered 1325 and then back to 325. *Both photos, Alco Historic Photos*

RIGHT. No. 413 was built by the Rhode Island Locomotive Works in October, 1892. *Alco Historic Photos*

ABOVE. No. 506 0-6-0 was built in 1901 by Richmond as a B-5 Class. BELOW. An 1898 Richmond product, this 4-6-0 had 64″ drivers. *Both photos, Alco Historic Photos*

BELOW. No. 754 was a Class F-5 built by Rhode Island in 1899 with a boiler pressure of 195 pounds and 26,593 pounds of tractive effort. Later it was rebuilt and renumbered to 573 and subsequently was sold in August of 1955 to the St. Louis Museum of Transport. *Alco Historic Photos*

TOP TO BOTTOM. No. 758 was a Class F-4 by Richmond and built in 1899. No. 900 was a Wabash-Pittsburgh Terminal engine of 1909. No. 918 is also a Wabash-Pittsburgh Terminal locomotive built in 1909. *All photos, Alco Historic Photos*

ABOVE. Schenectady built in 1923. 52″ drivers, 55,781 pounds of tractive effort. Scrapped in July, 1951. LEFT. The G-1 Class had 90 locomotives, built by either Rogers or Baldwin. No. 2065 was Rogers-built in 1907. *Both photos, Alco Historic Photos*

Another Wabash-Pittsburgh Terminal locomotive was this 0-6-0 No. 2201, a rather odd-looking engine built in 1905. *Alco Historic Photos*

Part of the K-3 Class was No. 2274, a 331,000 pound behemoth of the rails. Note the trolley at the right of the engine. *Alco Historic Photos*

A 1912 Richmond product, No. 2414 was sold in 1942 to the Seaboard. *Alco Historic Photos*

A K-5 2-8-2 with 64″ drivers, No. 2604 was Schenectady made in 1925. The K's were real workhorses on the Wabash. *Alco Historic Photos*

Another of the K Class is No. 2714, a K-4b with a booster. It's a long, sleek machine. *Alco Historic Photos*

No. 2735, a K-4 Class 2-8-2 built by Schenectady in 1925. *Alco Historic Photos*

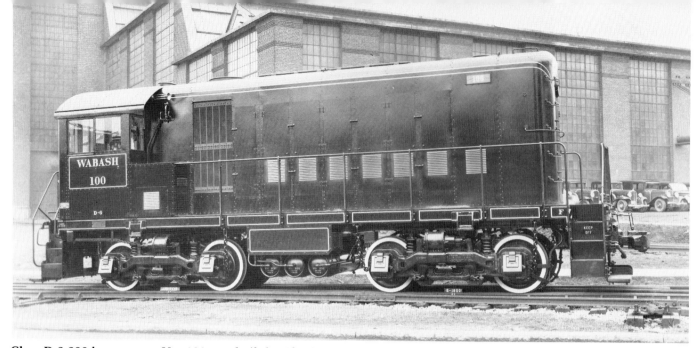

Class D-6 600 horsepower No. 100 was built by Alco in April, 1939. It was a unique-looking diesel, and one of the first diesels for the Wabash. It was scrapped in 1966. BELOW. No. 155 is an S-1 with 660 horsepower built in 1944. *Alco Historic Photos*

LEFT. No. 151, an Alco-GE S-1 was built in 1941. Photo shows unit enroute to delivery. *Louis Marre* NEXT PAGE. Class D-20 PA-2 2,000 horsepower is an Alco-GE locomotive of 1949. *Alco Historic Photos*

174

FA's were singularly attractive diesels to many fans. The FA-1 and FB-1's were the first units Alco made with a single large engine, and although they encountered several serious problems in service, they were nonetheless purchased by numerous railroads to replace steam locomotives. In all, nearly 700 units were built by Alco. Fifteen A and B units arrived on Wabash property between January and March of 1949. The A units were 51'6" in length over the couplers and 10' 6½" wide, with a wheelbase of 9'4". The B units were 50'2" in length. All 15 Wabash units were traded to GE in March and April of 1962. The trucks were used on Wabash GE U25B units Nos. 500-515, and the bodies were scrapped at Erie, Pennsylvania.

All photos, Alco Historic Photos

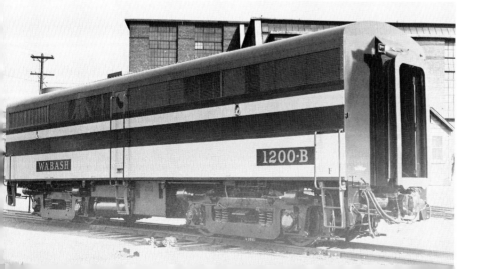

Baldwin Locomotive Works

ABOVE. No. 513 0-6-0 was built in November, 1903 with 58″ drivers and 165 pounds boiler pressure. It was part of an order of 16 B-6 engines. *H.L. Broadbelt collection*

RIGHT. One of the B-7 Class, No. 546 was built in 1907. *H.L. Broadbelt collection*

BELOW. The Class E-2's included No. 608 built in 1901. Note the flags alongside the Wabash name on the cab. *H.L. Broadbelt collection*

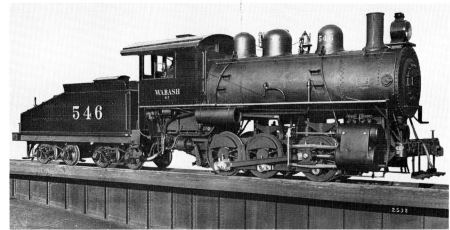

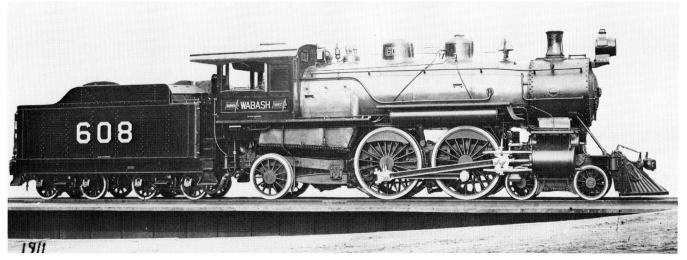

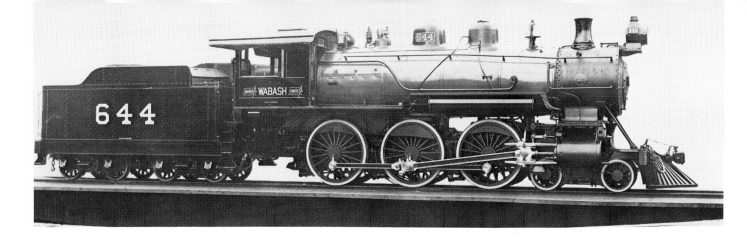

TOP. The Class H-12 locomotives included No. 644, built in 1904. These 4-6-0's had 74″ drivers and were later rebuilt. *H.L. Broadbelt collection* ABOVE. Class D-30 4-4-0's were high-stepping iron horses with 78″ drivers. Note the celestory cab roof. *H.L. Broadbelt collection*

RIGHT. In 1898, Baldwin produced five Class H-9's, Pittsburgh made five and Richmond made one. No. 705 was a Baldwin product. *H.L. Broadbelt collection*

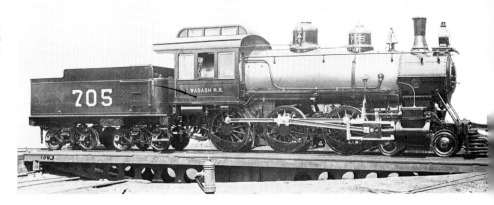

BELOW. F-4 Class 2-6-0 No. 774 was built in 1899 and scrapped in 1935. *H.L. Broadbelt collection*

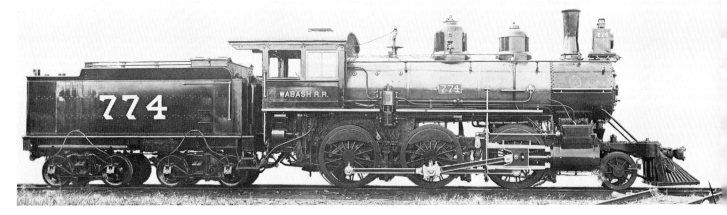

F-6 Class 2-6-0 No. 835 was built in July, 1903 and in November, 1917, rebuilt to a B-8 #487. *H.L. Broadbelt collection*

No. 2030 was a G-1 2-6-2 with 70″ drivers and 38,670 pounds of tractive effort. It was built in 1906. *H.L. Broadbelt collection* BELOW. No. 2806 was of the M-1 Class 4-8-2, built in 1930. *H.L. Broadbelt collection*

The Class O 4-8-4's were the heaviest class of power the Wabash had. They had 29x32″ cylinders, 70″ drivers and developed 70,817 pounds of tractive effort. They were built between 1930 and 1931. *H.L. Broadbelt collection*

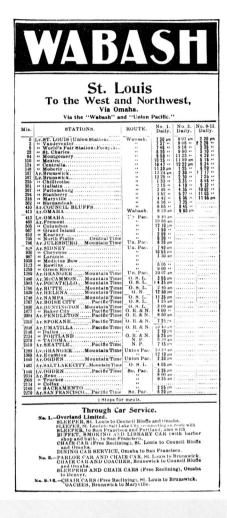

Electro-Motive Division (EMD)
of General Motors

Class D-10 NW-2 1,000 horsepower No. 351 was built in 1949.

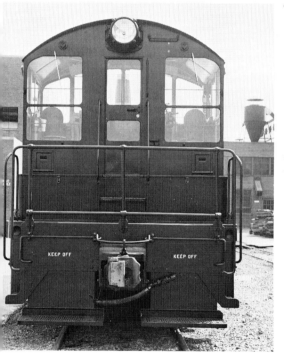

End view of No. 351 shows railings and part of the cab interior.

GP-7 1,500 horsepower diesel road switchers were 33 in number and built between 1950 and 1953.

Unless otherwise noted, all photos courtesy of EMD.

No. 454 was built in July of 1951, wrecked in August of 1959 and finally scrapped in June of 1960.

46-1580
E-662

No. 1101-A was built in 1949 and retired in 1964. Fresh from the factory, this three-piece machine was a classic.

No. 1143-A was built in June of 1950.

This builder's photo shows the F-7A No. 1104 and sister units in "mint" condition and ready for work.

The "BANNER BLUE LIMITED"

——— BETWEEN ———

ST. LOUIS and CHICAGO.

Inaugurated August 21st, 1904.

Leaves ST. LOUIS (Union Station),	-	11 00 a. m.	Leaves CHICAGO, - - - -	- 11 03 a. m.
Leaves ST. LOUIS (World's Fair Station),	-	11 14 a. m.	Arrives ST. LOUIS (World's Fair Station),	- 6 45 p. m.
Arrives CHICAGO, - - - -	-	7 00 p. m.	Arrives ST. LOUIS (Union Station),	- 7 03 p. m.

CONSIST OF TRAIN:

COMBINATION BAGGAGE AND SMOKING CAR,
COMBINATION DINING AND BUFFET CAR,
COMBINATION COACH AND CHAIR CAR,
COMBINATION OBSERVATION AND PARLOR CAR.

———

Painted in royal blue and gold; vestibuled throughout; lighted by electricity; cooled by electric fans; finished in African mahogany, inlaid with holly; windowed with bevel plate and cathedral jewel glass; furnished with Wilton carpets and upholstered with silk plush; Havlin china and Toledo cut glass; pantry, kitchen and chef's department specially designed; every car supplied with hot and cold water and heated by steam.

From September, 1904 Wabash timetable.

Lima Locomotive Works

Lima's only contribution to the Wabash steam locomotive roster was the C-4 switchers such as this No. 1564 0-8-0. These locomotives had 52″ drivers and 25x28″ cylinders and were all built in March and April of 1926.

Class D-12 1,200 horsepower yard switchers by Lima were Nos. 401-411, all built in 1950 and all retired in 1965 and 1966.

190

BARTON K DAVIS

WABASH

Chapter 10

Passenger trains

TOP. A 4-4-0 of the D-22 Class pauses at Peru, Indiana about 1900 during a passenger run. The fireman gazes out his window at the crowd. *M.D. McCarter collection* BELOW. No. 618, a 4-4-2 of the E-3 Class, highballs just west of Sadorus, Illinois around 1910 with a six-car train. *Frank Sadorus, collection of The Champaign County Historical Archives of The Urbana Free Library*

LEFT. Glistening under a warm morning sun in the Spring of 1944, the celebrated flagship of the Wabash passenger fleet, the *Banner Blue,* races through the Illinois countryside on its morning trip from Chicago to St. Louis with its charging M-1 4-8-2 Baldwin and its brass railed open platform Pullman observation car at the rear. Luxurious Sleepy Hollow seating, plantation cuisine, and easy going hospitality were the hallmarks of this once-famous name train in America's colorful parade of elegant varnish runs. *Charcoal by Barton K. Davis, 1984*

It's train time at Wabash, Indiana, and the Wabash passenger train is on time. *M.D. McCarter*

Train No. 13, a "no name" daily except Sunday train on the Wabash, that ran between Decatur and Chicago would, on signal, stop at Manhattan, Custer Park, Campus, Strawn, Foosland or Lodge, Illinois. Train is at 55th Street in Chicago in 1948. *Harold Stirton*

Presumably one of the local trains between Chicago and Decatur of 1947, this string of 3 cars and No. 665 slide down the mainline. *Collection of William Raia*

BELOW. A United States Army car rides at the headend of this train with No. 668 also at the headend. *Richard Ganger* BOTTOM. Northbound *Midnight Limited* with 10 cars opens up at 47th Street in Chicago on July 23, 1939. *Paul Eilenberger, collection of Harold Stirton*

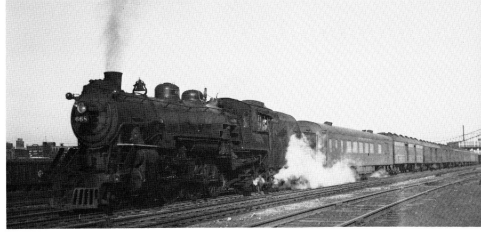

The *Red Bird,* a daily Chicago to Detroit Wabash train that included a parlor-lounge, drawing-room parlor car, diner, reclining chair cars, and observation-buffet car, holes up in Ft. Wayne on August 10, 1945 until passengers are loaded and unloaded. In Chicago, the train left from Union Station at Canal and Adams streets. In Detroit, it left from Fort Street Union Station. *Paul Eilenberger, Harold Stirton collection*

LEFT. The *Banner Blue* is being pulled by two J Class 4-6-2's. The dozen car train is southbound at Ashburn, Illinois in September of 1939. *Paul Eilenberger, collection of Harold Stirton*

BELOW. A 10-car *Banner Blue* hightails it out of Ashburn, Illinois in 1939 with a doubleheader doing the honors. *Paul Eilenberger, collection of Harold Stirton*

TOP. The *Blue Bird* rolls southbound at Englewood/63rd Street in Chicago at around 5 p.m. on May 25, 1947. The *Blue Bird* featured a dining car, reclining chair cars, drawing-room parlor car and parlor-lounge. *Harold Stirton* ABOVE. The St. Louis to Omaha *Omaha Limited* was carried over Union Pacific rails to Omaha and then on Southern Pacific rails to San Francisco. It featured 12-section drawing room sleepers, a cafe car and reclining chair cars. Here it's at Omaha with No. 691. *Collection of John Nixon*

Buffet Compartment Sleeping Cars.

A SNUG, richly furnished apartment, into which the traveler can lock himself or herself, and enjoy absolute privacy, brilliantly lighted by the Pintsch Gas System, supplied with lavatory and closet, having an electric bell for summoning attendant, should he be desired to perform any personal service or serve any order from the well-stocked buffet—this is what the Wabash offers its patrons in the way of Sleeping Car facilities, and at very reasonable prices. These superb compartment cars are run on night trains between St. Louis and Kansas City, St. Louis and Chicago, and Chicago and Detroit.

ABOVE. The *Detroit Limited* barrels eastbound through Adrian, Michigan with a 10-car train on October 3, 1948 with No. 700 4-6-4 pulling. The mighty power of the P Class locomotives shines through! *Harold Stirton* BELOW. Train Nos. 10 and 11 *Banner Blue* meet in Decatur on September 1, 1948. *Paul Stringham, collection of M.D. McCarter*

SERVING THE HEART OF AMERICA

The Peru, Indiana yard on August 25, 1947 was humming with activity, such as this Wabash passenger train featuring a troop sleeper at the headend. *M.D. McCarter*

WABASH RAILROAD

Harold Stirton snapped No. 705 heading up the seven car southbound *Banner Blue* at 21st Street, Chicago on August 1, 1948.

A fan trip on October 23, 1949 takes No. 817, a 2-6-0 from the F-6 Class out on the line. The train is at Pine, Indiana. *William Swartz, collection of M.D. McCarter*

BELOW. The conductor finds that it's cool riding on the rear platform as the hot sun starts to recede. The northbound *Banner Blue* is clicking away the miles from St. Louis and is now in the vicinity of Forrest, Illinois on September 27, 1948. *Harold Stirton*

The Wabash did a good business in tours and specials. On July 23, 1939 Banner Tours sponsored this excursion over Wabash rails. Here the 13-car train with a 4-8-4 leading heads southbound through Ashburn, Illinois. *Paul Eilenberger, collection of Harold Stirton*

An SW-8 has hold of a baggage car and a day coach, both of Canadian National origin, on July 20, 1953. The Wabash and CNR jointly operated mixed runs between St. Thomas and Jarvis, Ontario, each road underwriting the train for six months at a time. *Richard Ganger*

ABOVE. The 21.7 mile Centralia to Columbia, Missouri branch ran three passenger trains and three mixed trains every day between the two towns. The passenger equipment consisted of a baggage car used in Railway Express service and a coach named "City of Columbia." The passenger cars served as a caboose. *George Drake, collection of Louis Marre* LEFT. Nos. 486 and 485 GP-9's near Pine, Indiana haul a Detroit Railroad Club excursion from South Bend over the NJI&I on April 12, 1959. Note track speeder behind the train. *Louis Marre*

No. 486 and an N&W unit pull Wabash varnish out of the train shed on July 5, 1965 in Chicago. *William Raia*

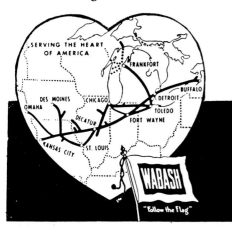

"CITY OF KANSAS CITY" — This completely new Wabash Streamliner offers you the ultimate in modern rail travel. Daily service between St. Louis and Kansas City. Diesel-powered, of course. *Extra* comfort . . . *but no extra fare.*

"CITY OF ST. LOUIS" — This sleek Wabash Streamliner, a companion train to the "City of Kansas City," is in daily service between St. Louis, Kansas City, Denver and the West Coast. Through sleeping cars and coaches to Los Angeles and Portland. Through sleeping car to San Francisco.

No. 1001 E-7 gets an inspection at Decatur as the train makes a stop. Date is 1959. *R.R. Wallin, collection of Louis Marre*

No. 1002 was a 2,000 hp E7 built by EMD for passenger service. It held 1,200 gallons of fuel, 400 gallons of cooling water and it stood 14′11″ above the rails. *Louis Marre collection*

This is the classic pose of the Wabash streamliner *Blue Bird,* with its four dome cars, including a dome-observation. *R.R. Wallin collection*

A seven car train heads through open countryside in a scene that was played over and over again when Wabash varnish was running. This day an E-8 No. 1003 (later renumbered to 3803 as an N&W unit) sports the train's flag. *Harry Zillmer, collection of M.D. McCarter*

BELOW. No. 1003 again at Lafayette, Indiana on May 24, 1964. *Louis Marre*

205

ABOVE. The *City of St. Louis,* with yellow cars, passes KCT Tower 8 eastbound at Kansas City on April 16, 1965. *Louis Marre* BELOW. Outbound *Banner Blue* at 15th Street in Chicago in February, 1962. *William Raia* NEXT PAGE. Bruce Meyer caught No. 1005 at Chicago in 1958.

No. 1011 rolls over the Penn Central diamond at Clymers, Indiana in September of 1963. *Louis Marre*

RIGHT. A winter's day in 1963 finds the *Banner Blue* in Chicago but making headway for St. Louis. *William Raia* BELOW. One of the *City* trains passes KCT Tower 8 westbound on December 18, 1959. *Louis Marre*

BRANCH LINES

CHAMPAIGN, MEREDOSIA, KEOKUK AND PITTSFIELD BRANCHES
FREIGHT AND PASSENGER:
   25 MPH, or 1 mile in 2 minutes 24 seconds.

STREATOR BRANCH
FREIGHT AND PASSENGER:
   30 MPH, or 1 mile in 2 minutes.

SULLIVAN BRANCH
FREIGHT AND PASSENGER:
   20 MPH, or 1 mile in 3 minutes.

EQUIPMENT RESTRICTIONS
   Passenger trains handling freight cars will observe freight train speeds.
   Trains, engines and self-propelled equipment must not exceed the following speeds when moving in automatic block signal or traffic control system, through interlocking or approaching highway crossings protected by automatic warning devices—

Single engine or unit of self-propelled equipment	20 MPH
Two units of engine or cars	30 MPH
Three units of engines or cars	40 MPH

D-20, D-22, or single unit of a D-30, D-45, or A and B unit of a D-45 running backwards, must not exceed 25 MPH.

Decatur Division Timetable, April 30, 1961

Wabash fans will recognize this location: Lake Decatur, a place where Wabash train watching and picture taking was always rewarding. *Harry Zillmer, M.D. McCarter collection*

The Continental Limited

Between

St. Louis and New York
and Chicago, New York and Boston

Is a solid fast through train, running every day in the year without change of cars between the cities named.

The equipment is as fine as is in use on any first class line.

All meals are served in dining cars, placed upon the train at convenient hours.

The dining cars serving this train are as fine as are made. They are mostly new, being electrically lighted and equipped with electric fans which are kept in motion when the temperature requires it. All the furnishings of these cars are very elaborate and beautiful, and the cuisine is equal to that of the best hotels. The time made by this train is very fast.

The Fast Mail

Between

Kansas City, Buffalo, New York and Boston.

The introduction of this train was one of the greatest boons to the business communities having interests between Kansas City and the East. It leaves Kansas City at the close of a business day (6.15 p. m.), arrives at Buffalo the evening of the following day (7.50 p. m.), at New York the second morning (7.45 a. m.) and at Boston 10.45 the second morning—thus occupying in its run only one full business day to Buffalo and New York City and but little more clear through to Boston.

It leaves Boston at 5.00 a. m. and New York at 10.00 a. m., arriving in Kansas City at 9.30 p. m. the following day. It is the fastest train running between Kansas City and New York and the only train by any line which does not require a change of cars between Kansas City and Buffalo.

209

You can just about hear the purr of the PA's as they idle at the Decatur station. There were only four PA's on the system. *W. Peters, collection of Louis Marre, Gordon Mott*

CHICAGO - ST. LOUIS—The Wabash fleet of fine trains is led by the Wabash Domeliner *Blue Bird*, called "the most beautiful train in America" and the only Dome train between these cities. The *Banner Blue* and the *Midnight* have also earned a reputation for speed and comfort.

DETROIT - ST. LOUIS—By day, the *Wabash Cannon Ball* offers fast modern service, with convenient connections to and from the West and Southwest at St. Louis. For overnight travel, there's the popular *Detroit Limited* and *St. Louis Limited*, with service to and from Toledo as well.

ST. LOUIS - KANSAS CITY—The ultra-modern Wabash Domeliner *City of Kansas City* features a luxurious Dome coach that lets you see more of Missouri than ever before! In addition, the streamliner *City of St. Louis* and the *Midnight Limited* both offer excellent service.

ST. LOUIS - WEST COAST—You can travel swiftly and directly to Denver, Los Angeles and San Francisco in the luxury streamliner *City of St. Louis*. Leaves St. Louis every afternoon—both coach and Pullman accommodations reserved in advance.

ST. LOUIS - OMAHA—Convenient overnight service with Pullman accommodations is provided between these cities.

RIGHT. The *Banner Blue* southbound at Chicago's 12th Street on August 28, 1958. *Bruce Meyer*

210

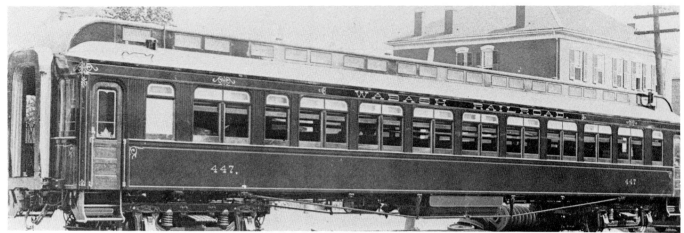

Information on this car, and others like it, is rare. It is, however, a turn of the century car. *ACF*

No. 1391 was built in 1912 as a buffet-chair car. *ACF*

In 1924, Wabash received this baggage car. Note it reads "American Railway Express" on the side. *ACF*

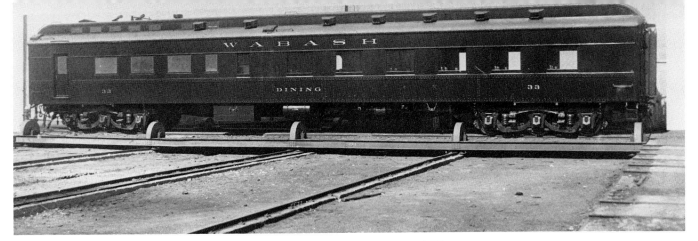

In 1923, ACF delivered No. 33. *ACF*

LEFT. Inside of Baggage car No. 340. *ACF*

BELOW. Chair car No. 1403 was constructed in 1927. *ACF*

BOTTOM. *Blue Boy* contained four bedrooms and 12 single roomettes. The car was made in 1950. *ACF*

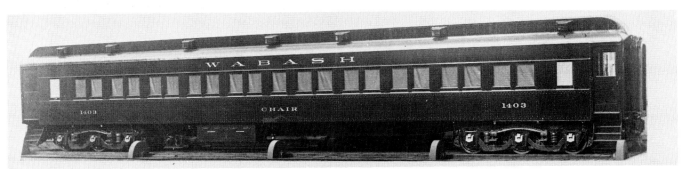

Western View was a 4 bedroom, 12 roomette sleeper in Union Pacific colors and Wabash lettering. It was constructed in January, 1950. *ACF*

City of Kansas City

In 1947 the Wabash put the streamline *City of Kansas City* into daily daytime service between St. Louis and Kansas City. The train was styled to provide an appearance of unity from locomotive to the observation end. Here is the baggage car. *Dick Kuelbs collection*

The two coaches made were identical on the exterior, but had different interior decorative treatment. The coach section sat 58, the smoking room eight. *ACF*

The buffet-coach sat 60 and also had a refreshment section in the center for serving soft drinks, ice cream and sandwiches. There were 10 bar stools for seating in this section. *Dick Kuelbs collection*

The observation-lounge was equipped with two settees for two persons each and six individual lounge chairs. All seating was Air-foam rubber with wine-colored leather upholstery. *Dick Kuelbs collection*

The observation-lounge featured blue carpeting, windows draped with tan Loomcraft with Da Lite control venetian blinds with wood slats painted oyster white and frames of golden bronze. In the table at the end were lockers underneath containing radio equipment, back-up equipment and Mars light control. *Dick Kuelbs collection*

Trucks on all the *City of Kansas City* cars were four-wheel with 6″ by 11″ Hyatt roller journal bearings on the two head-end cars and the dining car and 5½″ by 10″ on the coaches and parlor car. Wheels were 36″ rolled steel with treads ground after mounting to insure uniform size and concentricity. The Mars-Figure 8 red signal light on the rear car operated automatically with a service or emergency air brake application, and in emergency it could be operated manually. Exterior of the cars was aluminum and Wabash blue. *Dick Kuelbs collection*

Passenger Car Equipment

as of January, 1962

Car Number	Kind of Car	Year Built	Builder	Seating
400		1955	Decatur	
5		1924	AC&F Co.	
6		1911	AC&F Co	
	Rebuilt 1929	Decatur		
100		1924		
17	Safety/Freight clm	1923	AC&F Co.	44
		cnvt 1950 Decatur		
18	Eng. Ins. Car		Pullman Co.	16
		cnvt 1950 Decatur		
40	Dining-Tap	1927	Pullman Co.	36
50	Dining/Cocktail	1947	AC&F Co.	54
51	Dining/Cocktail	1949	Budd Co.	52
162	Postal	1913	AC&F Co.	
167	Postal	1914	AC&F Co.	
175	Postal	1915	AC&F Co.	
179	Postal	1916	AC&F Co.	
200	Chair Dome'D'	1950	Budd Co.	86
201	Chair Dome'D'	1950	Budd Co.	86
202	Chair Dome'D'	1950	Budd Co.	86
203	Chair Dome'D'	1958	Pullman	67
336	Baggage	1812	AC&F Co.	
		cnvt 1948		
340	Baggage	1925	AC&F Co.	
341	Baggage	1925	AC&F Co.	
342	Baggage	1925	AC&F Co.	
344	Baggage	1925	AC&F Co.	
345	Baggage	1925	AC&F Co.	
347	Baggage	1925	AC&F Co.	
348	Baggage	1926	AC&F Co.	
349*	Baggage	1926	AC&F Co.	
350	Baggage	1926	AC&F Co.	
351*	Baggage	1926	AC&F Co.	
352	Baggage	1926	AC&F Co.	
354	Baggage	1926	AC&F Co.	
355	Baggage	1926	AC&F Co.	
356	Baggage	1926	AC&F Co.	
357	Baggage	1926	AC&F Co.	
358*	Baggage	1926	AC&F Co.	
359*	Baggage	1926	AC&F Co.	
360	Baggage	1926	AC&F Co.	
361*	Baggage	1926	AC&F Co.	
363*	Baggage	1921	AC&F Co.	
364	Baggage	1926	AC&F Co.	
365S	Baggage	1926	AC&F Co.	
366*	Baggage	1926	AC&F Co.	
367	Baggage	1926	AC&F Co.	
369	Baggage	1925	AC&F Co.	
370	Baggage	1925	AC&F Co.	
372*	Baggage	1930	AC&F Co.	
		cnvt 1949		
373*	Baggage	1930	AC&F Co.	
		cnvt 1955		
375	Baggage	1947	AC&F Co.	
376*	Baggage	1927	AC&F Co.	
		cnvt 1952 Decatur		
377*	Baggage	1927	AC&F Co.	
		cnvt 1952 Decatur		
378*	Baggage	1927	AC&F Co.	
		cnvt 1952 Decatur		
379*	Baggage	1927	AC&F Co.	
		cnvt 1952 Decatur		
380*	Baggage	1928	AC&F Co.	
		cnvt 1956 Decatur		
381*	Baggage	1925	AC&F Co.	
		cnvt 1956 Decatur		
430	Bagg. & Mail	1917	AC&F Co.	
		cnvt 1923		
431	Bagg. & Mail	1917	AC&F Co.	
		cnvt 1923		

Car Number	Kind of Car	Year Built	Builder	Seating
435	Bagg. & Mail	1917	AC&F Co.	
		cnvt 1923		
441	Bagg. & Mail	1913	AC&F Co.	
		cnvt 1937		
442	Bagg. & Mail	1914	AC&F Co.	
		cnvt 1937		
444	Bagg. & Mail	1914	AC&F Co.	
		cnvt 1937		
445	Bagg. & Mail	1915	AC&F Co.	
		cnvt 1938		
446	Bagg. & Mail	1916	AC&F Co.	
		cnvt 1938		
448	Bagg. & Mail	1927	St.L. Car Co.	
		cnvt 1940		
598	Comb'D'	1925	AC&F Co.	24
609	Comb	1927	St.L. Car Co.	26
612*	Comb	1947	Pullman	44
613*	Comb	1947	Pullman	44
650	Bagg/Buffet/Lounge	1949	Budd	32
700	Storage Express	1959	Wabash	
701	Storage Express	1959	Wabash	
702	Storage Express	1959	Wabash	
703	Storage Express	1959	Wabash	
704	Storage Express	1959	Wabash	
705	Storage Express	1959	Wabash	
706	Storage Express	1959	Wabash	
707	Storage Express	1959	Wabash	
708	Storage Express	1959	Wabash	
709	Storage Express	1959	Wabash	
1222 City Coach	of Columbia	1912	AC&F Co.	88
1224	Chair 'D'	1923	AC&F Co.	58
1225	Chair 'D'	1923	AC&F Co.	58
1227	Chair 'D'	1923	AC&F Co.	68
1228	Chair 'D'	1923	AC&F Co.	58
1229	Chair 'D'	1923	AC&F Co.	58
1232	Chair 'D'	1927	AC&F Co.	58
1233	Chair 'D'	1927	AC&F Co.	58
1234	Chair 'D'	1927	AC&F Co.	58
1235	Chair 'D'	1927	AC&F Co.	68
1236	Chair 'D'	1927	AC&F Co.	58
1237	Chair 'D'	1927	AC&F Co.	68
1238	Chair 'D'	1927	AC&F Co.	58
1239	Chair 'D'	1927	AC&F Co.	68
1240	Chair 'D'	1927	AC&F Co.	68
1241	Chair 'D'	1927	AC&F Co.	68
1393	Chair 'D'	1925	AC&F Co.	68
1398	Chair 'D'	1925	AC&F Co.	68
1399	Chair 'D'	1925	AC&F Co.	68
1400	Chair 'D'	1925	AC&F Co.	68
1401	Chair 'D'	1925	AC&F Co.	68
1402	Chair 'D'	1927	AC&F Co.	68
1405	Chair 'D'	1927	AC&F Co.	68
1406	Chair 'D'	1927	AC&F Co.	61
1407	Chair 'D'	1927	AC&F Co.	61
1408	Chair 'D'	1927	AC&F Co.	61
1409	Chair 'D'	1927	AC&F Co.	61
1412	Chair 'D'	1927	Pullman	72
		cnvt 1942 Decatur		72
1417	Chair 'D'	1947	Pullman	66
1418	Chair 'D'	1947	Pullman	66
1419	Chair 'D'	1947	Pullman	66
1420	Chair 'D'	1947	Pullman	66
1421	Chair 'D'	1947	Pullman	66
1422	Chair 'D'	1947	Pullman	66
1423	Chair 'D'	1947	Pullman	66
1424	Chair 'D'	1947	Pullman	66
1425	Chair 'D'	1947	AC&F Co.	66
1426	Chair 'D'	1947	AC&F Co.	66
1427	Chair 'D'	1950	AC&F Co.	56
1428	Chair 'D'	1950	AC&F Co.	56

Car Number	Kind of Car	Year Built	Builder	Seating
1429	Chair 'D'	1950	AC&F Co.	56
1430	Chair 'D'	1950	AC&F Co.	56
1431	Chair 'D'	1950	AC&F Co.	52
1510	Lounge	1927	Pullman Co.	45
		cnvt 1933		
1525	Chair/Buffet/Deluxe	1947	AC&F Co.	72
1570	Cafe-Lounge	1947	Pullman Co.	41
1571	Cafe-Lounge	1947	Pullman Co.	41
1563	Cafe-Lounge	1927	Pullman Co.	36
		cnvt 1934		
1565	Cafe-Lounge	1923	AC&F Co.	33
		cnvt 1936		
1566	Cafe-Lounge	1923	AC&F Co.	33
		cnvt 1936		
1568	Cafe-Lounge	1927	Pullman	34
		cnvt. 1950 Decatur		
1569	Cafe-Lounge	1927	Pullman	34
		cnvt. 1950 Decatur		
City of Peru	Parlor	1925	Pullman	37
City of Decatur	Parlor 'D'	1927	Pullman	38
City of Lafayette	Parlor'D'/Observ.	1927	Pullman	36
City of Danville	Parlor 'D'	1927	Pullman	38
City of Wabash	Parlor 'D'/Observ.	1927	Pullman	36
1600	Parlor 'D'/Observ.	1947	AC&F Co.	47
1601	Parlor 'D' Dome/Observ.	1950	Budd	58
1602	Parlor 'D' Dome	1952	Pullman	56
Emerald Park	Sleeper	1917	Pullman	8-4
Clover Leaf	Sleeper	1911	Pullman	8-5
Clover Plateau	Sleeper	1913	Pullman	8-5
Western Lake	Sleeper	1950	AC&F Co.	4-12
Western Sunset	Sleeper	1950	AC&F Co.	4-12
Western View	Sleeper	1950	AC&F Co.	4-12
Blue Gazelle	Sleeper	1950	AC&F Co.	4-12
Blue Skies	Sleeper	1950	AC&F Co.	4-12
Blue Boy	Sleeper	1950	AC&F Co.	4-12
Blue Cloud	Sleeper	1950	AC&F Co.	4-12
Blue Horizon	Sleeper	1950	AC&F Co.	4-12
Blue Knight	Sleeper	1950	AC&F Co.	4-12
National Unity	Sleeper	1955	Pullman	4-6
National Homes	Sleeper	1955	Pullman	4-6
National Colors	Sleeper	1955	Pullman	4-6
New York University	Sleeper	1917	Pullman	12-2

*Sanitary Equipped
S-Storage

Dick Kuelbs collection

LEFT. An REA car at Decatur, April 22, 1967. *L.G. Issac*

BELOW. Wabash RPO No. 452 at St. Louis. *Wilbur Thurmon*

LEFT. No. 1235 was part of a steam special on May 25, 1966. William Raia photographed it in Indianapolis.

RIGHT. On that same steam special was No. 1401. BELOW. Coach No. 1406 in Chicago on July 6, 1967. *Both photos, William Raia*

RIGHT. Cafe-lounge No. 1568 is at Decatur on April 22, 1967. *L.G. Issac.* BELOW. The *City of Danville* rests in Landers Yard in Chicago, November, 1963. *William Raia.*

ABOVE. The parlor car *City of Peru* was built by Pullman in 1925. It seated six in the smoking section, 26 in the parlor room and five more in the drawing room. Previously it had been named the *Queen Anne. Wilbur Thurmon*

RIGHT. The observation-parlor *City of Wabash* was built in 1927. It seated 36 persons. Louis Marre photographed it at South Bend, Indiana, April 12, 1959 on the Detroit Railroad Club's Spring Rail Fan Trip.

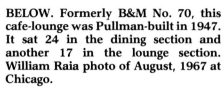
BELOW. Formerly B&M No. 70, this cafe-lounge was Pullman-built in 1947. It sat 24 in the dining section and another 17 in the lounge section. William Raia photo of August, 1967 at Chicago.

ABOVE. This baggage-buffet-lounge was Budd-built in 1949. Photo was taken in April of 1971 in Chicago. *William Raia*

ABOVE. This parlor-observation-dome car No. 1601 was Budd produced in 1950. Here it brings up the rear of the *Banner Blue* in 1963. *William Raia*

RIGHT. No. 1601 brings up the rear of the *Blue Bird*. *M.D. McCarter collection*

The *Banner Blue* was equipped with a dome, dining-lounge car, chair cars and this parlor-observation car. The February 1, 1962 Timetable listed the daily trains as Nos. 111-1 and 110, leaving Chicago at 10:30 a.m. and arriving in St. Louis at 4:15 p.m.; leaving St. Louis at 4 p.m. and arriving Chicago at 9:20 p.m. The *Banner Blue* was at 15th Street, Chicago, when this February, 1962 photo was taken. *William Raia*

WEST OR SOUTHWEST

GO

BELOW. No. 203 dome car was built by Pullman in 1958. This photo was taken a year later in St. Louis. *Bruce Meyer*

BOTTOM. Wabash No. 1427 was a chair car built by ACF in 1950. It seated 56. *Wilbur Thurmon*

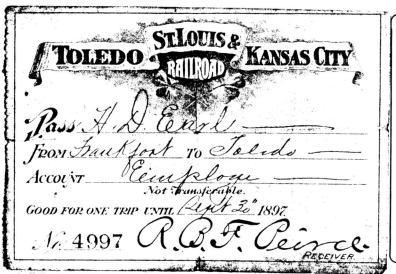

TOLEDO St.LOUIS & KANSAS CITY RAILROAD

Pass H. D. Earl

From Frankfort *to* Toledo

Account Employe

Not Transferable.

GOOD FOR ONE TRIP UNTIL *Sept 30"* 1897

N. 4997 R. B. F. Peirce

RECEIVER.

WABASH RAILROAD COMPANY

NOT GOOD ON BLUE BIRD OR CITY OF ST. LOUIS

1964-65-66-67-68 No. B 4711

PASS

Mrs. Henry Lischewski —————
Wife of Stockman

Good on trains 121, 128, 209 & 210

BETWEEN ALL STATIONS UNTIL DECEMBER 31, 1968
UNLESS OTHERWISE LIMITED ABOVE AND SUBJECT TO CONDITIONS ON BACK

ADDRESS Decatur, Ill. REQUESTED BY CEH

ACCEPTED BY ME FOR USE SUBJECT TO CONDITIONS ON BACK.

VICE-PRESIDENT AND GENERAL MANAGER

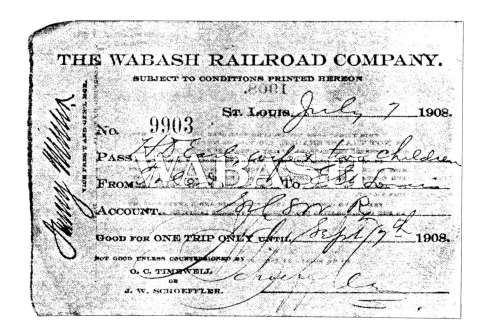

THE WABASH RAILROAD COMPANY.

SUBJECT TO CONDITIONS PRINTED HEREON

St. Louis July 7 1908.

No. 9903

PASS H. D. Earl wife & two children

FROM _____ To St. Louis

ACCOUNT Gen. Supt. R.

GOOD FOR ONE TRIP ONLY UNTIL Sept 7th 1908.

NOT GOOD UNLESS COUNTERSIGNED BY

O. C. TIMEWELL
OR
J. W. SCHOEFFLER.

WABASH RAILWAY COMPANY
TIME PASS 1920

No. T1814

PASS Mr. E. M. Doyle,----------

ACCOUNT Supv. of Track,
M. & St. L. RR.

BETWEEN Sta. in Ia. Ill. & Mo.

UNTIL Dec.31st 1920 { UNLESS OTHERWISE ORDERED AND SUBJECT TO CONDITIONS ON BACK

VALID WHEN COUNTERSIGNED BY
F. E. PESNELLE OR J. W. SCHOEFFLER

COUNTERSIGNED BY

PRESIDENT

1929 No. B 7980
WABASH RAILWAY COMPANY

PASS Miss Dorothy Earl........
Dep dtr of H. D. Earl, Gen. Manager
Texas & Pacific Ry. Co.

OVER ALL DIVISIONS UNTIL DECEMBER 31st UNLESS OTHERWISE
ORDERED AND SUBJECT TO CONDITIONS ON BACK

VALID WHEN COUNTERSIGNED BY R. E. DeGROAT. M. C. FUNCK OR D. L. PETERSON

COUNTERSIGNED BY

PRESIDENT

222

The Wabash Cannon Ball

There's a train that's still a runnin'
It's serving one and all,
Tis known throughout the country
as the "Wabash Cannon Ball."
She rolls right through the prairies
And the state of Illinois
With her soybeans and corn so tall,
Yes, sir, it's the "Wabash Cannon Ball."

She starts in ole St. Louis,
Through the woodlands by the shore
Of the muddy Mississippi
With its history galore.
It pauses at Decatur,
For an engine change and crew
Going on to Danville,
Next stop Peru.

To Ft. Wayne and Detroit,
That's as far as she will go.
She used to pull the Mail
Through the rain, sleet and snow.
She's had her share of hobos,
Some short and some tall,
But one thing they had in common,
They all rode the "Wabash Cannon Ball."

Many a man has pulled the throttle
Of this very famous train,
And when he had to leave her,
His heart was filled with pain.
He knew she'd keep on runnin'
For he heard the country's call,
To save this thing of beauty,
the "Wabash Cannon Ball."

By John W. Day
Retired Paint Foreman
Decatur Locomotive Shops

223

Freight cars

March, 1925

THE OFFICIAL RAILWAY EQUIPMENT REGISTER.

WABASH RAILWAY CO.

GENERAL OFFICERS.

W. H. WILLIAMS, Chman. of Board, New York, N.Y.
J. E. TAUSSIG, President............St. Louis, Mo.
W. C. MAXWELL, Vice-President in Charge of Traffic................ "
S. E. COTTER, Vice-President & General Manager.................... "
N. S. BROWN, Vice-President & General Solicitor.................... "
J. W. NEWELL, Vice-Pres. & Compt. "

G. E. FRANCISCO, Local Treasurer...St. Louis, Mo.
G. E. BRAMON, General Auditor....... "
W. J. TOBIN, Freight Claim Agent... "
G. H. SIDO, Supt. Transportation.... "
M. M. EIDSON, Gen. Car Accountant. "
G. F. HESS, Supt. Motive Power......Decatur, Ill.
R. H. HOWARD, Chief Engineer......St. Louis, Mo.
T. J. FRIER, Purchasing Agent...... "
C. H. STINSON, Frt. Traffic Mgr..... "

E. R. NEWMAN, Asst. Frt. Traf. Mgr..Chicago, Ill.
H. E. WATTS, Pass. Traf. Manager...St. Louis, Mo.
G. B. LINDSAY, Gen. Baggage Agt. & Gen. Agent Mail & Exp. Traffic.. "

Eastern District.

T. J. JONES, General Superintendent. St. Louis, Mo.

Western District.

E. A. SOLLITT, Gen. Superintendent..St. Louis, Mo.

GENERAL OFFICE, RAILWAY EXCHANGE BLDG, ST. LOUIS, MO. , NEW YORK OFFICE, 120 BROADWAY, NEW YORK CITY.

Miles of road operated, 2487.10. Gauge, 4 ft. 8½ in. Locomotives (coal burning), 645. American Railway Express Co. operates over this line. Pullman Sleeping Car Co. operates over this line.

FREIGHT EQUIPMENT.

The freight cars of this Company are numbered and classified as follows:

KIND OF CARS.		NUMBERS.	DIMENSIONS.												CAPACITY.		NO.
			Inside.			Outside.					Doors.						
								Height from Rail.			Side.		End.				
M. C. B. Designation	Class.		Length ft. in.	Width ft. in.	Height ft. in.	Length ft. in.	Width at Eaves or Platform ft. in.	To Eaves ft. in.	To Top of Platform or Runn'g Board ft. in.	To over all ft. in.	Width ft. in.	Height ft. in.	Width ft. in.	Height ft. in.	Cubic Feet Level Full.	Pounds or Gallons.	
XM..	Box............	63001 to 64000	36	8 4	7	36 9	10	11 7	12 3½	13 7	5 6	7 6⅛	......	......	2100	60000 lb.	69
XM..	"	64001 to 64500	36	8 4	7 9	36 9	10	12 4	13 0¾	14 2	5 6	7 6⅛	......	......	2325	60000 lb.	342
XM..	"	64501 to 68506	36	8 4	7 7	36 9	10	12 2	12 10½	14	5 6	7 6⅛	......	......	2275	60000 lb.	3045
XM..	"	71000 to 72999	40 5⅝	8 6⅛	9 3	41 2⅜	9 7	13 11	14 1¾	14 9	6	8 9¾	......	......	3186	80000 lb.	658
.....	" Steel.......	74000 to 74006	40 6	8 6	9	42 1½	9 3¼	12 8¾	13 6⅞	14 1¾	6	8 5⅞	......	......	3098	80000 lb.	3
XM..	" "	75000 to 76199	36 5⅝	8 6	8	37 4⅞	9 4¼	12 0½	12 10⅞	13 5⅝	6	7 7¾	......	......	2480	80000 lb.	1166
XM..	" "	76200 to 78199	36 5¾	8 6	8	38 5½	9 3	12 3½	13 0½	13 8½	6	7 7¾	......	......	2480	80000 lb.	1976
XM..	" "	78200 to 79699	40 6	8 6	9	42 1½	9 3¼	12 8¾	13 6⅞	14 1¾	6	8 5⅞	......	......	3098	80000 lb.	1499
XM...	" "	79700 to 80999	40 6	8 6	9	42 1½	9 3¼	12 8¾	13 6⅞	14 1¾	6	8 5⅞	......	......	3098	80000 lb	1300
XF...	Furniture, Steel Underframe	52000 to 52149	49 4	8 8	8 7½	50 4	10 2¾	12 9½	14 4½	14 4½	7 6	8 7½	......	......	3688	80000 lb.	142
SF...	Stock, Double Deck.	15000 to 15099	40 5⅝	8 3¾	7 3	41 0⅞	9 2⅝	11 8¼	12 4¼	13 5½	5 6	7	2 3	1 11	2439	80000 lb.	94
SM...	"	15100 to 15999	40 5⅝	8 3¾	7 3	41 0⅞	9 2⅝	11 8¼	12 4¼	13 5½	5 6	7	2 3	1 11	2439	80000 lb.	843
SF...	" Double Deck	16000 to 16299	40 5⅝	8 2¾	7 3	41 1	9 2½	12 4½	12 4	13 5½	5 6	1 7	2 6	1 8	2439	80000 lb.	295
XA...	Automobile	18700 to 18999	40 6	8 6	9 3	41 2	9 7	13 11	14 1¾	14 9	10	8 11	......	......	3186	80000 lb.	299
XA...	"	19000 to 19499	40 5⅝	8 6⅛	9 3	41 2⅜	9 7	13 11	14 1¾	14 9	10 5¾	8 8½	......	......	3186	80000 lb.	435
XA...	"	19750 to 19999	40 5⅝	8 6⅛	9 3	41 2⅜	9 7	13 11	14 1¾	14 9	10 5¾	8 8½	......	......	3186	80000 lb	236
XA...	" Steel	20000 to 20749	40 5⅝	8 6	10	42 6⅝	9 3¾	13 10	14 7	15 2½	10	9 8	......	......	3440	80000 lb.	736
XA...	"	21250 to 22999	40 6	8 6	9 2⅜	42	9 7	12 9¾	13 7 7/16	14 3½	10	8 5⅞	......	......	......	80000 lb.	1750
XA...	"	23000 to 24499	40 6	8 6	9	41 2	9 3¼	12 10½	13 8⅝	14 3½	10	8 5⅞	......	......	3098	80000 lb.	1500
FM...	Flat, Steel Underframe.	25000 to 25499	....	8 3	......	42	9 ...	3 8	3 8	3 8	......	......	......	......	......	80000 lb	487
GB...	Coal " ..	5000 to 6999	41	9 6	4 2½	43 10½	10 0½	8 0⅜	8 0⅜	9 0¾	......	......	......	......	1639	100000 lb.	519
GB...	" " ..	7000 to 9049	41 6	9 1⅝	4 6⅜	42 1	9 5⅛	8 4 9/16	8 4 9/16	8 4 13/16	......	......	......	......	1718	100000 lb	2050
GB...	" " ..	10000 to 10449	41 6	9 1⅝	4 6⅜	42 1	9 5⅛	8 4 9/16	8 4 9/16	8 4 13/16	......	......	......	......	1718	100000 lb.	116
.....	" " DropEnd	11000 to 11249	48 6	9 6	3 6	49 9	10 3¼	....	....	7 4½	......	......	......	......	1621	140000 lb.	250
GB...	" " ..	28000 to 29999	41	9 4	4 5	41 5¾	9 9¾	8 1¾	8 1¾	8 10½	......	......	......	......	1690	100000 lb	264
HT....	" Steel Hopper...	30001 to 30294	30	9 5½	9 1	31 6	10	10	10	10 8¼	......	......	......	......	1738	100000 lb.	291
HT...	" " " ...	31000 to 31749	30 6	9 5½	9 1	31 11	10 0¾	10	10	10 8¼	......	......	......	......	1688	100000 lb.	750
HT....	" " " ...	34001 to 34568	28	9 5½	8 7	28 10	10 1	9 6	9 6	10 0¾	......	......	......	......	1356	80000 lb.	557
HM..	" " " ...	35000 to 35999	30 6	9 5½	7 5	31 11	10 3¼	10 8	10 8	10 8	......	......	......	......	1880	110000 lb	1000
GB...	"	39501 to 39982	33 8	9 5	4 2	35	9 9	8 3½	....	9	......	......	......	......	1318	80000 lb.	295
NE...	Caboose.......	2000 to 2538	....	....	....	....	....	....	....	....	......	......	......	......	......	......	[illegible]
GA...	Cinder..........	96001 to 96035	36	9 7	4 2	38	9 8	7 9	....	8 6	......	......	......	......	1937	80000 lb	23
MWD.	Air Dump, Ballast.	96051 to 96058	26	9	1 9¾	31	10 4	....	....	7 11	......	......	......	......	424	60000 lb.	8
MWB.	Ballast..........	96500 to 96599	33 7	8 3	4	34	8 9	8 1½	....	....	......	......	......	......	1108	80000 lb.	[illegible]
GS...	Cinder..........	97000 to 97130	33	8 6	3 10	34 5	10 3	8 6	....	....	......	......	......	......	1075	60000 lb.	7
	Total																23354

PASSENGER EQUIPMENT.

M. C. B. Designation.	KIND.	SERIES OF NUMBERS.	SEATING CAP'CTY	LENGTH OF CAR.	No.	M. C. B. Designation.	KIND.	SERIES OF NUMBERS.	SEATING CAP'CTY	LENGTH OF CAR.	No.
PV.....	Business, Steel Undrfme.	1 to 4			4	DA	Dining............	29, 30			
PV.....	"	7			1	DA	" All Steel....	31 to 34			
....	" All Steel ..	5			1	DO....	Cafe, Observation	61 to 65			
IA.....	Instruction.......	400			1	PC....	Parlor, Steel Undrfme	80 to 84			
IA.....	Instruction.......	8, 9			2	PC....	"	85			1
IA.....	Dynamometer, Stl. Udfme	10			1	PC....	" Steel Underframe	86			
IA.....	Instruction.......	12			1	PC....	" Steel, Reinforced.	87			
DA	Dining............	20 to 24			3	MA....	Mail, All Steel....	162 to 180		60 ft. & under 70 ft.	18
DA	" Steel, Reinforced	25, 26			2	BE....	Bagg. & Exp......	200 to 306		Under 60 ft.	49
DA	"	27			1	BE....	" "	307 to 320		60 ft. & under 70 ft.	13
DA	" Steel, Reinforced.	28			1	BE....	" " Steel, Reinforced.	321, 322		60 ft. & under 70 ft.	

★ Denotes additions. ● Denotes increase. ▲ Denotes reduction.

PASSENGER EQUIPMENT—Continued.

M. C. B. Designation.	KIND.	SERIES OF NUMBERS.	SEATING CAP'CTY	LENGTH OF CAR.	No.
BE.....	Bagg. & Exp......	323 to 330		60 ft. & under 70 ft.	5
BE.....	" " Steel, Reinforced.	331		60 ft. & under 70 ft.	1
BE.....	Bagg. & Exp......	332		60 ft. & under 70 ft.	1
BE.....	" " Steel, Reinforced.	333 to 337		60 ft. & under 70 ft.	5
MBE...	Baggage & Mail ..	400 to 416		Under 60 ft.	6
MBE...	" "	417 to 435		60 ft. & under 70 ft.	15
CO.....	Pass., Mail & Bagg.	451		Under 60 ft.	1
MS.....	Pass. and Mail...	471 to 473		Under 60 ft.	3
CA.....	Pass. & Baggage.	502 to 535		Under 60 ft.	13
CA.....	" " ..	536		60 ft. & under 70 ft.	1
CA.....	" " ..	537		Under 60 ft.	1
CA.....	" " ..	551 to 588		60 ft. & under 70 ft.	25
CA.....	" " All Stl.	589 to 599		Over 70 ft.	8
PA.....	Coach	801 to 827	Under 70		3
PA.....	"	901 to 967	Under 70		19
PA.....	"	981	Under 70		1
PA.....	"	980, 982, 983	70 to 86		3
PB.....	"	1000 to 1030	Under 70		15
PB.....	"	1050 to 1066	70 to 86		17
PB.....	"	1070 to 1084	Over 86		13
PB.....	"	1100	Under 70		1
PB.....	"	1119 to 1140	70 to 86		20
PB.....	"	1200, 1201	70 to 86		2
PB.....	" Steel Underfrme	1202, 1203	70 to 86		2
PB.....	"	1204 to 1214	70 to 86		7
PB.....	" All Steel...	1218 to 1231	Over 86		13
PC.....	Chair............	1300 to 1364	Under 70		34
PC.....	" ..	1370 to 1380	Under 70		7
PC.....	" Steel Reinforced.	1381, 1382	Under 70		2
PC.....	" All Steel....	1383 to 1398	70 to 86		14
DB.....	Cafe—Coach......	1500, 1501	70 to 86		2
DB.....	" —Chair	1502 to 1506	Under 70		4
DB.....	" " All Steel	1507, 1508	Under 70		2
DB.....	Buffet—Chair	1515, 1516	Under 70		2
DB.....	" " All Steel	1517 to 1522	Under 70		6
	Total............				391

MISCELLANEOUS EQUIPMENT.

Caboose—2000 to 2538.................	314	
Box—02097 to 02099, 02136 to 02149, 02245 to 02249, 02448, 02495 to 02499, 4264...............	35	
Pile Driver—3000 to 3003..........	3	
" Derrick—3012, 3013..........	2	
" Bridge Crane—3014 to 3016.	3	
" Convoy—3020 to 3027......	5	
Steam Shovel—3040 to 3043.......	3	
Ice—3067 to 3079.................	5	
Interlocker—3080 to 3119.........	38	
Wheel—3120 to 3129..............	9	
Pick-up—3140 to 3148............	8	
Supply—3149 to 3157.............	2	
Water Tank—3130, 3131, 3158, 3159, 3160 to 3169.................	14	
Gas Tank—3741, 3742, 3743........	3	

Ditcher Convoy—3727 to 3729......	3
Derricks—3170 to 3184.............	14
Wreck Tools—3200 to 3299........	42
" Flat—3300 to 3399........	31
Co. Serv. Box—3400 to 3499.......	77
" Flat—3500 to 3599.......	37
" Box—3600 to 3699.......	78
Snow Plow—3700.................	1
Flanger—3705...................	1
Leveler—3717, 3718, 3719.........	3
Ditcher—3720 to 3726............	3
Locomotive Supply—3730 to 3749..	4
S. K. Supply—3750 to 3799........	20
S. S. Convoy—3060 to 3062.......	2
Hurdy.........................	6
Co. Serv. Box—3800 to 4299.......	318
Total..................1084	

RECAPITULATION OF CAR EQUIPMENT.

FREIGHT.

Automobile (XA)—
  Cars of 80,000 lbs. capacity.. 4956
Furniture (XF)—
  Cars of 80,000 lbs. capacity.. 142
Plain Box (XM)—
  Cars of 60,000 lbs. capacity.. 3456
  Cars of 80,000 lbs. " 6602
Total Box (All Class X and Class V cars, except XT)—
  Cars of 60,000 lbs. capacity.. 3456
  Cars of 80,000 lbs. " ...11700
Gondola, Flat Bottom (GB, GK, GM, GT)—
  Cars of 80,000 lbs. capacity— 295
  Cars of 100,000 lbs. " .. 2949
  Cars of 140,000 lbs. 250
Hopper (HD, HM, HT)—
  Cars of 80,000 lbs. capacity.. 557
  Cars of 100,000 lbs. " .. 1041
  Cars of 110,000 lbs. .. 1000

Total Open Top Cars (Includes all Class G and H cars)—
  Cars of 80,000 lbs. capacity.. 852
  Cars of 100,000 lbs. " .. 3990
  Cars of 110,000 lbs. " .. 1000
  Cars of 140,000 lbs. " .. 250
Stock, Single Deck (SM)—
  Cars of 80,000 lbs. capacity.. 843
Stock, Double Deck (SF)—
  Cars of 80,000 lbs. " .. 1232
Flat (all Class F cars)—
  Cars of 80,000 lbs. capacity.. 487
Total Revenue Freight Equipment—
  Cars of 60,000 lbs. capacity.. 3456
  Cars of 80,000 lbs. " ..14271
  Cars of 100,000 lbs. " .. 3990
  Cars of 110,000 lbs. " .. 1000
  Cars of 140,000 lbs. " .. 250
Non-Revenue Freight Equipment—
  Caboose.................... 349
  Ballast.................... 38
  Other freight cars.......... 1123

Total Freight Equipment Cars.................24090

PASSENGER.

Coaches....................	116	Combined Pass. and Bagg......	48
Chair.....................	57	Combined Pass., Bagg. and Mail	4
Dining....................	13	Postal....................	18
Cafe......................	5	Baggage..................	76
Club......................	16	Baggage—Mail............	21
Parlor....................	6	Official and Instruction........	11

Total Passenger Equipment Cars.................... 391

GRAND TOTAL, Freight and Passenger Cars.................... 24481

WABASH RAILROAD COMPANY.

January, 1955

FREIGHT EQUIPMENT.

The freight cars of this Company are marked "Wabash" and are numbered and classified as follows:

ITEM NUMBER.	A. A. R. Mech. Designation.	MARKINGS AND KIND OF CARS.	NUMBERS.	INSIDE. Length	INSIDE. Width	INSIDE. Height	OUTSIDE. LENGTH At Eaves or Top of Sides or Platform	OUTSIDE. WIDTH Extreme Width.	OUTSIDE. HEIGHT FROM RAIL. To Extreme Width.	OUTSIDE. HEIGHT To Eaves or Top of Sides or Platform	OUTSIDE. HEIGHT To Top of Running Board	OUTSIDE. HEIGHT To Extreme Height.	DOORS. SIDE. Width of Open'g	DOORS. SIDE. Height of Open'g	DOORS. END. Width of Open'g	DOORS. END. Height of Open'g	CAPACITY. Cubic Feet Level Full.	CAPACITY. Pounds or Gallons.	Number of Cars.
				ft. in.	ft. in.	ft. in.	ft. in.	ft. in.	ft. in.	ft. in.	ft. in.	ft. in.	ft. in.	ft. in.	ft. in.	ft. in.			
1	XM	Box, All Steel...	6000 to 6299	40 6	9 2	10 6	41 10	9 3	10 6	13 8	14 6	15 1	15 1	8	9 10	....		3892	100000 lb.	15
2	XAP	" " Note AA	"	"	"	"	"	"	"	"	"	"	"	"	"	....	....	"	"	9
3	XAP	" " Note LL	"	"	"	"	"	"	"	"	"	"	"	"	"	....	....	"	"	
4	XAP	" " Note RR	"	"	"	"	"	"	"	"	"	"	"	"	"	....	....	"	"	6
5	XME	" " Note BB	"	"	9 0½	"	"	"	"	"	"	"	"	"	"	....	....	3849	"	5

225

Item No.	A.A.R. Mech. Desig.	Markings and Kind of Cars	Numbers	Inside Length	Inside Width	Inside Height	Outside Length	Width at Eaves or Top of Sides	Extreme Width	To Extreme Width	To Eaves or Top of Sides	To Top of Running Board	To Extreme Height	Side Door Width of Open'g	Side Door Height of Open'g	End Door Width of Open'g	End Door Height of Open'g	Cubic Feet Level Full	Pounds or Gallons	No. of Cars
6	XM	" " ..	7000 to 7299	40 6	9 2	10 6	41 10	9 3	10 6	13 8	14 6	15 1	15 1	6	9 10			3892	100000 lb.	29
7	XAP	Auto., All Steel..Note S	8000 to 8299	40 7	9 2	10 6	41 10	9 3	10 6	13 8	14 6	15 1	15 1	11 11	9 10			4006	100000 "	28
11	XM	Box, All Steel. Note Z	" "	40 6	"	"	"	"	"	"	"	"	"					3892	"	
12	XME	" " Note X	9000 to 9199	40 6	9 2	10 4½	41 9	9 3	10 6	13 6	14 4	14 11	14 11	6	9 9			3801	100000 lb.	20
13	XME	" " Note X	9200 to 9224	40 6	9 2	10 6	41 10	9 3	10 6	13 8	14 6	15 1	15 1	6	9 10			3847	80000 lb.	2
14	XME	" " Note X	9225 to 9299	40 6	9 2	10 6	41 10	9 3	10 6	13 8	14 6	15 1	15 1	6	9 10			3847	100000 lb.	7
15	XME	" " Note X	9300 to 9362	40 6	9 2	10 4½	41 9	9 3	10 6	13 6	14 4	14 11	14 11	6	9 9			3801	100000 lb.	6
16	XME	" " Note X	9363 to 9436	40 6	9 2	10 6	41 10	9 3	10 6	13 8	14 6	15 1	15 1	6	9 10			3847	100000 lb.	7
17	XM	" {Stl. Underfr., S.S., Comp. Body.....}	74000 to 74389	40 6	8 6	10 ...	42 2	8 8	10 ...	13 6	14 3	14 7	14 8	6	9 8			3442	80000 lb.	34
21	XM	" "	76000 to 76999	40 6	9 ...	10 ...	42 1	9 2	10 5	13 8	14 3	14 9		6	9 8			3645	80000 lb.	22
22	XM	" {Stl. Underfr., D.S., Comp. Body....}	78200 to 80999	40 6	8 6	9 ...	42 1	8 8	9 10	12 3	13 2	13 7	14 2	6	8 5			3096	80000 lb.	
23	XM	" {Stagg. Doors, Stl. Underfr., D. S.,}	81000 to 81499	40 6	8 6	9 ...	42 1	8 9	10 1	12 5	13 4	13 9	14 4	6	8 5			3098	80000 lb.	17
24	XM	" {Comp. Body...) Steel	81502	40 6	8 6	9 2	42 2	8 9	10 1	12 5	13 3	13 8	13 9	6	8 5			3166		
25	XM	" Steel	81600 to 81684	40 6	8 9	9 2	42 2	8 8	10 ...	12 3	12 10	13 7	13 8	6	8 6			3254	80000 lb.	6
26	XM	" "	81900 to 81999	40 6	8 9	9 2	42 2	8 8	10 ...	12 3	12 10	13 7	13 8	6	8 6			3254	80000 lb.	7
31	XAP	" " Note M①	" "	"	8 10	"	"	"	"	"	"	"	"					3303		
32	XM	" "	82000 to 82506	40 6	8 9	9 2	......	8 8	10 ...	12 3	13 ...	13 7	13 8	6	8 6			3254	80000 lb.	11
33	XM	" "	82507 to 82599	40 6	8 9	9 2	42 2	8 8	10 ...	12 3	12 10	13 7	13 8	6	8 6			3254	80000 lb.	6
34	XAP	" " Note M②	" "	"	8 10	"	"	"	"	"	"	"	"					3303		
35	XM	"	82600 to 82849	40 6	8 10	9 2	42 1	9 3	10 1	12 4	12 10	13 8	13 8	6	8 6			3297	80000 lb.	23
36	XAP	" Note SS	" "	"	9 ...	"	"	"	"	"	"	"	"					3342		
37	XM	" "	82850 to 82999	40 6	9 ...	9 2	42 1	8 8	10 ...	12 3	13 ...	13 7	13 7	6	8 6			3254	80000 lb.	12
41	XAP	" " Note M③	" "	"	8 10	"	"	"	"	"	"	"	"					3303		
42	XM	" "	83000 to 83231	40 6	9 2	10 ...	42 ...	9 1	10 5	13 ...	13 3	14 5	14 5	6	9 4			3712	80000 lb.	22
43	XM	" "	83232 to 83481	40 6	9 2	10 4	42 ...	9 1	10 5	13 4	13 7	14 9	14 9	6	9 4			3835	80000 lb.	24
44	XM	" "	83500 to 83967	40 6	9 2	10 ...	42 ...	9 1	10 5	13 ...	13 4	14 5	14 5	6	9 4			3712	80000 lb.	45
45	XM	" "	84000 to 84543	40 6	9 2	10 4	42 ...	9 1	10 5	13 4	13 7	14 9	14 9	6	9 8			3835	80000 lb.	53
46	XM	" All Steel....	84600 to 84832	40 6	9 2	10 4	42 ...	9 1	10 5	13 4	13 7	14 9	14 9	6	9 8			3835	80000 lb.	22
47	XM	" Steel....	85000 to 85199	40 6	9 2	10 4	42 ...	9 1	10 5	13 4	13 7	14 9	14 9	6	9 8			3835	100000 lb.	19
51	XM	" All Steel....	86000 to 86874	40 6	9 2	10 4½	41 9	9 3	10 6	13 6	14 4	14 11	14 11	6	9 9			3835	100000 lb.	60
52	XM	" {Steel Underfr., S.S.,Comp.Body}	87000 to 87124	40 6	9 1	10 4	41 9	9 3	10 6	14 1	14 1	14 11	14 11	6	9 9			3788	100000 lb.	12
53	XM	" All Steel....	88000 to 88199	40 6	9 2	10 6	41 10	9 3	10 6	13 8	14 6	15 1	15 1	6	9 10			3892	80000 lb.	17
54	XM	" "	88200 to 88699	40 6	9 2	10 6	41 10	9 3	10 6	13 8	14 6	15 1	15 1	6	9 10			3892	100000 lb.	43
55	XM	" "	88700 to 89524	40 6	9 2	10 6	41 10	9 3	10 6	13 8	14 6	15 1	15 1	6	9 10			3892	100000 lb.	72
56	XAP	Auto., All Steel..Note T	89525 to 89599	40 7	9 3	10 6	41 10	9 3	10 6	13 8	14 6	15 1	15 1	6	9 10			4006	100000 lb.	7
57	SM	Stock, Steel Underfr., {Single Deck.}	15000 to 15399	40 6	8 6	10 ...	42 2	8 8	10 ...	13 6	14 3	14 7	14 8	6	9 8			3459	80000 lb.	39
61	SF	" Steel Underf., {Double Deck.}	16400 to 16599	40 6	8 6	{5 6 / 4 1}	42 2	8 8	10 ...	13 6	14 3	14 7	14 8	6	{5 2 / 4 2}			3355	80000 lb.	19
62	XM	Box, Stag. Doors, Steel Underfr., S.S., Com. Body, End Doors..	17000 to 17299	40 6	9 ...	10 3	41 11	9 3	10 5	13 4	14 6	14 11	15 ...	12	9 11	8 10	9 10	3736	80000 lb.	28
63	XM	Box, All Steel, End Doors.	18000 to 18024	50 6	9 2	10 4½	51 11	9 3	10 6	13 6	14 4	14 11	14 11	14 11	9 9	9 2	10 0¼	4803	100000 lb.	2
64	XME	" All Steel. Note V	19000 to 19124	50 6	9 2	10 4	52 ...	9 4	10 6	13 6	14 4	14 11	14 11	14 11	9 9			4803	100000 lb.	2
65	XAP	" " Note CC	" "	"	"	"	"	"	"	"	"	"	"							3
66	XAP	" " Note A	" "	"	"	"	"	"	"	"	"	"	"							1
71	XAP	" " Note L	" "	"	"	"	"	"	"	"	"	"	"							
72	XME	" " Note J	19125 to 19131	50 6	9 4	10 6	51 11	9 5	10 6	......				15 6	9 10			4954	100000 lb.	
73	XME	" " Note C	19132 to 19164	50 6	9 4	10 6	51 11	9 5	10 6	13 8	14 3	15 1	15 1	15 6	9 10			4954	100000 lb.	3
74	XME	" " Note C	19165 to 19299	50 6	9 4	10 6	51 11	9 5	10 6	13 8	14 3	15 1	15 1	7 9	9 10			4954	100000 lb.	13
75	XME	" " Note P	19300 to 19499	50 6	9 2	10 6	51 11	9 4	10 6	13 8	14 4	15 1	15 1	14 6	9 10			4900	100000 lb.	9
76	XAP	" " Note W	" "	"	8 11	"	"	"	"	"	"	"	"					4767	"	10
77	XME	" " Note B	19500 to 19779	50 6	9 0⅝	10 5½	51 10	9 5	10 6	13 6	14 4	15 1	15 1	15	9 10			4780	100000 lb.	28
81	XAP	" " Note S	19780 to 19799	50 6	9 2	10 5½	51 10	9 5	10 6	13 6	14 4	15 1	15 1	15	9 10			4850	100000 lb.	2
82	XM	"	19800 to 19999	50 6	9 2	10 5½	51 10	9 5	10 8	14 4	15 ...	15 1	15 1	15	9 10			4844	100000 lb.	3
83	XAP	" " Note MM	" "	"	"	"	"	"	"	"	"	"	"					4648		14
84	XAP	" " Note NN	" "	"	9 0⅝	"	"	"	"	"	"	"	"					4780		2
85	XAP	" " Note H	20000 to 20149	50 6	9 3⅝	10 5½	51 10	9 5	10 5	5 8	14 4	15 ...	15 1	15	9 10			4844	100000 lb.	15
86	XM	" "	20150 to 20199	50 6	9 3⅝	10 5½	51 10	9 5	10 5	5 8	14 4	15 ...	15 1	15	9 10			4890	100000 lb.	5
87	XML	Auto., Steel, Staggered Doors..Note QQ	21000 to 21015	50 6	9 2	10 5	51 9	10 ...	10 8	5 1	13 1	14 7	14 8	14 6	8 6			4629	100000 lb.	1
		Forward.....																		8881

DIMENSIONS.

Item No.	A.A.R. Mech. Desig.	Markings and Kind of Cars	Numbers	Inside Length	Inside Width	Inside Height	Outside Length	Width at Eaves or Top of Sides	Extreme Width	To Extreme Width	To Eaves or Top of Sides	To Top of Running Board	To Extreme Height	Side Door Width of Open'g	Side Door Height of Open'g	End Door Width of Open'g	End Door Height of Open'g	Cubic Feet Level Full	Pounds or Gallons	No. of Cars
		Brought forward.....																		8874
1	XML	Auto., Steel, Staggered Doors..Note QQ	21016 to 21062	50 6	9 2	10 5	51 9	10 ...	10 8	5 1	13 1	14 7	14 8	12	8 6			4629	100000 lb.	47
2	XML	Auto., Steel, Staggered Doors..Note QQ	21063 to 21070	50 6	9 2	10 7	51 10	8 11	10 8	5 1	14 6	15 3	15 3	14 6	9 7			4914	100000 lb.	8
3	XM	Box, {Stagg'd Doors, Steel Underfr. S.S. Comp. Body}	40000 to 40999	40 6	8 6	10 ...	42 2	8 8	10 ...	13 6	14 3	14 7	14 9	11	9 8			3425	80000 lb.	35
4	XM	" "	44001 to 44118	40 6	9 ...	10 ...	41 11	9 2	10 5	13 8	14 3	14 8	14 9	11	9 8			3645	80000 lb.	96
5	XM	" " ...	44119 to 44152	40 6	9 ...	10 3	41 11	9 3	10 5	13 4	14 6	14 11	15 ...	12	9 11			3736	80000 lb.	28

Item No.	A.A.R. Mech. Desig.	Markings and Kind of Cars	Numbers	Inside Length	Inside Width	Inside Height	Outside Length (At Eaves or Top of Sides or Platform)	Extreme Width	Ht. To Extreme Width	Ht. To Eaves or Top of Sides or Platform	Ht. To Top of Running Board	Ht. To Extreme Height	Door Side Width Open'g	Door Side Height Open'g	Door End Width Open'g	Door End Height Open'g	Cubic Feet Level Full	Pounds or Gallons	No. of Cars
6	XM	" " ..	45000 to 45399	40 6	9 ..	10 ..	42 1	9 2	10 5	18 8	14 8	14 8	14 9	11 ..	9 6			3645	80000 lb.	234
11	XAP Auto.	" Note D				9 8												3554	"	138
12	XM Box,	" All Steel	45400 to 46001	40 6	9 2	10 ..	42 1	9 2	10 5	13 8	14 3	14 8	14 9	11 ..	9 8			3713	80000 lb.	79
13	XAP "	" All Steel Note N	"		8 8													3510	"	232
14	XAP "	" Note KK	"		8 8													3510	"	113
15	XME "	" Note JJ	"		8 11													3611	"	147
16	XM "	" ..	46002 to 46999	40 6	9 ..	10 ..	42 1	9 2	10 5	13 8	14 3	14 8	14 9	11 ..	9 8			3645	80000 lb.	710
17	XM "	" ..	47000 to 47999	40 6	9 ..	10 ..	41 11	9 2	10 3	13 3	14 3	14 8	14 9	11 ..	9 8			3645	80000 lb.	879
21	XME Auto.	" Note G	"	"	"	"	"	"	"	"	"	"	"	"	"			"	"	57
22	XM Box,	" ..	48000 to 48999	40 6	9 ..	10 3	41 11	9 3	10 5	18 4	14 6	14 11	15 ..	12 ..	9 11			3736	80000 lb.	881
23	XAR Auto.,	" Note K	49000 to 49099	40 6	9 ..	{10 3 / 9 9}	41 11	9 3	10 5	13 4	14 6	14 11	15 ..	12 ..	9 11			{3736 / 3554}	80000 lb.	43
24	XAR Box,	" Note EE①	"	"	"	10 3	"	"	"	"	"	"	"	"	"			3736	"	51
25	XM "	" ..	49100 to 49199	40 6	9 ..	10 3	41 11	9 3	10 5	13 4	14 6	14 11	15 ..	12 ..	9 11			3736	80000 lb.	4
26	XAR Auto.	" Note U①	"	"	"	{10 3 / 9 9}	"	"	"	"	"	"	"	"	"			{3736 / 3554}	"	94
27	XAR "	" Note K	49200 to 49349	40 6	9 ..	{10 3 / 9 9}	41 11	9 3	10 5	13 4	14 6	14 11	15 ..	12 ..	9 11			{3736 / 3554}	80000 lb.	74
31	XM Box,	" Note EE②	"	"	"	10 3	"	"	"	"	"	"	"	"	"			3736	"	68
32	XM "	" Note F	49350 to 49450	40 6	9 ..	{10 3 / 9 9}	41 11	9 3	10 5	13 4	14 6	14 11	15 ..	12 ..	9 11			{3736 / 3554}	80000 lb.	14
33	XM "	" Note Q①	"	"	"	10 3	"	"	"	"	"	"	"	"	"			3736	"	80
34	XAR Auto.	" Note K	49451 to 49626	40 6	9 ..	{10 3 / 9 9}	41 11	9 3	10 5	13 4	14 6	14 11	15 ..	12 ..	9 11			{3736 / 3554}	80000 lb.	79
35	XM Box,	" Note EE③	"	"	"	10 3	"	"	"	"	"	"	"	"	"			3736	"	90
36	XM "	" Note F	49627 to 49651	40 6	9 ..	{10 3 / 9 9}	41 11	9 3	10 5	13 4	14 6	14 11	15 ..	12 ..	9 11			{3736 / 3554}	80000 lb.	5
37	XM "	" Note Q②	"	"	"	10 3	"	"	"	"	"	"	"	"	"			3736	"	20
41	XM "	" ..	49652 to 49699	40 6	9 ..	10 3	41 11	9 3	10 5	13 4	14 6	14 11	15 ..	12 ..	9 11			3736	80000 lb.	3
42	XAR Auto.,	" Note U③	"	"		{10 3 / 9 9}	"	"	"	"	"	"	"	"	"			{3736 / 3554}	"	43
43	XAR "	" Note K	49700 to 49799	40 6	9 ..	{10 3 / 9 9}	41 11	9 3	10 5	13 4	14 6	14 11	15 ..	12 ..	9 11			{3736 / 3554}	80000 lb.	80
44	XM Box,	" ..	74800 to 74813	40 6	8 6	10 ..	42 2	8 8	10 ..	13 6	14 3	14 8	14 9	11 ..	9 8			3425	80000 lb.	14
45	XM "	" ..	145400 to 145999	40 6	8 6	10 ..	42 1	8 8	10 ..	13 6	14 3	14 8	14 9	11 ..	9 8			3780	80000 lb.	3
46	XM "	" ..	147001 to 147119	40 6	9 ..	10 ..	41 11	9 2	10 5	13 8	14 3	14 8	14 9	11 ..	9 8			3645	80000 lb.	13
47	XM "	" ..	148001 to 148035	40 6	9 ..	10 3	41 11	9 3	10 5	13 4	14 6	14 11	15 ..	12 ..	9 11			3736	80000 lb.	4
51	GB	Coal, Steel, Drop Ends, Wood Floor	11000 to 11249	48 6	9 6	3 6	50 6	10 4	10 4	7 6	7 5		7 6					1621	140000 lb.	97
52	GB	Coal, Steel, Drop Ends, Steel Floor	12000 to 12049	65 6	7 9	3 6	67 11	8 7	9 ..	6 9	7 ..		7 3					1777	140000 lb.	50
53	GB	" "	12050 to 12099	65 6	7 9	3 6	67 4	8 6	8 6	7 ..	7 ..		7 ..					1777	140000 lb.	50
54	GB	Coal, Steel, Drop Ends	12100 to 12149	65 6	7 9	3 6	67 11	8 7	9 ..	6 9	7 ..		7 3					1777	140000 lb.	50
55	GB	Coal, Steel, Drop Ends, Wood Floor	12500 to 12599	52 6	9 5	3 6	54 11	10 3	10 9	5 2	7 3		7 6					1745	140000 lb.	2
56	GBS	" " Note DD①	"	"	"	"	"	"	"	"	"		"					"	"	98
57	GB	Coal, Steel, Drop Ends, Wood Floor	12600 to 12649	52 6	9 6	3 3	54 8	10 8	10 8	7 ..	7 ..		7 1					1660	140000 lb.	50
61	GB	" "	12650 to 12799	52 6	9 6	3 6	54 11	10 6	10 6	7 6	7 6		7 6					1745	140000 lb.	150
62	GB	Coal, Steel Underframe, Fixed Ends, Comp. Body, Wood Floor	13000 to 13249	41 6	9 5	4 8	42 11	10 7	10 7	8 4	8 4		8 4					1826	100000 lb.	231
63	GBS	" Note E	"	"	"	"	"	"	"	"	"		"					"	"	15
64	GB	Coal, Steel, Wood Floor	13500 to 14849	41 6	9 9	4 8	42 11	10 7	10 7	8 4	8 4		8 4					1896	100000 lb.	1144
65	GBS	" "	"	"	"	"	"	"	"	"	"		"					"	"	152
66	GBS	" " Wood Floor Note DD② Note HH	"	"	"	"	"	"	"	"	"		"					"	"	52
67	FD	Flat, Depressed, Steel Note Y	10, 11	{57 9 / 21 ..}	9 ..		58 4	9 ..	9 7	3 2	4 2		5 10						250000 lb.	2
68	FM	Flat..........	★ 100 to 149	53 6	10 6	4 1													100000 lb.	
71	FM	Flat, Steel......	25500 to 25549	53 6	10 6	3 5	54 3	...	10 8	5 8			5 8						140000 lb.	40
72	FMS	" Note FF	"	"	"	"	"	"	"	"			"						"	4
73	FC	" NoteGG	"	"	"	"	"	"	"	"			"						"	6
74	LO	Hopper, Covered ..	30000 to 30089	29 3	9 5	.....	35 3	9 3	10 2	11 9	12 7		13 ..					1958	140000 lb.	89
75	LO	" " ..	30090 to 30149	29 3	9 5	.....	35 3	9 3	10 2	11 9	12 7	12 10	13 ..					1958	140000 lb.	60
76	LO	" " ..	30150 to 30249	29 3	9 5	.....	31 11	10 1	10 2	10 10	10 8		10 10					1941	140000 lb.	100
77	LO	" " ..	30800 to 30844	35 9	10 2	.....	37 6	9 4	10 3	9 8	10 ..	10 9	10 11					1970	140000 lb.	45
81	LO	" " ..	31000 to 31039	41 1	9 6	.....	47 1	10 3	10 5	11 ..	12 3	14 2	14 2					2893	140000 lb.	40
		Forward.....																		15867

★ Denotes additions.   ◆ Denotes increase.   ↓ Denotes reduction.

Item Number	A.A.R. Mech. Designation	MARKINGS AND KIND OF CARS	NUMBERS	INSIDE Length	INSIDE Width	INSIDE Height	OUTSIDE Length (At Eaves or Top of Sides or Platform)	OUTSIDE Extreme Width	HEIGHT FROM RAIL To Extreme Width	HEIGHT FROM RAIL To Eaves or Top of Sides or Platform	HEIGHT FROM RAIL To Top of Running Board	HEIGHT FROM RAIL To Extreme Height	DOORS SIDE Width of Open'g	DOORS SIDE Height of Open'g	DOORS END Width of Open'g	DOORS END Height of Open'g	CAPACITY Cubic Feet Level Full	CAPACITY Pounds or Gallons	Number of Cars
				ft. in.	ft. in.	ft. in.	ft. in.	ft. in.	ft. in.	ft. in.	ft. in.	ft. in.	ft. in.	ft. in.	ft. in.	ft. in.			
		Brought forward																		15867
1	HM	Hopper, All Steel ..	36000 to 36424	33 ..	9 7		34 ..	10 6	10 7	10 8	10 8		10 10					2120	110000 lb.	17
2	HM	" " ..	36500 to 36624	33 ..	9 7		34 ..	10 6	10 7	10 8	10 8		10 10					2120	110000 lb.	121
3	HM	" " ..	36625 to 36742	33 ..	9 7		34 ..	10 6	10 7	10 8	10 8		10 10					2120	100000 lb.	116
4	HM	" " ..	37000 to 37799	33 ..	9 7		34 ..	10 6	10 7	10 8	10 8		10 10					2120	110000 lb.	766
5	HM	" Composite ..	39000 to 39399	33 ..	9 6		34 ..	10 5	10 5	10 8	10 8		10 9					1970	110000 lb.	398
		Total																		17285

227

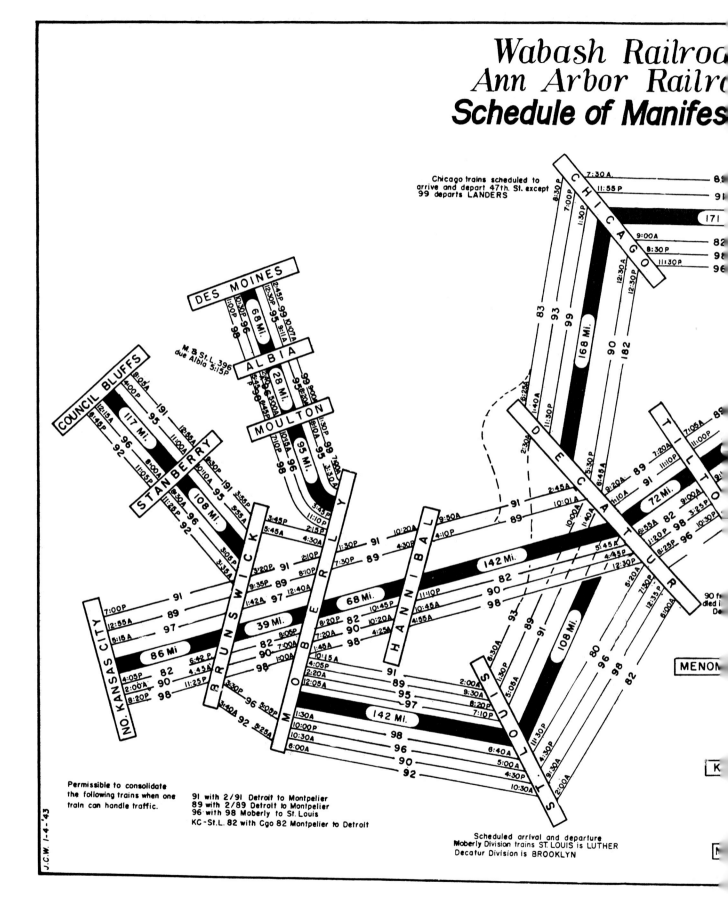

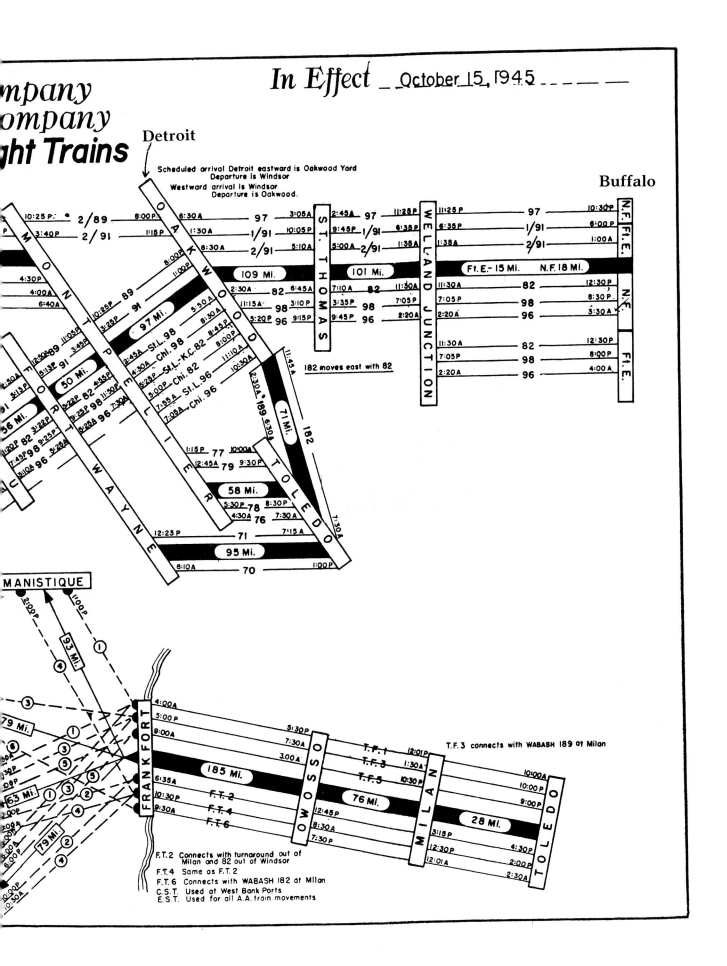

In July, 1905, ACF, formerly called American Car & Foundry, produced these wood-sided gondolas for the Wabash-Pittsburgh Terminal. *ACF*

Convertible Ballast & Coal Cars of 34 foot length were made by ACF for the Wabash. *ACF*

A low-sided gondola by ACF. *ACF*

Speeding Your Shipments

"The Conductor"

From November 12, 1930 Timetable

THE responsibility of speeding your shipments and maintaining fast *on time* schedules, rests largely with the Wabash conductor. He, being master of the train, is directly responsible for its movements and protection. It is he who co-ordinates the entire crew so that your Wabash Red Ball shipments arrive swiftly and safely at destination.

We pay tribute to Wabash freight conductors, for thru their alertness to duty and the skillful execution of their work, the Wabash Red Ball Freight Service holds an enviable position for speed, promptness and dependability.

ABOVE. An interesting-looking Wabash stock car with arch bar trucks. BELOW. A steel-underframe furniture car by ACF. *Both photos, ACF*

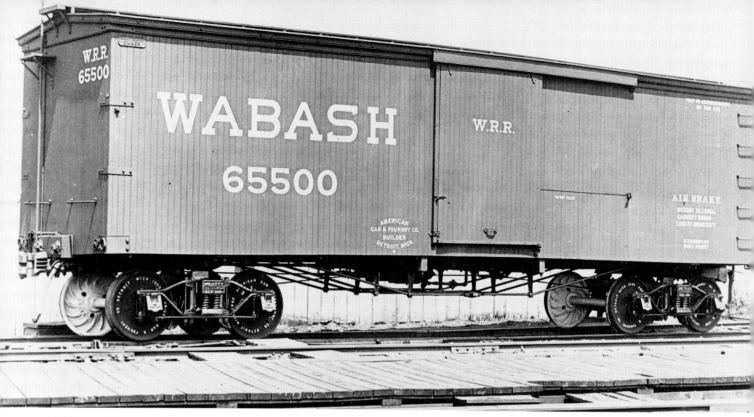

ABOVE. These short wood box cars were made by ACF. BELOW. "Post No Advertisements on This Car" reads the sign at the top right of car. BOTTOM. ACF-built automobile car. *All photos, ACF*

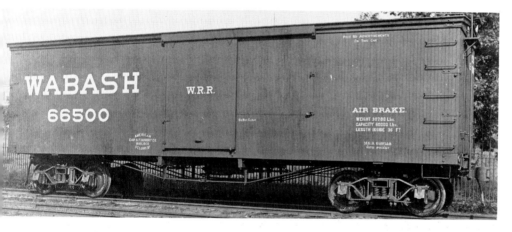

ABOVE. NO. 30477 was a 29-foot covered steel hopper. Here it's at Elkhart, Indiana. *John Nixon*

RIGHT. No. 3161 oil supply car at Decatur in 1973 shows some signs of wear. *Photo by D. Cycotte, collection of John Nixon*

RIGHT. Wabash No. 85265 was built in April of 1924 and rebuilt in 1947. It was used for flour loading. *John Nixon collection*

BELOW. No. 88556 was one of 340 cars of this type built. *John Nixon collection*

RIGHT. No. 90365 was a 40-ft. steel box in the 90,000-90,549 series. *William Raia* BELOW. An NJI&I 50-ft. box car rests in Sidney, Illinois in the summer of 1981. *Both photos, Don Heimburger*

The Wabash lettering at one time had been larger, but was replaced with smaller lettering on No. 5806, a 40-ft. box car now used in Maintenance-of-Way work. The car was photographed in the summer of 1981 at Tolono, Illinois. *Don Heimburger*

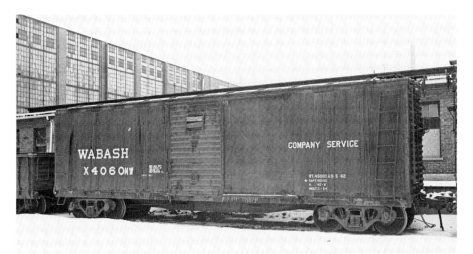

Wabash 40-ft. box car spotted behind the shops at Decatur in the winter of 1981. *Don Heimburger*

MIDDLE. Wabash BTTX No. 474602 double deck automobile carrier was photographed in October, 1963 at South Bend, Indiana. BOTTOM. Steam wrecker No. 3186 at Montpelier, Ohio in September of 1938. *Both photos, L.G. Issac*

All oversize cars on this page were made by Thrall Car Mfg. Co. Top car is a 60-ft., bottom is an 86-ft. *Photos collection of T.E. Nihiser*

Cabooses

It's January 19, 1943 in Peru, Indiana, and the wood cupola cabooses appear to be huddled together for warmth. *William Swartz, collection of M.D. McCarter*

Typical of the early Wabash cabooses (see dustjacket painting), this one features express trucks. Note the ornate cupola. *Collection of John Nixon*

LEFT. No. 2229 is now on display, and being preserved, at the St. Louis Museum of Transport. Photo taken summer of 1982. *Don Heimburger*

BELOW. No. 2520 is at Ft. Erie, Ontario, in August of 1958. This caboose has the old arch bar type trucks. *Richard Ganger*

THE WABASH RAILROAD CO.

RIGHT. A Wabash caboose with condensed lettering versus the more typical spaced out letter scheme. This caboose was at Ft. Erie, Ontario on May 3, 1958. *Richard Ganger*

LEFT. No. 2652 features large cupola windows. *John Nixon collection*

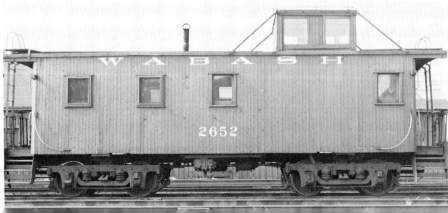

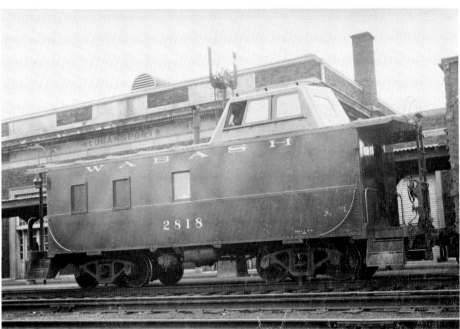

TOP. A Wabash caboose passes through Tolono, Illinois sometime in the 1960's. *Don Heimburger* LEFT, TOP. L.G. Isaac shot caboose No. 2799 at Tilton, Illinois in 1967. LEFT. No. 2818 passes Logansport, Indiana on August 16, 1953. *John Nixon collection*

RENT AN AUTO —Have it waiting at your destination for business or pleasure. Your Wabash agent has the details of this convenient Rail-Auto-Travel Plan.

CHARGE IT — Now you can charge your rail and Pullman tickets. Just ask your Wabash agent for a Rail Travel Card . . . good on Wabash and 48 other railroads.

PAY LATER — Pay after your trip . . . in small, convenient monthly installments. Your Wabash agent can complete arrangements in 24 hours. Ask him about the Traveloan Plan.

Yard caboose No. 02216 is at Chicago in 1965. *L.G. Issac*

Transfer caboose No. 02300 is at North Kansas City, Missouri on January 3, 1965. *Charles Winters, collection of Louis Marre*

LEFT. Crew car No. 5667 is now part of the MofW Department on the Wabash. But it once was a troop sleeper. L.G. Issac photo taken at Lafayette, Indiana in September of 1951. BELOW. One of the Wabash's early motorized vehicles was this low-sided truck. Photo was taken in Decatur. *Collection of Henry Lischawski family, courtesy Monticello Railway Museum*

BELOW. Switcher No. 536 spots No. 4001 gas-electric on the turntable at Hannibal, Missouri on June 29, 1948. *William Swartz, collection of M.D. Mc-Carter*

TOP. EMC photo of No. 4001 right after being made in early 1926. *Collection of Louis Marre* ABOVE. no. 4000 gas-electric and trailer at Ft. Wayne on April 27, 1935. *M.D. McCarter collection*

Chapter 12

Subsidiary lines

The Manistique & Lake Superior was reorganized in August of 1909 from the Manistique & Northern. Control of this tiny road (38.32 miles) was acquired by the Ann Arbor in 1911. The freight-only line ran from Manistique Michigan, to Doty in the upper peninsula. This photo of M&LS No. 1, an S-3, was taken at Manistique on August 30, 1964. *J. David Ingles, collection of Louis Marre*

The Lake Erie & Ft. Wayne was formerly the Fort Wayne Rolling Mill R.R. and the Wabash acquired control about 1929. Here VO-660 No.1 is enroute to be scrapped, says photographer Louis Marre who shot the unit at Ft. Wayne in 1967.

The New Jersey,Indiana and Illinois was acquired by the Wabash about 1926. The road was incorporated in 1902 and opened three years later. NJI&I No. 1 is an S-1. It's at South Bend, Indiana on November 1, 1958. *Louis Marre*

ABOVE. NJI&I No. 2, an NW-2 1,000 hp unit, is ex-Indiana Northern No. 100. Here it's at South Bend on October 10, 1962. BELOW. NJI&I No. 6, a 2-6-0, at South Bend in 1928. *Both photos, Louis Marre*

Chapter 13

Wabash Railroad stations

WABASH DEPOT   BEMENT, ILLINOIS   1955

WABASH DEPOT 1955
BLUE MOUND, ILL.

WABASH DEPOT 1955
BRUNSWICK, MISSOURI

WABASH DEPOT   BUFFALO, ILLINOIS   1955

WABASH DEPOT
BUTLER, IND.

WABASH DEPOT 1966
CARROLLTON, MO

WABASH DEPOT 1967
DANVILLE, ILLINOIS

WABASH DEPOT 1955
DECATUR, ILL.

WABASH DEPOT   DECATUR, ILL.   1907

WABASH DEPOT
EDON, OHIO

WABASH DEPOT 1955
EDWARDSVILLE, ILL.

WABASH DEPOT 1945
EFFINGHAM, ILLINOIS

WABASH DEPOT 1956
FAIRMOUNT, ILL.

WABASH DEPOT 1955
FORREST, ILL.

WABASH DEPOT
GALLATIN, MO.

WABASH DEPOT 1925
GILMORE, MO.

245

WABASH DEPOT   HOMER, ILLINOIS   1956

N&W DEPOT 1975
HUNTINGTON, IND.

WABASH DEPOT   LITCHFIELD, ILLINOIS   1955

WABASH DEPOT
LOGANSPORT, IND.

WABASH DEPOT 1966
LOVINGTON, ILL.

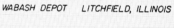

WABASH DEPOT 1968
MT OLIVE, ILLINOIS

WABASH DEPOT 1955
MADISON,   MISSOURI

246

WABASH DEPOT 1977
MOBERLY, MO.

WABASH DEPOT
MONTGOMERY, MO.

WABASH DEPOT 1908
MOULTON, IOWA

WABASH DEPOT 1955
MONTICELLO, ILL.

WABASH DEPOT 1955
PARIS, MO.

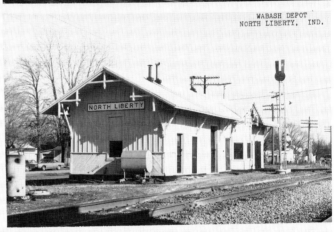

WABASH DEPOT
NORTH LIBERTY, IND.

WABASH DEPOT
PATTONSBURG, MO.

WABASH DEPOT   PHILO, ILLINOIS   1956

247

WABASH DEPOT   PONTIAC, ILLINOIS   1955

WABASH DEPOT 1955
SALISBURY, MISSOURI

WABASH DEPOT   SAUNEMIN, ILLINOIS   1957

WABASH DEPOT 1968
SHENANDOAH, IOWA

WABASH DEPOT 1964
STREATOR, ILLINOIS

WABASH DEPOT
TAYLORVILLE, ILL.

WABASH DEPOT
QUINCY, ILL.

248

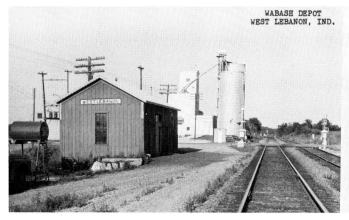

WABASH DEPOT
WEST LEBANON, IND.

WABASH DEPOT
WILLIAMSPORT, IND.

WABASH MERCER ST. TOWER
DECATUR, ILL.

WABASH WATCHMAN'S TOWER
HUNTINGTON, INDIANA 1911

WABASH TOWER 1955
REDDICK, ILLINOIS

MILEAGE OPERATED.

EASTERN DIVISION.

Toledo, O., to Tilton, Ill.	251	miles.
Detroit, Mich., to Peru, Ind.	195.2	”
Chicago, Ill., to Laketon Junction, Ind	122.7	”
Attica, Ind., to Covington, Ind	14.8	”
Chili, Ind., to Logansport (W. S.), Ind.	21.2	”
Montpelier, O., to Wolcottville, Ind.	39.7	”
Total	**644.6 miles.**	

WESTERN DIVISION.

St. Louis, Mo., to Kansas City, Mo.	276.8	miles.
Moberly, Mo., to Des Moines, Ia.	212.2	”
Brunswick, Mo., to Council Bluffs, Ia.	224.2	”
St. Louis, Mo. (Vine Street) to Ferguson, Mo.	10.7	”
Centralia, Mo., to Columbia, Mo.	21.6	”
Salisbury, Mo., to Glasgow, Mo.	14.8	”
Total	**760.3 miles.**	

MIDDLE DIVISION.

Tilton, Ill., to Hannibal, Mo	211.9	miles.
Chicago, Ill., to Effingham, Ill.	213.5	”
Shumway, Ill., to Altamont, Ill.	10.3	”
St. Louis, Mo., to Decatur, Ill.	112.5	”
Bluffs, Ill., to Quincy, Ill.	61.2	”
Clayton, Ill., to Keokuk, Ia.	42.3	”
Forrest, Ill., to Streator, Ill.	36.9	”
Sidney, Ill., to Champaign, Ill.	11.7	”
Maysville, Ill., to Pittsfield, Ill.	6.2	”
Edwardsville, Ill., to Edwardsville Crossing, Ill.	9.5	”
Total	**716.0 miles.**	

RECAPITULATION.

Eastern Division	644.6 miles.	
Middle Division	716.0	”
Western Division	760.3	”
Grand total—all lines	**2,120.9 miles.**	

Official Guide, 1893. Courtesy National Railway Publication Co.

John C. Gault at Toledo, Ohio. Collection of the late Charles F. Mensing. Photo courtesy Rev. Edward J. Dowling, S.J.

THE WABASH FLEET
Lake Erie Transportation Company
1879-1911

The Wabash Railway established its Great Lakes steamship line in 1879, thereby making freight connections with eastern railroads. Six package freighters and a tug were in the fleet; service began with two small chartered wooden freighters which were later purchased. Four larger ships were built for the fleet. Operations of the fleet were mostly between Toledo and Buffalo.

In 1911, operations ceased when the Wabash made through rail connections. The last two ships were sold to the Erie's Union Steamboat Line. Colors of the fleet were black hull, white cabins and yellow stack with black top.

John C. Gault. Wooden package freighter built in 1881.
George J. Gould. Steel package freighter built in 1893.

A.L. Hopkins. Wooden package freighter built in 1880.

Morley. Wooden package freighter built on speculation.

S.C. Reynolds. Iron package freighter built in 1890.

Russell Sage. Wooden package freighter built in 1881.

A.W. Colten. Iron tug built in 1881 named in honor of general manager of the Lake Erie Transportation Co.

—Rev. Edward J. Dowling, S.J.
University of Detroit

Wabash locomotive roster

This list is intended to include all motive power, both steam and diesel, owned by the Wabash and its predecessor lines. The time span extends from 1838 to 1964, when the Wabash became part of the Norfolk & Western. Locomotives are grouped together by type and class, rather than road number.

The Wabash classification scheme was adopted about 1897, when classes A to I were assigned to locomotives owned at that time. The other class designations were added in later years as locomotives with new wheel arrangements were acquired.

Narrow Gauge	-	2-6-2	Class	G -
0-4-0	Class A -	4-6-0	"	H -
0-4-6T Bogie		2-8-0	"	I -
0-6-0	Class B -	4-6-2	"	J -
0-8-0	Class C -	2-8-2	"	K -
4-2-0	--	2-10-2	"	L -
4-4-0	Class D -	4-8-2	"	M -
4-4-2	" E -	4-8-4	"	O -
2-6-0	" F -	4-6-4	"	P -

In the roster which follows, each engine is listed only once, except for engines rebuilt and hence reclassified. All renumbering is shown in chronological order for each engine. Specifications are presented in the following order: Cylinder diameter and stroke; driver diameter over tires; boiler pressure; engine weight excluding tender; and tractive effort. When column headings do not appear, data is presented in the following order: Numbering, Builder, Construction Number, Date Built, and Disposition.

Builders

ALCO = American Loco. Co.
BLW. = Baldwin Loco. Works
Manch. = Manchester Loco. Works
Pitts. = Pittsburg Loco. & Car Wks.
Schen. = Schenectady Loco. Works

Disposition

dr = Dropped from roster
RB = Rebuilt
RE = Renumbered
Ret = Retired
SS = Sold for scrap
SCR = Scrapped
So = Sold

The Wabash numbering system, such as it was, had its origin in 1856 with the formation of the first Toledo, Wabash & Western. All the earlier predecessor lines assigned names only to their power, a common practice in those early days. During the next 29 years, until 1885, as the identity of the first TW&W changed to the Toledo & Wabash, then the second TW&W, the Wabash, and finally the Wabash, St. Louis & Pacific, the locomotive numbers generally remained unchanged. As new power was added, vacancies were filled or the next higher available numbers were used. Engines acquired with other lines absorbed into the growing Wabash family were numbered in blocks, as shown in the following list:

Locomotive Numbering Scheme of the Early Wabash

Toledo, Wabash & Western R.R. 1856-1858.
Toledo & Wabash 1858-1865.
Toledo, Wabash & Western Ry. 1865-1877.
Wabash Railway 1877-1879.
Wabash, St. Louis & Pacific 1879-1885.

#	1-35	first used 1856 ex-LEW&St.L and Toledo & Illinois.
	36-100	first used 1862 to 1872 new power for TW&W and T&W.
	101-130	first used 1865 ex Great Western and Quincy & Toledo.
	131-191	first used 1866 to 1873 new power for TW&W.
	192-199	first used 1880 ex Chicago and Paducah.
	200-205	first used 1880 ex Havana, Rantoul & Eas. (excl. 201, 202)
	207-213	first used 1880 ex Eel River.
	215-323	first used 1880 ex St. Louis, Kansas City & Northern.
	324-399	first used 1880 to 1882 new power for WStL&P.
	400-402	first used 1880 ex Havana, Mason City, Lincoln & Eastern.
	403-406	first used 1880 ex Detroit, Butler & St. Louis.
	407-410	first used 1880 ex Quincy, Missouri & Pacific.
	411-454	first used 1880 ex Toledo, Peoria & Western.
	455-464	first used 1880 ex Missouri, Iowa & Nebraska.
	465	first used 1880 ex Springfield & North Western.
	466-482	first used 1881 new power for WStL&P.
	483-498	first used 1881 ex Peoria, Pekin & Jacksonville.
	499-532	first used 1881 ex Indianapolis, Peru & Chicago.
	533-539	first used 1881 ex Danville & South Western.
	540-555	first used 1881 ex Cairo & Vincennes.
	556-576	first used 1882 new power for WStL&P.
	577-584	first used 1882 ex St. Louis, Kansas City & Northern.

About 1885, all engines had 1000 added to their numbers, apparently as part of a numbering scheme to include all of the thousands of engines in the Gould System. After 1887, the 1000 was dropped on most engines, but not all. This should not be confused

with another renumbering after 1898, when 1000 was added to the three-digit numbers of Buffalo Division engines. This was done to simplify train dispatching between Windsor and Niagara Falls.

The roster which follows excludes power owned by two railroads sometimes considered parts of the Wabash but with separate numbering schemes. One was the Humeston & Shenandoah, which was jointly operated with the Burlington, for a time. H&S #6-20 were Pittsburgh 4-4-0's built in 1882-1883. The other was the Wabash-Pittsburgh Terminal, which operated many locomotives with the word Wabash stenciled on their cabs, but numbered in the Wheeling & Lake Erie series.

NARROW GAUGE LOCOMOTIVES (3 ft. Gauge)

N.G. Engines Acquired by Havana, Rantoul & Eastern (Leased 5/80 to WStL&P)

Orig.	Re'80	Re'84	Type	Specs.	Builder		New	Disp'n
1	200	1200	2-4-0	9x16- ?	Porter	230	9/75	dr by '86
2	204	1204	"		"	235	10/75	dr by '84
3	203	1203	4-4-0	11x22-44-32000	W.H.Bailey		12/77	RB'88 D-1
4	205	1205	"	"	"		2/78	"

N.G. Engines Acquired by Des Moines, Adel & Western (Leased '80 to WStL&P)

1	-	-	?	? ?				
2	?	?	2-4-0	8x14- ?	Porter	314	8/77	
2	?	?	2-6-0	11x16-42	Cooke	1092	1879	
3	?	?	4-4-0	11x18-42½	Pitts.	420	4/80	
4	?	?	"	12x18-42½	"	434	12/80	

Note: It is assumed that DMA&W power was renumbered into WStL&P 585 series.

Class A 0-4-0 Types
Early 0-4-0 Acquired by Toledo & Wabash (Consol. 7/65 into Tol.Wab. & Wes.)

Original	Re'85	Re'87	Note	Specs.	Builder	New	Disp'n
Ottumwa 36	-	-	(a)	10 x20-48-34100	Cooke	1862	Scr by'83
48 re 40	1040	40	(b)	13½x22-44-42000	Rogers	8/62	Scr '89

Early 0-4-0 Acquired by North Missouri (Reorg. as StLouis, K.C. & Nor.)

No.No.80re289	1289	289		14 x22-48-28000	BLW.	2152	5/70
"	81re290	1290	290	"	"	2147	?

Early 0-4-0 Acquired by Toledo, Peoria & Warsaw (Leased 5/80 to WStL&P) Re'87

TP&W *Hercules*	?	?	?	(c)	Rhode Is.	390	5/72	TP&W
" 46	?	?	"			677	6/76	"

Early 0-4-0 Acquired by Peoria, Pekin & Jacksonville (Leased '81 to WStL&P) Re'87

PP&J 1	483	1483	-		15 x22-48	Rogers	2/70	CP&StL
" 2	484	1484	-	(d)	? ?	?	?	"
" 3	485	1485	-	(e)	15 x22-60	Manch.	729	9/75	"

Early 0-4-0 Acquired by Indianapolis, Peru & Chicago (Leased 9/81 to WStL&P) Re'87

IP&C 11	511	1511	-		14 x22-44-50000	Cooke	1869	(RB'77)	LE&W62
" 14	514	1514	-		"	"	1870	(RB'81)	" 63
" 15	515	1515	-		"	"	"		" 61

Notes: a - Later 44" drivers
b - Later 57000 lb weight, tank type.
c - Reno. 1880 into WStL&P 411-454 series.
d - Purchased from CHICAGO & ROCK ISLAND.
e - Named *The Team*.

Class A-1 0-4-0 Tank Type: 13½x22-45-57000 (Orig. 13½x22-44-52320)

	Re'85		Re'87				
78	1078		78	TW&W	1871	Scr 7/07
79	1079		79	TW&W	1871	Scr '02
80	1080		80	TW&W	1871	RB '98,A-3
81	1081		81	TW&W	1871	RB '91,A-3

Class A-2 0-4-0: 16x24-52-60000 (Orig. 16x22-50)

356	1356		356	Pittsburgh	427	6/1880	Scr 1/16
357	1357		357	Pittsburgh	428	6/1880	Scr 1/16
358	1358		358	Pittsburgh	429	6/1880	Scr 1/16

Class A-3 0-4-0: 16x24-52-145-60000-14840 (See Note f)

		2	Moberly Shop	1888	Scr 2/16	
		7	Wabash RR	1885	So 3/17	(g)
11?	1011	11	Wabash RR	1882	Scr 1/16	
		15	Wabash RR	1887	So 4/22	(g)
		28	Wabash RR	1889	Scr 12/08	(h)
		30	Wabash RR	1887	Scr 10/10	
34?	1034	34	Wabash RR	1882	Scr 11/07	
35?	1035	35	Wabash RR	1881	Scr 7/25	
36?	1036	36	Wabash RR	1883	Scr 1/16	
37?	1037	37	Wabash RR	1883	Scr 9/14	
		40	Wabash RR	1891	Scr 2/16	
54?	1054	54	Wabash RR	1884	Scr 8/10	
		56	Wabash RR	1887	Scr 10/12	
57?	1057	57	Wabash RR	1882	Scr 6/16	
	(ex Class A-1)	80	Wabash RR	1890	Scr '10	
	(ex Class A-1)	81	Wabash RR	1891	Scr 8/10	
		103	Wabash RR	1889	Scr 8/10	
		106	Wabash RR	1888	Scr 6/16	
112?	1112	112	Wabash RR	1884	Scr 10/13	
114?	1114	114	Wabash RR	1883	Scr '02	
115?	1115	115	Wabash RR	1883	Scr 8/10	
	1116	116	Wabash RR	1885	Scr 1/16	
	1117	117	Wabash RR	1885	So 11/08	(i)
		119	Wabash RR	1887	Scr '02	
		120	Wabash RR	1888	Scr 1/16	
		157	Wabash RR	1888	Scr 8/10	
		159	Wabash RR	1888	Scr 8/10	
		178	Wabash RR	1889	Scr '12	
192	1192	192	Wabash RR	1880	Scr 10/12	
193	1193	193	Wabash RR	1883	Scr 2/16	
194	1194	194	Wabash RR	1882	Scr. 8/10	

* * * * * * *

Notes: f - This class contained three different types of 4-wheel switcher: 0-4-0 tank type without tender, 0-4-0 with tender, and 0-4-2 having trailing truck, with tender. According to available diagrams, all trailing trucks were removed by 1907. It is probable that most A-3's, but not *all*, were built with the 2-wheel trailing truck.
g - Sold to Carmichael Gravel Co.;   h - Sold to Fitzhugh-Luther
i - Sold to Lincoln Sand & Gravel Co.

Mason Bogie - 0-4-6 Type - Unclassified

0-4-6T Type: 15x22-48-55000

TW&W Hero	187	Mason	525	3/1874	Ret.by '84

Class B 0-6-0 Types

Class B-1 0-6-0: 16x22-49-75000

218	re 1218, 218	WStL&P	1882	Scr 3/09
223	re 1223, 223	WStL&P	1880	Scr '07

Class B-2 0-6-0: 17x24-52-150-92000-17340

4		Rhode Island	2592	6/1891	So 4/22 (g)
32	(ex DMURy. #1)	(Rhode Island	2093	10/1888)	Scr 10/24
105		Rhode Island	2593	6/1891	So 3/24 (j)
108		Rhode Island	2594	6/1891	Scr 6/27
109		Rhode Island	2595	6/1891	Scr 12/31
110		Rhode Island	2596	6/1891	Scr 7/25
111		Rhode Island	2597	6/1891	Scr 7/27
22		Rhode Island	2752	4/1892	Scr 12/22
121		Rhode Island	2753	4/1892	Scr 10/22
146		Rhode Island	2754	4/1892	Scr 10/22
162		Rhode Island	2755	4/1892	So 7/23 (k)
197		Rhode Island	2756	4/1892	Scr 10/23
198		Rhode Island	2757	4/1892	Scr 5/24
202		Rhode Island	2758	4/1892	Scr 6/22
215	(ex DMURy. #2)	(Rhode Island	2094	10/1888)	Scr 4/23
228		Rhode Island	2759	4/1892	Scr 3/23
431		Rhode Island	2773	11/1892	Scr 11/23
432		Rhode Island	2774	11/1892	Scr 12/25
433		Rhode Island	2775	11/1892	Scr 6/24
434		Rhode Island	2776	12/1892	Scr 3/22
435		Rhode Island	2777	12/1892	Scr 8/24

Class B-3 0-6-0: 19x22-52-170-89200-22952 (ex F-2 2-6-0)

268	(ex 1005)	Rebuilt		Scr 1/16
269	(ex 1026)	"		Scr 6/29
270	(ex 1029)	"		Scr 2/16
271	(ex 1032)	"		Scr 1/16
272	(ex 1101)	"		Scr 1/16
273	(ex 1102)	"		Scr '16
274	(ex 1107)	"		Scr 1/13
275	(ex 1113)	"		Scr 1/16
276	(ex 1214)	"		Scr 2/16

Notes: g - Sold to Carmichael Gravel Co.
  j - Sold to Northern Indiana Sand & Gravel Co.
  k - Sold to A. E. Staley Co.

Second Class B-3 - See Ann Arbor Class A

Class B-4 0-6-0: 18x24-52-160-92100-20730 (ex Wabash West. 1219-1222)

1219	re 219	Rhode Island	2204	3/1889	Scr 7/25
1220	re 220	Rhode Island	2205	3/1889	Scr '23
1221	re 221	Rhode Island	2206	4/1889	Scr '25
1222	re 222	Rhode Island	2207	4/1889	Scr 12/28

Class B-5 0-6-0: 18x24-52-185-102000-23976 RB - B.P. 165#, T.P. 20973

501		Rhode Island	3148	11/1899 to LE&FtW '29
502		Rhode Island	3149	11/1899	Scr 6/29
503		Rhode Island	3150	11/1899	Scr 3/33
504		Rhode Island	3151	11/1899	Scr 12/31
505		Richmond	3271	1901	Scr 6/27
506		Richmond	3272	1901	Scr 12/31
507		Richmond	3273	1901	Scr 12/33
508		Richmond	3274	1901	So 1/33 (k)

Class B-6 0-6-0: 19x28-58-165-143065-27403

509	Baldwin	23085	10/1903	Scr 8/35
510	Baldwin	23086	10/1903	Scr 12/35
511	Baldwin	23139	11/1903	Scr 11/40
512	Baldwin	23140	11/1903	Scr 12/31
513	Baldwin	23174	11/1903	Scr 5/36
514	Baldwin	23204	11/1903	Scr 12/41
515	Baldwin	24253	4/1904	Scr 2/36
516	Baldwin	24256	4/1904	Scr 12/41
517	Baldwin	24264	5/1904	Scr 11/47
518	Baldwin	24265	5/1904	Scr 1/41
519	Baldwin	24276	5/1904	So 6/41 (l)
520	Baldwin	24284	5/1904	Scr 7/34
521	Baldwin	24291	5/1904	Scr 8/34
522	Baldwin	24307	6/1904	So '36 (m)
523	Baldwin	24308	6/1904	Scr 11/40
524	Baldwin	24332	6/1904	So '48 (j)

Class B-7 0-6-0: 21x26-52-185-154040-34673

525		Rhode Island	41165	8/1906	Scr 1/53
526		Rhode Island	41166	8/1906	Scr 11/49
527		Rhode Island	41167	8/1906	Scr 1/51
528		Rhode Island	41168	8/1906	Scr 8/50
529		Rhode Island	41169	8/1906	Scr 7/49
530		Rhode Island	41170	8/1906	Scr 8/53
531		Rhode Island	41171	8/1906	So 12/51 (n)
532		Rhode Island	41172	8/1906	So '34 (o)
533		Rhode Island	41173	8/1906	Scr 2/54
534		Rhode Island	41174	8/1906	So '52 (p)
535		Rhode Island	41175	8/1906	Scr 1/51
536		Rhode Island	41176	8/1906	Scr 5/50
537		Baldwin (q)	31693	9/1907	Scr 9/50
538		Baldwin	31694	9/1907	Scr 11/49
539		Baldwin	31695	9/1907	Scr 12/50
540		Baldwin	31704	9/1907	So 4/54 (r)
541		Baldwin	31729	9/1907	Scr 4/53
542		Baldwin	31759	9/1907	Scr 7/53
543		Baldwin	31760	9/1907	Scr 3/52
544		Baldwin	31771	9/1907	Scr 7/53
545		Baldwin	31772	9/1907	Scr 3/52
546		Baldwin	31865	10/1907	Scr 4/53
547	(ex WPT 2207)	Rhode Island	41177	8/1906	Scr 11/51
548	(ex WPT 2208)	Rhode Island	41178	8/1906	Scr 8/50
549	(ex WPT 2209)	Rhode Island	41179	9/1906	Scr 3/51
550	(ex WPT 2210)	Rhode Island	41180	9/1906	Scr 4/51
551	(ex WPT 2211)	Rhode Island	41181	9/1906	Scr 2/51
552	(ex WPT 2212)	Rhode Island	41182	9/1906	Scr 7/51
553	(ex WPT 2213)	Rhode Island	41183	9/1906	Scr 2/50
554	(ex WPT 2214)	Rhode Island	41184	10/1906	Scr 4/51
555		Baldwin	37646	4/1912	Scr 3/52
556		Baldwin	37647	4/1912	So 12/50 (s)
557		Baldwin	37648	4/1912	So 3/54 (r)
558		Baldwin	37649	4/1912	Scr 12/49
559		Baldwin	37664	4/1912	Scr 1/50
560		Baldwin	37665	4/1912	Scr 7/51
561		Baldwin	37666	4/1912	Scr 12/50
562		Baldwin	37667	4/1912	Scr 1/50
563		Baldwin	37701	5/1912	So 9/51 (j)
564		Baldwin	37702	5/1912	Scr 2/51
565		Baldwin	37703	5/1912	Scr 2/51
566		Baldwin	37704	5/1912	Scr 2/51

Class B-8 0-6-0: 20x28-64-200-158100-29750 (ex F-7 2-6-0)

481	(ex 891)	Wabash RR	1923	Scr 12/31
482	(ex 801)	Wabash RR	1922	Scr 12/38
483	(ex 839)	Wabash RR	12/1918	Scr 12/31
484	(ex 902)	Wabash RR	12/1917	Scr 5/33
485	(ex 824)	Wabash RR	12/1917	Scr 9/35
486	(ex 804)	Wabash RR	12/1917	Scr 8/33
487	(ex 835)	Wabash RR	11/1917	Scr 11/35

Notes: j - Sold to Northern Indiana Sand & Gravel Co.
  k - Sold to A. E. Staley Co.
  l - Sold to Bates & Rogers Constr. Co.
  m - Sold to Peabody Coal Co.
  n - Sold to Neal Sand & Gravel Co.
  o - Sold to A. E. Staley Co. Repurchased 1942. Scrapped 4/50.
  p - 534 retired from LE&FtW, 3/57, donated to City of Fort Wayne and placed on exhibition in Swinney Park. The engine will be moved from Swinney Park in 1975 to a museum site of the Fort Wayne Railroad Historical Society at New Haven, Indiana.
  q - The ten Baldwin B-7's, 537-546, came from the builder with rectangular Baldwin plates, the same size as preceding group of Rhode Islands.
  r - 540, 557 sold to Missouri Aggregate Co.
  s - 556 sold to Neal Sand & Gravel Co., Mattoon, Illinois.

488	(ex 812)	Wabash RR	10/1917	Scr 12/33
489	(ex 819)	Wabash RR	11/1917	Scr 6/33
490	(ex 858)	Wabash RR	10/1917	Scr 11/33
491	(ex 880)	Wabash RR	9/1917	Scr 2/33
492	(ex 809)	Wabash RR	8/1917	Scr '35
493	(ex 827)	Wabash RR	8/1917	Scr 9/36
494	(ex 897)	Wabash RR	6/1917	Scr 5/33
495	(ex 856)	Wabash RR	5/1917	Scr 7/34
496	(ex 884)	Wabash RR	4/1917	Scr 7/34
497	(ex 864)	Wabash RR	3/1917	Scr 7/36
498	(ex 842)	Wabash RR	1/1917	Scr 12/31
499	(ex 845)	Wabash RR	2/1917	Scr 2/33

* * * * * * * *

Class C 0-8-0 Types

Class C-1 0-8-0: 22x28-58-215-183450-42700 (RB from I-2 2-8-0)

1501	(ex 2162)	Rebuilt	12/1917	Scr '47
1502	(ex 2156)	Rebuilt	12/1917	Scr '47

Class C-2 0-8-0: See Ann Arbor Class U

Class C-3 0-8-0: 25x28-52-195-217500-55781

1525	Schenectady	65086	9/1923	Scr 4/53
1526	Schenectady	65087	9/1923	Scr 3/54
1527	Schenectady	65088	9/1923	Scr 10/51
1528	Schenectady	65089	9/1923	Scr 4/51
1529	Schenectady	65090	9/1923	Scr 7/51
1530	Schenectady	65091	9/1923	Scr 5/53
1531	Schenectady	65092	9/1923	Scr 3/52
1532	Schenectady	65093	9/1923	Scr 8/51
1533	Schenectady	65094	9/1923	Scr 4/51
1534	Schenectady	65095	9/1923	Scr 2/53
1535	Schenectady	65096	9/1923	Scr 7/51
1536	Schenectady	65097	9/1923	Scr 2/53
1537	Schenectady	65098	9/1923	Scr 4/51
1538	Schenectady	65099	9/1923	Scr 7/51
1539	Schenectady	65100	9/1923	Scr 6/53
1540	Schenectady	65101	9/1923	Scr 8/53
1541	Schenectady	65102	9/1923	Scr 6/53
1542	Schenectady	65103	9/1923	Scr 7/51
1543	Schenectady	65104	9/1923	Scr 2/53
1544	Schenectady	65105	9/1923	Scr 12/53

Class C-4 0-8-0: 25x28-52-195-223800-55781

1545	Lima	7010	3/1926	Scr 8/51
1546	Lima	7011	3/1926	Scr 3/54
1547	Lima	7012	3/1926	Scr 7/51
1548	Lima	7013	3/1923	Scr 2/53
1549	Lima	7014	3/1926	Scr 4/53
1550	Lima	7015	3/1926	Scr 3/52
1551	Lima	7016	3/1926	Scr 6/53
1552	Lima	7017	3/1926	Scr 10/53
1553	Lima	7018	3/1926	Scr 12/53
1554	Lima	7019	3/1926	Scr 9/51
1555	Lima	7020	3/1926	Scr 1/54
1556	Lima	7021	3/1926	Scr 7/51
1557	Lima	7022	3/1926	Scr 7/51
1558	Lima	7023	3/1926	Scr 7/51
1559	Lima	7024	3/1926	Scr 7/51
1560	Lima	7025	4/1926	Scr 12/53
1561	Lima	7026	4/1926	So '54(t)
1562	Lima	7027	4/1926	Scr 7/51
1563	Lima	7028	4/1926	Scr 7/51
1564	Lima	7029	4/1926	Scr 11/51
1565	Lima	7030	4/1926	Scr 7/51
1566	Lima	7031	4/1926	Scr 3/53
1567	Lima	7032	4/1926	Scr 8/53
1568	Lima	7033	4/1926	Scr 7/51
1569	Lima	7034	4/1926	Scr 4/53

Note t - Sold to Sydney & Louisburg 85.

Early 4-2-0 Acquired by Northern Cross RR. (Became Sangamon & Morgan in 4/47)

Rogers (built as So. Caro. *Experiment*)	12x16-44-20000	Rogers	4	6/38	dr. '47
Illinois (not delivered, lost at sea)	12x16-44	BLW.	107	7/38	lost '38
Illinois	12x16-44	BLW.	127	5/39	dr. '47

Early 4-4-0 Acquired by Sangamon & Morgan RR. (Became Great Western in 2/53)

Pioneer		10½x20-60-24000	Rogers	135	7/48	dr.by '65
Sangamon	(re'65) TW&W "A"	"	"	140	8/48	dr.by '77
Morgan	" " "C" (a)	"	"	141	9/48	" "
Springfield	" " "B"	10½x18-60-24000	"	226	9/50	" "
Phoenix		? ? ?	Newell		1851	dr.by '65

Early 4-4-0 Acquired by Great Western Ry. of Illinois

(Consol. 7/65 into Tol., Wab. & Wes.)

	TW&W	Re'85	Re'87						
New England	101	—	—		13 x22-60-34000	Amoskeag	111	7/53	dr.by '84
New Hampshire	104	--	--		13½x22-54-34000	"	138	12/53	dr.by '84
New York	103	1103	103		14 x22-60-35000	Rogers	480	4/54	dr.by '89
New Jersey	102	—	—		14 x22-66-35000	"	485	4/54	dr.by '84
L.M.Wiley	105	--	—		14 x22-54-36000	Hinkley	568	9/55	dr.by '80
?	107	—	—		14½x20-60-36000	Souther		1855	dr.by '84
?	108	1108	108	(b)	15 x22-60-40000	Cooke		1855	Scr '89
?	113	—	—		16 x20-60-56000	Lawrence		1856	Ret.by'84
F.I.Carter	106	1106?	106		14½x20-60-36000	Rogers	644?	1/56	dr.by '88
J.M.Catlin	109	1109	109	(c)	16 x22-60-60000	"	673?	5/56	Scr '89
Savanna	110	1110	110	"	" " "	"	680?	6/56	Scr '89
Morris K.Jesup	111	1111	111	(d)	15 x22-60-40000	"	688?	8/56	Scr '89
J.L. Lamb	112	--	--		15½x22-60-41000	"	718?	12/56	Ret.by'84
Gov. Bissell	114	—	—		15 x22-60-48000	"	729?	1/57	dr.by '83
	115	--	--		15½x22-66-48000				Ret.by'83
	116	—	—		16 x22-60-62000				Ret.by'85
John Cooke	117	—	—		" " "	Rogers	791	8/57	Ret.by'85
Danville	118	1118	118	(e)	15 x22-60-48000	"	1071	5/63	Ret.by'92
Decatur	119	1119?	—		" " "	"	1074	"	dr.by '87
Hannibal	120	1120	120	(f)	" " "	"	1134	2/64	SS 4/88
Quincy	121	1121	121	"	" " "	"	1135	"	Scr '89
Keokuk	122	1122	122	"	" " "	"	1209	11/64	Scr '90
Bement	129	--	—		16 x22-60-58000	Mason	203	6/65	RB '81 See D-22
Homer	130	--	--		" " "	"	204	"	RB '83 See D-22

Note a - Later 11x22-48-57000; b - Later 15x22-64; c - Later 16x22-64-62000; d - 15x22-52-75000; e - Later 15x22-64-75000; f - Later 15x22-64-63000

Early 4-4-0 Acquired by Quincy & Toledo (Consol. 7/65 into Tol., Wab. & Wes.)

	TW&W							
(Ex Mad R.&L.E.)?	125	--	--	14x20-66-44000	(Lowell		1853)	dr. by '80
Mt. Sterling	126	—	—	13x20-60-35000	Rogers	1049	1/63	dr. by '80
?	127	—	—	14x20-66-44000	Souther		1863	dr. by '80
?	128	—	--	16x20-54-47000	Hinkley		"	RB '80 See D-22

Early 4-4-0 Acquired by Lake Erie, Wabash & St. Louis

(Consol. '56 into TW&W; Reorg. '58 as Toledo & Wabash)

	T&W	Re'81	Re'85	Re'87						
Titania	20 *	124	--			15x22-66-57800	Mason	33	12/55	RB '83 See D-22
Oberon	21	21	1021?			" " "	"	34	"	Scr '90
Diana	23	23	1023		(i)	" " "	"	35	1/56	Scr '89
Aurora	22	22	1022		(i)	" " "	"	36	"	Scr '92
Amazon	24	509	1509		(j)	15x22-72-57210	"	39	4/56	RB '87 LE&W 66
Nymph	25	520	1520	--	(j)	" " "	"	40	5/56	Re'87 LE&W 69
1	1	1	1001	1001	(n)	16x22-60-58170	Rogers	713	11/56	Ret. by '90
2	2	2	1002	1002	"	" " "	"	714	"	SS 4/88
3	3	3	1003	1003	"	" " "	"	731	1/57	SS 4/89
4? **	4	4	1004	4		16x22-60-62000	"	798	9/57	Scr '88
5	5	518	1518	—	(j)	15x22-60-54000	"	580	5/55	Re'87 LE&W 74
6	6	6	1006	—	(k)	" " "	"	584	6/55	So 8/87 Alaska
7	7	7	--	--		" " "	"	585	"	dr. by '84
8	8	8	—	—		" " "	"	588	"	dr. by '84
9	9	9	1009?	—	(l)	" " "	"	639	1/56	Ret. by '87
10	10	10	--	—		16x22-60-58170	"	643	"	Ret. by '83
11	11	11	1011?	11		" " "	"	674	5/56	Ret. by '88
12	12	12	1012	12	(m)	" " "	"	677	"	Scr '90
13	13	13	--	—	(o)	" " 60100	"	734	2/57	RB '84 D-22
14	14	14	?	?	(o)	" "	"	735	2/57	
15	15	15	1015?	--	(o)	" " 58170	"	805	10/57	Ret. by '87

* T&W 20 sold to Quincy & Toledo, re'65 to TW&W 124.
** (ord. as GW "L.A. Allen")

Notes: i - Later 15x22-70-60000 j - Later 15x22-60-61000
k - Later 15x22-60-73000 l - Later 16x22-60-58000
m - RB'71 to 16x24-66 n - Later 16x22-64-62000
o - #15 diverted from Miss. & Mo. *Nonesuch*; #13, 14 diverted from G.W. of I. *Thomas Condell* and *Gov. Moore*. Acquired 5/57.

Early 4-4-0 Acquired by Toledo & Illinois RR. (Consol.'56 into T.W.&W) (Reorg.'58 as Toledo & Wabash)

		Re'85	Re'87					
Ariel	30	1030	--	15x22-66-57800	Mason	23	7/55	Ret.by'87
Zephyr	16 re 508	1508	—	" " "	"	24	"	Re'87 LE&W 65
Atalanta	17 re 516	1516	--	" " "	"	25	8/55	Re'87 LE&W 67
Camilla	18	1018	18 (p)	" " "	"	26	"	Scr '06
Mazeppa	19	1019	1019 (q)	" " "	"	27	"	So 3/89
Boreas	26 re 530	1530	-- (j)	15x22-60-57210	Mason	55	11/56	Re'87 LE&W 71
Rushlight	27	1027	1027 "	" " "	"	56	"	SS 4/88
Fairy	28	1028	-- (r)	" " "	"	58	2/57	So 8/87 Alaska
Phantom	29	--	--	" " "	"	59	"	dr.by '84
?	35	--	--	16x22-60-57930	Springfield	-	6/55	Ret.by'81
?	33	1033	33 (s)	15x22-54-50100	Hinkley	558	"	Ret.by'99
?	34	—	— "	" " "	"	559	"	Ret.by'82
?	31	--	— "	" " "	"	574	11/55	RB '81 D-22
?	32	1032	32 "	" " "	"	575	"	RB '89 D-22

Early 4-4-0 Acquired by Toledo & Wabash (Consol. 7/65 into Tol.,Wab. & Wes.)

	Re'85	Re'87					
Bantam (re'65)"D"	--	—	9x20-54-24960	Mason	109	11/61	dr.by '77
Ex-? " "E"	--	—	12x18-54-26000	(Lowell		1853)	dr.by '77
37 (1st)	--	--	13x22-60-42400	Rogers	1015	4/62	dr.by '63
38 (1st)	—	—	" " "	"	1018	5/62	"
39 (1st)	—	--	" " "	"	1019	"	"
47 (1st) re 41	1041	41 (t)	" " "	"	1020	"	Scr '99
37 (2nd)	—	--	16x22-60-62000	Rogers	1078	6/63	Ret.by'83
38 (2nd)	--	—	" " "	"	1080	"	RB '79 D-22
39 (2nd)	1039	39	" " "	"	1082	7/63	Scr '98
41 re 14	—	—	" " "	"	1084	"	RB '84 D-22
42	--	—	" " "	"	1085	"	RB '79 D-22
43 *Boody*	1043	43 (u)	16x22-60-55900	Mason	135	6/63	?
44 *Colburn*	1044	44 (v)	" " "	"	136	"	So'01 Eel River
45 *Burrows*	1045	45 "	" " "	"	137	7/63	Scr '98
46 *John Ross*	1046	46 *	" " "	"	138	"	Scr '00
47 *George Cecil*	1047	47 (w)	" " "	"	202	6/65	Scr '00
48 *Wm. Kidd*	1048	48 "	" " "	"	205	"	Scr '00

*Class D-10

Note j - Later 15x22-60-60000 p - RB '79, later class D-2.
q - Later 15x22-70-68000 r - Later 15x22-72-58400
s - Later 15x24-60-50870 t - Later 13x22-60-62000
u - Later 16x22-64-60000 v - Later 16x22-74-60000
w - Later 16x22-60-63000

Early 4-4-0 Acquired by Toledo, Wabash & Western (Reorg. 1/77 as Wabash)

		Re'85	Re'87					
50 *John Knox*	re131	--	—	16x22-60-58170	Mason	209	8/65	RB '83 D-22
51 *J.N.Drummond*	re132	--	—	" " "	"	210	"	RB '81 D-22
52? *Delphi*	re145	1145	1145 (x)	15x24-68-57500	"	234	7/66	Scr '90
53? *Defiance*	re146	1146	146 (y)	" " "	"	235	"	Scr '90
54? *Tolono*	re147	1147	147 (z)	" " "	"	236	"	Ret.by'88
55 *Maumee*		1055	55 *	15x24-66-60600	"	232	6/66	Scr '00
56 *Wabash*		1056?	56	" " "	"	233	"	Ret.by'87
57		—	—	15x24-54-50100	Hinkley		1866	Ret.by'82
49		—	—	16x22-60-61200	Grant		6/66	RB '79 D-14
50		—	—	" " "	"		"	RB '80 D-22
51		—	—	" " "	"		"	" "
52		—	—	" " "	"		"	" "
53		—	—	" " "	"		"	RB '78 D-14
54	re499	1499	—	" " "	"		"	Re'87 LE&W 89
20		1020	—	15x22-66-57800	TW&W		1871	RB '86 D-12
138		—	—	16x24-62-65400	Cooke		1866	Ret.by'85
139				" " "	"		"	RB '84 D-22
140		1140	140**	" " "	"		"	Scr 1/00
141		1141	141	" " "	"		"	Scr '89
142		1142	142**	" " "	"		"	Scr '00
(49) re 136		—	—	16x24-60-65400	Schen.	423	7/66	Ret.by'84
(50) re 137		—	—	" " "	"	424	9/66	Ret.by'84
133		—	—	" " "	"	453	7/67	Ret.by'84
134		—	--	" " "	"	454	"	Ret.by'84
135		—	—	" " "	"	455	"	Ret.by'84
20 re 143		--	—	16x24-68-60400	Schen.	567	6/69	Ret.by'85
58 re 144		1144	1144 (x)	" " "	"	568	"	Scr '90
148		1148	148	" " "	"	561	"	Scr '89
149		1149	149	" " "	"	562	"	Scr '00
150		1150	150	" " "	"	560	"	RB '87 D-22
58		1058	58 (a)	16x24-60-65650	Pitts.	56	8/69	Scr '89
59		1059	59***	" " "	"	57	"	Scr 3/09
60		1060	60 "	" " "	"	58	9/69	Ret.by'02
61		1061	61 "	" " "	"	59	"	Scr '99
62		1062	62 "	" " "	"	60	"	Scr '99
63		—	—	" " "	"	95	8/70	RB '84 D-22
64		1064	64***	" " "	"	96	"	So '01 Eel River
65		1065	65 "	" " "	"	97	"	So '01 Eel River
66		1066	66 "	" " "	"	98	9/70	Scr 8/10
67		1067	67 "	" " "	"	99	"	Ret.by'99
68		1068	68 "	" " "	"	125	3/71	Scr '99

* Class D-2 ** Class D-19 *** Class D-4

Note x - Later 16x22-64-63000 y - Later 15x24-70-63000
z - Later 15x24-64-63000 a - Later 16x24-64-63000

69	--	—	16x24-60-65650	Pitts.	128	4/71	RB '84 D-22
70	1070	70 D-4	" " "	"	129	5/71	Scr 12/07
71	—	--	" " "	"	130	"	RB '84 D-22
72	1072	72 D-4	" " "	"	131	"	Scr '02
73	--	--	" " "	"	123	3/71	RB '79 D-12
74	1074	74	" " "	"	122	"	RB '88 D-22
75	—	—	" " "	"	124	"	RB '79 D-12
76	1076	76 D-4	" " "	"	126	4/71	Scr '02
77	--	—	" " "	"	127	"	RB '80 D-22
123	1123	123 (a)	" " 60100	Porter-Bell		1871	Ret.by'91
151	—	--	" " 62000	Mason	363	7/70	RB '85 D-21
152	--	--	" " "	"	364	"	RB '79 D-21
153	1153	—	" " "	"	366	8/70	RB '85 D-22
154	1154	—	" " "	"	367	"	RB '86 D-22
155	1155	155 D-10	" " "	"	368	"	Scr '00
156	1156	156 "	" " "	"	371	9/70	Scr 10/12
157	1157	157	" " "	"	372	"	Ret.by'88
158	1158	158	" " 65400	Schen.	653	9/70	Ret.by'90
159 re 532	1532	-- (b)	" " "	"	654	"	Re'87 LE&W 88
160	1160	160 (c)	" " "	"	655	"	Ret.by'91
161	1161	161	" " 62000	Mason	396	3/71	RB '89 D-22
162	1162	162 (c)	" " "	"	397	"	Scr '90
163	1163	163 D-7	" " "	"	398	4/71	Scr '95
164	1164	164 (c)	" " "	"	400	"	Scr '90
165	1165	165 "	" " "	"	401	"	Scr '90
166	1166	166 "	" " "	"	408	6/71	Scr '90
167	1167	—	" " "	"	409	"	RB '86 D-12
168	1168	168 (c)	" " "	"	413	"	Scr '90
169	1169	169	" " "	"	414	"	Scr '95
170	1170	170	" " "	"	415	"	Scr '00
171	1171	171 (d)	" " 65400	Schen.	688	8/71	Scr '00
172 re 531	1531	— "	" " "	"	689	"	Re '87 LE&W 87
173	1173	173 D-5	" " "	"	717	"	Scr 4/01
174	1174	174 (e)	" " "	"	718	"	Scr 7/89
175	1175	175 "	" " "	"	719	"	Scr '89
176	1176	176	" " "	"	720	"	RB '89 D-22
177	1177	177 (f)	" " "	"	721	"	Scr '89
178	1178	178 "	" " "	"	722	"	Scr 4/88
179	1179	179 D-5	" " "	"	723	"	Scr '95
180	1180	180 "	" " "	"	724	"	Scr '95

Notes

(a) Later 16x24-64-63000
(b) RB'85 (Rome) to 16x24-60-62000
(c) Later 16x24-64-65000
(d) Later 16x24-70-68000
(e) Later 16x24-60-68000
(f) Later 16x24-64-68000

	Re'80	Re'85	Re'87	Class					
82		—	—		16x24-60-60100	Rogers		6/71	RB '85 D-12
83		1083	83	D-3	" " "	"		7/71	So '01 Eel Riv.
84		1084	84	"	" " "	"		"	Scr '95
85		1085	85	"	" " "	"		"	Scr '95
86		1086	86	"	" " "	"		"	Ret.by'98
87		1087	87	"	" " "	"		"	Scr '95
88		--	--		" " "	"		"	RB '85 D-12
89		—	—		" " "	"		8/71	RB '85 D-12
90		1090	90	D-3	" " "	"		"	Scr '98
91		1091	91	"	" " "	"		"	Scr '00
92		—	—		" " "	Grant		1871	RB '85 D-22
93		--	—		" " "	"		"	RB '84 D-22
94		—	--		" " "	"		"	RB? D-22
95	re 500	1500	--		" " "	"		"	Re'87 LE&W 90
96		--	—		" " "	"		"	RB '84 D-22
97 **		1097	97	D-11	" " 75000	Pitts.	170	1/72	Scr by'02
98 ***		1098	98	D-7	" " "	Mason	450	4/72	Scr '95
99		1099	99	"	" " "	"	451	"	Scr '95
100		1100	100	"	" " "	"	452	"	Scr '00
201		1201	201	"	" " 68000	"	453	5/72	Scr 3/09
202		1202	202		" " "	"	454	"	Ret.by'92
181		1181	181	D-9	" " "	Pitts.	284	8/73	Scr 11/07
182		1182	—		" " "	"	285	"	RB '87 D-22
183		1183	183	D-9	" " "	"	286	"	Scr 3/09
184		1184	—		" " "	"	287	"	RB '86 D-22
185		1185	--		" " "	"	288	"	RB '85 D-22
186		1186	186	D-4	" " "	"	289	"	Scr '95
188		1188	188	D-11	" " "	"	281	7/73	Scr by'02
189		1189	189	D-4	" " "	"	282	"	Scr '92
190		1190	190	"	" " "	"	283	"	Scr by'02
191		1191	191	"	" " "	"	280	"	Scr by'02

Early 4-4-0 Acquired by Chicago & Paducah RR. (Merged 6/80 into WStL&P)

1	192	—	—		? ? ?	?	?	?	RB '80 A-3
2	193	—	—		15x24-60-60000	Cooke	935	8/73	RB '83 A-3
3	194	—	—		" " "	"	936	"	RB '82 A-3
4	195	1195	—		16x24-60-60000	"	937	9/73	RB '86 D-22
5	196	1196	196		" " "	"	938	"	Scr '95
6	197	1197	197		" " "	"	940	"	Scr '91
7	198	1198	198		" " "	"	941	"	Scr '90
8	199	1199	199	D-6	" " "	"	942	"	Scr '12

* Built as Mathias Chamberlin & Co. #1
***Gen. Gridley*

Early 4-4-0 Acquired with Eel River RR. (Leased 10/77 to Wabash Ry.)

6	207	1207	207	16x24-54-64000	Rhode Is.	314	10/71	So 12/01	PRR
7	208	1208	208	" " "	"	315	"	" "	"
8	209	1209	209	" " "	"	316	"	" "	"
9	210	1210	210	" " "	"	317	"	" "	"
10	211	1211	211	" " "	"	391	5/72	" "	"
11	212	1212	212	15x22?-60? "	"	411	8/72	" "	"
12	213	1213	213	" " "	"	421	"	" "	"

Note - #6-8 built for Detroit, Eel River & Illinois; 9-12 built for Detroit, Hillsdale & Indiana

Early 4-4-0 Acquired by North Missouri (5½'g.) - Reorg. 1/72 as St. Louis, Kan. City & Nor.

	Re'80	Re'85	Re'87	Class					
1 ?									dr.by '57
2 ?									" "
3 *Warren*									dr.by '77
4 *Audrain*									" "
5 *Montgomery*									" "
6 *Missouri*									" "
7 *Iowa*									dr.by '69
8 *Meteor*									dr.by '63
9 *Planet*									" "
10 *Schuyler*									dr.by '72
11 *Randolph*									dr.by '67
12 *Adair*									dr.by '72
13 *Boone*									" "
14 *Ariel*									" "
15 *President*									" "
16 ?									dr.by '64
17 *Mechanic*									dr.by '72
18 *Chief*									" "
19 *Minnesota*					? ?	Swinburne	49	'52	Scr.by'60
1 *St. Louis*	215	1215	215		16x24-60-68000	Taunton	232	7/57	Scr '87
2 *St. Charles*	216	1216	216		" " "	"	235	9/57	Ret.by'92
19 *Minnesota*	--	—	--		16x22-60-55000	Schen.	220	6/60	dr.by '72
20 *Dakota*	229	—	—	(g)	" " "	"	221	"	Ret.by'85
21 *Hercules*	230	1230	230	D-13	" " "	"	226	9/60	Scr '98
22 *Ajax*	—	—	—		16x22-60-55000	"	227	9/60	dr.by '72
8 *John O'Fallon* re *B.R. Bonner*	—	—	—		16x22-56	"	314	11/63	dr.by '69

Note g - RB'65 (St. Charles), renamed *Isaac H. Sturgeon.*

	Re'80	Re'85	Re'87	Class					
9 *John H.Lightner*	218	—	--		16x22-56-62000	Schen.	315	12/63	Ret.by'82
16 *J.S. Rollins*	225	—	--		16x24-56-61000	"	329	4/64	Ret.by'84
23 *U.S. Grant*	232	1232	232	D-13	" " "	"	362	1/65	Ret.by'02
24 *J.O. Farrar*	233	1233	233		16x22-54-60000	Rogers	1400?	10/66	Ret.by'92
25 *H. Overstolz*	234	—	—	(h)	" " "	"	1401?	"	So c.'90
26 *Henry Reed*	235	1235	235		15x22-60-63000	"	1453?	4/67	Ret.by'92
27 *E.W.Fox*	236	1236	236		" " "	"	1455?	5/67	Ret.by'92
28 *Jas H.Robinson*	237	1237	—		" " "	Mason	253	4/67	RB'85 D-20
29 *John R.Clark*	238	1238	238	D-2	" " "	"	255	"	Scr '92
30 *Chas.W.Irwin*	239	1239	239	"	" " "	"	257	5/67	Scr '95
31 *John Orric*	240	1240	240	"	" " "	"	258	"	Scr '95
32 *General Lyon*	241	1241	241	D-7	16x24-60-63000	"	260	"	Scr '98
33 *Frank Blair*	242	1242	242	"	" " "	"	261	"	Scr by'02
34 *General Pope*	243	1243	243	"	" " "	"	262	6/67	Scr '98
35 *Gen. Sherman*	244	1244	244	"	" " "	"	263	"	Scr '95
36 *Robert Tyler*	245	—	--		" " "	"	264	"	RB'79 D-15
37 *Nat.Paschall*	246	--	—		" " "	"	265	"	Ret.by'87
38 *Jay Cooke*	247	--	--		" " "	"	266	7/67	Ret.by'87
39 *John F.Hume*	248	1248	248	D-7	" " "	"	267	"	Scr '92
40 *Major Thomas*	249	1249	249	"	" " "	"	268	8/67	Scr '95
11 *N.B.Coates*	220	1220	220		" " "	"	269	"	Scr '88
41	250	1250	250		17x24-66-72000	?	(RB'84)		Ret.by'02
42	251	1251	251		16x22-60-72000	Norris	?		Ret.by'87
47	256	1256	256		16x24-54-61000	Rogers	1497	2/68	Ret.by'98
48	257	1257	257	D-3	" " "	"	1498	"	"
49	258	1258	258	"	" " "	"	1500A	"	"
50	259	1259	259	"	" " "	"	1503	3/68	"
51	260	1260	260	"	" " "	"	1634	8/69	. "
52	261	1261	261	"	" " "	"	1635	"	"
53	262	1262	262	"	" " "	"	1636	"	"
54	263	1263	263	" (i)	" " "	"	1637	"	"
55	264	1264	264	"	" " "	"	1644	9/69	"
56	265	1265	265	"	" " "	"	1645	"	"
58	267	1267	267		16x24-50	Schen.	579	8/69	dr.by '96
59	268	1268	268		" "	"	580	"	?
60	269	1269	269		" "	"	581	9/69	?
7	—	—	—		15x24-60-61000	"	587	10/69	dr.by '80
8	217	1217	217	(j)	" " "	"	588	"	Scr '98
64	273	1273	273	D-3	16x24-54-61000	Rogers	1693	2/70	Ret.by'98
65	274	1274	274	"	" " "	"	1694	"	"
66	275	1275	275	"	" " "	"	1695	"	"
67	276	1276	276	"	" " "	"	1696	"	"
68	277	1277	277	"	" " "	"	1698	"	"
69	278	1278	278	"	" " "	"	1699	"	"
70	279	1279	279	" (i)	" " "	"	1705	3/70	"

Note h - #234 sold to Clarinda & St. Louis　　i - Rebuilt Rome 1885
j - Later 16x24-54

	Re'80	Re'85	Re'87	Class					
71	280	1280	280	D-3	16x24-54-61000	Rogers	1706	3/70	Ret.by'98
72	281	1281	281	"	" " "	"	1709	"	"
73	282	1282	282	"	" " "	"	1710	"	"
74	283	1283	283	"	" " "	"	1711	"	"
75	284	1284	284	"	" " "	"	1719	4/70	"
76	285	1285	285	"	" " "	"	1723	5/70	"
77	286	1286	286	"	" " "	"	1728	"	"
78	287	1287	287	"	16x24-60-68000	"	1721	4/70	"
79	288	1288	288	"	" " "	"	1722	"	"
10	219	1219	219		17x24-60-70000	Schen.	755	2/72	Scr '88
12	221	1221	221		" " "	"	756	"	Scr. '88
13	222	1222	222		" " "	"	757	"	Scr '88
14	223	—	—		" " "	"	761	"	dr.by '80
15	224	1224	224		" " "	"	762	"	Ret.by'92
17	226	1226	226	D-16?	" " "	"	766	3/72	Scr '02
18	227	1227	227	" (i)	" " "	"	767	"	Scr '02
19	228	1228	228		" " "	"	769	"	Scr '89
22	231	1231	231	D-16?	" " "	"	770	"	Scr '02
84	293	1293	293		17x24-66?-72000	"	771	"	Ret.by'88

Early 4-4-0 Acquired by St. Louis, Kansas City & Northern (Consol.11/79 into WSt.L&P)

	85	294	1294	294	D-17	17x24-60-72000	Rhode Is	401	7/72	?
	86	295	1295	295	D-20	" " "	"	402	"	So 9/07-1
	87	296	1296	296	D-17	" " "	"	403	"	Scr '95
	88	297	1297	297	D-20	" " "	"	404	"	Scr '07
	89	298	1298	298	D-17	" " "	"	405	"	Ret.by'05
	90	299	1299	299	"	" " "	"	406	"	Ret.by'05
	91	300	1300	300	"	" " "	"	407	"	Ret.by'05
	92	301	1301	301	"	" " "	"	408	"	Scr '00
	93	302	1302	302	"	" " "	"	409	"	Ret.by'05
	94	303	1303	303	"	" " "	"	410	"	Scr '00
	95	304	1304	304	D-18	" " 70000	BLW.	4113	7/77	Scr 8/10
	96	305	1305	305	" (i)	" " "	"	4114	"	Scr '05
	97	306	1306	306	"	" " "	"	4120	"	Scr '05
	98	307	1307	307	"	" " "	"	4123	"	Scr 9/07
3 re	99	308	1308	308	"	" " "	"	4043	1/77	Scr 7/11
4 re	100	309	1309	309	" (i)	" " "	"	4044	"	Scr '05
5 re	101	310	1310	310	"	" " "	"	4051	2/77	Scr '05
6 re	102	311	1311	311	"	" " "	"	4052	"	Scr '05
	103	312	1312	312	D-26	" " 86500	Rhode Is	774	8/79	Note m
	104	313	1313	1313	"	" " "	"	775	"	Scr 10/13

Note i - Rebuilt Rome 1885　　1 - #295 sold to Dakota Central
m - Six class D-26 assigned 1887 to O&StL, of which four were rebuilt 1894, becoming class D-27 #262-265. All Scr 12/31.

Early 4-4-0 Acquired by St. Louis, Kansas City & Northern continued

105	314	1314	314	D-26	17x24-60-86500	Rhode Is	776	9/79	Scr 1/13
106	315	1315	315	"	" " "	"	777	"	Note m
107	316	1316	316	"	" " "	"	778	"	Scr 1/16
108	317	1317	317	"	" " "	"	779	10/79	Note m
109	318	1318	318	"	" " "	"	780	"	"
110	319	1319	319	"	" " "	"	781	"	Scr 3/16
111	320	1320	320	"	" " "	"	782	"	Note m
112	321	1321	1321	"	" " "	"	783	"	Scr 10/07
113	322	1322	322	"	" " "	"	784	11/79	Note m
114	323	1323	323	"	" " "	"	785	"	Scr 10/10
115	577	1577	577	"	18x24-66	"	786	"	Scr '16
116	578	1578	1578	"	" "	"	787	"	Scr '10
117	579	1579	579	D-28	" "	"	794	12/79	Scr '12

Early 4-4-0 Acquired by Wabash, St. Louis & Pacific (reorg. 3/87 as Wabash)

	Re'85	Re'87	Class					
324	1324	324	D-23	17x24-64-87000	Rogers	2617	7/80	Scr 1/16
325	1325	325	--	" " "	"	2618	"	Scr '91
326	1326	326	D-23	" " "	"	2612	"	Scr 10/13
327	1327	327	--	" " "	"	2614	"	Scr '91
328	1328	328	D-23	" " "	"	2616	"	Scr 3/09
329	1329	329	"	" " "	"	2584	4/80	Scr 9/07
330	1330	330	"	" " "	"	2585	"	Scr 10/13
331	1331	331	"	" " "	"	2587	"	Scr 9/14
332	1332	332	"	" " "	"	2591	5/80	Scr 9/07
333	1333	333	"	" " "	"	2592	"	Scr 10/13
334	1334	334	"	" " "	"	2594	"	Scr 2/16
335	1335	335	"	" " "	"	2597	"	Scr 3/09
336	1336	336	"	" " "	"	2599	"	Scr '05
337	1337	337	"	" " "	"	2601	"	Scr 3/09
338	1338	338	"	" " "	"	2603	6/80	Scr 4/16
339	1339	339	"	" " "	"	2605	"	Scr '07
340	1340	340	"	" " "	"	2606	"	Scr 9/07
341	1341	341	D-26	18x26-66-	Rhode Is	819	1/80	Scr 10/12
342	1342	342	D-28	" "	"	820	"	Scr 1/16
343	1343	343	"	" "	"	821	"	Scr 1/18
344	1344	344	"	" "	"	822	2/80	Scr 10/13
359	1359	359	D-8	16x24-64-73000	Hinkley		1880	(RB Rome '85)
360	1360	360	"	" " "	"		"	Scr 12/07
361	1361	361	"	" " "	"		"	Scr '05
362	1362	362	"	" " "	"		"	Scr 8/07
363	1363	363	"	" " "	"		"	Scr 2/15

Note m - Six class D-26 assigned 1887 to O&Stl, of which four were rebuilt 1894, becoming class D-27 #262-265. All Scr 12/31.

Early 4-4-0 Acquired by Wabash, St. Louis & Pacific continued

	364	1364	364	D-24	17x24-64-87000	Hinkley		1880	Scr 10/13
	365	1365	365	"	" " "	"		"	Scr 1/16
(exIB&W 66)	368	1368	368	D-3	" " 75000	(Rogers	2270	5/73)	Scr 7/11
(" 67)	369	1369	369	"	" " "	("	2275	")	Ret.by'98
(" 68)	370	1370	370	"	" " "	("	2273	")	Ret.by'98
	392	1392	1392	D-26	18x24-68	Rhode Is	926	1/81	Scr '16
	393	1393	1393	"	" "	"	927	"	Scr 10/13
	394	1394	394	D-28	" 64	"	928	"	Scr 1/13
	395	1395	395	D-26	" 68	"	929	"	Scr 1/16
	396	1396	396	"	" "	"	930	"	Scr 1/16
	397	1397	397	"	" "	"	931	"	Scr 6/16
(delv.as 91)	398	1398	398	"	17x24-60	"	1222	12/82	Scr 1/16
(" " 92)	399	1399	399	"	" "	"	1223	"	Scr 1/16

Early 4-4-0 Acquired by Havana, Mason City, Lincoln & Eastern (Leased'80 to WStL&P)

(exIB&W 18)	400	1400	--	--	15x22-60	(Rhode Is.	165	4/70)	IC 424
(" 20)	401	1401	--	--	" "	("	171	")	" 425
(" 32)	402	1402	--	--	" "	("	372	11/71)	" 426

Early 4-4-0 Acquired by Detroit, Butler & St. Louis (acquired '81 by WStL&P)

1	403	1403	403	D-25	17x24-64-75000	Manch.	831	8/80	Scr '11
2	404	1404	404	"	" " "	"	832	"	Scr by'13
3	405	1405	405	"	" " "	"	833	10/80	Scr '15
4	406	1406	406	" (i)	" " "	"	834	"	Scr '07

Early 4-4-0 Acquired by Quincy, Missouri & Pacific (leased '80 to WStL&P)

	Re'80	Re'85	Class					
1 *Tom Jasper*	407	1407	--	15x24-60	Manch.	376	8/71	Note n
2 *Henry Root*	408	1408	--	" "	"	377	8/71	"
3	409	1409	--	15x22-60	Rogers	2048	8/72	"
4	410	1410	--	16x24-64	?	?	?	RB'81 D-12

Note i - Rebuilt Rome 1885
n - Returned 1888 to QM&P, which became Quincy, Omaha & Kansas City.

Early 4-4-0 Acquired by Toledo, Peoria & Warsaw (Leased 5/80 to WStL&P)

Name	(Note o)			No.	Date	Note
Jacob Bunn	(Note o)		Portland	113	10/64	Note o
John V. Ayer	"			114	12/64	"
Portland	"	15x22-60		121	11/64	"
Rushnell	"	16x24-60	Rhode Is.	36	9/67	"
La Harpe	"	" " "		37	10/67	"
Canton	"			38		"
Judge Clifford	"	" " "	Portland	135	9/68	"
J.B. Brown	"	" " "		139		"
Falmouth	"	" " "		134	10/68	"
Falmouth	"	" " "		140	11/68	"
Z.Secor	"	" " "	Rhode Is.	70	10/68	"
Peoria	"	" " "		72	10/68	"
J.P. Drake	"	" " "		73		"
Ajax	"	15x24	"	74	"	"
Gen. Merritt	"	16x24-54	"	85	12/68	"
Ft. Madison	"	" " "	"	86	"	"
Burlington	"	" " "	"	88	"	"
City of Nebraska	"	" " "	"	89	1/69	"
Ft. Kearney	"	" " "	"	90	"	"
Farrington	"	" " "	"	91	"	"
Bloomfield	"	" " "	"	92	"	"
Centreville	"	" " "	"	93	2/69	"
California	"	" " "	"	94	"	"
Oregon	"	" " "	"	95	"	"
Conjden	"	16x24-60	"	98	4/69	"
Leon	"	" " "	"	102	"	"
.t. Aure	"	" " "	"	104	"	"
Beauford	"	" " "	"	106	5/69	"
Clarador	"	" " "	"	107	"	"

(+15 others, maybe not all 4-4-0. Nos. 1424,1432,1433 rebuilt Rome 1885)

Early 4-4-0 Acquired by Missouri, Iowa & Nebraska (Leased '80 to WStL&P)
Became Keokuk & Western

	Re'80	Re'85	Re'87	Class					
1	455	1455	--		17x24-61	Pitts.	108	3/71	Re.'87 K&W?
2	456	1456	--		" "	"	110	5/71	"
3	457	1457	--						"
4	458	1458	--						"
5	459	1459	--						"
6	460	1460	--						"
7	461	1461	--		17x24-63	Cooke	1095	10/79	"
8	462	1462	--		" "	"	1096	11/79	"
9	463	1463	--		" "	"	1097	10/80	"
10	464	1464	464	D-19	" "	"	1098	4/81	Ret.by'10

Note o - TP&W power ren. 1880 in WStL&P 411-454 series, ren. 1885 to 1411-1454, then returned to TP&W.

Early 4-4-0 Acquired by Springfield & Northwestern (Leased '80 to WStL&P)
(Sold 6/88 to Chicago, Peoria & St.Louis)

	Re'80	Re'85	Re'87	Class					
1	465	1465	--		14x24-60	Rhode Is.	286	7/71	Re CP&StL

Early 4-4-0 Acquired by Wabash, St. Louis & Pacific

466	1466	466	D-24	17x24-64-87000	Hinkley		1881	Scr '02
467	1467	467	D-25	" "	Manch.	914	3/81	Scr '02
468	1468	468	"	" "	"	915		Scr 7/11
469	1469	1469	D-22	" -70	"	916	6/81	" '10
470	1470	1470	"	" "	"	917	"	Scr '06
471	1471	471	D-25	" -64	"	918		Scr by'00
472	1472	472	D-22(i)	" -70	"	919	9/81	Scr 1/16
473	1473	473	D-25	" -64	"	920		Scr by'00
474	1474	474	D-22	" -70	"	921	9/81	Scr 1/16
475	1475	475	D-25	" -64	"	922		Scr 8/10
476	1476	476	"	" "	"	923		Scr 8/10

Early 4-4-0 Acquired by Peoria, Pekin & Jacksonville (Leased '81 to WStL&P)

	Re'81	Re'85						
4	486	1486		14x22-60	Rogers	1174	7/64	Re CP&StL
5	487	1487		" "	"	1180	8/64	"
6	488	1488		15x22-60	Portland	124	3/65	"
7	489	1489	(note p)					"
8	490	1490		15x24-60	Manch.	96	6/67	"
9	491	1491		16x24-60	"	105	2/68	"
10	492	1492		" "	"	109	9/68	"
11	493	1493		14x22-60	"	108	8/68	"
12	494	1494		16x24-62	Rogers	1671	12/69	"
13	495	1495		" "	"	1672		"
14	496	1496		" -60	"	1935	12/71	"
15	497	1497		" "	"	1940		"
16	498	1498		?	?	?	?	"

Note i - RB'85 Rome.
     p - Possibly ex-TP&W Portland.

Early 4-4-0 Acquired by Indianapolis, Peru & Chicago (Leased 9/81 to WStL&P)

	Re'81	Re'85						Re'87
1	--	--	(ex I&P)					
2	--	--	"					--
3	503	1503	"					--
4	504	1504	"	13x22-60	Rogers	1023	6/62	--
5	505	1505	" (note q)	15x22-54-60000	"	1060	3/63	LE&W 64
6	506	1506	"	" " "	"	1091	7/63	LE&W 75
7	507	1507	"	" " "	"	1279	7/65	LE&W 76
8	508	--	(ex U.S.M.R.)?		Cooke			dr.by'85
9	509	--	"					dr.by'81
10	510	1510?	"					dr.by'87
12	512	1512		15x22-55-62000	Cooke	1869		LE&W 72
16	516	--		" " " 58000	Pitts.	114	12/70	dr.by'85
17	517	1517		" " "	"	115	1/71	LE&W 73
18	518	--	(ex CC&L)	?	?	?	?	dr.by'85
19	519	1519		15x24-60-60000	Mason	284	7/68	LE&W 68
20	520	--		?	?	?	?	dr.by'85
21	521	1521		15x22-60-60000	Mason	300	1/69	LE&W 70
22	522	1522		16x24-55-67000	Pitts.	138	1/72	LE&W 77
23	523	1523		" " "	"	139		LE&W 78
24	524	1524		" " "	"	189	5/72	LE&W 80
25	525	1525		" " "	"	190		LE&W 81
26	526	1526		16x24-60-68000	Grant		1872	LE&W 85
27	527	1527	(RB 1880)					LE&W 86
1	501	1501					1873	LE&W 84
28	528	--		16x24-61-70000	Pitts.	318	6/75	LE&W 82
2	502	1502		" " "	"	319		LE&W 79
29	529	1529		" " "	"	361	10/77	LE&W 83

Early 4-4-0 Acquired by Danville & Southwestern (Leased '81 to WStL&P)

Paris & Dan.	D&SW	Re'81	Re'85					Re'88	
1 Danville	1	533	1533	15x24-62	BLW.	3653	9/74	CV&C	9
2 Paris	2	534	1534	" "	"	3654	10/74	"	10
3 Marshall	3	535	1535	" "	"	3671	12/74	"	11
4 Robinson	4	536	1536	15x24-57	"	3783	10/75	"	12
5	5	537	1537	" "	"	3950	7/76	"	13
	6	538	1538	16x24-63-76400	"	5007	3/80	"	14
	7	539	1539	" " "	"	4943	1/80	"	15

Note q - Rebuilt Peru 1872.

Early 4-4-0 Acquired by Cairo & Vincennes (Leased '81 to WStL&P)

Morgan Impr.Co.	C&V	Re'81	Re'85					Re'88	
1	1	540	1540	15x24-61-49000	BLW.	2389	3/71	CV&C	1
4	2	541	1541	" 57	"	2375	2/71	"	2
5	3	542	1542	" 62	"	2377		"	3
6	4	543	1543	" 67	"	2524	7/71	"	4
7	5	544	1544	16x24-55	"	2624	11/71	"	5
	6	545	1545	15x22-62	Grant		1872	"	6
	7	546	1546	" "	"		"	"	7
	8	547	1547					"	8
A.J.Thomas	12	549	1549	16x24-63-76400	BLW.	4795	9/79	"	16
	13	550	1550	" " "	"	4793		"	17
14?	551	1551		17x24-63	Grant		1880	"	19
	15	552	1552	" "	"		"	"	20
16?	-553	1553		" "	"		"	"	21
17?	554	1554		" "-76000	"			"	22
18?	555	1555		" " "	"			"	23
--	--		29	" "-81000	BLW.	7783	1/86	"	24

Class D-1 4-4-0: 13x20-44-37230 Rebuilt from H.R.&E. Narrow Gauge 4-4-0's.
   253? Rebuilt 1888 So 3/08;   254? Rebuilt 1888 So 11/07

Class D-2 4-4-0: 15x22-70-68000 (#238 Cylinders 16x24)
   See #18, 55, 238, 239, 240.

Class D-3 4-4-0: 16x24-64-68000 (#368-370 = 17x24-64-75000)
   See #83-87, 90, 91, 257-265, 273-288, 368-370.

Class D-4 4-4-0: 16x24-64-68000
   See #59-62, 64-68, 70, 72, 76, 186, 189, 190, 191.

Class D-5 4-4-0: 16x24-64-68000
   See #173, 179, 180.

Class D-6 4-4-0: 16x24-64-70000
   See #199.

Class D-7 4-4-0: 16x24-64-70000
   See #98-100, 163, 169, 170, 201, 241-244, 248, 249.

Class D-8 4-4-0: 16x24-64-73000
   See #359-363.

Class D-9 4-4-0: 16x24-64-79000
   See #181, 183.

Class D-10 4-4-0: 16x24-70-79000
   See #46; 155, 156.

Class D-11 4-4-0: 16x24-64-75000
   See #97, 188.

Class D-12 4-4-0: 16x24-64-87000 (#20, 73, 167 had 70" drivers)

Re'85	Re'87						Re'85	Re'87				
73	1073	73	Wab.	'79	Scr 12/07		88	1088	88	Wab.	'85	Scr '02
75	1075	75	"	"	Scr 8/10		89	1089	89	"	"	Scr 8/10
410	1410	410	"	'81	Ret.by'13		-	1020	20	"	'86	Scr 6/07
82	1082	1082	Rome	'85	Scr 8/10		-	1167	167	"	"	Scr 12/07

Class D-13 4-4-0: 16x24-64-62000
   See #230 and 232.

Class D-14 4-4-0: 17x22-70-87000
49 1049 49 Wab. '79 Scr 3/19; 53 1053 53 Wab. '78 Scr 1/16

Class D-15 4-4-0: 17x24-70-70000
245 1245 245 Wab. '79 Scr 9/09

Class D-16 4-4-0: 17x24-60-70000
   See #226, 227, 231.

Class D-17 4-4-0: 17x24-64-71000
   See #294, 296, 298-303.

Class D-18 4-4-0: 17x24-64-71000
   See #304-311.

Class D-19 4-4-0: 17x24-64-71000
   See #140, 142, 164.

Class D-20 4-4-0: 17x24-70-79000 (#10, 295 had 64" drivers) See also #295, 297

Re'85	Re'87						Re'85	Re'87				
10	1010	10	Wab.	'83	Scr 10/04			6		Wab.	'87	Scr '05
237	1237	237	"	'85	Scr 8/10			251		"	"	Scr 10/13

Class D-21 4-4-0: 17x24-64-87000
151 1151 151 Rome 1885 Scr '07 | 152 1152 152 Wab. 1879 Scr 1/16

Class D-22 4-4-0: 17x24-64-87000 (* had 70" drivers)

No	No	No	Builder	New	Disp'n		No	No	No	Builder	New	Disp'n
38	1038	38	Wab.	1879	Scr 1/16		94	1094	94	Wab.	?	Scr '98
42	1042	42	"	"	Scr 3/07		96	1096	96	"	1884	Scr '02
50	1050	1050	"	1880	Scr 10/10		139	1139	139	"	"	Scr 9/07
51	1051	51*	"	"	Scr 11/07			1092	92	Rome	1885	Scr '98
52	1052	52*	"	"	Scr 8/10			1153	153*	Wab.	"	Scr 1/16
77	1077	77*	"	"	Scr 1/16			1185	1185	"	"	Scr 10/07
125	1125	1125	"	"	Scr 11/07			1154	154*	"	1886	Scr 10/07
126	1126	126	"	"	Scr 2/13			1184	184*	"	"	Scr '07
127	1127	127	"	"	Scr 3/09			1195	1195*	"	"	Scr 2/13
128	1128	1128	"	"	Scr '02			1200	200	"	"	Scr 8/10
31	1031	31	"	1881	Scr 10/10				1030	"	1887	Scr 10/10
129	1129	129	"	So	'06(r)				1031*	"	"	Scr 10/10
132	1132	132	"	"	Scr '02				150*	"	"	Scr 10/13
206	1206	1206	"	"	Scr '07				182*	"	"	Scr 12/07
124	1124	1124	Wab.	1883	Scr 8/10				74*	Wab.	1888	Scr 7/07
130	1130	1130	"	"	Scr '07				19	"	1889	Scr 8/10
131	1131	1131	"	"	Scr 10/10				161	"	"	Scr 10/13
13	1013	13	"	1884	Scr 10/13				176	"	"	Scr 1/16
14	1014	14	"	"	Scr 1/16				1032	"	"	Scr c.'07?
63	1063	63	"	"	Scr 8/10				3	Moberly	'89	Scr '04
69	1069	69	"	"	Scr 8/10				1*	"	'90	Scr 11/07
71	1071	71*	"	"	Scr 6/16				12*	Wab.	1891	Scr 10/13
93	1093	93	"	"	Scr '12							

See also #1469*, 1470*, 472*, 474*.

Note r - #129 became Yosemite Valley 21.

Class D-23 4-4-0: 17x24-64-87000 (#326, 328 had 70" drivers)

See #324, 326, 328-340.

Class D-24 4-4-0: 17x24-64-87000

See #364, 365, 466.

Class D-25 4-4-0: 17x24-64-87000

See #403-406, 467, 468, 471, 473, 475, 476.

Class D-26 4-4-0: 17x24-70-150-87000-12816 (564,565 ex 18x24; 574,575 ex 6½ drivers)

No	No	No		Builder		New	Disp'n
564	1564	564		Rhode Is.	1122	3/82	Scr '16
565	1565	565	(Class D-28: 18x24)	"	1123	"	Scr '12
566	1566	566		"	1124	4/82	Scr '12
567	1567	567		"	1125	"	Scr '16
568	1568	568		"	1126	"	Scr 6/16
569	1569	1569		"	1127	"	Scr '16
570	1570	570		"	1128	5/82	So? Lincoln S&G
571	1571	1571		"	1129	"	Scr '15
572	1572	1572		"	1130	"	Scr 1/16
573	1573	1573		"	1131	"	Scr '15
574	1574	574	(ex 6½" drivers)	"	1132	10/82	Scr 1/13
575	1575	1575		"	1133	"	Scr '14

See also #312,314-320,322,323,341,395-399,577,1313,1321,1392,1393,1578.

Class D-27 4-4-0: 17x24-70-180-98000-15380

See #262-265, Rebuilt 1894 from Class D-26 returned from Omaha & St. Louis.

Class D-28 4-4-0: 18x24-64-150-91900-15379 (565, 579 had 70" drivers)

See #342, 343, 344, 394, 565, 579.

Class D-29 4-4-0: 17x24-70-170-98121-14318 (originally 18x24-175)

No	Builder	New	Disp'n		No	Builder	New		Disp'n
174	Fort Wayne	2/92	Scr 8/23		411	Rhode Is.	2785	10/92	Scr 12/28
118	" "	6/92	Scr 12/29		412	"	2786	"	Scr 12/28
177	" "	8/92	Scr 6/27		413	"	2787	"	Scr 12/31
					414	"	2788	"	Scr 10/23
214	Moberly	1/92	Scr '31		415	"	2789	"	Scr 6/27
216	"	5/92	Scr 6/27		416	"	2790	"	Scr 7/25
224	"	9/92	Scr 6/31		417	"	2791	"	Scr 2/24
					418	"	2792	"	Scr 2/24
175	Springfield	12/91	Scr 12/26		419	"	2793	11/92	Scr 12/28
325	"	4/92	Scr 12/26		420	"	2794	"	Scr 12/26
327	"	8/92	Scr 12/26		421	"	2795	"	Scr 6/26
					422	"	2796	"	Scr '24

Class D-30 4-4-0: 18½x26-78-185-122905-18173 (655-659) / 18½x26-74-185-122905-19168 (651-654)

No	Builder		New	Disp'n		No	Builder	New		Disp'n
651	Springfield		3/99	Scr 12/31		655	BLW.	17262	12/99	Scr 12/29
652	Rhode Is	3130	8/99	Scr 12/29		656	"	17263	"	Scr 12/31
653	"	3131	9/99	Scr 6/36		657	"	16916	7/99	Scr 11/35
654	"	3132	"	Scr 12/31		658	"	16917	"	Scr 12/31
						659	"	16918	"	Scr 9/33

(Note: 651 ex 17½x26-127800)

Class D-31 4-4-0: 19x26-74-185-126000-19945 (ex 13,22x26vc-77-190-20765)

255 (O&StL)	Wab.?	11/99	Scr 12/31	256 (O&StL)	Wab?	11/99	Scr 12/31

****

Class E 4-4-2 Types

Class E-1 4-4-2: 19x26-74-200-157900-21858 (note a)

No	ren.	Builder		New	Disp'n
601	ren. 1601	Baldwin	15791?	3/1898	Scr 6/31
602	ren. 1602	Baldwin	15792	3/1898	Scr 7/33
603	ren. 1603	Baldwin	15793	3/1898	Scr 6/33
604	ren. 1604	Baldwin	15794	3/1898	Scr 7/33
605	ren. 1605	Baldwin	15795	3/1898	Scr 12/31

Class E-2 4-4-2: 19x26-79-200-161600-20198

No	ren.	Builder		New	Disp'n
606	ren. 694,624	Richmond	3231	1901	Scr 12/31
607	ren. 695,625	Richmond	3232	1901	Scr 12/31
608	ren. 696,626	Richmond	3233	1901	Scr 5/33
609	ren. 697,627	Richmond	3234	1901	Scr 12/31
610	ren. 698,628	Richmond	3235	1901	Scr '33
611	ren. 699,629	Richmond	3236	1901	Scr 12/31

Note a - Class E-1 returned to U. S. operation in 1925, but remained in 1600 No. group.

Class E-3 4-4-2: 21x28-84-215-180700-25246: RB BP 200, TE 23205
(%) E-3s, Wt. 184000

No		Builder		New	Disp'n
612	(%)	Brooks	27682	1903	Scr 6/36
613	(%)	Brooks	27683	1903	Scr 1/44
614	(%)	Brooks	27684	1903	Scr 2/45
615		Brooks	27685	1903	Scr 10/33
616		Brooks	27686	1903	Scr 6/37
617	(%)	Brooks	27687	1903	Scr 1/45
618	(%)	Brooks	27688	1903	Scr 8/37
619		Brooks	27689	1903	Scr 10/45
620		Brooks	27690	1903	Scr 12/31
621	(%)	Brooks	27691	1903	Scr 12/45
622	(%)	Brooks	27692	1903	Scr 11/44
623	(%)	Brooks	27693	1903	Scr 10/33

Class E-4 4-4-2: 21x28-80-220-197820-30948: RB BP 210, TE 27551
(%) RB with Walschaert V.G. E-4w, Wt. 201820

No		Builder		New	Disp'n
602	(%)	Baldwin	24480	7/1904	Scr 3/49
603		Baldwin	24489	7/1904	Scr 12/42
604		Baldwin	24499	7/1904	Scr '40
605		Baldwin	24500	7/1904	Scr '40
606	(%)	Baldwin	24507	7/1904	Scr 2/47
607		Baldwin	24508	7/1904	Scr '40
608	(%)	Baldwin	24509	7/1904	Scr 3/47
609		Baldwin	24519	7/1904	Scr '41
610		Baldwin	24521	7/1904	Scr 4/44
611		Baldwin	24522	7/1904	Scr 6/36

Classes E-5 and E-6 4-4-2: See Ann Arbor Classes I and I-1

Class F 2-6-0 Types

Orig.	Rel880	Rel885	Re'87	Builder	New	Rebuilt	Disp'n

Early 2-6-0: 18x24-50

				Builder	New		Disp'n
			26	Baldwin	7694	10/1885	to CV&C 26, '87
			27	Baldwin	7789	2/1886	to CV&C 27, '87
			28	Baldwin	7792	2/1886	to CV&C 25, '87

Early 2-6-0: 17x24-54-98000: Acquired Second Hand from Indianapolis, Bloomington & Western

Orig.	Rel880	Rel885	Re'87	Builder	New	Disp'n
IB&W 52	371			Rogers	2241	4/1873	?
IB&W 47	372			Rogers	2218	3/1873	RB'81 to 4-6-0
IB&W 57	373			Rogers	2256	5/1873	" "
IB&W 58	374			Rogers	2263	5/1873	" "
IB&W 59	375			Rogers	2268	5/1873	" "
IB&W 46(a)	580	1580	580	Rogers	2216	3/1873	
IB&W 79(a)	581	1581	581	Rogers	2220	3/1873	
IB&W 51(a)	582	1582	582	Rogers	2239	3/1873	
IB&W 53(a)	583	1583	583	Rogers	2245	4/1873	
IB&W 63(a)	584	1584	584	Rogers	2287	6/1873	

Class F-1 2-6-0: 18x22-52-160-86000-19008 (Orig. 19x22-50)

				Builder	New		Disp'n
	1016	16		Rome	99	11/1884	Scr 2/16
	1017	17		Rome	100	12/1884	Scr 2/16
	1024	24		Rome	101	12/1884	Scr 1/16
	1025	25 (b)		Rome	102	12/1884	Scr 2/16
	1133	133		Rome	103	12/1884	Scr 3/16
	1134	134		Rome	104	12/1884	Scr 6/16
	1135	135		Rome	105	1/1885	Scr 6/16
	1136	136		Rome	106	1/1885	Scr 6/16
	1137	137		Rome	107	1/1885	Scr 6/16
	1138	138		Rome	108	1/1885	Scr 1/13
	1143	143		Rome	109	1/1885	Scr 1/16

Class F-2 2-6-0: 18x22-52-160-86000-19008 (Orig. 19x22-50)

		Builder		New		Disp'n
1005		Baldwin	7473	10/1884	(c)	to O&StL '88
1026		Baldwin	7475	10/1884	(c)	to O&StL '88
1029		Baldwin	7488	11/1884	(c)	to O&StL '88
1032		Baldwin	7491	11/1884	(c)	to O&StL '88
1101		Baldwin	7496	11/1884	(c)	to O&StL '89
1102		Baldwin	7495	11/1884	(c)	to O&StL '89
1104	104	Baldwin	7511	11/1884		Scr 1/16
1107		Baldwin	7512	11/1884	(c)	to O&StL '89
1113		Baldwin	7503	11/1884	(c)	to O&StL '89
1187	187	Baldwin	7506	11/1884		Scr 2/16
1204	204	Baldwin	7513	11/1884		Scr
1214		Baldwin	7514	11/1884	(c)	to O&StL '89
1225	225	Baldwin	7522	12/1884		to F-3 Class
1576	576	Baldwin	7515	12/1884		?

Class F-3 2-6-0: 19x22-52-160-86000-19855 (RB from F-2 class)

225 (Baldwin 7522 12/1884)	Scr 1/16

Note a - #580-584 ex St.Louis, Kansas City & Northern 118,119,120,122,121.
Note b - Numbered 1033 from 1899 to 1909.
Note c - Rebuilt to 0-6-0 class B-3 while on Omaha & St.Louis.

Class F-4 2-6-0: 19x28-64-190-123525-25507 (Orig. BP 195, TE 26593)

No	ren.	Builder		New		Disp'n
751	ren. 582	Rhode Isl.	3144	10/1899	12/14 So	(a)
756	ren. 576	Rhode Isl.	2857	1899	3/15	Scr 6/55
757	ren. 578	Richmond	2858	1899	2/15	Scr 11/33
758	ren. 581	Richmond	2859	1899	5/15	Scr 12/31
759	ren. 569	Rhode Isl.	3133	9/1899	1/16	Scr 6/55
760	ren. 588	Rhode Isl.	3134	9/1899	8/14	Scr '28
761	ren. 583	Rhode Isl.	3135	9/1899	12/14	Scr 12/31
762	ren. 574	Rhode Isl.	3136	9/1899	3/15	Scr 12/31
763	ren. 575	Rhode Isl.	3137	9/1899	3/15	Scr 7/29
764	ren. 580	Rhode Isl.	3138	10/1899	7/15	Scr 6/27
765	ren. 584	Rhode Isl.	3139	10/1899	12/14	Scr '28
766	ren. 587	Rhode Isl.	3140	10/1899	12/13	Scr 9/55
767	ren. 585	Rhode Isl.	3141	10/1899	10/14	Scr 7/29
768	ren. 589	Rhode Isl.	3142	10/1899	12/13 So	(a)
769	ren. 590	Rhode Isl.	3143	10/1899	12/13	Scr 7/29
770	ren. 591	Richmond	2852	1899	10/13	Scr '33
771	ren. 592	Richmond	2853	1899	8/13	Scr 12/31
772	ren. 593	Richmond	2854	1899	8/13	Scr 12/31
773	ren. 594	Richmond	2855	1899	7/13	Scr '28
774	ren. 596	Baldwin	16952	7/1899	5/13	Scr 8/35
775	ren. 595	Baldwin	16953	7/1899	5/13	Scr 12/31
776	ren. 597	Baldwin	16997	9/1899	6/13	Scr 1/33
777	ren. 598	Baldwin	16998	9/1899	5/13	Scr 2/33
778	ren. 599	Baldwin	16999	9/1899	5/13	Scr 1/33

Class F-5 2-6-0: 19½x32x28-64-195-124525-26593
Reb. simple, 19x28, BP 190, TE 25507, Class F-4

No	ren.	Builder		New		Disp'n
752	ren. 586	Rhode Isl.	3145	10/1899	8/14	Scr 12/33
753	ren. 579	Rhode Isl.	3146	11/1899	2/15	Scr 12/31
754	ren. 573	Rhode Isl.	3147	11/1899	5/15	(b)
755	ren. 571	Richmond	2856	1899	12/15	Scr 7/53

Class F-6 2-6-0: 20½x32x28-64-200-149524-27276
Reb. simple, 19x28, TE26849, Class F-7

No		Builder		New		Disp'n
801		Richmond	3237	1901	6/22	to B-8 482
802		Richmond	3238	1901		Scr 6/33
803		Richmond	3239	1901		Scr 3/33
804		Richmond	3240	1901	12/17	to B-8 486
805		Richmond	3241	1901		So NJI&I 805 '29
806		Richmond	3242	1901		Scr 4/34
807	ren.1807	Richmond	3243	1901		Scr 8/34
808		Richmond	3244	1901		Scr 2/36
809		Richmond	3245	1901	8/17	to B-8 492

810		Richmond	3246	1901	Scr 10/33
811		Richmond	3247	1901	Scr 6/31
812		Richmond	3248	1901	10/17 to B-8 488
813		Richmond	3249	1901	Scr 6/33
814		Richmond	3250	1901	Scr 12/30
815		Richmond	3251	1901	Scr 6/31

Note a - 582 sold NJI&I 6/28, 589 sold NJI&I 7/28.
Note b - 573 to St. Louis Museum of Transport 8/55.

816		Richmond	3252	1901	Scr 4/33
817		Richmond	3253	1901	trsf.NJI&I 817
818		Richmond	3254	1901	Scr 6/31
819		Richmond	3255	1901	11/17 to B-8 489
820		Richmond	3256	1901	Scr 6/31
821		Richmond	3257	1901	Scr 6/31
822		Richmond	3258	1901	Scr 6/31
823		Richmond	3259	1901	Scr 6/31
824		Richmond	3260	1901	12/17 to B-8 485
825		Richmond	3261	1901	Scr 12/31
826		Richmond	3262	1901	Scr '42
827		Richmond	3263	1901	8/17 to B-8 493
828		Richmond	3264	1901	Scr '42
829		Richmond	3265	1901	Scr 9/35
830		Richmond	3266	1901	Scr 6/33
831		Richmond	3267	1901	Scr '42
832	ren. 1832	Richmond	3268	1901	Scr 3/33
833		Richmond	3269	1901	Scr 6/31
834		Richmond	3270	1901	Scr 3/45
835		Baldwin	22551	7/1903	11/17 to B-8 487
836		Baldwin	22569	7/1903	Scr 6/31
837	ren. 1837	Baldwin	22580	7/1903	Scr 6/31
338		Baldwin	22589	8/1903	Scr 6/31
839		Baldwin	22590	8/1903	12/18 to B-8 483
840		Baldwin	22623	8/1903	Scr 8/33
841		Baldwin	22665	8/1903	Scr 6/31
842		Baldwin	22679	8/1903	1/17 to B-8 498
843		Baldwin	22817	9/1903	Scr 6/31
844		Baldwin	22836	9/1903	Scr 6/31
845		Baldwin	22849	9/1903	2/17 to B-8 499
846		Baldwin	22855	9/1903	Scr 11/36
847		Baldwin	22876	9/1903	Scr 6/31
848		Baldwin	22902	9/1903	Scr 6/50
849		Baldwin	22912	10/1903	Scr 4/33
850		Baldwin	22931	10/1903	Scr '40
851		Baldwin	22932	10/1903	Scr 10/34
852		Baldwin	22949	10/1903	So CA&S 852 6/35
853		Baldwin	22957	10/1903	Scr 8/33
854		Baldwin	22968	10/1903	Scr '41
855		Baldwin	22985	10/1903	Scr 12/31
856		Baldwin	22995	10/1903	5/17 to B-8 495
857		Baldwin	22996	10/1903	Scr 6/31
858		Baldwin	23012	10/1903	10/17 to B-8 490
859		Baldwin	23013	10/1903	Scr 12/52
860		Baldwin	23027	10/1903	Scr 6/31
861		Baldwin	23049	10/1903	Scr 6/31
862		Baldwin	23082	10/1903	Scr 6/31
863		Baldwin	23097	10/1903	Scr 8/33
864		Baldwin	23133	11/1903	3/17 to B-8 497
865		Baldwin	23176	11/1903	Scr 6/33
866		Baldwin	23203	11/1903	Scr 10/43

Class F-7 2-6-0: 19x28-64-200-148524-26849

867		Baldwin	24314	6/1904	Scr 9/34
868	ren. 1868	Baldwin	24315	6/1904	Scr '41
869	ren. 1869	Baldwin	24316	6/1904	Scr 6/31
870	ren. 1870	Baldwin	24325	6/1904	Scr 11/46
871	ren. 1871	Baldwin	24337	6/1904	Scr 6/31
872	ren. 1872	Baldwin	24338	6/1904	Scr 6/31
873	ren. 1873	Baldwin	24358	6/1904	Scr 6/31
874	ren. 1874	Baldwin	24359	6/1904	Scr 6/33
875		Baldwin	24360	6/1904	Scr 10/33
876	ren. 1876	Baldwin	24370	6/1904	Scr 10/33
877	ren. 1877	Baldwin	24381	6/1904	Scr 6/31
878	ren. 1878	Baldwin	24382	6/1904	Scr 6/31
879		Baldwin	24386	6/1904	Scr 9/33
880		Baldwin	24391	6/1904	9/17 to B-8 491
881		Baldwin	24397	6/1904	Scr 6/31
882		Baldwin	24398	6/1904	Scr 4/33
883	ren. 1883	Baldwin	24403	7/1904	Scr 2/33
884		Baldwin	24410	7/1904	4/17 to B-8 496
885	ren. 1885	Baldwin	24411	7/1904	Scr 6/31
886	ren. 1886	Baldwin	24416	7/1904	Scr 6/31
887	ren. 1887	Baldwin	24417	7/1904	Scr 8/33
888		Baldwin	24418	7/1904	Scr 7/33
889	ren. 1889	Baldwin	24437	7/1904	So CA&S 1889 '39
890	ren. 1890	Baldwin	24438	7/1904	Scr 9/46
891		Baldwin	24439	7/1904	5/23 to B-8 481
892	ren. 1892	Baldwin	24440	7/1904	Scr 11/47
893		Baldwin	24441	7/1904	Scr 12/31
894	ren. 1894	Baldwin	24442	7/1904	Scr 10/33
895		Baldwin	24448	7/1904	Scr 8/33
896		Baldwin	24449	7/1904	Scr 6/31
897		Baldwin	24467	7/1904	6/17 to B-8 494
898		Baldwin	24468	7/1904	Scr 6/31
899	ren. 1899	Baldwin	24475	7/1904	Scr 6/31
900	ren. 1900	Baldwin	24476	7/1904	Scr 11/33
901	ren. 1901	Baldwin	24491	7/1904	Scr 11/33
902		Baldwin	24501	7/1904	12/17 to B-8 484
903		Baldwin	24510	7/1904	Scr 6/31

****

Class G 2-6-2 Types

Class G-1 2-6-2: 23x28-70-215-228200-38670

(a) received new frames, Wt. 230100

Wabash No.		Builder		New	Disposition
2001		Baldwin	28731	8/1906	Scr 2/36
2002		Baldwin	28732	8/1906	Scr 10/38
2003		Baldwin	28780	8/1906	RB '26, J-2 683
2004		Baldwin	28781	8/1906	RB '26, J-2 684
2005	(a)	Baldwin	28830	8/1906	Scr 8/38
2006		Baldwin	28849	8/1906	Scr 7/36
2007		Baldwin	28850	8/1906	RB '23, J-2 691
2008		Baldwin	28865	8/1906	Scr 12/38
2009		Baldwin	28866	8/1906	Scr 2/36
2010		Baldwin	28896	8/1906	RB '25, J-2 685
2011		Baldwin	28897	8/1906	Scr 8/38
2012		Baldwin	28898	8/1906	Scr 9/34
2013		Baldwin	28899	8/1906	Scr 5/36
2014		Baldwin	28927	9/1906	Scr 12/35
2015		Baldwin	28928	9/1906	Scr 7/34
2016		Baldwin	28941	9/1906	RB '25, J-2 686
2017		Baldwin	28953	9/1906	Scr 11/35
2018		Baldwin	28975	9/1906	Scr 9/34
2019		Baldwin	29006	9/1906	RB '24, J-2 688
2020		Baldwin	29007	9/1906	Scr 5/36
2021	(a)	Baldwin	29017	9/1906	Scr 10/38
2022	(a)	Baldwin	29032	9/1906	Scr 3/44
2023		Baldwin	29033	9/1906	Scr 5/36
2024		Baldwin	29057	9/1906	Scr 8/36
2025	(a)	Baldwin	29058	9/1906	Scr 10/38
2026		Baldwin	29059	9/1906	Scr 2/37
2027	(a)	Baldwin	29075	9/1906	Scr 9/38
2028		Baldwin	29094	9/1906	Scr 3/37
2029		Baldwin	29166	9/1906	Scr 11/37
2030		Baldwin	29167	9/1906	Scr 9/39
2031		Rogers	43302	9/1907	RB '16, J-2 698
2032		Rogers	43303	9/1907	RB '24, J-2 687
2033		Rogers	43304	9/1907	RB '17, J-2 694
2034		Rogers	43305	9/1907	Scr 8/38
2035		Rogers	43306	9/1907	RB '16, J-2 699
2036	(a)	Rogers	43307	9/1907	Scr 9/38
2037		Rogers	43308	9/1907	RB '23, J-2 689
2038		Rogers	43309	9/1907	RB '17, J-2 697
2039		Rogers	43310	9/1907	RB '17, J-2 693
2040		Rogers	43311	9/1907	Scr 10/38
2041		Rogers	43312	9/1907	RB '23, J-2 690
2042		Rogers	43313	9/1907	Scr 2/36
2043		Rogers	43314	9/1907	Scr 9/38
2044		Rogers	43315	9/1907	RB '17, J-2 696
2045		Rogers	43316	9/1907	Scr 9/37
2046		Rogers	43317	9/1907	RB '23, J-2 692
2047		Rogers	43318	9/1907	RB '17, J-2 695
2048		Rogers	43319	9/1907	Scr 11/38
2049		Rogers	43320	9/1907	Scr 4/36
2050	(a)	Rogers	43321	9/1907	Scr 10/38
2051		Rogers	43322	9/1907	RB '17, J-2 1681
2052		Rogers	43323	9/1907	RB '16, J-2 1677
2053		Rogers	43324	9/1907	RB '16, J-2 1678
2054		Rogers	43325	9/1907	RB '17, J-2 1680
2055		Rogers	43326	9/1907	RB '16, J-2 1676
2056		Rogers	43327	9/1907	RB '17, J-2 1679
2057		Rogers	43328	9/1907	Scr 9/38
2058		Rogers	43329	9/1907	Scr 9/39
2059		Rogers	43330	9/1907	Scr 8/38
2060	(a)	Rogers	43331	9/1907	Scr 11/37

Class G-1 2-6-2: 23x28-64-215-228200-42295

2061		Rogers	43332	11/1907	Scr 4/37
2062		Rogers	43333	11/1907	Scr 5/37
2063	(a)	Rogers	43334	11/1907	Scr 9/44
2064		Rogers	43335	11/1907	Scr 8/49
2065		Rogers	43336	11/1907	Scr 11/35
2066		Rogers	43337	11/1907	Scr 6/37
2067		Rogers	43338	11/1907	Scr 9/50
2068		Rogers	43339	11/1907	Scr 12/38
2069		Rogers	43340	11/1907	Scr 1/51
2070		Rogers	43341	11/1907	Scr 11/38
2071		Rogers	43342	11/1907	Scr 2/37
2072		Rogers	43343	11/1907	Scr 5/37
2073	(a)	Rogers	43344	11/1907	Scr 1/51
2074		Rogers	43345	11/1907	Scr 9/50
2075		Rogers	43346	11/1907	Scr 8/49
2076		Rogers	43347	11/1907	Scr 7/37
2077		Rogers	43348	11/1907	Scr 12/38
2078	(a)	Rogers	43349	11/1907	Scr 3/45
2079		Rogers	43350	11/1907	Scr 12/38
2080		Rogers	43351	11/1907	Scr 7/37
2081		Rogers	43352	11/1907	Scr 9/50
2082		Rogers	43353	11/1907	Scr 6/37
2083		Rogers	43354	11/1907	Scr 3/37
2084		Rogers	43355	11/1907	Scr 7/37
2085		Rogers	43356	11/1907	Scr 2/47
2086		Rogers	43357	11/1907	Scr 3/37
2087	(a)	Rogers	43358	11/1907	Scr 2/49
2088		Rogers	43359	11/1907	Scr 5/37
2089		Rogers	43360	11/1907	So '38 to ?
2090		Rogers	43361	11/1907	Scr 10/39

****

Class H 4-6-0 Types

Orig. No.	WStL&P No. 1880	1885	Re'87	Builder		New	Rebuilt	Disp'n
Early 4-6-0: 16x24-54. Acquired by Cairo & Vincennes								
C&V 11	548	1548	-	BLW	3694	2/1875		to CV&C 18
Early 4-6-0: 16x22-54-72000 built for North Missouri								
NM 43	252	1252	252	Rogers		12/1868	'87	Scr '92
NM 44	253	1253	253	Rogers		12/1868	'87	Ret by'88 ?
NM 45	254	1254	254	Rogers		2/1869	'87	Ret by'88 ?
NM 46	255	1255	255	Rogers		2/1869		dr by '99
Early 4-6-0: 18x24-56-98000								
	372	1372	372	Rebuilt from 2-6-0		1881		?
	373	1373	373	"	"	"		?
	374	1374	374	"	"	"		?
	375	1375	375	"	"	"		?
Class H-1 4-6-0: 18x24-58-150-98000								
	376	1376	376	Rogers	2692	2/1881		Scr 9/14
	380	1380	380	Rogers	2710	3/1881		Scr 1/16
	381	1381	381	Rogers	2711	3/1881		Scr 1/16
Class H-1 4-6-0: 18x24-58-150-98000 (%) 17x24 TE 15247								
	377	1377	377	Rogers	2693	2/1881		Scr 1/16
(%)	378	1378	378	Rogers	2694	2/1881	'11	Scr 3/23
	379	1379	379	Rogers	2695	3/1881		Scr 1/16
Second Class H-1 4-6-0: See Ann Arbor Class F								
Class H-2 4-6-0: 18x24-70-160-98000-15327 (Rebuilt from H-6)								
			390	(Rhode Isl.	924	1/1881)		Scr 1/16
			1351	(Rhode Isl.	829	6/1880)		Scr 1/16
Class H-2 4-6-0: 18½x24-70-160-98000-16190 (Rebuilt from H-6)								
			1353	(Rhode Isl.	831	6/1880)		Scr 1/16
			1354	(Rhode Isl.	832	6/1880)		Scr 1/16
			1383	(Rhode Isl.	917	12/1880)		Scr 1/16
			1481	(Rhode Isl.	1014	7/1881)		Scr '16
			1563	(Rhode Isl.	1121	3/1882)		Scr '12
Second Class H-2 4-6-0: See Ann Arbor Class F-1								
Class H-3 4-6-0: 18x24-58-160-97000-18553								
			8	Wabash RR		1887		Scr 1/16
			9	Wabash RR		1887		Scr 1/16
			27	Wabash RR		1889		Scr 1/16
			203	Wabash RR		1888		Scr 1/16
			205	Wabash RR		1888		Scr 1/16

```
                  229    Wabash RR        1888      Scr 2/16
                  246    Wabash RR        1887      Scr 9/14
                  247    Wabash RR        1887      Scr 5/16
```

Second Class H-3 4-6-0: See Ann Arbor Class F-2

Class H-4 4-6-0: 18x24-70-160-101000-15323

```
           23    Springfield        1890      Scr 3/23
           95    Springfield       5/1890     Scr 5/23
         1144    Springfield       9/1891     Scr 5/24
         1145    Springfield       9/1891     Scr 7/24
```

Second Class H-4 4-6-0: See Ann Arbor Class F-3

Class H-5 4-6-0: 18x26-57-185-126000-23655: RB BP 170, TE 20987

```
O&StL 600 (re'01)  257  Baldwin  16426 12/1898   Scr 12/26
O&StL 601    "     258  Baldwin  16427 12/1898   Scr '28
O&StL 602    "     259  Baldwin  16428 12/1898   Scr 12/31
O&StL 603    "     260  Baldwin  16429 12/1898   Scr '20
O&StL 604    "     261  Baldwin  16430 12/1898   Scr 6/21
```

Class H-6 4-6-0: 19x24-64-160-98000-18703 (*) 18x24, TE 16786 (a)

```
              Re '85  Re '87
345     1345   345   Rhode Isl.  823  2/1880        Scr 1/16
346     1346   346   Rhode Isl.  824  3/1880        Scr 2/16
347     1347   347   Rhode Isl.  825  4/1880  6/99   to H-8
348 (*) 1348   348   Rhode Isl.  826  4/1880        Scr 1/16
349 (*) 1349   349   Rhode Isl.  827  4/1880        Scr 2/16
350 (*) 1350   350   Rhode Isl.  828  4/1880        Scr 3/16
351     1351  1351   Rhode Isl.  829  6/1880         to H-2
352 (*) 1352   352   Rhode Isl.  830  6/1880        Scr 1/16
353     1353  1353   Rhode Isl.  831  6/1880         to H-2
354     1354  1354   Rhode Isl.  832  6/1880         to H-2
355     1355   355   Rhode Isl.  833  6/1880        Scr 11/12
382     1382   382   Rhode Isl.  916 12/1880        Scr 1/16
383     1383  1383   Rhode Isl.  917 12/1880         to H-2
384     1384   384   Rhode Isl.  918 12/1880        Scr 2/16
385     1385   385   Rhode Isl.  919 12/1880        Scr 1/16
386     1386   386   Rhode Isl.  920 12/1880        Scr 2/16
387     1387   387   Rhode Isl.  920 12/1880        Scr 2/16
388 (*) 1388   388   Rhode Isl.  922 12/1880        Scr 1/16
389     1389   389   Rhode Isl.  923 12/1880 Rome '85 Scr 1/16
390     1390   390   Rhode Isl.  924  1/1881         to H-2
391     1391   391   Rhode Isl.  925  1/1881  8/99   to H-8
477 (*) 1477   477   Rhode Isl. 1010  7/1881        Scr 1/16
478     1478   478   Rhode Isl. 1011  7/1881        Scr 1/16
479     1479   479   Rhode Isl. 1012  7/1881        Scr 10/12
480 (*) 1480   480   Rhode Isl. 1013  7/1881        Scr 2/16
481     1481  1481   Rhode Isl. 1014  7/1881         to H-2
482 (*) 1482   482   Rhode Isl. 1015  7/1881        Scr 1/16
556     1556   556   Rhode Isl. 1114  3/1882        Ret by'12
557     1557   557   Rhode Isl. 1115  3/1882        Ret by'12
558     1558   558   Rhode Isl. 1116  3/1882        Ret by'12
559     1559   559   Rhode Isl. 1117  3/1882        Ret by'12
560 (*) 1560   560   Rhode Isl. 1118  3/1882        Ret by'12
561     1561   561   Rhode Isl. 1119  3/1882        Ret by'12
562     1562   562   Rhode Isl. 1120  3/1882        Ret by'12
563     1563  1563   Rhode Isl. 1121  3/1882         to H-2
```

Class H-7 4-6-0: 19x24-64-175-113000-20455: RB BP 170, TE 19446

```
  5    Rhode Isl. 2375  9/1890   Scr 12/20
 26    Rhode Isl. 2376  9/1890   Scr 6/26
 29    Rhode Isl. 2377  9/1890   Scr 12/20
 58    Rhode Isl. 2378  9/1890   Scr 4/23
101    Rhode Isl. 2379  9/1890   Scr '31
102    Rhode Isl. 2380  9/1890   Scr 12/24
107    Rhode Isl. 2381  9/1890   Scr 12/28
113    Rhode Isl. 2382  9/1890   Scr 12/30
123    Rhode Isl. 2641  9/1891   Scr 12/28
141    Rhode Isl. 2642  9/1891   Scr 7/27
147    Rhode Isl. 2383  9/1890   Scr 12/26
158    Rhode Isl. 2384  9/1891   Scr 5/23
160    Rhode Isl. 2643  9/1891   Scr 6/25
```

Note a - 477-482 orig. spec. 19x24-56; 556-563 orig. spec. 19x24-57

```
714    Richmond   2688  1898     Scr 12/31
715    Richmond   2689  1898     Scr 9/33
716    Richmond   2690  1898     Scr 9/33
717    Richmond   2691  1898     Scr 9/33
718    Richmond   2692  1898     Scr 12/31
719    Richmond   2693  1898     Scr 8/33
720    Richmond   2694  1898     Scr 12/31

164    Rhode Isl. 2644  9/1891   Scr 6/27
168    Rhode Isl. 2645  9/1891   Scr 5/22
172    Rhode Isl. 2646  9/1891   Scr 6/27
233    Rhode Isl. 2748  5/1892   Scr 12/20
234    Rhode Isl. 2749  5/1892   Scr 12/28
235    Rhode Isl. 2750  5/1892   Scr 12/28
236    Rhode Isl. 2751  5/1892   Scr 12/26
423    Rhode Isl. 2765  5/1892   Scr 6/23
424    Rhode Isl. 2766  5/1892   Scr 6/29
425    Rhode Isl. 2767  5/1892   Scr 6/27
426    Rhode Isl. 2768  5/1892   Scr 6/26
427    Rhode Isl. 2769  5/1892   Scr 12/29
428    Rhode Isl. 2770  5/1892   Scr 12/31
429    Rhode Isl. 2771  5/1892   Scr 12/31
430    Rhode Isl. 2772  5/1892   Scr 12/28
```

Class H-8 4-6-0: 19x24-70-185-128925-19745 (RB from H-6)

```
347    Moberly Shop   6/1899   Scr 1/23
391    Moberly Shop   8/1899   Scr 6/27
```

Class H-9 4-6-0: 19x26-64-200-155510-25327

```
701    Baldwin    15802  3/1898   Scr 5/33
702    Baldwin    15803  3/1898   Scr 12/28
703    Baldwin    15804  3/1898   Scr 12/31
704    Baldwin    15805  3/1898   Scr 3/33
705    Baldwin    15806  3/1898   Scr 12/28
706    Pittsburgh  1800  3/1898   Scr 12/31
707    Pittsburgh  1801  3/1898   Scr 12/28
708    Pittsburgh  1802  3/1898   Scr 8/33
709    Pittsburgh  1803  3/1898   Scr 3/33
710    Pittsburgh  1804  3/1898   Scr 6/29
711    Richmond    2685       1898   Scr 12/31
```

Class H-10 4-6-0: 20½x32½x26-64-200-158660-25327
Rebuilt simple, 19x26, Class H-9

```
712    Richmond   2686  1898   Scr 12/31
713    Richmond   2687  1898   Scr 12/31
```

Class H-11 4-6-0: 19x26-74-200-158600-21358 (Note b)

```
620 ren. 630,1630   Richmond  3225  1901   Scr '31
621 ren. 631,1631   Richmond  3226  1901   Scr '31
622 ren. 632,1632   Richmond  3227  1901   Scr '31
623 ren. 633,1633   Richmond  3228  1901   Scr '31
624 ren. 634,1634   Richmond  3229  1901   Scr '31
625 ren. 635,1635   Richmond  3230  1901   Scr '31
```

Class H-12 4-6-0: 21x28-74-220-193330-33500: RB BP 210, TE 29785
(*) had superheater, Wt. 197730

```
636        Baldwin 24526 8/1904   Scr 12/31
637        Baldwin 24534 8/1904   Scr 12/31
638 (*)    Baldwin 24535 8/1904   Scr 10/33
639        Baldwin 24536 8/1904   Scr 10/33
640 (*)(a) Baldwin 24544 8/1904   Scr 12/33
641 (*)    Baldwin 24545 8/1904   Scr 10/33
642        Baldwin 24547 8/1904   Scr 11/33
643        Baldwin 24560 8/1904   Scr 12/31
644        Baldwin 24567 8/1904   Scr 12/31
645 (c)    Baldwin 24608 8/1904   Scr 11/33
```

****

Class I 2-8-0 Types

Early 2-8-0: 20x24-50   Built for WStL&P

```
366 ren. 1366   Baldwin 5089 5/1880   to D&SW ? in 1888?
367 ren. 1367   Baldwin 5131 6/1880   to CV&C ? in 1888?
```

Class I-1 2-8-0: 20x24-52-132000   Built for Omaha & St.Louis

```
266 ex O&StL 16   Rhode Isl. 3092 11/1895   Scr 11/26
267 ex O&StL 17   Rhode Isl. 3093  1/1896
```

Class I-2 2-8-0: 19½x28-58-215-174500-33547   Purch. from DT&I in 1910

```
2150 ex DT&I 97    Brooks 38032 8/1905   Scr 10/50
2151 ex DT&I 99    Brooks 38034 8/1905   Scr 2/35
2152 ex DT&I 113   Brooks 38048 8/1905   Scr 12/35
2153 ex DT&I 110   Brooks 38045 8/1905   Scr 12/51
2154 ex DT&I 88    Brooks 38023 8/1905   Scr 12/34
2155 ex DT&I 100   Brooks 38035 8/1905   Scr 11/51
2156 ex DT&I 115   Brooks 38050 8/1905   RB C-1 1502
2157 ex DT&I 111   Brooks 38046 8/1905   Scr 9/34
2158 ex DT&I 102   Brooks 38037 8/1905   Scr 10/35
2159 ex DT&I 105   Brooks 38040 8/1905   Scr 12/35
2160 ex DT&I 93    Brooks 38028 8/1905   Scr 12/51
2161 ex DT&I 112   Brooks 38047 8/1905   Scr 9/35
2162 ex DT&I 101   Brooks 38036 8/1905   RB C-1 1501
2163 ex DT&I 89    Brooks 38024 8/1905   Scr 8/34
2164 ex DT&I 91    Brooks 38026 8/1905   Scr 8/34
2165 ex DT&I 92    Brooks 38027 8/1905   Scr 10/35
2166 ex DT&I 96    Brooks 38031 8/1905   Scr 10/35
```

Note a - Rebuilt with Walschaert Valve Gear.
b - Richmond records show Class H-11 built as 624-629.
c - Rebuilt with Baker Valve Gear

Class I-3 2-8-0: 22½x30-58-210-224100-46740   Purch. from W&LE 1910-11

```
2301 ex W&LE 2301  Baldwin 29129  9/1906   Scr 11/39
2302 ex W&LE 2302  Baldwin 29130  9/1906   Scr 10/47
2303 ex W&LE 2303  Baldwin 29158  9/1906   Scr '40
2304 ex W&LE 2304  Baldwin 29159 10/1906   Scr 11/39
2305 ex W&LE 2305  Baldwin 29175 10/1906   Scr 8/47
2306 ex W&LE 2306  Baldwin 29182 10/1906   Scr 4/47
2307 ex W&LE 2307  Baldwin 29183 10/1906   Scr 11/39
2308 ex W&LE 2308  Baldwin 29184 10/1906   Scr 3/46
2309 ex W&LE 2309  Baldwin 29196 10/1906   Scr 10/46
2310 ex W&LE 2310  Baldwin 29230 10/1906   Scr 4/46
2311 ex W&LE 2311  Baldwin 29246 10/1906   Scr 6/47
2312 ex W&LE 2312  Baldwin 29247 10/1906   Scr 5/47
2313 ex W&LE 2313  Baldwin 29248 10/1906   Scr 7/47
2314 ex W&LE 2314  Baldwin 29257 10/1906   Scr 9/39
2315 ex W&LE 2315  Baldwin 29270 10/1906   Scr 5/46
2316 ex W&LE 2316  Baldwin 29271 10/1906   Scr 7/47
2317 ex W&LE 2317  Baldwin 29272 10/1906   Scr 8/46
2318 ex W&LE 2318  Baldwin 29287 10/1906   Scr 4/47
2319 ex W&LE 2319  Baldwin 29296 10/1906   Scr 11/39
2320 ex W&LE 2320  Baldwin 29304 10/1906   Scr 7/44
2321 ex W&LE 2321  Baldwin 29305 10/1906   Scr 11/46
2322 ex W&LE 2322  Baldwin 29338 10/1906   So 8/47 (a)
2323 ex W&LE 2323  Baldwin 29339 10/1906   Scr 1/45
2324 ex W&LE 2324  Baldwin 29340 10/1906   Scr 9/39
2325 ex W&LE 2325  Baldwin 29341 10/1906   Scr 4/47
2326 ex W&LE 2326  Baldwin 29389 11/1906   Scr 6/46 (b)
2327 ex W&LE 2327  Baldwin 29406 11/1906   Scr 11/39
2328 ex W&LE 2328  Baldwin 29429 11/1906   Scr 7/46
2329 ex W&LE 2329  Baldwin 29495 11/1906   Scr '40
2330 ex W&LE 2330  Baldwin 29511 11/1906   Scr 12/39
```

Note a - to Mallinchrodt Chemical Co.
Note b - boiler sold to Moberly Milk Co.

Classes I-4, I-5, and I-6 2-8-0: See Ann Arbor Classes G, G-1, and G-2

Classes I-7 and I-8 2-8-0: See Ann Arbor Class E.

Classes I-9 and I-10 2-8-0: See Manistique & Lake Superior #8 and 13.

****

Class J 4-6-2 Types

| Wabash No. | Builder | New | Disp'n |

Class J-1 4-6-2: 24x26-74-215-248840-36984

```
660    Richmond 50635 2/1912   Scr 12/52
661    Richmond 50636 2/1912   Scr 7/51
662    Richmond 50637 2/1912   Scr 5/53
663    Richmond 50638 2/1912   Scr 3/53
664    Richmond 50639 2/1912   Scr 5/51
665    Richmond 50640 2/1912   Scr 7/51
666    Richmond 50641 2/1912   Scr 7/51
667    Richmond 50642 2/1912   Scr 12/54
668    Richmond 50643 2/1912   Scr 7/51
669    Richmond 50644 2/1912   Scr 4/53
670    Baldwin  37726 5/1912   Scr 9/53
671    Baldwin  37727 5/1912   Scr 7/51
672    Baldwin  37728 5/1912   Scr 7/51
673    Baldwin  37761 5/1912   Scr 2/54
674    Baldwin  37762 5/1912   Scr 5/51
675    Baldwin  37763 5/1912   Scr 10/51
```

Class J-2 4-6-2: 23x28-70-215-241000-38670

1676	ex G-1 2055	Wabash RR	10/1916	Scr 3/51
1677	ex G-1 2052	Wabash RR	11/1916	Scr 4/51
1678	ex G-1 2053	Wabash RR	12/1916	Scr 10/51
1679	ex G-1 2056	Wabash RR	2/1917	Scr 11/51
1680	ex G-1 2054	Wabash RR	8/1917	Scr 3/51
1681	ex G-1 2051	Wabash RR	12/1917	Scr 3/51
683	ex G-1 2003	Wabash RR	11/1926	Scr 7/49
684	ex G-1 2004	Wabash RR	4/1926	Scr 3/51
685	ex G-1 2010	Wabash RR	8/1925	Scr 3/50
686	ex G-1 2016	Wabash RR	7/1925	Scr 1/47
687	ex G-1 2032	Wabash RR	12/1924	Scr 4/50
688	ex G-1 2019	Wabash RR	10/1924	Scr 8/50
689	ex G-1 2037	Wabash RR	12/1923	Scr 3/50
690	ex G-1 2041	Wabash RR	12/1923	Scr 3/51
691	ex G-1 2007	Wabash RR	10/1923	Scr 2/52
692	ex G-1 2046	Wabash RR	9/1923	Scr 4/50
693	ex G-1 2039	Wabash RR	11/1917	Scr 10/49
694	ex G-1 2033	Wabash RR	10/1917	Scr 10/50
695	ex G-1 2047	Wabash RR	7/1917	Scr 9/49
696	ex G-1 2044	Wabash RR	6/1917	Scr 7/50
697	ex G-1 2038	Wabash RR	5/1917	Scr 10/49
698	ex G-1 2031	Wabash RR	5/1916	Scr 2/51
699	ex G-1 2035	Wabash RR	6/1916	Scr 5/50

****

Class K 2-8-2 Types

Class K-1 2-8-2: 26x30-64-210-266840-54408 (orig. 25½x30)

Wabash No.	Builder		New	Disp'n
2401	Richmond	50645	2/1912	Scr 11/51
2402	Richmond	50646	2/1912	Scr 2/51
2403	Richmond	50647	2/1912	So '41, A&S 21 (a)
2404	Richmond	50648	2/1912	Scr 2/51
2405	Richmond	50649	2/1912	So '41, A&S 23

Note a - A&S: Alton & Southern RR.

2406	Richmond	50650	2/1912	Scr 11/51
2407	Richmond	50651	2/1912	So '42, A&S 25
2408	Richmond	50652	2/1912	Scr 6/53
2409	Richmond	50653	2/1912	So '41, A&S 22
2410	Richmond	50654	2/1912	So '42, A&S 24
2411	Richmond	50655	2/1912	Scr '54
2412	Richmond	50656	2/1912	So '41, AC&HB 61(b)
2413	Richmond	50657	2/1912	Scr 12/53
2414	Richmond	50658	2/1912	So7/42,Seaboard 480
2415	Richmond	50659	2/1912	So7/42,Seaboard 481
2416	Baldwin	37757	5/1912	Scr '53
2417	Baldwin	37771	5/1912	Scr '53
2418	Baldwin	37772	5/1912	Scr 9/39
2419	Baldwin	37773	5/1912	So '41, AW&W (c)
2420	Baldwin	37774	5/1912	Scr 8/53
2421	Baldwin	37775	5/1912	Scr 8/53
2422	Baldwin	37776	5/1912	Scr 8/51
2423	Baldwin	37777	5/1912	Scr 7/53
2424	Baldwin	37778	5/1912	So7/42,Seaboard 482
2425	Baldwin	37779	5/1912	Scr '53
2426	Baldwin	37854	6/1912	AC&HB 60
2427	Baldwin	37855	6/1912	So7/42,Seaboard 483
2428	Baldwin	37856	6/1912	Scr 3/52
2429	Baldwin	37857	6/1912	Scr 3/51
2430	Baldwin	37858	6/1912	So '40, A&S 19
2431	Baldwin	37867	6/1912	Scr 4/53
2432	Baldwin	37868	6/1912	Scr 4/51
2433	Baldwin	37869	6/1912	Scr 4/51
2434	Baldwin	37870	6/1912	So7/42,Seaboard 484
2435	Baldwin	37871	6/1912	Scr 12/51
2436	Baldwin	37872	6/1912	Scr 8/51
2437	Baldwin	37873	6/1912	So '42,Seaboard 485
2438	Baldwin	37879	6/1912	Scr 5/53
2439	Baldwin	37880	6/1912	So7/42,Seaboard 486
2440	Baldwin	37881	6/1912	So7/42,Seaboard 487
2441	Baldwin	37882	6/1912	Scr 9/53
2442	Baldwin	37922	6/1912	Scr 12/51
2443	Baldwin	37923	6/1912	Scr 3/51
2444	Pitts.	52450	12/1912	Scr 4/51
2445	Pitts.	52451	12/1912	Scr 11/51
2446	Pitts.	52452	12/1912	Scr 2/54
2447	Pitts.	52453	12/1912	So '41, A&S 20
2448	Pitts.	52454	12/1912	So '40, A&S 18
2449	Pitts.	52455	12/1912	Scr 1/54
2450	Pitts.	52456	12/1912	Scr 12/51
2451	Pitts.	52457	12/1912	Scr 4/53
2452	Pitts.	52458	12/1912	Scr 4/51
2453	Pitts.	52459	12/1912	Scr 3/51
2454	Pitts.	52460	12/1912	Scr 3/52
2455	Pitts.	52461	12/1912	So '45, AC&HB 63
2456	Pitts.	52462	12/1912	Scr 6/43 (d)
2457	Pitts.	52463	12/1912	So 1/45, AC&HB 64
2458	Pitts.	52464	12/1912	So 1/46, AC&HB 66
2459	Pitts.	52465	12/1912	Scr 11/54
2460	Pitts.	52466	12/1912	So '40, AC&HB 62
2461	Pitts.	52467	12/1912	Scr 5/53
2462	Pitts.	52468	12/1912	Scr 4/53
2463	Pitts.	52469	12/1912	So 2/45, AC&HB 65

Note b - AC&HB: Algoma Central & Hudson Bay RR.
Note c - AW&W: Algers Winslow & Western RR (Enosville, Indiana).
Note d - 2456 wrecked in head-on crash with 2262 at Moulton, Ontario, 6/42, scrap at St. Thomas.

Class K-2 2-8-2: 26x30-64-200-292000-53868 USRA

2201		Schenectady	59660	11/1918	Scr 7/51
2202		Schenectady	59661	11/1918	Scr 11/49
2203		Schenectady	59662	11/1918	Scr '53
2204		Schenectady	59663	11/1918	Scr 5/51
2205		Schenectady	59664	11/1918	Scr 8/51
2206		Schenectady	59665	11/1918	Scr 5/51
2207		Schenectady	59666	11/1918	Scr 7/51
2208		Schenectady	59667	11/1918	Scr '53
2209		Schenectady	59668	11/1918	Scr '53
2210		Schenectady	59669	11/1918	Scr 11/51
2211		Schenectady	59670	11/1918	Scr '53
2212		Schenectady	59671	11/1918	Scr 11/51
2213		Schenectady	59672	11/1918	to PM RR 1025 10/19
2213	ex WP 321	Baldwin	50804	12/1918	Scr 3/52
2214		Schenectady	59673	11/1918	to PM RR 1026 10/19
2214	ex WP 322	Baldwin	50805	12/1918	Scr 12/51
2215		Schenectady	59674	11/1918	to PM RR 1027 10/19
2215	ex WP 323	Baldwin	50806	12/1918	Scr 7/51
2216		Schenectady	59675	11/1918	Scr '53
2217		Schenectady	59676	11/1918	Scr '53
2218		Schenectady	59677	11/1918	to PM RR 1028 10/19
2218	ex WP 324	Baldwin	50807	12/1918	Scr 8/51
2219		Schenectady	59678	11/1918	to PM RR 1029 10/19
2219	ex WP 325	Baldwin	50808	12/1918	Scr 7/51
2220		Schenectady	59679	11/1918	Scr 7/51

Class K-3 2-8-2: 27x32-64-210-325000-65063

2250	Schenectady	65056	12/1923	Scr 11/51
2251	Schenectady	65057	12/1923	Scr 7/51
2252	Schenectady	65058	12/1923	Scr 7/51
2253	Schenectady	65059	12/1923	Scr 7/51
2254	Schenectady	65060	12/1923	Scr 9/44
2255	Schenectady	65061	12/1923	Scr 7/51
2256	Schenectady	65062	12/1923	Scr 8/55
2257	Schenectady	65063	12/1923	Scr 7/51
2258	Schenectady	65064	12/1923	Scr '53
2259	Schenectady	65065	12/1923	Scr 12/52
2260	Schenectady	65066	12/1923	Scr 11/51
2261	Schenectady	65067	12/1923	Scr 9/50
2262	Schenectady	65068	12/1923	Scr 7/51
2263	Schenectady	65069	12/1923	Scr 7/51
2264	Schenectady	65070	12/1923	Scr 12/51
2265	Schenectady	65071	12/1923	Scr 7/51
2266	Schenectady	65072	12/1923	Scr 1/55
2267	Schenectady	65073	12/1923	Scr 3/55
2268	Schenectady	65074	12/1923	Scr 7/51
2269	Schenectady	65075	12/1923	Scr 7/51

Class K-3 2-8-2: 27x32-64-210-331000-65063

2270	Schenectady	65076	12/1923	Scr 9/55
2271	Schenectady	65077	12/1923	Scr 7/51
2272	Schenectady	65078	12/1923	Scr '54
2273	Schenectady	65079	12/1923	Scr 8/55
2274	Schenectady	65080	12/1923	Scr 5/51

Class K-3b 2-8-2: 27x32-64-210-341000-76899 w/booster

2275	Schenectady	65081	12/1923	Scr 6/51
2276	Schenectady	65082	12/1923	Scr 5/51
2277	Schenectady	65083	12/1923	Scr 7/51
2278	Schenectady	65084	12/1923	Scr 6/51
2279	Schenectady	65085	12/1923	Scr 3/52

Class K-4b 2-8-2: 27x32-64-210-346480-76899 w/booster

2700	Schenectady	66138	2/1925	Scr 2/53
2701	Schenectady	66139	2/1925	Scr 3/52
2702	Schenectady	66140	2/1925	Scr 7/51
2703	Schenectady	66141	2/1925	Scr 7/51
2704	Schenectady	66142	2/1925	Scr 7/51
2705	Schenectady	66143	2/1925	Scr 7/51
2706	Schenectady	66144	2/1925	Scr 7/51
2707	Schenectady	66145	2/1925	Scr 8/51
2708	Schenectady	66146	2/1925	Scr 8/51
2709	Schenectady	66147	2/1925	Scr 12/51
2710	Schenectady	66148	2/1925	Scr 11/51
2711	Schenectady	66149	2/1925	Scr 8/51
2712	Schenectady	66150	2/1925	Scr 8/51
2713	Schenectady	66151	2/1925	Scr 8/51
2714	Schenectady	66152	2/1925	Scr 8/51
2715	Schenectady	66153	2/1925	Scr 8/51
2716	Schenectady	66154	2/1925	Scr 8/51
2717	Schenectady	66155	2/1925	Scr 8/51
2718	Schenectady	66156	2/1925	Scr 2/53
2719	Schenectady	66157	2/1925	Scr 12/51

Class K-4 2-8-2: 27x32-64-210-338580-65063

2720	Schenectady	66128	1/1925	Scr 8/51
2721	Schenectady	66129	1/1925	Scr 12/51
2722	Schenectady	66130	1/1925	Scr 10/51
2723	Schenectady	66131	1/1925	Scr 2/51 (e)
2724	Schenectady	66132	1/1925	Scr 7/51
2725	Schenectady	66133	1/1925	Scr 7/51
2726	Schenectady	66134	1/1925	Scr 12/51
2727	Schenectady	66135	1/1925	Scr 7/51
2728	Schenectady	66136	1/1925	Scr 3/53
2729	Schenectady	66137	2/1925	Scr 7/51

Note e - 2723 destroyed in wreck near West Unity, O., 6/48. Not rebuilt. Boiler scrapped Montpelier.

Class K-4 2-8-2: 27x32-64-210-333730-65063

2730	Schenectady	66113	1/1925	Scr 12/51
2731	Schenectady	66114	1/1925	Scr 8/51
2732	Schenectady	66115	1/1925	Scr 8/51
2733	Schenectady	66116	1/1925	Scr 12/51
2734	Schenectady	66117	1/1925	Scr 8/51
2735	Schenectady	66118	1/1925	Scr 12/51
2736	Schenectady	66119	1/1925	Scr 12/51
2737	Schenectady	66120	1/1925	Scr 7/51
2738	Schenectady	66121	1/1925	Scr 12/51
2739	Schenectady	66122	1/1925	Scr 3/53
2740	Schenectady	66123	1/1925	Scr 11/51
2741	Schenectady	66124	1/1925	Scr 12/51
2742	Schenectady	66125	1/1925	Scr 8/51
2743	Schenectady	66126	1/1925	RB '47, P-1 706
2744	Schenectady	66127	1/1925	RB '46, P-1 705

Class K-5 2-8-2: 1-23x28-64-210-340490-67869
2-23x32

2600	Schenectady	66158	2/1925	RB '43, P-1 700
2601	Schenectady	66159	2/1925	RB '43, P-1 701
2602	Schenectady	66160	2/1925	RB '44, P-1 702
2603	Schenectady	66161	2/1925	RB '44, P-1 703
2604	Schenectady	66162	2/1925	RB '44, P-1 704

Classes K-6 and K-7 2-8-2: See Ann Arbor Classes H and H-1

Class L 2-10-2 Types

Class L-1 2-10-2: 29x32-64-210-395000-75079

Wabash No.	Builder		New	Disposition
2501	Brooks	57553	7/1917	So 12/47, C&IM 656
2502	Brooks	57554	7/1917	So 8/42, MoP 1715
2503	Brooks	57555	7/1917	Scr 6/50
2504	Brooks	57556	7/1917	So 5/42, KCS 200
2505	Brooks	57557	7/1917	So 8/42, MoP 1716
2506	Brooks	57558	7/1917	So 5/42, KCS 205
2507	Brooks	57559	7/1917	Scr 3/51
2508	Brooks	57560	7/1917	So 5/42, KCS 201
2509	Brooks	57561	7/1917	So '42, C&EI 4001(a)
2510	Brooks	57562	7/1917	So '41, C&IM 651
2511	Brooks	57563	7/1917	So 5/42, KCS 204
2512	Brooks	57564	7/1917	So 8/42, MoP 1717
2513	Brooks	57565	7/1917	So '42, C&EI 4000(a)
2514	Brooks	57566	7/1917	So '41, C&IM 652
2515	Brooks	57567	7/1917	So '50, C&IM 658
2516	Brooks	57568	7/1917	So 8/42, MoP 1718
2517	Brooks	57569	7/1917	So '42, C&IM 654
2518	Brooks	57570	7/1917	So '42, C&IM 655
2519	Brooks	57571	7/1917	So '50, C&IM 659

2520		Brooks	57572	7/1917	So	7/50, C&IM*
2521		Brooks	57573	7/1917	So	5/42, KCS 202
2522		Brooks	57574	7/1917	So	6/42, MoP 1719
2523		Brooks	57575	7/1917	So	'42, C&IM 653
2524		Brooks	57576	7/1917	So	12/47, C&IM 657
2525		Brooks	57577	7/1917	So	5/42, KCS 203

Note a - These engines to Chesapeake & Ohio 4000-4001.

* for parts only

Class L-2 2-10-2: See Ann Arbor Class L

Class M 4-8-2 Types
Class M-1 4-8-2: 29x32-70-245-406400-67400

2800	Baldwin	61149	1/1930	Scr 2/53
2801	Baldwin	61150	1/1930	Scr 2/53
2802	Baldwin	61151	1/1930	Scr 3/53
2803	Baldwin	61152	1/1930	Scr 9/55
2804	Baldwin	61153	1/1930	Scr 3/53
2805	Baldwin	61154	1/1930	Scr 9/55
2806	Baldwin	61155	1/1930	Scr 4/53
2807	Baldwin	61156	1/1930	Scr 3/53
2808	Baldwin	61157	1/1930	Scr 6/55
2809	Baldwin	61158	1/1930	Scr 3/53
2810	Baldwin	61177	2/1930	Scr 3/53
2811	Baldwin	61178	2/1930	Scr 3/53
2812	Baldwin	61179	2/1930	Scr 3/53
2813	Baldwin	61180	2/1930	Scr 4/53
2814	Baldwin	61181	2/1930	Scr 3/53
2815	Baldwin	61182	2/1930	Scr 3/53
2816	Baldwin	61183	2/1930	Scr 2/53
2817	Baldwin	61200	2/1930	Scr 12/55
2818	Baldwin	61201	2/1930	Scr 2/53
2819	Baldwin	61202	2/1930	Scr 9/55
2820	Baldwin	61203	2/1930	Scr 2/53
2821	Baldwin	61204	2/1930	Scr 2/53
2822	Baldwin	61205	2/1930	Scr 9/55
2823	Baldwin	61206	3/1930	Scr 12/53
2824	Baldwin	61207	3/1930	Scr 2/53

Class O 4-8-4 Types

Wabash No.	Builder	New	Disposition

Class O-1 4-8-4: 29x32-70-250-454090-70817

2900	Baldwin	61417	8/1930	Scr 1/56
2901	Baldwin	61418	8/1930	Scr 11/55
2902	Baldwin	61435	8/1930	Scr 11/55
2903	Baldwin	61436	8/1930	Scr 11/55
2904	Baldwin	61437	8/1930	Scr 11/55
2905	Baldwin	61438	8/1930	Scr 10/55
2906	Baldwin	61482	10/1930	Scr 1/56
2907	Baldwin	61483	10/1930	Scr 1/56
2908	Baldwin	61484	10/1930	Scr 10/55
2909	Baldwin	61485	10/1930	Scr 10/55
2910	Baldwin	61516	11/1930	Scr 1/56
2911	Baldwin	61517	11/1930	Scr 2/56
2912	Baldwin	61518	11/1930	Scr 1/56
2913	Baldwin	61519	11/1930	Scr 1/56
2914	Baldwin	61520	11/1930	Scr 2/56
2915	Baldwin	61521	11/1930	Scr 1/56
2916	Baldwin	61567	12/1930	Scr 11/55
2917	Baldwin	61568	12/1930	Scr 1/56 (a)
2918	Baldwin	61572	12/1930	Scr 1/56
2919	Baldwin	61588	1/1931	Scr 12/55
2920	Baldwin	61589	1/1931	Scr 11/55
2921	Baldwin	61590	1/1931	Scr 11/55
2922	Baldwin	61591	1/1931	Scr 1/56
2923	Baldwin	61592	1/1931	Scr 11/55
2924	Baldwin	61593	1/1931	Scr 11/55

Note a - 2917 wrecked in boiler explosion 1/3/37 at Adrian, Michigan. Rebuilt with new Baldwin boiler, Extra Order 5808 1937.

Class P 4-6-4 Types

Wabash No.	Builder	New	Disposition

Class P-1 4-6-4: 26x28-80-220-374680-44244

700	ex 2600	Decatur	8/1943	Scr 5/56
701	ex 2601	Decatur	11/1943	Scr 9/56
702	ex 2602	Decatur	2/1944	Scr 8/56
703	ex 2603	Decatur	5/1944	Scr 6/56
704	ex 2604	Decatur	9/1944	Scr 9/56
705	ex 2744	Decatur	1946	Scr 7/56
706	ex 2743	Decatur	1947	Scr 9/56

Wabash diesels

Wabash Number	N&W Number	Builder	New	Disposition

Class D-3 B-B Diesel Switcher: GE Model 44 Ton 350 HP 87000 Wt.

51	--	Gen. Elec.	12496	7/1939	So	'61 Merrilees Equip Co. to L. Ont. St. Co.

Class D-6 B-B Diesel Switcher: ALCO Model HH600 600 HP 197000 Wt.

100	--	ALCO	69083	4/1939	Ret., Scr 4/66
150	--	ALCO	69254	3/1940	Ret. 12/66

Class D-6 B-B Diesel Switcher: ALCO-GE Model S-1 660 HP 198000 Wt.

1	--Acq.1/62	ALCO	69190	5/1940	ex Des Moines Union #1, Scr 10/62
2	--Acq. '61	ALCO	69196	6/1940	ex NJI&I #1, Scr 12/66
151	--	ALCO	69495	7/1941	Ret. 11/66
152	--	ALCO	69607	1/1942	Ret. 12/66

153	--	ALCO	72695	9/1944	So	'66 to Precision Eng. Co., Resold '67 Green River Steel #153
154	--	ALCO	72696	9/1944	Ret.	9/66
155	--	ALCO	72839	9/1944	Ret.	5/66
156	--	ALCO	75127	2/1947	So	3/62 Birm. Rail & Loco.Co.
157	--	ALCO	75128	2/1947	Ret.	4/66
158	--	ALCO	75646	3/1948	So	3/62 Birm. Rail & Loco.Co.
159	--	ALCO	75647	3/1948	So	3/62 Birm. Rail & Loco.Co.

Class D-6 B-B Diesel Switcher: EMD Model SW-1 600 HP 193130 Wt.

101	--	EMC	880	4/1939	So	'60 Peabody Coal Co. #101
102	--	EMC	881	6/1939	So	10/61 Bon. & Hat. Sou. #2
103	--	EMC	882	6/1939	So	10/61 Bon. & Hat. Sou. #1
104	--	EMD	1024	2/1940	So	7/60 Peabody Coal Co. #104
105	--	EMD	1075	5/1940	So	3/60 Tulsa-Sapulpa Un. #105
106	--	EMD	1197	11/1940	So	7/61 Granite City Steel #106
107	--	EMD	1388	11/1945	So	8/61 Granite City Steel #602
108	--	EMD	4730	4/1947	So	4/64 Tulsa-Sapulpa Un. #108
109	3109	EMD	7533	6/1949		
110	3110	EMD	7741	6/1949	So Anderson Corp., Bayport, Minn.	
111	--	EMD	7742	6/1949	So	7/64 Granite City Steel #111

Class D-6 B-B Diesel Switcher: Baldwin Model VO 660 660 HP 198000 Wt.

200	--	Baldwin	62497	7/1941	Leased '65 LE&FtW #1, Ret. 5/68

Class D-6 B-B Diesel Switcher: Baldwin Model DS4-4-660 660HP 198010 Wt.

201	--	Baldwin	73363	2/1947	Ret. 3/64
202	--	Baldwin	73364	3/1947	Ret. 3/64

Class D-8 B-B Diesel Switcher: EMD Model SW-8 800HP 232100 Wt.

120	3120	EMD	9045	10/1950	
121	3121	EMD	9046	10/1950	
122	3122	GMD	A-145	12/1950	
123	3123	GMD	A-146	12/1950	
124	3124	GMD	A-147	1/1951	
125	3125	EMD	14418	9/1951	
126	3126	EMD	14419	9/1951	
127	3127	GMD	A-278	8/1951	
128	3128	EMD	17589	2/1953	
129	3129	EMD	17590	2/1953	
130	3130	EMD	17591	2/1953	
131	3131	EMD	17592	2/1953	
132	3132	EMD	17593	2/1953	

Class D-10 B-B Diesel Switcher: Baldwin Model VO 1000 1000HP 242730 Wt.

300	--	Baldwin	64425	9/1942	Ret. 3/64
301	--	Baldwin	70151	2/1944	Ret. 3/64
302	--	Baldwin	70152	2/1944	Ret. 9/66
303	--	Baldwin	72229	6/1944	Ret. 11/66

Class D-10 B-B Diesel Switcher: BLW-West Model DS-4-4-1000 1000HP 241730 Wt.

304	--	BLW-West.	73955	1/1949	RB after wreck to cabless booster Ret. 3/64

Class D-10 B-B Diesel Switcher: ALCO-GE Model S-2 1000HP 231830 Wt.

310	--	ALCO	69910	8/1942	Ret. 7/66
311	--	ALCO	69911	8/1942	Ret. 12/66
312	--	ALCO	70226	11/1943	Ret. '66
313	--	ALCO	70245	4/1944	Ret. 11/66
314	--	ALCO	70201	4/1944	Ret. 4/67
315	--	ALCO	70202	3/1944	Ret. 9/68
316	--	ALCO	72063	6/1944	Ret. 11/66
317	--	ALCO	72064	6/1944	1000th ALCO Diesel: Ret. 7/66
318	--	ALCO	74491	7/1946	Ret. 12/66
319	--	ALCO	74492	7/1946	
320	3320	ALCO	76762	5/1949	
321	3321	ALCO	76763	5/1949	
325	--	ALCO	69928	7/1942	Ex Nickel Plate #5; acq.5/64;Ret. 3/66

Class D-10 B-B Diesel Switcher: ALCO-GE Model S-4 1000HP 238570 Wt.

322	3322	ALCO	80610	6/1953	
323	3323	ALCO	80611	6/1953	
324	3324	ALCO	80612	6/1953	

Class D-10 B-B Diesel Switcher: EMD Model NW-2 1000HP 249000 Wt.

346	--	EMD	1423	8/1941	Ex NKP #98; ex W&LE D-1; to DMU IC/61
347	--	EMD	998	4/1940	Ex NKP #95; ex W&LE D-1; to DMU #6
348	3348	EMD	1089	7/1940	Ex NKP #96; ex W&LE D-2; So 3/68 to Island Creek Coal
349	3349	EMD	1422	6/1941	Ex NKP #97; ex W&LE D-3; So 10/66 to Celanese Co.
350	3350	EMD	4159	12/1946	Trsf. 10/66 DMU #7
351	3351	EMD	7531	7/1949	
352	3352	EMD	7532	7/1949	
353		EMD	7898	5/1948	(a)

Note a - Orig. Indiana Northern #100; to NJI&I #2 in 1961.

Class D-10 B-B Diesel Switcher: F-M Model ALT 100.6a 1000HP (1) 242230 Wt.
(2) 244300 Wt.

380	3380	F-M	L1021	11/1946	Ret. 3/66 (1)
381	3381	F-M	L1022	11/1946	Ret. 6/66 (1)
382	3382	F-M	10L101	3/1949	Ret. '70 (2)
383	3383	F-M	10L102	3/1949	Ret. 6/66 (2)

Class D-10 B-B Diesel Switcher: Lima-Hamilton Yd. Sw. 1000HP 239410 Wt.

400	--	Lima-Ham.	9395	3/1950	Ex L-H Demo.#1002; RB to 1200HP

Class D-12 B-B Diesel Switcher: B-L-H-W Model S-12 1200HP 239950 Wt.

305	--	BLHW	75062	1951	
306	--	BLHW	75063	1951	
307	--	BLHW	75823	2/1953	So 4/67 Calif.Western #54, Wrecked 1/14/70, Scrapped
308	--	BLHW	75824	2/1953	Ret. 6/67
309	--	BLHW	75825	2/1953	Ret. 8/66

Class D-12 B-B Diesel Switcher: EMD Model SW-7 1200HP 247540 Wt.

355	3355	EMD	9037	7/1950	
356	3356	EMD	9038	7/1950	
357	3357	EMD	9039	7/1950	
358	3358	EMD	9040	7/1950	
359	3359	EMD	9041	7/1950	
360	3360	EMD	9042	7/1950	
361	3361	EMD	9043	7/1950	
362	3362	EMD	9044	7/1950	

Class D-12 B-B Diesel Switcher: EMD Model SW-9 1200HP 247860 Wt.

363	3363	EMD	12622	4/1951
364	3364	EMD	12623	4/1951
365	3365	EMD	12624	5/1951
366	3366	EMD	12625	5/1951
367	3367	EMD	15058	2/1952
368	3368	EMD	15059	2/1952
369	3369	EMD	15060	2/1952
370	3370	EMD	15061	2/1952
371	3371	EMD	15062	2/1952
372	3372	EMD	17580	3/1953
373	3373	EMD	17581	3/1953
374	3374	EMD	17582	3/1953

Class D-12 B-B Diesel Switcher: EMD Model SW-1200 1200HP 247350 Wt.

375	3375	EMD	18877	1/1954
376	3376	EMD	18878	1/1954
377	3377	EMD	18879	1/1954
378	3378	EMD	18880	1/1954
379	3379	EMD	23297	1/1957

Class D-12 B-B Diesel Switcher: F-M Model H-12-44 1200HP 244880 Wt.

384	3384	F-M	12L744	3/1953	Ret. '71
385	3385	F-M	12L745	3/1953	Ret. '71
386	3386	F-M	12L746	3/1953	Ret. '70

Class D-12 B-B Diesel Switcher: Lima-Hamilton Yd.Sw. 1200HP
Wt.: (1) 247900 (2) 240510 (3) 246480

401 (1)	--	Lima-Ham.	9417	4/1950	RB ALCO 1200HP eng. Ret. 10/65
402 (1)	--	Lima-Ham.	9418	4/1950	RB ALCO 1200HP eng. Ret. 5/65
403 (1)	--	Lima-Ham.	9419	4/1950	RB ALCO 1200HP eng. Ret. 2/66
404 (1)	--	Lima-Ham.	9420	5/1950	RB ALCO 1200HP eng. Ret. 2/66
405 (1)	--	Lima-Ham.	9421	5/1950	RB ALCO 1200HP eng. Ret. 2/66
406 (1)	--	Lima-Ham.	9422	5/1950	RB ALCO 1200HP eng. Ret. 2/66
407 (2)	--	Lima-Ham.	9397	8/1950	Ex L-H Demo.#1003; RB with ALCO 1200HP eng. Ret. 2/66
408 (3)	--	Lima-Ham.	9508	11/1950	RB ALCO 1200HP eng. Ret. 9/65
409 (3)	--	Lima-Ham.	9509	11/1950	RB ALCO 1200HP eng. Ret. 7/66
410 (3)	--	Lima-Ham.	9510	11/1950	RB ALCO 1200HP eng. Ret. 7/65
411 (3)	--	Lima-Ham.	9511	11/1950	RB ALCO 1200HP eng. Ret. 2/66

Class L-15 B-B Diesel Road Switcher: EMD Model GP-7 1500HP
Wt.: (1) 237350 (2) 252835

450	(1)	3450	EMD	11993	8/1950	
451	(1)	3451	EMD	11994	8/1950	
452	(1)	3452	EMD	11995	9/1950	
453	(2)	3453	GMD	A-148	1/1951	
454	(2)	--	EMD	14408	7/1951	Wrecked 8/59, Scr 6/60
455	(2)	3455	EMD	14409	7/1951	
456	(2)	3456	EMD	14410	7/1951	
457	(2)	3457	EMD	14411	7/1951	Ret. 4/67
458	(2)	3458	EMD	14412	7/1951	
459	(1)	3459	EMD	14413	7/1951	
460	(1)	3460	EMD	14414	7/1951	Ret. 5/67
461	(1)	3461	EMD	14415	7/1951	
462	(1)	3462	EMD	14416	7/1951	
463	(1)	3463	EMD	14417	7/1951	
464	(2)	3464	EMD	15048	2/1952	
465	(1)	3465	EMD	15049	2/1952	
466	(1)	3466	EMD	15050	2/1952	
467	(1)	3467	EMD	15051	2/1952	
468	(1)	3468	EMD	15052	2/1952	
469	(1)	3469	EMD	15053	2/1952	
470	(1)	3470	EMD	15054	2/1952	
471	(1)	3471	EMD	15055	2/1952	
472	(1)	3472	EMD	15056	2/1952	
473	(1)	3473	EMD	15057	2/1952	
474	(2)	3474	EMD	17080	8/1952	
475	(1)	3475	EMD	17076	8/1952	
476	(1)	3476	EMD	17077	8/1952	
477	(1)	3477	EMD	17078	8/1952	
478	(1)	3478	EMD	17079	8/1952	
479	(2)	3479	EMD	17571	1/1953	
480	(2)	3480	EMD	17572	1/1953	
481	(2)	3481	EMD	17573	1/1953	
482	(2)	3482	EMD	17574	1/1953	
483	(1)	3483	EMD	17575	1/1953	

Class D-15 B-B Diesel Freight: EMD Model F-7A & F-7B 1500HP 231460 Wt.

Wabash Number	Re'61	N&W Number	Builder		New	Disposition
1100B	600	--	EMD	7616	8/1949	Ret. 2/64
1101B	601	--	EMD	7617	8/1949	So 10/63 - Ann Arbor
1102B	602	--	EMD	7618	8/1949	Ret. 2/64
1103B	603	--	EMD	7621	8/1949	Ret. 3/64
1104B	604	--	EMD	7615	8/1949	Ret. 3/64
1105B	605	--	EMD	7628	8/1949	Ret. 4/64
1106B	606	--	EMD	7629	8/1949	Ret. 7/65
1107B	607	--	EMD	7630	8/1949	Ret. 2/64
1108B	608	--	EMD	11295	6/1950	Ret. 4/65
1100	609	--	EMD	7609	8/1949	Ret. 8/64
1100A	610	--	EMD	7610	8/1949	Ret. 7/64
1101	611	--	EMD	7611	8/1949	Ret. 7/65
1101A	612	--	EMD	7612	8/1949	Ret. 8/64
1102	613	--	EMD	7613	8/1949	Ret. 4/65
1102A	614	--	EMD	7614	8/1949	So 10/63 - Ann Arbor
1103	615	--	EMD	7619	8/1949	Ret. 8/64
1103A	616	--	EMD	7620	8/1949	Ret. 4/65
1104	617	--	EMD	7607	8/1949	Ret. 8/64
1104A	618	--	EMD	7608	8/1949	Ret. 2/64
1105	619	--	EMD	7622	8/1949	Ret. 4/64
1105A	620	--	EMD	7623	8/1949	So 10/63 - Ann Arbor
1106	621	--	EMD	7624	8/1949	Ret. 4/65
1106A	622	--	EMD	7625	8/1949	Ret. 7/64
1107	623	--	EMD	7626	8/1949	Ret. 5/65
1107A	624	--	EMD	7627	8/1949	Ret. 7/64
1108	625	--	EMD	9061	6/1950	Ret. 7/65
1108A	626	--	EMD	9062	6/1950	Ret. 7/65
1140	627	--	EMD	9047	6/1950	Ret. 4/65
1140A	628	--	EMD	9048	6/1950	Ret. 4/65
1141	629	--	EMD	9049	6/1950	Wrecked 8/59, RB F-9A 11/59, Ret. '66
1141A	630	--	EMD	9050	6/1950	Ret. '66
1142	631	--	EMD	9051	6/1950	Ret. 4/66
1142A	632	--	EMD	9052	6/1950	Ret. 4/65
1143	633	--	EMD	9053	6/1950	Ret. 4/65
1143A	634	--	EMD	9054	6/1950	Ret. 5/65
1144	635	--	EMD	9055	6/1950	Ret. 4/65
1144A	636	--	EMD	9056	6/1950	Ret. 8/65
1145	637	--	EMD	9057	6/1950	Ret. 10/65
1145A	638	--	EMD	9058	6/1950	Ret. 7/65
1146	639	--	EMD	9059	6/1950	Ret. 8/66
1146A	640	--	EMD	9060	6/1950	Ret. 4/65
1147	641	--	EMD	9063	6/1950	Ret. 5/66
1147A	642	--	EMD	9064	6/1950	Ret. 4/65
1148	643	--	EMD	9065	7/1950	Ret. 5/65
1148A	644	--	EMD	9066	7/1950	Ret. 10/65
1149	645	--	EMD	9067	7/1950	Ret. 4/65
1149A	646	--	EMD	9068	7/1950	Ret. 4/65
1150	647	--	EMD	9069	7/1950	Ret. 7/66
1150A	648	--	EMD	9070	7/1950	Ret. 10/65
1151	649	--	EMD	9071	7/1950	Ret. 9/65
1151A	650	--	EMD	9072	7/1950	Ret. 5/66
1152	651	--	EMD	9073	7/1950	Ret. 10/65
1152A	652	--	EMD	9074	7/1950	Ret. 5/66
1153	653	--	EMD	11293	7/1950	Ret. 7/65
1153A	654	--	EMD	11294	7/1950	Ret. 8/65
1154	655	--	EMD	12305	7/1950	Ret. 6/66
1154A	656	--	EMD	12306	7/1950	Ret. 4/65
1155	657	3657	GMD	A-125	12/1950	(a)
1155A	658	3658	GMD	A-126	12/1950	
1156	659	3659	GMD	A-127	12/1950	
1156A	660	3660	GMD	A-128	12/1950	
1157	661	3661	GMD	A-129	12/1950	
1157A	662	3662	GMD	A-130	12/1950	
1158	663	3663	GMD	A-131	1/1951	Ret. 7/66

Note a - GMD units 1155-1164 Wt. 229000.

1158A	664	3364	GMD	A-132	1/1951	Ret. 8/66
1159	665	3665	GMD	A-133	1/1951	Ret. 6/67
1159A	666	3666	GMD	A-134	1/1951	
1160	667	3667	GMD	A-135	1/1951	
1160A	668	3668	GMD	A-136	1/1951	Ret. 8/66
1161	669	3669	GMD	A-137	1/1951	Ret. 8/67
1161A	670	3670	GMD	A-138	1/1951	Ret. 7/66
1162	671	3671	GMD	A-139	1/1951	
1162A	672	3672	GMD	A-140	1/1951	Ret. 8/67
1163	673	3673	GMD	A-141	1/1951	Ret. 10/66
1163A	674	3674	GMD	A-142	1/1951	Ret. 8/67
1164	675	3675	GMD	A-143	1/1951	Ret. 6/67
1164A	676	3676	GMD	A-144	1/1951	Ret. 6/67
1165	677	3677	EMD	9020	6/1951	Ret. 7/65
1165A	678	3678	EMD	9021	6/1951	Ret. 6/67
1166	679	3679	EMD	9022	6/1951	Ret. 4/65
1166A	680	3680	EMD	9023	6/1951	Ret. 5/66
1167	681	3681	EMD	9024	6/1951	Ret. 4/65
1167A	682	3682	EMD	9025	6/1951	Ret. 4/65
1168	683	3683	EMD	9026	6/1951	Wrecked 4/65
1168A	684	3684	EMD	9027	6/1951	Ret. 10/65
1169	685	3685	EMD	9028	6/1951	Ret. 3/67
1169A	686	3686	EMD	9029	6/1951	Ret. 7/66
1170	687	3687	EMD	9030	7/1951	Wrecked 4/65
1170A	688	3688	EMD	9031	7/1951	Ret. 6/66
1171	689	3689	EMD	9032	7/1951	Leased to CNJ
1171A	690	3690	EMD	9033	7/1951	Leased to CNJ
1172	691	3691	EMD	9034	7/1951	Ret. 5/66
1172A	--	--	EMD	9035	7/1951	Wrecked, Scr 11/59
1173	693	3693	EMD	9036	7/1951	Ret. 7/65
1173A	694	3694	EMD	12612	7/1951	Ret. 6/67
1174	695	3695	EMD	12613	7/1951	
1174A	696	3696	EMD	12614	7/1951	Ret. 10/65
1175	697	3697	EMD	12615	7/1951	Leased to CNJ
1175A	698	3698	EMD	12616	7/1951	Ret. 10/65
1176	699	3699	EMD	12617	7/1951	Ret. 10/65
1176A	700	3700	EMD	12618	7/1951	Ret. 9/66
1177	701	3701	EMD	15036	1/1952	Ret. 8/66
1177A	702	3702	EMD	15037	1/1952	Ret. 6/67
1178	703	3703	EMD	15038	1/1952	Leased to CNJ
1178A	704	3704	EMD	15039	1/1952	Ret. 6/67
1179	705	3705	EMD	15040	1/1952	Leased to CNJ
1179A	706	3706	EMD	15041	1/1952	
1180	707	3707	EMD	15042	1/1952	Ret. 6/66
1180A	708	3708	EMD	15043	1/1952	Wrecked 4/65
1181	709	3709	EMD	15044	1/1952	
1181A	710	3710	EMD	15045	1/1952	Ret. 10/67
1182	711	3711	EMD	15046	1/1952	
1182A	712	3712	EMD	15047	1/1952	Leased to CNJ
1183	713	3713	EMD	17068	9/1952	So 11/63 - Ann Arbor
1183A	714	3714	EMD	17069	9/1952	Leased to CNJ
1184	715	3715	EMD	17070	9/1952	Leased to CNJ
1184A	716	3716	EMD	17071	9/1952	
1185	717	3717	EMD	17072	9/1952	Leased to CNJ
1185A	718	3718	EMD	17073	9/1952	Leased to CNJ
1186	719	3719	EMD	17074	9/1952	
1186A	720	3720	EMD	17075	9/1952	
1187	721	3721	EMD	17576	1/1953	
1187A	722	3722	EMD	17577	1/1953	
1188	723	3723	EMD	17578	1/1953	
1188A	724	3724	EMD	17579	1/1953	Ret. 8/67
1189	725	3725	GMD	A-487	4/1953	
1189A	726	3726	GMD	A-488	4/1953	

Class D-15 B-B Diesel Freight: ALCO-GE Model FA-1 & FB-1 1500HP 231775 Wt.
Trucks used on GE U25B Units 500-515: bodies scrapped at Erie

	Re'61					
1200B	800	--	ALCO	76712	2/1949	Traded 4/62 - GE
1201B	801	--	ALCO	76724	3/1949	Traded 4/62 - GE
1202B	802	--	ALCO	76725	3/1949	Traded 3/62 - GE
1203B	803	--	ALCO	76726	3/1949	Traded 4/62 - GE
1204B	804	--	ALCO	76866	3/1949	Traded 4/62 - GE
1200	805	--	ALCO	76664	1/1949	Traded 4/62 - GE
1200A	806	--	ALCO	76665	1/1949	Traded 4/62 - GE
1201	807	--	ALCO	76696	3/1949	Traded 3/62 - GE
1201A	808	--	ALCO	76697	3/1949	Traded 3/62 - GE
1202	809	--	ALCO	76698	3/1949	Traded 3/62 - GE
1202A	810	--	ALCO	76699	3/1949	Traded 4/62 - GE
1203	811	--	ALCO	76700	3/1949	Traded 3/62 - GE
1203A	812	--	ALCO	76701	3/1949	Traded 4/62 - GE
1204	813	--	ALCO	76702	3/1949	Traded 4/62 - GE
1204A	814	--	ALCO	76703	3/1949	Traded 3/62 - GE

Class D-16 B-B Diesel Freight: ALCO-GE Model FA-2 1600HP 243270 Wt.

820 ex AA 52A	(Acq'63)	ALCO	78384	12/1950	Traded 7/65 - ALCO
821 ex AA 55A	"	ALCO	78480	12/1950	Traded 7/65 - ALCO
822 ex AA 50A	"	ALCO	78380	12/1950	Traded 7/65 - ALCO
823 ex AA 55	"	ALCO	78479	12/1950	Traded 7/65 - ALCO

Class D-17 B-B Diesel Road Sw.: EMD Model GP-9 1750HP
Wt.: (1) 252835 (2) 246820 (3) 254940

484	(1)	3484	EMD	18871	1/1954
485	(1)	3485	EMD	18872	1/1954
486	(1)	3486	EMD	18873	1/1954
487	(1)	3487	EMD	18874	1/1954
488	(1)	3488	EMD	18875	1/1954
489	(1)	3489	EMD	18876	1/1954
490	(2)	3490	EMD	21216	4/1956
491	(2)	3491	EMD	21217	4/1956
492	(2)	3492	EMD	21215	4/1956
493	(3)	3493	EMD	21212	4/1956
494	(3)	3494	EMD	21213	4/1956
495	(3)	3495	EMD	21214	4/1956

Class D-20 A1A-A1A Diesel Passenger: EMD Model E-7A 2000HP
Wt.: (1) 309710 (2) 315715

1000 re.1002A, re'61 1017	--	EMD	3226	8/1946	(2)	Ret. '65
1001A re. '61 1016	--	EMD	4085	4/1947	(1)	Ret. 10/65
1001	--	EMD	4084	4/1947	(1)	Ret. 10/65
1002	--	EMD	6499	3/1949	(2)	Ret. 10/65

Class D-20 A1A-A1A Diesel Passenger: ALCO-GE Model PA-2 2000HP 309110 Wt.

	re'61					
1020	1050	--	ALCO	77081	5/1949	Ret. 3/65
1020A	1051	--	ALCO	77082	5/1949	Ret. 3/64
1021	1052	--	ALCO	77083	5/1949	Ret. 3/65
1021A	1053	--	ALCO	77084	5/1949	Ret. 3/65

Class D-22 A1A-A1A Diesel Passenger: EMD Model E-8A 2250HP
Wt.: (1)304225 (2)331255 (3)337570

1000 (1)	3800	EMD	15063	10/1951	Ret. 9/67
1003 (2)	3803	EMD	7812	11/1949	Ret. 7/65
1004 (2)	3804	EMD	7813	11/1949	Ret. 7/65
1005 (2)	3805	EMD	7814	11/1949	Ret. 10/65
1006 (2)	3806	EMD	7815	11/1949	Ret. 9/67
1007 (2)	3807	EMD	7816	11/1949	Ret. 6/66
1008 (2)	3808	EMD	7817	11/1949	Ret. 6/70
1009 (1)	3809	EMD	14420	6/1951	Ret. 8/66
1010 (1)	3810	EMD	14421	10/1951	Ret. 4/66
1011 (1)	3811	EMD	14422	10/1951	Ret. 10/65
1012 (1)	3812	EMD	14423	6/1951	Ret. 8/67
1013 (1)	--	EMD	14424	6/1951	Wrecked, Scr 8/61
1014 (3)	--	EMD	17565	1/1953	Wrecked, Scr 8/61
1015 (3)	3815	EMD	17566	1/1953	Ret. 6/70

Class D-23 C-C Diesel Freight: F-M Model H-24-66 2350 HP 375000 Wt.

592 ex 552	3592	F-M	24L891	4/1956	
593 ex 553	3593	F-M	24L893	4/1956	
594 ex 554	3594	F-M	24L895	5/1956	
595 ex 552A,555	3595	F-M	24L892	4/1956	
596 ex 553A,556	3596	F-M	24L894	5/1956	
597 ex 554A,557	3597	F-M	24L896	5/1956	
598 ex 550	3598	F-M	24L730	1954	
599 ex 551	3599	F-M	24L731	1954	

Class D-24 C-C Diesel Freight: F-M Model H-24-66 2400HF 378400 Wt.
Orig. FM demonstrators TM-1 and TM-2

550 re '64 598	3598	F-M	24L730	2/1954	RB ALCO-Rerated 2350HP
551 re " 599	3599	F-M	24L731	2/1954	RB ALCO "

Class D-48 C-C Diesel Freight: F-M Model H-24-66 2400HF 315715 Wt.

552 re'64 592	3592	F-M	24L891	4/1956	RB ALCO-Rerated 2350HP
552A re'61 555,595	3595	F-M	24L892	4/1956	RB ALCO "
553 re'64 593	3593	F-M	24L893	5/1956	RB ALCO "
553A re'61 556,596	3596	F-M	24L894	5/1956	RB ALCO "
554 re'64 594	3594	F-M	24L895	5/1956	RB ALCO "
554A re'61 557,597	3597	F-M	24L896	5/1956	RB ALCO "

Class D-24 B-B Diesel Freight: ALCO Model DL-640A 2400HP 256300 Wt.
Built orig. for NdeM, used as booster units on Wabash

Re'70

B900	3900-421	ALCO	3372-01	3/1964	
B901	3901-422	ALCO	3372-02	3/1964	
B902	--	ALCO	3372-03	3/1964	Wrecked 10/64, Scr
B903	3903-423	ALCO	3372-04	3/1964	
B904	3904-424	ALCO	3372-05	3/1964	
B905	3905-425	ALCO	3372-06	3/1964	
B906	3906-426	ALCO	3372-07	3/1964	

Class D-25 B-B Diesel Freight: GE Model U-25B 2500HP 266760 Wt.
Built on ALCO FA trucks

N&W

Re'64 Re'70

500	3529-8152	GE	34254	5/1962	
501	3522-8145	GE	34522	8/1962	
502	3520-8143	GE	34256	5/1962	
503	3518-8141	GE	34257	5/1962	
504	3517-8140	GE	34258	5/1962	
505	3524-8147	GE	34259	5/1962	
506	3526-8149	GE	34519	8/1962	
507	3523-8146	GE	34520	8/1962	
508	3521-8144	GE	34521	8/1962	
509	3516-8139	GE	34524	8/1962	
510	3525-8148	GE	34523	8/1962	
511	3528-8151	GE	34525	8/1962	
512	--	GE	34526	8/1962	Wrecked 10/64, Scr
513	3519-8142	GE	34527	8/1962	
514	3527-8150	GE	34255	5/1962	
--	3515-8138	GE	35581	2/1965	Repl. for 512

Class D-25 B-B Diesel Freight: EMD Model GP-35 2500HP (540-547 258400 Wt.)
548-554 ordered by Wabash; delv. under N&W Nos. (548-554 257000 Wt.)

Re'64 Re'70

540	3540 2911	EMD	29468	4/1964	
541	3541 2912	EMD	29469	4/1964	
542	3542 2913	EMD	29471	4/1964	
543	3543 2914	EMD	29472	4/1964	
544	3544 2915	EMD	29473	4/1964	
545	3545 2916	EMD	29474	4/1964	
546	3546 2917	EMD	29475	4/1964	
547	3547 2918	EMD	29476	4/1964	

Gas-Electric

4000		EMC	140	2/1926	RB'37 to MofW 4297
4001		EMC	139	1/1926	So'56 Consol.Ry.Equip.

****

Note - N&W 1302-1308 (GP-35) built by EMD 11/64, ordered as WAB. 548-554.
Also - N&W 1000-1007 (DL-425) built by ALCO 11/64, ordered as WAB. 582-589.

Ann Arbor steam

Original	Ann Arbor Number	Wabash Number	Builder		New	Disposition

Class A 0-6-0: Wabash B-3: 18x24-51-160-96000-20736

	1	300	Pittsburgh 1586	2/1898	Scr 1/33

Class B 4-4-0: 16x24-60-75000

F&SE	1	2	Rhode Isl. 2236	5/1889	Scr 6/13 (a)
F&SE	2	3	Rhode Isl. 2237	5/1889	So 10/03 (a)

Class B 4-4-0: 16x24-63-81600

T&AA	4	4	Rogers 3692	10/1886	Scr 6/13
T&AA	5	5	Rogers 3693	10/1886	Scr 6/13
T&AA	6	6	Rogers 3694	10/1886	Scr 6/13

Class B 4-4-0: 16x24-63-81600 RB 17x24

TAA&NM	7	7	Rogers 3780	7/1887	Scr 5/25
TAA&NM	8	8	Rogers 3811	8/1887	So to DT&I4 4/09
TAA&NM	9	9	Rogers 3819	10/1887	Scr 5/25
TAA&NM	10	10	Rogers 3839	10/1887	Scr 10/11
TAA&NM	11	11	Rogers 3850	11/1887	So to DT&I5 4/09
TAA&NM	12	12	Rogers 3879	12/1887	So to Day., Leb. & Cinn.12 /09

Class B 4-4-0: 17x24-58-76900 (%) RB to 62"

TAA&NM	8	22		Pittsburgh 582	10/1882	Scr 5/06 (b)
TAA&NM	9	23,29		Pittsburgh 583	10/1882	Scr 12/10
TAA&NM	10	24	(%)	Pittsburgh 623	2/1883	Scr 2/05
TAA&NM	11	25,30		Pittsburgh 779	3/1885	Scr 12/10
TAA&NM	12	26	(%)	Pittsburgh 647	6/1884	Scr 5/06
TAA&NM	13	13,25		Pittsburgh 648	9/1884	Scr 12/10
TAA&NM	14	14		Pittsburgh 780	3/1885	So J.C.Carland 9/01
TAA&NM	15	15		Pittsburgh 788	3/1886	So to DT&I 15 7/08
TAA&NM	16	16,26		Pittsburgh 801	4/1886	Scr 12/10
TAA&NM	17	17,27		Pittsburgh 802	4/1886	Scr 12/10
TAA&NM	18	18		Pittsburgh 803	9/1886	So to D&TSL 11 4/01
TAA&NM	19	19		Pittsburgh 828	9/1886	Scr 5/09 (c)
TAA&NM	20	20		Pittsburgh 831	12/1886	Scr 6/13
TAA&NM	21	21,28		Pittsburgh 832	12/1886	Scr 2/10

(a) Frankfort & Southeastern #1-2 were named *Frankfort* and *Benzonia*; #3 was sold to Kelley's Creek & Northwestern.
(b) There is evidence that TAA&NM #22-26 were built under #8-12 and renumbered after delivery.
(c) #19 destroyed in head-on crash with #103, 9/17/08, Mt.Pleasant, Mich.

Class C 2-6-0: 17x24-50-140-88000-16184

TAA&NM	27	27,50	Pittsburgh 1038	3/1889	Scr 6/13
TAA&NM	28	28,51	Pittsburgh 950	11/1887	Scr 11/19
TAA&NM	29	29,52	Pittsburgh 951	11/1887	Scr 6/13
TAA&NM	30	30,53	Pittsburgh 952	11/1887	Scr 11/19
TAA&NM	31	31,54	Pittsburgh 953	11/1887	Scr 6/13
TAA&NM	32	32,55	Pittsburgh 954	12/1887	Scr 10/16

Class D 4-6-0: 18x24-54-150-90000

AM	19	33,75	Baldwin 10576	1/1890	to M&LS 9 6/13
AM	18	34,76	Baldwin 10577	1/1890	to M&LS 10 8/13
AM	20	35,77	Baldwin 10609	1/1890	Scr 5/25
AM	21	36,78	Baldwin 10611	1/1890	So 9/10 (d)

Early 2-8-0: (39-44 Vauclain compound)

	37	19x24 50	Baldwin 13037	11/1892		(e)
	38	" "	Baldwin 13038	11/1892		
	39	13,22x24-50	Baldwin 13040	11/1892		
	40	" "	Baldwin 13053	11/1892		
	41	" "	Baldwin 13224	2/1893		
	42	" "	Baldwin 13227	2/1893		
	43	" "	Baldwin 13252	2/1893		
	44	" "	Baldwin 13257	2/1893		

Class E 2-8-0: Wabash I-8: 20x24-51

C&BI	43	140	2375	Baldwin 12509	2/1892	(f)

Class E 2-8-0: Wabash I-7: 18x24-51-180-106000-23328

	37,125	2139	Baldwin 14348	7/1895	to M&LS 12 3/20
	38,126	2140	Baldwin 14349	7/1895	to M&LS 2140 9/39
	39,127	2141	Baldwin 14578	12/1895	Scr 1/33
	40,128	2142	Baldwin 14579	12/1895	Scr 1/33

Early 4-6-0: 18x24-56-111600

TAA&NM	47	47	Cooke 2091	9/1891	(g)
TAA&NM	48	48	Cooke 2092	9/1891	

(d) #78 sold to Arcadia & Betsey River RR #4. Rebuilt at Baldwin with Extra Order Plate #10750.
(e) First 37-44 repossessed during receivership of 1894. Sold to Canadian Pacific in 1898. CPR #497-504,1310-17,3110-17.
(f) Calumet & Blue Island #43 to EJ&E #503 and sold by J.G. Gardner 8/17 to Ann Arbor. Rented to the M&LS 3/20.
(g) First 47-48 returned to builder, rebuilt and sold to W&LE, 9/94, as #72 and #71.

Class F 4-6-0: Wabash H-1: 19x26-63-180-125000-22794

	41,100	120	Baldwin 16405	12/1898	Scr 4/51
	42,101	121	Baldwin 16406	12/1898	to stat. boiler, at Frankfort

Class F-1 4-6-0: Wabash H-2: 19x26-63-180-131240-22794

	43,102	130	Baldwin 16025	7/1898	Scr 11/44
	44,103	131	Baldwin 16026	7/1898	Scr 10/41

Class F-2 4-6-0: Wabash H-3: 19x26-63-180-140000-22794

	45,104	140	Pittsburgh 2162	10/1900	Scr 3/33
	46,105	141	Pittsburgh 2163	10/1900	Scr 8/40

Class F-3 4-6-0: Wabash H-4: 19x26-63-170-140000-21528

	47,106	140	Baldwin 19988	1/1902	Scr 11/28
	48,107	150	Baldwin 19989	1/1902	?
	49,108	151	Baldwin 21526	1/1903	Scr 3/51
	50,109	152	Baldwin 21570	1/1903	Scr 3/33
	51,110	153	Baldwin 23202	11/1903	Scr 12/48
	52,111	154	Baldwin 23212	11/1903	Scr 2/33

Class G 2-8-0: Wabash I-4: 22x30-57-200-216000-43305

	150	2170	Schenectady 45772	10/1908	Scr 7/51
	151	2171	Schenectady 45773	10/1908	Scr 7/51
	152	2172	Schenectady 45774	10/1908	Scr 7/51
	153	2173	Schenectady 45775	10/1908	Scr 12/50
	154	2174	Schenectady 45776	10/1908	Scr 11/50
	155	2175	Schenectady 45777	10/1908	Scr 11/50
	156	2176	Schenectady 45778	10/1908	Scr 6/48
	157	2177	Schenectady 45779	10/1908	Scr 7/51
	158	2178	Schenectady 45780	10/1908	Scr 9/40

Class G-1 2-8-0; Wabash I-5: 22x30-57-200-221000-43305

	159	2180	Schenectady	46212	12/1909	Scr	3/51
	160	2181	Schenectady	46213	12/1909	Scr	1/51
	161	2182	Schenectady	46214	12/1909	Scr	12/35
	162	2183	Schenectady	46215	12/1909	Scr	6/48

Class G-2 2-8-0; Wabash I-6: 25x30-57-180-231000-50328

	170	2350	Brooks	51507	1912	Scr	11/40
	171	2351	Brooks	51508	1912	Scr	10/40
	172	2352	Brooks	51509	1912	Scr	10/46

Class H 2-8-2; Wabash K-6: 27x30-63-185-294500-54588

	180	2480	Brooks	56592	12/1916	Scr	3/52
	181	2481	Brooks	56593	12/1916	Scr	3/52
	182	2482	Brooks	56594	12/1916	Scr	3/52

Class H-1 2-8-2; Wabash K-7: 27x30-63-200-298000-59014

	183	2490	Brooks	64308	7/1923	Scr	3/52
	184	2491	Brooks	64309	7/1923	Scr	7/51
	185	2492	Brooks	64310	7/1923	Scr	7/51
	186	2493	Brooks	64902	10/1923	Scr	7/51
	187	2494	Brooks	64903	10/1923	Scr	7/51

Class I 4-4-2; Wabash E-5: 19x26-69-200-161300-23125

	200	1610	Schenectady	43298	11/1907	Scr	11/36
	201	1611	Schenectady	43299	11/1907	Scr	2/51
	202	1612	Schenectady	43300	11/1907	Scr	1/51
	203	1613	Schenectady	43301	11/1907	Scr	12/33

Class I-1 4-4-2; Wabash E-6: 19x26-69-200-161300-23125

	204	1614	Schenectady	46202	6/1909	Scr	3/51

Class L 2-10-2; Wabash L-2: 27x32-57-200-352000-69575

	190	2550	Baldwin	52248	9/1919	So 9/42	KCS 220
	191	2551	Baldwin	52279	9/1919	So 9/42	KCS 221
	192	2552	Baldwin	52280	9/1919	So 9/42	KCS 222
	193	2553	Baldwin	52281	9/1919	So 9/42	KCS 223

Class U 0-8-0; Wabash C-2: 22½x28-51-190-200000-44887

	50	1520	Brooks	61984	9/1920	Scr	1/53
	51	1521	Brooks	61985	9/1920	Scr	8/52

General Note: Ann Arbor engines were renumbered and reclassed during 1932-1933 to fit in with Wabash numbers and classification. These engines continued to carry the Ann Arbor name although the Wabash paint scheme was adopted - name on cab and numbers on tender.

T&AA - Toledo & Ann Arbor   TAA&NM - Toledo Ann Arbor & North Michigan
AM - Alabama Midland   D&TSL - Detroit & Toledo Shore Line

Ann Arbor diesels
LE&FW, M&LS, NJI&I

Ann Arbor Number	Builder		New	Disposition

Class D-3 B-B Diesel Switcher: Whitcomb Model 44DE 22 386HP 85600 Wt.

1	Whitcomb	60035	1/1941	So 10/65 Dundee Cement Co. #951901

Class D-6 B-B Diesel Switcher: ALCO-GE Model S-1 660HP 198000 Wt.

2	ALCO	70051	7/1944	Traded 3/70 EMD
3	ALCO	71663	9/1944	Traded 3/70 EMD

Class D-6 B-B Diesel Switcher: ALCO-GE Model S-3 660HP 197750 Wt.

4	ALCO	78400	11/1950	Traded 3/70 EMD
5	ALCO	78401	11/1950	So '69 George Sillcott
6	ALCO	78402	11/1950	
7	ALCO	78403	11/1950	

Class D-6 B-B Diesel Switcher: ALCO-GE Model S-3 660HP 196210 Wt.

10	ALCO	80289	10/1952	Acquired 12/68 from M&LS #1

Class D-10 B-B Diesel Road Switcher: ALCO-GE Model RS-1 1000HP 240230 Wt. (MU)

20	ALCO	78374	11/1950	
21	ALCO	78375	11/1950	

Class D-32 B-B Diesel Freight: ALCO-GE Model FA-2 1600HP 243270 Wt.

50	ALCO	78379	12/1950	Traded '64 EMD
50A	ALCO	78380	12/1950	to Wabash 822 '63
51	ALCO	78381	12/1950	Traded '64 EMD
51A	ALCO	78382	12/1950	Traded '64 EMD
52	ALCO	78383	12/1950	Traded '64 EMD
52A	ALCO	78384	12/1950	to Wabash 820 '63
53	ALCO	78385	12/1950	Traded '64 EMD
53A	ALCO	78476	12/1950	Traded '64 EMD
54	ALCO	78477	12/1950	Traded '64 EMD
54A	ALCO	78478	12/1950	Traded '64 EMD
55	ALCO	78479	12/1950	to Wabash 823 '63
55A	ALCO	78480	12/1950	to Wabash 821 '63
56	ALCO	78481	12/1950	Traded '64 EMD
56A	ALCO	78482	12/1950	Traded '64 EMD

Class D-25 B-B Diesel Freight: EMD Model GP-35 2500HP 257500 Wt. on ALCO trucks

385	EMD	28991	1964
386	EMD	28992	1964
387	EMD	28993	1964
388	EMD	28994	1964
389	EMD	28995	1964
390	EMD	28996	1964
391	EMD	28997	1964
392	EMD	28998	1964
393	EMD	28999	1964
394	EMD	29000	1964

Class D-15 B-B Diesel Freight: EMD Model F-7A&B 1500HP 231460 Wt.
Acquired from Wabash '63; Traded '64 on D-25 units

601	EMD	7617	8/'1949	ex Wabash 601,1101B
614	EMD	7614	8/'1949	ex Wab. 614,1102A
620	EMD	7623	8/'1949	ex Wabash 620,1105A
713	EMD	17068	9/'1952	ex Wabash 713,1183

****

LAKE ERIE & FORT WAYNE RAILROAD

Locomotive Roster

LE&FW No.	Date Acq.	Type	Specs	Builder		New	
1st 1	'06	0-4-0	15x24-46	Brooks	480	12/1880	ex LSMS 4080, orig. LE&W 42
2nd 1	'52	0-6-0	21x26-52-154040	Rhode Isl.	41174	8/1906	ex Wab. 534 (a)
3rd 1	'57	DE Sw.	660HP 198000	Baldwin	62497	7/1941	ex Wab. 200 (b)
1st 2	'06	0-4-0	14x22-50	Cooke		1870	ex LSMS 4082, ex LE&W 63, orig. IP&C 15
2nd 2	'09	0-6-0	18x24-52-85000	LS&MS?		1885?	ex LSMS 4348, 266 B-52
3	'13	0-6-0	17x24-44-169300	Lima	1324	1913	(c)
?	'29	0-6-0	18x24-52-102000	Rhode Isl.	3148	11/1899	ex Wab. 501

Note - LE&FtW was formerly the Fort Wayne Rolling Mill RR.

(a) Retired 3/57, placed on permanent exhibition. See B-7 Class Note (c).
(b) Retired 5/68, thereafter switching was done by the Nickel Plate.
(c) Sold ca. 1930 to Northern Indiana Gravel Co. (Wolcottville, Ind.).

****

MANISTIQUE & LAKE SUPERIOR RAILROAD

Locomotive Roster

M&LS No.	Type	Specs.	Builder		New	
1	2-6-0	15x24-50	Baldwin	8120	9/1886	ex Manistique Ry. 1
2	2-6-0	15x24-50	Baldwin	9083	2/1888	ex Manistique Ry. 2
3	2-6-0	16x24-50	Baldwin	10892	5/1890	ex Manistique Ry. 3
4	2-6-0	16x24-50	Baldwin	15307	4/1897	ex Manistique Ry. 4
5	?					
6	?					
7	?					
8	2-8-0	19x24-50	(Baldwin	18777	3/1901)	ex Atlantic Min.Co. 8 ren.2380 I-9, Scr '51
9	4-6-0	18x24-54-90000	(Baldwin	10576	1/1890)	ex Ann Arbor 75,Acq.6/13
10	4-6-0	18x24-54-90000	(Baldwin	10577	1/1890)	ex Ann Arbor 76,Acq.8/13
11	2-8-0	20x24-51	(Baldwin	12509	2/1892)	ex Ann Arbor 140,Acq.3/20 ren.2375 I-8
12	2-8-0	18x24-51-106000	(Baldwin	14348	7/1895)	ex Ann Arbor 125,Acq.3/20 ren.2139,2370 I-7, Scr '51
13	2-8-0	20x28-50-148000	(Pitts.	1615	6/1896)	ex LS&I 13, (a) ren. 2390 I-10
1	B-B (S-3)	660HP 196210	ALCO-GE	80289	10/1952	ren. AA10 in 12/68

(a) M&LS #13 is uncertain. The engine may have been ren. from LS&I #13 to #2390. Purchased by M&LS in 1951. Destroyed in roundhouse fire in 1952 and scrapped 1953.

****

NEW JERSEY INDIANA & ILLINOIS RAILWAY

Locomotive Roster

NJI&I No.	Date Acq.	Type	Specs	Builder		New	
1							
2							
3		2-6-0	120000	ALCO-B	54537	1/1914	'31 Binkley Coal Co.
4							
5	'02	4-4-0					ex Penn.
6	'28	2-6-0	19x28-64-123525	Rhode Isl.	3144	10/1899	ex Wab. 582
7	'28	2-6-0	19x28-64-123525	Rhode Isl.	3142	10/1899	ex Wab. 589
8	'29	2-6-0	19x28-64-149524	Richmond	3241	1901	ex Wab. 805

In addition to the above, F-7 826 was assigned to the NJI&I, replaced by F-7 817 in 1942 but neither engine was renumbered.

Diesels

1	'40	S-1	660HP 198000	Schen.	69196	6/1940	to Wab. 2 '61
2	'59	NW-2	1000HP 247000	EMD	7898	5/1948	(a)

(a) ex Ind. Nor. #100, (to NJI&I #2), to Wabash #353.

****

General arrangement drawings of steam, diesel locomotives and miscellaneous

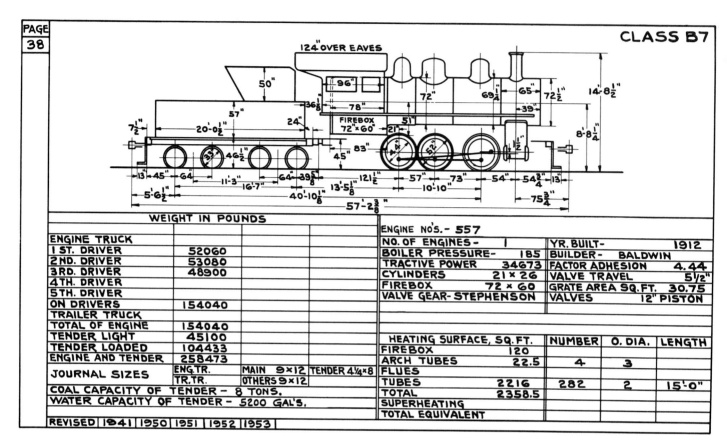

CLASS B7

124" OVER EAVES

FIREBOX 72"×60"

WEIGHT IN POUNDS			
ENGINE TRUCK			
1ST. DRIVER	52060		
2ND. DRIVER	53080		
3RD. DRIVER	48900		
4TH. DRIVER			
5TH. DRIVER			
ON DRIVERS	154040		
TRAILER TRUCK			
TOTAL OF ENGINE	154040		
TENDER LIGHT	45100		
TENDER LOADED	104433		
ENGINE AND TENDER	258473		
JOURNAL SIZES	ENG.TR.	MAIN 9×12	TENDER 4¼×8
	TR.TR.	OTHERS 9×12	
COAL CAPACITY OF TENDER - 8 TONS.			
WATER CAPACITY OF TENDER - 5200 GAL'S.			

ENGINE NO'S. - 557

NO. OF ENGINES -	1	YR. BUILT-	1912
BOILER PRESSURE-	185	BUILDER- BALDWIN	
TRACTIVE POWER	34673	FACTOR ADHESION	4.44
CYLINDERS	21×26	VALVE TRAVEL	5½"
FIREBOX	72×60	GRATE AREA SQ.FT.	30.75
VALVE GEAR- STEPHENSON		VALVES	12" PISTON

HEATING SURFACE, SQ. FT.		NUMBER	O. DIA.	LENGTH
FIREBOX	120			
ARCH TUBES	22.5	4	3	
FLUES				
TUBES	2216	282	2	15'-0"
TOTAL	2358.5			
SUPERHEATING				
TOTAL EQUIVALENT				

REVISED | 1941 | 1950 | 1951 | 1952 | 1953

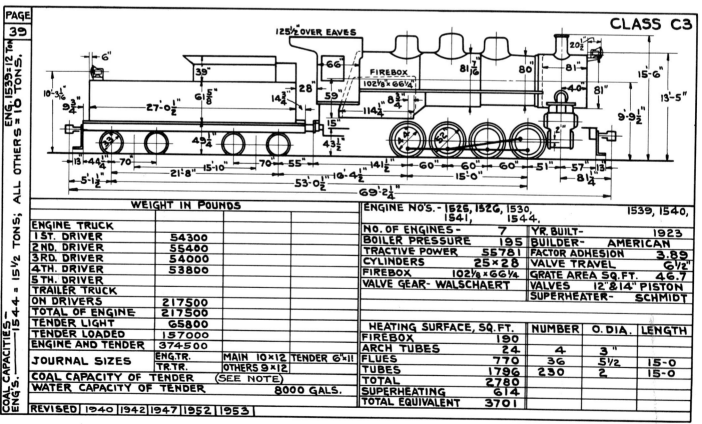

CLASS C3

125½" OVER EAVES

FIREBOX 102⅛×66¼"

COAL CAPACITIES- ENG'S.- 1544 = 15½ TONS; ALL OTHERS = 16 TONS. ENG. 1539=12 TONS.

WEIGHT IN POUNDS			
ENGINE TRUCK			
1ST. DRIVER	54300		
2ND. DRIVER	55400		
3RD. DRIVER	54000		
4TH. DRIVER	53800		
5TH. DRIVER			
TRAILER TRUCK			
ON DRIVERS	217500		
TOTAL OF ENGINE	217500		
TENDER LIGHT	65800		
TENDER LOADED	157000		
ENGINE AND TENDER	374500		
JOURNAL SIZES	ENG.TR.	MAIN 10×12	TENDER 6"×11
	TR.TR.	OTHERS 9×12	
COAL CAPACITY OF TENDER		(SEE NOTE)	
WATER CAPACITY OF TENDER			8000 GALS.

ENGINE NO'S. - 1525, 1526, 1530, 1541, 1544. 1539, 1540,

NO. OF ENGINES -	7	YR. BUILT-	1923
BOILER PRESSURE	195	BUILDER- AMERICAN	
TRACTIVE POWER	55781	FACTOR ADHESION	3.89
CYLINDERS	25×28	VALVE TRAVEL	6½"
FIREBOX	102⅛×66¼	GRATE AREA SQ.FT.	46.7
VALVE GEAR- WALSCHAERT		VALVES	12"&14" PISTON
		SUPERHEATER-	SCHMIDT

HEATING SURFACE, SQ. FT.		NUMBER	O. DIA.	LENGTH
FIREBOX	190			
ARCH TUBES	24	4	3 "	
FLUES	770	36	5½	15-0
TUBES	1796	230	2	15-0
TOTAL	2780			
SUPERHEATING	614			
TOTAL EQUIVALENT	3701			

REVISED | 1940 | 1942 | 1947 | 1952 | 1953

NOTE- THESE ENGINES HAVE BUILT-UP TENDER FRAMES AND COMMONWEALTH TENDER TRUCKS.

CLASS E4

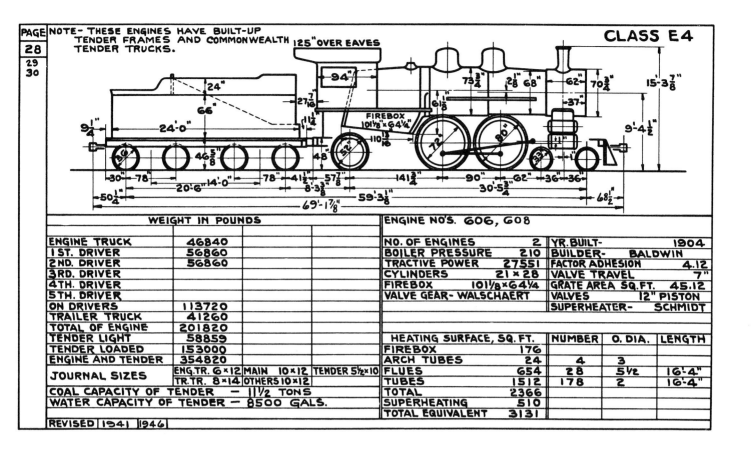

WEIGHT IN POUNDS				ENGINE NO'S. 606, 608			
ENGINE TRUCK	46840			NO. OF ENGINES	2	YR.BUILT-	1904
1ST. DRIVER	56860			BOILER PRESSURE	210	BUILDER-	BALDWIN
2ND. DRIVER	56860			TRACTIVE POWER	27551	FACTOR ADHESION	4.12
3RD. DRIVER				CYLINDERS	21×28	VALVE TRAVEL	7"
4TH. DRIVER				FIREBOX	101⅛×64¼	GRATE AREA SQ.FT.	45.12
5TH. DRIVER				VALVE GEAR- WALSCHAERT		VALVES	12" PISTON
ON DRIVERS	113720					SUPERHEATER-	SCHMIDT
TRAILER TRUCK	41260						
TOTAL OF ENGINE	201820						
TENDER LIGHT	58859			HEATING SURFACE, SQ. FT.		NUMBER	O. DIA.	LENGTH
TENDER LOADED	153000			FIREBOX	176			
ENGINE AND TENDER	354820			ARCH TUBES	24	4	3	
JOURNAL SIZES	ENG.TR. 6×12	MAIN 10×12	TENDER 5½×10	FLUES	654	28	5½	16'-4"
	TR.TR. 8×14	OTHERS 10×12		TUBES	1512	178	2	16'-4"
COAL CAPACITY OF TENDER — 11½ TONS				TOTAL	2366			
WATER CAPACITY OF TENDER — 8500 GALS.				SUPERHEATING	510			
				TOTAL EQUIVALENT	3131			

REVISED 1941 1946

CLASS F4

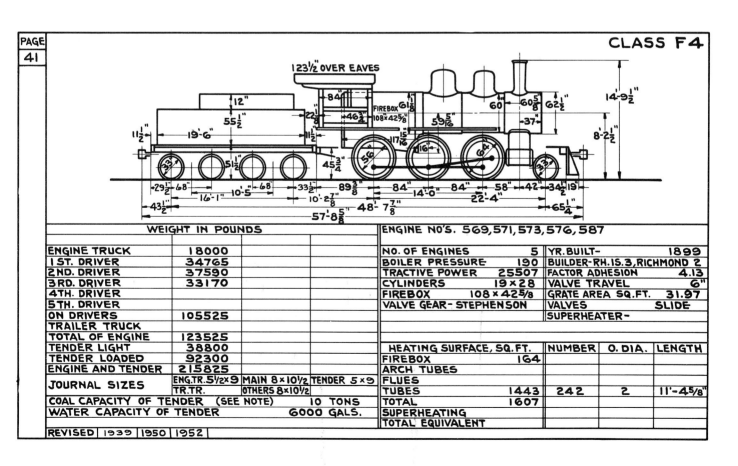

WEIGHT IN POUNDS				ENGINE NO'S. 569,571,573,576,587			
ENGINE TRUCK	18000			NO. OF ENGINES	5	YR.BUILT-	1899
1ST. DRIVER	34765			BOILER PRESSURE	190	BUILDER-RH.15.3,RICHMOND 2	
2ND. DRIVER	37590			TRACTIVE POWER	25507	FACTOR ADHESION	4.13
3RD. DRIVER	33170			CYLINDERS	19×28	VALVE TRAVEL	6"
4TH. DRIVER				FIREBOX	108×42⅝	GRATE AREA SQ.FT.	31.97
5TH. DRIVER				VALVE GEAR- STEPHENSON		VALVES	SLIDE
ON DRIVERS	105525					SUPERHEATER-	
TRAILER TRUCK							
TOTAL OF ENGINE	123525						
TENDER LIGHT	38800			HEATING SURFACE, SQ.FT.		NUMBER	O. DIA.	LENGTH
TENDER LOADED	92300			FIREBOX	164			
ENGINE AND TENDER	215825			ARCH TUBES				
JOURNAL SIZES	ENG.TR. 5½×9	MAIN 8×10½	TENDER 5×9	FLUES				
	TR.TR.	OTHERS 8×10½		TUBES	1443	242	2	11'-4⅝"
COAL CAPACITY OF TENDER (SEE NOTE) 10 TONS				TOTAL	1607			
WATER CAPACITY OF TENDER 6000 GALS.				SUPERHEATING				
				TOTAL EQUIVALENT				

REVISED 1939 1950 1952

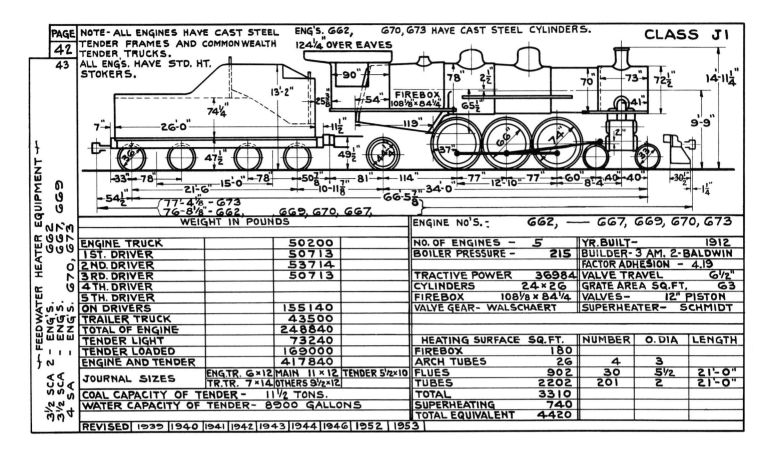

CLASS J1

NOTE- ALL ENGINES HAVE CAST STEEL TENDER FRAMES AND COMMONWEALTH TENDER TRUCKS. ALL ENGS. HAVE STD. HT. STOKERS.

ENG'S. G62, G70, G73 HAVE CAST STEEL CYLINDERS.

124¼" OVER EAVES

FIREBOX 108⅛ × 84¼

77'-4⅞ - G73
76'-8⅛ - G62, G69, G70, G67,

FEEDWATER HEATER EQUIPMENT —
2 — ENG'S. G62, G67, G69
2 — ENG'S. G70, G73
3½ SCA
3½ SCA
4 SA

WEIGHT IN POUNDS		
ENGINE TRUCK	50200	
1ST. DRIVER	50713	
2ND. DRIVER	53714	
3RD. DRIVER	50713	
4TH. DRIVER		
5TH. DRIVER		
ON DRIVERS	155140	
TRAILER TRUCK	43500	
TOTAL OF ENGINE	248840	
TENDER LIGHT	73240	
TENDER LOADED	169000	
ENGINE AND TENDER	417840	
JOURNAL SIZES	ENG.TR. 6×12 MAIN 11×12	TENDER 5½×10
	TR.TR. 7×14 OTHERS 9½×12	
COAL CAPACITY OF TENDER - 11½ TONS.		
WATER CAPACITY OF TENDER- 8900 GALLONS		

ENGINE NO'S.: G62, — G67, G69, G70, G73

NO. OF ENGINES - 5		YR. BUILT- 1912	
BOILER PRESSURE - 215		BUILDER- 3 AM. 2- BALDWIN	
		FACTOR ADHESION - 4.19	
TRACTIVE POWER 36984		VALVE TRAVEL 6½"	
CYLINDERS 24×26		GRATE AREA SQ.FT. 63	
FIREBOX 108⅛×84¼		VALVES- 12" PISTON	
VALVE GEAR- WALSCHAERT		SUPERHEATER- SCHMIDT	

HEATING SURFACE SQ. FT.		NUMBER	O. DIA	LENGTH
FIREBOX	180			
ARCH TUBES	26	4	3	
FLUES	902	30	5½	21'-0"
TUBES	2202	201	2	21'-0"
TOTAL	3310			
SUPERHEATING	740			
TOTAL EQUIVALENT	4420			

REVISED | 1939 | 1940 | 1941 | 1942 | 1943 | 1944 | 1946 | 1952 | 1953

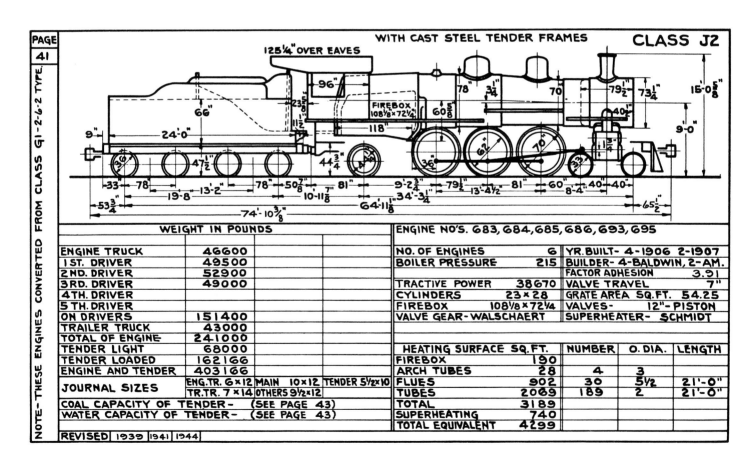

CLASS J2

WITH CAST STEEL TENDER FRAMES

125¼" OVER EAVES

FIREBOX 108⅛ × 72¼

NOTE-THESE ENGINES CONVERTED FROM CLASS G1-2-6-2 TYPE.

WEIGHT IN POUNDS		
ENGINE TRUCK	46600	
1ST. DRIVER	49500	
2ND. DRIVER	52900	
3RD. DRIVER	49000	
4TH. DRIVER		
5TH. DRIVER		
ON DRIVERS	151400	
TRAILER TRUCK	43000	
TOTAL OF ENGINE	241000	
TENDER LIGHT	68000	
TENDER LOADED	162166	
ENGINE AND TENDER	403166	
JOURNAL SIZES	ENG.TR. 6×12 MAIN 10×12	TENDER 5½×10
	TR.TR. 7×14 OTHERS 9½×12	
COAL CAPACITY OF TENDER - (SEE PAGE 43)		
WATER CAPACITY OF TENDER - (SEE PAGE 43)		

ENGINE NO'S. 683, 684, 685, 686, 693, 695

NO. OF ENGINES 6		YR. BUILT- 4-1906 2-1907	
BOILER PRESSURE 215		BUILDER- 4-BALDWIN, 2-AM.	
		FACTOR ADHESION 3.91	
TRACTIVE POWER 38670		VALVE TRAVEL 7"	
CYLINDERS 23×28		GRATE AREA SQ.FT. 54.25	
FIREBOX 108⅛×72¼		VALVES- 12"- PISTON	
VALVE GEAR-WALSCHAERT		SUPERHEATER- SCHMIDT	

HEATING SURFACE SQ.FT.		NUMBER	O. DIA.	LENGTH
FIREBOX	190			
ARCH TUBES	28	4	3	
FLUES	902	30	5½	21'-0"
TUBES	2069	189	2	21'-0"
TOTAL	3189			
SUPERHEATING	740			
TOTAL EQUIVALENT	4299			

REVISED | 1939 | 1941 | 1944

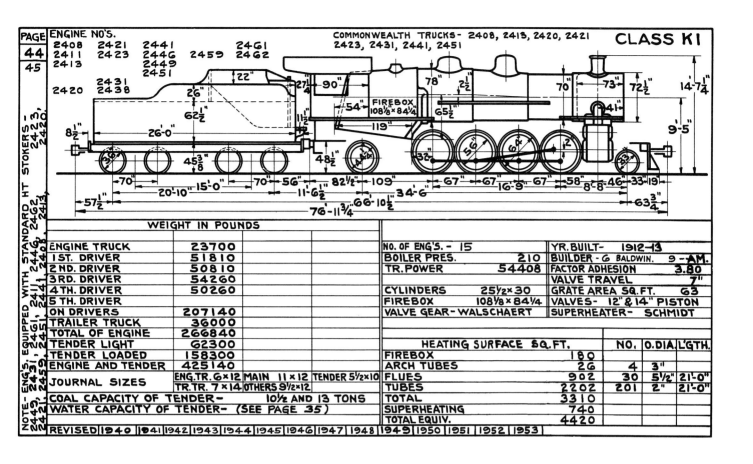

PAGE 44 45

ENGINE NO'S.
2408 2421 2441 2461
2411 2423 2446 2459 2462
2413 2449
2451
2431
2420 2438

COMMONWEALTH TRUCKS- 2408, 2413, 2420, 2421
2423, 2431, 2441, 2451

CLASS K1

NOTE- ENG'S. EQUIPPED WITH STANDARD HT STOKERS - 2449, 2431, 2461, 2411, 2446, 2462, 2423, 2421, 2459, 2451, 2441, 2408, 2413, 2420.

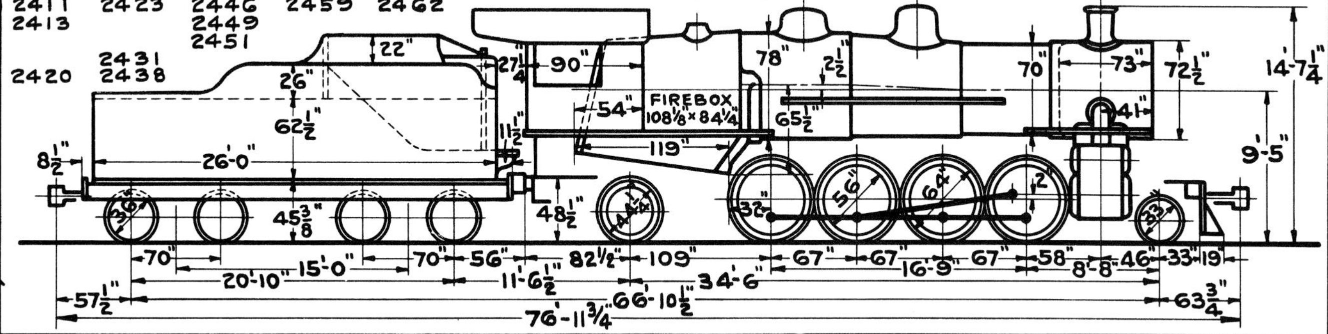

WEIGHT IN POUNDS			
ENGINE TRUCK	23700		
1ST. DRIVER	51810		
2ND. DRIVER	50810		
3RD. DRIVER	54260		
4TH. DRIVER	50260		
5TH. DRIVER			
ON DRIVERS	207140		
TRAILER TRUCK	36000		
TOTAL OF ENGINE	266840		
TENDER LIGHT	62300		
TENDER LOADED	158300		
ENGINE AND TENDER	425140		
JOURNAL SIZES	ENG.TR. 6×12	MAIN 11×12	TENDER 5½×10
	TR.TR. 7×14	OTHERS 9½×12	
COAL CAPACITY OF TENDER-	10½ AND 13 TONS		
WATER CAPACITY OF TENDER- (SEE PAGE 35)			

NO. OF ENG'S. - 15		YR. BUILT-	1912-13
BOILER PRES.	210	BUILDER - G BALDWIN.	9 - AM.
TR. POWER	54408	FACTOR ADHESION	3.80
		VALVE TRAVEL	7"
CYLINDERS	25½×30	GRATE AREA SQ.FT.	63
FIREBOX	108⅛×84¼	VALVES-	12" & 14" PISTON
VALVE GEAR- WALSCHAERT		SUPERHEATER-	SCHMIDT

HEATING SURFACE SQ.FT.		NO.	O.DIA.	L'GTH.
FIREBOX	180			
ARCH TUBES	26	4	3"	
FLUES	902	30	5½"	21'-0"
TUBES	2202	201	2"	21'-0"
TOTAL	3310			
SUPERHEATING	740			
TOTAL EQUIV.	4420			

REVISED | 1940 | 1941 | 1942 | 1943 | 1944 | 1945 | 1946 | 1947 | 1948 | 1949 | 1950 | 1951 | 1952 | 1953

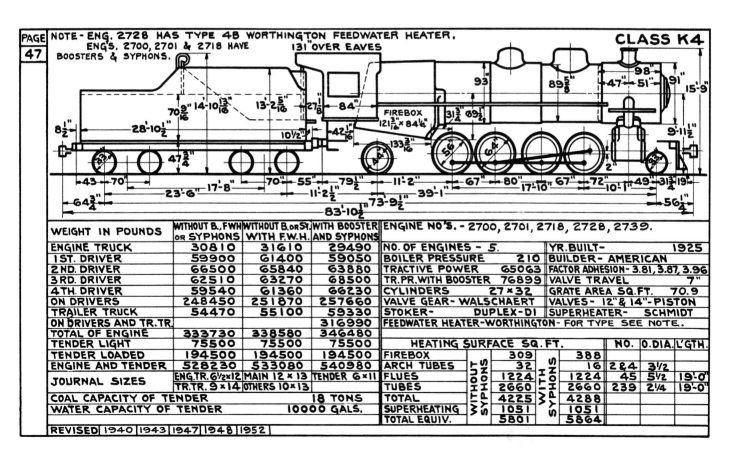

PAGE 47

NOTE - ENG. 2728 HAS TYPE 4B WORTHINGTON FEEDWATER HEATER.
ENG'S. 2700, 2701 & 2718 HAVE BOOSTERS & SYPHONS.

CLASS K4

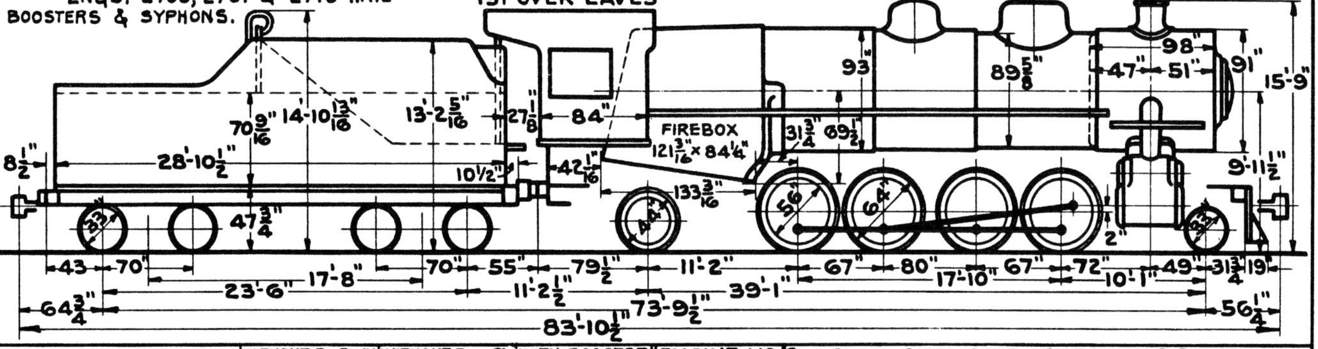

WEIGHT IN POUNDS	WITHOUT B., FWH OR SYPHONS	WITHOUT B. OR SY. WITH F.W.H.	WITH BOOSTER AND SYPHONS
ENGINE TRUCK	30810	31610	29490
1ST. DRIVER	59900	61400	59050
2ND. DRIVER	66500	65840	63880
3RD. DRIVER	62510	63270	68500
4TH. DRIVER	59540	61360	66230
ON DRIVERS	248450	251870	257660
TRAILER TRUCK	54470	55100	59330
ON DRIVERS AND TR.TR.			316990
TOTAL OF ENGINE	333730	338580	346480
TENDER LIGHT	75500	75500	75500
TENDER LOADED	194500	194500	194500
ENGINE AND TENDER	528230	533080	540980
JOURNAL SIZES	ENG.TR. 6½×12	MAIN 12×13	TENDER 6×11
	TR.TR. 9×14	OTHERS 10×13	
COAL CAPACITY OF TENDER		18 TONS	
WATER CAPACITY OF TENDER		10000 GALS.	

ENGINE NO'S. - 2700, 2701, 2718, 2728, 2739.

NO. OF ENGINES - 5.		YR. BUILT-	1925
BOILER PRESSURE	210	BUILDER- AMERICAN	
TRACTIVE POWER	65063	FACTOR ADHESION-	3.81, 3.87, 3.96
TR.PR. WITH BOOSTER	76899	VALVE TRAVEL	7"
CYLINDERS	27×32	GRATE AREA SQ.FT.	70.9
VALVE GEAR- WALSCHAERT		VALVES-	12" & 14"-PISTON
STOKER-	DUPLEX-D1	SUPERHEATER-	SCHMIDT
FEEDWATER HEATER-WORTHINGTON- FOR TYPE SEE NOTE.			

HEATING SURFACE SQ.FT.	WITHOUT SYPHONS	WITH SYPHONS	NO.	O.DIA.	L'GTH.
FIREBOX	309	388			
ARCH TUBES	32	16	2&4	3½	
FLUES	1224	1224	45	5½	19'-0"
TUBES	2660	2660	239	2¼	19'-0"
TOTAL	4225	4288			
SUPERHEATING	1051	1051			
TOTAL EQUIV.	5801	5864			

REVISED | 1940 | 1943 | 1947 | 1948 | 1952

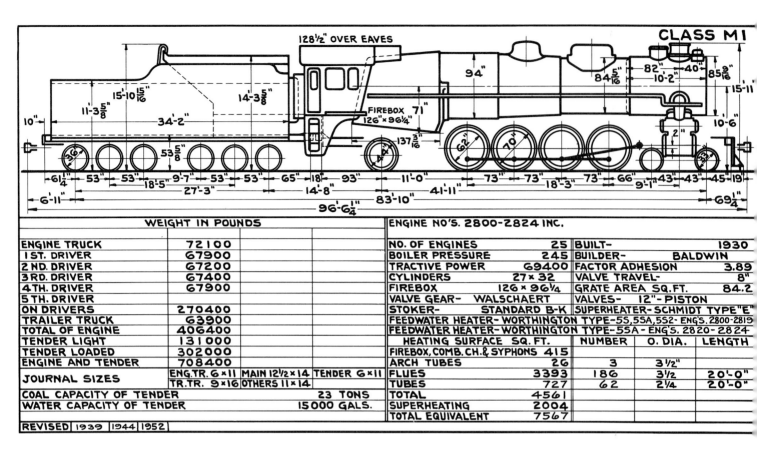

CLASS M1

WEIGHT IN POUNDS		
ENGINE TRUCK	72100	
1ST. DRIVER	67900	
2ND. DRIVER	67200	
3RD. DRIVER	67400	
4TH. DRIVER	67900	
5TH. DRIVER		
ON DRIVERS	270400	
TRAILER TRUCK	63900	
TOTAL OF ENGINE	406400	
TENDER LIGHT	131000	
TENDER LOADED	302000	
ENGINE AND TENDER	708400	
JOURNAL SIZES	ENG.TR. 6×11 MAIN 12½×14	TENDER 6×11
	TR.TR. 9×16 OTHERS 11×14	
COAL CAPACITY OF TENDER		23 TONS
WATER CAPACITY OF TENDER		15000 GALS.

REVISED 1939 1944 1952

ENGINE NO'S. 2800-2824 INC.

NO. OF ENGINES	25	BUILT-	1930
BOILER PRESSURE	245	BUILDER-	BALDWIN
TRACTIVE POWER	69400	FACTOR ADHESION	3.89
CYLINDERS	27×32	VALVE TRAVEL-	8"
FIREBOX	126×96¼	GRATE AREA SQ.FT.	84.2
VALVE GEAR-	WALSCHAERT	VALVES-	12"-PISTON
STOKER-	STANDARD B-K	SUPERHEATER-SCHMIDT TYPE "E"	
FEEDWATER HEATER-WORTHINGTON TYPE-5S,5SA,5S2- ENGS.2800-2819			
FEEDWATER HEATER-WORTHINGTON TYPE-5SA - ENG'S. 2820-2824			

HEATING SURFACE SQ. FT.	NUMBER	O. DIA.	LENGTH
FIREBOX,COMB. CH.& SYPHONS 415			
ARCH TUBES 26	3	3½"	
FLUES 3393	186	3½	20'-0"
TUBES 727	62	2¼	20'-0"
TOTAL 4561			
SUPERHEATING 2004			
TOTAL EQUIVALENT 7567			

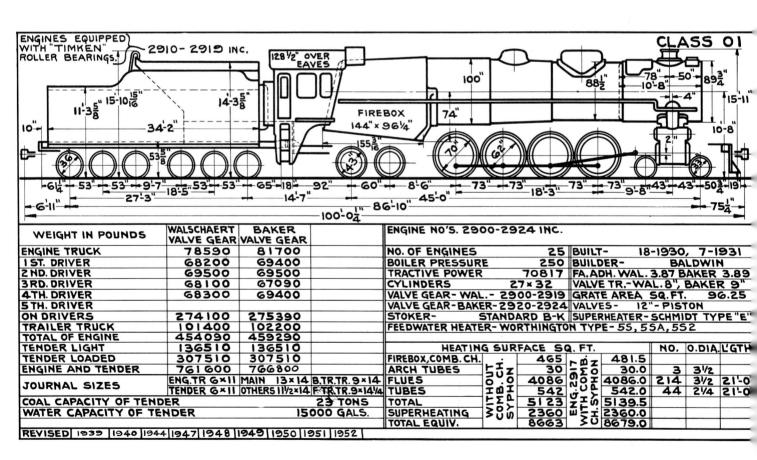

ENGINES EQUIPPED WITH "TIMKEN" ROLLER BEARINGS. 2910-2919 INC.

CLASS O1

WEIGHT IN POUNDS	WALSCHAERT VALVE GEAR	BAKER VALVE GEAR	
ENGINE TRUCK	78590	81700	
1ST. DRIVER	68200	69400	
2ND. DRIVER	69500	69500	
3RD. DRIVER	68100	67090	
4TH. DRIVER	68300	69400	
5TH. DRIVER			
ON DRIVERS	274100	275390	
TRAILER TRUCK	101400	102200	
TOTAL OF ENGINE	454090	459290	
TENDER LIGHT	136510	136510	
TENDER LOADED	307510	307510	
ENGINE AND TENDER	761600	766800	
JOURNAL SIZES	ENG.TR 6×11 MAIN 13×14	B.TR.TR. 9×14	
	TENDER 6×11 OTHERS 11½×14	F.TR.TR.9×14¼	
COAL CAPACITY OF TENDER			23 TONS
WATER CAPACITY OF TENDER			15000 GALS.

REVISED 1939 1940 1944 1947 1948 1949 1950 1951 1952

ENGINE NO'S. 2900-2924 INC.

NO. OF ENGINES	25	BUILT-	18-1930, 7-1931
BOILER PRESSURE	250	BUILDER-	BALDWIN
TRACTIVE POWER	70817	FA. ADH. WAL. 3.87 BAKER 3.89	
CYLINDERS	27×32	VALVE TR.-WAL.8", BAKER 9"	
VALVE GEAR- WAL.- 2900-2919		GRATE AREA SQ.FT.	96.25
VALVE GEAR-BAKER-2920-2924		VALVES-	12"-PISTON
STOKER-	STANDARD B-K	SUPERHEATER-SCHMIDT TYPE "E"	
FEEDWATER HEATER-WORTHINGTON TYPE- 5S, 5SA, 5S2			

HEATING SURFACE SQ. FT.	WITHOUT COMB.CH. SYPHON	ENG.2917 WITH COMB. CH. SYPHON	NO.	O.DIA.	L'GTH
FIREBOX, COMB. CH.	465	481.5			
ARCH TUBES	30	30.0	3	3½	
FLUES	4086	4086.0	214	3½	21'-0
TUBES	542	542.0	44	2¼	21'-0
TOTAL	5123	5139.5			
SUPERHEATING	2360	2360.0			
TOTAL EQUIV.	8663	8679.0			

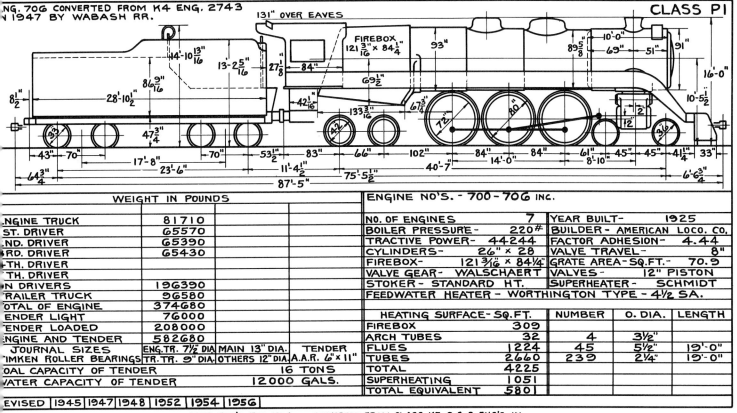

ENG. 70G CONVERTED FROM K4 ENG. 2743 IN 1947 BY WABASH RR.

WEIGHT IN POUNDS	
ENGINE TRUCK	81710
1ST. DRIVER	65570
2ND. DRIVER	65390
3RD. DRIVER	65430
4TH. DRIVER	
5TH. DRIVER	
ON DRIVERS	196390
TRAILER TRUCK	96580
TOTAL OF ENGINE	374680
TENDER LIGHT	76000
TENDER LOADED	208000
ENGINE AND TENDER	582680
JOURNAL SIZES	ENG.TR. 7½ DIA MAIN 13" DIA. TENDER
TIMKEN ROLLER BEARINGS	TR.TR. 9" DIA. OTHERS 12" DIA. A.A.R. 6"x 11"
COAL CAPACITY OF TENDER	16 TONS
WATER CAPACITY OF TENDER	12000 GALS.

REVISED 1945 1947 1948 1952 1954 1956

ENGINE NO'S. - 700-70G INC.			
NO. OF ENGINES	7	YEAR BUILT-	1925
BOILER PRESSURE-	220#	BUILDER- AMERICAN LOCO. CO.	
TRACTIVE POWER-	44244	FACTOR ADHESION-	4.44
CYLINDERS-	26" x 28	VALVE TRAVEL-	8"
FIREBOX-	121 3/16 x 84¼	GRATE AREA-SQ.FT.-	70.9
VALVE GEAR- WALSCHAERT		VALVES-	12" PISTON
STOKER- STANDARD HT.		SUPERHEATER-	SCHMIDT
FEEDWATER HEATER - WORTHINGTON TYPE - 4½ SA.			

HEATING SURFACE-SQ.FT.		NUMBER	O. DIA.	LENGTH
FIREBOX	309			
ARCH TUBES	32	4	3½"	
FLUES	1224	45	5½"	19'-0"
TUBES	2660	239	2¼"	19'-0"
TOTAL	4225			
SUPERHEATING	1051			
TOTAL EQUIVALENT	5801			

NOTE- ENG'S. 700-704 INC. CONVERTED FROM CLASS K5 2-8-2 ENG'S. IN 1943-44. ENG. 705 CONVERTED FROM CLASS K4 2-8-2 ENG. 2744 IN 1946 BY WABASH RR.

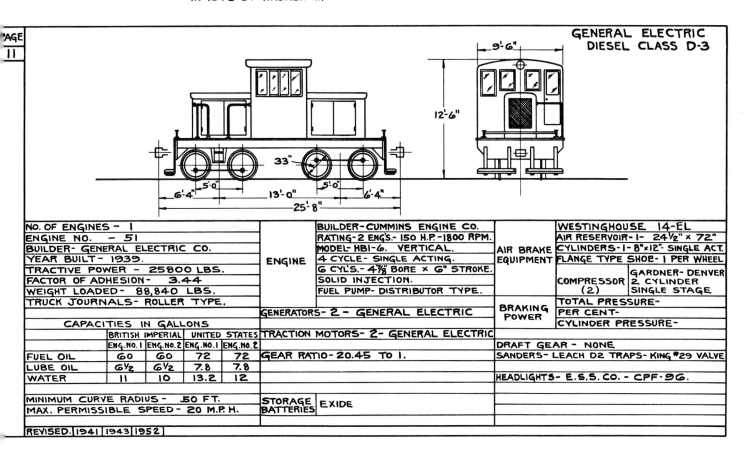

GENERAL ELECTRIC DIESEL CLASS D-3

NO. OF ENGINES - 1					
ENGINE NO. - 51					
BUILDER- GENERAL ELECTRIC CO.					
YEAR BUILT - 1939.					
TRACTIVE POWER - 25800 LBS.					
FACTOR OF ADHESION- 3.44					
WEIGHT LOADED- 88,840 LBS.					
TRUCK JOURNALS- ROLLER TYPE.					

ENGINE	BUILDER-CUMMINS ENGINE CO.
	RATING-2 ENG'S.- 150 H.P. -1800 RPM.
	MODEL- HBI-6. VERTICAL.
	4 CYCLE- SINGLE ACTING.
	6 CYL'S.- 4⅞ BORE x 6" STROKE.
	SOLID INJECTION.
	FUEL PUMP- DISTRIBUTOR TYPE.

GENERATORS- 2 - GENERAL ELECTRIC

TRACTION MOTORS- 2- GENERAL ELECTRIC

GEAR RATIO- 20.45 TO 1.

CAPACITIES IN GALLONS				
	BRITISH IMPERIAL		UNITED STATES	
	ENG.NO.1	ENG.NO.2	ENG.NO.1	ENG.NO.2
FUEL OIL	60	60	72	72
LUBE OIL	6½	6½	7.8	7.8
WATER	11	10	13.2	12

MINIMUM CURVE RADIUS - 50 FT.
MAX. PERMISSIBLE SPEED - 20 M.P.H.

STORAGE BATTERIES - EXIDE

AIR BRAKE EQUIPMENT	WESTINGHOUSE 14-EL
	AIR RESERVOIR- 1- 24½" x 72"
	CYLINDERS-1- 8"x12"- SINGLE ACT.
	FLANGE TYPE SHOE- 1 PER WHEEL

COMPRESSOR (2)	GARDNER- DENVER 2 CYLINDER SINGLE STAGE

BRAKING POWER	TOTAL PRESSURE-
	PER CENT-
	CYLINDER PRESSURE-

DRAFT GEAR - NONE
SANDERS- LEACH D2 TRAPS- KING #29 VALVE

HEADLIGHTS- E.S.S. CO. - CPF-9G.

REVISED. 1941 1943 1952

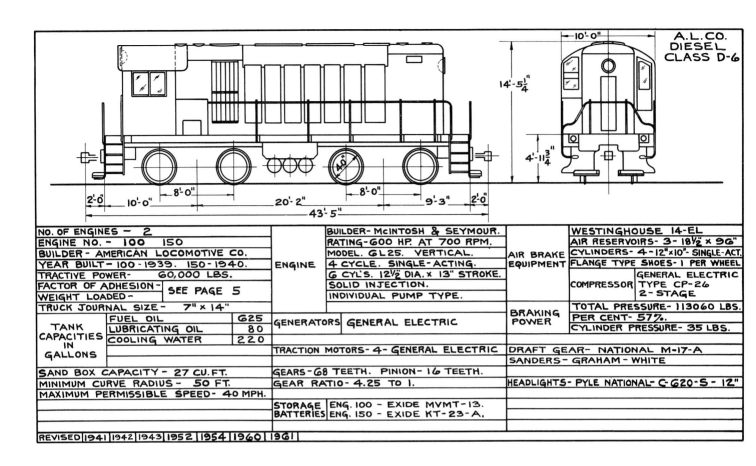

NO. OF ENGINES – 2	ENGINE	BUILDER– McINTOSH & SEYMOUR.	AIR BRAKE EQUIPMENT	WESTINGHOUSE 14-EL
ENGINE NO. – 100 150		RATING–600 HP. AT 700 RPM.		AIR RESERVOIRS– 3–18½" x 96"
BUILDER– AMERICAN LOCOMOTIVE CO.		MODEL. GL25. VERTICAL.		CYLINDERS– 4–12"x10"– SINGLE-ACT.
YEAR BUILT– 100-1939. 150-1940.		4 CYCLE. SINGLE-ACTING.		FLANGE TYPE SHOES– 1 PER WHEEL
TRACTIVE POWER– 60,000 LBS.		6 CYL'S. 12½ DIA. x 13" STROKE.	COMPRESSOR	GENERAL ELECTRIC TYPE CP-26 2-STAGE
FACTOR OF ADHESION– SEE PAGE 5		SOLID INJECTION.		
WEIGHT LOADED–		INDIVIDUAL PUMP TYPE.		
TRUCK JOURNAL SIZE– 7" x 14"			BRAKING POWER	TOTAL PRESSURE– 113060 LBS.
TANK CAPACITIES IN GALLONS	FUEL OIL 625	GENERATORS GENERAL ELECTRIC		PER CENT– 57%.
	LUBRICATING OIL 80			CYLINDER PRESSURE– 35 LBS.
	COOLING WATER 220			
		TRACTION MOTORS– 4– GENERAL ELECTRIC	DRAFT GEAR– NATIONAL M-17-A	
SAND BOX CAPACITY – 27 CU. FT.		GEARS–68 TEETH. PINION– 16 TEETH.	SANDERS– GRAHAM– WHITE	
MINIMUM CURVE RADIUS – 50 FT.		GEAR RATIO– 4.25 TO 1.	HEADLIGHTS– PYLE NATIONAL– C-620-S – 12"	
MAXIMUM PERMISSIBLE SPEED– 40 MPH.				
		STORAGE BATTERIES	ENG. 100 – EXIDE MVMT–13.	
			ENG. 150 – EXIDE KT-23-A.	

REVISED|1941|1942|1943|1952|1954|1960|1961|

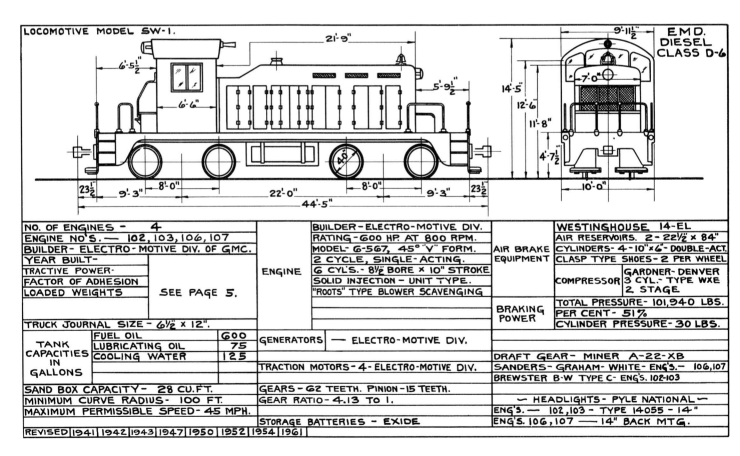

LOCOMOTIVE MODEL SW-1.

NO. OF ENGINES – 4	ENGINE	BUILDER– ELECTRO-MOTIVE DIV.	AIR BRAKE EQUIPMENT	WESTINGHOUSE 14-EL
ENGINE NO'S.– 102,103,106,107		RATING–600 HP. AT 800 RPM.		AIR RESERVOIRS. 2–22½" x 84"
BUILDER– ELECTRO-MOTIVE DIV. OF GMC.		MODEL– 6-567, 45° "V" FORM.		CYLINDERS– 4–10"x6"– DOUBLE-ACT.
YEAR BUILT–		2 CYCLE, SINGLE-ACTING.		CLASP TYPE SHOES–2 PER WHEEL
TRACTIVE POWER–		6 CYL'S.– 8½" BORE x 10" STROKE	COMPRESSOR	GARDNER-DENVER 3 CYL.– TYPE WXE 2 STAGE
FACTOR OF ADHESION	SEE PAGE 5.	SOLID INJECTION – UNIT TYPE.		
LOADED WEIGHTS		"ROOTS" TYPE BLOWER SCAVENGING		
			BRAKING POWER	TOTAL PRESSURE– 101,940 LBS.
TRUCK JOURNAL SIZE – 6½" x 12".				PER CENT– 51%
TANK CAPACITIES IN GALLONS	FUEL OIL 600	GENERATORS — ELECTRO-MOTIVE DIV.		CYLINDER PRESSURE– 30 LBS.
	LUBRICATING OIL 75			
	COOLING WATER 125		DRAFT GEAR– MINER A-22-XB	
		TRACTION MOTORS– 4– ELECTRO-MOTIVE DIV.	SANDERS– GRAHAM- WHITE– ENG'S.– 106,107	
			BREWSTER B-W TYPE C– ENG'S. 102-103	
SAND BOX CAPACITY – 28 CU. FT.		GEARS – 62 TEETH. PINION–15 TEETH.		
MINIMUM CURVE RADIUS– 100 FT.		GEAR RATIO– 4.13 TO 1.	— HEADLIGHTS– PYLE NATIONAL —	
MAXIMUM PERMISSIBLE SPEED– 45 MPH.			ENG'S. — 102,103 – TYPE 14055 – 14"	
		STORAGE BATTERIES – EXIDE	ENG'S. 106,107 —— 14" BACK MTG.	

REVISED|1941|1942|1943|1947|1950|1952|1954|1961|

270

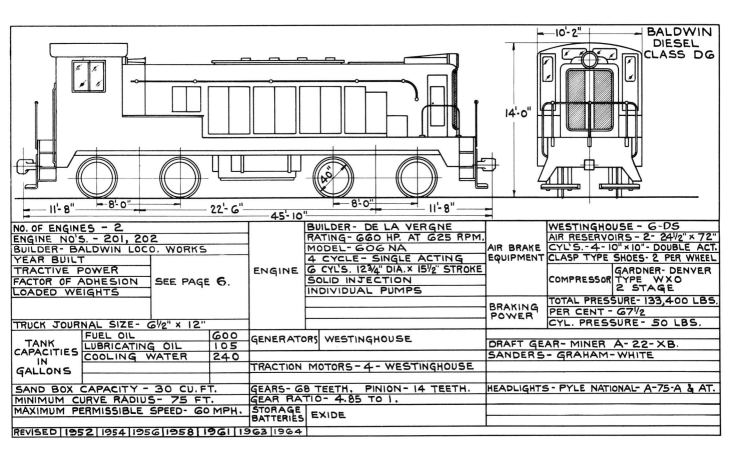

BALDWIN
DIESEL
CLASS D6

NO. OF ENGINES - 2			BUILDER- DE LA VERGNE		AIR BRAKE EQUIPMENT	WESTINGHOUSE - 6-DS
ENGINE NO'S. - 201, 202			RATING- 660 HP. AT 625 RPM.			AIR RESERVOIRS - 2- 24½" x 72"
BUILDER- BALDWIN LOCO. WORKS			MODEL- 606 NA			CYL'S.-4-10"x10"-DOUBLE ACT.
YEAR BUILT	SEE PAGE 6.	ENGINE	4 CYCLE - SINGLE ACTING			CLASP TYPE SHOES- 2 PER WHEEL
TRACTIVE POWER			6 CYL'S. 12¾" DIA. x 15½" STROKE			COMPRESSOR	GARDNER- DENVER TYPE WXO 2 STAGE
FACTOR OF ADHESION			SOLID INJECTION			
LOADED WEIGHTS			INDIVIDUAL PUMPS			
					BRAKING POWER	TOTAL PRESSURE- 133,400 LBS.
TRUCK JOURNAL SIZE- 6½" x 12"						PER CENT - 67½
TANK CAPACITIES IN GALLONS	FUEL OIL	600	GENERATORS	WESTINGHOUSE		CYL. PRESSURE- 50 LBS.
	LUBRICATING OIL	105				DRAFT GEAR- MINER A-22-XB.
	COOLING WATER	240				SANDERS- GRAHAM-WHITE
			TRACTION MOTORS-4-WESTINGHOUSE			
SAND BOX CAPACITY - 30 CU. FT.			GEARS- 68 TEETH. PINION- 14 TEETH.			HEADLIGHTS- PYLE NATIONAL- A-75-A & AT.
MINIMUM CURVE RADIUS- 75 FT.			GEAR RATIO- 4.85 TO 1.			
MAXIMUM PERMISSIBLE SPEED- 60 MPH.			STORAGE BATTERIES	EXIDE		

REVISED | 1952 | 1954 | 1956 | 1958 | 1961 | 1963 | 1964

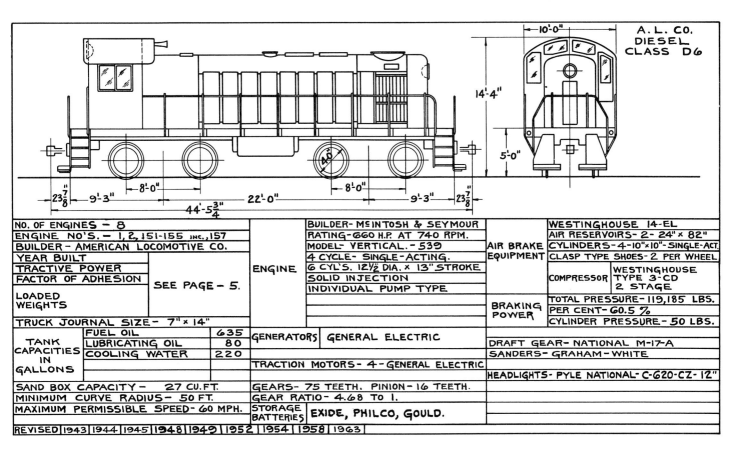

A. L. CO.
DIESEL
CLASS D6

NO. OF ENGINES - 8			BUILDER- McINTOSH & SEYMOUR		AIR BRAKE EQUIPMENT	WESTINGHOUSE 14-EL
ENGINE NO'S. - 1, 2, 151-155 INC.,157			RATING-660 H.P. AT 740 RPM.			AIR RESERVOIRS- 2- 24" x 82"
BUILDER - AMERICAN LOCOMOTIVE CO.			MODEL- VERTICAL. - 539			CYLINDERS-4-10"x10"-SINGLE-ACT.
YEAR BUILT	SEE PAGE - 5.	ENGINE	4 CYCLE- SINGLE-ACTING.			CLASP TYPE SHOES-2 PER WHEEL
TRACTIVE POWER			6 CYL'S. 12½" DIA. x 13" STROKE			COMPRESSOR	WESTINGHOUSE TYPE 3-CD 2 STAGE
FACTOR OF ADHESION			SOLID INJECTION			
LOADED WEIGHTS			INDIVIDUAL PUMP TYPE			
					BRAKING POWER	TOTAL PRESSURE-119,185 LBS.
TRUCK JOURNAL SIZE- 7" x 14"						PER CENT-60.5 %
TANK CAPACITIES IN GALLONS	FUEL OIL	635	GENERATORS	GENERAL ELECTRIC		CYLINDER PRESSURE-50 LBS.
	LUBRICATING OIL	80				DRAFT GEAR- NATIONAL M-17-A
	COOLING WATER	220				SANDERS- GRAHAM-WHITE
			TRACTION MOTORS- 4-GENERAL ELECTRIC			
SAND BOX CAPACITY - 27 CU. FT.			GEARS- 75 TEETH. PINION-16 TEETH.			HEADLIGHTS- PYLE NATIONAL-C-620-CZ-12"
MINIMUM CURVE RADIUS- 50 FT.			GEAR RATIO- 4.68 TO 1.			
MAXIMUM PERMISSIBLE SPEED- 60 MPH.			STORAGE BATTERIES	EXIDE, PHILCO, GOULD.		

REVISED | 1943 | 1944 | 1945 | 1948 | 1949 | 1952 | 1954 | 1958 | 1963

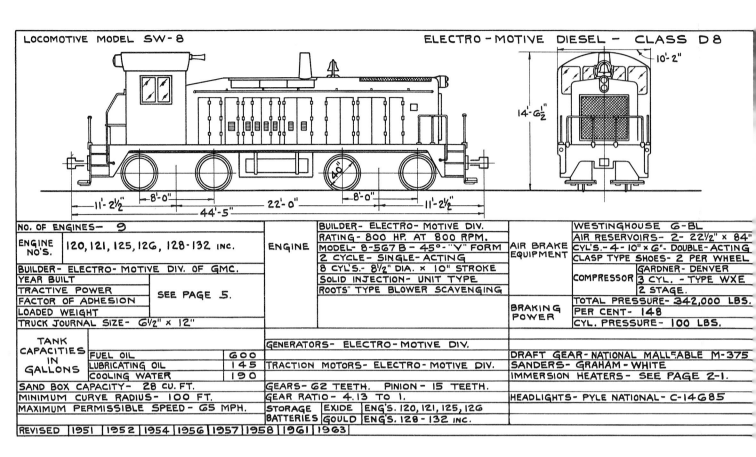

LOCOMOTIVE MODEL SW-8   ELECTRO-MOTIVE DIESEL - CLASS D8

10'-2"

14'-6½"

11'-2½" 8'-0"   22'-0"   8'-0" 11'-2½"
              44'-5"

40"

NO. OF ENGINES- 9						
ENGINE NO'S.	120, 121, 125, 126, 128-132 INC.	ENGINE	BUILDER- ELECTRO-MOTIVE DIV. RATING- 800 HP. AT 800 RPM. MODEL- 8-567 B - 45°- "V" FORM 2 CYCLE- SINGLE-ACTING 8 CYL'S.- 8½" DIA. × 10" STROKE SOLID INJECTION- UNIT TYPE ROOTS" TYPE BLOWER SCAVENGING	AIR BRAKE EQUIPMENT	WESTINGHOUSE 6-BL AIR RESERVOIRS- 2- 22½" × 84" CYL'S.- 4- 10" × 6"- DOUBLE-ACTING CLASP TYPE SHOES- 2 PER WHEEL	
BUILDER- ELECTRO-MOTIVE DIV. OF GMC.						
YEAR BUILT	SEE PAGE 5.				COMPRESSOR	GARDNER - DENVER 3 CYL. - TYPE WXE 2 STAGE.
TRACTIVE POWER						
FACTOR OF ADHESION						
LOADED WEIGHT				BRAKING POWER	TOTAL PRESSURE- 342,000 LBS.	
TRUCK JOURNAL SIZE- 6½" × 12"					PER CENT- 148	
					CYL. PRESSURE- 100 LBS.	
TANK CAPACITIES IN GALLONS	FUEL OIL	600	GENERATORS- ELECTRO-MOTIVE DIV.		DRAFT GEAR-NATIONAL MALLEABLE M-375	
	LUBRICATING OIL	145	TRACTION MOTORS- ELECTRO-MOTIVE DIV.		SANDERS- GRAHAM-WHITE	
	COOLING WATER	190			IMMERSION HEATERS- SEE PAGE 2-1.	
SAND BOX CAPACITY- 28 CU. FT.			GEARS- 62 TEETH. PINION - 15 TEETH.			
MINIMUM CURVE RADIUS- 100 FT.			GEAR RATIO - 4.13 TO 1.		HEADLIGHTS- PYLE NATIONAL- C-14685	
MAXIMUM PERMISSIBLE SPEED - 65 MPH.			STORAGE BATTERIES	EXIDE	ENG'S. 120, 121, 125, 126		
				GOULD	ENG'S. 128 - 132 INC.	

REVISED |1951|1952|1954|1956|1957|1958|1961|1963|

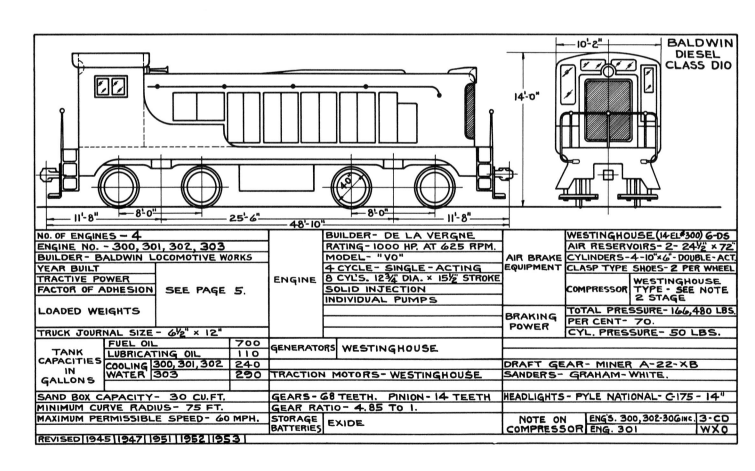

BALDWIN DIESEL CLASS D10

10'-2"

14'-0"

11'-8" 8'-0"   25'-6"   8'-0" 11'-8"
              48'-10"

40"

NO. OF ENGINES - 4						
ENGINE NO. - 300, 301, 302, 303			BUILDER- DE LA VERGNE RATING- 1000 HP. AT 625 RPM. MODEL- "VO" 4 CYCLE- SINGLE-ACTING 8 CYL'S. 12¾" DIA. × 15½" STROKE SOLID INJECTION INDIVIDUAL PUMPS	AIR BRAKE EQUIPMENT	WESTINGHOUSE (14-EL#300) 6-DS AIR RESERVOIRS- 2- 24½" × 72" CYLINDERS- 4- 10" × 6"- DOUBLE-ACTING CLASP TYPE SHOES- 2 PER WHEEL	
BUILDER- BALDWIN LOCOMOTIVE WORKS		ENGINE				
YEAR BUILT	SEE PAGE 5.				COMPRESSOR	WESTINGHOUSE TYPE - SEE NOTE 2 STAGE
TRACTIVE POWER						
FACTOR OF ADHESION						
LOADED WEIGHTS				BRAKING POWER	TOTAL PRESSURE- 166,480 LBS.	
					PER CENT- 70.	
TRUCK JOURNAL SIZE - 6½" × 12"					CYL. PRESSURE- 50 LBS.	
TANK CAPACITIES IN GALLONS	FUEL OIL		700	GENERATORS	WESTINGHOUSE	
	LUBRICATING OIL		110			
	COOLING WATER	300, 301, 302	240	TRACTION MOTORS- WESTINGHOUSE	DRAFT GEAR- MINER A-22-XB	
		303	290		SANDERS- GRAHAM-WHITE.	
SAND BOX CAPACITY- 30 CU. FT.				GEARS- 68 TEETH. PINION- 14 TEETH	HEADLIGHTS- PYLE NATIONAL- C-175 - 14"	
MINIMUM CURVE RADIUS- 75 FT.				GEAR RATIO- 4.85 TO 1.		
MAXIMUM PERMISSIBLE SPEED - 60 MPH.				STORAGE BATTERIES	EXIDE	NOTE ON COMPRESSOR	ENG'S. 300, 302-306 INC.	3-CD
						ENG. 301	WXO

REVISED |1945|1947|1951|1952|1953|

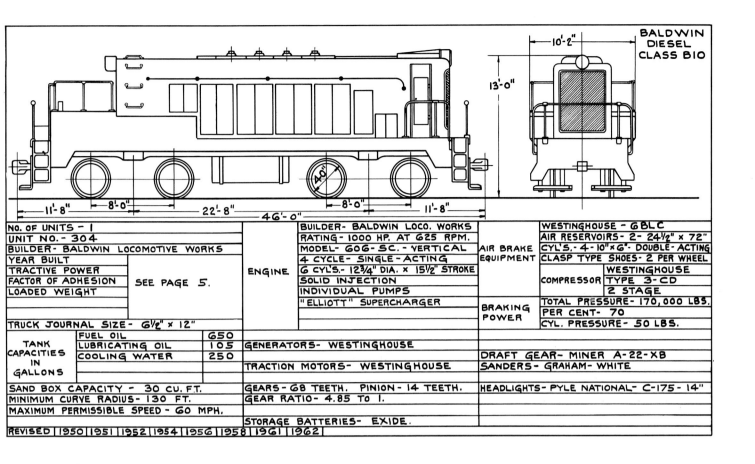

BALDWIN
DIESEL
CLASS B10

NO. OF UNITS - 1			ENGINE	BUILDER- BALDWIN LOCO. WORKS	AIR BRAKE EQUIPMENT	WESTINGHOUSE - 6BLC
UNIT NO.- 304				RATING - 1000 HP. AT 625 RPM.		AIR RESERVOIRS- 2- 24½" x 72"
BUILDER- BALDWIN LOCOMOTIVE WORKS				MODEL- 606- SC. - VERTICAL		CYL'S.- 4- 10"x6"- DOUBLE-ACTING
YEAR BUILT	SEE PAGE 5.			4 CYCLE- SINGLE-ACTING		CLASP TYPE SHOES- 2 PER WHEEL
TRACTIVE POWER				6 CYL'S.- 12¾" DIA. x 15½" STROKE	COMPRESSOR	WESTINGHOUSE
FACTOR OF ADHESION				SOLID INJECTION		TYPE 3-CD
LOADED WEIGHT				INDIVIDUAL PUMPS		2 STAGE
				"ELLIOTT" SUPERCHARGER	BRAKING POWER	TOTAL PRESSURE- 170,000 LBS.
TRUCK JOURNAL SIZE- 6½" x 12"						PER CENT- 70
TANK CAPACITIES IN GALLONS	FUEL OIL	650				CYL. PRESSURE- 50 LBS.
	LUBRICATING OIL	105	GENERATORS- WESTINGHOUSE			
	COOLING WATER	250				DRAFT GEAR- MINER A-22-XB
			TRACTION MOTORS- WESTINGHOUSE			SANDERS- GRAHAM- WHITE
SAND BOX CAPACITY - 30 CU. FT.			GEARS - 68 TEETH. PINION - 14 TEETH.			HEADLIGHTS- PYLE NATIONAL- C-175- 14"
MINIMUM CURVE RADIUS- 130 FT.			GEAR RATIO- 4.85 TO 1.			
MAXIMUM PERMISSIBLE SPEED - 60 MPH.						
			STORAGE BATTERIES- EXIDE.			
REVISED |1950|1951|1952|1954|1956|1958|1961|1962|						

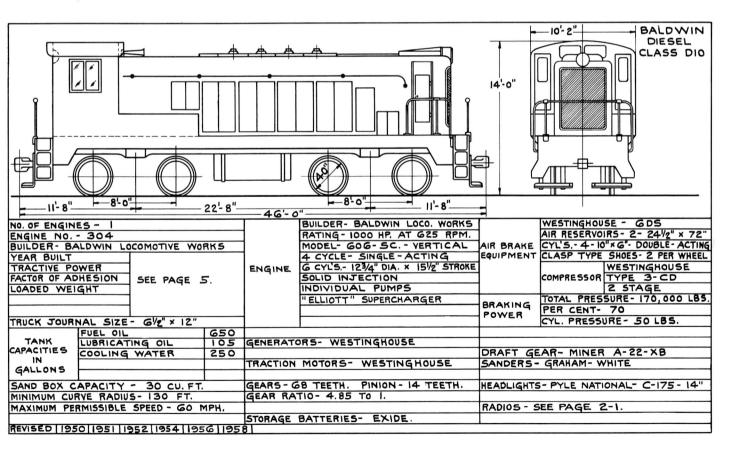

BALDWIN
DIESEL
CLASS D10

NO. OF ENGINES - 1			ENGINE	BUILDER- BALDWIN LOCO. WORKS	AIR BRAKE EQUIPMENT	WESTINGHOUSE - 6DS
ENGINE NO. - 304				RATING - 1000 HP. AT 625 RPM.		AIR RESERVOIRS- 2- 24½" x 72"
BUILDER- BALDWIN LOCOMOTIVE WORKS				MODEL- 606- SC. - VERTICAL		CYL'S.- 4- 10"x6"- DOUBLE-ACTING
YEAR BUILT	SEE PAGE 5.			4 CYCLE- SINGLE-ACTING		CLASP TYPE SHOES- 2 PER WHEEL
TRACTIVE POWER				6 CYL'S.- 12¾" DIA. x 15½" STROKE	COMPRESSOR	WESTINGHOUSE
FACTOR OF ADHESION				SOLID INJECTION		TYPE 3-CD
LOADED WEIGHT				INDIVIDUAL PUMPS		2 STAGE
				"ELLIOTT" SUPERCHARGER	BRAKING POWER	TOTAL PRESSURE- 170,000 LBS.
TRUCK JOURNAL SIZE- 6½" x 12"						PER CENT- 70
TANK CAPACITIES IN GALLONS	FUEL OIL	650				CYL. PRESSURE- 50 LBS.
	LUBRICATING OIL	105	GENERATORS- WESTINGHOUSE			
	COOLING WATER	250				DRAFT GEAR- MINER A-22-XB
			TRACTION MOTORS- WESTINGHOUSE			SANDERS- GRAHAM- WHITE
SAND BOX CAPACITY - 30 CU. FT.			GEARS - 68 TEETH. PINION - 14 TEETH.			HEADLIGHTS- PYLE NATIONAL- C-175- 14"
MINIMUM CURVE RADIUS- 130 FT.			GEAR RATIO- 4.85 TO 1.			
MAXIMUM PERMISSIBLE SPEED - 60 MPH.						RADIOS - SEE PAGE 2-1.
			STORAGE BATTERIES- EXIDE.			
REVISED |1950|1951|1952|1954|1956|1958|							

273

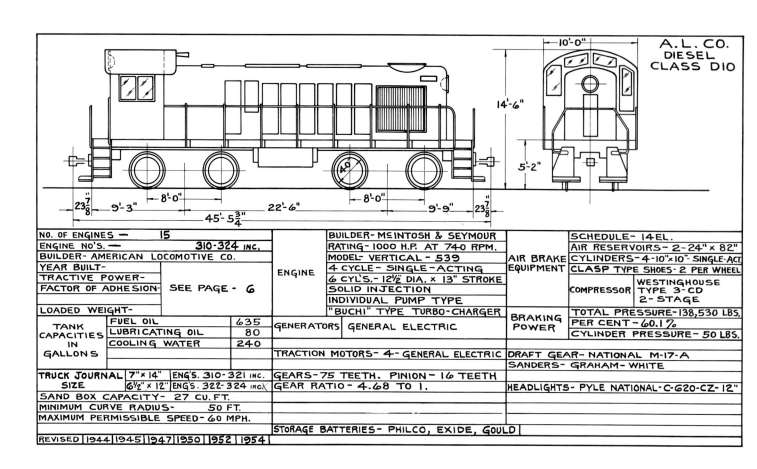

A.L.CO. DIESEL CLASS D10

NO. OF ENGINES — 15		BUILDER- McINTOSH & SEYMOUR	SCHEDULE- 14EL.
ENGINE NO'S. — 310-324 INC.		RATING- 1000 H.P. AT 740 RPM.	AIR RESERVOIRS- 2-24"x 82"
BUILDER- AMERICAN LOCOMOTIVE CO.		MODEL- VERTICAL - 539	CYLINDERS- 4-10"x10"- SINGLE-ACT.
YEAR BUILT-		4 CYCLE - SINGLE - ACTING	CLASP TYPE SHOES- 2 PER WHEEL
TRACTIVE POWER-	SEE PAGE - 6	6 CYL'S. - 12½" DIA. x 13" STROKE	COMPRESSOR WESTINGHOUSE TYPE 3-CD 2-STAGE
FACTOR OF ADHESION-		SOLID INJECTION	
		INDIVIDUAL PUMP TYPE	
LOADED WEIGHT-		"BUCHI" TYPE TURBO-CHARGER	BRAKING POWER: TOTAL PRESSURE-138,530 LBS.
TANK CAPACITIES IN GALLONS: FUEL OIL 635, LUBRICATING OIL 80, COOLING WATER 240		GENERATORS GENERAL ELECTRIC	PER CENT- 60.1%
			CYLINDER PRESSURE- 50 LBS.
		TRACTION MOTORS- 4- GENERAL ELECTRIC	DRAFT GEAR- NATIONAL M-17-A
TRUCK JOURNAL SIZE: 7"x14" ENG'S. 310-321 INC. / 6½"x12" ENG'S. 322-324 INC.		GEARS- 75 TEETH. PINION - 16 TEETH	SANDERS- GRAHAM-WHITE
		GEAR RATIO - 4.68 TO 1.	HEADLIGHTS- PYLE NATIONAL-C-G20-CZ-12"
SAND BOX CAPACITY- 27 CU. FT.			
MINIMUM CURVE RADIUS- 50 FT.			
MAXIMUM PERMISSIBLE SPEED- 60 MPH.			
		STORAGE BATTERIES- PHILCO, EXIDE, GOULD	
REVISED 1944 1945 1947 1950 1952 1954			

AIR BRAKE EQUIPMENT

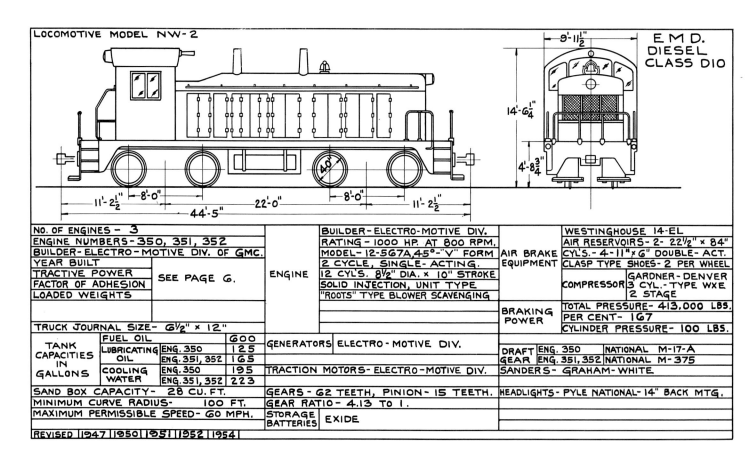

LOCOMOTIVE MODEL NW-2

E.M.D. DIESEL CLASS D10

NO. OF ENGINES - 3		BUILDER- ELECTRO-MOTIVE DIV.	WESTINGHOUSE 14-EL
ENGINE NUMBERS- 350, 351, 352		RATING- 1000 H.P. AT 800 RPM.	AIR RESERVOIRS- 2- 22½"x 84"
BUILDER- ELECTRO-MOTIVE DIV. OF GMC.		MODEL- 12-567A, 45°-"V" FORM	CYL'S.- 4-11"x 6" DOUBLE- ACT.
YEAR BUILT		2 CYCLE, SINGLE-ACTING.	CLASP TYPE SHOES- 2 PER WHEEL
TRACTIVE POWER	SEE PAGE 6.	12 CYL'S. 8½" DIA. x 10" STROKE	COMPRESSOR GARDNER-DENVER 3 CYL.- TYPE WXE 2 STAGE
FACTOR OF ADHESION		SOLID INJECTION, UNIT TYPE	
LOADED WEIGHTS		"ROOTS" TYPE BLOWER SCAVENGING	
			BRAKING POWER: TOTAL PRESSURE- 413,000 LBS.
			PER CENT- 167
TRUCK JOURNAL SIZE- 6½" x 12"			CYLINDER PRESSURE- 100 LBS.
TANK CAPACITIES IN GALLONS: FUEL OIL 600; LUBRICATING OIL ENG.350 125, ENG.351,352 165; COOLING WATER ENG.350 195, ENG.351,352 223		GENERATORS ELECTRO-MOTIVE DIV.	DRAFT GEAR ENG. 350 NATIONAL M-17-A / ENG.351,352 NATIONAL M-375
		TRACTION MOTORS- ELECTRO-MOTIVE DIV.	SANDERS- GRAHAM-WHITE
SAND BOX CAPACITY- 28 CU. FT.		GEARS - 62 TEETH, PINION- 15 TEETH.	HEADLIGHTS- PYLE NATIONAL-14" BACK MTG.
MINIMUM CURVE RADIUS- 100 FT.		GEAR RATIO - 4.13 TO 1.	
MAXIMUM PERMISSIBLE SPEED- 60 MPH.		STORAGE BATTERIES EXIDE	
REVISED 1947 1950 1951 1952 1954			

AIR BRAKE EQUIPMENT

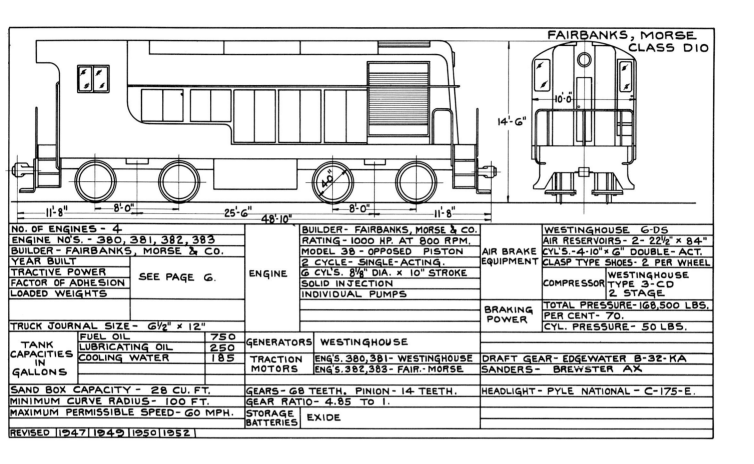

FAIRBANKS, MORSE CLASS D10

Dimensions: 14'-6", 10'-0", 11'-8", 8'-0", 25'-6", 48'-10", 8'-0", 11'-8", 40"

			ENGINE	BUILDER - FAIRBANKS, MORSE & CO.	AIR BRAKE EQUIPMENT		WESTINGHOUSE 6-DS
NO. OF ENGINES - 4				RATING - 1000 HP. AT 800 RPM.			AIR RESERVOIRS - 2- 22½" x 84"
ENGINE NO'S. - 380, 381, 382, 383				MODEL 38 - OPPOSED PISTON			CYL'S.- 4-10" x 6" DOUBLE - ACT.
BUILDER - FAIRBANKS, MORSE & CO.				2 CYCLE- SINGLE-ACTING.			CLASP TYPE SHOES- 2 PER WHEEL
YEAR BUILT	SEE PAGE 6.			6 CYL'S. 8⅛" DIA. x 10" STROKE		COMPRESSOR	WESTINGHOUSE TYPE 3-CD 2 STAGE
TRACTIVE POWER				SOLID INJECTION			
FACTOR OF ADHESION				INDIVIDUAL PUMPS			
LOADED WEIGHTS					BRAKING POWER		TOTAL PRESSURE-168,500 LBS.
							PER CENT- 70.
TRUCK JOURNAL SIZE - 6½" x 12"							CYL. PRESSURE- 50 LBS.
TANK CAPACITIES IN GALLONS	FUEL OIL	750	GENERATORS	WESTINGHOUSE			
	LUBRICATING OIL	250	TRACTION MOTORS	ENG'S. 380, 381- WESTINGHOUSE	DRAFT GEAR- EDGEWATER B-32-KA		
	COOLING WATER	185		ENG'S. 382, 383- FAIR.- MORSE	SANDERS- BREWSTER AX		
SAND BOX CAPACITY - 28 CU. FT.			GEARS- 68 TEETH. PINION - 14 TEETH.	HEADLIGHT- PYLE NATIONAL - C-175-E.			
MINIMUM CURVE RADIUS- 100 FT.			GEAR RATIO- 4.85 TO 1.				
MAXIMUM PERMISSIBLE SPEED- 60 MPH.			STORAGE BATTERIES	EXIDE			
REVISED 1947 1949 1950 1952							

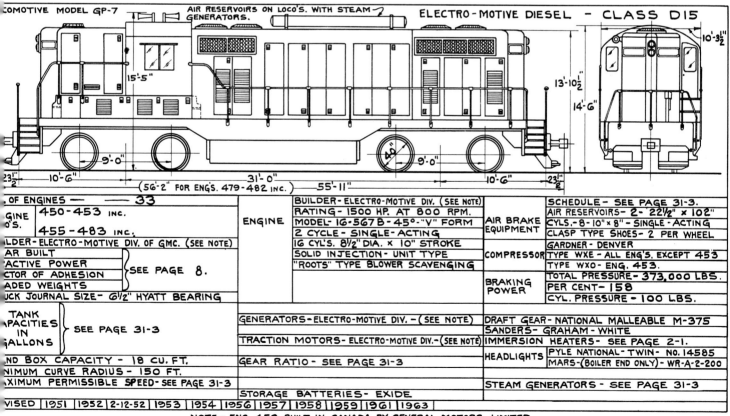

LOCOMOTIVE MODEL GP-7
AIR RESERVOIRS ON LOCO'S. WITH STEAM GENERATORS.
ELECTRO-MOTIVE DIESEL - CLASS D15

Dimensions: 15'-5", 10'-3½", 13'-10½", 14'-6", 23½", 10'-6", 31'-0", (56'-2" FOR ENG'S. 479-482 INC.), 55'-11", 9'-0", 40", 9'-0", 10'-6", 23½"

			ENGINE	BUILDER- ELECTRO-MOTIVE DIV. (SEE NOTE)	AIR BRAKE EQUIPMENT		SCHEDULE - SEE PAGE 31-3.
NO. OF ENGINES — 33				RATING - 1500 HP. AT 800 RPM.			AIR RESERVOIRS- 2- 22½" x 102"
ENGINE NO'S. 450-453 INC. 455-483 INC.				MODEL- 16-567 B - 45°-"V" FORM			CYLS.- 8-10" x 8" - SINGLE-ACTING
				2 CYCLE- SINGLE-ACTING			CLASP TYPE SHOES - 2 PER WHEEL
BUILDER- ELECTRO-MOTIVE DIV. OF GMC. (SEE NOTE)				16 CYL'S. 8½" DIA. x 10" STROKE	COMPRESSOR		GARDNER - DENVER TYPE WXE - ALL ENG'S. EXCEPT 453
YEAR BUILT	SEE PAGE 8.			SOLID INJECTION- UNIT TYPE			TYPE WXO - ENG. 453.
TRACTIVE POWER				"ROOTS" TYPE BLOWER SCAVENGING			
FACTOR OF ADHESION					BRAKING POWER		TOTAL PRESSURE- 373,000 LBS.
LOADED WEIGHTS							PER CENT- 158
TRUCK JOURNAL SIZE- 6½" HYATT BEARING							CYL. PRESSURE - 100 LBS.
TANK CAPACITIES IN GALLONS	SEE PAGE 31-3		GENERATORS- ELECTRO-MOTIVE DIV. - (SEE NOTE)		DRAFT GEAR- NATIONAL MALLEABLE M-375		
					SANDERS- GRAHAM - WHITE		
			TRACTION MOTORS- ELECTRO-MOTIVE DIV.- (SEE NOTE)		IMMERSION HEATERS- SEE PAGE 2-1.		
SAND BOX CAPACITY - 18 CU. FT.			GEAR RATIO - SEE PAGE 31-3		HEADLIGHTS		PYLE NATIONAL- TWIN- NO. 14585
MINIMUM CURVE RADIUS - 150 FT.							MARS-(BOILER END ONLY)- WR-A-2-200
MAXIMUM PERMISSIBLE SPEED- SEE PAGE 31-3					STEAM GENERATORS - SEE PAGE 31-3		
REVISED 1951 1952 2-12-52 1953 1954 1956 1957 1958 1959 1961 1963			STORAGE BATTERIES- EXIDE				

NOTE- ENG. 453 BUILT IN CANADA BY GENERAL MOTORS, LIMITED.

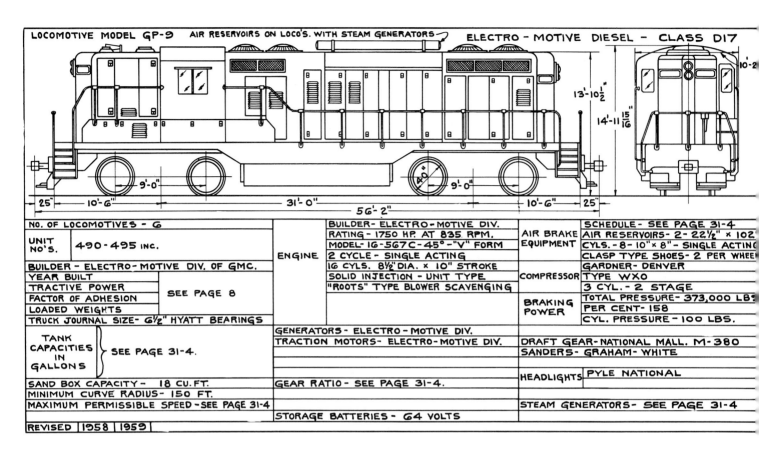

LOCOMOTIVE MODEL GP-9   AIR RESERVOIRS ON LOCO'S. WITH STEAM GENERATORS   ELECTRO-MOTIVE DIESEL - CLASS D17

13'-10½"
14'-11 15/16"
10'-2"
9'-0"
40"
9'-0"
25" 10'-6" 31'-0" 10'-6" 25"
56'-2"

NO. OF LOCOMOTIVES - 6			ENGINE	BUILDER- ELECTRO-MOTIVE DIV. RATING - 1750 HP. AT 835 RPM. MODEL- 16-567C-45°-"V" FORM 2 CYCLE - SINGLE ACTING 16 CYLS. 8½" DIA. × 10" STROKE SOLID INJECTION - UNIT TYPE "ROOTS" TYPE BLOWER SCAVENGING	AIR BRAKE EQUIPMENT	SCHEDULE - SEE PAGE 31-4
UNIT NO'S.	490-495 INC.					AIR RESERVOIRS- 2- 22½" × 102"
						CYLS. - 8 - 10"× 8" - SINGLE ACTING
BUILDER - ELECTRO-MOTIVE DIV. OF GMC.						CLASP TYPE SHOES- 2 PER WHEEL
YEAR BUILT	SEE PAGE 8				COMPRESSOR	GARDNER- DENVER
TRACTIVE POWER						TYPE WXO
FACTOR OF ADHESION						3 CYL. - 2 STAGE
LOADED WEIGHTS					BRAKING POWER	TOTAL PRESSURE- 373,000 LBS.
TRUCK JOURNAL SIZE- 6½" HYATT BEARINGS						PER CENT- 158
TANK CAPACITIES IN GALLONS	SEE PAGE 31-4.					CYL. PRESSURE - 100 LBS.
			GENERATORS - ELECTRO-MOTIVE DIV.		DRAFT GEAR-NATIONAL MALL. M-380	
			TRACTION MOTORS- ELECTRO-MOTIVE DIV.		SANDERS- GRAHAM-WHITE	
					HEADLIGHTS	PYLE NATIONAL
SAND BOX CAPACITY - 18 CU. FT.			GEAR RATIO - SEE PAGE 31-4.			
MINIMUM CURVE RADIUS- 150 FT.						
MAXIMUM PERMISSIBLE SPEED -SEE PAGE 31-4					STEAM GENERATORS- SEE PAGE 31-4	
			STORAGE BATTERIES - 64 VOLTS			
REVISED	1958	1959				

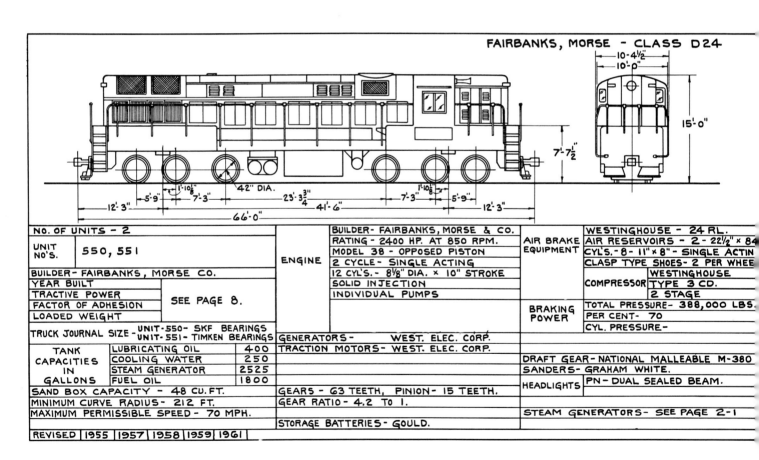

FAIRBANKS, MORSE - CLASS D24

10'-4½"
10'-0"
15'-0"
7'-7½"
42" DIA.
12'-3" 5'-9" 1'-10⅛" 7'-3" 23'-3¾" 7'-3" 1'-10⅛" 5'-9" 12'-3"
41'-6"
66'-0"

NO. OF UNITS - 2			ENGINE	BUILDER- FAIRBANKS, MORSE & CO. RATING - 2400 HP. AT 850 RPM. MODEL 38 - OPPOSED PISTON 2 CYCLE - SINGLE ACTING 12 CYL'S.- 8⅛" DIA. × 10" STROKE SOLID INJECTION INDIVIDUAL PUMPS	AIR BRAKE EQUIPMENT	WESTINGHOUSE - 24 RL.
UNIT NO'S.	550, 551					AIR RESERVOIRS - 2- 22½"× 84"
						CYL'S.- 8 - 11"× 8" - SINGLE ACTING
BUILDER- FAIRBANKS, MORSE CO.						CLASP TYPE SHOES- 2 PER WHEEL
YEAR BUILT	SEE PAGE 8.				COMPRESSOR	WESTINGHOUSE TYPE 3 CD. 2 STAGE
TRACTIVE POWER						
FACTOR OF ADHESION						
LOADED WEIGHT					BRAKING POWER	TOTAL PRESSURE- 388,000 LBS.
TRUCK JOURNAL SIZE- UNIT-550- SKF BEARINGS UNIT-551- TIMKEN BEARINGS						PER CENT- 70
			GENERATORS- WEST. ELEC. CORP.			CYL. PRESSURE-
TANK CAPACITIES IN GALLONS	LUBRICATING OIL	400	TRACTION MOTORS- WEST. ELEC. CORP.			
	COOLING WATER	250			DRAFT GEAR- NATIONAL MALLEABLE M-380	
	STEAM GENERATOR	2525			SANDERS- GRAHAM WHITE.	
	FUEL OIL	1800			HEADLIGHTS	PN - DUAL SEALED BEAM.
SAND BOX CAPACITY - 48 CU. FT.			GEARS - 63 TEETH, PINION - 15 TEETH.			
MINIMUM CURVE RADIUS- 212 FT.			GEAR RATIO - 4.2 TO 1.			
MAXIMUM PERMISSIBLE SPEED - 70 MPH.					STEAM GENERATORS- SEE PAGE 2-1	
			STORAGE BATTERIES - GOULD.			
REVISED	1955	1957	1958	1959	1961	

276

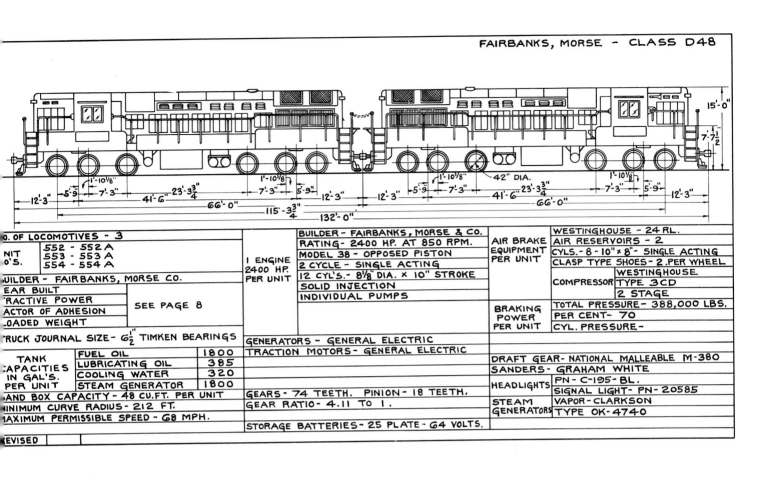

NO. OF LOCOMOTIVES - 3			I ENGINE 2400 HP. PER UNIT	BUILDER - FAIRBANKS, MORSE & CO.	AIR BRAKE EQUIPMENT PER UNIT	WESTINGHOUSE - 24 RL.
UNIT NO'S.	552 - 552 A 553 - 553 A 554 - 554 A			RATING- 2400 HP. AT 850 RPM.		AIR RESERVOIRS - 2
				MODEL 38 - OPPOSED PISTON		CYLS.- 8 -10"× 8"- SINGLE ACTING
BUILDER - FAIRBANKS, MORSE CO.				2 CYCLE - SINGLE ACTING		CLASP TYPE SHOES - 2 PER WHEEL
YEAR BUILT		SEE PAGE 8		12 CYL'S - 8⅛" DIA. × 10" STROKE		COMPRESSOR - WESTINGHOUSE TYPE 3CD 2 STAGE
TRACTIVE POWER				SOLID INJECTION		
FACTOR OF ADHESION				INDIVIDUAL PUMPS		
LOADED WEIGHT					BRAKING POWER PER UNIT	TOTAL PRESSURE - 388,000 LBS.
TRUCK JOURNAL SIZE - 6½" TIMKEN BEARINGS						PER CENT- 70
				GENERATORS - GENERAL ELECTRIC		CYL. PRESSURE -
TANK CAPACITIES IN GAL'S. PER UNIT	FUEL OIL	1800		TRACTION MOTORS - GENERAL ELECTRIC		
	LUBRICATING OIL	385				DRAFT GEAR - NATIONAL MALLEABLE M-380
	COOLING WATER	320				SANDERS - GRAHAM WHITE
	STEAM GENERATOR	1800			HEADLIGHTS	PN - C-195- BL.
SAND BOX CAPACITY - 48 CU.FT. PER UNIT				GEARS - 74 TEETH. PINION - 18 TEETH.		SIGNAL LIGHT- PN - 20585
MINIMUM CURVE RADIUS - 212 FT.				GEAR RATIO- 4.11 TO 1.	STEAM GENERATORS	VAPOR - CLARKSON
MAXIMUM PERMISSIBLE SPEED - 68 MPH.						TYPE OK- 4740
				STORAGE BATTERIES - 25 PLATE - 64 VOLTS.		
REVISED						

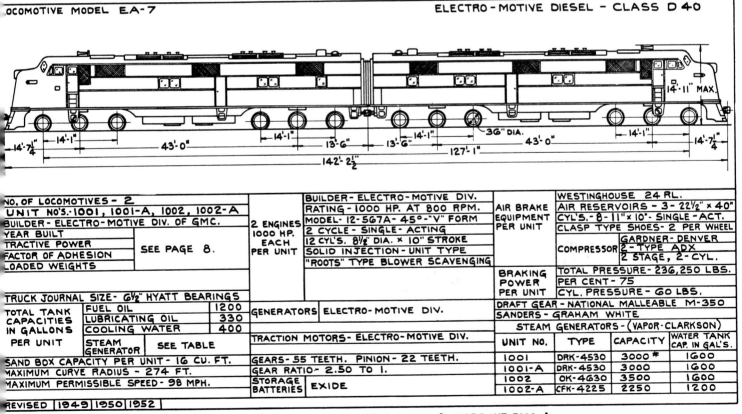

NO. OF LOCOMOTIVES - 2			2 ENGINES 1000 HP. EACH PER UNIT	BUILDER - ELECTRO-MOTIVE DIV.	AIR BRAKE EQUIPMENT PER UNIT	WESTINGHOUSE 24 RL.
UNIT NO'S. 1001, 1001-A, 1002, 1002-A				RATING - 1000 HP. AT 800 RPM.		AIR RESERVOIRS - 3 - 22½" × 40"
BUILDER - ELECTRO-MOTIVE DIV. OF GMC.				MODEL - 12-567A - 45°- "V" FORM		CYL'S.- 8 -11"× 10"- SINGLE - ACT.
YEAR BUILT				2 CYCLE - SINGLE - ACTING		CLASP TYPE SHOES- 2 PER WHEEL
TRACTIVE POWER		SEE PAGE 8.		12 CYL'S. 8½" DIA. × 10" STROKE		COMPRESSOR - GARDNER - DENVER - TYPE ADX - 2 STAGE, 2- CYL.
FACTOR OF ADHESION				SOLID INJECTION - UNIT TYPE		
LOADED WEIGHTS				"ROOTS" TYPE BLOWER SCAVENGING		
					BRAKING POWER PER UNIT	TOTAL PRESSURE- 236,250 LBS.
TRUCK JOURNAL SIZE - 6½" HYATT BEARINGS						PER CENT - 75
TOTAL TANK CAPACITIES IN GALLONS PER UNIT	FUEL OIL	1200		GENERATORS - ELECTRO-MOTIVE DIV.		CYL. PRESSURE - 60 LBS.
	LUBRICATING OIL	330				DRAFT GEAR - NATIONAL MALLEABLE M-350
	COOLING WATER	400				SANDERS - GRAHAM WHITE
	STEAM GENERATOR	SEE TABLE		TRACTION MOTORS - ELECTRO-MOTIVE DIV.		STEAM GENERATORS - (VAPOR-CLARKSON)

SAND BOX CAPACITY PER UNIT - 16 CU. FT.	GEARS - 55 TEETH. PINION - 22 TEETH.			UNIT NO.	TYPE	CAPACITY	WATER TANK CAP. IN GAL'S.
MAXIMUM CURVE RADIUS - 274 FT.	GEAR RATIO - 2.50 TO 1.			1001	DRK-4530	3000 *	1600
MAXIMUM PERMISSIBLE SPEED - 98 MPH.	STORAGE BATTERIES	EXIDE		1001-A	DRK-4530	3000	1600
				1002	OK-4630	3500	1600
REVISED 1949 1950 1952				1002-A	CFK-4225	2250	1200

HEADLIGHTS - PYLE NATIONAL - 14590 EST. & MARS WR-5000-A.

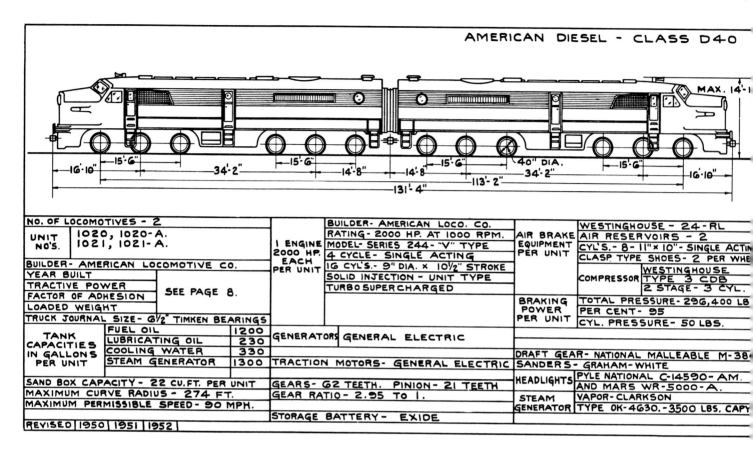

MAX. 14'-1

16'-10" · 15'-6" · 34'-2" · 15'-6" · 14'-8" · 14'-8" · 15'-6" · 40" DIA. · 34'-2" · 15'-6" · 16'-10"

113'-2"

131'-4"

NO. OF LOCOMOTIVES - 2							
UNIT NO'S.	1020, 1020-A. 1021, 1021-A.		1 ENGINE 2000 HP. EACH PER UNIT	BUILDER- AMERICAN LOCO. CO. RATING- 2000 HP. AT 1000 RPM. MODEL- SERIES 244- "V" TYPE 4 CYCLE - SINGLE ACTING 16 CYL'S.- 9" DIA. × 10½" STROKE SOLID INJECTION - UNIT TYPE TURBO SUPERCHARGED	AIR BRAKE EQUIPMENT PER UNIT	WESTINGHOUSE - 24-RL AIR RESERVOIRS - 2 CYL'S.- 8 - 11"× 10"- SINGLE ACTIN CLASP TYPE SHOES- 2 PER WHE	
BUILDER- AMERICAN LOCOMOTIVE CO. YEAR BUILT TRACTIVE POWER FACTOR OF ADHESION LOADED WEIGHT		SEE PAGE 8.				COMPRESSOR	WESTINGHOUSE TYPE 3 CDB 2 STAGE- 3 CYL.
					BRAKING POWER PER UNIT	TOTAL PRESSURE- 296,400 LB PER CENT- 95 CYL. PRESSURE- 50 LBS.	
TRUCK JOURNAL SIZE- 6½" TIMKEN BEARINGS							
TANK CAPACITIES IN GALLONS PER UNIT	FUEL OIL	1200	GENERATORS	GENERAL ELECTRIC			
	LUBRICATING OIL	230					
	COOLING WATER	330				DRAFT GEAR- NATIONAL MALLEABLE M-38	
	STEAM GENERATOR	1300	TRACTION MOTORS- GENERAL ELECTRIC		SANDERS - GRAHAM-WHITE		
SAND BOX CAPACITY - 22 CU.FT. PER UNIT			GEARS- 62 TEETH. PINION- 21 TEETH		HEADLIGHTS	PYLE NATIONAL C-14590- AM. AND MARS WR-5000-A.	
MAXIMUM CURVE RADIUS - 274 FT.			GEAR RATIO- 2.95 TO 1.		STEAM GENERATOR	VAPOR-CLARKSON TYPE OK-4630.-3500 LBS. CAPY	
MAXIMUM PERMISSIBLE SPEED- 90 MPH.							
			STORAGE BATTERY- EXIDE				
REVISED 1950 1951 1952							

LOCOMOTIVE MODEL F7

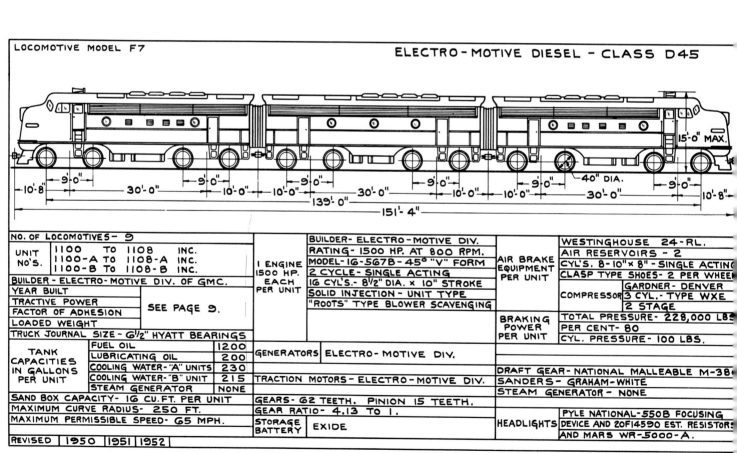

15'-0" MAX.

10'-8" · 9'-0" · 30'-0" · 9'-0" · 10'-0" · 10'-0" · 9'-0" · 30'-0" · 9'-0" · 10'-0" · 10'-0" · 9'-0" · 40" DIA. · 30'-0" · 9'-0" · 10'-8"

139'-0"

151'-4"

NO. OF LOCOMOTIVES- 9							
UNIT NO'S.	1100 TO 1108 INC. 1100-A TO 1108-A INC. 1100-B TO 1108-B INC.		1 ENGINE 1500 HP. EACH PER UNIT	BUILDER- ELECTRO-MOTIVE DIV. RATING- 1500 HP. AT 800 RPM. MODEL- 16-567B-45° "V" FORM 2 CYCLE- SINGLE ACTING 16 CYL'S.- 8½" DIA. × 10" STROKE SOLID INJECTION - UNIT TYPE "ROOTS" TYPE BLOWER SCAVENGING	AIR BRAKE EQUIPMENT PER UNIT	WESTINGHOUSE 24-RL. AIR RESERVOIRS - 2 CYL'S. 8-10"× 8"- SINGLE ACTING CLASP TYPE SHOES- 2 PER WHEE	
BUILDER - ELECTRO-MOTIVE DIV. OF GMC. YEAR BUILT TRACTIVE POWER FACTOR OF ADHESION LOADED WEIGHT		SEE PAGE 9.				COMPRESSOR	GARDNER - DENVER 3 CYL.- TYPE WXE 2 STAGE
					BRAKING POWER PER UNIT	TOTAL PRESSURE- 228,000 LBS PER CENT- 80 CYL. PRESSURE- 100 LBS.	
TRUCK JOURNAL SIZE - 6½" HYATT BEARINGS							
TANK CAPACITIES IN GALLONS PER UNIT	FUEL OIL	1200	GENERATORS	ELECTRO-MOTIVE DIV.			
	LUBRICATING OIL	200					
	COOLING WATER-"A" UNITS	230				DRAFT GEAR- NATIONAL MALLEABLE M-38	
	COOLING WATER-"B" UNIT	215	TRACTION MOTORS - ELECTRO-MOTIVE DIV.		SANDERS - GRAHAM-WHITE		
	STEAM GENERATOR	NONE			STEAM GENERATOR - NONE		
SAND BOX CAPACITY- 16 CU. FT. PER UNIT			GEARS- 62 TEETH. PINION 15 TEETH.				
MAXIMUM CURVE RADIUS- 250 FT.			GEAR RATIO- 4.13 TO 1.		HEADLIGHTS	PYLE NATIONAL-550B FOCUSING DEVICE AND 20F14590 EST. RESISTORS AND MARS WR-5000-A.	
MAXIMUM PERMISSIBLE SPEED- 65 MPH.			STORAGE BATTERY	EXIDE			
REVISED 1950 1951 1952							

NOTE-
ENG'S. 1140-1154 INC. AND 1165-1186 INC. INCLUDING GENERATORS & MOTORS BUILT BY ELECTRO-MOTIVE DIV.
ENG'S. 1155-1164 INC. INCLUDING GENERATORS AND MOTORS BUILT BY GENERAL MOTORS LIM. CANADA.
AIR COMPRESSOR ON UNITED STATES ENGINES IS TYPE WXE, ON CANADIAN ENGINES WXO.

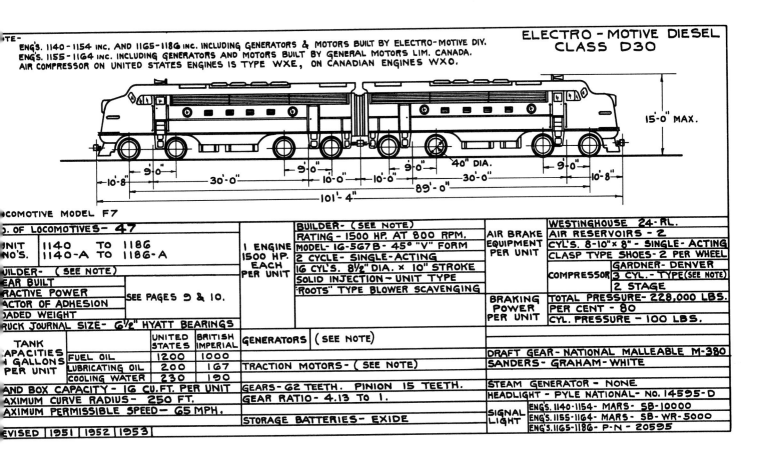

LOCOMOTIVE MODEL F7

NO. OF LOCOMOTIVES- 47

| UNIT NO'S. | 1140 TO 1186 | | |
| | 1140-A TO 1186-A | | |

| | | UNITED STATES | BRITISH IMPERIAL |

BUILDER- (SEE NOTE)
GEAR BUILT
TRACTIVE POWER — SEE PAGES 9 & 10.
FACTOR OF ADHESION
LOADED WEIGHT
TRUCK JOURNAL SIZE- 6½" HYATT BEARINGS

TANK CAPACITIES IN GALLONS PER UNIT		UNITED STATES	BRITISH IMPERIAL
	FUEL OIL	1200	1000
	LUBRICATING OIL	200	167
	COOLING WATER	230	190

SAND BOX CAPACITY - 16 CU.FT. PER UNIT
MAXIMUM CURVE RADIUS- 250 FT.
MAXIMUM PERMISSIBLE SPEED- 65 MPH.

REVISED | 1951 | 1952 | 1953

1 ENGINE 1500 HP. EACH PER UNIT	BUILDER- (SEE NOTE)
	RATING - 1500 HP. AT 800 RPM.
	MODEL- 16-567B - 45° "V" FORM
	2 CYCLE- SINGLE-ACTING
	16 CYL'S. 8½" DIA. × 10" STROKE
	SOLID INJECTION - UNIT TYPE
	"ROOTS" TYPE BLOWER SCAVENGING

GENERATORS (SEE NOTE)

TRACTION MOTORS- (SEE NOTE)

GEARS- 62 TEETH. PINION 15 TEETH.
GEAR RATIO- 4.13 TO 1.

STORAGE BATTERIES- EXIDE

AIR BRAKE EQUIPMENT PER UNIT	WESTINGHOUSE 24-RL.
	AIR RESERVOIRS - 2
	CYL'S. 8-10"× 8" - SINGLE-ACTING
	CLASP TYPE SHOES- 2 PER WHEEL
	COMPRESSOR GARDNER- DENVER 3 CYL. - TYPE (SEE NOTE) 2 STAGE

BRAKING POWER PER UNIT	TOTAL PRESSURE- 228,000 LBS.
	PER CENT - 80
	CYL. PRESSURE - 100 LBS.

DRAFT GEAR- NATIONAL MALLEABLE M-380
SANDERS- GRAHAM-WHITE

STEAM GENERATOR - NONE
HEADLIGHT - PYLE NATIONAL- NO. 14595-D

SIGNAL LIGHT	ENG'S. 1140-1154- MARS- SB-10000
	ENG'S. 1155-1164- MARS- SB-WR-5000
	ENG'S. 1165-1186- P-N- 20595

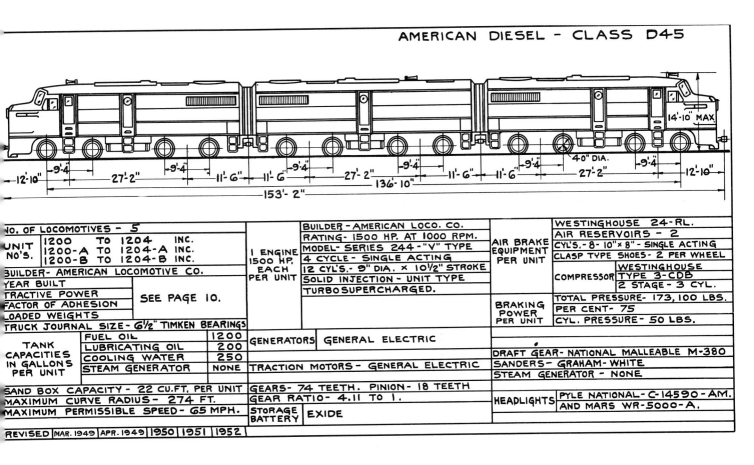

NO. OF LOCOMOTIVES - 5

UNIT NO'S.	1200 TO 1204 INC.
	1200-A TO 1204-A INC.
	1200-B TO 1204-B INC.

BUILDER- AMERICAN LOCOMOTIVE CO.
YEAR BUILT
TRACTIVE POWER — SEE PAGE 10.
FACTOR OF ADHESION
LOADED WEIGHTS
TRUCK JOURNAL SIZE- 6½" TIMKEN BEARINGS

TANK CAPACITIES IN GALLONS PER UNIT	FUEL OIL	1200
	LUBRICATING OIL	200
	COOLING WATER	250
	STEAM GENERATOR	NONE

SAND BOX CAPACITY - 22 CU.FT. PER UNIT
MAXIMUM CURVE RADIUS - 274 FT.
MAXIMUM PERMISSIBLE SPEED- 65 MPH.

STORAGE BATTERY | EXIDE

REVISED | MAR. 1949 | APR. 1949 | 1950 | 1951 | 1952

1 ENGINE 1500 HP. EACH PER UNIT	BUILDER - AMERICAN LOCO. CO.
	RATING- 1500 HP. AT 1000 RPM.
	MODEL- SERIES 244 -"V" TYPE
	4 CYCLE - SINGLE ACTING
	12 CYL'S. 9" DIA. × 10½" STROKE
	SOLID INJECTION - UNIT TYPE
	TURBO SUPERCHARGED.

GENERATORS | GENERAL ELECTRIC

TRACTION MOTORS - GENERAL ELECTRIC

GEARS- 74 TEETH. PINION- 18 TEETH
GEAR RATIO- 4.11 TO 1.

AIR BRAKE EQUIPMENT PER UNIT	WESTINGHOUSE 24-RL.
	AIR RESERVOIRS - 2
	CYL'S. - 8- 10"× 8" - SINGLE ACTING
	CLASP TYPE SHOES- 2 PER WHEEL
	COMPRESSOR WESTINGHOUSE TYPE 3-CDB 2 STAGE - 3 CYL.

BRAKING POWER PER UNIT	TOTAL PRESSURE- 173,100 LBS.
	PER CENT- 75
	CYL. PRESSURE- 50 LBS.

DRAFT GEAR- NATIONAL MALLEABLE M-380
SANDERS- GRAHAM-WHITE
STEAM GENERATOR - NONE

| HEADLIGHTS | PYLE NATIONAL- C-14590-AM. |
| | AND MARS WR-5000-A. |

279

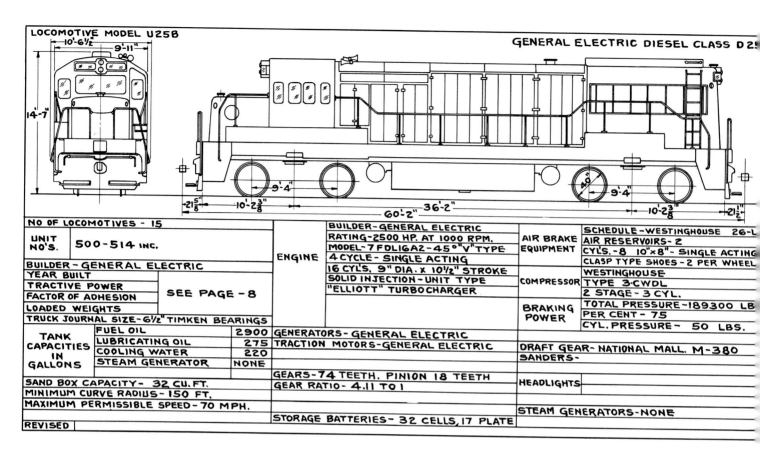

LOCOMOTIVE MODEL U25B

GENERAL ELECTRIC DIESEL CLASS D 25

NO OF LOCOMOTIVES - 15							
UNIT NO'S.	500-514 INC.		ENGINE	BUILDER - GENERAL ELECTRIC	AIR BRAKE EQUIPMENT	SCHEDULE - WESTINGHOUSE 26-L	
				RATING - 2500 HP. AT 1000 RPM.		AIR RESERVOIRS - 2	
BUILDER - GENERAL ELECTRIC				MODEL - 7 FDL16A2 - 45°"V" TYPE		CYL'S. - 8 10"×8" - SINGLE ACTING	
YEAR BUILT	SEE PAGE - 8			4 CYCLE - SINGLE ACTING		CLASP TYPE SHOES - 2 PER WHEEL	
TRACTIVE POWER				16 CYL'S, 9" DIA. × 10½" STROKE	COMPRESSOR	WESTINGHOUSE	
FACTOR OF ADHESION				SOLID INJECTION - UNIT TYPE		TYPE 3-CWDL	
LOADED WEIGHTS				"ELLIOTT" TURBOCHARGER		2 STAGE - 3 CYL.	
TRUCK JOURNAL SIZE - 6½" TIMKEN BEARINGS					BRAKING POWER	TOTAL PRESSURE - 189300 LB	
TANK CAPACITIES IN GALLONS	FUEL OIL	2900	GENERATORS - GENERAL ELECTRIC			PER CENT - 75	
	LUBRICATING OIL	275	TRACTION MOTORS - GENERAL ELECTRIC			CYL. PRESSURE - 50 LBS.	
	COOLING WATER	220			DRAFT GEAR - NATIONAL MALL. M-380		
	STEAM GENERATOR	NONE			SANDERS -		
SAND BOX CAPACITY - 32 CU. FT.			GEARS - 74 TEETH. PINION 18 TEETH		HEADLIGHTS		
MINIMUM CURVE RADIUS - 150 FT.			GEAR RATIO - 4.11 TO 1				
MAXIMUM PERMISSIBLE SPEED - 70 MPH.					STEAM GENERATORS - NONE		
REVISED			STORAGE BATTERIES - 32 CELLS, 17 PLATE				

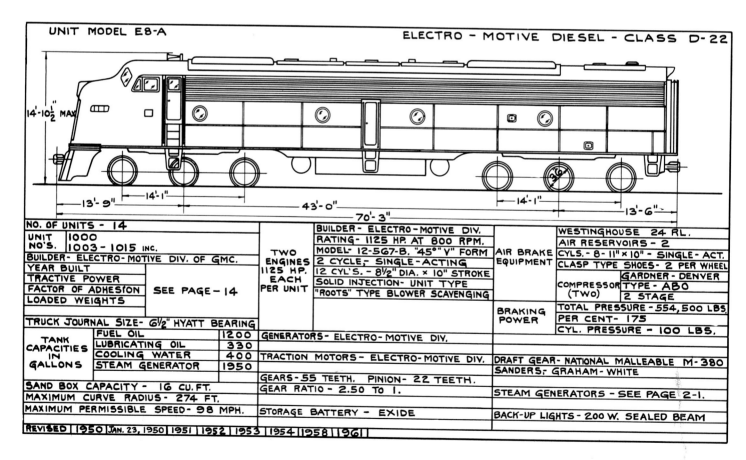

UNIT MODEL E8-A

ELECTRO - MOTIVE DIESEL - CLASS D-22

NO. OF UNITS - 14							
UNIT NO'S.	1000 1003 - 1015 INC.		TWO ENGINES 1125 HP. EACH PER UNIT	BUILDER - ELECTRO-MOTIVE DIV.	AIR BRAKE EQUIPMENT	WESTINGHOUSE 24 RL.	
				RATING - 1125 HP. AT 800 RPM.		AIR RESERVOIRS - 2	
BUILDER - ELECTRO-MOTIVE DIV. OF GMC.				MODEL - 12-567-B. "45°"V" FORM		CYLS. - 8 - 11"×10" - SINGLE - ACT.	
YEAR BUILT	SEE PAGE - 14			2 CYCLE - SINGLE - ACTING		CLASP TYPE SHOES - 2 PER WHEEL	
TRACTIVE POWER				12 CYL'S. - 8½" DIA. × 10" STROKE	COMPRESSOR (TWO)	GARDNER - DENVER	
FACTOR OF ADHESION				SOLID INJECTION - UNIT TYPE		TYPE - A80	
LOADED WEIGHTS				"ROOTS" TYPE BLOWER SCAVENGING		2 STAGE	
TRUCK JOURNAL SIZE - 6½" HYATT BEARING					BRAKING POWER	TOTAL PRESSURE - 554,500 LBS.	
TANK CAPACITIES IN GALLONS	FUEL OIL	1200	GENERATORS - ELECTRO-MOTIVE DIV.			PER CENT - 175	
	LUBRICATING OIL	330				CYL. PRESSURE - 100 LBS.	
	COOLING WATER	400	TRACTION MOTORS - ELECTRO-MOTIVE DIV.		DRAFT GEAR - NATIONAL MALLEABLE M-380		
	STEAM GENERATOR	1950			SANDERS - GRAHAM - WHITE		
SAND BOX CAPACITY - 16 CU. FT.			GEARS - 55 TEETH. PINION - 22 TEETH.				
MAXIMUM CURVE RADIUS - 274 FT.			GEAR RATIO - 2.50 TO 1.		STEAM GENERATORS - SEE PAGE 2-1.		
MAXIMUM PERMISSIBLE SPEED - 98 MPH.			STORAGE BATTERY - EXIDE				
REVISED 1950 JAN. 23, 1950 1951 1952 1953 1954 1958 1961					BACK-UP LIGHTS - 200 W. SEALED BEAM		

280

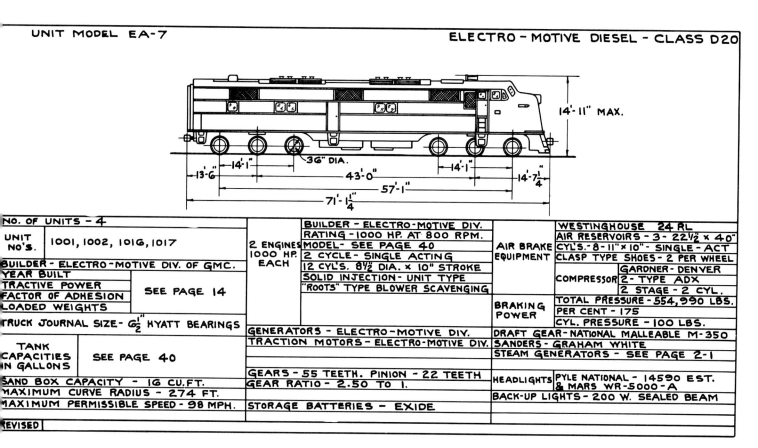

UNIT MODEL EA-7

ELECTRO - MOTIVE DIESEL - CLASS D20

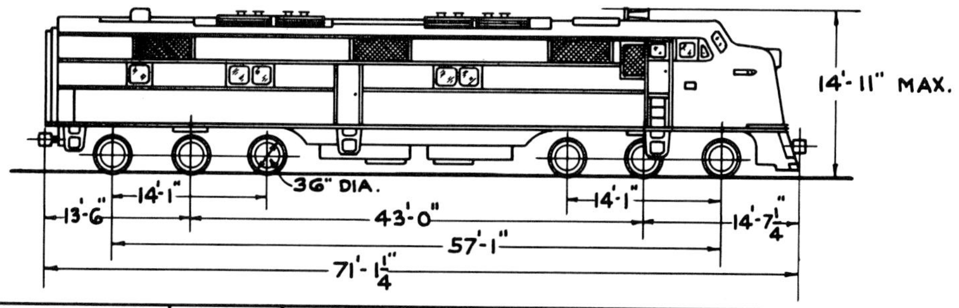

NO. OF UNITS - 4		2 ENGINES 1000 HP. EACH	BUILDER - ELECTRO-MOTIVE DIV.	AIR BRAKE EQUIPMENT	WESTINGHOUSE 24 RL
UNIT NO'S.	1001, 1002, 1016, 1017		RATING - 1000 HP. AT 800 RPM.		AIR RESERVOIRS - 3 - 22½ × 40"
BUILDER - ELECTRO-MOTIVE DIV. OF GMC.			MODEL - SEE PAGE 40		CYL'S. - 8 - 11" × 10" - SINGLE - ACT
YEAR BUILT	SEE PAGE 14		2 CYCLE - SINGLE ACTING		CLASP TYPE SHOES - 2 PER WHEEL
TRACTIVE POWER			12 CYL'S. 8½ DIA. × 10" STROKE	COMPRESSOR	GARDNER - DENVER
FACTOR OF ADHESION			SOLID INJECTION - UNIT TYPE		2 - TYPE ADX
LOADED WEIGHTS			"ROOTS" TYPE BLOWER SCAVENGING		2 STAGE - 2 CYL.
TRUCK JOURNAL SIZE - 6½" HYATT BEARINGS				BRAKING POWER	TOTAL PRESSURE - 554,990 LBS.
					PER CENT - 175
					CYL. PRESSURE - 100 LBS.
TANK CAPACITIES IN GALLONS	SEE PAGE 40	GENERATORS - ELECTRO-MOTIVE DIV.		DRAFT GEAR - NATIONAL MALLEABLE M-350	
		TRACTION MOTORS - ELECTRO-MOTIVE DIV.		SANDERS - GRAHAM WHITE	
				STEAM GENERATORS - SEE PAGE 2-1	
SAND BOX CAPACITY - 16 CU. FT.		GEARS - 55 TEETH. PINION - 22 TEETH		HEADLIGHTS	PYLE NATIONAL - 14590 EST. & MARS WR-5000-A
MAXIMUM CURVE RADIUS - 274 FT.		GEAR RATIO - 2.50 TO 1.			
MAXIMUM PERMISSIBLE SPEED - 98 MPH.		STORAGE BATTERIES - EXIDE		BACK-UP LIGHTS - 200 W. SEALED BEAM	
REVISED					

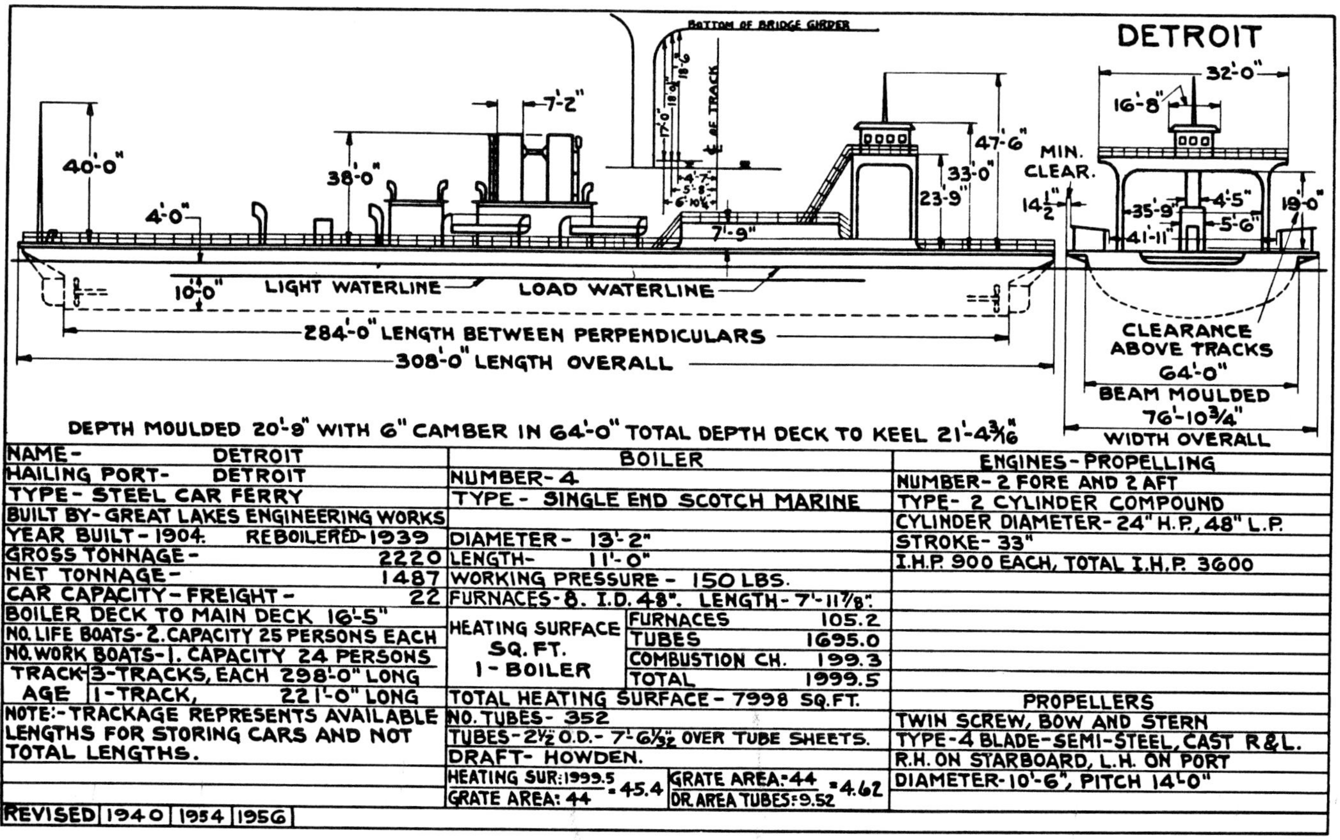

DEPTH MOULDED 20'-9" WITH 6" CAMBER IN 64'-0" TOTAL DEPTH DECK TO KEEL 21'-4 3/16"

		BOILER		ENGINES - PROPELLING
NAME -	DETROIT			
HAILING PORT -	DETROIT	NUMBER - 4		NUMBER - 2 FORE AND 2 AFT
TYPE - STEEL CAR FERRY		TYPE - SINGLE END SCOTCH MARINE		TYPE - 2 CYLINDER COMPOUND
BUILT BY - GREAT LAKES ENGINEERING WORKS				CYLINDER DIAMETER - 24" H.P., 48" L.P.
YEAR BUILT - 1904	REBOILERED - 1939	DIAMETER - 13'-2"		STROKE - 33"
GROSS TONNAGE -	2220	LENGTH - 11'-0"		I.H.P. 900 EACH, TOTAL I.H.P. 3600
NET TONNAGE -	1487	WORKING PRESSURE - 150 LBS.		
CAR CAPACITY - FREIGHT -	22	FURNACES - 8. I.D. 48". LENGTH - 7'-11⅞".		
BOILER DECK TO MAIN DECK 16'-5"		HEATING SURFACE SQ. FT. 1 - BOILER	FURNACES 105.2	
NO. LIFE BOATS - 2. CAPACITY 25 PERSONS EACH			TUBES 1695.0	
NO. WORK BOATS - 1. CAPACITY 24 PERSONS			COMBUSTION CH. 199.3	
TRACKAGE	3 - TRACKS, EACH 298'-0" LONG		TOTAL 1999.5	
	1 - TRACK, 221'-0" LONG	TOTAL HEATING SURFACE - 7998 SQ. FT.		PROPELLERS
NOTE:- TRACKAGE REPRESENTS AVAILABLE LENGTHS FOR STORING CARS AND NOT TOTAL LENGTHS.		NO. TUBES - 352		TWIN SCREW, BOW AND STERN
		TUBES - 2½ O.D. - 7'-6 1/32 OVER TUBE SHEETS.		TYPE - 4 BLADE - SEMI - STEEL, CAST R & L.
		DRAFT - HOWDEN.		R.H. ON STARBOARD, L.H. ON PORT
		HEATING SUR: 1999.5 / GRATE AREA: 44 = 45.4	GRATE AREA: 44 / DR. AREA TUBES: 9.52 = 4.62	DIAMETER - 10'-6", PITCH 14'-0"
REVISED	1940 1954 1956			

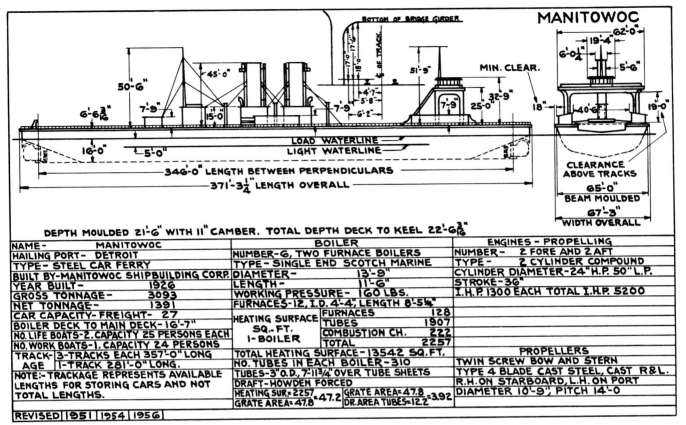

MANITOWOC

DEPTH MOULDED 21'-6" WITH 11" CAMBER. TOTAL DEPTH DECK TO KEEL 22'-6 3/16"

NAME- MANITOWOC	BOILER	ENGINES – PROPELLING
HAILING PORT- DETROIT	NUMBER-6, TWO FURNACE BOILERS	NUMBER- 2 FORE AND 2 AFT
TYPE- STEEL CAR FERRY	TYPE- SINGLE END SCOTCH MARINE	TYPE- 2 CYLINDER COMPOUND
BUILT BY-MANITOWOC SHIPBUILDING CORP.	DIAMETER- 13'-9"	CYLINDER DIAMETER-24"H.P. 50"L.P.
YEAR BUILT- 1926	LENGTH- 11'-6"	STROKE-36"
GROSS TONNAGE- 3093	WORKING PRESSURE- 160 LBS.	I.H.P. 1300 EACH TOTAL I.H.P. 5200
NET TONNAGE- 1391	FURNACES-12, I.D. 4'-4", LENGTH 8'-5¼"	
CAR CAPACITY-FREIGHT- 27	HEATING SURFACE SQ.-FT. 1-BOILER	FURNACES 128	
BOILER DECK TO MAIN DECK-16'-7"		TUBES 1907	
NO. LIFE BOATS-2. CAPACITY 25 PERSONS EACH		COMBUSTION CH. 222	
NO. WORK BOATS-1. CAPACITY 24 PERSONS		TOTAL 2257	
TRACK- 3-TRACKS EACH 357'-0" LONG AGE 1-TRACK 281'-0" LONG.	TOTAL HEATING SURFACE-13542 SQ.FT.	PROPELLERS
	NO. TUBES IN EACH BOILER-310	TWIN SCREW BOW AND STERN
NOTE:- TRACKAGE REPRESENTS AVAILABLE LENGTHS FOR STORING CARS AND NOT TOTAL LENGTHS.	TUBES-3"O.D., 7'-11¾" OVER TUBE SHEETS	TYPE 4 BLADE CAST STEEL, CAST R&L.
	DRAFT-HOWDEN FORCED	R.H. ON STARBOARD, L.H. ON PORT
	HEATING SUR=2257 =47.2 GRATE AREA=47.8 =.392	DIAMETER 10'-9", PITCH 14'-0
	GRATE AREA=47.8 DR. AREA TUBES=12.2	

NOTE-
EQUIPPED WITH PEABODY TYPE ML-13-½" FORCED DRAFT
REGISTERS, SWING FRONTS WITH TYPE "A" WIDE RANGE
MECHANICAL ATOMIZING OIL BURNER UNITS.
SIMPLEX ENGINEERING CORP.- DETROIT, MICH.
DATE APPLIED- DEC. 1950.

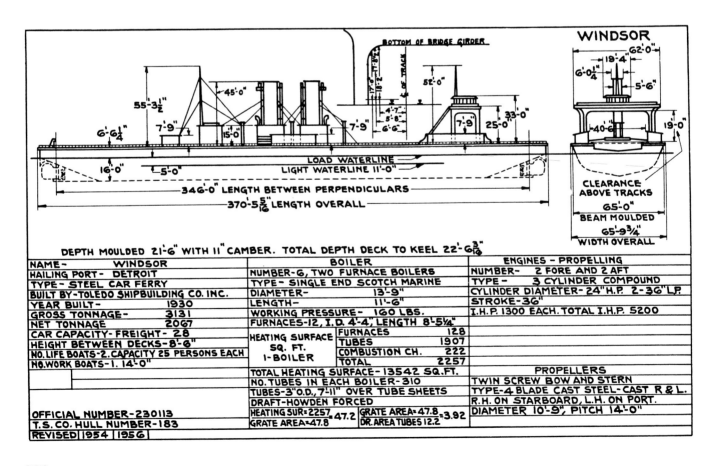

WINDSOR

DEPTH MOULDED 21'-6" WITH 11" CAMBER. TOTAL DEPTH DECK TO KEEL 22'-6 3/16"

NAME- WINDSOR	BOILER	ENGINES – PROPELLING
HAILING PORT- DETROIT	NUMBER-6, TWO FURNACE BOILERS	NUMBER- 2 FORE AND 2 AFT
TYPE- STEEL CAR FERRY	TYPE- SINGLE END SCOTCH MARINE	TYPE- 3 CYLINDER COMPOUND
BUILT BY-TOLEDO SHIPBUILDING CO. INC.	DIAMETER- 13'-9"	CYLINDER DIAMETER-24"H.P. 2-36"L.P.
YEAR BUILT- 1930	LENGTH- 11'-6"	STROKE-36"
GROSS TONNAGE- 3131	WORKING PRESSURE- 160 LBS.	I.H.P. 1300 EACH. TOTAL I.H.P. 5200
NET TONNAGE 2067	FURNACES-12, I.D. 4'-4", LENGTH 8'-5¼"	
CAR CAPACITY-FREIGHT- 28	HEATING SURFACE SQ. FT. 1-BOILER	FURNACES 128	
HEIGHT BETWEEN DECKS-8'-6"		TUBES 1907	
NO. LIFE BOATS-2. CAPACITY 25 PERSONS EACH		COMBUSTION CH. 222	
NO. WORK BOATS-1. 14'-0"		TOTAL 2257	
	TOTAL HEATING SURFACE-13542 SQ.FT.	PROPELLERS
	NO. TUBES IN EACH BOILER-310	TWIN SCREW BOW AND STERN
	TUBES-3"O.D., 7'-11" OVER TUBE SHEETS	TYPE-4 BLADE CAST STEEL-CAST R & L.
	DRAFT-HOWDEN FORCED	R.H. ON STARBOARD, L.H. ON PORT.
OFFICIAL NUMBER-230113	HEATING SUR=2257 =47.2 GRATE AREA=47.8 =3.92	DIAMETER 10'-9", PITCH 14'-0"
T.S. CO. HULL NUMBER-183	GRATE AREA=47.8 DR. AREA TUBES 12.2	

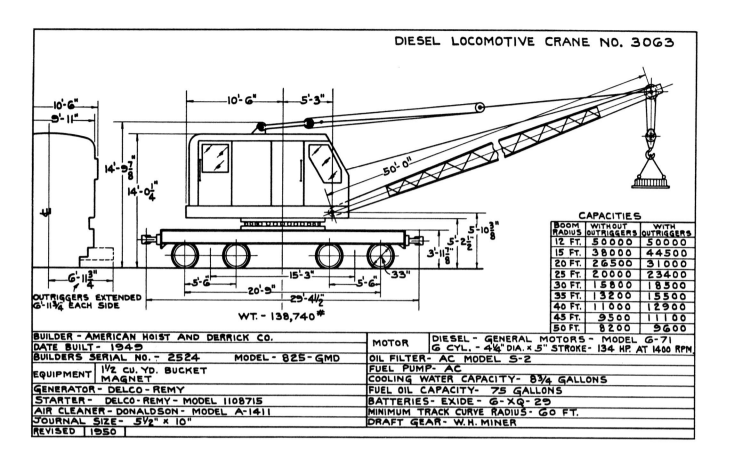

DIESEL LOCOMOTIVE CRANE NO. 3063

WT. - 138,740 #

OUTRIGGERS EXTENDED
6'-11¾" EACH SIDE

CAPACITIES

BOOM RADIUS	WITHOUT OUTRIGGERS	WITH OUTRIGGERS
12 FT.	50000	50000
15 FT.	38000	44500
20 FT.	26500	31000
25 FT.	20000	23400
30 FT.	15800	18500
35 FT.	13200	15500
40 FT.	11000	12900
45 FT.	9500	11100
50 FT.	8200	9600

BUILDER - AMERICAN HOIST AND DERRICK CO.
DATE BUILT - 1949
BUILDERS SERIAL NO. - 2524   MODEL - 825-GMD
EQUIPMENT 1½ CU. YD. BUCKET / MAGNET
GENERATOR - DELCO-REMY
STARTER - DELCO-REMY - MODEL 1108715
AIR CLEANER - DONALDSON - MODEL A-1411
JOURNAL SIZE - 5½" x 10"
REVISED | 1950

MOTOR DIESEL - GENERAL MOTORS - MODEL G-71
6 CYL. - 4¼" DIA. x 5" STROKE - 134 H.P. AT 1400 RPM.
OIL FILTER- AC MODEL S-2
FUEL PUMP- AC
COOLING WATER CAPACITY- 8¾ GALLONS
FUEL OIL CAPACITY- 75 GALLONS
BATTERIES- EXIDE- 6-XQ-29
MINIMUM TRACK CURVE RADIUS- 60 FT.
DRAFT GEAR- W.H. MINER

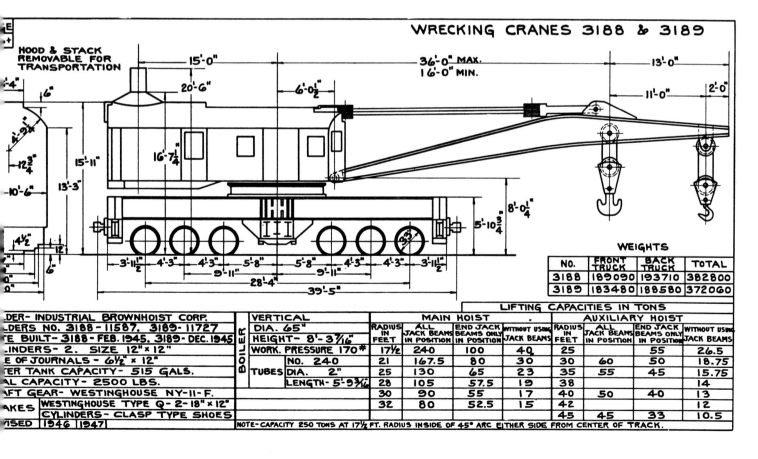

WRECKING CRANES 3188 & 3189

HOOD & STACK REMOVABLE FOR TRANSPORTATION

36'-0" MAX.
16'-0" MIN.

WEIGHTS

NO.	FRONT TRUCK	BACK TRUCK	TOTAL
3188	189090	193710	382800
3189	183480	188580	372060

BUILDER- INDUSTRIAL BROWNHOIST CORP.
BUILDERS NO. 3188 - 11587, 3189 - 11727
DATE BUILT- 3188 - FEB. 1945, 3189 - DEC. 1945
CYLINDERS- 2. SIZE 12" x 12"
SIZE OF JOURNALS - 6½" x 12"
WATER TANK CAPACITY- 515 GALS.
COAL CAPACITY- 2500 LBS.
DRAFT GEAR- WESTINGHOUSE NY-11-F.
BRAKES WESTINGHOUSE TYPE Q-2-18" x 12"
CYLINDERS- CLASP TYPE SHOES
REVISED | 1946 | 1947

BOILER
VERTICAL
DIA. 65"
HEIGHT- 8'-3 7/16"
WORK. PRESSURE 170 #
TUBES NO. 240
DIA. 2"
LENGTH- 5'-9 3/16"

LIFTING CAPACITIES IN TONS

	MAIN HOIST				AUXILIARY HOIST			
RADIUS IN FEET	ALL JACK BEAMS IN POSITION	END JACK BEAMS ONLY IN POSITION	WITHOUT USING JACK BEAMS		RADIUS IN FEET	ALL JACK BEAMS IN POSITION	END JACK BEAMS ONLY IN POSITION	WITHOUT USING JACK BEAMS
17½	240	100	40		25		55	26.5
21	167.5	80	30		30	60	50	18.75
25	130	65	23		35		55	15.75
28	105	57.5	19		38			14
30	90	55	17		40	50	40	13
32	80	52.5	15		42			12
					45	45	33	10.5

NOTE- CAPACITY 250 TONS AT 17½ FT. RADIUS INSIDE OF 45° ARC EITHER SIDE FROM CENTER OF TRACK.

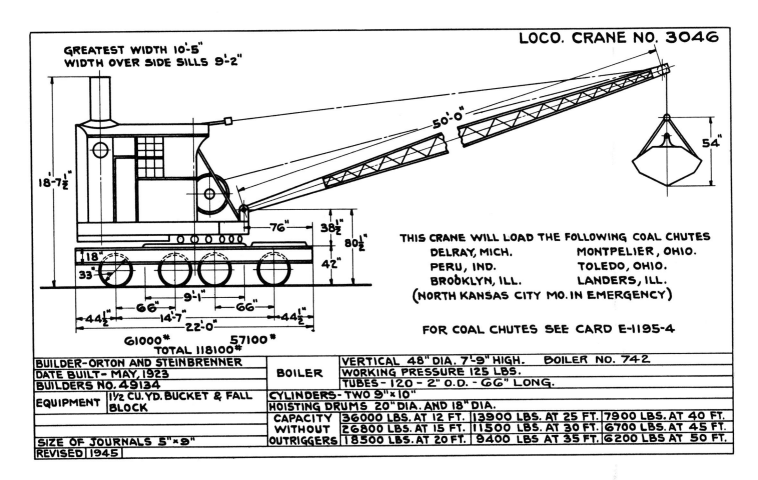

LOCO. CRANE NO. 3046

GREATEST WIDTH 10'-5"
WIDTH OVER SIDE SILLS 9'-2"

THIS CRANE WILL LOAD THE FOLLOWING COAL CHUTES
DELRAY, MICH.   MONTPELIER, OHIO.
PERU, IND.   TOLEDO, OHIO.
BROOKLYN, ILL.   LANDERS, ILL.
(NORTH KANSAS CITY MO. IN EMERGENCY)

FOR COAL CHUTES SEE CARD E-1195-4

BUILDER—ORTON AND STEINBRENNER		BOILER	VERTICAL 48" DIA. 7'-9" HIGH. BOILER NO. 742
DATE BUILT— MAY, 1923			WORKING PRESSURE 125 LBS.
BUILDERS NO. 49134			TUBES - 120 - 2" O.D. - 66" LONG.
EQUIPMENT	1½ CU. YD. BUCKET & FALL BLOCK	CYLINDERS— TWO 9"x10"
		HOISTING DRUMS 20" DIA. AND 18" DIA.
		CAPACITY WITHOUT OUTRIGGERS	36000 LBS. AT 12 FT.	13900 LBS. AT 25 FT.	7900 LBS. AT 40 FT.
SIZE OF JOURNALS 5"x 9"			26800 LBS. AT 15 FT.	11500 LBS. AT 30 FT.	6700 LBS. AT 45 FT.
REVISED 1945			18500 LBS. AT 20 FT.	9400 LBS AT 35 FT.	6200 LBS. AT 50 FT.

TURNTABLE INFORMATION

PAGE 80

LOCATION	LENGTH	POWER	LONGEST ENGINE	LOCATION	LENGTH	POWER	LONGEST ENGINE
Ft. Erie	85'-0"	Air & Electric	P-1	Luther	80'-0"	Electric	K-4
Niagara Falls	90'-0"	Air & Electric	O-1	Vandeventer	90'-0"	Electric	O-1
St. Thomas	71'-1"	Air	K-1	Moulton	70'-0"	Air	K-2
Windsor	90'-0"	Electric	O-1	Ottumwa	60'-0"	Hand	F-7
				Des Moines	80'-0"	Electric	K-4
Delray	105'-0"	Electric	O-1	N. Kansas City	100'-0"	Electric	O-1
Toledo	100'-0"	Electric	O-1	Stanberry	69'-2"	Hand	K-1
Montpelier	100'-0"	Electric	O-1	East Switch	85'-0"	Hand	P-1
Ft. Wayne	70'-0"	Electric	K-1				
Peru	100'-0"	Electric	O-1				
Tilton	74'-6"	Electric	K-4		ANN ARBOR RR. CO.		
				Toledo	90'-0"	Electric	K-7
Landers	90'-4"	Electric	O-1	Ann Arbor	80'-0"	Hand	K-7
Forrest	90'-0"	Electric	O-1	Owosso	75'-0"	Electric	K-7
Decatur	100'-0"	Electric	O-1	Cadillac	Wye		K-7
Brooklyn	90'-2"	Electric	O-1	Frankfort	75'-0"	Electric	K-7
Bluffs	69'-6"	Air	K-1	Mt. Pleasant	Wye		K-7
Quincy	70'-2"	Hand	K-1				
Hannibal	100'-2"	Electric	O-1		MANISTIQUE & LAKE SUPERIOR RR. CO.		
				Manistique	55'-0"	Air	I-7
					N. J. I. & I. RR. CO.		
Moberly	100'-0"	Electric	O-1	South Bend	70'-0"	Electric	K1-Wab.
Columbia	70'-0"	Hand	K-1				

Revised   1941   1944   1946   1952

284

Selections from First Annual Report of the Wabash Railway Company, fiscal year ended December 31, 1916.

WABASH RAILWAY COMPANY

To the Stockholders of the Wabash Railway Company:

The Board of Directors submit the following report of the operations for the year ended December 31, 1916:

Average Mileage Operated	2,519.06
Operating Revenues:	
Freight	$ 27,609,740.86
Passenger	7,024,228.52
Mail	785,480.41
Express	1,072,573.61
Miscellaneous	603,743.58
Incidental	564,306.97
Joint Facility	61,030.54
Total Operating Revenues	$ 37,721,104.49
Operating Expenses:	
Maintenance of Way and Structures	$ 3,796,801.79
Maintenance of Equipment	5,662,908.88
Traffic	1,109,933.48
Transportation	13,364,775.63
Miscellaneous Operations	208,911.72
General	824,345.25
Transportation for Investment—Cr.	93,259.68
Total Operating Expenses	$ 24,874,417.07
Net Revenue from Railway Operations	$ 12,846,687.42
Railway Tax Accruals	$ 1,169,380.37
Uncollectible Railway Revenues	5,857.88
Total	$ 1,175,238.25
Total Operating Income	$ 11,671,449.17
Nonoperating Income	$ 509,772.00
Gross Income	$ 12,181,221.17
Deductions from Gross Income	6,790,312.96
Net Income	$ 5,390,908.21
Disposition of Net Income:	
Income applied to Sinking and Other Reserve Funds	$ 84,410.00
Income Balance Transferred to Profit and Loss	$ 5,306,498.21

5

WABASH RAILWAY COMPANY
TRANSPORTATION STATISTICS
Year Ended December 31, 1916, Compared with Previous Year

	1916	1915	Amount Increase	Amount Decrease	Per Cent Increase	Per Cent Decrease
TRAIN MILES						
Revenue Service:						
Freight Train Miles	8,487,969	7,910,670	577,299		7.3	
Passenger Train Miles	7,537,839	7,252,211	285,628		3.9	
Mixed Train Miles	95,875	96,181		306		.3
Special Train Miles	8,296	8,856		560		6.3
Total Revenue Service	16,129,979	15,267,918	862,061		5.6	
Non-Revenue Train Miles	251,455	265,899		14,444		5.4
Total Train Miles	16,381,434	15,533,817	847,617		5.5	
CAR MILES						
Revenue Service:						
Freight Train Car Miles:						
Loaded	224,162,458	188,587,441	35,575,017		18.9	
Empty	75,006,669	90,091,103		15,084,434		16.7
Caboose	8,552,392	7,940,901	611,491		7.7	
Total	307,721,519	286,619,445	21,102,074		7.4	
Passenger Train Car Miles:						
Coach and Chair Car Miles	17,074,135	15,956,610	1,117,525		7.0	
Parlor and Observation Car Miles	630,263	629,383	880		.1	
Sleeping Car Miles	9,334,969	8,725,089	609,880		7.0	
Baggage, Mail and Express Car Miles	10,153,063	8,991,386	1,161,677		12.9	
Dining Car Miles	1,677,400	1,500,249	177,151		11.8	
Official Car Miles	156,950	139,174	17,776		12.8	
Total	39,026,780	35,941,891	3,084,889		8.6	
Special Train Car Miles:						
Freight—Loaded	125,255	120,360	4,895		4.1	
Freight—Empty	259	908		649		71.5
Caboose	8,361	8,952		591		6.6
Total	133,875	130,220	3,655		2.8	
Total Revenue Service Car Miles	346,882,174	322,691,556	24,190,618		7.5	
Non-Revenue Train Car Miles	1,341,628	2,028,580		686,952		33.9
Total Train Car Miles	348,223,802	324,720,136	23,503,666		7.2	
Miscellaneous Freight:						
Foreign Loaded Car Miles	194,817,094	136,679,003	58,138,091		42.5	
Foreign Empty Car Miles	58,947,654	63,422,671		4,475,017		7.1
Total Foreign Car Miles	253,764,748	200,101,674	53,663,074		26.8	
Wabash Loaded Car Miles	29,470,619	52,028,798		22,558,179		43.4
Wabash Empty Car Miles (including Caboose)	24,620,027	34,619,193		9,999,166		28.9
Total Wabash Car Miles	54,090,646	86,647,991		32,557,345		37.6
Average number of Wabash Cars in Service (exclusive of Work Trains) per day	18,293	21,768		3,475		16.0
Average number of Wabash Cars on other Roads per day	9,959	6,584	3,375		51.3	
Miles per Car per Day Wabash Cars on Wabash Road	17.92	16.82	1.10		6.5	
Average number of Foreign Cars on Wabash Road per Day	16,662	11,412	5,250		46.0	
Miles per Car per Day Foreign Cars on Wabash Road	41.61	48.04		6.43		13.4
Average Revenue Freight Train Miles per Day	23,453	21,937	1,516		6.9	
Average Loaded Cars per Train Mile	26.11	23.55	2.56		10.9	
Average Empty Cars (excluding Caboose) per Train Mile	8.74	11.25		2.51		22.3
Average Loaded and Empty Cars per Train Mile	34.85	34.80	.05		.1	
Average Total Cars (including Caboose) per Train Mile	35.85	35.80	.05		.1	
Per Cent of Loaded Car Miles to Total Car Miles	72.85	65.80	7.05		10.7	
PASSENGER						
Total Wabash Passenger Train Car Miles	36,617,114	34,300,054	2,317,060		6.8	
Total Foreign Passenger Train Car Miles	2,409,666	1,641,837	767,829		46.8	
Average Revenue Passenger Train Miles per Day	20,857	20,133	724		3.6	
Average number of Cars per Passenger Train Mile	5.11	4.89	.22		4.5	

WABASH RAILWAY COMPANY
TRAFFIC AND GENERAL STATISTICS
Year Ended December 31, 1916, Compared with Previous Year

	1916	1915	Amount Increase	Amount Decrease	Per Cent Increase	Per Cent Decrease
FREIGHT TRAFFIC.						
Number of Tons Carried:						
Revenue Freight	17,236,884	14,304,775	2,932,109		20.5	
Company Freight	3,195,984	2,893,866	302,118		10.4	
Total	20,432,868	17,198,641	3,234,227		18.8	
Number of Tons Carried One Mile:						
Revenue Freight	4,440,861,488	3,436,000,964	1,004,860,524		29.2	
Company Freight	351,219,122	370,901,081		19,681,959		5.3
Total	4,792,080,610	3,806,902,045	985,178,565		25.9	
Number of Tons Carried One Mile per Mile of Road:						
Revenue Freight	1,762,904	1,364,001	398,903		29.2	
Company Freight	139,425	147,238		7,813		5.3
Total	1,902,329	1,511,239	391,090		25.9	
Number of Tons per Loaded Car Mile:						
Revenue Freight	19.81	18.22	1.59		8.7	
Company Freight	1.57	1.97		.40		20.3
Total	21.38	20.19	1.19		5.9	
Number of Tons per Train Mile:						
Revenue Freight	517.35	429.13	88.22		20.6	
Company Freight	40.92	46.32		5.40		11.7
Total	558.27	475.45	82.82		17.4	
Average Haul per Ton (in miles):						
Revenue Freight	257.64	240.20	17.44		7.3	
Company Freight	109.89	128.17		18.28		14.3
Total	234.53	221.35	13.18		6.0	
Revenue per Ton—Revenue Tons	$ 1.6018	$ 1.5387	$ .0631		4.1	
Revenue per Ton per Mile—Revenue Tons	.006217	.006406		$ .000189		3.0
Revenue per Loaded Car Mile	.1232	.1167	.65		5.6	
Revenue per Train Mile	3.2165	2.7491	.4674		17.0	
Revenue per Mile of Road Operated	10,960.33	8,737.90	2,222.43		25.4	
PASSENGER TRAFFIC.						
Passengers Carried	5,932,117	5,446,255	485,862		8.9	
Passengers Carried One Mile	364,774,714	304,389,264	60,385,450		19.8	
Passengers Carried One Mile per Mile of Road Operated	144,806	120,834	23,972		19.8	
Number of Passengers per Passenger Car Mile	13.49	12.03	1.46		12.1	
Number of Passengers per Train Mile	47.78	41.42	6.36		15.4	
Average Distance per Passenger	61.49	55.89	5.60		10.0	
Revenue per Passenger	$ 1.1841	$ 1.1117	$ .0724		6.5	
Revenue per Passenger and Sleeping Car Mile	$ .2598	$ .2392	$ .0206		8.6	
Revenue per Passenger Mile	$ .01926	$ .01989		$ .00063		3.2
Revenue per Passenger Train Mile	$ .9202	$ .8240	$ .0962		11.7	
Passenger Train Revenue per Passenger Train Mile	$ 1.1856	$ 1.0618	$ .1238		11.7	
Passenger Train Revenue per Mile of Road Operated	$ 3,592.83	$ 3,097.32	$ 495.51		16.0	
GENERAL						
Total Traffic Train Miles	16,121,683	15,259,062	862,621		5.7	
Operating Revenues per Traffic Train Mile	$ 2.2740	$ 1.9199	$ .3541		18.4	
Operating Expenses per Traffic Train Mile	$ 1.5429	$ 1.5053	$ .0376		2.5	
Net Operating Revenue per Traffic Train Mile	$ 0.7311	$ 0.4146	$ .3165		76.3	
Miles of Road Operated	2,519.06	2,519.06				
Operating Revenue per Mile of Road Operated	$ 14,974.28	$ 12,182.05	2,792.23		22.9	
Operating Expenses per Mile of Road Operated	$ 9,874.48	$ 9,279.81	594.67		6.4	
Net Operating Revenue per Mile of Road Operated	$ 5,099.80	$ 2,902.24	$ 2,197.56		75.7	

28

WABASH RAILWAY COMPANY

REVENUE FREIGHT TRAFFIC STATISTICS

Year Ended December 31, 1916, Compared with Previous Year

	1916		1915		Increase		Decrease	
	Tons	Per Cent of Total	Tons	Per Cent of Total	Tons	Per Cent	Tons	Per Cent
PRODUCTS OF AGRICULTURE:								
Grain	1,990,003	11.54	1,665,425	11.64	324,578	19.5		
Flour	285,726	1.66	243,428	1.70	42,298	17.4		
Other Mill Products	375,226	2.18	311,167	2.18	64,059	20.1		
Hay	140,157	.81	175,386	1.23			35,229	20.1
Tobacco	9,396	.05	5,601	.04	3,795	67.8		
Cotton	57,480	.34	51,505	.36	5,975	11.6		
Fruit and Vegetables	417,763	2.42	382,620	2.67	35,143	9.2		
Other Products of Agriculture	152,921	.89	125,164	.87	27,757	22.2		
Total	3,428,672	19.89	2,960,296	20.69	468,376	15.8		
PRODUCTS OF ANIMALS:								
Live Stock	447,874	2.60	428,148	2.99	19,726	4.6		
Dressed Meats	253,916	1.47	173,190	1.21	80,726	46.6		
Other Packing House Products	201,443	1.17	247,995	1.74			46,552	18.8
Poultry, Game and Fish	116,657	.68	84,895	.59	31,762	37.4		
Wool	20,708	.12	11,922	.08	8,786	73.7		
Hides and Leather	58,095	.34	65,177	.46			7,082	10.9
Other Products of Animals	121,077	.70	90,633	.63	30,444	33.6		
Total	1,219,770	7.08	1,101,960	7.70	117,810	10.7		
PRODUCTS OF MINES:								
Anthracite Coal	377,110	2.19	425,598	2.98			48,488	11.4
Bituminous Coal	3,532,071	20.49	3,001,103	20.98	530,968	17.7		
Coke	81,458	.47	59,849	.42	21,609	36.1		
Ores	87,506	.51	48,699	.34	38,807	79.7		
Stone, Sand and other like Articles	894,771	5.19	870,001	6.08	24,770	2.8		
Other Products of Mines	841,175	4.88	638,258	4.46	202,917	31.8		
Total	5,814,091	33.73	5,043,508	35.26	770,583	15.3		
PRODUCTS OF FORESTS:								
Lumber	966,522	5.61	885,327	6.19	81,195	9.2		
Other Products of Forests	97,580	.56	107,678	.75			10,098	9.4
Total	1,064,102	6.17	993,005	6.94	71,097	7.2		
MANUFACTURES:								
Petroleum and Other Oils	433,743	2.51	261,585	1.82	172,158	65.8		
Sugar	111,445	.65	94,608	.66	16,837	17.8		
Naval Stores	25,663	.15	23,767	.17	1,896	8.0		
Iron, Pig and Bloom	179,260	1.04	118,818	.83	60,442	50.9		
Iron and Steel Rails	88,078	.51	32,487	.23	55,591	171.1		
Other Castings and Machinery	484,929	2.81	295,002	2.06	189,927	64.4		
Bar and Sheet Metal	302,678	1.76	223,958	1.57	78,720	35.1		
Cement, Brick and Lime	661,221	3.84	612,436	4.28	48,785	8.0		
Agricultural Implements	52,692	.30	44,663	.31	8,029	18.0		
Wagons, Carriages, Tools, etc.	216,546	1.26	167,688	1.17	48,858	29.1		
Wines, Liquors and Beers	119,706	.69	105,616	.74	14,090	13.3		
Household Goods and Furniture	88,618	.52	79,615	.56	9,003	11.3		
Other Manufactures	1,181,152	6.85	936,378	6.55	244,774	26.1		
Total	3,945,731	22.89	2,996,621	20.95	949,110	31.7		
Merchandise (less than carload Freight)	1,286,733	7.47	928,684	6.49	358,049	38.6		
Miscellaneous (other Commodities not mentioned above)	477,785	2.77	280,701	1.97	197,084	70.2		
Total	17,236,884	100.00	14,304,775	100.00	2,932,109	20.5		

29

WABASH RAILWAY COMPANY

PERFORMANCE OF LOCOMOTIVES

Year Ended December 31, 1916, Compared with Previous Year

	1916	1915	Increase	Decrease
MILEAGE:				
Freight Locomotive Miles	8,816,107	8,214,927	601,180	
Passenger Locomotive Miles	7,712,933	7,453,228	259,705	
Mixed Locomotive Miles	98,028	99,568		1,540
Special Locomotive Miles	8,443	9,049		606
Switching Locomotive Miles	4,217,822	3,840,668	377,154	
Total Revenue Locomotive Miles	20,853,333	19,617,440	1,235,893	
Non-Revenue Service Locomotive Miles	395,176	335,335	59,841	
Total Locomotive Miles	21,248,509	19,952,775	1,295,734	
Average Mileage per Locomotive in Service for Year	43,188	40,309	2,879	
Average Monthly Mileage per Locomotive in Service	3,599	3,359	240	
Tons of Coal Consumed	1,719,665	1,629,306	90,359	
Average Cost per Ton of Coal on Tender. . . .	$1.60	$1.45	$0.15	
Average Miles Run to One Ton of Coal	12.36	12.25	.11	
EXPENSE OF OPERATING LOCOMOTIVES.				
Repairs:				
Labor	$ 1,693,922.07	$ 1,554,628.33	$ 139,293.74	
Material	735,643.69	667,506.15	68,137.54	
Lubricants . . . . :	41,490.56	26,420.99	15,069.57	
Fuel	2,751,366.79	2,364,660.38	386,706.41	
Enginemen	2,116,139.76	1,848,689.83	267,449.93	
Enginehouse Expense	641,811.12	507,129.12	134,682.00	
Total	$ 7,980,373.99	$ 6,969,034.80	$ 1,011,339.19	
COST PER 100 MILES RUN:				
Repairs	$ 11.44	$ 11.14	$ .30	
Lubricants	.19	.13	.06	
Fuel	12.95	11.85	1.10	
Enginemen	9.96	9.27	.69	
Enginehouse Expense	3.02	2.54	.48	
Total	$ 37.56	$ 34.93	$ 2.63	
LOCOMOTIVES REPAIRED:				
Locomotives Receiving Light Repairs	536	524	12	
Locomotives Receiving Medium Heavy Repairs	289	280	9	
Locomotives Receiving General Overhauling . .	422	363	59	
Total	1,247	1,167	80	
Average Cost of Repairs per Locomotive. . . .	$ 4,076.45	$ 3,248.73	$ 827.72	

NOTE.—Tons of coal consumed includes wood and fuel oil used in firing up engines.

NOTE.—Light repairs includes locomotives receiving less than $250.00. Medium heavy repairs includes locomotives receiving $250.00 to $1,000.00. General overhauling includes locomotives receiving over $1,000.00.

30

WABASH RAILWAY COMPANY

EQUIPMENT INVENTORY

December 31, 1916, Compared with Previous Year

	On Hand December 31, 1915	Changed, Built or Purchased	Destroyed, Sold or Changed	On Hand December 31, 1916	INCREASE	DECREASE
LOCOMOTIVES:						
Freight	360		6	354		6
Passenger	107	5		112	5	
Switch	122	1		123	1	
Total	589	6	6	589		
Average Tractive Power (lbs.)	30,201			30,317	116	
FREIGHT TRAIN CARS:						
Automobile	747	500	3	1,244	497	
Box	8,120	1,000	838	8,282	162	
Furniture	356		1	355		1
Stock	995		6	989		6
Coal	5,816		351	5,465		351
Flat and Cable	730		9	721		9
Caboose Box	17	4		21	4	
Caboose Standard	292	9	5	296	4	
Total	17,073	1,513	1,213	17,373	300	
PASSENGER TRAIN CARS:						
Dining and Cafe	17			17		
Parlor	7			7		
Postal	37	6	11	32		5
Baggage	71	4	1	74	3	
Baggage and Mail	14	9	2	21	7	
Baggage, Passenger and Mail	1	1		2	1	
Passenger and Mail	7		2	5		2
Combination	57		1	56		1
Coaches	135		2	133		2
Chair and Club	64			64		
Total	410	20	19	411	1	
FLOATING EQUIPMENT:						
Ferry Boats	3			3		
WORK EQUIPMENT:						
Business	3	1		4	1	
Pay	1			1		
Enginemen's Instruction Cars	2			2		
Dynamometer	1			1		
Valuation	1			1		
Shop Train Coaches	9			9		
Cinder	112		11	101		11
Ballast	87			87		
Company Service	339	221	6	554	215	
Total	555	222	17	760	205	
TOTAL CARS	18,038	1,755	1,249	18,544	506	
Average Capacity of Revenue Freight Cars	78,532 lbs.			78,934 lbs.	402 lbs.	

NOTE.—500 Box Cars were converted into Automobile Cars.
219 Box Cars were converted into Company Service Cars.
332 Coal Cars were retired from service.

31

1925 Annual Report

WABASH RAILWAY COMPANY

INVENTORY OF EQUIPMENT

Year Ended December 31, 1925, Compared with Previous Year

	On Hand December 31, 1925	Changed Built or Purchased	Destroyed Sold or Changed	On Hand December 31, 1924	In-crease	De-crease
LOCOMOTIVES:						
Freight	426	50	6	382	44	
Passenger	118	2	1	117	1	
Switch	138		8	146		8
TOTAL	682	52	15	645	37	
Average Tractive Power (Lbs.)	38,737			36,240	2,497	
FREIGHT TRAIN CARS:						
Automobile	5,946	1,075	85	4,956	990	
Box	9,680	52	431	10,059		379
Furniture	142			142		
Stock	1,228		4	1,232		4
Coal	6,163	425	470	6,208		45
Flat	487			487		
Caboose Box	37	2		35	2	
Caboose Standard	328	27	4	305	23	
TOTAL	24,011	1,581	994	23,424	587	
PASSENGER TRAIN CARS:						
Dining and Cafe	20	2		18	2	
Parlor	6			6		
Postal	18			18		
Baggage	83	10	3	76	7	
Baggage and Mail	21			21		
Baggage, Passenger and Mail	1			1		
Combination	50	3		47	3	
Passenger and Mail	3			3		
Coaches	102		14	116		14
Chair—Coaches	3			3		
Chair	55	5	2	52	3	
Chair—Cafe	6			6		
Chair—Buffet	8			8		
Coach—Cafe	2			2		
TOTAL	378	20	19	377	1	
FLOATING EQUIPMENT:						
Ferry Boats	3			3		
WORK EQUIPMENT:						
Business Cars	6			6		
Pay Cars	1			1		
Enginemen's Instruction Cars	2			2		
Apprentice Instruction Cars	1			1		
Dynamometer Cars	1			1		
Shop Train Coaches			6	6		6
Cinder Cars	10		20	30		20
Ballast Cars	8			8		
Company Service Cars	798	78	18	738	60	
TOTAL	827	78	44	793	34	
TOTAL CARS	25,216	1,679	1,057	24,594	622	
Average Capacity of Revenue Freight Cars (Lbs.)	82,767			82,508	259	

29

WABASH CITY TICKET OFFICE, 511 JEFFERSON STREET, TOLEDO, OHIO. PHONE ADAMS 4184.

WABASH RAILWAY COMPANY

GENERAL OFFICES: - - - - Railway Exchange Building, ST. LOUIS, MO.
NEW YORK OFFICE: - - - - - 120 Broadway, NEW YORK CITY

WILLIAM H. WILLIAMS, Chairman of the Board...................New York, N. Y.
J. E. TAUSSIG, President...St. Louis, Mo.

W. C. MAXWELL, Vice-President in charge of Traffic....St. Louis, Mo.	G. H. SIDO, General Manager...St. Louis, Mo.
S. E. COTTER, Vice-President ....St. Louis, Mo.	E. A. SOLLITT, General Superintendent, Western District....St. Louis, Mo.
WINSLOW S. PIERCE, General Counsel...................New York, N. Y.	V. PARVIN, General Superintendent, Eastern District........St. Louis, Mo.
N. S. BROWN, Vice-President and General Solicitor. ......St. Louis, Mo.	FRED MEYERS, Superintendent Transportation................St. Louis, Mo.
J. W. NEWELL, Vice-President...........................St. Louis, Mo.	G. F. HESS, Superintendent Motive Power....................Decatur, Ill.
A. K. ATKINSON, Vice-President, Secretary and Treasurer. New York, N. Y.	P. F. SCHOWENGERDT, Dir. of Agricultural Development....St. Louis, Mo.
W. D. STEELE, Assistant Secretary and Assistant Treasurer. New York, N. Y.	T. J. FRIER, Purchasing Agent................................St. Louis, Mo.

TRAFFIC DEPARTMENT

W. C. MAXWELL, Vice-President in Charge of Traffic.........St. Louis, Mo.

FREIGHT

C. H. STINSON, Freight Traffic Manager...................St. Louis, Mo.
G. G. EARLY, Freight Traffic Manager.....................St. Louis, Mo.
H. G. HOLDEN, Assistant Freight Traffic Manager..........St. Louis, Mo.
SIDNEY KING, Assistant Freight Traffic Manager...........St. Louis, Mo.
R. A. BELDING, General Freight Agent.....................St. Louis, Mo.
C. J. SAYLES, General Freight Agent......................St. Louis, Mo.
T. R. FARRELL, Assistant General Freight Agent...........St. Louis, Mo.
W. A. HOPKINS, Assistant General Freight Agent...........St. Louis, Mo.
F. G. MAXWELL, Assistant General Freight Agent...........St. Louis, Mo.
C. N. RICHARDS, Assistant General Freight Agent..........St. Louis, Mo.
B. H. COYLE, Assistant General Freight Agent.............St. Louis, Mo.
P. A. SPIEGELBERG, Assistant General Freight Agent.......St. Louis, Mo.
L. W. COLE, Assistant General Freight Agent..............St. Louis, Mo.
J. A. SULLIVAN, Assistant Freight Traffic Manager........Detroit, Mich.
R. A. WALTON, Assistant Freight Traffic Manager..........Chicago, Ill.
J. J. MOSSMAN, Assistant General Freight Agent...........Buffalo, N. Y.

FREIGHT—(Continued)

W. E. ALDERSON, Assistant General Freight Agent......Kansas City, Mo.
D. E. GILBERT, Assistant General Freight Agent............Toledo, Ohio
L. E. CLARAHAN, General Industrial Agent.................St. Louis, Mo.
W. C. STREIT, Assistant to Vice-President.................St. Louis, Mo.

PASSENGER

H. E. WATTS, Passenger Traffic Manager ....St. Louis, Mo.
L. W. BADE, Assistant Passenger Traffic Manager..........St. Louis, Mo.
L. A. BLATTERMAN, General Passenger Agent.............St. Louis, Mo.
FD. HAMMER, Assistant General Passenger Agent..........Detroit, Mich.
F. L. McNALLY, Assistant General Passenger Agent.........St. Louis, Mo.
H. L. PIGOTT, Assistant General Passenger Agent..........Chicago, Ill.
J. C. HETHERINGTON, General Advertising Agent...........St. Louis, Mo.
G. B. LINDSAY, General Baggage Agent....................St. Louis, Mo.
G. B. LINDSAY, General Agent, Mail and Express Traffic....St. Louis, Mo.
G. M. HART, Superintendent Dining Cars..................St. Louis, Mo.

TRAFFIC REPRESENTATIVES

City	Representatives	Address
Atlanta, Ga....	C. R. CHESNEY......Dist. Pass. Agt. I. L. WADE, JR.......Trav. Frt. Agt.	620 Healey Bldg.
Birmingham, Ala.	W. G. KIDD......Gen. Agt. R. G. McCLURE......Trav. Frt. Agt. L. W. JONES......Trav. Frt. and Pass. Agt.	701-2 Watts Bldg.
Boston, Mass.	C. B. HOXIE......Gen. Agt. W. F. WARD......Dist. Pass. Agt. H. P. HORNE......Trav. Frt. Agt. R. C. DREW......Trav. Frt. Agt.	331-332 Chamber of Commerce Bldg.
Buffalo, N. Y..	J. R. BECK......Div. Pass. Agt. City Ticket Office...... Wabash Passenger Station...... H. A. LEE......Trav. Frt. Agt. E. P. BECKER......Trav. Frt. Agt.	880 Ellicott Square Bldg. Pearl and Church Sts. No. 1 Main St. 880 Ellicott Square Bldg.
Chicago, Ill.	G. G. KOTTENSTETTE. Div. Pass. Agt. H. J. DWYER......Trav. Pass. Agt. City Ticket Office...... Ticket Office Dearborn Station...... E. R. NEWMAN......Special Traffic Rep. E. H. GEORGE......Special Traffic Rep. FRANK GAGE......Div. Frt. Agt. E. E. ELVIDGE......Trav. Frt. Agt. C. H. STRATHMAN......Trav. Frt. Agt. J. A. HOLMGREN......Trav. Frt. Agt. A. H. MOONEY......Perishable Trf. Agt.	144 S. Clark St. Polk and Dearborn Sts. 1620 Utilities Bldg., La Salle & Van Buren 608 Produce Exch. Bldg. 1425 So. Racine Ave.
Cincinnati, Ohio.	C. P. WILCOX......Dist. Pass. Agt. J. D. LUND......Gen. Agt. Frt. Dept. L. E. MERCER......Trav. Frt. Agt.	319-320 Dixie Terminal Bldg.
Cleveland, Ohio	J. C. O'BOYLE......Gen. Agt. Frt. Dept. M. C. SAUNDERS......Trav. Frt. Agt.	2110-11 Terminal Tower.
Dallas, Tex ...	G. C. BROOK......Act'g Dist. Pass. Agt. C. M. BROWN......Gen. Agt. Frt. Dept. H. W. COOK......Trav. Frt. Agt.	1207 Kirby Bldg.
Decatur, Ill.	G. N. LOVELL......Div. Pass. Agt. L. F. BOSS......Div. Frt. Agt. J. F. CRINIGAN......Trav. Frt. Agt. J. E. DOOLEY......Trav. Frt. Agt.	
Denver, Colo.	C. J. HELBER......Gen. Agt. G. W. TERRY......Trav. Frt. Agt.	303 Denver National Bldg.
Des Moines, Iowa	H. P. GARDNER......Div. Pass. Agt. City Ticket Office...... Ticket Office Union Station...... PHIL. SCHORR......Div. Frt. Agt. P. A. ZIEHLKE......Trav. Frt. Agt.	Union Station 501 Locust St. 5th and Cherry Sts. Union Station
Detroit, Mich ..	H. F. BOBBITT......Div. Pass. Agt. H. W. WILSON......Trav. Pass. Agt. City Ticket Offices...... Ticket Office Union Station...... T. R. COCHRANE......Div. Frt. Agt. THOS. O'CONNELL......Trav. Frt. Agt. B. H. LEWIS......Trav. Frt. Agt.	1731 First Nat. Bk. Bldg. 228 Michigan Ave. and G'n'l Motors Bldg. Fort and 3rd Sts. 1731 First Nat. Bk. Bldg.
E. St. Louis, Ill.	J. R. HUNDLEY......Dist. Frt. Agt. R. F. STAPLETON......Trav. Frt. Agt.	308 Spivey Bldg.
Ft. Wayne, Ind.	O. W. BRAUNGART......Pass. and Ticket Agt. A. L. GILBERT......Dist Frt. Agt.	Wabash Pass. Station 244 Utility Bldg.
Hannibal, Mo.	F. H. WEGENER......Div. Frt. and Pass. Agt.	
Harlingen, Tex.	G. F. HARRIGAN ......Perishable Frt. Agt.	201 First St. Reese-Wil-Mond Hotel
Houston, Tex...	V. W. BAKER......Dist. Pass. Agt. P. L. JOHNSON......Gen. Agt. Frt. Dept. W. L. KNIPE......Trav. Frt. Agt.	1029 Bankers Mortgage Bldg.
Indianapolis, Ind.	R. F. WALLER......District Pass. Agt. A. S. BIRCHETT......Gen. Agt. Frt. Dept. C. E. ALWES......Trav. Frt. Agt.	420-21 Merchants Bank Bldg.
Kansas City, Mo.	J. J. SHINE......Div. Pass. Agt. W. L. HIGGINS......Trav. Pass. Agt. City Ticket Office...... R. W. OWENS......Special Traffic Rep. G. D. WRIGHT......Traveling Frt. Agt. A. A. McKOWEN......Trav. Frt. Agt.	721 Walnut St. 319 Railway Ex. Bldg.
Keokuk, Iowa.	W. A. BRIDGMAN......Div. Frt. and Pass Agt.	
Little Rock, Ark.	W. D. WOOD......Dist. Pass. Agent. T. G. SMITH......Gen. Agt. Frt. Dept. L. E. CLARK......Trav. Frt. Agent.	315-316 Gazette Bldg.
Los Angeles, Cal.	R. B. NELSON......Dist. Pass. Agt. C. V. ECCLESTONE......Gen. Agt. Frt. Dept. F. X. BELL......Trav Frt. Agent	930 Van Nuys Bldg.
Memphis, Tenn.	OSCAR PLUNKET......Gen. Agt. Frt. Dept. C. A. ROSE......Trav. Frt. Agt.	620-21 Exchange Bldg.
Milwaukee, Wis.	W. S. TURNBULL......Dist. Pass. Agt. G. W. CALLEN......Gen. Agt. Frt. Dept. G. D. VALELLY......Trav. Frt. Agt. F. J. RAHNER......Traveling Frt. Agt.	1406 Majestic Bldg.
Minneapolis, Minn.	G. J. LOVELL......Dist. Pass. Agt. R. P. McCUNE......Gen. Agt. Frt. Dept. J. P. MULLEN......Trav. Frt. Agt.	616 Metropolitan Life Bldg.
Moberly, Mo.	L. R. WILSON......Div. Frt. and Pass. Agt. P. R. HOLMES......Trav. Frt. and Pass. Agt. S. G. BROTHERS......Trav. Frt. and Pass. Agt. B. F. RICE......Trav. Frt. and Pass. Agt.	
New Orleans, La.	J. M. COUSINS......Gen. Agt. J. S. MASON......Trav. Frt. and Pass. Agt.	1411-12 American Bank Bldg.
New York, N. Y.	L. C. BOSTWICK......Gen. Agt. A. S. DUNBAR......Dist. Pass. Agt. JEROME F. HART......Trav. Pass. Agent. F. C. FOLEY......Asst. Gen. Agt. Frt. Dept. W. F. VAIL......Trav. Frt. Agt. W. J. DUNCAN......Trav. Frt. Agent.	816 Singer Bldg.
Omaha, Neb.	T. C. HAYDEN......Div. Pass. Agt. City Ticket Office...... Ticket Office Wabash Station...... WM. CULP......Div. Frt. Agt. F. A. RIASKI......Trav. Frt. Agt.	1907 Harney St. 311 S. 16th St. 10th and Marcy Sts. 1907 Harney St.
Ottumwa, Iowa.	G. B. CHAPMAN......Dist. Pass. Agt.	
Peoria, Ill.	C. T. CHAPMAN......Gen. Agt.	828 Jefferson Bldg.
Philadelphia, Pa.	W. McCRACKAN......Gen. Agt. CHARLES HAMILTON. Dist. Pass. Agt. B. M. PILATZ......Trav. Frt. and Pass. Agt.	1206 Widener Bldg.
Pittsburgh, Pa.	CHARLES HAMILTON. Dist. Pass. Agt. G. N. THOMAS......Gen. Agt. Frt. Dept. C. B. HENTHORNE......Trav. Frt. Agt.	1720 Oliver Bldg.
Phoenix, Ariz.	M. A. CARROLL......Gen. Agent.	219 Security Bldg.
Portland, Ore.	R. D. FARRELL......Dist Frt. & Pass. Agt.	517 Pacific Bldg.
Quincy, Ill.	G. C. OSBORN......Div. Frt. and Pass. Agt. O. M. HUGHES......Trav. Frt. and Pass. Agt.	
St. Louis, Mo..	F. L. McNALLY......Asst. Gen. Pass. Agt. W. D. LIVINGSTON......Trav. Pass. Agt. City Ticket Office...... Delmar Blvd. Station...... G. L. KAESHOEFER......Div. Frt. Agt.	1450 Railway Exc. Bldg. 328 N. Broadway 6001 Delmar Blvd. 324 Pierce Bldg.
Salt Lake City, Utah.	A. P. MacINNIS......Gen. Agt. A. J. CARLBERG......Trav. Frt. and Pass. Agt.	206 Judge Bldg.

WABASH CITY TICKET OFFICES {228 MICHIGAN AVE. (BOOK-CADILLAC HOTEL), DETROIT. PHONE CADILLAC 0900
GENERAL MOTORS BLDG., WEST GRAND BLVD. AND CASS AVE., DETROIT. PHONE EMPIRE 9405}

WABASH RAILWAY COMPANY

TRAFFIC REPRESENTATIVES—Concluded

City	Name	Title	Address
St. Thomas, Ont.	R. A. SNYDER	Dist. Frt. Agt.	
San Antonio, Texas	A. B. GREEN	Gen. Agt. Frt. Dept	717 Majestic Bldg.
	H. L. JOHNSTON	Trav. Frt. Agt	
San Francisco, Cal.	H. E. DIXON,	Dist. Pass. Agt	917 Monadnock Bldg.
	W. N. PRICE	Gen. Agt. Frt. Dept	
	L. H. JONES	Trav. Frt. Agt	
	R. I. LYNAS	Trav. Frt. Agt	
	C. L. NELSON	Perishable Frt. Agt	
Seattle, Wash.	J. E. HOLTON	Gen. Agt	333 Henry Bldg.
	R. L. CRUSEN	Trav. Frt. and Pass. Agt.	
	H. S. HEMINGWAY	Trav. Frt. and Pass. Agt.	
Springfield, Ill.	M. G. CLARK	Div. Frt. Agt	Wabash Pass. Station
	R. B. HALL	Trav. Frt. Agt	
Toledo, Ohio	T. B. O'CONNOR	Div. Pass. Agt	511 Jefferson St.
	City Ticket Office		
	Ticket Office Union Station		Foot of Knapp St.
	G. C. KNICKERBOCKER	Acting Div. Frt. Agt	440 Spitzer Bldg.
	J. REDDING	Dist. Frt. Agt	
	A. R. DAVIS	Trav. Frt. Agt	
Toronto, Ont	J. R. BECK	Dist. Pass. Agt	1101 Royal Bank Bldg.
	T. L. COCHRANE	Gen. Agt. Frt. Dept	
	A. W. WHISKIN	Trav. Frt. Agt	
Tulsa, Okla.	R. V. MILLER	Gen. Agt. Frt. Dept	316 Kennedy Bldg.
	R. C. HUGHES	Trav. Frt. Agt	

STATION INDEX

Each time table is numbered. The figures opposite the stations in Index refer to the time table.
For example: Chillicothe, Mo., is carried in Time Table No. 4, and Jacksonville, Ill., in Time Table No. 12.

Station	Table No.
Aboite, Ind	5
Adelphi, Iowa	2
*Ackley, Iowa	2
Adrian, Mich	5, 11
Ætna, Ind	11
Aladdin, Ill	12
Albany, Mo	4
*Albert Lea, Minn	2
Albia, Iowa	2
*Albia, Iowa	2
Alderney, Mo	1
Alexander, Ill	12
Alpine, Ill	10
Altamont, Ill	17
Alvordton, Ohio	5, 11
Andrews, Ind	5
Andrews Yard, Ind	5
Antwerp, Ohio	8, 9
Arnold, Ill	12
Artic, Ind	5
Ashburn, Ill	10
Ashley-Hudson, Ind	11
Atlanta, Mo	2
Attica, Ind	5, 8, 9, 20
Axtell, Mo	2
Aylmer, Ont	5
Bairds, Ont	5
Ballou, Ill	10
Barry, Ill	12
Bates, Ill	12
Baylis, Ill	12
Bedford, Mo	4
Bedison, Mo	4
Belknap, Iowa	2
Belleville, Mich	5, 11
Belle River, Ont	5
Bement, Ill	5, 10, 17
Bentley, Ill	14
Benton, Ind	11
Benton City, Mo	1
Bingham, Iowa	4
xBinghamton, N. Y.	5
Birmingham, Mo	1
Black Rock, N. Y.	5, 11
Blacks, Ill	14
Blakesley, Ohio	5
Blanchard, Iowa	4
Bloomfield, Iowa	2
Blue Mound, Ill	5, 10
Blue Point, Ill	17
Blue Ridge, Ill	10
Bluff Hall, Ill	13
Bluffs, Ill	12, 14
Boody, Ill	5, 10
Bothwell, Ont	5
Bowen, Ill	14
‡Bowling Green, Mo	1
Brailey, Ohio	5, 6
Bridgeburg, Ont	5
Brisbane, Ill	10
Britton, Mich	5, 11
Brooklyn, Ill	5, 10
Brown's, Mo	3
Brown's Crossing, Ill	12
Bruce, Ill	17
Brunswick, Mo	1, 4, 12
Buck Creek, Ind	5
Buffalo, Ill	12
Buffalo, N. Y.	5, 11, 12
Burlington Junc., Mo	4
Burrows, Ind	5
Bussey, Iowa	2
Butler, Ind	5
Cairo, Mo	2
Calumet, Ind	11
Camden, Mo	1
Camp Dodge, Iowa	2
Camp Point, Ill	12
Campus, Ill	10
Canfield Junc., Ont	5
Carbon, Iowa	2
Cardiff, Ill	10
Carlow, Mo	4
Carpenter, Ill	5, 10
Carrollton, Mo	1, 12
Carthage, Ill	14
Catlin, Ill	5
Cayuga, Ont	5
Cecil, Ohio	8, 9
Centralia, Mo	1, 3
Cerro Gordo, Ill	5, 10
Champaign, Ill	5, 19
Chapin, Ill	12
Chatham, Ont	5, 11
Chatton, Ill	14
Chicago, Ill	10, 11, 12,
Chicago, Ill. (Forty-seventh St.)	10, 11
Chicago Ridge, Ill	10
Chillicothe, Mo	4
Clapper, Mo	12
Clark, Mo	1
Clarksdale, Ill	5, 10
Clayton, Ill	14
Clifton, Mo	1
Clyde, Mo	4
Clymers, Ind	5
Coatesville, Mo	2
Coin, Iowa	4
Colburn, Ind	5
Colton, Ohio	8, 9
Columbia, Mo	1, 3
Conception, Mo	4
Cone, Mich	5, 11
Cooley Lake, Mo	4A
Cordova, Iowa	2
Corinth, Ont	5
Cornell, Ill	18
Council Bluffs, Iowa	4
Courtland, Ont	5
Covington, Ind	20
Crocker, Ind	11
Curran, Ill	12
Cushman, Ill	17
Custer Park, Ill	10
Dalton, Mo	1
Danville, Ill	5, 8, 9
Darling Road, Ont	5
Darlington, Mo	4
Dawson, Ill	12
Dawsonville, Mo	4
Decatur Ill	5, 8, 9, 10, 12
Deer's, Ill	19
Defiance, Ohio	8, 9
Delhi, Ont	5
Delphi, Ind	5
Delray, Mich	5, 11
Delta, Ohio	6, 7
†Denver, Col	1
Denver, Ill	14
Des Moines, Iowa	2
*Des Moines, Iowa	2
Detroit, Mich	5, 11, 12
De Witt, Mo	1
Dillon, Ind	11
Diltz, Ont	5
Dumfries, Iowa	4
Dunreath, Iowa	2
East Chicago, Ind	11
East Decatur, Ill	5, 10
East Des Moines, Iowa	2
East Hannibal, Ill	13
East St. Louis, Ill	5, 10
East Switch, Iowa	4
Eckley, Ohio	6, 7
Eden, Mo	1
Eddy, Ind	11
Edon, Ohio	11
Edwardsville, Ill	5, 10
Effingham, Ill	17
Ekfrid, Ont	5
Elmira, Ohio	6, 7
xElmira, N. Y.	5, 11
Elmo, Mo	4
Elvaston, Ill	14
Emington, Ill	10
Emmett, Ohio	8, 9
Englewood, Ill	10, 11
Essex, Ill	10
Evansville, Mo	12
Excello, Mo	2
Excelsior Spgs., Mo	1, 4A
Excelsior Springs Junc., Mo	1, 4A
Fairbury, Ill	18
Fairmount, Ill	5
Fall Creek, Ill	13
Ferguson, Mo	1
Fifield, Iowa	2
Fleming, Mo	1
Flint, Ind	5
Foosland, Ill	10
Foraker, Ind	11
Forest Green, Mo	15
Foristell, Mo	1
Forrest, Ill	10, 18
Fort Wayne, Ind	5, 6, 7, 8, 9
Fountain Ind	20
Fountain Grove, Mo	4
Franklin, Ohio	5, 11
French Landing, Mich	5, 11
Galesville, Ill	10
Gallatin, Mo	4
Garber, Ill	10
Gar Creek, Ind	8, 9
Gardnerville, Mo	1
Gary, Ind	11
Gibson City, Ill	10
*Gifford, Iowa	2
Gilbirds, Ill	14
Gilmore, Mo	1
Glasgow, Mo	15
Glencoe, Ont	5, 11
Glen Echo, Mo	1
Glenwood, Mo	2
Glenwood Junc., Mo	2
Golden, Ill	14
Goss, Mo	12
Grabill, Ind	5
Granite City, Ill	5, 10
Granite City, Ill., (Yard Office)	5, 10
Green Top, Mo	2
Griggsville, Ill	12
Grinnell, Iowa	2
Hadley, Ill	12
Hallsville, Mo	3
Hamilton, Ill	14
Hamilton, Iowa	2
Hamilton, Ind	11
Hammond, Ill	17
Hammond, Ind	11
*Hampton, Iowa	2
Hand, Mich	5, 11
Hannibal, Mo.	12, 13, 16
Hardin, Mo	1
Harristown, Ill	12
Harvel, Ill	5, 10
Harvey, Iowa	2
Hassard, Mo	12
Hastie, Iowa	2
Haydens	10
Helmer, Ind	11, 21
Henrietta, Mo	1
Herborn, Ill	17
Hersman, Ill	14
Hiattsville, Iowa	2
High Hill, Mo	1
Hildreth, Mo	2
xHoboken, N. Y.	5, 11
Holliday, Mo	12
Holloway, Mich	5, 11
Homer, Ill	5
Homewood, Ohio	8, 9
Honey Bend, Ill	5, 10
Howell, Iowa	2
Hulls, Ill	12
Huntington, Ind	5, 8, 9
Huntington, Mo	12
Huntsville, Mo	1
Illiopolis, Ill	12
Imogene, Iowa	4
Island Grove, Ill	12
Ivesdale, Ill	5
Jacksonville, Ill	12
Jacksonville, Mo	2
Jameson, Mo	4
Jarvis, Ont	5
Jewell, Ohio	8, 9
Johnsonville, Ind	5
Jonesburg, Mo	1
Julesburg, Mo	2
Kansas City, Mo	1, 2, 12, 4A.
†Kansas City, Mo	1
Karnes, Ill	5, 10
Keokuk, Iowa	12, 14
Keytesville, Mo	1
Kinderhook, Ill	12
Kingsbury, Ind	11
Kinloch Park, Mo	1
Kirksville, Mo	2
Knights, Ill	5, 10
Knoxdale, Ohio	8, 9
Kunkle, Ohio	5, 11
LaFayette, Ind	5, 8, 9
Lagro, Ind	5
Lakeville, Ind	11
Landers, Ill	10
Lanesville, Ill	12
La Plata, Mo	2
Lawrence, Ont	5
Lewis Mill, Mo	15
Liberty Center, Ohio	8, 9
Litchfield, Ill	5, 10
Lock Springs, Mo	4
Lodemia, Ill	18
Lodge, Ill	10
Logansport, Ind.	5, 8, 9
†Los Angeles, Cal	1
Lotus, Ill	10
Love Lake, Mo	2
Lovilia, Iowa	2
Lovington, Ill	17
Macon, Mo	2
Madison, Mo	12
Magee, Ind	11
Malvern, Iowa	4
Manhattan, Ill	10
Mansfield, Ill	10
Manville, Ill	18
Marble Head, Ill	13
Mardenis, Ind	5
Markham, Ill	12
Marley, Ill	10
*Marshalltown, Iowa	2
Marshfield, Ind	5
Marshville, Ont	5
Martinsburg, Mo	1
Maryville, Mo	4
*Mason City, Iowa	2
Maumee, Ohio	6, 7, 8, 9
Maysville, Ill	12, 16
McCurry, Mo	4
McDowell, Ill	18
McFall, Mo	4
Meredosia, Ill	14
Mexico, Mo	1
Miami, Mo	1
Middlemiss, Ont	5
Midway, Ohio	6, 7
Milan, Mich	5, 11
Millard, Mo	2
Millersburg, Ind	11
Milmine, Ill	5, 10
Miltondale, Mo	4A
Mineola, Iowa	4
*Minneapolis, Minn.	2
Mira, Ill	19
Missouri City, Mo	1
Mitchell, Ill	5, 10
Moberly, Mo	1, 2, 4, 12
Monclova, Ohio	6, 7
Monroe City, Mo	12
Montgomery, Mo	1
Monticello, Ill	10
Montpelier, Ohio	5, 6, 7, 11.
Moore's Switch, Mo.	3
Moravia, Iowa	2
Morgan, Ill	12
Morris, Ind	11
Morrisonville, Ill	5, 10
Moulton, Iowa	2
Moulton, Ont	5
Mount Olive, Ill	5, 10
Mount Sterling, Ill	14
Munson, Mich	5, 11
Nameoki, Ill ¶	5, 10
Naples, Ill	12
Napoleon, Ohio	8, 9
Nebeker's, Ind	20
Neely's, Ill	12
Nelles Corners, Ont.	5
Neoga, Iowa	4
xNewark, N. J	5, 11
Newbury, Ont	5
New Berlin, Ill	12
New Florence, Mo	1
New Haven, Ind	5, 8, 9
New Lenox, Ill	10
New Paris, Ind	11
New Salem, Ill	12
New Sarum, Ont	5
New Waverly, Ind	5
xNew York, N. Y.	5, 11
Niantic, Ill	12
Nimrod, Mo	1
Nixon, Ont	5
Norborne, Mo	1
North Kansas City, Mo	1
North Liberty, Ind.	11
North Morenci, Mich	5, 11
Northwood, Ont	5
Norville, Mo	4
Oak Lawn, Ill	10
Oakley, Ill	5, 10
Oakwood, Mich	5, 11
O'Fallon, Mo	1
Oil City, Mo	15
Okolona, Ohio	8, 9
Omaha, Neb	4
†Omaha, Neb	4
Orland Park, Ill	10
Orleans, Ill	12
Orrick, Mo	1
*Oskaloosa, Iowa	2
Osman, Ill	10
Ottumwa, Iowa	2
Palemon, Mo	1
Palmer, Ill	5, 10
Palos Park, Ill	10
Paris, Mo	12
Pattonsburg, Mo	4
Paynes, Ont	5
Peacock, Ind	20
Pendleton, Mo	1
Percy, Iowa	2
Perry Springs, Ill	14
Persinger, Mo	3
Peru, Ind	5, 8, 9
Philo, Ill	5
Platt, Ind	5
Pine, Ind	11
Pittsfield, Ill	12, 16
Poag, Ill	5, 10
Pontiac, Ill	18
†Portland, Ore	4
Prairie Switch, Ind	5
Preston, Mich	5, 11
Proctor, Ill	10
Queen City, Mo	3
Quincy, Ill	12, 13, 16
Raisin Center, Mich.	6, 11
Randolph, Mo	1
Raymond, Ill	5, 10
Reddick, Ill	10
Renick, Mo	1
Renolett, Ohio	8, 9
Rensselaer, Mo	12
Renton, Ont	5
Rich Valley, Ind	5
Ritchie, Ill	10
Riverside, Ind	5
Riverton, Ill	12
Roanoke, Ind	5
Robertson, Mo	1
Rockfield, Ind	5
Romulus, Mich	5, 11
Rowe, Ill	18
Runnells, Iowa	2
St. Charles, Mo	1
St. Joe, Ind	5
St. Louis, Mo., (Union Station)	1, 2, 3, 5, 7, 8, 9, 10.
St. Louis, Mo. (City) Delmar Boulevard	1, 2, 4, 5, 10.
Ewing Avenue	1
Vandeventer Ave	1, 5, 10
Washington Ave.	5, 10
*St. Paul, Minn	2
St. Peters, Mo	1
St. Thomas, Ont	5, 11
St. Vincent's, Mo	1
Sadorus, Ill	5
†Salt Lake City, Utah	1
Salisbury, Mo	1, 15
Sampsel, Mo	4
Sand Creek, Mich	5, 11
‖San Francisco, Cal.	1
Sangamon, Ill	5, 10
Sanger, Ill	12
Saunemin, Ill	10
xScranton, Pa	5, 11
†Seattle, Wash	1, 4
Selection, Iowa	2
Seneca, Mich	5, 11
Shadeland, Ind	5
Shannondale, Mo	15
Shelby's, Ind	20
Shenandoah, Iowa	4
Shops, Ill	12
Shumway, Ill	17
Sibley, Ill	10
Sidney, Ill	5, 19
Silver City, Iowa	4
Simcoe, Ont	5, 11
Solomon, Iowa	4
§South Bend, Ind	11
South Liberty, Mo	1
South Milford, Ind.	11
Southmoor	10
Spencerville, Ind	5
Springfield, Ill	12
Stanberry, Mo	4
Starne, Ill	12
State Line, Ind	5
Station 15, Ohio (Neapolis)	8, 9
Staunton, Ill	5, 10
Steele, Ill	10
Stephens, Mo	3
Steubenville, Ind	11
Stewardson, Ill	17
Stoney Point, Ont	5
Stonington, Ill	5, 10
Stoutsville, Mo	12
Strahan, Iowa	4
Strasburg, Ill	17
Strawn, Ill	10
Streator, Ill	18
Stroh, Ind	21
Sturgeon, Mo	1
Sublette, Mo	2
Sullivan, Ill	17
Summit, Iowa	4
Sumner, Mo	4
Switzler, Mo	3
Symerton, Ill	10
†Tacoma, Wash	1, 4
Taylorville, Ill	10
Thames River, Ont.	5
Thamesville, Ont	5
Thompson, Mo	1
Thurman, Ind	5
Tillsonburg, Ont	5
Tilton, Ill	5
Timewell, Ill	14
Toledo, Ohio	6, 7, 8, 9, 12.
Toledo, Ohio (Yards)	8
Tolleston, Ind	11
Tolono, Ill	5
Topeka, Ind	11
Tracy, Iowa	2
Triplett, Mo	4
Truesdale, Mo	1
Udell, Iowa	2
Urbana, Ill	5, 19
Valley City, Ill	5, 12
Venice, Ill	10
Versailles, Ill	14
Voorhies, Ill	17
Wabash, Ind	5, 8, 9
Wakarusa, Ind	11
Wakenda, Mo	1
Wakerton, Ont	5
*Waseca, Minn	2
Warrenton, Mo	1
*Waterville, Iowa	2
Wauseon, Ohio	6, 7
Wea, Ind	5
Welland Junc., Ont	5, 11
Wellsville, Mo	1
Wentzville, Mo	1
Western Indiana Junc., Ill	10
West Grove, Iowa	2
West Lebanon, Ind	5
West Peru, Ind	5
West Point, Ind	5
West Unity, Ohio	6, 7
Westville, Ind	11
†West Yellowstone	
White Cloud, Iowa	4
White House, Ohio	8, 9
Whittaker, Mich	5, 11
Whitham, Mo	4
Whitten, Mo	4
Wilcox, Mo	4
Willeys, Ill	5, 10
Williamsport, Ind	5
Willis, Mich	5, 11
Willow Creek, Ind	11
Windsor, Ont	5, 11
Windsor, Ill	17
Wing, Ill	10
Wolcottville, Ind	11
Woodburn, Ind	8, 9
Worden, Ill	5, 10
Worth, Ill	10
Wright, Mo	1
Wyatt, Ind	11
Wyckles, Ill	12

x D. L. & W. R. R. stations.
§ N. J. I. & I. Railroad Station.
‖ Southern Pacific stations.
* Minneapolis & St. Louis Railroad stations.
† Union Pacific System stations.
¶ Freight Station.

Through Car Service and Equipment

ST. LOUIS AND KANSAS CITY

Miles	STATIONS	3 Daily	9 Daily	17 Daily	ROUTE
.0	St. Louis (Union Station).....Lv.	9 03 AM	2 00 PM	11 45 PM	Wabash
5.6	St. Louis (Delmar Blvd.)....Lv.	9 17 AM	2 15 PM	12 01 AM	"
109.8	Mexico...................Ar.	11 51 AM	4 45 PM	2 40 AM	......
123.9	Centralia.................Ar.	12 15 PM	5 10 PM	3 10 AM	Wabash
147.8	Moberly..................Ar.	12 50 PM	6 47 PM	3 50 AM	Wabash
278.7	Kansas City..............Ar	4 33 PM	9 20 PM	7 30 AM	Wabash

No. 3— Observation-Parlor Car....St. Louis to Kansas City—D. R.
 Dining Car...............St. Louis to Kansas City.
 Reclining Chair Car.....St. Louis to Kansas City.
No. 9— Observation-Parlor Car....St. Louis to Kansas City.
 Sleeping Car............St. Louis to Kansas City—12 Sects.—D. R.—Compts. (To San Francisco via Un. Pac.).
 Sleeping Car............St. Louis to Kansas City.—12 Sects.—D. R.—(To West Yellowstone effective June 18th, via Un. Pac.).
 Dining Car..............St. Louis to Kansas City.
 Reclining Chair Car.....St. Louis to Kansas City.
No. 17—Club Lounge Car.........St. Louis to Kansas City.
 Sleeping Car............St. Louis (Delmar Blvd. Station) to Kansas City—12 Sects.—D. R. (Open 9:30 p. m.).
 Sleeping Car............St. Louis to Kansas City—16 Sects.
 Sleeping Car............St. Louis to Kansas City—10 Sects.—D. R.—Compts.
 Sleeping Car............St. Louis to Kansas City—12 Sects.—D. R. (To Denver via Un. Pac.).
 Sleeping Car............St. Louis to Kansas City—8 Sects.—D. R.—Compts. (To Los Angeles via Santa Fe every 3rd day, see page 7.) (Sleepers open 10:00 p. m.).
 Reclining Chair Cars.....St. Louis to Kansas City.

Miles	STATIONS	2 Daily	12 Daily	4-18 Daily	18 Daily	ROUTE
.0	Kansas City.................Lv.	9 00 AM	3 00 PM	9 30 AM	11 55 PM	Wabash
131.1	Moberly...................Lv.	12 28 PM	6 19 PM	3 20 AM	3 20 AM	Wabash
155.0	Centralia.................Lv.	1 03 PM	6 55 PM	4 02 AM	4 02 AM	Wabash
169.1	Mexico...................Lv.	1 24 PM	7 18 PM	4 25 AM	4 25 AM	"
273.3	St. Louis (Delmar Blvd.).......	3 59 PM	9 58 PM	7 05 AM	7 05 AM	"
278.7	St. Louis (Union Station).....Ar.	4 20 PM	10 20 PM	7 30 AM	7 30 AM	Wabash

No. 2 —Observation-Parlor Car....Kansas City to St. Louis.
 Sleeping Car............Kansas City to St. Louis—12 Sects.—D. R.—Compt. (From San Francisco via Un. Pac.).
 Sleeping Car............Kansas City to St. Louis—12 Sects.—D. R.—(From West Yellowstone, effective June 21st, via Un. Pac.).
 Reclining Chair Car.....Kansas City to St. Louis.
 Dining Car..............Kansas City to St. Louis.
No. 12—Observation-Parlor Car....Kansas City to St. Louis—D. R.
 Reclining Chair Cars....Kansas City to St. Louis.
 Dining Car..............Moberly to St. Louis.
No. 4-18—Sleeping Car...........Kansas City to St. Louis—12 Sects.—D. R. (From Denver via Un. Pac.).
 Reclining Chair Cars....Kansas City to St. Louis.
No. 18—Club Lounge Car.........Kansas City to St. Louis.
 Sleeping Car............Kansas City to St. Louis—16 Sects.
 Sleeping Car............Kansas City to St. Louis—10 Sects.—D. R.
 Sleeping Car............Kansas City to St. Louis—12 Sects.—D. R.
 Sleeping Car............Kansas City to St. Louis—8 Sects.—D. R.—Compts. (From Los Angeles via Santa Fe every 3rd day, see page 7.) (Sleepers open 10:00 p. m.).
 Reclining Chair Car.....Kansas City to St. Louis.

ST. LOUIS—KANSAS CITY—DENVER—LOS ANGELES—SAN FRANCISCO—PORTLAND—SEATTLE

WESTBOUND

Miles	STATIONS	Pacific Coast Ltd	Exam.	Pacific Coast Ltd.	Exam	Denver Exp.	Exam	St. Louis-Colo. Ltd.	Exam	ROUTE
.0	St. Louis (Union Sta.)....Lv.	2 00	Sun.	2 00	Sun.	11 45	Sat.	9 03	Sun.	Wab.
.6	St. Louis (Delmar Blvd.)..Lv.	2 15	"	2 15	"	12 01	"	9 17	"	Wab.
279	Kansas City............Ar.	9 20	Sun.	9 20	Sun.	7 30	Sun.	4 33	Sun.	Wab.
279.0	Kansas City (C.T.)......Lv.	10 00	Sun.	10 00	Sun.	10 40	Sun.	6 15	Sun.	U.P.S.
918.0	Denver (Mtn.T.)........Ar.	1 00	Mon.	1 00	Mon.	7 00	Mon.	9 45	Mon.	U.P.S.
918.0	Denver................Lv.	1 30	Mon Via Borie.	1 30	Mon.	1 30	Mon. Via Borie.	......	......	U.P.S.
102.4	Cheyenne..............Lv.									U.P.S.
156.4	Pocatello..............Lv.									U.P.S.
1722.0	West Yellowstone......Ar.	2 25	Effective	June 18th	to	Sept 16th.				U.P.S.
1496.0	Ogden.................Ar.	10 45	Tues.	6 15	Tues.	6 15	Tues.			U.P.S.
1496.0	Ogden.................Lv.	10 05	Tues.	9 55	Tues.	9 55	Tues.			S.P.
2279.0	San Francisco..........Ar.	8 30	Wed.	8 10	Wed.	8 10	Wed.			S.P.
1496.0	Ogden.................Lv.	6 40	Tues.	6 40	Tues.	6 40	Tues.			U.P.S.
1532.0	Salt Lake City.........Ar.	7 30	"	7 30	"	7 30	"			U.P.S.
1532.0	Salt Lake City.........Lv.	8 00	"	8 00	"	8 00	"			U.P.S.
1807.0	Cedar City (to Zion)....Ar.	4 00	Tues.	4 00	Tues.	4 00	Tues.			U.P.S.
2316.0	Los Angeles...........Ar.	8 15	Wed.	8 15	Wed.	8 15	Wed.			U.P.S.
918.0	Denver................Lv.	4 30	Mon.	6 15	Mon.					U.P.S.
1024.0	Cheyenne..............Ar.	7 30	"	9 15	"					U.P.S.
1564.0	Pocatello..............Ar.	9 50	Tues.	5 40	Tues.					U.P.S.
2280.0	Portland (Pac.T.)......Ar.	7 45	Wed.	5 30	Wed.					U.P.S.
2425.0	Tacoma...............Ar.	1 04	Wed.	4 50	Thur.					U.P.S.
2463.0	Seattle...............Ar.	2 20	Wed.	6 30	Thur.					U.P.S.

▲Motor Bus.

EASTBOUND

STATIONS	Pacific Coast Ltd.	Exam.	Portland Pacific Coast Ltd.	Exam.	St Louis-Colo. Ltd.	Exam.	St Louis Exp.	Exam.	Midnight Ltd.	Exam.	ROUTE
San Francisco........Lv.	9 00	Sun.									S.P.
Ogden...............Ar.	9 35	Mon.									"
Los Angeles.........Lv.	8 30	Sun.			10 00	Sun.				U.P.S.
Cedar City (to Zion Pk.)Lv.	1 20	Mon.								U.P.S.
Salt Lake City........Ar.	9 45	Mon.			12 15	Mon.				U.P.S.
Salt Lake City........Lv.	10 05	Mon.			12 30	Mon.				"
Ogden...............Lv.	10 55	Mon.			1 30	Mon.				"
Ogden...............Lv.	11 20	Mon.			2 10	Mon.				"
Cheyenne............Lv.	Via Borie.				6 45	Tues.				"
Denver...............Ar.	2 30	Tues.			10 00	Tues.				"
Seattle..............Lv.			12 01	Sun.	11 15	Sat.				U.P.S.
Tacoma..............Lv.			1 17	"	12 40	Sun.				"
Portland.............Lv.			9 30	Sun.	9 40	"				U.P.S.
West Yellowstone.....Lv.	1 25	Effective June 21st to Sept. 19th								U.P.S.
Green River..........Lv.	4 05	Tues.	1 20	Tues.	7 45	Mon.				U.P.S.
Cheyenne............Lv.	Via Borie.		8 50	Tues.	6 45	Tues.				"
Denver...............Ar.	2 30	Tues.	11 50	Tues.	10 00	Tues.				"
Denver...............Lv.	3 00	Tues.	3 00	Tues.	11 00	Wed.	10 00	10 00	Sun.	
Kansas City..........Ar.	8 00	Wed.	8 00	Wed.	7 50	Thur.	4 10	4 10	Mon.	U.P.S.
Kansas City..........Lv.	9 00	Wed.	9 00	Wed.	9 00	Thur.	9 30	11 55	Mon.	Wab.
St. Louis (Delmar Blvd.).Ar.	3 59	"	3 59	"	3 59	"	7 05	7 05	Tues.	"
St. Louis (Union Sta.)...Ar.	4 20	Wed.	4 20	Wed.	4 20	Thur.	7 30	7 30	Tues.	"

▲Motor Bus.

EQUIPMENT:

Pacific Coast Limited
 Observation-Parlor Car....St. Louis to Kansas City.
 Limousine Lounge Car.....Kansas City to Los Angeles—D. R.—Compt.
 Sleeping Car...............St. Louis to San Francisco—12 Sects.—D. R.—Compt.
  St. Louis to Los Angeles (via Omaha in No. 11 and Un. Pac. No. 7.) See table on page 7.
 Sleeping Car...............St. Louis to West Yellowstone—12 Sects.—D. R.—June 18th to Sept. 16th.
  Kansas City to Portland—16 Sects.
  Kansas City to Los Angeles—12 Sects.—D. R.
 Tourist Sleeping Car......Denver to San Francisco and Los Angeles.
 Reclining Chair Car.......St. Louis to Kansas City—Denver to San Francisco.
 Coach......................Kansas City to Los Angeles.
 Dining Car Service.

Denver Express
 Club Lounge Car..........St. Louis to Kansas City.
 Sleeping Cars.............St. Louis to Denver—12 Sects.—D. R.
  Denver to San Francisco and Los Angeles.
 Tourist Sleeping Car......Kansas City to San Francisco—Ogden to Los Angeles.
 Reclining Chair Car.......St. Louis to Kansas City, Denver to Cheyenne, Cheyenne to Los Angeles and San Francisco.
 Coach......................Kansas City to Denver.
 Dining Car Service.

St. Louis-Colorado Limited
 Observation-Parlor Car....St. Louis to Kansas City—D. R.
 Observation-Sleeping Car..Kansas City to Denver.
 Sleeping Car...............Kansas City to Denver.
 Reclining Chair Car.......St. Louis to Kansas City, Kansas City to Denver.
 Dining Car Service.

For equipment between St. Louis and Kansas City, see equipment at top of this page.

Note.—See Table on page 7 for service, St. Louis via Omaha to and from Los Angeles.

EQUIPMENT:

Pacific Coast Limited
 Limousine Lounge Car....Los Angeles to Kansas City—D. R.—Compts.
 Observation-Parlor Car....Kansas City to St. Louis.
 Sleeping Cars.............San Francisco to St. Louis—12 Sects.—D. R.—Compt.
 Sleeping Car...............West Yellowstone to St. Louis—12 Sects.—D. R.—Effective June 21st to Sept. 19th.
  Los Angeles to St. Louis (Un. Pac. to Omaha and No. 14 to St. Louis). See table on page 7.
 Tourist Sleeping Car......Los Angeles and Portland to Kansas City.
 Reclining Chair Car.......Los Angeles to Ogden—San Francisco to Kansas City.
 Coach......................Kansas City to St. Louis.
 Dining Car Service.........Los Angeles to Kansas City.

Portland Rose (connection enroute with thru equipment in Pacific Coast Limited.)
 Club Lounge Observation Car.....Portland to Cheyenne.
 Parlor Car................Cheyenne to Denver.
 Standard Sleeping Cars....Seattle to Cheyenne.
  Portland to Cheyenne.
  Denver to Kansas City.
 Tourist Sleeping Car......Denver to Kansas City.
 Reclining Chair Car.......Denver to St. Louis.
 Coach......................Denver to Kansas City.
 Dining Car Service.

St. Louis-Colorado Limited
 Observation-Parlor Car....Kansas City to St. Louis—D. R.
 Sleeping Car...............Portland to Denver and Denver to Kansas City—D. R.
 Reclining Chair Car.......Denver to Kansas City, Kansas City to St. Louis.
 Dining Car Service.

St. Louis Express
 Observation Sleeping Car...Denver to Kansas City.
 Club Lounge Car..........Kansas City to St. Louis.
 Sleeping Car...............Denver to St. Louis—12 Sects.—D. R.
 Reclining Chair Car.......Denver to Kansas City.
 Coach......................Denver to Kansas City.
 Dining Car Service.

Midnight Limited—For equipment see St. Louis Express; also equipment of Kansas City-St. Louis No. 4-18 shown on this page.
 For equipment between Kansas City and St. Louis, see schedules at top of this page.

Through Car Service and Equipment

ST. LOUIS, OMAHA, SAN FRANCISCO, LOS ANGELES

Miles	STATIONS	Los Angeles Limited Daily	Route	San Francisco Limited Daily	Route	Example
0	St. Louis (U.Sta.)....Lv.	7 30PM	Wab. 11	7 30PM	Wab. 11	Sun.
5.6	St. Louis (Delmar) Lv.	7 44PM	"	7 44PM	"	Mon.
410.8	Council Bluffs.....Ar.	7 45AM	"	7 45AM	"	"
413.6	Omaha..........Ar.	8 00AM	Wab. 11	8 00AM	Wab. 11	"
413.6	Omaha..........Lv.	10 07AM	U.P. 7	10 10AM	U.P. 27	"
1403.6	Ogden..........Ar.	9 20AM	"	10 45AM	"	Tue.
2185.6	San Francisco.....Ar.	....	....	8 30AM	S.P. 27	Wed.
1403.6	Ogden..........Lv.	9 45AM	U.P. 7	....	....	Tue.
1440.6	Salt Lake City....Ar.	10 35AM	"	....	....	"
2223.6	Los Angeles.....Ar.	8 30AM	"	....	....	Wed.

Los Angeles Limited.
Club car.....................St. Louis to Omaha.
Sleeping car.................St. Louis to Los Angeles—10 Sects.—D. R.—2 Compts.
Sleeping car.................St. Louis to Omaha— 12 Sects.—D. R.
Reclining Chair car..........St. Louis to Omaha.
Club Observation car and
　Dining car...............West of Omaha.
San Francisco Limited.
Sleeping car.................St. Louis to San Francisco—12 Sects.—D. R.
See Equipment of Los Angeles
　Limited for equipment.....St. Louis to Omaha.
Club Observation car and
　Dining car...............West of Omaha.

LOS ANGELES, SAN FRANCISCO, OMAHA, ST. LOUIS

Miles	STATIONS	Los Angeles Limited Daily	Route	San Francisco Limited Daily	Route	Example
0	Los Angeles......Lv.	6 05PM	U.P. 8	....	....	Sun.
783	Salt Lake City....Lv.	5 35PM	"	....	....	Mon.
819.3	Ogden..........Ar.	6 30PM	"	....	....	"
0	San Francisco.....Lv.	....	....	6 00PM	S.P. 28	Sun.
782	Ogden..........Lv.	6 55PM	U.P. 8	6 40PM	U.P. 28	Mon.
1810	Omaha..........Ar.	8 15PM	"	8 10PM	"	Tues.
1810	Omaha..........Lv.	8 30PM	Wab. 14	8 30PM	Wab. 14	"
	Council Bluffs....Lv.	8 45PM	"	8 45PM	"	"
	St. Louis (Delmar) Ar.	8 09AM	"	8 09AM	"	Wed.
	St. Louis (U.Sta.)..Ar.	8 30AM	"	8 30AM	"	"

Los Angeles Limited.
Sleeping car.................Los Angeles to St. Louis—10 Sects.—D. R.—2 Compts.
Sleeping car.................Omaha to St. Louis—12 Sects.—D. R.
Club car.....................Omaha to St. Louis.
Reclining Chair car..........Omaha to St. Louis.
Club Observation car and
　Dining car...............West of Omaha.
San Francisco Limited.
Sleeping car.................San Francisco to St. Louis—12 Sects.—D. R.
Club Observation car and
　Dining car...............West of St. Louis.
See Los Angeles Limited
　Equipment...............Omaha to St. Louis.

ST. LOUIS TO LOS ANGELES
Via Santa Fe Every Third Day

Read Down No. 17	Miles	STATIONS	Read Up No. 18
11 45PM	0.0	Lv........St. Louis (Union Station)..........Ar.	7 30AM
12 01AM	5.6	Lv........St. Louis (Delmar Blvd.)..........Ar.	7 05AM
7 30AM	278.7	Ar..............Kansas City..............Lv.	11 55PM
5 55AM	1998.2	Ar...........San Bernardino.............Lv.	8 05PM
8 15AM	2058.2	Ar..............Los Angeles...............Lv.	6 15PM

No. 17—Sleeping car.................St. Louis to Los Angeles—D. R.—2 compts.
No. 18—Sleeping car.................Los Angeles to St. Louis—D. R.—2 compts.
Leaves St. Louis and Los Angeles, May 25, 28, 31, June 3, 6, 9, 12, 15, 18, 21, 24, 27, 30,
July 3, 6, 9, 12, 15, 18, 21, 24, 27, 30, and every third day thereafter.
(St. Louis sleeper open 10:00 P. M.)

ST. LOUIS TO DES MOINES

Read Down 11 Daily	Miles	STATIONS	14 Daily	Read Up ROUTE
7 30PM	.0	Lv. St. Louis (Union Sta)..........Ar.	8 30AM	Wabash
7 44PM	5.6	Lv. St. Louis (Delmar Blvd.)......Ar.	8 09AM	"
11 25PM	147.8	Ar. Moberly...................Lv.	4 50AM	"
6 50AM	340.1	Ar. Des Moines................Lv.	9 45PM	Wabash

No. 11—Observation Sleeping Car.....St. Louis to Des Moines—10 Sects.
　　　　Sleeping Car.................St. Louis to Des Moines—12 Sects.—D. R.
　　　　Cafe Car....................St. Louis to Moberly (to Omaha).
　　　　Reclining Chair Car..........St. Louis to Des Moines.
No. 14—Observation Sleeping Car.....Des Moines to St. Louis—10 Sects.
　　　　Sleeping Car.................Des Moines to St. Louis—12 Sects.—D. R.
　　　　Cafe Car....................Albia to St. Louis.
　　　　Reclining Chair Car..........Des Moines to St. Louis.

ST. LOUIS TO MINNEAPOLIS AND ST. PAUL

Miles	STATIONS	9-19 Daily	ROUTE
.0	St. Louis..................Lv.	2 00PM	Wabash
5.6	St. Louis (Delmar Blvd.).........	2 15PM	"
147.8	Moberly.....................	5 52PM	"
243.6	Moulton.....................	8 53PM	"
271.8	Albia.....................Ar.	9 45PM	Wabash
295.3	Oskaloosa..................Ar.	10 42PM	M. & St. L.
352.7	Marshalltown.................	12 25AM	"
440.5	Mason City..................	3 07AM	"
447.4	Albert Lea..................	4 10AM	"
584.6	Minneapolis.................	7 35AM	"
596.4	St. Paul...................	8 15AM	M. & St. L.

No. 9-19—The North Star Limited.
Sleeping car.................St. Louis to Minneapolis-St. Paul—12 Sects.—D. R.
Cafe car....................St. Louis to Albia and Marshalltown to Minneapolis
　　　　　　　　　　　　　and St. Paul.
Reclining Chair car........St. Louis to Albia and Albia to Minneapolis-St. Paul.

ST. PAUL AND MINNEAPOLIS TO ST. LOUIS

Miles	STATIONS	14 Daily	ROUTE
.0	St. Paul...................Lv.	2 00PM	M. & St. L.
11.8	Minneapolis.................	2 45PM	"
119.0	Albert Lea..................	5 55PM	"
155.9	Mason City..................	7 00PM	"
243.7	Marshalltown.................	9 45PM	"
301.1	Oskaloosa...................	11 35PM	"
324.6	Albia.....................Lv.	12 35AM	Wabash
352.8	Moulton....................	1 28AM	"
448.6	Moberly....................	4 50AM	"
590.6	St. Louis (Delmar Blvd.).......	8 09AM	"
596.4	St. Louis..................Ar.	8 30AM	Wabash

No. 14—The North Star Limited.
Sleeping car..................St. Paul and Minneapolis to St. Louis—12 Sects.—D.R.
Cafe car.....................St. Paul and Minneapolis to Marshalltown and Albia
　　　　　　　　　　　　　to St. Louis.
Reclining Chair car.........St. Paul and Minneapolis to Albia and Albia to St.Louis

CENTRAL STATES LIMITED

KANSAS CITY TO DETROIT

Miles	STATIONS	28 Daily	ROUTE
.0	Kansas City................Lv.	5 45PM	Wabash
200.1	Hannibal...................Lv.	10 50PM	"
267.9	Jacksonville................Lv.	12 50AM	"
301.8	Springfield.................Lv.	1 47AM	"
340.4	Decatur...................Ar.	2 57AM	"
414.3	Danville...................Ar.	4 55AM	"
460.5	Lafayette..................Ar.	6 11AM	"
497.5	Logansport.................Ar.	7 07AM	"
513.4	Peru.....................Ar.	7 30AM	"
545.5	Huntington.................Ar.	8 25AM	"
569.5	Ft. Wayne.................Ar.	8 57AM	"
618.6	Montpelier.................Ar.	10 25AM	"
618.6	Montpelier.................Lv.	10 30AM	"
715.6	Detroit (Fort St. Station) (Central Time)...Ar.	12 45PM	"
715.6	Detroit (Fort St. Station) (Eastern Time)......Ar.	1 45PM	Wabash

No. 28—Central States Limited.
　Observation sleeping car.......Kansas City to Detroit—10 Sects.
　Sleeping car,..................Kansas City to Detroit—10 Sects.—D. R.—2 Compts.
　Reclining Chair car,...........Kansas City to Detroit.—(Club Smoking Room)
　Dining car...................Kansas City to Detroit.

DETROIT TO KANSAS CITY

Miles	STATIONS	29 Daily	ROUTE
.0	Detroit (Fort St. Station) (Central Time).........Lv.	10 30PM	Wabash
.0	Detroit (Fort St. Station) (Eastern Time)..........	11 30PM	"
146.1	Ft. Wayne..................Ar.	2 05AM	"
170.1	Huntington.................Ar.	2 50AM	"
202.2	Peru.....................Ar.	3 45AM	"
218.1	Logansport.................Ar.	4 15AM	"
255.1	Lafayette..................Ar.	5 15AM	"
301.3	Danville...................Ar.	6 40AM	"
375.2	Decatur...................Ar.	8 20AM	"
413.8	Springfield.................Ar.	9 35AM	"
447.7	Jacksonville................Ar.	10 36AM	"
515.4	Hannibal...................Ar.	12 38PM	Wabash
534.3	Quincy....................Lv.	11 30AM	Wabash
534.3	Quincy....................Ar.	1 40PM	Wabash
515.5	Hannibal...................Lv.	12 38PM	Wabash
715.6	Kansas City................Ar.	5 45PM	Wabash

No. 29—Central States Limited.
　Observation Sleeping Car.....Detroit to Kansas City—10 Sects.
　Sleeping car.................Detroit to Kansas City—10 Sects.—D. R.—2 Compts.
　Dining car..................Ft. Wayne to Moberly.
　Reclining Chair Car (Club Smoking Room)....Detroit to Kansas City (sleepers
　　　　　　　　　　　　　　　　　　　　　　open 10 P. M.—E. T.
　Coach.

7　　　　　　　8

Through Car Service and Equipment

CHICAGO—DECATUR—ST. LOUIS

Miles	STATIONS	11 Daily	21-1 Daily	17 Daily	ROUTE
.0	Chicago (Dearborn Station).Lv.	11 30 PM	3 15 PM	11 50 PM	...... Wabash
4.4	Chicago (47th Street)......Lv.	a11 40 AM	a3 24 PM	a12 00 AM	"
6.5	Englewood (63rd & Wallace).Lv.	11 45 AM	3 29 PM	12 05 AM	"
172.5	Decatur.................Ar.	3 07 PM	6 45 PM	4 10 AM	"
......	St. Louis (Washington Ave.).Ar.	......	......	......	"
......	St. Louis (Delmar Blvd.)....Ar.	6 39 PM	9 34 PM	7 18 AM	"
285.7	St. Louis (Union Station)....Ar.	6 00 PM	9 55 PM	7 39 AM	...... Wabash

a Stops to receive revenue passengers.

No. 11—St. Louis "Banner Blue Limited"
Observation-Parlor car.....Chicago to St. Louis.
Drawing-room Parlor car.....Chicago to St. Louis.
Dining car............Chicago to St. Louis.
Reclining Chair car........Chicago to St. Louis.

No. 21-1—St. Louis Special.
Sleeping car............Chicago to St. Louis—10 Sects.—D. R.—Compts. (To Hot Springs).
Parlor car............Chicago to St. Louis—Drawing-room.
Reclining Chair car.......Chicago to St. Louis.
Cafe car............Chicago to St. Louis.
Dining car............Decatur to St. Louis.

No. 17—St. Louis "Midnight Limited"
Club Lounge car.........Chicago to St. Louis.
Sleeping car............Chicago to St. Louis—10 Sects.—3 Single Bed Rooms.
Sleeping car............Chicago to St. Louis—12 Sects.—D. R.—Compt.
Sleeping car............Chicago to St. Louis—12 Sects.—D. R.
Sleeping car............Chicago to Decatur—12 Sects.—D. R. (In No. 3 to Quincy).
Sleeping car............Chicago to Decatur—16 Sects. (Passengers can remain in sleeper until 8:00 a. m. on arrival at Decatur). (Sleepers open 10 p. m.).
Reclining Chair car.......Chicago to St. Louis.

ST. LOUIS—DECATUR—CHICAGO

Miles	STATIONS	4-24 Daily	10 Daily	18 Daily	ROUTE
.0	St. Louis (Union Station)....Lv.	8 47 AM	12 05 PM	11 55 PM	...... Wabash
.0	St. Louis (Delmar Blvd.)....Lv.	......	12 20 PM	12 10 AM	"
.0	St. Louis (Washington Ave.).Lv.	......	......	......	"
113.2	Decatur.................Ar.	11 20 AM	2 47 PM	2 50 AM	"
279.1	Englewood (63rd & Wallace) Ar.	3 01 PM	6 18 PM	7 17 AM	"
281.1	Chicago (47th Street)......Ar.	e3 06 PM	c6 23 PM	c7 22 AM	"
285.7	Chicago (Dearborn Station)..Ar.	3 17 PM	6 35 PM	7 35 AM	...... Wabash

c Stops to discharge revenue passengers.

No. 4-24—Chicago Special
Parlor car...............St. Louis to Chicago—Drawing-room.
Reclining Chair car.......St. Louis to Chicago.
Cafe car............St. Louis to Chicago.
Dining car............St. Louis to Decatur.

No. 10—Chicago "Banner Blue Limited"
Observation-Parlor car.....St. Louis to Chicago.
Drawing-room Parlor car....St. Louis to Chicago.
Dining car............St. Louis to Chicago.
Reclining Chair car........St. Louis to Chicago.

No. 18—Chicago "Midnight Limited"
Club car............St. Louis to Chicago.
Sleeping car............St. Louis (Delmar Blvd. Station) to Chicago—12 Sect.—D. R. (Open 9:30 p. m.).
Sleeping car............St. Louis to Chicago—10 Sects.—3 Single Bed Rooms.
Sleeping car............St. Louis to Chicago—12 Sects.—D. R.—Compt. (Sleepers open 10:00 p. m.).
Sleeping car............St. Louis to Chicago—10 Sects.—D. R.—Compt. (From Hot Springs via Mo. Pac.).
Reclining Chair car........St. Louis to Chicago.

CHICAGO AND DETROIT, BUFFALO AND NEW YORK

Miles	STATIONS	6 Daily	12 Daily	ROUTE
.0	Chicago (Dearborn Station)..........Lv.	10 30 AM	11 30 PM	Wabash
4.4	Chicago (47th Street)..............Lv.	10 40 AM	11 40 PM	"
6.5	Englewood (63rd & Wallace)..........Lv.	10 45 AM	11 45 PM	"
272.1	Detroit (Central Time)...............Ar.	5 30 PM	6 55 AM	"
272.1	Detroit (Eastern Time)...............Ar.	6 30 PM	7 55 AM	"
272.1	Detroit (Central Time)...............Lv.	5 55 PM	......	"
272.1	Detroit (Eastern Time)...............Lv.	6 55 PM	......	"
513.4	Buffalo......................Ar.	2 40 AM	......	Wabash
513.4	Buffalo......................Lv.	4 00 AM	......	D. L. & W.
659.9	Elmira......................Ar.	8 15 AM	......	"
716.8	Binghamton...................Ar.	9 43 AM	......	"
775.5	Scranton....................Ar.	11 20 AM	......	"
900.8	Newark.....................Ar.	3 15 PM	......	"
907.8	Hoboken....................Ar.	3 30 PM	......	"
909.6	New York (E. T.)...............Ar.	3 50 PM	......	"
909.6	Barclay St....................Ar.	3 50 PM	......	"
909.6	West 23rd St...................Ar.	3 50 PM	......	D. L. & W.

Miles	STATIONS	1-11 Daily	5 Daily	ROUTE
.0	New York (E. T.)...........Lv.	2 00 PM	......	D. L. & W.
.0	West 23rd St..............Lv.	2 00 PM	......	"
.0	Barclay St................Lv.	......	......	"
1.0	Hoboken.................Lv.	2 20 PM	......	"
8.8	Newark..................Lv.	2 35 PM	......	"
134.1	Scranton.................Lv.	6 40 PM	......	"
192.7	Binghamton...............Lv.	8 15 PM	......	"
249.7	Elmira..................Lv.	9 43 PM	......	"
396.2	Buffalo.................Ar.	1 05 AM	......	D. L. & W.
396.2	Buffalo.................Lv.	1 15 AM	......	Wabash
637.5	Detroit (Central Time)........Ar.	7 35 AM	......	"
637.5	Detroit (Eastern Time)........Ar.	8 35 AM	......	"
637.5	Detroit (Central Time)........Lv.	9 50 AM	11 45 PM	"
637.5	Detroit (Eastern Time)........Lv.	10 50 AM	12 45 AM	"
903.1	Englewood (63rd & Wallace).......Ar.	4 32 PM	6 57 AM	"
......	Chicago (47th Street)..........Ar.	4 37 PM	7 02 AM	"
909.6	Chicago (Dearborn Station)......Ar.	4 50 PM	7 15 AM	Wabash

No. 6 —Detroit Special
Sleeping car............Chicago to New York—12 Sects.—D. R.
Dining car............Chicago to St. Thomas.
Dining car............Elmira to Hoboken.
Coach..............Chicago to New York.

No. 12—Detroit Midnight Limited
Club Lounge car........Chicago to Detroit.
Sleeping car............Chicago to Detroit—10 Sects.—3 single Bed Rooms.
Sleeping car............Chicago to Detroit—12 Sects.—D. R. (Sleepers ready for occupancy 10:00 p. m.).
Reclining Chair car.......Chicago to Detroit.

No. 1-11—Chicago Special
Sleeping car............New York to Chicago—12 Sects.—D. R.
Dining car............Hoboken to Binghamton.
Dining car............St. Thomas to Chicago.
Coach..............New York to Chicago.

No. 5 —Chicago Midnight Limited
Club Lounge car........Detroit to Chicago.
Sleeping car............Detroit to Chicago—10 Sects.—3 single Bed Rooms.
Sleeping car............Detroit to Chicago—12 Sects.—D. R. (Open 10:00 p. m. E. T.).
Reclining Chair car.......Detroit to Chicago.

DECATUR-CHICAGO

No. 12 Daily	Miles	STATIONS	No. 17 Daily	ROUTE
1 05 AM	0	Lv. Decatur.................Ar.	4 10 AM	Wabash
		Ar. Chicago.................Lv.		"
6 38 AM	165.9	... Englewood (63rd & Wallace)...Lv.	12 05 AM	"
6 43 AM	167.9	... 47th Street..............Lv.	12 00 MN	"
6 55 AM	172.5	... Dearborn Station...........Lv.	11 50 PM	"

Sleeping Car between Decatur and Chicago—12 Sects.—D. R. (Open at Decatur 9:00 P. M.—at Chicago 10:00 P. M.—available until 8:00 A. M. on arrival at Decatur.)
Coach service.........Decatur to Chicago.
Reclining Chair car.....Chicago to Decatur.

CHICAGO—HANNIBAL—QUINCY

17-3 Daily	Miles	STATIONS	12 Daily	ROUTE
11 50 PM	.0	Lv. Chicago (Dearborn Station)....Ar.	6 55 AM	Wabash
12 05 AM	6.5	Lv. Englewood (63rd & Wallace)...Ar.	6 38 AM	"
4 45 AM	172.5	Lv. Decatur..................Lv.	1 05 AM	"
5 55 AM	211.5	Ar. Springfield...............Lv.	10 48 PM	"
7 00 AM	245.2	Ar. Jacksonville..............Lv.	9 35 PM	"
9 45 AM	312.8	...Hannibal................Lv.	6 25 PM	Wabash
10 45 AM	331.6	Ar. Quincy.................Lv.	5 30 PM	Wabash

Sleeping car between Chicago and Quincy—12 Sects.—D. R.
Coach service between Decatur, Hannibal and Quincy.
Reclining Chair car Chicago-Decatur.
Sleeper at Chicago open 10:00 p. m.

9   10

Through Car Service and Equipment

ST. LOUIS, TOLEDO, DETROIT, BUFFALO—NEW YORK

Miles	EAST-BOUND	4 Daily	2 Daily	18-28-6 Daily	ROUTE
.0	St. Louis (Union Station).....Lv.	8 47AM	6 30PM	11 55PM	Wabash
.0	St. Louis (Delmar Blvd.)........	.....	.....	12 10AM	"
113.2	Decatur.............................	11 30AM	9 10PM	3 15AM	"
187.1	Danville............................	1 20PM	10 50PM	4 55AM	"
233.3	Lafayette..........................	2 34PM	12 01AM	6 11AM	"
270.3	Logansport........................	3 34PM	12 59AM	7 07AM	"
286.2	Peru...............................	4 05PM	1 30AM	7 35AM	"
318.3	Huntington........................	4 58PM	2 17AM	8 25AM	"
342.3	Ft. Wayne.........................Ar.	5 30PM	2 55AM	8 57AM	Wabash
437.0	Toledo (Central Time)........Ar.	8 40PM	7 00AM	.....	Wabash
437.0	Toledo (Eastern Time)........Ar.	9 40PM	8 00AM	.....	Wabash
342.3	Ft. Wayne.........................Lv.	5 40PM	3 10AM	9 05AM	Wabash
429.6	Adrian.............................	8 05PM	5 20AM	11 20AM	"
488.8	Detroit (Central Time)......Ar.	9 30PM	6 45AM	12 45PM	"
488.8	Detroit (Eastern Time)......Ar.	10 30PM	7 45AM	1 45PM	Wabash
488.8	Detroit (Eastern Time)......Lv.	.....	.....	6 55PM	Wabash
729.7	Buffalo............................Ar.	.....	.....	2 40AM	Wabash
1125.9	New York..........................Ar.	.....	.....	.....	D. L. & W.
1125.9	Barclay St.........................	.....	.....	3 50PM	"
1125.9	West 23rd St.......................	.....	.....	3 50PM	D. L. & W.

No. 4—Parlor car............St. Louis to Detroit—Drawing-room.
   Dining car................St. Louis to to Montpelier.
   Coach......................
   Coach connection......Fort Wayne to Toledo.

No. 2—Observation Sleeping car.St. Louis to Detroit—10 Sects.—Drawing-room.
   Sleeping cars............St. Louis to Detroit—12 Sects.—Drawing-room.
   Sleeping car..............St. Louis to Detroit—4 private sections.
   Sleeping car..............St. Louis to Toledo—12 Sects.—Drawing-room.
       (in No. 12 from Fort Wayne.)
   Dining car................St. Louis to Decatur—Montpelier to Detroit.
   Cafe car..................Ft. Wayne to Toledo (in No. 12 from Fort Wayne.)
   Reclining Chair car......St. Louis to Detroit.
   Coach......................Fort Wayne to Toledo (in No. 12 from Fort Wayne.)

No. 18-28—6—Club Lounge car....St. Louis to Detroit
   Sleeping car..............St. Louis to Detroit—12 Sects.—D. R. (Open 10:00 p. m.)
   Sleeping car..............Detroit to New York—12 Sects. (From Chicago.)
   Dining car................Decatur to Detroit—Detroit to St. Thomas and Elmira to Hoboken.
   Coach......................Detroit to New York (From Chicago.)
   Reclining Chair car......St. Louis to Detroit.

Miles	WEST-BOUND	1 Daily	3-13-3 Daily	29-9 Daily	ROUTE
.0	New York..........................Lv.	.....	.....	.....	D. L. & W.
.0	Barclay St.........................	2 00PM	.....	.....	"
.0	West 23rd St.......................	2 00PM	.....	.....	D. L. & W.
396.2	Buffalo (Eastern Time)......Lv.	1 15AM	.....	.....	Wabash
637.1	Detroit (Central Time)......Ar.	7 35AM	.....	.....	Wabash
637.1	Detroit (Central Time)......Lv.	9 00AM	6 00PM	10 30PM	Wabash
637.1	Detroit (Eastern Time)......Lv.	10 00AM	7 00PM	11 30PM	"
696.3	Adrian.............................	10 23AM	7 26PM	11 58PM	"
783.6	Ft. Wayne.........................Ar.	12 25PM	9 30PM	2 05AM	Wabash
.....	Toledo (Central Time)........Lv.	9 30AM	6 25PM	.....	Wabash
.....	Toledo (Eastern Time)........Lv.	10 30AM	7 25PM	.....	Wabash
783.6	Ft. Wayne.........................Lv.	12 35PM	9 45PM	2 15AM	Wabash
807.6	Huntington........................	1 12PM	10 19PM	2 50AM	"
839.7	Peru...............................	2 05PM	11 10PM	3 50AM	"
855.6	Logansport........................	2 29PM	11 37PM	4 15AM	"
892.0	Lafayette..........................	3 32PM	12 45AM	5 15AM	"
939.8	Danville...........................	4 55PM	2 10AM	6 40AM	"
1012.7	Decatur............................	6 50PM	3 55AM	8 35AM	"
1125.9	St. Louis (Delmar Blvd.)......Ar.	9 34PM	.....	.....	"
1125.9	St. Louis (Union Station)......Ar.	9 55PM	7 15AM	11 45AM	Wabash

No. 1—Sleeping car............New York to Detroit—12 Sects.—D. R. (No. 11 to Chicago).
   Dining car................Hoboken to Binghamton—St. Thomas to Detroit—Detroit to Decatur.
   Parlor car................Detroit to St. Louis—Drawing room.
   Coach......................New York to Detroit (in No. 11 to Chicago.)
   Coach......................Detroit to St. Louis.
   Coach connection......Toledo to Fort Wayne.

No. 3-13-3—Observation Sleeping car Detroit to St. Louis—10 Sects.
   Sleeping cars............Detroit to St. Louis—D. R.
   Sleeping car..............Detroit to St. Louis—10 Sects.—4 private sections.
   Sleeping car..............Toledo to St. Louis—12 Sects.—D. R. (No. 13 from Toledo).
   Dining car................Detroit to Ft. Wayne—Decatur to St. Louis.
   Cafe car..................Detroit to Fort Wayne (in No. 13 from Toledo via Defiance).
   Reclining Chair car......Detroit to St. Louis.
   Coach......................Toledo to Fort Wayne (in No. 13 from Toledo via Defiance).

No. 29-9—Club Lounge car......Detroit to St. Louis
   Sleeping car..............Detroit to St. Louis—12 Sects.—D. R.—(Open 10 p. m. E. T.)
   Dining car................Ft. Wayne to Decatur—Decatur to St. Louis.
   Reclining Chair car......Detroit to St. Louis.

DETROIT—EVANSVILLE

3-9 Daily	Miles	STATIONS	10-28 Daily	ROUTE
6 00PM	.0	Lv. Detroit (Fort St. Sta.) (C. T.)...Ar.	12 45PM	Wabash
7 00PM	.0	Lv. Detroit (Fort St. Sta.) (E. T.)...Ar.	1 45PM	"
9 45PM	146.5	Lv. Ft. Wayne.....................Ar.	8 57AM	"
2 10AM	301.7	Ar. Danville......................Lv.	4 55AM	"
3 00AM	301.7	Ar. Danville......................Lv.	3 10AM	C&E I!ls.
4 25AM	356.0	Ar. Terre Haute..................Lv.	1 34AM	"
5 16AM	382.2	Ar. Sullivan......................Lv.	.....	"
5 57AM	413.2	Ar. Vincennes....................Lv.	12 03AM	"
6 40AM	437.6	Ar. Princeton.....................Lv.	11 20PM	"
7 40AM	465.0	Ar. Evansville....................Lv.	10 40PM	C&E Ills.

Sleeping Car—between Detroit and Evansville.—12 Sects.—D. R.

DETROIT—SOUTH BEND

6 Daily	Miles	STATIONS	12 Daily	ROUTE
11 45 PM	.0	Lv. Detroit (Fort St. Sta.) (C. T.)...Ar.	6 55AM	Wabash
12 45 AM	.0	Lv. Detroit (Fort St. Sta.) (E. T.)...Ar.	7 55AM	"
5 45 AM	197.9	Ar. South Bend (C. T.).........Lv.	1 15AM	N. J. I. & I.

Sleeping car—between Detroit and South Bend—12 Sects.—D. R.
Club Car—between Detroit and Pine.
Reclining Chair Car between Detroit and Pine.
Sleepers ready for occupancy: at Detroit 10:00 P. M. (E.T.), at South Bend 9:00 P. M. (C.T.).

CHICAGO—ST. LOUIS—LITTLE ROCK—HOT SPRINGS

21-1 Daily	Miles	STATIONS	18 Daily	ROUTE
3 15PM	0	Lv. Chicago (Dearborn Sta.).......Ar.	7 35AM	Wabash
3 29PM	6.5	Lv. Englewood (63rd & Wallace)....Ar.	7 17AM	"
9 34PM	.....	Ar. St. Louis (Delmar Blvd.)......Lv.	12 10AM	"
9 55PM	285.7	Ar. St. Louis......................Lv.	11 55PM	"
10 35PM	285.7	Lv. St. Louis......................Ar.	11 33PM	Mo. Pac.
7 45AM	634.7	Ar. Little Rock....................Lv.	3 00PM	"
9 50AM	688.7	Ar. Hot Springs...................Lv.	12 55PM	Mo. Pac.

Through Sleeping car between Chicago and Hot Springs—10 Sects.—D. R.—Compts.

DETROIT, CINCINNATI, ATLANTA, JACKSONVILLE, ST. PETERSBURG, TAMPA, SARASOTA

Read Down   Read Up

"The Southland" 29 Daily	Exam.	STATIONS	"The Southland" Exam.	50 Daily	ROUTE
11 30PM	Sun.	Lv. Detroit (E. T.)...........Ar.	Tues.	8 35AM	Wabash
10 30PM	"	Lv. Detroit (C. T.)...........Ar.	"	7 35AM	"
2 05AM	Mon.	Ar. Ft. Wayne (C. T.).......Lv.	Tues.	3 30AM	"
8 30AM	Mon.	Ar. Cincinnati (E. T.)........Lv.	Mon.	11 45PM	Penn.
9 00AM	Mon.	Lv. Cincinnati (E. T.)........Lv.	Mon.	10 00PM	L. & N.
10 03AM	"	Ar. Paris (C. T.)............Lv.	"	6 46PM	"
10 53AM	Mon.	Ar. Lexington................Lv.	Mon.	5 50PM	L. & N.
10 30AM	Mon.	Ar. Winchester..............Lv.	Mon.	6 21PM	L. & N.
3 47PM	"	Ar. Knoxville................Lv.	"	12 55PM	"
8 50PM	Mon.	Ar. Atlanta (Union Station)..Lv.	Mon.	7 50AM	"
9 10PM	Mon.	Lv. Atlanta (Terminal Station).Ar.	Mon.	7 25AM	C. of Ga.
11 45PM	Mon.	Lv. Macon (C. T.)...........Ar.	"	4 40AM	"
8 30AM	Tues.	Ar. Jacksonville (E. T.)......Lv.	Sun.	9 00AM	A. C. L.
3 35AM	Tues.	Lv. Albany (E. T.)..........Ar.	Mon.	2 50AM	A. C. L.
5 00AM	"	Ar. Thomasville..............Lv.	"	1 20AM	"
9 07AM	"	Ar. Dunnellon...............Lv.	Sun.	8 54PM	"
10 13AM	"	Ar. Trilby....................Lv.	"	7 49PM	"
11 35AM	"	Ar. Tarpon Springs.........Lv.	"	6 23PM	"
11 59AM	"	Ar. Clearwater..............Lv.	"	6 01PM	"
12 40PM	Tues.	Ar. St. Petersburg..........Lv.	Sun.	5 30PM	"
11 40AM	Tues.	Ar. Tampa...................Lv.	Sun.	6 35PM	A. C. L.
c 6 45PM	Tues.	Ar. Sarasota (E. T.)........Lv.	Sun.	c 9 10AM	A. C. L.

Sleeping Car—Between Detroit, Cincinnati and Tampa—8 Sects.—D. R.—Compts. (Open 10:00 p. m. E. T.)
Sleeping Car—Cincinnati to Jacksonville—12 Sects.—D. R.
Coach Service.   Dining Car serving all meals.
cBy connecting Train.

11   12

Read Down.   ST. LOUIS, KANSAS CITY, DENVER AND PACIFIC COAST POINTS   Read Up.

13 Mixed Ex. Sun.	51 Daily	29 Daily	11 Daily	17 Daily	9 Daily	3 Daily	Miles	Table 1	2 Daily	12 Daily	18 Daily	4-18 Daily	14 Daily	14 Daily	14 Daily	50 Mixed Ex. Sun.	28 Daily	74 Freight Ex. Sun.	64 Freight Ex. Sun.
AM 6 00	AM		PM 7 30	PM 11 45	PM 2 00	AM 9 03	0	Lv......St. Louis......Ar	PM 4 20	PM 10 20	AM 7.30	AM 7 30	AM 8 30	AM 8 30	AM 8 30	AM 11 37			
6 09			7 44	12 01	2 15	d 9 17	1.1	....Ewing Avenue....Lv								11 20			
6 17						d	2.2	..Vandeventer Avenue....								11 12			
f						d	5.6	...Delmar Blvd. 2, 3...	3 59	9 58	7.05	7 05	8 09	8 09	8 09	11 12			
f 6 24						d	7.6	......Eden......								f			
						d	8.3	...St. Vincent's...								f			
						d	8.8	...Glen Echo...								11 05			
6 40						c 9 31	9.9	...Aldernay...											
f 6 45						d	12.1	...Ferguson...		v 6 49	v 6 49					10 55			
6 55					k 2 34	d	13.9	...Kinloch Park...								f 10 42			
						d	16.2	...Robertson...		v 6 41	v 6 41					10 37			
								Lambert-St. Louis' FlyingField											
7 23			g 8 16	m12 40	2 48	9 51	23.0	...St. Charles...	3 28	9 27	t 6 24	t 6 24				10 15			
f 7 33						d	26.5	...Gardnerville...								f 9 57			
7 42						d	31.6	...St. Peters...								9 41			
7 52						d	36.1	...O'Fallon...								9 30			
8 06						d	41.8	...Gilmore...								9 16			
8 16						d	44.3	...Wentzville...								9 08			
8 29						d	50.1	...Foristell...								8 53			
8 42						d	53.6	...Wright...								8 42			
8 55			g 9 07			d	59.7	...Truesdale...		o 8 33	s 5 32	s 5 52				8 29			
8 59						d	60.7	...Warrenton...								8 24			
9 10						d	65.4	...Pendleton...								8 15			
9 20						d	69.9	...Jonesburg...								8 05			
9 35						d	74.5	...High Hill...								7 55			
9 50						d	78.5	...New Florence...								7 45			PM
10 11			g 9 43			11 11	84.0	...Montgomery...		7 56	s 5 32	s 5 52				7 30			6 05
10 27			g 9 55			11 23	91.6	...Wellsville...	1 48		s 4 48	s 4 48				7 10			f 5 45
10 39			p 10 02			l 11 30	96.3	...Martinsburg...			• 4 42	• 4 42				6 58			f 5 30
10 51						d	103.0	...Benton City...								6 45			f 5 10
11 05			10 23	2 40	4 45	11 51	109.8	...Mexico...	1 24	7 18	4 25	4 25	• 5 47	• 5 47	• 5 47	6 30			f 4 32
11 16						d	115.4	...Thompson...								6 10			f 4 00
11 36			g 10 45	3 10	5 10	12 15	123.9	Ar...Centralia 3...Lv	1 03	6 55	4 02	4 02	• 5 27	• 5 27	• 5 27	5 55			f 3 40
2 05				4 10	6 00	2 05	145.6	Ar...Columbia 3...(Lv	11 10	6 02	2 00	2 00	4 15	4 15	4 15	4 15			3 25
				2 00	4 05	11 10	145.6	Lv...(Ar	2 05	7 55			6 50	6 50	6 50				
11 36			g 10 45	3 10	5 10	12 15	123.9	Lv...Centralia 3...Ar	1 03	6 55	4 02	4 02	• 5 27	• 5 27	• 5 27	5 55			3 25
11 52						12 25	131.7	...Sturgeon...								5 34			2 41
12 05						d	136.5	...Clark...								5 24			2 30
12 17							142.0	...Renick...								5 12			2 22
12 35	6 00	2 45	11 25	3 50	5 47	12 50	147.8	Ar...Moberly 2, 4, 12...(Lv	12 28	6 19	3 20	3 20	4 50	4 50	4 50	5 00			2 15
AM	6 12		11 30	3 55	5 55	12 58	147.8	Lv...(Ar	12 23	6 16	3 15	2 05		4 30		AM	8 45	PM	PM
6 48	6 24		.b.				154.6	...Huntsville...Lv		6 03		1 30		a 4 10				1 05	
7 05	6 37					1 27	161.3	...Clifton...				1 18						12 45	
7 25	6 49		b . p			1 36	168.8	...Salisbury 15...	11 47	5 43		1 07	a 3 52					12 25	
7 45	6 55						175.8	...Keytesville...		f 5 33		f 12 50	a 3 43					11 57	
7 55	7 10					1 55	179.7	...Dalton...				f 12 40						11 42	
8 25	7 22		12 25		6 49		186.8	...Brunswick 4, 12...	11 21	5 19		12 25	3 29					11 21	
8 45	7 28		AM				193.3	...De Witt...				f 12 08	AM					10 35	
8 55	7 39						197.1	...Miami...				f 12 02						10 20	
9 15	7 55						203.6	...Wakenda...				f 11 54						9 55	
9 35	f 8 07			5 30	7 21	2 30	210.6	...Carrollton 12...	10 47	4 44	1 35	11 40						9 35	
f 10 00	8 14						216.7	...Palemon...				f						f	
10 20						z 2 47	220.6	...Norborne...				11 17						8 50	
f 10 30							224.9	...Nimrod...										f	
10 50	8 29				z 3 00	3 10	229.2	...Hardin...				11 03						8 20	
11 15	8 40			p 6 08	e 7 58	3 10	235.3	Ar...Henrietta...Lv	10 09	4 08	n 12 59	10 52						8 00	
								(Manley Motor Service)											
				6 10	8 15			Lv...Henrietta...Ar				10 45							
				7 00	9 00			Ar...Excelsior Springs..Lv				9 30							
11 40	8 51						240.9	...Camden...				f 10 41						7 38	
f 11 47	f 8 57						243.2	...Fleming...				f 10 35						7 25	
11 55	9 05						246.5	...Orrick...				10 31						7 20	
12 20	9 25					3 38	253.1	Ar Excelsior Sprgs Jct. 4A Lv	9 45	3 42		f 10 19						6 55	
	10 26					4 18	261.8	Ar Excelsior Springs 4A (Lv	9 05	3 00									
	9 05					3 00	0	Lv...(Ar	10 26	4 18									
12 20	9 25					3 38		Lv.Excelsior Springs Jct.Ar	9 45	3 42		f 10 19							
12 30	9 31						256.1	Lv...Missouri City...Lv				10 14						6 45	
f 12 45	f 9 41						262.1	...South Liberty...				f 10 03						6 25	
f 1 00	f 9 47						266.6	...Birmingham...										6 15	
1 05	f						270.2	...Randolph...										f	
	10 00				p		273.3	...North Kansas City...		f		v							
	10 20		5 45	7 30	9 20	4 33	278.7	Ar...Kansas City...Lv	9 00	3 00	11 55	9 30				5 45			
PM	AM		6 15	10 40	10 00	6 15		Lv Kansas City (U. P. Sys) Ar	8 00	7 50	4 10	4 10				4 10			
			9 45	7 00	1 00	9 45	919	Ar...Denver (U. P. Sys).Lv	3 00	11 00	10 00	10 00				10 00			
			7 30	7 30	7 30	7 30	1532	Ar Salt Lake City(U.P.S).Lv	10 05	12 30									
			8 15	8 15	8 15	8 15	2315	Ar Los Angeles (U. P. Sys) Lv	8 30	10 00									
			x 8 15				2064	Ar Los Angeles (Santa Fe) Lv			x 6 15	x See Page 7 for schedule of date and departure of							
	8 10		8 10	8 10	8 30	8 10	2278	Ar San Francisco(So.Pac) Lv	9 00	11 20		thru service.							
Effective June 18th to Sept. 16th.				2 25			1721.7	Ar W.Yellowstone (U.P.S)Lv	1 25	Effective June 21st to Sept. 10th.									
	7 45		7 45	7 45	7 45		2280	Ar...Portland (U. P. Sys).Lv	9 30	9 40									
	1 04		1 04	1 04	1 04		2425	Ar.Tacoma (U. P. Sys).Lv	1 17	12 40									
	2 20		2 20	2 20	2 20		2463	Ar..Seattle (U. P. Sys)..Lv	12 01	11 15									

Reference Marks.—a Stops on signal to discharge revenue passengers from west of Brunswick. b Stops on signal for revenue passengers for points west of Stanberry. c Stops on signal to receive revenue passengers for Kansas City. d Stops on signal on Sunday to discharge passengers from beyond St. Louis, or to receive passengers for beyond Moberly. e Stops on signal to discharge revenue passengers from points east and north of Moberly and revenue passengers for Excelsior Springs. f Flag stop. g Stops on signal to receive or discharge paying passengers. j Stops on signal to receive revenue passengers for Ft. Wayne and east, or to discharge revenue passengers from Kansas City. k Stops on signal to receive revenue passengers for Kansas City or Albia or beyond. l Stops on signal on Sunday to receive or discharge revenue passengers. m Stops on signal to receive revenue passengers for Moberly and beyond. n Stops on signal to receive revenue passengers for points east and north of Moberly. o Stops on signal to discharge revenue passengers from Kansas City and to receive revenue passengers for St. Louis. p Stops to discharge revenue passengers from St. Louis. r Stops on signal to discharge revenue passengers from Kansas City, Des Moines, Albia and beyond. s Stops on signal to discharge revenue passengers or to receive revenue passengers for St. Louis. t Stops on signal to discharge revenue passengers. u Stops on signal to discharge revenue passengers from Omaha, Albia or beyond. v Stops on signal to discharge revenue passengers from Kansas City. z Stops on signal to discharge paying passengers from points east of Moberly and to receive paying passengers for Kansas City. •Stops on signal to receive revenue passengers for St. Louis. ■Stops on signal to discharge revenue passengers from Chillicothe, Macon or beyond.

13   14

ST. LOUIS, KANSAS CITY DES MOINES, MINNEAPOLIS AND ST. PAUL

Read Down. Read Up.

71 Freight Ex. Sun	9-19 Daily	11-28 Daily	Miles	Table 2	14-51 Daily	12-9 Daily	70 Freight Ex. Sun
	PM	PM			AM	PM	
	2 00	7 30	0	Lv......St. Louis......Ar	8 30	10 20	
	2 15	7 44	5.6	Lv...Delmar Blvd....Ar	8 09	9 58	
	5 47	11 25	147.8	Ar..Moberly 1, 4, 12..Lv	4 50	6 19	
		5 45	0	Lv...Kansas City....Ar	10 20	9 20	
AM		8 45	130.8	Ar..Moberly 1, 4, 12..Lv	6 00	5 55	PM
	5 52	11 30	147.8	Lv..Moberly 1, 4, 12..Ar	4 45	5 30	
7 15	f 6 04		154.4	.........Cairo.........	c 4 28	5 02	12 10
7 28	f 6 13		159.8	......Jacksonville.......	c 4 16	4 52	11 52
7 38	f 6 18		162.9	.........Excello.........	c 4 10	4 45	11 38
	f		169.4	.........Hildreth.........		f	
8 01	6 30	12 21	170.4	.........Macon.........	3 55	4 29	11 13
f 8 27	f 6 41		176.1	.........Axtell.........	c 3 44	f 4 16	f10 48
8 50	f 6 53		182.2	.........Atlanta.........	c 3 32	4 03	10 33
f 9 02	f 6 59		185.7	.........Love Lake.........	c 3 25	f 3 55	f10 24
9 25	7 09	1 05	190.9	.........La Plata.........	3 15	3 44	10 10
9 57	f 7 19		196.9	.........Millard.........	c 3 04	3 32	9 57
10 40	7 34	1 35	204.8	.........Kirksville.........	2 48	3 15	9 20
f10 57	f 7 48		212.6	.........Sublette.........	c 2 31	2 57	f 8 26
11 05	f 7 54		215.7	.........Green Top.........	c 2 24	2 50	8 18
11 17	f 8 02		220.0	.........Queen City.........	c 2 15	2 40	8 08
f11 34	f 8 10		224.5	.........Julesburg.........	c 2 06	f 2 30	f 7 58
11 47	f 8 18		229.0	.........Glenwood.........	c 1 57	2 20	7 48
11 50	8 21	a 2 40	230.1	...Glenwood Junction...	1 54	2 17	7 45
12 08	f 8 33		235.3	.....Coatesville, Mo.....	c 1 42	2 04	7 18
12 30	8 50	3 04	243.6	Ar...Moulton, Iowa...Lv	1 28	1 48	7 00
9 00			243.6	Lv......Moulton......Ar			3 30
9 22			251.4	.......West Grove.......			2 43
9 47			258.9	.......Bloomfield.......			2 05
10 05			264.1	.......Belknap.......			1 44
f10 23			270.0	.......Carbon.......			f 1 23
11 30			279.7	Ar......Ottumwa......Lv			12 50
	8 53	3 09	243.6	Lv......Moulton......Ar	1 24	1 44	
	f 9 06		251.1	.........Udell.........	c 1 12	1 29	
	f 9 15		256.6	......Hiattsville......	c 1 02	f 1 19	
	f 9 22		260.8	........Moravia........	c12 54	1 11	
	f 9 33		267.2	........Selection........	c12 43	f12 59	
	9 45	4 14	271.8	Ar......Albia......Lv	12 35	12 50	
		4 14	271.8	Lv......Albia......Ar	12 15		
			281.9	.........Lovilia.........			
			284.2	.........Hamilton.........			
			286.8	.........Bussey.........			
	Via Albia	f 4 57	292.1	.........Tracy.........	d11 20		
		f 5 04	295.7	.........Harvey.........	d11 13		
		f 5 14	300.7	.........Howell.........	d11 03		
			305.6	.........Fifield.........			
		f 5 30	308.6	.........Cordova.........	d10 50		
		f 5 38	312.3	.........Dunreath.........	d10 44		
		f 5 49	317.8	.........Percy.........	d10 34		
		f 6 02	324.2	.........Runnells.........	d10 22		
			328.6	.........Adelphi.........			
			332.8	.........Hastie.........			
		6 45	339.6	....East Des Moines....	9 50		
		6 50	340.1	Ar....Des Moines....Lv	9 45		
		AM			PM	PM	
		† 7 30	340.1	Lv....Des Moines....Ar		M. &	
		†10 50	428.1	Ar.....Fort Dodge....Lv		St. L.	
	9 55	† 5 45	271.8	Lv.......Albia.......Ar	12 30	«	
	10 42	6 30	295.3	Ar.....Oskaloosa.....Lv	11 35	«	
	11 45	7 35	327.1	.........Grinnell.........	10 32	«	
	12 25	8 20	352.7	......Marshalltown......	9 45	«	
	f 1 09	9 16	374.6	.........Gifford.........		«	
	1 50	10 02	395.8	.........Ackley.........	8 17	«	
	2 15	10 30	411.7	.........Hampton.........	7 49	«	
	3 07	11 25	440.5	.......Mason City.......	7 00	«	
	4 10	‖12 25	447.4	Ar.....Albert Lea.....Lv	5 55	«	
	4 20	† 2 40	447.4	Lv.....Albert Lea.....Ar	5 50	M. &	
	5 10	3 32	508.8	.........Waseca.........	5 00	St. L.	
	8 30	* 7 30	573.8	Ar.....Rochester.....Lv.		C. &	N.W.
	f 5 28	3 50	519.5	.......Waterville.......	f 4 41		
	7 35	5 55	584.6	Lv. Minneapolis (Gt. N. Un. St.) Lv.	2 45	M. &	
	8 15	† 6 35	596.4	Ar......St. Paul....Lv.	2 00	St. L.	
	AM	PM			PM		

CENTRALIA AND COLUMBIA

Read Down. Read Up.

No. 41 Mixed Daily	No. 39 Pass. Daily	No. 37 Mixed Daily	No. 35 Mixed Daily	No. 33 Mixed Daily	Miles	Table 3	No. 32 Mixed Daily	No. 34 Mixed Daily	No. 36 Mixed Daily	No. 38 Mixed Daily	No. 40 Pass. Daily
PM	PM	PM	AM	AM			AM	AM	PM	PM	PM
6 55	5 10	1 05	5 35	3 10	0.	Lv Centralia Ar	3 00	5 15	12 10	5 05	6 55
f 7 15	5 27	1 25	5 55	f 3 27	8.7	...Hallsville...	f 2 26	f 4 40	11 37	4 32	f 6 27
f 7 25	5 36	1 35	6 07	f 3 36	13.9	...Browns...	f 2 16	f 4 31	11 27	4 22	f 6 18
			f 6 10		15.4	...Stephens...			f11 24		
			f 6 13		16.7	...Switzler...			f11 22		
					17.6	...Persinger...					
					18.7	Moores Switch					
7 55	6 00	2 05	6 50	4 10	21.7	Ar Columbia Lv	2 00	4 15	11 10	4 05	6 02
PM	PM	PM	AM	AM			AM	AM	AM	PM	PM

ST. LOUIS, OMAHA, DENVER AND PACIFIC COAST POINTS

Read Down. Read Up.

71 Frt. Mon. Wed. Fri.	13 Daily	3 Daily	11 Daily	Miles	Table 4	14 Daily	2 Daily	12 Daily	70 Frt. Tue. Thur. Sat.
		AM	PM			AM	PM		
		9 03	7 30	0	Lv......St. Louis......Ar	8 30	4 20		
		9 17	7 44	5.6	Lv...Delmar Blvd....Ar	8 09	3 59		
		12 58	11 30	147.8	Lv..Moberly 1, 2, 12..Ar	4 30	12 23		
AM		1 55	12 25	186.8	Ar...Brunswick 1, 12..Lv	3 29	11 21		PM
7 30	NOTE—Train No. 3 will stop at Magill Switch on signal.	2 05	12 25	186.8	Lv..Brunswick 1, 12...Ar	3 29	11 05	NOTE—Train No. 2 will stop at Magill Switch on signal.	2 05
7 48		2 18		194.1	.........Triplett.........		10 43		1 45
f 7 56		2 25		198.0	.........Whitham.........		10 33		f 1 35
8 20		2 40		205.5	.........Sumner.........		10 20		1 16
f 8 34		2 50		210.9	.....Fountain Grove.....		10 09		f 1 02
f 8 43		2 58		214.6	.........Bedford.........		10 01		f12 50
f 8 58		f 3 07		219.8	.........Norville.........		f 9 51		f12 34
9 40		3 25	1 32	225.0	.......Chillicothe.......	2 33	9 40		12 18
f10 16		3 41		233.8	.........Sampsel.........		9 13		f11 55
10 38		3 49	e1 53	238.1	......Lock Springs......	m2 09	9 04		11 30
f11 05		3 57		241.9	.........Carlow.........		8 57		f11 05
11 42		4 15	2 19	250.2	.........Gallatin.........	1 48	8 40		10 45
12 03		4 30	e2 32	256.9	.........Jameson.........	m1 36	8 28		9 50
12 28		4 50	2 50	266.4	......Pattonsburg......	1 20	8 09		9 30
12 52		5 10	e3 05	273.5	.........McFall.........		7 56		9 05
f 1 07		f 5 19		279.0	.........Whitten.........		f 7 45		f 8 45
f 1 17		5 26	e3 21	282.5	.........Albany.........	n12 52	7 35		f 8 24
1 29		5 35		285.9	.......Darlington.......		7 28		8 14
f 1 35		f 5 40		287.8	.......McCurry.......		f 7 23		f 8 03
1 55		5 55	3 45	294.3	Ar....Stanberry....Lv	12 33	7 13		7 50
8 00	AM 5 00	6 05	3 50	294.3	Lv....Stanberry....Ar	12 28	7 08	PM 10 00	1 35
8 17	5 15	6 22		302.8	.........Clyde.........		6 49	9 40	1 19
8 27	5 25	6 30	4 10	304.1	.......Conception.......		6 43	9 33	1 13
f 8 39	5 39	6 42		309.9	.........Bedison.........		6 35	9 20	f12 53
9 30	5 57	7 00	4 40	318.1	.........Maryville.........	11 46	6 20	9 05	12 30
f 9 46	6 11			324.4	.........Wilcox.........			8 48	f12 05
10 05	6 27		g5 01	331.3	...Burlington Junction...			8 34	11 45
f10 10	f 6 31			333.5	.......Dawsonville.......			f 8 26	f11 38
10 21	6 40			337.4	.......Elmo, Mo.......			8 18	11 30
10 43	6 56			344.7	Ar...Blanchard, Iowa..Lv			8 03	11 11
10 58	7 09		g5 31	350.1	.........Coin.........			7 50	10 58
f11 22	f 7 24			357.6	.........Bingham.........			f 7 33	f10 40
12 00	7 40		5 56	362.6	......Shenandoah......	10 24		7 20	10 15
f12 14	f 7 49			367.3	.........Summit.........			f 7 00	f 9 27
12 29	7 58			371.5	.........Imogene.........			6 50	9 12
f12 35	f 8 03			373.7	.........Solomon.........			f 6 45	f 9 06
f12 47	8 12			378.3	.........Strahan.........			6 35	f 8 50
f12 56	f 8 18			381.0	......White Cloud......			f 6 30	f 8 40
1 09	8 28		g6 41	385.1	.........Malvern.........			6 21	8 28
1 30	8 45			393.1	.......Silver City.......			6 05	8 08
1 43	8 58			397.4	.........Mineola.........			5 54	7 56
f 1 55	f 9 10			401.2	.........Dumfries.........			5 45	f 7 47
f 2 11	f 9 20			406.3	.........Neoga.........			f 5 32	f 7 36
2 20	9 26			408.9	.......East Switch.......			5 25	7 30
	9 45		7 45	410.8	......Council Bluffs......	8 45		5 15	
			8 00	413.6	Ar......Omaha......Lv	8 30			
			7 15	973.6	Ar. Denver (U.P.Sys.).Lv	11 30			
			7 45	2197.6	Ar. Portland (U.P.Sys.).Lv	9 30			
			1 04		Ar. Tacoma (U.P.Sys.).Lv	1 17			
			2 20		Ar. Seattle (U.P.Sys.).Lv	12 01			
			10 35	1440.6	Ar. Salt Lake City (UPS).Lv	5 35			
			8 30	2223.6	Ar. Los Angeles (UPS).Lv	6 05			
			8 30	2185.6	Ar San Francisco (SoPac) Lv	6 00			
PM	AM	PM	AM			PM	AM	PM	AM

KANSAS CITY AND EXCELSIOR SPRINGS

Read Down. Read Up.

12-34 Daily	2-32 Daily	Miles	Table 4-A	35-3 Daily	33-51 Daily
3 00	9 00	0	Lv. Kansas City 1, 2, 12. Ar	4 33	10 20
3 42	9 45	25.4	Ar. Excelsior Springs Junction 1 Lv	3 38	9 25
3 42	9 50	25.4	Lv. Excelsior Springs Junction 1 Ar	3 30	9 25
f 3 45	f 9 53	26.0	......Cooley Lake......	f 3 24	f 9 21
f 3 48	f 9 57	27.4	.......Miltondale.......	f 3 20	f 9 19
4 18	10 26	34.5	Ar. Excelsior Springs 1. Lv	3 00	9 05

Reference Marks—*Daily. †Daily, except Sunday. ‖Meals. a Stops on signal to receive revenue passengers for Des Moines. c Stops on signal to discharge revenue passengers from west of Albia. d Stops on signal to discharge revenue passengers from Des Moines or to receive revenue passengers for stations east of Albia. e Stops on signal to discharge revenue passengers from St. Louis and to receive revenue passengers for Omaha. f Flag stop. g Stops to discharge revenue passengers from St. Louis. m Stops to discharge revenue passengers from west of Stanberry. n Stops on signal to discharge revenue passengers from Omaha and to receive revenue passengers for St. Louis.

Time from 12.01 midnight to 12.00 noon is shown by LIGHT faced figures, and time from 12.01 noon to 12.00 midnight by HEAVY faced figures.

ST. LOUIS, DETROIT, BUFFALO AND NEW YORK

Table 5

Read Up

Trains (Read Up): 71 Fri./Mon./Wed./Fri., 73 Frt. Ex. Sun., 71 Frt. Ex. Sun., 21-1 Daily, 11 Daily, 17 Daily, 51 Daily Note, 29-9 Daily, 3 Daily, 1 Daily

Read Down

Trains (Read Down): 4 Daily, 2 Daily, 18-28 Daily, 10 Daily, 18 Daily, 50 Daily Note, 4-24 Daily, 70 Frt. Tues./Thur./Sat., 70 Frt. Ex. Sun., 72 Frt. Ex. Sun.

Miles	Stations	1 Daily PM	3 Daily AM	29-9 Daily AM	51 Daily AM	4 Daily AM	2 Daily PM	50 Daily AM
0	Lv. St. Louis (Un. Sta.) .. Ar.	9 55	7 15	11 45	8 04	8 47	8 30	8 59
2.0	Lv. Vandeventer Ave. .. Lv.	9 34	7 04	11 34	7 53	9 12	8 55	9 07
5.0	Lv. Delmar Boulevard .. Lv.	9 07		11 15	7 34			9 28
6.0	Ar. Granite City 10 .. Lv.				7			9 50
8.3	Lv. Washington Avenue .. Ar.							9 59
	Lv. East St. Louis 10 .. Ar.							10 06
	Brooklyn 10							10 16
11.3	Venice 10			r1055	7x26	r9 27		10 26
13.8	Ar. Granite City 10 .. Lv.		6 26	r1039	7 13			10 41
15.7	Mitchell 10		5 57	10 30	r7 00	r9 47		10 51
21.8	T Nameoki 10				6 51			11 01
23.3	Edwardsville 10				6 42			11 06
28.3	Carpenter 10		5 46	10 18	6 32	r9 54		11 20
32.6	Worden 10		5 35	10 08	f6 03	10 04		11 27
38.5	Staunton 10			9 56	5x158			11 33
44.2	Mount Olive 10			9 50	5 50			11 48
47.2	Litchfield 10	8 07		9 44	5x145	7 47	8 29	11 57
53.1	Hitch Bend 10			9 36	15 41			12 15
58.0	Raymond 10			9 31	5 23			12 26
63.3	Harvel 10				5 16			
66.6	Morrisonville 10			9 19	5 08			12 50
72.6	Palmer 10							
79.4	Clarkdale 10		4 41					
84.8	Taylorville 10	7 25			4 45	10 42	10 42	7 47
89.6	Willeys 10			9 06	4 40			7 47
93.5	Stonington 10			8 58				8 07
99.6	Blue Mound 10			8 50				8 16
104.0	Boody 10							
109.6	Knights 10							
113.2	Ar. Decatur 8, 9, 10, 12 Lv.	6 50	3 55	8 35	4 45	11 20	9 05	12 50
113.7	Lv. Decatur 8, 9, 10, 12 Ar.	6 35	3 50	8 20	4 20	11 30	9 10	Note
114.1	East Decatur 10						11 30	N
118.2	Sangamon 10							
121.1	Oakley 10							
125.1	Cerro Gordo 10							
129.4	Milmine 10							
133.4	Ar. Bement 10, 17 .. Lv.	8 07			6 03		8 29	7 47
133.7	Lv. Bement 10, 17 .. Ar.	5 46	3 01	7 31	3 18	12 21	9 58	48 18
140.2	Ivesdale							
146.9	Sadorus							
150.8	Tolono		3 01	7 31		12 10	9 58	48 07
156.6	Lv. Illini Coach Co.	4 53			3 50	11 28	8 58	
161.7	Urbana	5 15			43 01	11 45	9 11	7 47
161.2	Champaign	5 36			43 01	12 10	9 58	48 16
161.2	Lv. Illini Coach Co.							
167.3	Tolono							
171.1	Ar. Tolono (Wabash) .. Ar.	5 51		7 35	3 50	12 25	10 01	8 35
184.9	Philo	6 27	2 10	7 20	3 37	12 45	10 37	48 56
187.1	Sidney	5 46		8 12	3 01	12 55	12 55	49 07
187.1	Sidney 19			7 31		12 36	9 58	
194.5	Fairmount							
197.4	Homer							
199.3	Catlin							
209.0	Tilton	4 55	2 10	6 40	1 55	1 20	55 00	9 30
211.9	Ar. Danville 8, 9 Lv.	4 55	2 10	6 40	1 18	1 20	55 00	9 46
219.9	State Line, Ind.							
216.5	Johnsonville				11 05		11 26	10 02
223.4	Marshfield							10 17
228.5	West Lebanon							
233.3	Attica 8, 9, 20	4 13	v1 18	t5 49	11 05	1 53	d5 33	10 36
233.3	Riverside	4 05			12 45	2 00		
241.3	Ar. West Point .. Lv.				12 20			
244.9	Shadeland				12 01			11 08
250.1	Ar. LaFayette Lv.	3 32	12 45	5 15	12 01	2 34	6 11	11 08
250.1		3 32	12 45	5 15	11 20	2 34	6 11	11 42
256.6	Buck Creek							
260.9	Colburn							
264.4	Delphi	3 00	12 v05	4 45	10 45	3 00	p6 35	12 25
273.3	Rockfield						d2 25	12 39
282.9	Burrows	2 29	11 37	4 15	10 15	3 34	7 07	12 55
285.8	Clymers		11 10	3 50	10 10	4 00	7 30	1 20
286.2	Logansport	2 05	11 05	3 45	9 48	4 05	7 35	
294.5	West Peru	2 00	10 43	3 18		4 27	k1 50	
299.0	Ar. Peru .. Lv.	1 39						
305.6	Rich Valley	1 12	10 19	2 50	9 15	4 44	2 17	1 50
311.6	Wabash					4 58		
318.3	Andrews Yard, Andrew, Huntington							

From Chicago, see Table 10.
To Chicago, see Table 10.

NOTE—No. 51 stops at Granite City Yard Office—Coach service only from Detroit to St. Louis.

NOTE—No. 50 stops at Granite City Yard Office—Coach service only from St. Louis to Detroit.

Banner Blue Limited (trains 11 and 10)

17   18

300

Nos. 21-1 and 13-3 will stop on signal at Renollet.
Note—Carries Cafe Car Toledo to Ft. Wayne.

LIGHT faced figures and time from 12.01 noon is shown by
Time from 12.01 midnight to 12.00 noon is shown by | HEAVY faced figures.

TOLEDO TO MONTPELIER

Table 7

		21-1 Daily	13-3 Note
0	Toledo E. T. Lv		
1	Toledo C. T.	10 30	6 25
5	Maumee 8,9	9 30	
9	Monclova	9 48	6 42
13	Midway		
17	Brailey		
23	Delta	10 03	6 55
34	Wauseon	10 10	
40	Elmira	10 17	
43	West Unity	10 24	7 15
59	Montpelier 5, 6, 11 ...... Ar	10 35	7 30

TOLEDO TO FT. WAYNE AND ST. LOUIS

Table 9

		71 Fri. Ex. Su.
0	Toledo E. T. Lv	7 00
	Toledo C. T.	7 20
9	Maumee Yard	7 30
17	Defiance	7 45
21	Station 15, Ohio (Neapolis)	7 55
26	Colton	8 05
29	Liberty Center	8 18
36	Napoleon	8 30
42	Okolona	9 00
46	Jewell	9 20
57	Defiance	9 35
64	Emmett	9 48
64	Knoxdale	11 38
72	Antwerp, Ohio	8 18
76	Woodburn, Ind.	8 32
89	Gar Creek	8 44
95	New Haven 5, Lv	8 59
95	Fort Wayne 5, Ar	9 15
119	Wabash	9 45
137	Huntington	10 10
151	Peru	10 43
204	Logansport	11 10
270	Attica	11 37
294	Danville	12 45
324	Decatur	3 12
437	St. Louis	7 15

MONTPELIER TO TOLEDO

Table 6

		72
0	Ft. Wayne Lv	
0	Montpelier 5, 7, 11 Lv	
9	West Unity	
19	Elmira	
25	Wauseon	
36	Delta	
41	Brailey	
42	Midway	
46	Monclova	
50	Maumee 8, 9	
58	Toledo Yard	
59	Toledo C. T.	
59	Toledo E. T. ...... Ar	

ST. LOUIS AND FORT WAYNE TO TOLEDO

Table 8

		70 Fri. Ex. Su.
0	St. Louis Lv	
113	Decatur	
187	Danville	
212	Attica	
233	LaFayette	
270	Logansport	
296	Peru	
300	Wabash	
342	Huntington	
342	Fort Wayne, Ar	
348	Fort Wayne 5, Lv	
354	Gar Creek	
358	Woodburn, Ind.	
365	Antwerp, Ohio	
369	Knoxdale	
373	Emmett	
376	Defiance	
386	Jewell	
391	Okolona	
395	Napoleon	
401	Liberty Center	
411	Colton	
416	Station 15, Ohio (Neapolis)	
420	White House	
424	Homewood	
428	Maumee 5, 11	
436	Maumee Yard	
437	Toledo C.T.	
437	Toledo E.T. ...... Ar	

Note§—No. 2-12, Carries Cafe Car Ft. Wayne to Toledo.

Numbers opposite stations refer to tables showing connecting trains.

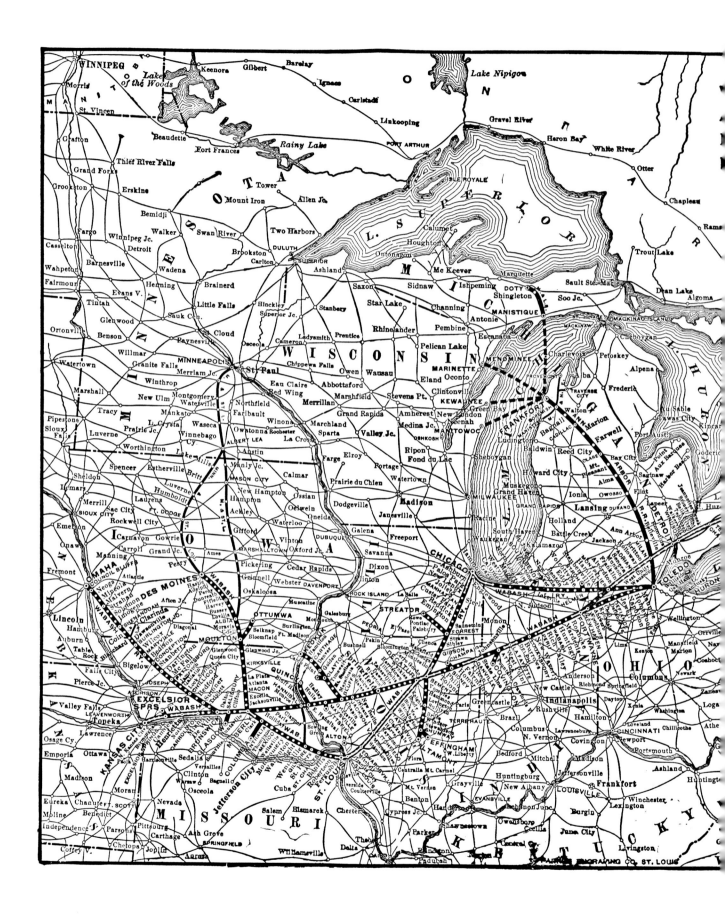

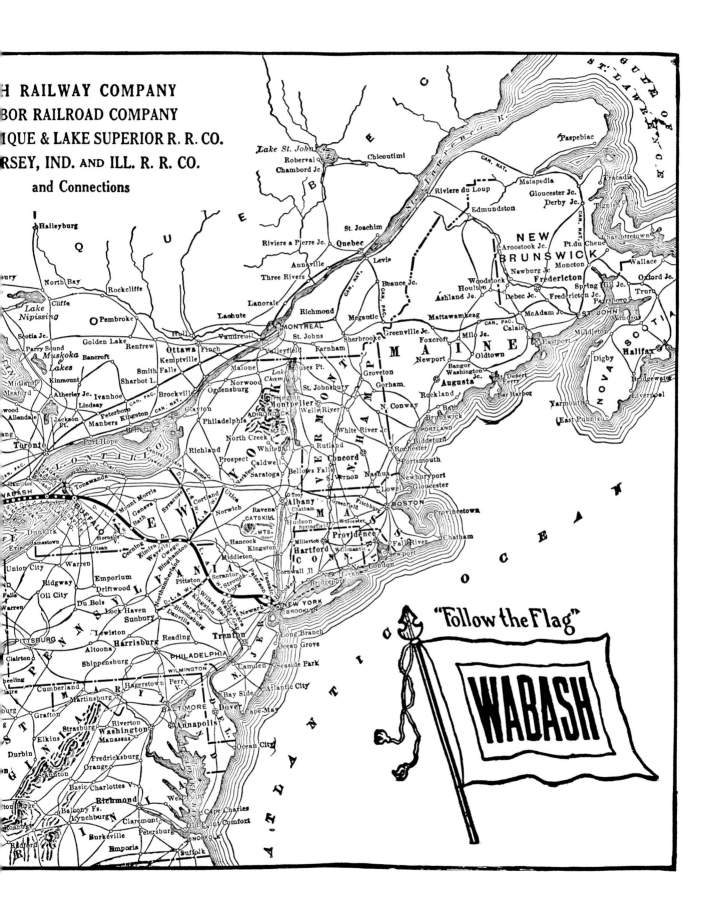

H RAILWAY COMPANY
BOR RAILROAD COMPANY
IQUE & LAKE SUPERIOR R. R. CO.
RSEY, IND. AND ILL. R. R. CO.
and Connections

"Follow the Flag"

WABASH

303

ST. LOUIS AND CHICAGO

Read Down.   Read Up

Notes: *Note—No. 50 stops at Granite City Yard Office.*   *Note—No. 51 makes regular stop at Granite City Yard Office.*   *To Detroit, see Table 5.*   *To Buffalo, see Table 5.*   *From Buffalo, see Table 5.*   *From Detroit, see Table 5.*

70 Frt Ex.Sun	70 Frt Tu Th Sa	72 Frt Ex.Sun	18-28	2	50	4	18	12	10	4-24	Miles	Table 10	11	21-1	13	17	3	51	9	1	73 Frt Ex.Sun	71 Frt Ex.Sun	71 Frt M W F
		PM 11 55		PM 6 30	PM 8 59	AM 8 47	PM 11 55	AM	PM 12 05	AM 8 47	0	Lv. St. Louis (Un. Sta.) Ar	PM 6 00	9 55	AM 7 39		AM 7 15	AM 8 04	AM 11 45	PM 9 55			
												Lv. Vandeventer Ave. A											
			12 10				12 10		12 20			.. Delmar Boulevard ..	5 39	9 34			7 18			9 34			
								b12 47				Ar .. Granite City 5 .. Lv	n 5 12	d9 07			x 6 51			m			
					9 07						2.0	Lv. Washington Ave. Ar					7 04	7 53	11 34				
			Via Delmar Blvd	Via Merchants Bridge	Via Merchants Bridge	Via Merchants Bridge	Via Delmar Blvd	Via Delmar Blvd	Via Delmar Blvd	Via Merchants Bridge	3.2	Lv. East St. Louis 5 Ar	Via Delmar Blvd	Via Delmar Blvd		Via Delmar Blvd	Via Merchants Bridge	Via Merchants Bridge	Via Merchants Bridge	Via Delmar Blvd			
											5.0	.. Brooklyn 5 ..											
											6.0	.. Venice 5 ..											
											8.3	Ar .. Granite City 5 .. Lv											
					9 28			b12 47	9 12		8.3	Lv. Granite City 5 Ar	n 5 12	d9 07			x 6 51	7 34	11 15	m			
					f 9 33						11.3	¶ Nameoki 5 ..											
					f 9 38						13.8	.. Mitchell 5 ..						m					
											17.7	.. Poag 5 ..											
					9 50				b 9 27		21.8	.. Edwardsville 5 ..						7 13	f10 55		9 30		
					9 59						28.3	.. Carpenter 5 ..						7 00			8 45		
					a10 06						32.6	.. Worden 5 ..						6 51	f10 39		8 30		
					10 16				b 9 47		38.5	.. Staunton 5 ..						6 42	10 30		8 00		
											42.9	.. Karnes 5 ..									7 35		
								9 54	b 9 54		44.3	.. Mount Olive 5 ..						6 32	10 18		7 00		
AM 7 45	1 15	1 35		7 47	10 41	10 04	1 35	ra1 35		10 04	52.3	.. Litchfield 5 ..	nd4 23	8 07			5 45	5 35	6 22	8 07	7 00		11 20
f8 00	PM				f10 51						58.0	.. Honey Bend 5 ..							f 9 56		AM		f10 50
8 30					a11 01						63.3	.. Raymond 5 ..						f 6 03					10 35
8 45					a11 08						66.6	.. Harvel 5 ..						n 5 58	f 9 44				10 10
9 08					a11 20						72.6	.. Morrisonville 5 ..						5 50					9 36
9 25					a11 27						76.4	.. Palmer 5 ..						n 5 45	f 9 31				8 55
9 35					f11 33						79.4	.. Clarksdale 5 ..						f 5 41					8 30
10 15			8 29	11 48	10 42		rb2 12		10 42		84.8	.. Taylorville 5 ..	nc3 46	7 25			k 4 57	5 33	9 19	7 25			8 15
f10 48				f11 57							89.6	.. Willeys 5 ..						f 5 23					7 30
11 15				12 04							93.5	.. Stonington 5 ..						5 16					7 15
11 54				a12 15							99.0	.. Blue Mound 5 ..						5 08					6 55
12 45				12 26							104.9	.. Boody 5 ..											6 35
f 1 00											109.6	.. Knights 5 ..						f 8 50					f 6 15
1 30											113.2	Ar } .. Decatur .. { Lv	3 10	6 50			4 15	3 55	4 45	8 35	6 50		6 00
	2 50	9 05	12 50	11 20	2 50			2 47	11 20		113.2	Lv } 5, 8, 9, 12, 18 { Ar	3 07	6 45	3 20	4 10	3 50	4 20	8 20	6 35			
	3 15	9 10	7 10	11 30	2 55	1 05		2 50	11 25		114.3	.. East Decatur 5 ..									PM 12 15		
6 00											118.2	.. Sangamon 5 ..									11 45		
6 20	To Detroit, see Table 5.	To Buffalo, see Table 5.	7 31								121.0	.. Oakley 5 ..									11 30		
6 40								b 1 23			125.1	.. Cerro Gordo 5 ..			f 3 02						11 05		
7 00											129.4	.. Milmine 5 ..									10 45		
7 30			7 47				1 35	b11 49			133.4	Ar } .. Bement .. { Lv		2 50		3 50							
7 15			m				1 35	b11 49			133.4	Lv } 5, 17 { Ar		2 50							12 30		
7 55			To Detroit, see Table 5.	r 3 36			1 52	r 3 23	11 59		140.7	.. Monticello ..	na2 29	6 10	2 34	na3 26	From Detroit, see Table 5.	From Detroit, see Table 5.	From Detroit, see Table 5.	From Buffalo, see Table 5.	11 50		
8 15				f 2 03							144.4	.. Lodge ..		f 2 22							11 10		
8 35				f 2 12							149.6	.. Galesville ..		f 2 12							10 55		
9 00				f 2 22							154.5	.. Mansfield ..		2 03							10 00		
9 15				f 2 32							158.4	.. Blue Ridge ..		f 1 55							9 50		
9 30				f 2 41							160.6	.. Osman ..		f 1 51							9 40		
9 55											162.3	.. Lotus ..		f 1 48							9 30		
10 05											165.5	.. Foosland ..		f 1 41							8 03		
10 20												.. Proctor ..		f 1 33							7 50		
11 05				b 4 28	3 04			r12 39			173.6	.. Gibson City ..		na 535	1 26	na2 44					7 40		
11 30				f 3 10							176.8	.. Garber ..		f 1 19							7 00		
12 00				f 3 19							181.7	.. Sibley ..		f 1 10									
12 30				f 3 28							186.3	.. Strawn ..		f12 59									
6 45				5 00	3 41	c 4 28	c 1 08				193.3	Ar } .. Forrest 18 { Lv	c 1 25	c 5 10	12 45	2 13					2 30		
7 05				5 03	3 46	c 4 28	c 1 08				193.3	Lv } { Ar	c 1 25	c 5 10	12 40	2 10					2 05		
7 30					3 58						198.3	.. Wing ..		f12 29							1 27		
7 50					f 4 09						203.3	.. Saunemin ..		f12 20							12 45		
8 10					f 4 20						209.1	.. Emington ..		f12 09							12 22		
8 25					f 4 29						213.5	.. Campus ..		f12 00							12 02		
8 35					f 4 32						215.7	.. Cardiff ..		f11 55							11 25		
9 00					f 4 41						219.7	.. Reddick ..		f11 48							11 25		
9 37					f 4 52						225.9	.. Essex ..		f11 38							10 17		
9 55					f 5 03						231.5	.. Custer Park ..		f11 24							10 05		
10 05					f 5 06						232.8	.. Ritchie ..		f11 20									
10 20					f 5 10						234.6	.. Ballou ..		f11 13							9 53		
11 55					f 5 18						238.7	.. Symerton ..		11 01	n 1 02						9 28		
12 23					f 5 33						246.1	.. Manhattan ..		f10 49							8 58		
f12 29					f 5 43						251.2	.. Brisbane ..		f10 46									
12 39					f 5 44						252.1	.. Steele ..		f10 44							8 28		
12 53					f 5 49						252.5	.. New Lenox ..		f10 40							8 20		
1 10					f 5 54						255.6	.. Marley ..		f10 34							8 10		
1 30					p 6 00						259.2	.. Alpine ..		f10 34							8 00		
1 40					p..						262.5	.. Orland Park ..		10 25							7 43		
f 1 47					p 6 10						265.8	.. Palos Park ..		10 19							7 31		
1 55					p..						267.9	.. Worth ..		10 13							7 25		
2 00											269.3	.. Chicago Ridge ..		10 08							7 10		
											270.9	.. Oak Lawn ..		10 03							7 00		
											273.5	.. Ashburn ..		9 58									
											274.9	.. Landers ..											
											277.7	.. Western Indiana Junc. ..											
				7 17	6 38	6 18	3 01				279.1	Englewood (63rd & Wallace)	11 45	ce1140	3 29	9 45	12 05						
				t 7 22	6 43	t 6 23	t 3 06				281.1	.. Forty-seventh Street ..	ce1140	ce3 24	9 40	c=1200							
				7 35	6 55	6 35	3 17				285.7	Ar .. Chicago .. Lv	11 30	3 15	9 30	11 50							
				AM	AM	PM	PM					(Dearborn Sta. Polk & Dearborn)	AM	PM	PM	PM							

Footnote legend: a Stops daily and stops on signal on Sunday. b Stops on signal to discharge and receive revenue passengers for Chicago. c Stops on signal to discharge revenue passengers. ce Will stop on signal to receive revenue passengers from Chicago and Detroit and beyond. d Stops on signal to discharge revenue passengers from Chicago. f Flag stop. g Stops on signal on Sunday to discharge revenue passengers for Chicago. h Will stop on signal to discharge revenue passengers for points north of Decatur. k Will stop to discharge revenue passengers from Chicago and receive passengers for St. Louis. m See Table 5. n Stops on signal to receive revenue passengers for St. Louis. nd Stops on signal to discharge revenue passengers for Litchfield and St. Louis. p Stops on signal on Sunday to discharge revenue passengers for Chicago. q Will stop on signal on Sunday to discharge revenue passengers for Decatur and beyond. r Stops on signal to discharge revenue passengers for Taylorville, Decatur and Chicago. ra Stops on signal from St. Louis and Litchfield and receive revenue passengers. rb Stops on signal to discharge revenue passengers for Chicago. t Stops on signal for Decatur and Chicago. x Stops on signal to discharge revenue passengers from Chicago and Taylorville.

The columns marked "10" (down) and "11" (up) are the **BANNER BLUE LIMITED**.

Time from 12.01 midnight to 12.00 noon is shown by LIGHT faced figures, and time from 12.01 noon to 12.00 midnight by HEAVY faced figures.

CHICAGO, DETROIT, BUFFALO AND NEW YORK

Read Down. **Read Up.**

Table 11

12 Mxd Ex. Sun.	70 Frt. Ex. Sun.	4 Daily	28 Daily	2 Daily	50 Daily	12 Daily	6 Daily	Miles	Stations	11 Daily	5 Daily	29 Daily	1 Daily	3 Daily	51 Daily	73 Mxd Ex. Sun.	71 Frt. Ex. Sun.
	AM					PM	AM		Dearborn Sta., Polk & Dearb'n		AM						
						11 30	10 30	0	Lv.........Chicago.........Ar	4 50	7 15						
						11 40	10 40	4.6	...Forty-seventh Street..	4 37	7 02						
						11 45	10 45	6.6	Lv.Englewood (63d & Wallace)Lv	4 32	6 57						
								10.8	Lv.........Landers.........Ar								
						12 13	f11 13	20.3	Lv.....Hammond, Ind.....Lv	f 6 28							
						12 19	..*.	22.1	......East Chicago......	f 6 22							
								28.8	........Tolleston.......								
						12 40	11 35	30.6	..........Gary..........	3 40	6 05						
								32.9	.........Aetna..........								
								35.8	........Calumet........								
								38.4	......Willow Creek.....								
	9 30							41.7	........Crocker........								8 47
	f 9 52							49.3	.........Morris........								f 8 30
	10 07					1 17		55.0	........Westville.......	3 03	f 5 23						8 19
	f10 27							62.6	.........Magee.........								f 8 04
	f10 33							64.8	........Kingsbury......								f 7 58
	f10 52							71.8	.........Dillon........								f7 45
	11 10					1 53	12 45	79.2	Ar } ..North Liberty.... { Lv	2 28	4 42					PM	7 30
7 30	AM					1 58	12 50	79.2	Lv } .... { Ar	2 23	4 37					12 10	AM
7 50						2 13		84.8	Ar..........Pine.......Lv		4 28					f11 53	
						1 15			Lv.......South Bend....Ar		5 45						
									(N. J. I. & I. Ry.)								
7 50						2 13		84.8	Lv,.........Pine.......Ar		4 28					11 53	
7 59								87.3	........Lakeville......							11 44	
f 8 14								93.0	.........Wyatt.........							11 27	
8 35								100.9	.......Wakarusa.......		h 4 03					11 03	
f 8 50								105.5	........Foraker........							10 49	
9 05						k 2 55	k 1 39	110.7	.......New Paris.......	h 1 39						10 34	
9 14								114.1	.........Benton........							10 24	
f 9 26								118.1	.......Millersburg.....							10 12	
9 49						k 3 18		126.1	.........Topeka........		h 3 32					9 49	
f10 00								131.4	..........Eddy.........							f 9 32	
10 15						3 33	2 12	135.4	.......Wolcottville.....	1 04	3 14					9 18	
f10 30								140.3	......South Milford....							9 02	
10 45								145.7	........Helmer 21......							8 42	
11 00								150.7	.....Ashley-Hudson....							8 30	
f11 10	70 Frt. Ex. Sun.							153.4	......Steubenville.....							8 23	
11 40								158.9	.......Hamilton, Ind...							8 08	
12 22								166.8	........Edon, Ohio.....							7 49	
1 00	AM	AM	AM	AM	AM	4 35	3 10	175.1	Ar } ...Montpelier 5, 6, 7.. { Lv	12 10	2 15	AM	AM	PM	PM	7 30	PM
PM	7 00	7 10	10 30	4 30	4 50	4 40	3 15	175.1	Lv } .... { Ar	12 05	2 10	12 55	11 15	8 20	6 15	AM	1 25
	7 20							182.2	........Kunkle 5.......						6 00		12 54
	7 40							186.4	.......Alvordton 5.....						6 49		12 35
	7 45				x 5 09			187.3	.....Franklin, Ohio 5..						f 5 45		12 30
	f 8 02				x 5 18			192.6	.....Munson, Mich. 5..						5 35		f12 07
	8 23				x 5 26		k 3 45	198.9	....North Morenci 5...	h11 30	m1 32				5 24		f11 40
	f 8 33							201.9	.........Seneca 5......						5 18		f11 26
	8 50							206.5	.......Sand Creek 5....						5 10		f10 50
	9 25	8 05	11 20	5 20	5 53	5 30	4 05	213.3	Ar } ....Adrian...... { Lv	11 13	1 13	11 58	10 23	7 26	4 58		10 23
	9 25	8 05	11 20	5 20	5 53	5 30	4 05	213.3	Lv } .... { Ar	11 13	1 13	11 58	10 23	7 26	4 58		10 23
	f 9 50							217.4	......Raisin Center....						f 4 45		f 9 48
	f10 00							219.6	........Holloway 5.....						4 40		f 9 39
	10 25				6 13			225.2	........Britton 5.......						4 31		9 18
	f10 45							229.9	..........Cone 5.......						4 23		f 9 00
	11 10		n 5 48	6 31	p 5 58	k 4 33	234.8	.........Milan 5.......	10m44	12 43			f 9 54	c 6 57	4 15		8 42
	f11 35				x 6 38			240.6	........Whittaker 5....						4 04		f 8 20
	f11 59							243.4	.........Willis 5.......						3 58		f 8 10
	12 18				6 52			248.3	.......Belleville 5.....						3 50		7 52
	12 28							250.6	....French Landing 5...						f 3 45		7 43
	12 36							253.1	........Romulus 5......						3 40		7 34
								257.2	.........Preston.......						f		
	f 1 00							259.7	..........Hand 5.......						3 29		f 7 10
	1 30							265.1	........Oakwood 5......						3 20		6 55
	PM							267.9	.........Delray 5.......								AM
	9 30	12 45	6 45	7 35	6 55	5 30	272.1	Ar ..Detroit, Mich. (CT).. Lv	9 50	11 45	10 30	9 00	6 00	3 00		
	10 30	1 45	7 45	8 35	7 55	6 30	272.1	Ar Un. Sta. Fort & 3rd St. (ET) Lv	10 50	12 45	11 30	10 00	7 00	4 00		
	PM	5 55	AM	AM	AM	5 55	272.1	Lv.....Central Time.....Ar	7 35	AM	PM	7 35	PM	PM		
		6 55				6 55	273.1	Lv.....Eastern Time.....Ar	8 35			8 35				
		8 05				8 05	273.1	.......Windsor, Ont.....	7 35			7 35				
		9 15				9 15	318.7	.........Chatham 5......	6 25			6 25				
		10 45				10 45	380.4	.....St. Thomas 5.f.....	4 55			4 55				
		f11 55				f11 55	426.2	........Simcoe 5.......	f 3 46			f 3 46				
							481.4	.....Welland Junction 5....								
		1 55				1 55	498.8	........Black Rock 5....	1 55			1 55				
		2 40				2 40	513.4	Ar.Buffalo (D. L. & W. Sta.) Lv	1 15			1 15				
		4 00				4 00	513.4	Lv..Buffalo (D. L. & W.)..Ar	1 05			1 05				
		8 00				8 00	659.9	.........Elmira......Lv	9 43			9 43				
		11 30				11 30	775.5	........Scranton.......	6 40			6 40				
		3 15				3 15	900.8	.........Newark........	2 35			2 35				
		3 30				3 30	907.8	.........Hoboken.......	2 20			2 20				
							909.6	Ar New York (E.T.)a Lv								
		3 50				3 50	909.6	..Barclay St.	2 00			2 00				
		3 50				3 50	909.6	..West 23rd St.	2 00			2 00				
		PM				PM			PM			PM				

Vertical column notes between Adrian/Montpelier area: From St. Louis—Quincy, see Tables 5 and 12. From St. Louis—Kansas City, see Tables 5 and 12. From St. Louis, see Table 5. From St. Louis, see Table 5. Central States Limited. To St. Louis and Kansas City, see Tables 5 and 12. To St. Louis, see Tables 5 and 12. To St. Louis—Quincy, see Tables 5 and 12. Central States Limited. 71 Frt. Ex. Sun.

Numbers opposite stations refer to tables showing connecting trains.

REFERENCE MARKS—*Daily. †Daily, except Sunday. ‖Meals. f Flag stop. a Will stop on signal to discharge revenue passengers from Detroit. b Stops on signal to discharge revenue passengers from Chicago and to receive revenue passengers for Montpelier and points beyond. c Will stop on signal to receive revenue passengers for Danville or beyond. h Stops on signal to discharge revenue passengers from Detroit and to receive revenue passengers for Chicago and beyond. k Will stop on signal to discharge revenue passengers from Chicago and to receive revenue passengers for Detroit and beyond. m Stop on signal to receive revenue passengers for Chicago. n See Table No. 5. p Stops to discharge revenue passengers from Chicago. s No ferry service to or from Christopher St. on Sunday. x Stops on signal to receive revenue passengers for Detroit and beyond. For Local Time between Detroit and Buffalo, see Table 5.

Time from 12.01 midnight to 12.00 noon is shown by LIGHT faced figures, and time from 12.01 noon to 12:00 midnight by HEAVY faced figures.

27   28

KANSAS CITY, MOBERLY, QUINCY, HANNIBAL, KEOKUK, DECATUR, TOLEDO AND DETROIT

BRANCH LINES

Table 12

Read Down / Read Up

50 Mxd. Ex. Sun.	12 Daily	28 Daily	Miles	Table 12	29 Daily	3 Daily	3 Mixd. Ex.Sun.	71 Frt. Ex.Sun.
	PM	PM			PM	PM		
		5 45	0	Lv.....Kansas City.....Ar	5 45			
		d 7v21	68.0	....Carrollton.....				
			91.8	....Brunswick.....				
AM		8 45	130.8	Ar....Moberly....Lv	2 45			
6 10		8 50	130.8	Lv....Moberly....Ar	2 37		1 50	
6 27			138.8	....Evansville.....			1 32	
6 47		a 9 11	144.1	....Madison.....	a 2 14		12 55	
7 01			148.9	....Holliday.....			12 40	
7 26		a 9 30	156.6	....Paris.....	a 1 54		12 15	
f 7 38			161.0	....Goss.....			11 43	
7 51			166.5	....Stoutsville.....			11 28	
8 04			168.9	....Clapper.....			f11 15	
8 24		a10 06	178.2	....Monroe City.....	a 1 21		10 58	
f 8 33			182.0	....Hassard.....			f10 46	
f 8 42			185.4	....Huntington.....			f10 37	
8 50			188.3	....Rensselaer.....			10 28	
			198.0	....Outer Depot.....			f10 03	
9 30		10 50	200.1	Ar.....Hannibal.....Lv	12 38		9 50	
	5 30		0	Lv.....Quincy.....Ar	1 40	10 45		
	6 15		18.8	Ar.....Hannibal.....Lv	12 45	9 55		
9 55			0	Lv.....Hannibal.....Ar	12 20			
10 45			18.8	Ar.....Quincy.....Lv	11 30			
7 40	6 25	10 50	200.1	Lv..Hannibal, Mo.13,16..Ar	12 38	9 45		1 05
7 55	f 6 32		201.7	....East Hannibal, Ill.....		9 35		12 55
f8 03			203.5	....Aladdin.....				f12 27
8 35	6 50		210.1	....Hulls.....		9 22		12 12
8 50	6 56		212.9	....Kinderhook.....		9 15		11 41
9 45	7 12	z11 29	219.4	....Barry.....	z11 57	9 02		11 10
10 05	f 7 20		223.2	....Hadley.....		f 8 55		10 05
10 30	7 30		227.2	....Baylis.....		8 48		9 43
10 45	7 37		231.1	....New Salem.....		8 39		9 18
11 15	7 45		233.7	Ar....Maysville 16....Lv		8 31		8 43
			6.2	Ar Pittsfield 16..... Lv				
§†1035	† 8 10		6.2			§†7 40		
	7 00			Lv		§†8 55		
11 15	7 45		233.7	Lv....Maysville 16....Ar		8 43		8 43
11 30	7 55	z11 58	237.1	....Griggsville.....	z11 30	8 18		8 18
12 18	8 05		242.0	....Valley City.....		8 05		7 18
1 28	f 8 15		246.5	....Naples.....		7 55		6 58
1 45	8 21		250.3	Ar.....Bluffs 14.....Lv	y11 05	7 46		6 45
	3 15		75.8	Lv.....Keokuk 14.....Ar		12 00		
	7 45		75.8	Ar.....Bluffs 14.....Lv		7 45		
6 30	8 41		250.4	Lv.....Bluffs.....Ar	y11 05	7 33	2 00	
6 f45	f 8 50		253.7	....Neely's.....		f 7 26	1 45	
			256.3	....Morgan.....				
7 19	8 59		257.9	....Chapin.....		7 19	1 20	
7 f34	f 9 10		262.8	....Markham.....		f 7 08	1 03	
8 59	9 35	12 50	267.9	....Jacksonville.....	10 36	7 00	12 48	
9 f40	f 9 45		272.8	....Arnold.....		f 6 46	9 40	
9 56	f 9 51		276.3	....Orleans.....		f 6 41	9 23	
10 39	9 55		278.4	....Alexander.....		6 37	9 05	
10 56	f10 03		282.6	....Island Grove.....			8 f34	
11 15	10 08		285.2	....New Berlin.....		6 26	8 28	
11 29	f10 23		288.5	....Bates.....		f 6 20	8 13	
11 49	f10 23		292.8	....Curran.....		6 14	8 01	
11 59			295.7	....Sanger.....			7 f49	
12 20	f10 38		301.1	....Shops.....			7 30	
	10 48	1 47	301.8	Ar.....Springfield.....Lv	9 35	5 55		
AM			304.9	....Starne.....				
8 00	†11 05		308.5	....Riverton.....		5 31	2 30	
8 41	†11 13		312.9	....Dawson.....		5 26	2 10	
9 07	†11 18		315.8	....Buffalo.....		5 22	1 45	
9 30	†11 24		319.0	....Lanesville.....		5 17	1 30	
10 18	†11 40		324.7	....Illiopolis.....		5 10	1 10	
10 35	†11 46		328.6	....Niantic.....		5 05	12 56	
11 05	†11 50		333.0	....Harristown.....		4 59	12 31	
f 11 50	†11 50		335.9	....Wyckles.....			12 23	
12 40	12 08	2 57	340.4	Ar..Decatur 5,8,9,10,18.Lv	8 30	4 45	12 01	
PM	6 55		512.0	Ar.Chicago(DearbornSta.).Lv		11 50		
74 Frt. Tue. Thur. Sat.		3 15	340.4	Lv.....Decatur.....Ar	8 20	3 50	75 Frt. Mon. Wed. Fri.	
		4 55	414.3	....Danville.....	6 40	2 10		
s 5 33			439.1	....Attica, Ind.....	t 5 49	k 1 18		
		6 11	460.5	....Lafayette.....	5 15	12 45		
		7 07	497.5	....Logansport.....	4 15	11 37		
		7 35	513.4	....Peru.....	3 50	11 19		
		8 25	545.5	....Huntington.....	2 50	10 19		
		8 57	569.5	Ar....Ft. Wayne....Lv	2 15	9 45		
			664.0	Ar....Toledo (C. T.)....Lv		6 25		
			664.0	Ar....Toledo (E. T.)....Lv		7 25		
		9 05	569.5	Lv....Ft. Wayne....Ar	2 05	9 30		
		10 30	618.6	Lv...Montpelier, Ohio..Lv	1 00	8 25		
		11 20	656.8	Lv...Adrian, Mich.....Lv	11 58	7 26		
		12 45	715.6	ArDetroit,Mich.(U.Sta.C.T.)Lv	10 30	6 00		
		1 45	715.6	ArDetroit,Mich.(U.Sta.E.T.)Lv	11 30	7 00		
		2 40	956.9	ArBuffalo,N.Y.(DL&WSta.)Lv				
			1352.9	Ar.....New York.....Lv				
		3 50	1352.9	Ar....West 23rd St.....Lv				
		3 50	1352.9	Ar....Barclay St.....Lv				

(Column headed "CENTRAL STATES LIMITED" appears vertically under train 72 Frt. Ex. Sun. and No. 10 Freight and under column 29.)

QUINCY AND HANNIBAL

Read Down / Read Up

Table 13

37 Daily	35 Daily	Miles	Table 13	32 Daily	34 Daily
PM	AM			AM	PM
5 30	11 30	0	Lv..Quincy, Ill. 12, 16...Ar	10 45	1 40
f	f	6.6	....Marble Head.....	f	f
f	f	9.5	....Bluff Hall.....	f	f
f	f	12.4	....Fall Creek.....	f	f
6 05	12 09	17.2	....East Hannibal.....	10 05	12 55
6 15	12 20	18.8	Ar.Hannibal, Mo. 12, 16..Lv	9 55	12 45

BLUFFS AND KEOKUK

Read Down / Read Up

Table 14

76 Frt. Ex. Sun. and Tues.	12 Daily	Miles	Table 14	3 Daily	77 Frt. Ex. Sun
AM	PM			PM	PM
8 20	3 15	0	Lv.....Keokuk 12.....Ar	12 00	3 05
8 40	3 25	1.3	....Hamilton.....	11 46	2 20
9 00	3 50	7.8	....Elvaston.....	11 26	2 00
9 25	4 10	13.2	....Carthage.....	11 06	1 35
9 45	4 26	18.3	....Bentley.....	10 50	1 15
10 05	4 40	22.2	....Denver.....	10 35	1 00
10 20	4 55	26.9	....Bowen.....	10 20	12 35
f10 50	5 10	32.7	....Chatton.....	10 05	f12 15
11 20	5 20	35.6	....Golden.....	9 55	12 05
f11 45	f5 30	38.5	....Blacks.....	f 9 45	f11 45
12 01	5 45	42.3	Ar.....Clayton.....Lv	9 35	11 30
12 01	5 45	42.3	Lv.....Clayton.....Ar	9 35	11 30
12 20	6 00	47.2	....Timewell.....	9 21	11 00
12 45	6 25	53.2	....Mount Sterling.....	9 05	10 35
1 05	6 35	55.8	....Hersman.....	8 54	10 05
f 1 15	f6 45	59.1	....Gilbirds.....	f 8 44	f 9 50
1 52	6 56	62.2	....Versailles.....	8 34	9 35
2 05	7 05	65.8	....Perry Springs.....	8 17	9 10
2 25	7 25	69.8	....Meredosia.....	8 02	8 50
3 15	7 45	75.8	Ar.....Bluffs 12.....Lv	7 45	8 05
PM	PM			AM	AM

SALISBURY AND GLASGOW

Read Down / Read Up

Table 15

33 Mixed Daily	31 Mixed Daily	Miles	Table 15	30 Mixed Daily	32 Mixed Daily
PM	AM			PM	PM
1 35	9 00	0	Lv.....Salisbury 1.....Ar	12 05	3 40
1 58	9 20	5.5	....Shannondale.....	11 29	3 15
f2 02	f9 25	6.5	....Oil City.....	f11 20	f3 10
2 11	9 35	8.8	....Forest Green.....	11 13	3 05
2 27	9 45	12.9	....Lewis Mill.....	11 00	2 55
2 35	10 20	15.1	Ar.....Glasgow.....Lv	10 55	2 50
PM	AM			AM	PM

QUINCY—HANNIBAL—PITTSFIELD

Table 16

70 Frt. Ex. Su.	12 Daily	35 Ex. Su.	33 Ex. Su.	Miles	Table 16	32-3 Daily	34 Ex. Su.	71 Frt. Ex. Su.
	5 30			0	Lv.....Quincy 12, 13.....Ar	10 45		
7 40	6 25			18.8	Lv.....Hannibal 12, 13,...Ar	9 45		1 05
11 15	7 45			52.4	Ar.....Maysville 12.....Lv	8 31		8 43
		† 7 50	†11 10	52.4	Lv.....Maysville 12.....Ar	†8 00	10 55	
		‡ 8 10	†11.25	58.6	Ar.....Pittsfield 12.....Lv	†7 40	10 35	

Numbers opposite stations refer to tables showing connecting trains.

a Stops on signal to receive or discharge revenue passengers. d Stops on signal to receive revenue passengers for Ft. Wayne or east. e Will stop on signal to discharge revenue passengers from Decatur and beyond. h Stops on signal to discharge paying passengers from Moberly, or to receive paying passengers for Ft. Wayne or beyond. f Flag stop. k Stops on signal to discharge revenue passengers from Toledo, Detroit and East and receive revenue passengers for St. Louis and beyond. m Will stop on signal to discharge revenue passengers from points west of Springfield, and to receive revenue passengers for points east or north of Bement. s Stops on signal to discharge revenue passengers from St. Louis, Hannibal or beyond and to receive revenue passengers for Detroit or beyond. t Stops to discharge revenue passengers from Detroit or beyond and to receive revenue passengers for St. Louis, Hannibal or beyond. v Stops on signal to discharge revenue passengers from Kansas City. x Stops on signal to discharge revenue passengers from St. Louis and to receive revenue passengers for Toledo and Detroit or beyond.

y Stops on signal to receive revenue passengers for Kansas City and beyond.

z Stops on signal to receive and discharge revenue passengers to and from regular stops.

NOTE—Freight Trains Nos. 70 and 71 will stop on signal at Magner.

■NOTE—For schedules From Decatur to Chicago and intermediate points, see Table 10. To Detroit and Buffalo see Tables 5 and 11. From Fort Wayne to Toledo, see Table 8. Between Moberly and Kansas City, see Table 1.

REFERENCE MARKS—*Daily. †Daily, except Sunday. ‖Meals. §Wabash Service. ‡Pittsfield Transpth. Motor Service.

Time from 12.01 midnight to 12.00 noon is shown by LIGHT faced figures, and time from 12.01 noon to 12.00 midnight by HEAVY faced figures.

29   30

306

WABASH CITY TICKET OFFICES { 328 NORTH BROADWAY (COR. LOCUST), ST. LOUIS. PHONE, CHESTNUT 4700. / 6001 DELMAR BOULEVARD, ST. LOUIS. PHONE, CHESTNUT 4700.

BRANCH LINES

BEMENT AND EFFINGHAM — Table 17

73 Frt. Ex. Sun.	71 Frt. Ex. Sun.	Miles	Table 17	70 Frt. Ex. Sun.	72 Frt. Ex. Sun.
	AM			PM	
	8 30	0	Lv....Bement 5, 10....Ar	12 20	
	f 8 42	3.8	Voorhies	f12 05	
	9 00	8.5	Hammond	11 50	
	9 20	14.7	Lovington	11 30	
	9 35	18.7	Cushman	11 15	
	11 30	22.8	Sullivan	11 00	
	11 50	28.7	Bruce	10 25	
	12 10	34.4	Windsor	10 05	
	12 35	40.6	Strasburg	9 45	
	f12 45	44.2	Herborn	f 9 30	
	1 10	46.9	Stewardson	9 20	
	1 30	52.7	Ar....Shumway....Lv	9 00	
	1 55	59.9	Ar....Effingham....Lv	7 00	
7 30		0	Lv....Shumway....Ar		8 45
7 47		5.0	Ar....Blue Point....Ar		8 29
8 01		9.4	Ar....Altamont....Lv		8 15
AM	PM			AM	AM

(Left margin) Nos. 70 and 71 will stop at Lanton and Kirk on signal.

BRANCH LINES

FORREST AND STREATOR — Table 18

NOTE—All trains will stop on signal at Champlin, Pontiac Junction and Dimmick.

72 Frt. Ex. Sun.	Miles	Table 18	73 Frt. Ex. Sun.
PM			PM
11 25	0	Lv....Forrest 10....Ar	10 30
11 50	5.6	Fairbury	9 50
f12 10	11.0	Lodemia	f 9 20
12 20	12.8	McDowell	9 10
1 25	16.8	Pontiac	8 50
1 40	21.3	Rowe	8 10
2 00	26.3	Cornell	7 50
2 20	31.2	Manville	7 27
3 00	36.9	Ar....Streator....Lv	7 00
AM			PM

SIDNEY AND CHAMPAIGN — Table 19

33 Ex. Sun.	31 Ex. Sun.	Miles	Table 19	30 Ex. Sun.	32 Ex. Sun.
AM	AM			AM	AM
9 15	5 30	0	Lv......Sidney 5......Ar	5 15	9 00
f9 26	f5 41	3.4	Deer's	4 55	f8 40
f9 36	f5 51	6.3	Mira	f 4 40	f8 25
9 52	6 07	9.5	Urbana 5	4 25	8 10
10 05	6 20	11.7	Ar....Champaign 5....Lv	4 00	7 45
AM	AM			AM	AM

ATTICA AND COVINGTON — Table 20

SERVICE IRREGULAR

Miles	
0	Lv. Attica 5 9 8. Ar
0.4	Peacock
7.2	Fountain
9.7	Neleker's
12.3	Shelly's.
14.8	Ar..Covington..Lv

SERVICE IRREGULAR

HELMER AND STROH — Table 21

SERVICE IRREGULAR

Miles	
0	Lv Helmer 11 Ar
4.6	Ar..Stroh..Lv

SERVICE IRREGULAR

RATES FOR LOWER BERTHS IN PULLMAN STANDARD SLEEPERS, INCLUDING SURCHARGE.

Published as a matter of information only and subject to change without notice.

BETWEEN	Buffalo Lower	Buffalo Drawing Room	Chicago Lower	Chicago Drawing Room	Danville Lower	Decatur Lower	Des Moines Lower	Des Moines Drawing Room	Detroit Lower	Detroit Drawing Room	Ft. Wayne Lower	Hannibal Lower	Jacksonville Lower	Kansas City Lower	LaFayette Lower	Mexico Lower	Moberly Lower	Omaha Lower	St. Louis Lower	St. Louis Drawing Room	Springfield Lower	Toledo Lower	Toledo Drawing Room
Atlanta..........Ga.									8.25	30.00				12.00				12.00	9.75	34.50			
Binghamton......N.Y.	3.00	10.50	7.50	27.00					5.25	19.50	6.38			12.00				12.00	9.75	34.50			
Chicago.........Ill.	5.63	21.00				3.50			†3.75	13.50		3.75	3.75	4.50				4.13	†3.75	13.50	3.75	3.75	13.50
Cincinnati.......Ohio									3.75	13.50													
Dallas..........Tex.	15.00	52.50	10.50	37.50			9.00		12.75	45.00				6.38					8.25	30.00	9.00	12.75	45.00
Danville........Ill.	6.00	21.00				*.75	7.50	27.00	3.75	13.50	3.00	3.75	3.00	4.50	*.75	3.75	3.75	7.50	3.75	13.50	*.90	3.75	13.50
Decatur.........Ill.	6.38	22.50	3.50	12.50	*.75		7.50	27.00	4.13	15.00	3.75	3.00	*.75	3.75	3.00	3.75		7.50	3.00	10.50	*.75	3.75	13.50
Denver..........Colo.	16.50	58.50	10.88	39.00	10.38	10.13	8.25	30.00	13.50	48.00	12.75	9.38	10.13	6.38	10.88	8.63	8.25	6.38	10.13	36.00	10.13	13.50	48.00
Des Moines......Iowa	9.38	33.00		13.50	7.50	7.50			7.50	27.00	9.00		6.75	7.50	3.75	3.75	3.00	3.75		13.50	7.13	9.75	34.50
Detroit.........Mich.	3.00	10.50	†3.75	13.50	3.75	4.13	7.50	27.00			3.00	4.50	4.50	7.50	3.75	5.63	6.38	8.25	4.50	16.50		4.50	10.50
Elmira..........N.Y.	3.00	10.50							6.38	22.50													
Evansville......Ind.									5.63	21.00	3.75	3.75											
Ft. Worth.......Tex.	15.00	52.50	10.50	37.50			9.00		12.75	45.00				6.38					8.25	30.00	9.00	12.75	45.00
Frankfort.......Mich.			6.00	6.38							4.13			5.63					6.38	22.50			
Galveston.......Tex.	16.88	60.00	12.75	45.00					14.25	51.00				9.00					9.75	34.50	10.88	14.25	51.00
Hannibal........Mo.	7.50	27.00	3.75	13.50	3.75	3.00			4.50	16.50	3.75		*.75	3.00	3.75	*.75	.75					9.00	33.00
Hot Springs.....Ark.	12.00	43.50	7.50	27.00	8.25	6.00			9.00	33.00	8.25			8.25					4.50	16.50		9.00	33.00
Houston.........Tex.	16.88	60.00	12.38	43.50		10.50			14.25	51.00				9.00					9.75	34.50	10.50	14.25	51.00
Indianapolis....Ind.									12.75	45.00													
Jacksonville....Fla.									12.75	45.00													
Jacksonville....Ill.	7.50	27.00	3.75	13.50	3.00	*.75	6.75	24.00	4.50	16.50	3.75	*.75		3.75	3.38	3.00		7.13			*.75	4.50	16.50
Kansas City.....Mo.	10.13	36.00	4.50	16.50	4.50	3.75			7.50	27.00	6.38	3.00	3.75		4.50	3.00	3.00		†3.75	13.50	3.75	7.50	27.00
Little Rock.....Ark.	11.63	42.00	6.38	22.50	7.88	5.63			8.63	31.50	7.88			7.88					4.13	15.00		8.63	31.50
Los Angeles.....Cal.	28.88	102.00	23.63	84.00	24.38	23.63	21.38	75.00	27.00	94.50	26.25	22.88	23.63	19.88	24.38		21.38	19.88	22.50	79.50	23.63	27.00	94.00
Louisville......Ky.									4.50	16.50													
Macon...........Ga.									9.00	31.50													
Mexico..........Mo.	9.00	31.50	3.75	13.50					5.63	21.00	5.25		3.00	3.75	*.75		3.75		*.75			6.00	21.00
New York........N.Y.	3.75	13.50	9.00	31.50			9.00	10.13	12.75	45.00	6.38		22.50	7.50	10.88	10.88	13.50	9.00	12.00	13.50		10.88	10.88
Omaha...........Neb.	10.13	36.00			7.50	7.50	3.00	10.50	8.25	30.00	9.38		7.13	7.88	3.75	3.75			4.50	16.50	7.50	8.25	30.00
Quincy..........Ill.	7.50	27.00	3.75	13.50	3.75	3.00			4.50	16.50	3.75		*.75			3.75					.90	4.50	16.50
Sarasota........Fla.									15.00	52.50													
Scranton........Pa.	3.00	10.50	8.25	30.00					5.63	21.00	6.75			12.75				12.75	10.13	36.00			
St. Louis.......Mo.	7.50	27.00	†*3.75	13.50					3.75	13.50	3.00		3.75	*.75	4.50	†3.75	13.50	3.00			4.50	4.50	16.50
St. Paul........Minn.	9.00	31.50	3.75	13.50	8.25	8.25	3.75	13.50	7.50	27.00	9.75		7.50	5.63	8.25	5.63	4.50	3.75	5.63	21.00	7.88	7.50	27.00
St. Petersburg..Fla.									14.63	52.50													
Salt Lake.......Utah	21.00	73.50	15.38	54.00	17.25	16.50	13.13	46.50	19.13	67.50	19.13	15.75	16.50	12.75	17.25	14.63	14.25	12.00	15.38	54.00	16.50	19.13	67.50
San Antonio.....Tex.	18.00	63.00	13.50	48.00		11.25			15.38	54.00				9.00					10.88	39.00	11.25	15.38	54.00
San Francisco...Cal.	28.88	102.00	23.63	84.00	24.38	23.63	21.38	75.00	27.00	94.50	26.26	22.88	23.63	19.88	24.38	21.75	21.38	19.88	22.50	79.50	23.63	27.00	94.00
South Bend......Ind.	5.25	19.50	3.00	10.50					3.75	13.50									7.50				
Springfield.....Ill.	7.50	27.00	3.75	13.50	*.90	*.75	7.13		4.50	16.50	3.75	*.75	*.75			3.00	3.38	7.50				4.13	15.00
Tampa...........Fla.									14.63	52.50													
Toledo..........Ohio	13.50	3.75	3.75	3.00	3.75	3.75	7.50	27.00	3.00	10.50	3.00	4.50	4.50	7.50	3.38	6.00	6.00	8.25	4.50	16.50	4.13		
W. Yellowstone..Mont.														12.75				15.38	14.63			15.38	54.00

THE FOLLOWING ARE COMPARTMENT RATES BETWEEN POINTS SHOWN:

Between St. Louis, Mo., and Kansas City, Mo.	$10.50
St. Louis, Mo., and Denver, Colo.	28.50
St. Louis, Mo., and Los Angeles, Cal.	63.00
St. Louis, Mo., and San Francisco, Cal.	63.00
St. Louis, Mo., and Chicago, Ill.	10.50
Between Kansas City, Mo., and Detroit, Mich.	$21.00
Kansas City, Mo., and Ft. Wayne, Ind.	18.00
Chicago, Ill., and Detroit, Mich.	10.50
Chicago, Ill., and Little Rock, Ark.	18.00
Chicago, Ill., and Hot Springs, Ark.	21.00

Number of tickets required for exclusive occupancy of Sections, Compartments or Drawing Rooms, see page 40.

▲(Single Room in Bed Room Cars.) For this privacy, the cost is only $7.50 for each room, plus one and one-quarter railroad fare.

Upper berth charge will be 80 per cent of the lower berth charge. A section occupied by one passenger, will be the lower berth rate, plus 40% for two or more passengers, charge will be the sum of lower and upper berth rates.—Rates for berth, compartment or Drawing Room space from points not shown in the above table can be obtained on application to Wabash Agents.   *Seat Fare.   †Pullman Parlor Car Seat Fare $1.50.

TERMINAL CONNECTIONS

CONNECTIONS AT BUFFALO

Railroad	Station					
Buffalo, Rochester and Pittsburgh.	Buffalo............Lv	* 9 15	*10 25		* 5 05	
Lackawanna Terminal.	East Salamanca.....Ar	10 57	12 05		7 02	
	Bradford	11 34	12 50		7 38	
	DuBois	1 48	3 06		9 55	
	Pittsburgh..........Ar	5 45	7 05			
Delaware, Lackawanna & Western.	Buffalo............Lv	* 4 00	* 9 30	6 00	*8 30	11 00
D. L. & W. Depot,	Binghamton........Ar	9 30	2 07	12 05	1 07	3 30
Foot of Main Street.	Scranton	11 20	3 37	2 15	2 41	5 02
	Stroudsburg	1 12	5 08	4 03	4 25	6 40
	New York E. T......Ar	3 50	7 30	6 45	7 15	9 15
Erie.	Buffalo............Lv	* 5 10	* 9 30	11 00		
Erie Depot, Corner Michigan Avenue and Exchange Street.	Hornell	8 25	11 57	1 30		
	Elmira.............Ar	10 10	1 16	2 48		
	Binghamton	11 55	2 34	4 07		
	Port Jervis	3 25	5 43	7 18		
	New York..........Ar	6 14	8 24	9 37		
Lehigh Valley.	Buffalo E.T.........Lv	* 6 25	* 9 45	* 7 45	10 15	*11 10
Lehigh Valley Depot, Corner Main, Scott and Washington Streets.	Rochester	7 15	10 35	8 40		
	Wilkes-Barre	12 26	3 35	2 07		4 51
	Philadelphia.........Ar	4 55	7 41	6 51	7 45	9 10
	New York (Penna.Sta.)..Ar	5 40	8 15	7 20	8 10	9 40
New York Central.	Buffalo............Lv	* 8 00	* 7 50	*12 10		
Central Terminal.	Rochester..........Ar	9 27	9 13	1 32		
	Albany	2 49	2 35	6 06		
	Boston					
	New York E.T.......Ar	6 40	6 00	9 30		
Pennsylvania.	Buffalo............Lv	* 9 15	* 9 00	*11 00		
Central Terminal.	Harrisburg..........Ar	5 06	5 05	6 22		
	Philadelphia	7 45	7 46	9 01		
	Baltimore	7 48	7 40	9 05		
	Washington.........Ar	8 50	8 40	10 05		

CONNECTIONS AT CHICAGO

Railroad	Station							
Atchison, Topeka & Santa Fe.	Chicago.......Lv	10 20	10 15		*7 00	9 05	11 00	11 00
Dearborn Station, Dearborn and Polk Sts.	Kansas City...Lv	10 10	10 00		8 25	8 45	9 50	10 50
	Denver........Ar	7 00			10 00		Ex-	10 00
	Williams......Ar	3 10	10 15			f6 05	tra	2 05
	Grand Canyon.Ar	6 30	8 00			7 40	Fare	8 00
	Los Angeles....Ar	7 00	12 15			8 15	5 00	5 45
	San Diego.....Ar	12 15	5 00			12 15	9 30	9 30
	San Francisco..Ar	7 00				7 00	8 15	8 15
Chicago, Burlington & Quincy.	Chicago........Lv	11 30	10*30	11 00		*6 30	10 30	10 45
Union Passenger Station, Canal and Adams Sts.	St. Paul........Ar			9 20		7 00	8 20	8 35
	Minneapolis			9 55		7 35	9 00	9 20
	Omaha	3 50	11 24					
	Denver	7 15	1 05					
	Seattle			7 30			8 45	8 00
	Portland			7 35			7 35	7 35

Railroad	Station					
Chicago Great Western.	Chicago..............Lv	*8 00	*11 30			
Grand Central Station, Harrison and Wells Sts.	Dubuque..............Ar	12 26	4 58			
	Rochester	7 00				
	St. Paul	7 30				
	Minneapolis	8 10				
	Waterloo	4 17	8 30			
	Des Moines	7 20	11 55			
	St. Joseph	11 40				
	Leavenworth	12 55				
	Kansas City	1 40				
	Fort Dodge					
	Omaha..............Ar					

Railroad	Station							
Chicago, Milwaukee, St. Paul and Pacific R. R.	Chicago.......Lv	* 1 55	*5 45		*10 30	* 6 45	*10 45	
Union Station, Canal St. and Jackson Blvd.	Milwaukee	4 00			12 30	9 00	12 45	
	St. Paul......Ar.	2 45	8 20		8 50	7 00	8 35	
	Minneapolis	3 35	9 05		9 35	7 35	9 15	
	Butte						12 19	
	Spokane						9 40	
	Seattle........Ar						8 00	
	Tacoma						9 30	
	Chicago.......Lv		* 5 45		* 6 00	* 6 00		*10 30
	Des Moines					6 15		9 20
	Omaha........Ar					7 35		12 50
	Sioux City					7 50		1 40
	Sioux Falls		9 30					
	Kansas City...Ar				8 30			

Chicago....Lv	1*55	7 30	9 20	10*30	11†30	12 30	†2 10	3*20	5*05		*6 45	10*15	10*45
Milwaukee.Ar	3 45	9 15	11 05	12 20	1 15	2 15	4 00	5 05	6 50		8 45	12 05	12 35

Railroad	Station							
Chicago, Rock Island & Pacific	Chicago.......Lv	10*30	8 45	*6 00	8 25	11*30		
La Salle Street Station, La Salle and Van Buren Streets.	Omaha.........Ar	11 15			8 37	12 40		
	Kansas City		9 00	8 00				
	Fort Worth			6 45				
	Dallas			7 59				
	Denver	1 05				7 25		
	Los Angeles		7 45	8 55				
	San Diego		10 30	10 30				
	San Francisco..Ar	4 15	11 00	7 45		8 30		
Grand Trunk—Canadian National	Chicago.......Lv	† 8 05	* 9 05	*12 45	* 7 15	*10 00	11*45	
Station, Dearborn and Polk Streets	South Bend....Ar	11 11	11 21	3 28	9 35	12 29	2 18	
	Battle Creek...Ar	1 35	1 00	5 20	11 15	2 10	4 05	
	Lansing........Ar	2 58	1 59	6 30	12 18	3 20	5 14	
	Flint...........Ar	4 46	3 08	7 51	1 30		6 35	
	Port Huron....Ar	* 6 50	4 30	*9 25	2 55		8 35	
	Toronto.......Ar		*10 20		8 25		3 40	
	Montreal......Ar		* 7 00		4 00		10 00	

CONNECTIONS AT CHICAGO—Continued

Railroad	Station							
Chicago & North Western.	Chicago.......Lv	* 1 55	*10 30	* 5 40	* 8 00	* 8 30	*10 15	
C.&N.W.Terminal, Madison and Canal Sts.	Milwaukee....Lv		12 30		10 20	10 55		
	Madison......Lv	7 00		9 25			1 15	
	St. Paul.......Ar	4 10	8 50	7 25		7 25	8 05	
	Minneapolis...Ar	4 45	9 25	8 00		8 00	8 40	
	Duluth........Ar			* 8 15		*12 20	12 20	
	Rochester.....Ar		* 8 55		* 7 05		* 9 45	
a Daily will operate tri-weekly. Will leave Chicago Mon., Wed. and Sat. Arrive San Francisco Wed., Fri. and Mon.	Chicago.......Lv	a10 30	*10 35	* 2 30	* 9 30	* 9 35	10 15	*11 20
	Clinton........Ar	1 35	2 00	6 00	12 35	12 45	1 35	2 20
	Boone.........Ar	6 15	7 10	11 25	5 25	5 35	6 15	7 25
	Omaha........Ar	10 05	11 25	3 05	9 35	9 40	9 45	12 25
	Salt Lake City.Ar	Extra Fare		7 30	10 35			4 55
	Los Angeles...Ar			8 15	8 30			5 30
	San Francisco..Ar	a 4 30		8 10		8 30		* 4 50
	Portland......Ar						7 45	5 30
	Seattle........Ar						2 20	* 6 30
	Denver		1 10					

Chicago..Lv	1*50	7†00	8*00	*9 00	10*30	12†01	12†01	2†00	3*00	4†01	5*00	6*00	*8 00	8 30	*9 30
Milwaukee Ar	4 00	9 00	9 45	11 10	12 25	1 55	2 10	4 15	4 4[illegible]	6 15	7 05	8 05	10 05	10 45	11 35

Railroad	Station								
Chicago, North Shore & Milwaukee R. R.	Chicago...Lv.	*7 05	8 05	10 05	11 05	12 05	3 05	5 05	6 05
Adams St. and Wabash Ave.	Milwaukee.Ar.	9 14	9 57	12 12	1 14	2 12	4 57	7 14	8 14

"In addition to the above, trains leave Adams and Wabash station every hour at five minutes after the hour." Daylight saving time.

Railroad	Station						
Illinois Central	Chicago............Lv	*12 30	*10 10	* 3 00	* 6 00		
Central Station, Roosevelt Rd. (12th St.) and Michigan Ave.	Dubuque...........Ar	6 00	3 10	8 40	10 32		
	Omaha	4 15			8 15		
	Sioux City.........Ar	5 05			8 00		
Michigan Central.	Chicago.......Lv	† 9 05	*12 20	* 5 10	*10 00	*11 30	
Central Station, Michigan Ave. and Roosevelt Rd. (12th St.)	Grand Rapids..Ar	1 45	* 4 50	10 05		5 35	
	Lansing		† 6 45		4 55	† 6 55	
	Saginaw		† 8 40		6 30	† 8 55	
	Bay City		† 9 10		7 00	† 9 25	
	Mackinaw City.Ar		6 30	6 50	8 40	† 8 40	
Minneapolis, St. Paul Sault Ste. Marie.	Chicago.......Lv		* 1 00	* 7 30	* 5 30		
Grand Central Station, South Wells and Harrison Streets.	Oshkosh.......Lv		7 04	12 34	10 48		
	St. Paul		4 30	8 25		* 1 50	1 20
	Minneapolis		5 35	9 20		1 20	2 05
	Duluth.........Ar				8 05	5 50	8 10
Pere Marquette.	Chicago............Lv	† 8 45	*12 00	† 5 00	*11 45		
Grand Central Station, Harrison St. and So. Wells St.	Muskegon..........Ar		† 5 15		6 40		
	Grand Rapids	2 50	* 4 35	9 50	5 50		
	Thompsonville.......Lv.	(Via Ann					
	Frankfort...........Ar.	Arbor R. R.)					
	Traverse City		9 10		12 30		
	Petoskey...........Ar				† 3 35		

CONNECTIONS AT DETROIT

Railroad	Station					
Baltimore & Ohio.	Detroit (E. T.)......Lv	*11 05	* 8 20	*12 25		
Union Station, Fort and Third Streets.	Dayton.............Lv	5 20	1 55	5 34		
	Hamilton...........Lv	-6 10	2 45	6 25		
	Cincinnati..........Ar	7 25	3 40	7 15		
	Louisville (C. T.)....Ar	10 35	6 30	9 50		
Canadian Pacific.	Detroit (East. Time).Lv	Trains Leave Detroit from Fifteenth and Michigan Ave.	* 2 15	* 4 40	* 8 30	
	Toronto (East. Time).Ar		* 8 15	*10 35	* 3 15	
	Ottawa		* 2 50	* 6 30	* 9 15	
	Montreal		* 3 45	* 7 25	* 9 45	
	Quebec		* 8 30	* 2 00	* 6 15	
	St. John		*11 00	† 5 10		
	Halifax		* 9 50	† 5 35		
	Portland			† 7 05		
	Boston.............Ar		* 6 30	* 6 30		
Grand Trunk—Candian National	Detroit......E. T......Lv	*11 45	*12 00	* 4 00	* 8 30	
Grand Trunk Depot, Foot Brush Street.	London (C.N.R.)........Ar	3 12	4 00	7 06	11 45	
	Toronto (C.N.R.)	7 15	* 8 00	10 20	* 3 40	
	Montreal (C.N.R.)	4 00	* 6 30	7 00	*10 00	
	St. John, N.B. (C.N.R.)	† 8 20		† 1 50		
	Halifax, N.S. (C.N.R.)	9 50		† 5 35		
	Quebec (C.N.R.)	9 40		* 2 15		
	Portland (G.T.R.)	†10 00		* 5 45		
	Boston (B.&M.).........Ar	* 6 45		* 7 10		
Michigan Central.	Detroit.............Lv		*7 45		* 3 10	† 5 15
Michigan Central Terminal.	Saginaw............Ar		*10 55		12 05	7 45
	Bay City		*11 30		12 40	8 15
	Mackinaw City......Ar		* 8 40		6 30	
Pere Marquette.	Detroit............Lv	*11 10	† 7 55	* 4 45		
Union Depot, Fort and Third Streets.	Plymouth..........Ar	11 58	8 43	5 26		
§Sunday only.	Flint	1 32	10 20	6 38		
	Saginaw	3 05	11 25	7 45		
	Bay City...........Ar	4 00	12 15	8 35		
	Detroit............Lv	† 7 50	†12 40	* 4 30		
	Lansing...........Ar	9 49	† 2 46	* 6 33		
	Grand Rapids......Ar	†11 20	† 4 10	* 8 00		

CONNECTIONS AT KANSAS CITY

Railroad	Station							
Atchison, Topeka & Santa Fe.	Kansas City...Lv	8 45	8 20	10 50	10 05	9 40	11 35	10 00
Union Station.	Newton........Ar	2 00	3 35	4 35	2 10	4 00	5 00	3 10
	Oklahoma City.Ar		10 50		7 35		1 00	
	Fort Worth....Ar		6 15		1 25		7 55	
	Galveston.....Ar		8 45				9 35	
	Albuquerque...Lv	8 30						10 20
	Ash Fork......Ar	7 00		3 05		4 00		11 25
	Los Angeles...Ar	8 15		5 45		7 00		12 15
	San Francisco..Ar	7 00		8 15		7 00		
Chicago, Burlington & Quincy.	Kansas City..........Lv	*10 30	* 9 30	*10 30	7 00			
Union Station.	Billings.............Ar			6 15	5 30			
	Seattle			7 30	8 45			
	Portland			7 35	7 35			
	Denver.............Ar	7 40	1 15					

TERMINAL CONNECTIONS

CONNECTIONS AT KANSAS CITY—Continued.

Chicago, Rock Island & Pacific. Union Station.

Kansas City...Lv	*8 45	*9 40	2 00	8 10	
Topeka...Ar	10 20	11 20	3 35	9 50	
Fort Worth			6 45	1 50	
Dallas			7 59	3 10	
El Paso	9 55	8 30			
Los Angeles	8 55	7 45			
San Diego	10 30	10 30			
San Francisco..Ar	7 45	11 00			

Kansas City Southern. Union Station.

Kansas City...Lv	5 25	9 45
Joplin...Ar	9 30	2 20
Fort Smith	2 45	8 15
Texarkana	6 40	3 50
Shreveport	9 15	6 50
Port Arthur...Ar	5 20	8 00

Missouri Pacific. Union Station.

Kansas City...Lv	*11 25	*5 00	5 30	*9 10	*11 30
Osawatomie...Ar	1 12	6 45			
Independence	4 15	10 10			
Coffeyville	4 40	10 38			
Wichita	7 15				
Carthage			10 03	2 05	5 45
Joplin...Ar			10 35	2 40	6 30

Missouri-Kansas-Texas. Union Station.

Kansas City...Lv	4 30	10 10
Parsons	8 30	1 30
Oklahoma City...Ar		7 45
Muskogee...Ar	11 55	5 10
Denison	4 35	9 20
Wichita Falls...Ar		2 10
Dallas...Ar	8 10	12 25
Fort Worth...Ar	7 55	12 40
Waco...Ar	11 40	3 00
Austin...Ar	3 10	6 01
San Antonio...Ar	6 15	8 30
Houston...Ar	7 30	

St. Louis-San Francisco. Union Station.

Kansas City...Lv	*6 15	*11 50	*11 45	*10 30	*10 30
Memphis...Ar	8 00	6 00			10 50
Birmingham	3 20				7 00
Pensacola...Ar					12 55
Jacksonville	7 30				3 24
Joplin		6 25			
Tulsa		2 45	7 00	5 15	
Oklahoma City		8 50	10 30	8 50	
Dallas				7 50	
Fort Worth...Ar				8 05	

Union Pacific. Union Station. a—Via Borie.

Kansas City...Lv	*10 40	*10 40	*6 15	6 15	10 00	10 00
Topeka...Lv	12 40	12 40	7 45	7 45	11 28	11 28
Denver...Ar	7 00	7 00	9 45	9 45	1 00	1 00
Cheyenne	7 30	7 30	a	9 15	a	
Ogden	6 15	9 20	6 15	3 45	10 45	6 15
Salt Lake City	7 30	10 35	7 30	4 55	7 30	7 30
San Francisco	8 10	8 30	8 10	4 50	8 30	8 10
Los Angeles	8 15	8 30	8 15	5 30	8 15	8 15
Portland		7 45	7 45	5 30	7 45	7 45
Tacoma		1 04	1 04	4 50	1 04	1 04
Seattle...Ar		2 20	2 20	6 30	2 20	2 20

CONNECTIONS AT OMAHA

Chicago, Burlington & Quincy. Burlington Depot, Tenth and Mason Streets.

Omaha...Lv	*4 25	*4 25	*11 50	*11 50
Deadwood...Ar	1 30			
Billings	6 15			5 30
Seattle	7 30			8 45
Denver...Ar		7 15	1 05	

Chicago & North Western. Union Station, Tenth and Marcy Streets.

Omaha...Lv	*7 35	*5 00	9 30	7 35
Sioux City...Ar	10 30		12 30	10 25
Fremont		6 16		
Winner (S. D.)				
Lander (Wyo.)		† 5 30		
Hot Springs (S.D.)		*9 15		
Rapid City		9 55		
Deadwood				

Union Pacific. Union Station, Tenth and Marcy Streets.

Omaha	11 50	3 25	10 07	10 10	10 05	12 55	4 25
Grand Isl'd.Lv	3 10	6 45	1 20	1 30	1 10	4 25	8 20
Denver...Ar	1 10				7 15		
Green River	12 40	4 10	5 25	3 40	9 55		
Butte		4 50	4 50				
Portland		7 45	5 30				
Tacoma		1 04	4 50				
Seattle		2 20	6 30				
Ogden	6 15	9 20	10 45	3 45			
Salt Lake City	7 30	10 35		4 55			
San Francisco	8 10	8 30		4 50			
Los Angeles.Ar	8 15	8 30		5 30			

CONNECTIONS AT ST. LOUIS

Baltimore & Ohio. Union Station, 18th and Market Streets.

St. Louis (C. T.)...Lv	*9 10	*12 40	*9 47
Louisville...Ar	6 30	9 50	6 40
Cincinnati (E. T.)	6 30	9 50	7 55
Pittsburgh	8 32	8 30	7 50
Washington	8 50	11 00	2 30
Baltimore	9 55	11 58	3 43
Philadelphia	1 56	6 06	
New York E.T. Jersey City Ar	2 08	3 56	8 25

Cleveland, Cincinnati, Chicago & St. Louis. Union Station, 18th and Market Streets.

St. Louis...Lv	*8 40	*9 04	*12 10	*12 12	*6 00	*10 00
Indianapolis...Ar	2 20	1 40	5 05	5 50	10 50	4 15
Cincinnati (E.T.)...Ar	6 05			9 30		7 55
Cleveland (E.T.)..Ar		8 15	11 30	2 12	5 30	3 45
New York...Ar		9 05	12 00	5 05	6 50	
Boston...Ar		11 55	3 10		9 40	

CONNECTIONS AT ST. LOUIS—Continued.

Illinois Central. Union Station, 18th and Market Streets. a Sleeping car passengers only.

St. Louis...Lv	*8 10	*1 00	*4 35	*11 30
Memphis...Ar	6 50	10 40	12 31	7 30
New Orleans...Ar	7 45	9 45	9 30	7 50
Birmingham				4 40
Jacksonville				7 15

Louisville & Nashville. Union Station, 18th and Market Streets. a—This train carries Coach passengers

St. Louis...Lv	8 40	3 05	9 15	a10 40
Evansville...Ar	2 00	7 55	2 25	3 25
Louisville	6 50			7 15
Nashville...Ar	7 30	1 00	7 45	10 50
Atlanta	6 30	8 20	6 45	6 55
Jacksonville (via Atlanta)		8 50		7 15
Birmingham	5 27	8 13		2 45
Jacksonville (via Mont'y)				7 15
Miami	7 00			7 45
Pensacola...Ar	3 30			5 50
Mobile	4 10			2 15
New Orleans...Ar	8 30			6 50

Missouri Pacific. Union Station, 18th and Market Streets.

St. Louis...Lv	11 59	*9 00	*10 10	6 20	2 02
Sedalia...Ar	4 50	1 56	4 05	10 44	6 46
Joplin...Ar	2 40	10 35		6 30	
Wichita...Ar				7 45	
St. Louis...Lv	11 30	8 55	*6 30	*10 35	1 40	2 00
Memphis...Ar	7 30	6 35				
Little Rock...Ar		6 30	2 50	7 45	10 40	10 45
Hot Springs		8 50		9 50		12 30
New Orleans			6 30			6 50
Texarkana	11 40	7 10	12 45	2 15	2 40	
Dallas	7 05	12 25		7 45	8 50	
Fort Worth	8 25	1 25		8 25	10 00	
El Paso...Ar	7 45				4 30	
Palestine...Ar	7 00	12 20		7 20	10 35	
Beaumont	3 25				5 12	
Houston	4 30		11 45	2 40		
Galveston	6 00		2 30	9 35		
San Antonio	8 30		4 20	8 20		
Laredo	2 00			2 00		
Mexico City...Ar	7 35			9 40		

Missouri-Kansas-Texas. Union Station, 18th and Market Streets.

St. Louis...Lv	8 58	*1 40	*6 30	9 03
Sedalia...Ar	3 48			3 25
Parsons...Ar	8 35			7 45
Oklahoma City...Ar				3 45
Muskogee...Ar	11 55	12 50	5 30	11 25
McAlester...Ar	1 45	2 35	7 14	1 30
Wichita Falls...Ar			2 10	
Dallas...Ar	8 10	7 45	12 25	8 30
Fort Worth...Ar	7 55	7 55	12 40	8 15
Waco...Ar	11 40	11 40	3 00	1 30
Austin...Ar	3 10	3 10	6 01	5 10
San Antonio...Ar	6 15	6 15	8 30	7 45
Houston...Ar	7 30	7 30		8 10
Galveston...Ar				10 00

Mobile & Ohio. Union Station, 18th and Market Streets.

St. Louis...Lv	8 30	10 10
Cairo...Ar	1 15	3 14
Jackson	5 05	6 50
Mobile		5 10
New Orleans		7 20
Montgomery		5 35

Pennsylvania. Union Sta., 18th & Market Sts. *Daily. a Stops to discharge passengers and pick up passengers for Piqua and beyond. b Stops to discharge passengers and to receive for points east of Pittsburgh. c Stops to discharge passengers. p Arrives in North Philadelphia. x Extra fare train.

St. Louis...Lv	*9 10	x9*02	*12x02	*12x10	*4x45	*6x00	12*03
Terre Haute...Ar	12 51	12 20	3 23	4 43	8 49	9 26	5 05
Indianapolis	2 35	1 45	5 39	6 40	9 45	10 50	7 00
Dayton	6 30	5 14		11 30	1 45		12 00
Columbus	8 10	6 47	9 39	1 15	3 30	4 05	1 40
Pittsburgh	1 50	11 20	2 13	6 40	8 40	8 45	6 57
Washington	3 15	8 45	11 15		6 35	6 35	7 55
Philadelphia	12p39	7pc16	p10 09		p3 25	p5 02	4p22
New York E. T. Ar	2 25	9 02	11 52	6 20	7 10	6 50	6 25

Southern Railway System. Union Station, 18th and Market Streets.

St. Louis...Lv	8 50	8 50	*11 00	8 50
Louisville...Ar	6 20	6 20	7 05	6 20
Knoxville		5 05		
Chattanooga	3 55	3 55	4 00	4 55
Atlanta...Ar	8 15	8 15	8 20	

St. Louis-San Francisco. Union Station, 18th and Market Streets.

St. Louis...Lv	*4 00	*11 40				
Memphis...Ar	11 20	7 35				
Pensacola...Ar	12 55					
St. Louis...Lv	1 40	10 00	6 58	6 30	8 45	11 57
Springfield...Ar	7 45	5 55	1 45	12 35	3 27	7 35
Ft. Smith	1 00	8 45			12 00	
Joplin	12 20				6 50	
Wichita					1 35	
Tulsa	12 40	5 10			2 45	
Oklahoma City	5 50	10 30			8 50	
Dallas	7 45	8 10	12 25			
Fort Worth	7 55	10 20	12 40			
San Antonio	8 45	8 30				
Houston...Ar	7 15	7 40				

St. Louis Southwestern. Union Station, 18th and Market Streets.

St. Louis...Lv	11 30		Stuttgart...Ar	11 36
Paragould...Ar	6 42		Pine Bluff...Ar	12 50
Jonesboro...Ar	7 20		Texarkana...Ar	5 05

CONNECTIONS AT TOLEDO

Ann Arbor. Ann Arbor Sta., Cherry St.

Toledo (E. T.)...Lv	*7 30
Ann Arbor (C. T.)...Ar	8 05
Durand	9 42
Frankfort	5 30

Baltimore & Ohio. Union Station.

Toledo (E. T.)...Lv	*1 05	*8 00	10 20	2 15
Dayton	5 20	2 10	1 55	5 34
Cincinnati...Ar	7 25	4 10	3 40	7 15
Louisville (C. T.)...Ar	10 35	4 10	6 30	9 50

REFERENCE MARKS.—*Daily. †Daily, except Sunday. §Sunday only. ‡Except Mon. Time from 12.01 midnight to 12.00 noon is shown by LIGHT faced figures, and time from 12.01 noon to 12.00 midnight by HEAVY faced figures. *Tuesday, Thursday, Sat.

See additional Toledo Connections on pages 37 and 38.

CONNECTIONS AT TOLEDO—Continued.

Cleveland, Cincinnati, Chicago & St. Louis. Union Station.								New York Central. (Ohio Central Lines) Union Station.						
Toledo (E. T.).....Lv	* 1 05	* 9 55	* 1 40	....	....			Toledo (E. T.).......Lv	* 9 55	* 3 10	* 8 55	7 00	1 00	
Springfield..........Ar	5 00	1 00	4 45	....	....			Sandusky...........Ar	10 55	4 15	10 00	8 20	2 05	
Dayton..............Ar	5 45	1 40	5 25	....	....			Cleveland...........Ar	12 28	5 45	11 35	10 05	3 45	
Cincinnati.........Ar	7 20	3 00	7 00	....	....			Youngstown(ErieR.R)Ar	4 00	7 40			5 45	

Chesapeake & Ohio. Union Station.														
Toledo (E. T.).....Lv	* 4 00	* 2 20	* 8 00	6 15	....			Toledo (E. T.).......Lv	* 9 50	* 1 50	* 5 50	3 45	....	
Marion (E. T.)..........	6 20	4 32	9 52	8 15	....			Columbus (E. T.).....Ar	1 50	5 10	9 10	7 15	....	
Columbus (E. T.)......	7 30	5 50	11 00	9 20	....			Charleston (E. T.)...Ar				3 50	....	
Athens (E. T.)..........	11 02	8 35			....									
Pomeroy (E. T.).....Ar	† 1 00				....			Wheeling & Lake Erie. aCherry Street Depot.						

								aToledo (E.T.).......Lv	† 1 35 E. T.					
								Wheeling...........Ar	9 10 E. T.					

CONNECTIONS TO AND FROM THE PACIFIC COAST

ATCHISON, TOPEKA & SANTA FE RAILWAY.

19	21	23	3	9	STATIONS	2	24	4	22	20	8	2-6
9 50	10 30	10 00	8 45	11 35	Lv...Kansas City...Ar	7 15	5 15	9 45	7 15	8 55	10 10	8 40
					Lv....Topeka.....Lv		7 55					6 25
2 05	4 50	3 20	2 10	5 15	Lv....Newton.....Lv	2 30	12 40	4 15		4 30	5 50	2 55
4 25		6 05	4 50		Lv..Dodge City..Lv		7 45	11 35		12 10	11 55	8 30
8 40		10 30	9 10		Ar..La Junta..Lv		3 00	7 10		7 50	7 20	3 55
	4 00				Lv...La Junta...Ar					1 55	1 40	
	5 40				Ar....Pueblo....Lv					12 25	11 05	
	7 15				Lv..Colorado Springs..Lv					11 20	10 45	
	10 00				Ar.....Denver....Lv					9 00	8 30	
2 35		5 05	3 20		Ar...Las Vegas...Lv		8 25	12 30		1 25	11 55	9 30
6 45		9 55	7 50		Ar..Albuquerque..Lv		4 15	8 15		9 00	7 10	5 30
f4 10	2 15	10 15	f6 05	3 10	Ar....Williams....Lv	5 00	5 30	10 45	4 10	12f15	7 30	5 00
8 00	8 00	8 00		6 30	Ar...Grand Canyon..Lv Bus Service	7 45	7 45		10 15	10 15	10 15	7 45
4 55		11 20	7 00	4 00	Ar.....Ash Fork....Lv	3 30	4 00	9 40	3 00	11 10	5 35	3 30
2 35		2 35	5 56	4 50	....Prescott.....Lv	12 32	12 32	12 38			12 38	12 32
		8 00	8 00	10 45	....Phoenix.....Lv	7 00	7 00	7 00	7 45		7 45	7 00
12 40	12 30	7 35	3 20	2 05	Ar....Barstow.....Lv	3 30	5 05	10 40	2 50	1 00	4 30	3 30
3 05	3 35	10 10	5 55	4 50	...San Bernardino....	12 50	2 25	8 05	12 05	10 35	1 45	12 50
4 25	5 10	11 40	7 42	6 19	....Pasadena.....	10 25	1 00	6 43		9 15	12 05	10 25
5 00	5 45	12 15	8 15	7 00	...Los Angeles...	9 45	12 30	6 15	9 45	8 45	11 30	9 45
9 30	9 30	5 00	12 15	12 45	...San Diego...	8 30	8 30	2 30	2 30	2 30	7 05	8 30
3 25	3 25		4 20	4 20	Lv....Barstow....Ar	1 00		10 20	10 20			1 00
11 30	11 30		12 01	12 01	Ar....Fresno.....Lv	5 00		3 08	3 08			5 00
2 25	2 28		1 43	1 43	...Merced....	3 25		1 38	1 38			3 25
4 45	4 45		3 35	3 35	...Stockton....	1 40		11 52	11 52			1 40
8 11	8 11		6 58	6 58	...Oakland....	10 15		8 45	8 45			10 15
8 15	8 15		7 00	7 00	Ar..San Francisco..Lv	10 30		9 00	9 00			10 30

CHICAGO, BURLINGTON & QUINCY RAILROAD.

43	41	15	17	STATIONS	16	14	42	44
* 7 00	* 10 30	* 9 30	10 * 30	Lv...Kansas City...Ar	8 40	2 00	* 8 40	....
	1 15	7 40		Ar......Denver.....Lv	8 00	2 00		....
11 50	4 25	11 50	4 25	Lv.....Omaha.....Ar	3 25	6 30	3 25	....
	1 05	7 15		Ar.....Denver.....Lv	11 30	3 45		....
2 30	6 30			Lv.....Lincoln....Ar			1 00	....
	1 30			Ar....Deadwood...Lv			2 10	....
5 30	R 6 15			Ar.....Billings....Lv			8 00	....
9 40	R 6 30			....Spokane....			8 05	....
8 45	7 30			....Seattle....			7 00	....
7 35	7 35	S. P. & S. RR		....Portland...			9 30	....

MISSOURI PACIFIC RAILROAD.

31	11	Miles	STATIONS	12	32
8 00	* 9 25	0	Lv...Kansas City...Ar	8 30	5 15
2 58	1 24	178	Ar...Herington...Lv	4 25	
11 24	5 54	424	....Scott City....	10 05	2 17
7 00	10 45	640	Ar....Pueblo....Lv	5 30	8 00
	2 15	757	Ar....Denver....Lv	2 00	
11 50		640	Lv..Pueblo (D.R.& G.W.)..Lv	5 10	
8 30		1262	Ar..Salt Lake City..Lv	9 45	
9 45			Ar..San Francisco (W.P.)..Lv	6 30	

REFERENCE MARKS.—*Daily. †Daily except Sunday. ¶Meals.
Time from 12.01 midnight to 12.00 noon is shown by LIGHT faced figures, and time from 12.01 noon to 12.00 midnight by HEAVY faced figures.

UNION PACIFIC SYSTEM.

21-7	21-17	101-27	19	103-21	STATIONS	8-22	18-22	28	20-128	104
10 00	10 00	6 15		10 40	Lv...Kansas City...Ar	8 00	8 00	8 00	7 50	4 10
11 28	11 28	7 45		12 40	....Topeka....Lv	6 10	6 10	6 10	5 45	2 15
1 00	1 00	9 45		7 00	Ar....Denver....Lv	3 00	3 00	3 00	11 00	10 00
10 07	10 05	10 12	12 55	3 25	Lv.....Omaha....Ar	8 15	8 25	8 10	5 40	....
1 20	1 10	1 30	4 25	6 45	Lv Grand Island Lv	5 05	5 25	3 46		....
4 15	4 05	4 25	8 00	10 10	Ar. North Platte.Lv	2 15	2 35	2 00	10 35	....
4 30	b1 30	4 30	6 15	1 30	Lv.....Denver....Ar	11 50	c2 30	11 50	10 00	7 05
7 30	a	7 30	9 15	a	Ar..Cheyenne..Lv	8 50	a	8 50	6 45	4 05
9 00		9 20	1 25	3 40	Lv..Cheyenne..Ar	8 05	a	7 50	3 35	....
4 10	12 40	4 25	5 55	12 40	Ar.Green River.Lv	12 05		11 50	7 45	....
	9 50		5 40		Ar..Pocatello..Lv		6 50		11 35	....
	8 05		3 55		...Huntington...		10 20		12 50	....
	*2 50		7 10		...Spokane...		*2 00		7 25	....
	7 45		5 30		...Portland....		9 30		9 40	....
	1 04		4 50		...Tacoma...		1 17		12 40	....
	2 20		6 30		Ar....Seattle...Lv		12 01		11 15	....
9 20	6 15	10 45	3 45	6 15	Ar....Ogden....Lv	6 55	11 20	5 20	2 10	....
	4 35	5 20	1 20	4 35	ArSac'mto (S.P.)Lv		12 15	9 35	2 35	....
	10 35	8 30	4 50	8 10	ArSanFrancisco(S.P.)Lv		9 00	6 00	11 20	....
10 35	7 30		4 55	7 30	Ar.Salt Lake..Lv	5 35	10 05		12 30	....
11 00	8 00		5 15	8 00	Lv..Salt Lake..Ar	5 15	9 45		12 15	....
8 30	8 15		8 15	8 15	Ar...Los Angeles...Lv	6 00	8 30		10 00	....

(a) Via Borie. (b) Portland connection leaves 4;30 P. M. via Cheyenne
(c) Portland-Kansas City car arrives 11:50 A. M. ▲Motor coach connection.

CHICAGO, ROCK ISLAND & PACIFIC RAILROAD.

5	7	STATIONS	8	6	8-224 14
*2 00	11 *40	Lv.....Omaha....Ar	2 20	3 35	....
3 45	1 15	....Lincoln....	12 35	2 00	....
2 00		Lv..Kansas City..Ar		4 30	7 15
3 35		Ar.....Topeka.....Lv		2 40	5 15
7 30	12 45	..Colorado Springs..	11 00	10 45	11 00
7 25	1 05	....Denver....	11 00	11 00	11 00
11 50	5 30	Lv..Pueblo (D.& R.G.)..Ar	7 00	5 10	....
1 05	6 43	Lv...Canon City...Lv	5 25	3 46	....
9 00	1 35	Ar....Glenwood....Lv	9 16	8 48	....
8 30	2 00	..Salt Lake City..	7 35	9 45	....
10 05		Lv..Ogden (Sou. Pac.)..Lv	6 15	8 20	....
11 20	9 50	....Reno....	8 30	3 25	....
8 30	8 15	Ar San Francisco (Sou. Pac.) Lv	9 00	6 00	....

3		11			4		12
9 40		8 45	Lv....Kansas City....Ar		8 15		5 00
11 30		10 30	Lv.....Topeka.....Lv		6 15		3 00
3 25		2 50	...Hutchinson...		2 10		10 15
8 30		9 55	Ar.....El Paso.....Lv		7 33		12 35
4 45		6 25	Ar..Tucson (So. Pac.)..Lv	11 00		3 40	
7 45		8 55	...Los Angeles...		6 15		12 05
10 30		10 30	...San Diego...		4 15		....
11 00		7 45	Ar...San Francisco...Lv	6 00		8 20	

EXPRESS SERVICE VIA WABASH RAILWAY

From all stations along this railroad, shipments by express may be sent over the shortest and most direct routes to any of the 26,700 points in the United States, and Canada, served by the Railway Express Agency.

The Railway Express Agency will pick up and deliver shipments within its designated limits at no extra cost.

A duplicate system of receipts to the shipper and from the consignee insure safety.

Shipments are accepted either prepaid or with charges collect and C. O. D. Remittances promptly returned.

Free liability for full value up to $50.00 for 100 lbs. or less—and at same ratio for heavier shipments.

Prompt notification if shipments cannot be delivered.

For details of rates, advice in regard to packing and marking, or for vehicle call, telephone the Railway Express Agent nearest you.

General Information

Not Responsible—The Wabash Railway Company does not hold itself responsible for errors in time tables, inconvenience or damage resulting from delayed trains or failure to make connections; schedules herein are subject to change without notice.

Freight Trains—The Wabash Railway Company does not wish to carry passengers upon way-freight trains, and does so only as an accommodation to the public. These trains cannot stop at the station platforms, and all persons who ride on them must do so with the understanding that they must get on or off where the cars may chance to stop, and that they assume all inconvenience and risk in getting to or from the cars. Baggage can be checked on these trains but delivery must necessarily be made at destination wherever the train may stop. Tickets must be purchased before taking these trains. Cash fares will not be accepted for passage. Passengers should apply to agents for full particulars.

Buy Tickets before boarding trains and avoid payment of extra charge.

Children under 5 years of age free when accompanied by parent or guardian; 5 years of age and under 12, one-half fare; 12 years of age or over, full fare.

Tickets Must be Used Within Limit—Local one-way tickets will be honored only for continuous passage to destination or stopover point, commencing within one day from date of sale. Passengers holding interline tickets must reach destination not later than midnight of date punched in margin or indicated on stopover paster.

Stop-over Privileges—Stop-overs will be allowed without deposit of ticket on one-way tickets sold at regular one-way fare and on round-trip tickets sold at double regular one-way fare, all-year tourist, summer tourist, winter tourist, European Trans-Pacific and around-the-world tickets at any station en route within final limit of ticket. Passenger must notify conductor before arrival at stop-over point and conductor will endorse train number, date and station name or number on ticket to show that passenger has stopped over at such point. Stop-over may be made at as many points as passenger desires, provided ticket is valid through such points, but such non-deposit stop-overs will not under any circumstances be permitted to extend the final limit of ticket. A passenger having availed of the non-deposit stop-over privilege at one or more points, must therefore resume the use of the ticket in time to reach destination before expiration of limit or to reach first deposit stop-over point en route (additional stop-over points are as shown below) where ticket may be deposited prior to its expiration, and a further stop-over and extension of not to exceed ten days (not including date of deposit) may be obtained.

Buffalo, N. Y.	Des Moines, Iowa	Omaha, Neb.
■Centralia, Mo.	Detroit, Mich.	Quincy, Ill.
Champaign, Ill.	★Excelsior Springs Jct., Mo.	St. Louis, Mo.
Chicago, Ill.	Ft. Wayne, Ind.	Shenandoah, Iowa
Council Bluffs, Iowa	Hannibal, Mo.	Sidney, Ill.
Danville, Ill.	Huntington, Ind.	Springfield, Ill.
Decatur, Ill.	Kansas City, Mo.	Toledo, Ohio

■Stopover allowed for Columbia, Mo. ★Stopover allowed for Excelsior Springs, Mo. free side trip, on all year, Winter and Summer Tourist tickets.

Adjustment of Fares—In cases of dispute with Conductors or Agents, pay the fare required, take receipt and communicate with the General Passenger Agent, St. Louis, Mo.

Redemption of Tickets—Tickets unused or partly used will be redeemed under tariff regulations at proper value. Apply to Agent or the General Passenger Agent, St. Louis, Mo.

Baggage—150 pounds of baggage will be carried free on each whole ticket and 75 pounds on each half ticket.

Baggage Maximum—No single piece of baggage exceeding 250 pounds in weight or single shipment 72 inches in greatest dimension, or exceeding $2,500.00 in value will be checked. Free allowances subject to tariff stipulations as to contents, weight, value and size.

Liability Limited—Excess value to be declared and paid for at time of checking.

Bicycles (not motorcycles), **Baby Carriages, Dogs and Guns** are transported in baggage cars subject to tariff regulations.

Hand-Baggage in Pullman Cars is restricted to what can be conveniently placed in the berth seat or other accommodations purchased by the passenger.

Lost Articles to be inquired for of Division Superintendents or through the nearest ticket agent.

No Responsibility Is Assumed for unchecked articles left in stations or cars.

Representatives of National Travelers Aid Society are at many of the larger stations, for purposes of relief of distress and assistance of unprotected. Those in need of such service should inquire of the station force for a National Travelers Aid Society representative.

The Parmelee Company, Passenger and Baggage Transfer in Chicago—A uniformed agent of THE PARMELEE COMPANY boards all incoming trains of the Wabash Railway before arrival at terminal Station. Passengers may arrange with him for transfer of themselves and their baggage to other STATIONS or LOOP HOTELS, also for the handling of their baggage to or from railway stations to any city address.

Western Union Telegraph Service—The Time Saving Facilities of the Western Union Telegraph Service are at the disposal of our patrons at Wabash stations, to enable you to keep in constant touch with your home or business affairs. These offices offer you every type of telegraph service: TELEGRAMS, NIGHT LETTERS, CABLEGRAMS, DAY LETTERS, NIGHT MESSAGES.

Have you wired ahead for hotel accommodations? **Western Union Blanks** will be found in all Pullman Cars.

FOR EXCLUSIVE OCCUPANCY OF SECTIONS, SINGLE ROOMS, COMPARTMENTS OR DRAWING ROOMS. THE FOLLOWING MINIMUM NUMBER OF ADULT RAILROAD TICKETS WILL BE REQUIRED.

Section............One ticket.....Between all stations.
(Berth or seat service)

Compartment or Drawing-Room.....Two tickets... Between all stations east of and including St. Louis, Mo., Hannibal, Mo., Quincy, Ill., Keokuk, Ia., and Chicago, Ill., except does not apply locally between stations in Canada, between stations in Illinois or between stations in Illinois and St. Louis, Mo., Hannibal, Mo., and Keokuk, Ia., see arrangements below.
(Berth or seat service)

Compartment.......One and one-half tickets
(Berth or Seat Service)
Drawing-Room.....Two tickets....
(Berth or Seat service)
Between stations in Illinois, between stations in Illinois, and all stations West of Mississippi River, also between stations West of Mississippi River.

Single Rooms...........1¼ tickets Between St. Louis and Chicago.

Optional Routes—The geographical location of the Wabash Railway permit the offer of a number of attractive optional routes, without additional charge, between the various commercial centers served by it. The following are a few available. For detailed information of additional routes consult your local agent, or any representative or conductor of the Wabash Railway.

Via Chicago or Ft. Wayne—When tariffs provide that fares apply via either Route, tickets reading between Bement, Ill. and stations west, and Montpelier Ohio and stations east, will be honored via Ft. Wayne, Ind., or via Chicago, Ill. Tickets from New York, N. Y., to St. Louis, Mo., containing coupons reading to and from Chicago, will be honored as routed or via Ft. Wayne at option of the passenger.

Toledo Tickets Honored to or From Detroit—Tickets reading via Wabash Railway to or from Toledo, Ohio, will be honored to or from Detroit, Mich., upon payment of $2.07 to conductor in charge of train (eastbound) into Detroit or (westbound) out of Detroit.

Detroit Tickets Honored to or from Toledo—Tickets (all classes) reading via Wabash Railway between Detroit, Mich., (or points east) and New Haven, Ind., or Montpelier, Ohio (or points west), will be honored to or from Toledo, Ohio, according to direction of travel, without extra charge.

Via Hannibal, Mo., or St. Louis, Mo., Tickets Reading Between Kansas City, Mo., and Chicago, Ill., Decatur, Ill., and Points East—Unless ticket is indorsed to the contrary, tickets of Wabash Railway issue or tickets of other lines' issue reading via Wabash Railway between Kansas City, Mo., and points east of and including Chicago or Decatur, Ill. (including stations between Chicago and Decatur, Ill.), in either direction will be honored via St. Louis, Mo., or via Hannibal, Mo.

Free Side Trips—Buffalo to Niagara Falls and Return—Passengers holding one-way or round trip tickets reading Wabash Railway via Buffalo from St. Thomas, Ont., and points west to Rochester, N. Y., Elmira, N. Y., or Emporium, Pa., and points east, or the reverse, may secure free side trip Buffalo to Niagara Falls and return, via International Railway, if desired. Passengers desiring this side trip should apply to Conductor, Wabash Railway into Buffalo, or to Agents Wabash Railway at Buffalo, N. Y., Chicago, Ill., or Detroit, Mich.

Excelsior Springs Jct., Mo., to Excelsior Springs, Mo., and Return—Passengers holding All Year, Winter and Summer Tourist tickets reading via Wabash Railway from St. Louis, Hannibal and East to Kansas City and West, or the reverse, may secure free side trip tickets to Excelsior Springs and return, upon application to agent Excelsior Springs Jct., and deposit of ticket with agent at that point.

39   40

Round Trip Summer Excursion Fares
FOR
VACATION TOURS

TO THE EAST

FROM	Toronto, Ontario	Montreal, Quebec	Niagara Falls, N. Y.	Holland, Michigan	Pt. Huron, Michigan	St. Paul and Minneapolis, Minn.	Alexandria Bay, New York	Charlevoix, Michigan	Grand Haven, Michigan	Minocqua, Wisconsin	Bigwin Inn, Ontario	Frankfort, Michigan	Bala, Ontario	Quebec, Quebec
Return Limit	Oct. 31	Oct. 31	Oct. 31	Oct. 31	Oct. 31	Oct. 31	Oct. 31	Oct. 31	Oct. 31	Oct. 31	Oct. 31	Oct. 31	Oct. 31	Oct. 31
Chicago .... Ill.	$26.57	$43.82	$28.98	$....	$....	$....	$37.52	$....	$....	$....	$37.37	$....	$32.52	$52.32
Danville .... Ill.	29.25	46.50	30.50	....	21.20	32.85	40.20	27.20	....	....	40.05	24.12	35.20	55.00
Decatur .... Ill.	33.49	50.74	34.74	18.90	25.60	30.45	44.44	31.40	20.15	29.40	44.29	28.60	39.44	59.24
Detroit ..... Mich.	[1]15.25	[1]29.10	14.40	....	....	[7]44.24	[1]22.80	....	....	35.35	26.05	15.25	[1]21.20	[1]37.60
Ft. Wayne ..... Ind.	20.29	37.54	21.54	....	12.25	....	31.24	20.89	....	....	31.09	17.05	26.24	46.04
Hannibal .... Mo.	41.72	58.97	44.13	25.70	34.15	30.45	52.90	38.20	26.95	36.20	52.52	35.40	47.67	67.47
Jacksonville .... Ill.	37.70	54.95	38.95	21.60	29.75	30.45	48.65	34.10	22.85	32.10	48.50	31.30	43.65	63.45
Kansas City .... Mo.	53.07	70.32	54.20	35.65	39.55	26.35	65.15	48.15	36.90	42.10	63.87	45.35	59.02	78.82
Kirksville ...... Mo.	47.12	64.37	49.53	29.70	39.55	26.35	61.47	42.20	30.95	40.20	57.92	39.40	53.07	72.87
La Fayette ..... Ind.	26.57	43.82	27.83	....	18.82	....	37.52	24.55	....	....	37.37	21.80	32.52	52.32
Litchfield ...... Ill.	37.00	54.25	38.26	22.50	29.10	30.45	47.95	35.00	23.75	33.00	47.80	32.20	42.95	62.75
Logansport .... Ind.	24.43	41.68	25.70	....	16.68	....	35.38	22.40	....	....	35.23	19.62	30.38	50.18
Mexico .... Mo.	45.07	62.32	46.29	27.65	37.50	29.09	57.57	40.15	28.90	38.15	55.87	37.35	51.02	70.82
Moberly .... Mo.	46.72	63.97	48.47	29.70	39.15	26.35	57.90	42.20	30.95	40.20	57.92	39.40	51.07	72.47
Omaha .... Neb.	55.27	72.52	56.40	37.85	47.70	....	67.35	50.35	39.10	....	66.07	47.55	61.22	81.02
Quincy .... Ill.	41.72	58.97	44.13	25.70	34.15	30.45	52.90	38.20	26.95	36.20	52.52	35.40	47.67	67.47
St. Louis ...... Mo.	40.27	57.52	40.07	25.85	31.75	30.45	51.22	38.35	27.10	36.35	51.07	35.55	46.22	66.02
Springfield ..... Ill.	35.75	53.00	36.98	19.85	27.80	30.45	46.70	32.35	21.10	30.35	46.55	29.55	41.70	61.50

TO THE WEST

FROM	Denver, Colorado Springs and Pueblo, Colo.	Ogden and Salt Lake City, Utah	San Francisco, Los Angeles, and San Diego, Cal., via Direct Route	Portland, Ore. Seattle, Wash., and Vancouver, B. C.	San Francisco, Cal., via Portland, Ore., or Seattle, Wash., in One Direction	YELLOWSTONE NATIONAL PARK — Both Ways via Yellowstone, Mont. (Western Entrance)	Going via Yellowstone, Mont. (West Entrance) Returning via Gardner, Mont. (Nor. Entrance)
Return Limit	October 31	October 31	October 31	October 31	October 31	See Note A	See Note A
Buffalo .... N. Y.	$68.70	$84.20	$113.70	$113.70	$131.70	$138.20	$138.20
Carrollton .... Mo.	30.60	55.25	78.35	[7]78.35	96.36	109.25	109.25
Chapin .... Ill.	37.65	58.30	86.65	[9]86.65	104.66	113.35	113.35
Chicago .... Ill.	43.05	59.35	90.30	90.30	108.30	113.35	113.35
Chillicothe ...... Mo.	30.10	52.50	79.25	[7]79.25	97.26	106.50	106.50
Conception ..... Mo.	30.10	52.50	75.60	[7]75.60	93.60	106.50	106.50
Danville .... Ill.	44.95	62.67	91.35	91.35	109.36	117.25	117.25
Decatur .... Ill.	40.20	59.30	89.70	[10]89.70	107.70	113.35	113.35
Defiance .... Ohio	51.98	67.48	96.98	96.98	114.98	121.48	121.48
Detroit .... Mich.	56.70	72.20	101.70	101.70	119.70	126.20	126.20
Des Moines ..... Iowa	32.35	55.75	83.50	[7]83.50	100.53	109.75	109.75
Fort Wayne ..... Ind.	49.53	65.03	94.53	94.53	112.53	119.03	119.03
Hannibal .... Mo.	34.10	57.25	83.95	[7]83.95	101.96	111.25	111.25
Jacksonville ..... Ill.	37.65	58.30	86.95	[7]86.95	104.96	113.35	113.35
Kansas City ..... Mo.	27.85	52.50	75.60	[7]75.60	93.60	106.50	106.50
Kirksville .... Mo.	32.35	55.75	83.10	[7]83.10	101.10	109.75	109.75
LaFayette .... Ind.	47.40	62.90	92.40	92.40	110.40	117.41	117.41
Litchfield .... Ill.	38.65	58.80	88.00	88.00	106.00	115.95	115.95
Logansport ...... Ind.	47.80	63.30	92.80	92.80	110.80	117.41	117.41
Macon .... Mo.	31.80	55.75	82.05	[7]82.05	100.06	109.75	109.75
Mexico .... Mo.	33.10	57.30	82.40	[7]82.40	100.40	111.30	111.30
Moberly .... Mo.	31.80	55.75	81.10	[7]81.10	99.10	109.75	109.75
Monroe City ..... Mo.	31.85	56.00	83.10	[7]83.10	101.10	110.00	110.00
Moravia .... Iowa	32.35	55.75	83.50	[7]83.50	101.50	109.75	109.75
Omaha .... Neb.	27.85	48.30	75.60	[7]75.60	93.60	102.30	102.30
Pattonsburg ..... Mo.	30.10	52.50	78.50	[7]78.50	96.50	106.50	106.50
Quincy .... Ill.	34.30	57.40	85.00	[7]85.00	103.00	111.40	111.40
St. Louis .... Mo.	37.80	58.80	85.60	85.60	103.60	115.95	115.95
Shenandoah ..... Iowa	30.10	49.10	75.60	[7]75.60	93.60	103.10	103.10
Springfield ...... Ill.	38.65	58.30	88.05	[7]88.05	106.06	113.35	113.35
Toledo .... Ohio	54.48	69.98	99.48	99.48	117.48	123.98	123.98
Tolono .... Ill.	42.79	60.49	90.30	90.30	108.30	114.49	114.49

Round Trip Summer Tourist tickets at fares named above will be on sale daily, effective May 15, 1931, except to destinations in Colorado, Utah and Wyoming, effective June 1, 1931, to September 30, 1931, inclusive, with final return limit to reach original starting point prior to midnight of October 31, 1931, except as noted above.

[1] Via Buffalo, N. Y. [2] To Minneapolis, $45.02 [3] To Vancouver, $81.60 [4] To Vancouver, $85.60 [5] To Vancouver, $81.55.
[6] To Vancouver, $87.15. [7] To Vancouver, $89.65. [8] To Vancouver, $84.35. [9] To Vancouver, $83.85. [10] To Vancouver, $90.30.

Stop-overs will be allowed on tickets sold at the above fares at all stations on either going or returning trip, within final limit of the ticket, upon application to conductor.

NOTE A.—To Yellowstone Park, fares in effect daily June 1st to September 13th, 1931, limit October 31st, 1931. Fare includes automobile transportation and hotel accommodations in the park for four and one-half day tour.

On application to local agents or any representative of the Wabash Railway (see pages 1 to 4) through fares can be obtained from and to points not shown above.

41   42

Relations with Other Companies—In 1927, the company bought $11,565,950 stock or 231,319 shares of Lehigh Valley R. R. at a cost of $23,232,118 or $100.43 average per share. During the same year, the Delaware & Hudson Co. bought $15,226,950 Lehigh Valley R. R. stock or 304,539 shares at $72.51 average cost, also $6,650,000 common and $15,070,000 preferred A stock of Wabash Ry. at average costs of $70.91 and $95.77 per share, respectively. In 1927, the Pennsylvania Co. purchased $19,190,000 common and $13,170,000 preferred A stock of Wabash Ry. at $68.25 and $90.33 average costs. In April, 1928, the Pennsylvania R. R. arranged with the Delaware & Hudson Co. to buy its holdings of Lehigh Valley R. R. and Wabash Ry. stocks for about $63,000,000. As of December 31, 1937, the Pennsylvania Co. held $18,251,950 Lehigh Valley R. R. stock (cost $43,551,208) and $36,290,000 common (cost $29,958,195) and $31,290,000 preferred A (cost $33,-083,353) Wabash Ry. stock. This was 30.2% of Lehigh Valley stock and 48.8% of Wabash Ry. stock. In addition, Wabash Ry. at the close of 1937 held $12,946,450 (21.4%) of Lehigh Valley R. R. stock carried at a book value of $24,726,199. In addition, Pennroad Corp. held $90,000 stock of Lehigh Valley R. R.

The Wabash Ry. enters Chicago over the Chicago & Western Indiana R. R., of whose stock one-fifth, or $1,000,000, is owned. From Delray, west of Detroit, into Buffalo, the Wabash Ry. operates over the tracks of other companies, chiefly Canadian National Ry. Agreement for use of Grand Trunk Ry. (Canadian National Ry.) tracks, Windsor to Black Rock, runs to 1940 at rental of $275,000 annually plus expenses. Net payment for joint facility rentals in 1937 was $1,668,898 and for lease of road and equipment $364,298.

Control of Ann Arbor R. R.—In May, 1925, the Wabash Ry. was reported to have acquired from bankers a block of the stock of Ann Arbor R. R. at a cost of $62.50 a share for preferred and $35 a share for common stock. In July, 1925, the Wabash Ry. applied to the I. C. C. for authority to acquire 8,400 shares of preferred and 6,935 shares of common stock of Ann Arbor R. R. in addition to 10,929 shares of preferred and 13,352 shares of common stock then held. The Wabash Ry. offered to purchase additional preferred stock at 70 and common stock at 45 until April 1, 1926. During 1926, $2,094,000 stock was purchased for $1,245,575, and during 1927, $80,000 additional at $48,900 cost. In June, 1930, the company paid initial annual dividends of $6.00 on the common stock and $5.00 on the preferred stock. On December 31, 1930, a special dividend of $27.00 a share on common and $5.00 a share on preferred was declared out of surplus, totaling approximately $1,075,000. Ann Arbor's balance sheet under current liabilities showed this under Dividends Matured Unpaid—Wabash included this under Dividend Income but in their balance sheet under Dividends Receivable. In 1936, this dividend was cancelled by a credit to surplus. At December 31, 1937, holdings were $7,209,200 preferred and common stock which cost $4,190,852 and were 99.43% of total.

On December 4, 1931, Ann Arbor R. R. went into receivership.

Rail Statement—Rail in main track at December 31, 1937, included:

233 miles of 112-pound rail,	32 miles of 75-pound rail,
686 " " 110- " "	29 " " 70- " "
3 " " 100- " "	90 " " 63- " "
794 " " 90- " "	48 " " 60- " "
10 " " 85- " "	9 " " 59- " "
438 " " 80- " "	12 " " 52- " "

The following indicates maintenance work in recent years:

	1931	1932	1933	1934	1935	1936	1937
Miles 112-lb. Rail Laid..	0	0	0	22	28	87	103
Miles 110-lb. Rail Laid..	7	23	34	46	0	1	0
Miles Track Ballasted..	1	2	7	1	1	2	5
Miles Track Reballasted	50	57	84	74	40	44	75
Miles Ditching	34	26	40	41	80	255	57
Miles Fences Built, Rebuilt or Repaired.....	69	95	123	149	131	170	145
Miles Siding and Spurs Built	3	5	2	1	2	6	4

From June 13, 1939 Wabash timetable.

DEPENDABLE FREIGHT SERVICE

SHIP BY WABASH RED BALL SERVICE

The Wabash has established an enviable reputation for on-time performance of Red Ball fast merchandise trains. This is due to the combination of powerful high-speed locomotives, splendid roadbed, heavy rails, modern equipment, fast train schedules, and a very high degree of efficiency in operation.

DIVERSION OF PERISHABLES DAY AND NIGHT SERVICE

Wabash Diversion Bureau at St. Louis, operating 24 hours a day, enables shippers to exercise diversion privileges on carload traffic from one market to another upon request.

A request by telegraph, stating shipment is to be diverted, will be given immediate attention, day or night.

A request for information regarding freight shipments, by phone or letter, to any of the forty-four Wabash offices shown on the opposite pages of this folder will be given prompt attention.

Wabash Rebuilds 3-Cylinder Steam Locomotive at Decatur Shops

First of five locomotives is converted from 2-8-2 to a modern 4-6-4 type adapted for hauling high-speed trains in either passenger or freight service.

FOR some time the Wabash has felt the need for more powerful passenger locomotives which can be interchanged with fast-freight power. During 1925, 50 heavy 2-8-2 freight locomotives were built for the Wabash by the American Locomotive Company. Forty-five of these locomotives were of the two-cylinder type and the other five were of the three-cylinder type. These five locomotives, Nos. 2600 to 2604, inclusive, were operated in fast-freight service between St. Louis and Chicago. Business was at such low ebb during depression years that most of the heavy Mikado locomotives were set aside and performed no service for several years. They were, however, given general repairs and gradually returned to service with the increasing business due to war-time conditions, with the exception of the three-cylinder locomotives which were not designed for the increased speed now required.

The boilers of the three-cylinder locomotives were in good condition and have a steam generating capacity 48 per cent greater than the existing Wabash class J-1 Pacific-type passenger power. They are fitted with 45-unit Type A superheaters and have 40-in. combustion chambers. It was decided that, as they are not adaptable to present needs, they should be reconstructed into 4-6-4 type locomotives, usable in heavy fast passenger and in fast freight service, by applying the boiler and cab to a new locomotive bed casting and modernizing, as to details and economy appliances.

The original tender of the three-cylinder locomotive is used, but with water capacity increased from 10,000 to 12,000 gal. by adding 16 in. of water space to the top of the tank and by removing tool and supply boxes from the front water legs.

The drivers are 80 in. in diameter as compared with 64 in. for the old locomotive and 74 in. for the class J-1 passenger locomotive; tractive force, 44,200 lb., against 36,984 lb. for the class J-1. The Walschaert valve gears are used, with 12-in. piston valves, 8-in. valve travel, and McGill needle bearings for link block, link trunnions, link foot and combination lever bearings. Roller bearings are used for all drivers, and for engine and trailer trucks. Two 32-pint mechanical lubricators are installed, one using valve oil for main valves, cylinders, feed-water heater and guides; the other using car oil to lubricate truck pedestals, shoe and wedge faces, valve-stem crosshead guides, equalizer pins, expansion pads, cylinder center plate, trailer radius-bar center plate and the slide bearing at the back end of each valve-motion radius bar. The multiple-bearing crosshead guides are

supported from the cross-brace casting instead of in the conventional manner from the guide yoke and back cylinder head.

The engine truck is of special design using coil springs that carry 70 per cent of the weight and semi-elliptic springs carrying the other 30 per cent. Trailer truck brakes are used, with the brake cylinders and rigging easily accessible from the outside. The cast-steel engine bed weighs 59,000 lb. complete. Cast integral with it are the cylinders and back cylinder heads, with high cylinder saddle and inside steam pipes, and the main air reservoir. There are integral brackets at the front for the air compressor and feedwater-heater hot-water pump, and a bracket at the rear on the left side for the stoker engine.

One sliding boiler support is placed between the cylinders and the rear expansion pad. This incorporates box-type welded construction and also serves as a power-reverse-gear bracket and speedometer drive-wheel bracket. The main rods and side rods are of alloy steel, railroad design, made at Decatur shops. Valve-motion parts are low carbon steel, also manufactured at the railroad company shops.

The main wheels are cross-counterbalanced with separate primary and secondary balances, the weights being calculated with due consideration to the different effects of the right and left eccentric cranks and rods. The main wheels carry 120 lb. overbalance. The front and back wheels are statically balanced for rotating weights and carry 150 lb. overbalance, each. The total overbalance per side is 420 lb. and amounts to 28 per cent of the reciprocating weights. The dynamic augment at the diameter speed of 80 m.p.h. is 5,400 lb. for the main wheels and 6,700 lb. for the front and back wheels.

The locomotive is designed to operate on maximum curves of 20 deg., or 288 ft. radius. One thing particularly stressed in the design has been the provision of well-rounded and streamlined steam and exhaust passages. The latter are unusually liberal in size and average 14 per cent of the cylinder area in all sections between the main valves and the exhaust-stand base. A Master Mechanic's front end is installed, with Goodfellow nozzle and cylindrical box-type spark arrester.

The body of the locomotive and tender, driving wheels and running gear are painted a deep blue. There is a 24-in. skirt, the full length of the running board and a 24-in. wide band continuing back over the cab and tender. The skirt and band are painted aluminum white and edged, at top and bottom, with a 1-in. red stripe. The lettering and numbering are in blue. Rods and valve-motion parts are polished.

Article courtesy Railway Age, October 23, 1943.

This locomotive will be used in passenger service on the heavy night trains of the Wabash between St. Louis, Mo., and Detroit, Mich., on fast-passenger trains between St. Louis and Kansas City, Mo., on troop trains, and to a considerable extent in fast-freight service.

Principal Dimensions of the New Wabash Class P-1 Locomotive Compared with a K-5 (3-cylinder) and a J-1 (4-6-2) Passenger Locomotive

	P-1	K-5	J-1
Type	4-6-4	2-8-2	4-6-2
Boiler pressure, lb.	220	210	215
Cylinders, diameter and stroke, in.	26 x 28	2-23 x 32 1-23 x 28	24 x 26
Diameters of drivers, in.	80	64	74
Tractive force, lb.	44,200	67,869	36,984
Factor of adhesion	4.44	3.76	4.20
Total weight of engine, lb.	374,690	340,490	248,840
Weight of drivers, lb.	196,390	251,215	155,140
Wheel base, engine, ft.-in.	40—7	39—1	34—0
Wheel base, engine and tender, ft.-in.	75—5½	73—9½	66—5⅞
Overall length, ft.-in.	87—5	83—10½	76—7⅝
Tender capacity:			
Coal, tons	16	18	11½
Water, gals.	12,000	10,000	8,800
Boiler dia. 1st. course inside, in.	88	88	68⅝
Firebox length, inside, in.	121 3/16	121 3/16	108⅛
Firebox width, inside, in.	84¼	84¼	84¼
Grate areas, sq. ft.	70.9	70.9	63
Heating surface, total evaporative, sq. ft.	4,225	4,225	3,310
Heating surface, superheater, sq. ft.	1,051	1,051	740
Heating surface, total equivalent, sq. ft.	5,801	5,801	4,420
Piston valve diameter, in.	12	12	12
Valve travel, in.	8	6½	6½

New Materials and Equipment on the P-1 Locomotive Not on the Original K-5 Locomotive

Locomotive bed frame, engine truck, trailer truck, Boxpok driving—wheel centers, swing coupler pilot	General Steel Castings Corporation, Eddystone, Pa.
Roller bearings, all locomotive wheels	Timken Roller Bearing Company, Canton, Ohio
Needle bearings, valve motion	Pilliod Company, New York
Feedwater heater 4½ S.A.	Worthington Pump and Machinery Corporation, Harrison, N. J.
Mechanical lubricators	Detroit Lubricator Company, Detroit, Mich.
Stoker, H.D.	The Standard Stoker Company, Inc., New York
Air brakes, No. 8 ET	Westinghouse Air Brake Company, Wilmerding, Pa.
Radial buffer, Type E2	Franklin Railway Supply Company, Inc., New York
Foameter	Electro-Chemical Engineering Corporation, Chicago
Cylinder protection valves	The Prime Manufacturing Company, Milwaukee, Wis.
Grates, 12-in. Tuyere type	Hulson Grate Company, Keokuk, Ia.
Speed recorder	Chicago Pneumatic Tool Company, Chicago
Cast air radiation elements	Wilson Engineering Corporation, Chicago
Injector, Type S.R.	William Sellers & Co., Inc., Philadelphia, Pa.
Cylinder packing	The Locomotive Finished Material Company, Atchison, Kan.
Driver brake beams—Widdicombe	Sivyer Steel Casting Co., Milwaukee, Wis.

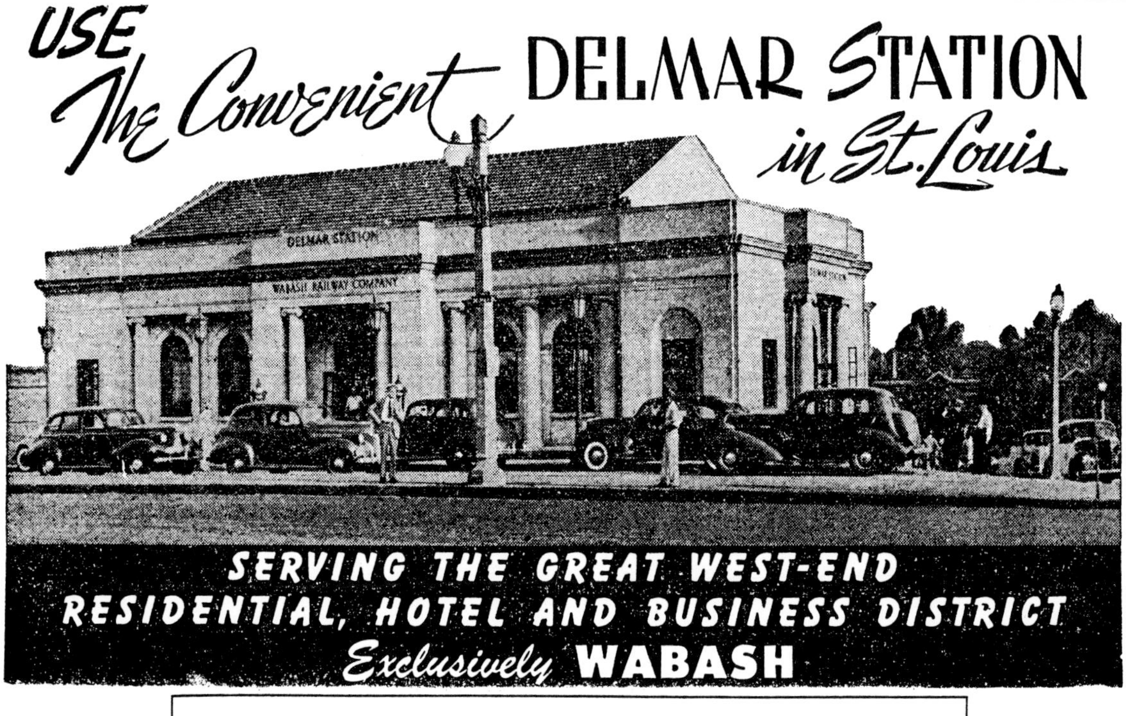

My Fellow Employees:

I take this opportunity to welcome the employees of the Nickel Plate, Wabash, Pittsburgh and West Virginia, Akron, Canton & Youngstown, and the Sandusky Line, as well as the Norfolk and Western, into the new Norfolk and Western unified company.

I am well acquainted with a great many of the officers and employees of most of these companies. I know them to be loyal and dedicated to their former companies. I have the greatest confidence that this loyalty and dedication will come to the new company.

All of the companies in the new Norfolk and Western enjoy a reputation for good service and prompt attention to the requirements of their patrons. It is now our job, not only to continue this good service, but to improve upon it and continue to give the most prompt and satisfactory solutions to the problems of our old patrons, as well as our new patrons, that it is humanly possible to do.

The new N&W is an aggressive, energetic company that has a tremendous potential for proving the advantages of rail service at a time when we are surrounded by many forms of rugged competition, and yet, the climate is in our favor.

It will be our endeavor to furnish our organization with the best tools, power and equipment with which to work, but these are of no value without the reliable and dedicated performance of every single member of this new organization. Every person in this organization is important.

We must keep in mind that we are being watched closely by our competitors, as well as shippers, so that we must have good performance from the start.

You are with a property of which you can be proud. With the loyalty that you have already demonstrated to your former company continuing, we can make the new Norfolk and Western the most efficient and respected transportation agency in this country.

Sincerely,

Herman H. Pevler

President

November, 1964 Norfolk & Western Magazine "Welcome address" by N&W President Herman H. Pevler

Acknowledgements

Wabash material wasn't hard to find in preparing this book, but I learned that one must be dogged and look in many places to find material on a railroad that is no longer a corporate entity.

Large portions of the material in this book came from Wabash fans from all over the country who wanted to see a tribute to the railroad in book form. Artists, photographers, historians, librarians and many others have helped make this book a representative sampling of the Wabash Railroad throughout its lifetime. Their help is truly appreciated and acknowledged.

As you might expect, I talked to and corresponded with hundreds of people about the Wabash, and everyone deserves my hearty thanks for sharing their time and information. It is impossible to include everyone who contributed to this book, but I have listed, to the best of my knowledge, those persons or groups who were very helpful over the past several years as I was preparing this book.

Alco Historic Photos
Allen County Historical Society
William Arland
Arthur Bixby Sr.
Kenneth Borg
H.L. Broadbelt
E.A. Burkhardt
Lewis Concklin
Harold Conner
Barton Davis
John Day
Dale Doud
Rev. Edward Dowling, S.J.
W.D. Edson
Charles Felstead

Robert Fiedler
Kermit Gaines
Richard Ganger
Ross Grenard
Donald Gruber
F.H. Gwinn
L.G. Issac
J. David Ingles
E.F. Jurow
John Keller
Reid Kenedy
John Krause
Robert Laidlaw
Earl Larson

Ted Lemen
Donald Mather
M.D. McCarter
Russell McDaniel
Bruce Meyer
Max Miller
Miner Enterprises
Marion Moore
T.E. Nihiser
John Nixon
Mike Pearsall
Tony Perles
James Platt
Robert Post
William Raia

Frederick Schlipf
Harold Scott
Paul Slager
Robert Sloan
Harold Stirton
R. Brooks Stover
E.F. Striplin Jr.
William Swartz
Wilbur Thurmon
Dick Voght
R.R. Wallin
Bill Wallace
David Withall
Doug Wornam
Frank Yeakel

The joint Wabash-Illinois Central railroad depot at Tolono, Illinois as it looked on May 2, 1894. With nearly 20 years of financial turmoil behind it, the Wabash was optimistic as it faced the 1890's, years that would bring the Columbian Exposition to Chicago and continued expansion of lines to the east. *Photo courtesy collection of Marion Moore*

Bibliography

Books

Munday's Earning Power of Railroads, 1938, James H. Oliphant & Co., New York and and Chicago

The Nickel Plate Story, John A. Rehor, Kalmbach Publishing Co., 1965

The Wabash Railroad, William Swartz, Railroad History, No. 133, Fall, 1975, Railway & Locomotive Historical Society, Inc.

Diesel Locomotive Rosters, Wayner Publications, p. 115

The Wabash Club Silver Jubilee souvenir book, 1911-1936

Magazines

Collector's Items, William Baldwin, Forbes, December 19, 1983

Modern Mixed Train Daily, Ken Heinen, Model Railroader, January 1966, p. 38

Missouri Mixeds, J. David Ingles, Trains, October, 1973, p. 18

Wabash, David P. Morgan, Trains, July 1950

Norfolk & Western Magazine, November 1964, December 1964 and June 15, 1976

New Passenger Car Repair Shops & Stores Buildings for Wabash Railway, Railway Review, February 7, 1925

Newspapers

Decatur Salutes Wabash Centennial, Decatur Herald & Review, May 9, 1954

Annual Reports

The Wabash Railroad, June 30, 1908

Wabash Railway Company, June 30, 1916

Wabash Railway Company, December 31, 1916

Wabash Railway Company, December 31, 1925

Wabash Railway Company, December 31, 1931

Wabash Documents

Freight Car Equipment Guide, January 1, 1956

The History of the Wabash Railroad, Advertising & Public Relations Department, August, 1959

Norfolk & Western Documents

Wabash Railroad Company Freight Car Equipment, December 1, 1964

Equipment Guide, January 1, 1956

And the notes, timetables, letters, brochures and personal experiences of dozens of former Wabash employees, and Wabash fans, who graciously shared them with me for use in this book.

Graying skies and melting snow, Green things hint of more below and all seems full of promise.

Photo by Frank Sadorus, courtesy of The Champaign County Historical Archives of the Urbana Free Library

317

Index

A fast J-1 Class 4-6-2 built by Richmond Locomotive Works rolls through Decatur with a passenger train and two express cars. *Dick Wallin collection*